KU-626-749

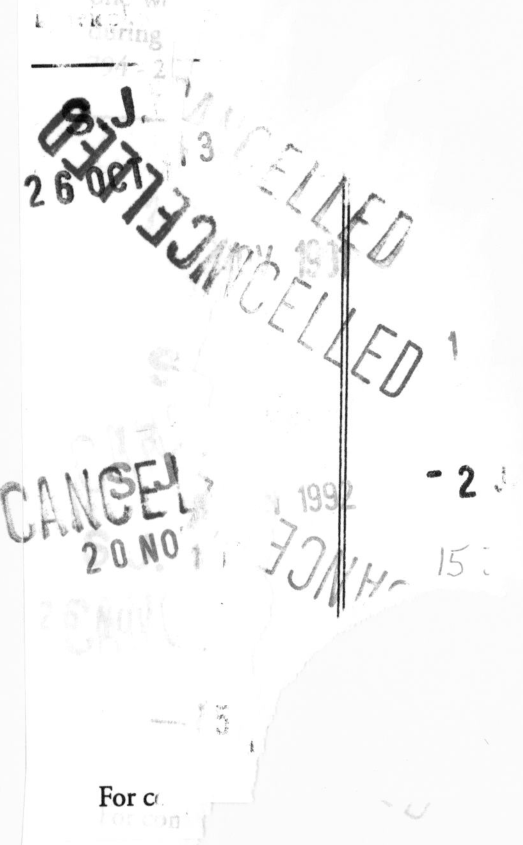

Economics for a Developing World

Michael P. Todaro

Economics for a Developing World

An introduction to principles, problems and policies for development

Second edition

Longman
London and New York

Longman Group UK Limited
Longman House, Burnt Mill, Harlow,
Essex CM20 2JE, England
and Associated Companies throughout the world

First published 1977
Second edition 1982
Second impression 1985
Third impression 1986
Fourth impression 1988

British Library Cataloguing in Publication Data
Todaro, Michael P.
Economics for the developing world. – 2nd ed.
1. Underdeveloped areas – Economic conditions
I. Title
330.9172.4 HC59.7

ISBN 0-582-64343-0

Produced by Longman Singapore Publishers (Pte) Ltd.
Printed in Singapore.

Contents

List of figures

List of tables

Preface to the First Edition

Teachers of the introductory economics course at universities throughout the developing world have long been aware of the need for a relevant, comprehensive introductory text oriented towards the critical issues of economic and social development. In Africa, Asia, Latin America and the Middle East, local instructors often have little choice but to use so-called 'international student editions' of 'Western' introductory texts. Their students are thus subjected to lengthy discourses on the functioning of the US Federal Reserve System, the industrial structure of the British economy and/or the range of contemporary economic problems experienced by advanced market economies – topics of only limited relevance to developing nations. Moreover, the institutional assumptions and theoretical models put forward in these texts often bear little resemblance to the structural and economic realities of the developing world.

To give some examples, unemployment, typically, is ascribed to a deficiency of Keynesian aggregate demand, while inflation arises because of an excess of aggregate demand. Structural problems on the supply side are for the most part neglected. The high productivity agricultural sector which is fully commercialised and sparsely populated in most developed countries is relatively insignificant and therefore given limited coverage. And yet in developing nations agriculture is by far the most important economic activity and its low productivity is a major source of concern. Similarly, foreign trade is often treated as only marginally significant since most rich nations can deal with periodic balance of payments crises by applying an appropriate mixture of fiscal, monetary and commercial policies. The phenomenon of international economic dependence so central to much of the developing world is rarely mentioned.

In addition, most Western texts do not treat rapid population growth as a serious problem. Environmental decay is considered much more important. Yet the reverse is true in most developing countries. Self-sustaining technological progress and continuous economic growth are taken for granted in most standard texts, whereas in developing nations these are priority goals. The availability of skilled human resources and management expertise are also assumed, whereas a major task of development is to create such human resources and to foster such expertise. Finally, problems of widespread poverty and growing income inequality, if discussed at all in standard texts, are treated as relatively minor aberrations of a smoothly functioning, highly integrated, industrially advanced market economy, rather than as endemic manifestations of a highly fragmented and dualistic economy in the process of transition from subsistence to modernisation. One could cite numerous other examples of the very limited relevance of these standard texts for understanding the unique problems of underdevelopment in Africa, Asia and Latin America.

There is thus an urgent need to produce more appropriate and meaningful introductory economics books for students in developing nations. While such a need has long been recognised, its fulfilment has rarely been attempted. Leading Third World economists typically and understandably are often too busy with their heavy load of teaching, research and government advising, and the incentives, both professional and financial, are not sufficiently attractive. The most that local economists usually do is to put together mimeographed books of readings or collections of individually written chapters on the economy of the local country or region.[1] Often faculty lecture notes are passed out to students and used to supplement standard texts. Although such collections of readings and notes are valuable improvements on the wholesale, uncritical importation of standard Western texts, the fact remains that there have been few, if any, successful attempts to prepare a comprehensive introductory economics text for widespread use in developing nations. There is a need for one which tries simultaneously to focus on development problems and issues of vital national

[1] A leading example of the former is the set of readings on East Africa put together by the staff of Makerere University in Uganda during the 1960s while an outstanding example of the latter is a recently published collection of articles on the Philippine economy with contributions by a number of leading Philippine economists.

and regional importance while still providing students with a solid foundation of meaningful and relevant economic concepts and principles. The present book is designed specifically to meet this need.[2]

[2] See the Foreword for a more detailed description of the orientation, scope and organisation of the text.

Acknowledgements

A number of people, many more than I can mention, have helped me both directly and indirectly in the process of writing this book. First to my students and colleagues, especially in Africa but also in Latin America and Asia, I owe a debt of gratitude for encouraging me to undertake such a major effort. Their probing questions and challenging criticisms of the orthodox introductory economics material persuaded me of the urgent need for a new approach. Among my students I would like to mention particularly Mr J.M. Obiri and Mr G.S. Mwabu of Kenya for their comments on earlier drafts and for their assistance in preparing the Glossary. Among my colleagues, I am particularly grateful to Philip W. Bell, Edgar O. Edwards and Lloyd G. Reynolds for their early and continuous prodding and to Kenneth W. Thompson for encouraging me to take a broader view of international affairs. To my friends and colleagues in the Third World, especially Aklilu Habte, Denisard Alves, Romeo Bautista, Amado Castro, Claudio Castro, Jorge Cauas, Victor Diejomaoh, Jose Encarnacion, Sunday Essang, Luis Fuenzalida, Dharam Ghai, Joseph Maitha, Philip Ndegwa, Alfonso Ocampo, Harry Oshima, Justinian Rweyemamu, Marcello Selowsky, William Senga, Soedjatmoko, Gabriel Velasquez, Flavio Versiani, Vinyu Vicit-Vadakan and many, many others, I give a special note of thanks for innumerable conversations that helped to influence my thinking on the teaching of economics to students in developing countries.

Finally, a very special note of indebtedness to my wife, Donna Renée, for the inspiration, encouragement and intellectual and spiritual support to persevere in very trying circumstances. If ever a cliché were true, it would be that without her, this book would never have been possible.

Summary of major concepts and theoretical frameworks covered in the Book

Concept or theory	*Location*
Scarcity, demand, supply, market price determination, demand curves, price and income elasticity of demand, normal and inferior goods, shifting demand curves, supply curves, supply elasticity, surplus labour, rationing, non-market pricing	Ch. 3
Production theory, resources and factors of production, neo-classical production functions, diminishing returns to variable factors, factor prices and appropriate technology, cost curves and supply, demand and revenue, simple profit maximisation, savings and investment, present vs. future consumption, income distribution, private vs. social costs and benefits, externalities in production and consumption, prices and imperfect markets	Ch. 4
Linear stages theory of development, Harrod-Domar growth model, structural theories, neo-Marxist theories, dualistic theories	Ch. 6
Diminishing returns, marginal costs and supply curves, production-possibility curves and opportunity costs, factor intensities and increasing costs, unemployment and social opportunity costs, theory of economic growth, physical and human capital, technological progress – neutral, labour and capital saving, shifts in production – possibility curves	Ch. 7
Size and functional distributions of income, Lorenz curves, Gini coefficients, factor shares distribution theory, theories of growth vs. distribution, welfare indices – GNP, poverty and equal weights	Ch. 9 and Ch. 10
Theory of demographic transition, Malthusian population theory, microeconomic theory of household behaviour and fertility choices, marginal utility and demand curves, work and leisure (labour supply curves), demand for children (quantity and quality trade-offs)	Ch. 12
Concepts of unemployment and underemployment, free market, competitive model, Keynesian theory of employment, factor-price distortions and choice of technology, price incentive model – shadow prices	Ch. 13
Lewis dual economy model, Todaro migration model,	Ch. 14
Theory of firm (farm) Subsistence agriculture and risk theory, rural development – integrated approaches	Ch. 15 and Ch. 16
Theory of human capital and education, economics of education, 'brain drain' – external and internal	Ch. 17 and Ch. 18
Theories of international trade – Ricardo comparative advantage model, Hecksher-Ohlin factor proportions model, classical and neoclassical models of trade and development	Ch. 19
Commercial policy – theory and practice, import substitution, export promotion, currency devaluation, tariffs, quotas etc., theory of economic integration, custom unions, free trade areas, common markets.	Ch. 21
Multinational corporations, 'two-gap' models, theories of foreign aid	Ch. 22
Theory of planning, planning models – aggregate growth, sectoral projection and input output models, project appraisal and cost/benefit analysis	Ch. 23
Policy economics – theory of monetary and fiscal policy, theories of inflation and taxation	Ch. 24
Aggregating demand curves, prices and rationing again, international resource supply curves, New International Economic Order propositions	Ch. 25

To Donna Renée

Foreword The nature, purpose and design of this new text

This book has been written for use by first-year economics students at universities throughout Africa, Asia, Latin America and the Middle East. For too many years, students in these developing nations have had to rely on 'Western' economics textbooks written primarily for their counterparts in North America and Western Europe. Although such books may claim to be universal in scope, in reality they are typically oriented towards the unique institutional, social and economic structures of the industrially advanced economies of the West. Students in developing countries are often therefore forced to absorb a broad spectrum of economic concepts, principles and theories and to analyse a wide range of contemporary problems and issues which may have little or no relationship to the institutional and economic realities of their own societies.

The few textbooks that have been developed for use by students in poor nations have invariably used the same conceptual approaches and the same sets of principles and problems as those intended for their counterparts in rich countries. The only differences have been minor modifications for local conditions and the occasional substitution of local examples and some local data for the advanced country material. Such texts are improvements on the uncritical importation of 'international student editions' of developed country books, but usually they simply do not go far enough. Often they fail to modify, and/or discriminate among, 'received' theories in light of the institutional and structural realities of many 'Third World' nations.[1] Nor do they treat pervasive development problems such as population growth, poverty, inequality, unemployment, illiteracy and rural stagnation in sufficient detail and with a broad enough geographical coverage to excite and challenge the student to examine the common nature of these problems and to reach an independent and informed judgment as to their possible solution.

Having therefore to rely almost exclusively on imported Western texts, introductory economics courses in developing nations too often become no more than disguised versions in scope and content of courses used in developed countries. Thus they naturally tend to give undue emphasis to economic models and contemporary problems important to the developed countries to the neglect of those which may be more appropriate for the developing world. Although the thought processes and certain basic economic concepts and principles should be largely the same for both the developed and the developing world,[2] the differences in institutional assumptions, problem areas and policy options relevant to a better understanding of the economics of developing nations warrant a new approach to teaching introductory economics in such countries: one that represents a radical departure from the traditional Western approach still widely used

[1] The 143 African, Asian and Latin American member countries of the United Nations often collectively refer to themselves as the 'Third World'. They do this primarily to distinguish themselves from the economically advanced 'Capitalist' ('First World') and 'Socialist' ('Second World') countries. Although the precise origin of the term 'Third World' is obscure, it has become widely accepted and utilised by economically poor nations themselves, especially in their negotiations with economically rich nations on critical international controversies relating to international trade, foreign aid, oil and other natural resource depletion and dwindling world food supplies. While it is unfortunate that numbers such as 'First', 'Second' and 'Third' occasionally bear the regrettable connotation of superiority and inferiority when used in reference to different groups of nations, the fact remains that the term 'Third World' *is* widely used among developing nations in a concerted effort to generate and represent a new sense of common identity and a growing unity of purpose. Accordingly, we will often use the expression 'Third World' when referring to the developing countries as a whole with the clear understanding at the outset that the expression is always being used in its *positive* sense of a common identity and a growing unity of purpose.

[2] In Chapters 3 and 4 we will attempt to identify and delineate such a common core of relevant economic concepts and principles for developing nations.

throughout much of Africa, Asia and Latin America.[3]

The present text represents an attempt to devise such a new approach. It may be distinguished from existing introductory texts, both foreign and local, used in developing countries, in the following eight ways:

1. It is oriented exclusively towards the teaching of economics within the context of **the major problems of development and underdevelopment** in Third World nations. It focuses on these countries in their capacity as independent nation states, in relation to one another, and in their interaction with rich nations, both capitalist and socialist.
2. It recognises the necessity of treating the problems of development and underdevelopment from an **institutional** as well as an economic perspective with appropriate modifications of the received 'general' economic principles, theories and policies.
3. It views development and underdevelopment in both a domestic and global context, stressing the **increasing interdependence of the world economy** in areas such as food, energy, natural resources, technology and financial flows.
4. It takes a **problem-oriented approach** to the teaching of economics on the dual assumption that
   (*a*) students can best grasp important economic concepts when these are discussed in the context of familiar 'real world' development problems:
   (*b*) a central aim of any introductory economics course should be the development of a student's ability to understand contemporary economic problems and to reach independent judgments about their possible solution.

   Rather than presenting economic principles as a set of abstract concepts applicable to any and all societies, this book draws on appropriate and relevant traditional economic concepts to illuminate real development problems.[4] To do otherwise would be just as inappropriate a 'transfer of technology' as to import massive northern hemisphere tractors with heaters under the driver's seat for use on small family farms in tropical Africa.
5. It approaches development problems systematically by following a **standard procedure** with regard to the analysis and exposition of each problem. Each chapter begins by stating the general nature of the problem (e.g. population, poverty, education, income distribution, unemployment, etc.), its principal issues and how it is manifested in the various less developed countries. It goes on to discuss main goals and possible objectives, the role of economic principles in illuminating the problem, and some possible policy alternatives and their likely consequences. We believe that this approach will assist students to think systematically about major current development issues. Perhaps more importantly, it will provide them with a methodology and operating procedure for analysing and reaching policy conclusions about other contemporary and future development problems which may be peculiar to their own countries or regions.
6. It is based on the conviction that it is possible to design and structure an economics textbook for simultaneous use in the various countries of Africa, Asia, Latin America and the Middle East by using the best available cross-section of data. Ideally, each problem-oriented chapter could be supplemented with local data for each country or region in which the book is used.[5] While recognising that problems will differ in both scope and magnitude when dealing with such diverse

[3] It seems rather absurd that in many Third World university economics departments a course in 'development economics' is often offered as a 'speciality' or even as an 'option' for advanced undergraduate students. In reality, the introductory course should be *the* basic 'development' course with most other courses having a similar development orientation. Courses based on typical Western introductory texts might then be offered as an option to students interested in the 'economics of advanced capitalist societies'.

[4] As Professor Rendigs Fels, a former chairman of the American Economic Association's Committee on Economic Education, has correctly pointed out, 'The test of whether to include or omit a particular concept (in an elementary economics text) is not its importance to the professional economist nor its profundity nor its place in an esthetically elegant theoretical structure. The test is its usefulness to the layman in comparison with the time and effort he must take to learn it': R. Fels, 'Developing Independent Problem-solving Ability in Elementary Economics', *American Economic Review*, lxiv, 2 (1974), 404.

[5] For example, teachers of the introductory course in African nations may wish to supplement this book with the low priced (for students, libraries and faculties) *Surveys of African Economics* published by the International Monetary Fund, Washington DC. These surveys provide a valuable compilation of published statistics and descriptions of the institutional and structural framework of the economies concerned.

countries as India, Indonesia, Lebanon, Kenya, Nigeria, Egypt, Brazil, Mexico and Guatemala, the fact remains that all these countries face very similar development problems. Widespread poverty and growing income and asset inequalities; rapid population growth; low levels of literacy and nutritional intake; rising levels of urban unemployment and under-employment; stagnating agriculture and relative rural neglect; inadequate and often inappropriate educational systems and health services; inflexible institutional and administrative structures; significant vulnerability to external economic, technological and cultural forces of dominance and dependence; and the difficult choices regarding trade-offs between 'modernisation' and cultural preservation: these and other problems are pervasive phenomena and, in fact, often define the very nature of underdevelopment even in culturally diverse and physically varied Third World nations.

7. It views the many economic, social and institutional problems of underdevelopment as highly interrelated and requiring simultaneous and co-ordinated approaches to their solution at both the national and international levels. It is based on the premise that economic development, even when defined in terms of both the rapid growth and more equitable distribution of national incomes and opportunities, is a necessary but not sufficient condition for 'development'. The problem is that one simply cannot talk about economics for development without placing economic variables squarely in the context of sociopolitical systems and institutional realities. To ignore 'non-economic' factors in an analysis of so-called 'economic' problems such as poverty, unemployment and inequality, both within and between nations, would do students a great disservice. Worse still, it could close their minds to the whole picture when they eventually assume positions of responsibility for the development of their nations.
8. Finally, this book is intended to give all students who take an introductory course in economics a sufficient breadth of knowledge not only about major development issues in their own nations but similar ones in other Third World countries. It is hoped that this will enable them to maximise the real world value of other university courses, whether in the the social sciences, engineering, medicine, agriculture or law. Ultimately, it will help to make them more informed and responsible citizens. Most students who take a first course in economics will not go on to specialise in it. It is therefore up to the author of an introductory text to cater for their needs as well as for those of aspiring young economists, even if it means trading a little esoteric elegance for a lot of mundane reality (a trade-off with a very large 'net benefit' to my mind!).

Organisation and Orientation

The book is organised into four Parts. Part One focuses on the nature and meaning of underdevelopment and its manifestations in different Third World nations. It also expounds selected economic principles and concepts which appear to be particularly relevant for an understanding of problems of international development. Each of these basic principles and concepts is described within the context of actual issues and problems of developing nations.

Parts Two and Three form the core of the book. Part Two focuses on major **domestic** development problems and policies while Part Three examines the place of Third World nations in the **international** economy. Topics for analysis and review (at the end of each chapter) include economic growth, poverty and income distribution, population, unemployment, migration, agriculture and rural development, education, international trade, private foreign investment and foreign aid. Throughout Parts Two and Three, the problem discussions draw on the relevant fundamental principles and concepts expounded in Part One.

Finally, Part Four reviews the possibilities and prospects for Third World development. After discussing the theory and practice of development planning and the role and limitation of public economic policy, it analyses the evolving world economy of the 1980s and the place of less developed nations in an increasingly interdependent but highly unequal global economic system. The impact of the recent energy, food and debt crises on the economies of developing nations is closely examined, and growing Third World demands for a 'new international economic order' in the context of greater collective self-reliance are reviewed and analysed.

An extensive glossary provides a quick reference for definitions and explanations of various terms and concepts used throughout the book.

In all four Parts of the book, we ask the fundamental questions: what kind of development is most desirable, and how can Third World nations best achieve these economic and social objectives, either individually or, better, in co-operation with one another and, it may be hoped, with appropriate and meaningful assistance from the more developed countries of the world?

In our discussion and analysis of critical development problems we give the diverse and often conflicting viewpoints of development economists, other social scientists, planners and those actually on the 'firing line' in Third World government ministries and/or departments. If we reveal a bias, it is probably in trying always to put forward the viewpoints of Third World social scientists and development practitioners who, in the 1970s, began to articulate their shared perceptions of the meaning of development as never before.[6]

The locus of intellectual influence on development thinking is rapidly shifting from the First and Second Worlds to the Third World. It is in these nations that the ultimate answers must be found and appropriate strategies formulated. And it will be the nationals of these countries who will increasingly exert the major influence on the form and content of these strategies. We hope that the present text may make a modest contribution to the formulation of such future strategies and to the fostering of a better understanding of the diverse problems of underdevelopment by providing Third World students with an introduction to economics which has both relevance and meaning.

---

[6] See, for example, Padma Desai, 'Third World Social Scientists in Santiago', *World Development*, i, 9 9 (1973); 'Self-reliance and International Reform', *Overseas Development Council Communique*, 24, June 1974; Mahbub ul Haq, 'Crisis in Development Strategies', *World Development*, i. 7, July 1973; and the 'Communiqué' of fifty leading economists from the developing countries who met for the first time as members of the Third World Forum in Karachi, Pakistan, in January 1975.

Part One Principles and concepts

Chapter 1 Economics: its nature and importance for developing nations

The ideas of economists and political philosophers both when they are right and when they are wrong are more powerful than is commonly understood. Indeed the world is ruled by little else.
John Maynard Keynes, 1936

The Third World,[1] with 70 per cent of the world population, subsists on only 20 per cent of the world income – and even this meagre income is so maldistributed internally as to leave the bulk of its population in abject poverty.
Santiago Declaration of Third World Economists, 1973

Introduction

Poverty and affluence in an interdependent world

Throughout the world people wake each morning to face a new day in very different circumstances. Some live in comfortable homes with many rooms. They have more than enough to eat, are well clothed, in good health and can look forward to a reasonable degree of financial security. Others – and these constitute more than two-thirds of the earth's four and a half billion peoples – are much less fortunate. They may have little or no shelter and inadequate food. Their health is poor, they cannot read or write, they are unemployed, and their prospects for a better life are bleak or uncertain at best. Let us, therefore, begin our study of economics by examining a sample of these living conditions in different parts of the world. To facilitate this examination, let us imagine that we are travellers in an aircraft equipped with technology enabling us to circle our planet and to observe how the earth's various inhabitants live. What would we see? What might be our reactions?

Suppose we focused first on an average family in North America. It is probably a family of four with an annual income of approximately $16 000. They live in a comfortable suburban house purchased with a large bank loan, called a 'mortgage', and probably have two motor cars, one each for the husband, who works full-time in a nearby office building, and the wife, who works part-time in the local library. Their house has many comfortable features, including separate bedrooms for each of the two children. It is filled with numerous items such as a washing machine, refrigerator, television, radio and other electrical appliances known as 'consumer goods', many of which were manufactured outside North America in countries like South Korea, Argentina and Taiwan. The family has three meals every day including one to two portions each of meat or fish, green and yellow vegetables, fruit, bread and milk. The food comes from many other parts of North America and many items come from overseas; for example, coffee from Brazil, Kenya or Colombia; tinned fish and fruit from Peru, Japan and Australia; and bananas and other tropical fruits from Central America. All these items were probably purchased at a large supermarket where many appliances and other household goods and clothing are also sold. Both children are healthy and at school. They can expect to go to university and choose almost any career to which they are attracted, and to live to an average age of 74 years.

On the surface, this family, which is typical of many rich nations, appears to have a good life. The parents have the education and ability to secure well-paid jobs, to shelter, clothe, feed and educate their children and to save some money each year for later life. But against these 'economic' benefits, there are always 'non-economic' costs. The competitive pressures to succeed financially are very strong, and

[1] For a discussion of the meaning of 'Third World' and the context in which the term is used throughout this book, see footnote 1 on page xxi of the Foreword.

the mental strain and physical pressure of trying to provide for a family at levels that the community regards as desirable can take its toll on the health of both the father and the mother. Their ability to relax, to enjoy the simple pleasures of a country stroll and to breathe clean air, drink pure water and see a crimson sunset are rapidly disappearing with the onslaught of economic progress. But, on the whole, theirs is an economic status and life style towards which many millions of other less fortunate people throughout the world seem to be aspiring.

Now let us focus on a typical family in rural Asia. It is a family of ten: parents and five children, two grandparents and an uncle. They have a combined annual income, both in money and in kind (i.e. they consume a share of the food they grow), of $150. They all live in a one-room poorly constructed shelter as tenant farmers on a large agricultural estate owned by an absentee landlord who lives in the nearby city. The father, mother and uncle, as well as the older children, must work all day on the land. None of the adults can read or write, and of the five school-age children, only one attends regularly and he cannot expect to proceed beyond four or five years. There is only one meal a day. It rarely changes nor is it usually sufficient to alleviate the constant hunger pains experienced by all the children. The house has no electricity, sanitation or fresh water supply. There is much sickness, but qualified doctors and medical practitioners are far away in the cities. The work is hard, the sun is hot and aspirations for a better life are constantly being suffocated. The daily struggle for physical survival in this part of the world finds its only relief in the spiritual traditions of its people.

Shifting position in our aircraft, we find ourselves over another continent, setting our sights on a city beautifully situated along the coast of South America. It is a large and sprawling area but from our high perspective, we can discern what appear to be two cities within one boundary. There is a modern stretch of tall buildings and wide tree-lined boulevards along the edge of a gleaming white beach. However, just a few hundred metres back and up the side of a steep hill, squalid shanty houses are pressed together in precarious balance. We decide that it might be interesting to observe two families at the same time – one living in a multi-room complex on the top floor of a beautiful building overlooking the sea and the other cramped tightly into a small makeshift shack in a *favella* or squatter slum on the hill behind that sea front building.

It is Saturday evening and both families are preparing for dinner. In the penthouse flat a long table with expensive dishes from Germany, silverware from England and fine linen from Ireland is being set by one of three servants. Russian caviar, French champagne and Spanish olives will constitute the first of five courses. Guests will be arriving soon so the family's three children are hurrying to get dressed. The eldest is home from his university in North America while the other two are on vacation from their boarding schools in France and Switzerland. The father is a prominent surgeon trained in the United States, with a clientele of wealthy local and foreign dignitaries and businessmen. Annual vacations abroad, imported luxury automobiles, and the finest food and clothing are commonplace amenities for this family in their penthouse flat.

And what about the family on the hill? They too can see the water, but somehow, it does not seem so beautiful or relaxing. The stench of open sewers makes enjoyment rather remote. There is no long dinner table in this shack on the hill. In fact, there is no dinner. Most of the seven illiterate children are out on the streets begging for money, shining shoes or occasionally even trying to steal purses from unsuspecting persons as they stroll along the boulevard. The father migrated to the city from the rural hinterland a few years ago and the rest of the family recently followed. He has had part-time jobs over the years but nothing permanent. The family income is less than $170 per year. The children have been in and out of school many times, as most are forced to help out financially in any way they can. Occasionally the eldest teenage daughter who lives with 'friends' across town seems to have some extra money, but no one ever asks where it comes from or how it is obtained.

One could easily be confused and disturbed by the sharp contrast between the luxurious life in the penthouse by the sea and the stark existence of life in that shack on the hill. However, had we looked at almost any other major city in Latin America, Asia and Africa, the contrasting scene would have been much the same, although the degree of income inequality might be less pronounced.

As a final aspect of this brief videoscan of life on the planet below, our camera is now turned towards a large land mass across the ocean, focusing on a small cluster of tiny huts in a dry and barren land. It is eastern Africa and we have isolated a remote and nomadic tribal village. Rather than a single family, there appear to be a group of families here, all participating in and sharing the work. There is no money income as such here, because all food, clothing, shelter and wordly goods are made and consumed by the people themselves: theirs is a 'subsistence' economy. There are no roads, schools, hospitals, electricity or water supplies and life here seems to have been unchanged for thousands of years. In many respects it is as stark and difficult an existence as that of the people in that Latin American favella across the ocean. Both share in a common struggle for survival. But it is not as psychologically troubling because there is no luxurious penthouse to emphasise the relative deprivation of the poor. Life here seems to be external and unchanging, but not for much longer.

A hundred kilometres away a road is being built which will pass near this village. No doubt it will bring with it the means for prolonging life through improved medical care. But it will also inexorably bring information about the world outside along with the gadgets of modern civilisation. The possibilities of a 'better' life will be promoted and the opportunities for such a life will become feasible. Aspirations will be raised, but so will frustrations. In short, the 'development' process will have been set in motion. Before long, exportable tropical fruits and vegetables will probably be grown in this now sparsely settled region. They may even end up on the dinner table of the South American family in the penthouse. Meanwhile transistor radios, made at the other end of the earth in south-east Asia and playing music recorded in northern Europe, will become a prized possession in this African village. Throughout the world remote subsistence villages such as this one are gradually but inexorably being linked up with modern civilisation. The process is now well under way and will become even more intensified in the coming years.

Having had this first fleeting glimpse of life in various parts of our planet, we might naturally be a bit confused and begin to ask questions. How can such obvious wealth coexist with such dire poverty, not only across different continents but also within the same country or even the same town or village? How are these societies and nations organised economically to satisfy the wants and desires of their inhabitants? How are these economic wants translated into the production of goods and services? Who decides what is to be produced? On what basis are they distributed? Why can't everybody have everything they desire? If this is not possible, why do some get so much and others so little? By what process and under what conditions do rural subsistence families such as those in remote regions of Nigeria, Mexico, Brazil, Egypt or the Philippines evolve into commercial farmers selling their produce in return for the means by which they can purchase goods produced outside their immediate environment?

Many similar questions concerning international and national differences and potentialities in levels of living, including, among other things, health and nutritional conditions, educational facilities, employment opportunities, population growth rates, and life expectancies, might be posed on the basis of even this very superficial look at life on our earth below.

However, there is no need to travel in a space vehicle to be aware of or to formulate and seek answers to such 'real world' questions. Important insights into the origins, nature and possible solutions of these and many other development problems can be gained from an introductory course in economics which focuses on the two-thirds of the world's population where poverty and low levels of living are a way of life. If nothing else, our planetary excursion has given us the advantage of viewing the earth as a whole. What it does *not* reveal is that as our earth shrinks with the spread of modern transport and communications, the futures of all peoples on this small planet are becoming increasingly interdependent. What happens to the health and economic welfare of that poor rural family and many others in South Asia will in one way or another, directly or indirectly, affect the health and economic welfare of their counterparts in North America, and vice versa. The 'hows' and 'whys' of this interdependence will unfold in the remaining chapters. But it is within this context of a common future for all mankind in the rapidly shrinking world of the 1980s that we now begin our study of economics.

What traditional economics is about: its scope and limitations

It is neither easy nor desirable to give a strict

definition of economics. The concepts and thought processes of economics have a wide range of applications in so many aspects of life. Basically, however, economics is the study and exercise of **choice.** It is concerned with the manner in which the **wants** and desires of people are converted into a limited number of material **goods** (such as rice, maize, radios, bicycles and clothes) and **services** (such as medical care, education, police protection, music and dance) through the judicious use of scarce productive **resources** (including land, mechanical capital goods, labour, materials, managerial, technical and administrative know-how). People have many basic wants such as hunger, thirst and sensitivity to climate. These become revealed as desires for goods like food, drink, shelter and clothing. In the most elementary subsistence economy, like the African village described earlier, basic needs are met entirely by those who experience them. Consumers and producers are one and the same. Simple tools are fashioned to turn the soil or to construct a house. Technical know-how derives primarily from oral tradition as each generation passes on its knowledge to the next. Most important, human labour constitutes the essential productive resource used to produce basic foodstuffs, simple clothing and adequate houses.

But even in this most primitive society, the forces of economics are at work. Given scarce and therefore costly resources, choices must be made regarding **what** goods to produce, **how much** of each good to produce, **how** (i.e. with what combination of resources) and **for whom**. These questions, as we shall soon see, are basic to any economic system from the richest industrial nation to the poorest and most primitive subsistence society. Increasingly, however, an additional question is assuming major importance in the world's economies: how shall scarce economic goods (e.g. world food supplies) and productive resources (e.g. oil and industrial raw materials) be rationed and distributed both within and among nations?[2] In other words, who shall have **access** to these scarce goods and resources, and on what basis shall such access be determined?

Rather than burden the student at this early stage with complicated and often confusing definitions, let us see how economics and economic thought processes permeate everyday life in the less developed countries (LDCs). On what economists call the 'micro' level ('micro-economics' is concerned with **individual** economic units such as the small farmer, the shop-owner, the individual consumer, the family, etc.), rice growers in Thailand and Nigeria, maize farmers in Mexico and Kenya, or wheat producers in Argentina and India often face many of the following difficult choices:

1. how much of their commercial crop to attempt to produce in a particular growing season;
2. whether or not to hire wage labour;
3. whether the extra probable **output** of the crop would be worth the cost of purchasing and applying physical **inputs** such as new seeds, pesticides and fertilisers;
4. whether or not to borrow money from commercial lending institutions (banks) or, if this is not possible, from individual money lenders who may charge exorbitant rates or interest; and
5. whether or not to **risk** the uncertain prospects of crop failure for the **reward** of a promised higher yield of output if new seed varieties of hybrid corn, rice or wheat are planted in place of the traditional varieties.

All these are real and difficult economic problems which must be faced by farmers and other producers, small or large, throughout the world. They involve the essential ingredients of every economic decision: the **choice** of how to utilise scarce (i.e. not free) resources – in these cases primarily financial and physical resources: money and land – in the best possible combinations in order to get the greatest output or satisfaction. It is **scarcity** which gives rise to choice, and choices involve **trade-offs** – giving up something (goods or money) to get something else. A Kenyan maize farmer or Indian wheat grower knows that if he uses his limited financial resources to irrigate his land, he will not be able to purchase a small tractor. If his objective is to increase yields, a choice must be made whether the trade-off involved in foregoing the installation of irrigation ditches in favour of purchasing a small tractor for the same expenditure will result in a higher or lower per-hectare yield of output. If yields increase, the trade-off is usually worth it; if they do not, then it is not advisable.

The above example illustrates a concept fundamental to all economics – the so-called

[2] See Chapter 2 for a further elaboration of these central economic questions facing all societies.

'law', or rather, the 'principle', of economy.[3] This principle states that when choosing among a number of alternative possibilities, a private individual or public agency acting rationally should choose that alternative which **minimises** the cost of achieving a desired benefit or, alternatively, **maximises** the benefit or satisfaction derived from a given cost. For example, a famer whose objective is to maximise crop yields should choose that type of seed or fertiliser which for a given expenditure, say 500 rupees, will result in the greatest output per hectare of his land. If he has a different objective, such as greater crop diversification and/or meeting minimum subsistence requirements for his family, he might allocate his money in different ways. A family with a small monthly budget for food consumption should choose that good or combination of goods which will best alleviate their hunger while still providing adequate nutrition. A person building a house should choose those materials and that quantity of labour which will minimise the cost of securing adequate shelter and necessary comfort. A government faced with the decision whether to utilise a given amount of tax revenue to build more schools or hospitals, in the city or in rural areas, should attempt to balance the potential 'benefits' (however defined) against expected 'costs' so as to make the decision that yields the greatest 'social' benefit (i.e. the overall benefit to society as a whole) per unit cost or, alternatively, that minimises the expected cost of achieving a desired social benefit.[4]

All these are examples of the principle of economy. It serves as a general rule of choice in economics and is, therefore, central to a thorough understanding of economic analysis and policy formulation. But the decision to maximise benefits or minimise costs at both the private and public level is not as simple and straightforward as it might appear on the surface, or, for that matter, in most traditional economics textbooks.

The concept of 'economy' or 'economising', involving as it does the act of rational choice, is derived from a set of explicit and implicit assumptions about human behaviour and motivations which may or may not be valid for all societies and at all times. Moreover, as the guiding principle for private and collective economic decisions, it may be subject to such qualifications and/or modifications that it loses much of its theoretical 'purity' and intellectual simplicity. To illustrate the point, the concept of economy assumes that individuals and groups of individuals have some clear notion of what they want which can readily be translated into a set of well-ordered 'preferences'. For example, if A (apple) is preferred to B (banana) and B is preferred to C (carrot), then A (apple) will **always** be preferred to C (carrot). Here we immediately come up against the problem that people, and particularly governments, cannot always rank their preferences according to some unique, non-contradictory ordering. As a result, complex decisions involving a range of conflicting objectives and opposing forces often have to be reached through some judicious combination of intuition and guesswork. Moreover, the actual decision will often be influenced more by the relative power of certain dominant individuals or interest groups than by any rational calculation of social benefits and costs. In 'simple' choices where individuals or groups have all the necessary accurate information at hand (which they rarely do), where their preferences are really their own and not dictated by external forces such as corporations and governments (a fairly uncommon occurrence in both developed and less developed countries), and where their decisions are not only in their own best private interest but also do not adversely affect others (an unusual phenomenon in both rich and poor nations), then in these very special cases it can be said that the principle of economy will be the guiding force for private and public decision-making.

However, most decisions at both the individual and group level are very complex. Typically, they involve weighing opposing and often contradictory interests against rules of procedure for arriving at decisions which may be far from the economist's definition of 'rational'. Some economists have been too slow to recognise the quite common contradictions of the human personality or to admit that

[3] As we shall soon discover, there really are no 'laws' of economics in the sense of their being universally applicable with the same results in all societies and at all times. In fact, in economics there are only 'tendencies' which can give 'probable' directions and orders of magnitude when certain conditions are fulfilled.

[4] In Chapter 4, we will discuss in greater detail the important concept of 'social' as opposed to 'private' benefits and costs.

'economic' decisions are often reached through less than economically rational institutional processes. Specifically, the failure to incorporate risk, uncertainty and imperfect knowledge at the private level and the phenomenon of 'power' (political and economic) at both the public and private level into the analysis of 'real world' decision-making has greatly weakened the applicability of the traditional economic approach, especially in the institutional and social context of many developing nations. For example, to understand why in most Third World countries small farmers or individual businessmen are often reluctant to experiment with new production techniques, why individual consumers may resist new and cheaper varieties of their staple food, why disparities in personal incomes between rich and poor have widened in the past and will probably continue to do so in the future, why technologically sophisticated and very costly urban industrial projects have often been promoted at the expense of improving small-farm agriculture and/or stimulating a 'people-oriented' rural development, why the majority of hospitals, better schools and other government services and facilities are concentrated in urban centres where typically less than 20 per cent of most LDC populations reside, and finally why most attempts at land reform and rural reconstruction fail to achieve their stated objective of helping the rural poor, it is necessary to go beyond the principle of economy, though it still provides a useful intellectual framework with which to analyse and evaluate the 'economic' effects of various public policies.

We might, therefore, restate this principle in terms which make it more appropriate for understanding the decision-making process at all levels in many developing (and, indeed, developed) nations. For example, if we recognise, as we should, the important and pervasive interconnections between economics and power and incorporate this notion of power into the principle of economy, it might usefully be reformulated on the following lines:

An individual entity **acting rationally in isolation** and with **sufficient** and **accurate information** will **tend** to choose that course of action which **maximises** its personal satisfaction (income) derived at a given cost or, alternatively, that which **minimises** the cost of achieving any desired level of satisfaction (income); but when a **group** of individuals or entities with **differing objectives and/or preferences** are parties, either directly or indirectly, to a decision affecting the 'social' welfare of a larger population, they will often choose that course of action which **for almost any politically acceptable social cost** will maximise the satisfaction (or income) of certain **elite power groups** who will in fact be instrumental either in making or influencing the overall decision.

In short, economic decisions cannot be divorced from their political, social, institutional and cultural context. They can and often will be influenced by the relative power of small yet dominant elite interest groups (e.g. wealthy landlords, the ruling oligarchy, local large business interests, the military, foreign investors, etc.) whose first concern may be economic aggrandisement and political self-protection rather than any generalised concern for the 'social good'.

Throughout this book we shall give numerous examples of the validity of this 'reformed' principle of economy. We will discover, for example, that relative economic power affects a wide range of actual development situations, including, among others, the system of international trade and aid relations between rich and poor nations, the structure of land ownership and its impact on food production, the organisation and orientation of the formal educational system, the relationship between the choice of technology and the problem of unemployment, and the geographic and sectoral priorities of national economic plans. For the present, however, our intention has been merely to alert the student to the broader social and institutional context in which all economic decisions must normally be made and to the many ways in which the phenomenon of power can compromise the strict 'rationality' criteria of the principle of economy.[5]

The meaning and significance of 'Third World' economics

Economics in its traditional sense, therefore, is

[5] For a penetrating and perceptive analysis of the role and influence of power in the ordinary economic processes of developed nations, see John Kenneth Galbraith, 'Power and the Useful Economist'. *American Economic Review*, lxiii, 1, March 1973.

concerned primarily with the efficient (i.e. least-cost) utilisation of scarce productive resources and with the optimal growth of these resources over time, so as to produce an ever expanding range of goods and services. **Political economy**, on the other hand, goes beyond simple economics to study among other things the social and institutional processes through which certain groups of (mainly) economic and political elites choose to allocate scarce productive resources now and in the future for their own benefit or for that plus the wider benefit of the larger population. It is therefore concerned with the interaction between politics and economics.

Development, or 'Third World' economics, however, goes even further. In addition to the efficient allocation of existing scarce (or idle) productive resources and their sustained growth over time, and the political content of economic decisions, it is concerned with the **economic, social** and **institutional mechanisms**, both public and private, necessary for bringing about **rapid (at least by historical standards) and large scale improvements in levels of living** for the masses of poverty-stricken, malnourished and illiterate peoples of Africa, Asia and Latin America. Thus, Third World economics, to a greater extent than 'traditional' economics or even political economy, is concerned with the economic and political processes necessary for effecting **rapid structural and institutional transformations of entire societies in a manner that will most efficiently bring the fruits of economic progress to the broadest segments of their populations.** As such, the role of government and the need for some degree of centralised or at least coordinated economic planning and broad-based economic policies to bring about such rapid change becomes a vital component of Third World economics.

Economic **principles** are those **tools of analysis** which permit us in a simplified yet realistic way to understand why various socio-economic changes take place and/or to predict how they can be brought about by the conscious manipulation or independent alteration of one or more of the primary economic and/or institutional variables – e.g. savings and interest rates, wage levels, agricultural commodity prices, land-tenure systems, credit allocations, individual and corporate tax structures.

Finally, economic **policies** are those decisions and actions taken primarily by government ministries and public officials which are deliberately designed to bring about rapid improvements in some of the principal components of Third World development – e.g. the level and distribution of national income, the prices of key commodities, the level of employment, the availability and quality of rural health, education and other social services, the productivity of small scale agriculture, the level of saving and investment and the ownership and distribution of land and other valuable physical assets. Although such policies may be, and often ostensibly are, designed to benefit primarily the rural and urban poor, the ultimate beneficiaries, as we have seen, often turn out to be those who already represent the economic elites of developing nations.

Why study economics?

There are several reasons why so many students in developing nations study economics. It is clearly the most popular subject among the social sciences (sociology, history, psychology, political science and anthropology) and, with the exception of Latin America and parts of the Arab world where medicine, law and engineering still dominate career choices, economics is rapidly becoming the most popular of all university courses. This is not surprising because economic problems and issues directly and in a most significant way touch the lives of each and every individual in Africa, Asia, the Middle East and Latin America.

Students, therefore, often choose to study economics in the hope of finding answers to vital questions such as the following:

1. What do we really mean by 'development' and how can economic principles and theories contribute to a better understanding of the development process?
2. What are the sources of national and international economic growth? Who benefits most from such growth and why? Why do some countries and groups of people continue to get richer while others remain very poor?
3. Why is there so much unemployment, especially in the cities, and why do people continue to flock into the cities from rural areas even though their chances of finding a job are very slim?

4. Should the rich be taxed more than the poor and how should government tax revenues be spent in order to improve standards of living for all people?
5. What is development planning all about? Why plan at all?
6. Should foreign private corporations be encouraged to invest in the economies of poor nations and, if so, under what conditions?
7. What about 'foreign aid' from rich country governments? Should it be sought after, under what conditions, and for what purposes?
8. Should exports of primary products such as agricultural commodities be promoted or should all LDCs attempt to industrialise by developing their own heavy manufacturing industries as rapidly as possible?
9. What is a 'balance of payments' problem? When and under what conditions should the government adopt a policy of exchange control, raise tariffs and/or set quotas on the importation of certain goods in order to improve balance of payments deficits?
10. Is international trade desirable from the point of view of the development of poor nations? Who really gains from trade and how are the advantages distributed among nations?
11. What has been the impact of the rapid rise in international oil prices on the economies of less developed nations? And, what future role might the now wealthy OPEC oil nations play in furthering the development of other Third World nations?
12. What is the best way to promote agricultural and rural development where 60 to 80 per cent of most LDC populations still reside?
13. How does the spread of inflation and unemployment among the economies of rich nations affect the levels of living of people in poor nations? Do poor nations have any recourse, or must they be passive but vulnerable spectators at an international economic power game?
14. Are there economic factors influencing levels of fertility (birth rates) in poor nations? What are the economic and social consequences of rapid population growth? Is the population problem simply a question of numbers or is it also related to the impact of rising affluence in developed nations on resource depletion throughout the world?
15. Will there be chronic world food shortages? If so, which nations will be most adversely affected and how might such shortages best be avoided in the future?
16. Do contemporary Third World educational systems really promote economic development or do they simply act as a rationing or screening device by which certain select groups or classes of people are perpetuated in positions of wealth, power and influence?
17. What is the origin and basis of growing Third World demands for a 'new international economic order'? Is such a new world order possible, and, if so, what might be its main features?

These and many other similar questions are analysed and explored in the following chapters. The answers are often more complex than you might think. Remember that the overriding purpose of any course in economics should be to train you to **think systematically** about economic problems and issues and to formulate judgments and conclusions on the basis of the application of 'relevant' analytical principles and 'reliable' statistical information. Since many problems of development are unique in the modern world and not easily understood through the use of traditional Western economic theories (see Chapter 3, pp. 27–30, for an explanation of the nature of traditional economic theory), we may need unconventional approaches to what may appear to be conventional problems such as unemployment, income distribution, inflation, rural–urban migration and agricultural versus industrial expansion. Traditional economic principles have an important role to play in enabling us to improve our understanding of world development problems, but they should not blind us to the realities of local conditions. They often need to be modified in both assumptions and procedures before they can shed light adequately on complicated and economically unprecedented development issues.

Another reason why students enrol in an economics course is because economics is a field in great demand offering a wide range of career opportunities. Economists are regularly employed in government planning and finance ministries, in central and commercial banks, in public and private industries, in universities and research institutes and, finally, in international agencies such as the International Bank for Reconstruction and Development (World Bank), the International Labour Organisation (ILO), the International Monetary

Fund (IMF), the United Nations Economic Commission for Africa (ECA), for Asia and the Pacific (ESCAP) and for Latin America (ECLA), the United Nations Development Program (UNDP), the various regional Development Banks as well as numerous other international assistance agencies.[6]

There are now and will continue to be many challenging and rewarding opportunities for Asian, African, Middle Eastern and Latin American economists to make significant contributions to the promotion of economic and social development of their own countries and regions. However, to be really effective in their jobs economists, or for that matter any professional (doctor, lawyer, civil servant, engineer, architect or businessman) or ordinary educated citizen, should have a thorough understanding of the nature and causes of 'underdevelopment' and a grasp of how certain economic principles and policies can be used to assist nations and people to escape from poverty and improve their conditions. The purpose of this book is to provide the basis for such an understanding.

The important role of values in economics

Economics is a social science. It is concerned with man and the social systems by which he organises his activities to satisfy basic material needs (food, shelter, clothing, etc.) and non-material wants (education, knowledge, leisure, spiritual fulfilment, etc.). Economists are social scientists who are in the unusual position that the objects of their studies – human beings in the ordinary business of life – and their own activities are rooted in the same social context. Unlike the physical sciences, the social science of economics can claim neither scientific 'laws' nor 'universal truths'. In economics there can only be tendencies; and even these are subject to great variations in different countries and cultures and at different times. Many so-called 'general' economic models and 'objective' studies are often based on a set of implicit assumptions about human behaviour and economic relationships which may have little or no connection with the realities of developing economies. To this extent, their 'objectivity' may be more assumed than real. Economic investigations and analyses cannot simply be lifted out of their institutional, social and political context, especially when one must deal with the human dilemmas of hunger, poverty and ill-health which plague two-thirds of the world's population.

It is necessary, therefore, to recognise from the outset that ethical or normative 'value' premises about what is or is not desirable are central features of the economic discipline in general, and of development economics in particular. The very concepts of 'economic development' and 'modernisation' represent implicit as well as explicit value premises about desirable goals for achieving what Mahatma Gandhi once called the 'realisation of the human potential'. Objectives such as economic and social equality, the elimination of poverty, universal education, rising levels of living, national independence, modernisation of institutions, political and economic participation, grass roots democracy, self-reliance and personal fulfilment all derive from subjective value judgments about what is good and desirable and what is not. So also for that matter are opposite values – for example, the sanctity of private property and the right of individuals to accumulate unlimited personal wealth, the preservation of traditional social institutions and rigid, inegalitarian class structures, and the supposed 'natural right' of some to lead while others follow.

When we deal in Parts Two and Three with such major problems and issues of development as poverty, inequality, unemployment, population growth, rural stagnation and international 'dependence', the mere identification of these topics as 'problems' conveys the value judgment that their improvement or elimination is desirable and therefore good. The fact that there is widespread agreement among many diverse groups of people – politicians, academics and ordinary citizens – that these *are* desirable goals does not alter the fact that they arise not only out of a reaction to objective, 'positive', scientific analysis of 'what is' but also from a subjective, 'normative', value judgment of 'what should be'.

It follows that value premises, however carefully disguised, are an integral component both of economic analysis and economic policies. Economics cannot be 'value-free' in the same sense

[6] For a brief description of the nature and purposes of each of these international agencies, see the Glossary at the end of the book.

as, say, physics or chemistry. The validity of economic analysis and the correctness of prescriptions, therefore, should always be evaluated in the light of the nature of the underlying assumptions and/or value premises. Once these subjective values have been agreed upon by a nation or, more specifically, by those charged with the responsibility for national decision-making, then specific development goals (e.g. greater income equality) and corresponding public policies (e.g. taxing higher incomes at higher rates) can be pursued. However, where serious value conflicts and disagreements exist among decision-makers, the possibilities of a consensus either about desirable objectives or appropriate policies will be considerably diminished. In either case, it is essential that value premises, especially in the field of development economics, be specified carefully and not hidden behind a smokescreen of 'pseudo-scientific' jargon or the excessive mathematication of simple economic concepts.[7]

Summary and conclusions

In this introductory chapter, we started by posing the hypothetical question of what we might see and how we might react if we were able to view the wide variety of living conditions on the planet earth. Striking differences in levels of living including incomes, consumption standards, health and nutritional levels, family size variances and levels of education were found to exist not only between rich and poor nations around the world but also between rich and poor groups of people within the same nation. At the same time, a visual perspective from above can help us to understand, as no verbal description can, the ultimate interdependence of all nations and peoples of the world.

We next described the nature, scope and limitations of traditional economics. Basically, traditional economics focuses on the question of choice and the ways in which scarce physical and human resources are organised and best developed through a variety of national and international institutional and social arrangements to provide adequate and rising levels of living, now and in the future, for diverse groups of people. The concept of 'economy' or 'economising' (minimising the cost of achieving a desired benefit or maximising the benefit derived from a given cost) is a central principle of traditional economics. But as a general proposition it needs to be amended to take account of the important influence of 'power', both economic and political, in the real world of economic decisions and choices in developed and developing countries. Political economy, therefore, goes beyond traditional economics by studying the interconnections between economic decisions affecting whole societies and the political power of small elites and other vested interest groups both within and outside these societies to promote their own welfare, often at the expense of the larger indigenous population.

'Third World' or 'development' economics is a distinct yet very important extension of both traditional economics and political economy. While it is concerned with efficient resource allocation and the growth of aggregate output over time, Third World economics also focuses primarily on those needed economic, social and institutional mechanisms required to bring about rapid and large-scale improvements in levels of living for the masses of poor people in developing nations. As such, Third World economics must be concerned with the formulation of appropriate public policies designed to effect major economic, institutional and social transformations of entire societies in the shortest possible time. Otherwise the gap between development aspirations and world realities will continue to widen with each passing year. For this reason the public sector and the role of the state in the overall economic system is a much more important factor in Third World economics than in traditional Western economics.

There are many reasons for studying economics: searching for explanations and possible answers to vital development problems: the widespread demand for the career services of economists in governments, commercial banks, universities, private industries and international aid agencies; and the importance of some knowledge of economics for any well-balanced education.

As a social science, economics is concerned with people and how best to provide them with the material means to help them realise their full

[7] For an excellent dissection of the role of values in development economics, see Gunnar Myrdal, *The Challenge of World Poverty*, Pantheon, 1970, Ch. 1.

human potentials. But the question, 'What constitutes the good life?' is perennial, and economics must of necessity be concerned with values. Our very concern with promoting development represents an implicit value choice about good (development) and evil (underdevelopment). But 'development' may mean a lot of different things to a lot of different people. Therefore, the nature and character of that development and the meaning we attach to it needs to be carefully defined. This will be our object in Chapter 6 and at numerous other points throughout the book.

Concepts for review

'Traditional' Western economics	values and value premises
political economy	income in 'kind'
'Third World' or development economics	money income
	subsistence economy
economic goods and services	rational choice
	economic variables
resources – physical and human	levels of living
	political and economic elites
trade-off	
principle of economy	vested interests
economic principles	'positive' versus 'normative' economics
economic policies	
social science	
laws versus tendencies	

Questions for discussion

1. Why do you think the study of economics is so central to an understanding of the problems of development? Give some examples of its role and usefulness.
2. Do you think that the wide diversity of living conditions found by our brief trip around the world can also be found within most developing countries? What do we mean by the notion of different levels of living?
3. What distinguishes economics, which is known as a 'social' or 'soft' science, from a discipline like physics which is usually referred to as a 'physical' or 'hard' science?
4. Can you summarise the conceptual distinction between 'traditional' economics and 'Third World' economics as we have defined these fields of study in the text? To what extent is traditional economics a component of 'Third World' economics and not the reverse? Explain.
5. What do you hope to gain from this course (besides an examination pass)?
6. Why are values and value premises so important in economics? Can economics ever be really 'value free'? Why or why not?
7. Can you identify the basic values which guide the development policies of your own nation? Are these values widely held by the population? Discuss.

Further reading

For a lively, layman's discussion of the nature of traditional, Western economics see ROBERT A. MUNDELL, *Man and Economics*, McGraw-Hill, New York, 1968, chs 1–3. On the role of values in economics see GUNNAR MYRDAL, *The Challenge of World Poverty*, Pantheon, New York, 1970, Part One.

Chapter 2 Economic systems and Third World economies

Capitalism is the exploitation of man by man;
communism is the reverse.
Anonymous

Introduction

The central economic problems of all societies

Three basic tasks

Every economy, whether rich or poor, capitalist, socialist or a mixture of both, has to accomplish three basic tasks. First, it has to determine **what** goods and services are required and **how much** of each, and **where** (in what regions of the country) and in **what manner** they could best be produced. Second, it has to allocate the aggregate or total amount of goods and services produced, that is, the Gross Domestic Product, or GDP, among **consumption** by private individuals (food, bicycles, haircuts, radios, clothing, etc.), consumption by society as a whole in the form of **government expenditures** (police protection, national defence, provision of clean water and sanitation, road and transport construction, public health and education facilities, etc.), replacement of capital stocks used up in the course of production (buildings, roads, machinery and equipment, etc.), and future growth of the economy through new **investment** or 'net' additions to that capital stock. Third, it has to decide how to **distribute** its total material benefits (the 'national income') among the various members of society – in the form of wages, interest payments, rents and profits (whether public, private or both).

In this chapter we explore how different societies, both capitalist and socialist, set about the task of resolving these fundamental issues.

A survey of the various definitions of national income and output

First, however, let us briefly examine the different ways in which a nation can statistically measure its national output. For any country, national output, national expenditure and national income all refer to roughly the same total, but looked at from different perspectives. Thus, the **Gross Domestic Product** (GDP) refers to the total monetary value of all goods and services produced within the geographic boundaries of a nation during a given year. It is calculated simply by valuing the outputs of all 'final' goods and services at 'market' prices (i.e. the actual prices at which they are bought and sold) and then adding the total. Note that the market value of all 'intermediate' products – those used to produce the final output like cotton for clothes or steel for bicycles – is excluded from the calculation of GDP since the values of intermediate goods are already implicitly included in the market prices of the final goods. The word 'gross' implies that not all this output was available for private or public consumption and investment, since a small part was needed to replace or maintain worn-out capital equipment – factories, houses, machinery, railway lines, roads, etc. The word 'domestic' implies that only the income produced in that country is accounted for. Thus, the income that arises from investments and possessions owned abroad is not included in GDP estimates.

Gross National Product (GNP) or **National Income**, on the other hand, refers only to that part of GDP which is actually produced and earned by or transferred to resident nationals of that country.[1]

[1] In many cases, there are sizable numbers of nationals of one country working temporarily in a neighbouring nation (e.g. Colombians in Venezuela, Pakistanis and Indians in Saudi Arabia, Mexicans in the USA, Upper Voltans in the Ivory Coast, etc.). The earnings which they transfer back to relatives in their home country would normally be estimated and counted as part of that country's GNP.

The earnings of foreigners which arise out of their domestic economic activities are thus excluded. It follows that where there is substantial foreign participation in the economy and a large part of the total domestic income is earned and repatriated by foreigners and foreign corporations as it is in many LDCs, GDP will be much larger than GNP and the growth of the former may not be correlated with the growth of the latter. As a result, statistics of GDP growth may give a false impression of the economic performance of a particular developing nation. Since we are more concerned with the income earned by the nationals of a country, we will tend to use GNP or national income as the more appropriate measure throughout most of the book.

If we next want to know how this national output is used, we may refer to the pattern of 'national expenditure' – i.e. how much of it is used for private consumption, government expenditure, investment in capital equipment and exports minus imports. Finally, we may want to know how this national output (or income, or expenditure) is earned, for example, by wage-earners, farmers, businessmen and other individuals who may own productive assets such as land, capital goods or financial resources (e.g. money in banks). This provides us with one measure of the distribution of personal incomes (see Chapter 9 for an explanation of the various measures of income distribution as well as data on income distribution for a wide range of

Table 2.1
Gross domestic product, national income and the principal components of national expenditure: a sample of ten selected Third World nations

Country (year) (currency units)	Gross domestic product	National income	National Expenditure – Percentage distribution of GDP: Private final consumption	Government final expenditure	Gross fixed capital formation	Net exports of goods and services
1. Brazil (1977) (1,000 million cruzeiros)	2,352·8	2,197·0	69	9	22	0
2. Egypt (1977) (million E. pounds)	7,341	7,139	66	21	24	−11
3. India (1975) (1,000 million rupees)	729·5	683·0	73	9	18	0
4. Kenya (1977) (million pounds)	1,832·7	1,762·0	59	17	21	3
5. Mexico (1976) (1,000 million pesos)	1,227·9	1,091·6	66	13	22	−1
6. Nigeria (1975) (million nairas)	15,449	n.a.	53	13	31	3
7. Pakistan (1975) (million rupees)	130·1	125·2	77	11	18	−6
8. Peru (1975) (1,000 million soles)	605·8	528·4	78	12	19	−9
9. Philippines (1977) (1,000 million pesos)	153·1	137·5	69	11	24	−4
10. Tanzania (1977) (million T. shillings)	28,270	26,973	72	14	17	−3

Source: United Nations *Statistical Yearbook 1978*, New York, 1979, Tables 185 and 186.
Note that the values shown for each country's gross domestic product and national income are *not* comparable since the figures are expressed in each country's own (different) domestic currency units. To make them comparable, all figures would have to be expressed in the same currency, e.g. dollars. In the Appendices to Chapter 5 such comparable figures are presented for all Third World nations.

Third World nations). The meaning of these various output, expenditure and income concepts will become clearer as we use them at various stages throughout the book. For the students' information, however, Table 2.1 provides some summary data on GDP, national income and the breakdown of national expenditure for ten selected Third World nations during the latter half of the 1970s.

Distribution – domestic and international

There are numerous ways of accomplishing the three basic societal tasks outlined in the introduction. These range from complete decentralisation of decision-making on the basis of the private ownership of resources (market capitalism) to total central planning and control over publicly owned resources (the 'command' socialist economy). These 'institutional' arrangements, that is the norms, rules of conduct, or established ways of doing things in a society – are known as **economic systems.** The nations of the world, including those of the Third World, reveal a great diversity of economic systems.

Given the political nature of economic systems and, more important, the power structures which pervade all societies, there is clearly a need for a fourth question: who makes the decisions about the production and distribution of national output, and for whom are these decisions made? Often the three basic tasks or decisions facing every economy referred to in the beginning of this chapter are largely determined by the answer to this question. For example, if a nation is ruled by a powerful but small elite combination of, say, urban industrialists (many of whom may be foreigners), trade unionists and large rural landowners, then the quantities and types of goods produced, the place where they are produced, the technological manner of production and the distribution of its benefits (both domestic and international) may cater for the needs and wishes of this small group to an extent that is grossly out of proportion to their numbers. Our fourth question, therefore, represents an important ethical or value issue, the answer to which may largely determine whether the benefits of development accrue to the masses or simply to a small but powerful political and economic elite.

A fifth and final question, mentioned briefly in Chapter 1, relates to the global economic system: how shall the emerging global economic scarcity of essential commodities such as world grain and fish supplies, necessary agricultural inputs such as fertilisers, and important natural resources such as petroleum, minerals and other industrial raw materials, be distributed or rationed among nations, and who will ultimately make these allocations? Many spokesmen from developing countries argue that wealthy capitalist and socialist nations will for the most part make these vital decisions of life and death, while the less developed countries are once again disregarded and even victimised. But much will depend, as we shall see in later chapters, on the relative bargaining powers of rich and poor nations. Moreover, it may also depend on the ability or inability of Third World countries to consolidate and co-ordinate their joint bargaining positions *vis-à-vis* the developed world.

Economic systems: idealised prototypes and real world structures

In the preceding section we emphasised that every society has to accomplish certain basic tasks. Each has to decide what kind and how much of economic goods and services it will produce, where, and in what manner these goods and services (the GDP) will be produced and distributed both among alternative uses (private consumption and investment or public consumption and investment) and among different individuals or groups. Different societies have different ways of accomplishing these tasks. In the most primitive subsistence societies every household or village attempts to take care of its own needs directly, probably with some internal exchange but with little or no contact with the outside world. Such a society produces its own food, clothing and shelter and distributes these primarily in accordance with social customs and tradition. Although such purely subsistence economies are rapidly disappearing, there are still many parts of the developing world where this oldest of economic organisations prevails in one form or another.

But most contemporary economies and economic systems are more complex than this. There is a greater interdependence among different regions and industries, and questions such as what, where, how and how much is to be produced are determined, either spontaneously through what is called the 'market mechanism' with little central direction and planning, or on the basis of careful planning with a greater degree of central control. As we shall shortly see, however, the distinction between market spontaneity and careful planning becomes blurred when dealing with the realities of economic activity in most contemporary economies.

To illustrate these points, let us briefly examine some alternative ways of organising economies. In doing so we shall distinguish among such often confusing and confused concepts as 'capitalism' as opposed to 'socialism', and market-oriented as opposed to centrally planned or mixed market planned economies. Our purpose here is not to compare economic systems or to ask which is 'best', but to describe the essential characteristics of different economic systems and to analyse the place of most Third World economies within this broad framework.

Economic systems are typically classified into five broad categories:

- the pure market (capitalist) economy
- the developed market (or advanced) capitalist economy
- the market socialist economy
- the command (or centrally planned) socialist economy
- the mixed market (capitalist) and planned (socialist) economy.[2]

The pure market capitalist economy

This is the Western economist's idealised prototype of an economy which never really existed except in economics textbooks. It is primarily set forth as a model of economic efficiency and as a standard by which to judge the actual performance of real world economies and economic policies. It is characterised by the **private ownership** of all productive assets (land, factories, machinery and equipment, etc.). The private owner's motivating economic objective, whether he is a small farmer or wealthy industrialist, is assumed to be the earning of as much profit (i.e. excess of total revenues over total costs) as possible from the use of his productive assets and the sale of his product in competitive markets. Thus, the four principal characteristics of market capitalism are: (1) the institution of **private ownership** backed up by legal guarantees; (2) the pervasiveness of **free enterprise and competition**; (3) the preponderance of commercial **production for sale** in these competitive markets (as opposed to subsistence production which could include private ownership); and (4) the overriding behavioural objective of **maximising profits** for producers and satisfaction for consumers.

Productive resources as well as economic goods and services are allocated and distributed among various activities and uses by what is known as the 'market mechanism' in capitalist societies. This mechanism, sometimes called the 'price system', also brings about efficient resource allocation and economic growth. It has three basic characteristics:

1. Decisions as to what, where, how and how much are produced and consumed are taken by individual economic units: the household, the business firm or the commercial farm.
2. Those individual units base their decisions on alternatives available to them as reflected by the market prices of goods, services and resources which they confront but cannot influence. (We use the word 'price' here in its broadest sense, to include not only the price of goods such as rice and radios or services such as haircuts and railway tickets but also to the 'price' of labour, capital, land and other productive resources; in Chapter 3 we discuss the role and meaning of these prices in much greater detail.)
3. Prices are determined by the forces of demand and supply for all individual goods, services and productive resources and adjust to changes in that demand and/or supply.

Prices, therefore, serve two principal functions: (1) they supply information to individual economic units on which they base their decisions; (2) they are the sources, direct and indirect, of individual and corporate incomes.

One final point about the pure capitalist model is its emphasis on 'perfect' competition and the 'invisible hand'. It is assumed that all production and consumption takes place under perfectly competitive conditions in the sense that each of thousands of individual economic units (producers

[2] For a more comprehensive review of alternative economic systems but without explicit reference to Third World countries, the interested student is referred to Gregory Grossman, *Economic Systems*, second edition. Prentice-Hall, New Jersey, 1974.

and consumers) is so small in relation to the market as a whole that it cannot influence the price it pays for goods and factors or the price it receives for the sale of its goods or productive resources. Every economic unit is also assumed to possess 'perfect knowledge' of all alternatives (prices) and to be guided by the desire to maximise profits for producers and satisfaction for consumers. Furthermore, it is argued that in a world of perfect competition, if each individual economic unit pursues its own self-interest its actions will be guided as if by an invisible hand[3] to promote the overall welfare of society as a whole. In short, **the pursuit of self-interest in the capitalist system is supposed to promote the national interest.**

Since the concept of the market mechanism and the perfectly competitive model looms so large in the thinking of most Western economists and has, as a result, been applied, often uncritically and unwisely, to analyse economic phenomena in developing countries, we return to look more carefully at this notion primarily in Chapter 3 but also at various other points throughout the remainder of this book.

The developed market (or advanced) capitalist economy

Whereas the idealised prototype of a 'pure' capitalist, market economy rests on the basic assumption of total private ownership and use of resources and decision-making by individual private economic units, in reality most of the so-called First World or developed, capitalist, market economies (those of North America, Western Europe, Israel, South Africa, Australia, New Zealand and Japan) are mixtures of both private and public resource ownership and private and public economic decision-making. Over the years their governments have assumed increasing control over aggregate economic activity, not only through the use of so-called monetary and fiscal policies, but also through their growing direct participation in economic activities in the form of nationalised industries, public enterprises, and public investment programmes. Moreover, as these capitalist societies have deviated more and more from the idealised world of competition and smallness of economic units, their governments have increasingly been called on to moderate and regulate the activities and the undesirable consequences of the growth of giant, monopolist corporations.

Today, in most market-oriented developed nations, governments perform a wide range of direct and indirect economic roles. They are active in the areas of economic planning, regulating private corporate activities, taxing private individuals and corporations, allocating public expenditure, engaging in direct investments, managing and running public corporations, conducting and regulating foreign trade, manipulating and controlling wages, interest rates and other prices, redistributing incomes and a host of other diverse activities. Thus, although the institution of private property and the notion of individual economic freedom still permeate the rhetoric of advanced capitalist societies, the distinction between public and private economic activities, between market determined and non-market determined wages and prices, and between private interest and public interest has become increasingly blurred. In many respects the 'invisible hand' of the market mechanism has been replaced by the 'guiding hand' of the central government as the principal economic force in these capitalist societies.

The 'market' socialist economy

For many years, economists found themselves with conflicting opinions about the social implications of the pure market economy model. On the one hand, the 'automatic' adjustment mechanism of competitive prices (whereby prices serve to allocate resources, goods and services, and automatically rise or fall to balance supply and demand – see Chapter 3) with its efficiency-promoting signals and incentives for individual economic units was thought to be an important and useful device for the functioning of an economy. On the other hand, private ownership of resources, and especially the tendency of such ownership to become increasingly concentrated in a few hands, with the result that market forces could lead to highly unequal distributions of income and power, led a number of economists to advocate the abolition of private (non-labour) resource ownership while retaining the

[3] The concept of the 'invisible hand' was first expounded by Adam Smith, often referred to as the founder or father of economics, in his famous treatise, *The Wealth of Nations*, published in 1776.

essential features of the market mechanism. The resulting system has come to be known as 'market socialism' or 'decentralised socialism' in the sense that the socialist ideal of public resource ownership is combined with the capitalist ideals of the decentralised price-oriented and profit-motivated decisions of individual economic units.

In short, market socialist economic systems try to get the best of both worlds: the price mechanism and economic efficiency of market capitalism and the egalitarianism of socialist production and distribution. Yugoslavia probably provides the closest real world example of a market-oriented socialist economy, though even here central government planning assumes a much more important and directly controlling role than in any capitalist market economy.

The 'command' (or centrally planned) socialist economy

At the opposite end of the spectrum to the market capitalist economy is the command socialist economy. This is most widely associated with the economy of the Soviet Union and other centrally planned economies of Eastern Europe including Albania, Bulgaria, Czechoslovakia, the German Democratic Republic, Hungary, Poland and Romania. The command socialist (Second World) economy is based not only on the public ownership of all productive resources but also on the complete replacement of the market price mechanism by the central planning of all economic activities. The whole Soviet economy, for example, can be depicted as a bureaucratic pyramid in which, with the exception of the household sector, all significant production and distribution decisions are made by a central planning commission at the top. The bottom of the pyramid consists of hundreds of thousands of individually operated but publicly owned firms and farms whose main task is to carry out the directives and fulfil the production targets set from above.

Since command economies must still operate with money, prices are necessary to provide material incentives and to account for the flow of goods and resources. However, instead of being determined by market forces of demand and supply, these prices are centrally determined. Comprehensive national and regional plans are drawn up every year, setting production targets and resource requirements for practically every sector of the economy. Resource needs and availabilities are brought into balance by centrally determined allocations, as opposed to the price signals of the market system.

The unique characteristic of the command socialist economy and the one which has spurred the most interest in variants of this form of economic organisation among Third World nations is its presumed ability to mobilise scarce economic resources (especially capital) effectively and to channel them into their most productive long-term uses. The spectacular industrial growth of the Soviet Union during the first few decades of command rule is often referred to as an example of the effectiveness of central planning. In Chapter 23 we examine the pros and cons of this proposition as well as the broader question of economic planning and its role and limitations in promoting Third World development in the light of recent experience.

Perhaps a more relevant example of the command socialist economy for developing nations is the People's Republic of China. China has abolished most forms of private ownership and relies heavily on the efficacy of comprehensive planning in place of the market mechanism. Four kinds of ownership remain in China's socialist system: private, communal, co-operative and state. **Private** ownership is very limited (though it is rapidly reappearing in various forms in the 1980s) and consists mainly of hand tools, rural houses, some urban housing and a small but increasing number of privately owned plots of farm land. **Communal** ownership encompasses most rural land, the means of agricultural production and all commune-owned industries. **Co-operative** ownership covers non-rural economic activities, mostly trade and processing, with all employees sharing the ownership of these activities. Finally, **state** ownership extends to all land and means of production not owned by the commune or the co-operatives.

The major difference between Chinese planning procedure and that of the the Soviet Union is that the former relies to a much greater extent on planning from the bottom up: that is to say, Chinese planning is less centralised and occurs mostly at the level of the People's Communes in accordance with their specific production and consumption needs. We discuss the Chinese socialist system further in the context of the problem of rural development in Chapter 16.

The mixed market (capitalist) and planned (socialist) economy

Most developing countries, with the exception of Cuba, China, North Korea and a few others, can be classified basically as mixed capitalist–socialist systems. Varying degrees of private ownership of resources exist side by side with substantial public ownership and participation in economic activities. Resources are often jointly owned by public and private interests. Some countries (e.g. Brazil, Mexico, Lebanon, Kenya, Taiwan and South Korea) have substantial private sectors while others (e.g. Peru, Ecuador, Zaïre, Tanzania, Uganda, India, Algeria, Libya, Egypt and Bangladesh) have large and influential public sectors. On the whole the state plays a much more decisive role in all Third World economies than in the advanced capitalist societies.

Another major element of the LDC mixed economy is the juxtaposition of resource and product allocation by market and publicly determined prices and the central planning and guidance of overall economic activity by the state. Thus, most LDCs have tried to borrow some features of both capitalist 'market' and socialist 'planned' economies. Often, however, the results have been less than spectacular. As one influential Asian economist has observed.

> In most cases, such a choice [of the 'mixed' economy] has combined the worst, not the best, features of capitalism and socialism. It has often prevented the developing countries from adopting honest-to-goodness economic incentives and using the free functioning of the price system to achieve efficiency in the capitalist framework, if not equity. In reality, there have been too many inefficient administrative controls and price distortions. At the same time, the choice of the mixed economy has prevented these societies from pursuing their goals in a truly socialistic framework, since mixed economy institutions have often been more capitalist than not. The end result, therefore, has been that they have fallen between two stools, combining weak economic incentives with bureaucratic socialism.[4]

Other observers have reached different conclusions and the verdict on the performance of these mixed systems is far from clear. We return to this central issue in Part Three, in the context of our discussion of critical development problems.

Some conclusions about economic systems

We conclude this brief discussion by stressing once again the amorphous nature of the boundary lines separating so-called capitalist, socialist and mixed systems. Planning, whether centralised or decentralised, plays an important though different role in almost every nation of the world. The extent of public versus private ownership of resources is an important distinguishing characteristic of different countries and different systems. But how those resources are used and how their benefits are distributed is sometimes a more important economic and social issue than who owns them. Yet as we shall see in Chapters 9 and 10, the relationship between highly unequal resource ownership and highly unequal income distribution is very close in most non-socialist economies. While market-determined prices may not play a crucial role in advanced socialist economies, incentives in one form or another are always in evidence. In advanced capitalist economies like those in Western Europe and the United States, market prices and general economic activities are often being modified or controlled by planned government intervention at the same time that centrally planned economies like that of the Soviet Union are moving inexorably towards the adoption of some forms of market pricing and decentralised, individual decision-making. Thus, while labels such as capitalist, socialist and communist still pervade public rhetoric and academic writings, it is more important for students to judge a particular economy and its economic system by the manner in which it is actually organised and the way in which diverse economic decisions are reached, than by reference to outmoded stereotyped labels. Ideologies do play an important role in economic activities, but the gap between ideological pronouncements and actual practice is often substantial. We may conclude by citing an anonymous yet famous epigram once pinned on a bulletin board of Warsaw University in Poland. It said: 'Capitalism is the exploitation of man by man; communism is the reverse.'

[4] Mahbub ul Haq, 'Crisis in Development Strategies', *World Development*, i, 7, July 1973, p. 31.

The diverse structure of Third World economies

It is hazardous to try to generalise too much about the 143 developing nations that constitute the 'less developed countries' of the Third World. While almost all are poor in money terms they are diverse in culture, economic conditions and social and political structures. Thus, for example, low income countries include India with over 680 million people and 22 states as well as Gambia with less than 600 000 people, fewer than a single borough of New York City. Large size entails complex problems of national cohesion and administration while offering the benefits of relatively large markets, a wide range of resources, and the potential for self-sufficiency and economic diversity. On the other hand, most small countries present quite different problems, including limited markets, shortages of skills, scarce physical resources, weak bargaining power and little prospect of significant economic self-reliance.

Analysts, therefore, sometimes prefer to distinguish among **three** major groups of countries within the Third World: the 31 poorest countries designated by the United Nations as 'least developed',[5] the 99 non-oil exporting 'developing' nations and the 13 petroleum-rich OPEC countries whose national incomes increased dramatically during the 1970s. Appendix II to Chapter 5 provides a complete listing of all 143 Third World countries classified by income groups as well as the 29 developed nations with important economic and social data for each. Despite their obvious diversity, however, most Third World nations share a set of common and well defined goals. These include among others the reduction of poverty, inequality and unemployment, the provision of minimum standards of education, health, housing and food to every citizen, the broadening of economic and social opportunities and the forging of a cohesive nation-state.

Related to these economic, social and political goals are the common problems shared in varying degrees by most developing countries – e.g. widespread and chronic absolute poverty, high and rising levels of unemployment and underemployment, wide and growing disparities in the distribution of income, low and stagnating levels of agricultural productivity, sizable and growing imbalances between urban and rural levels of living and economic opportunities, antiquated and inappropriate educational and health systems, and substantial and increasing dependence on foreign and often inappropriate technologies, institutions and value systems. It is therefore useful to talk about critical and similar development problems faced by the Third World as a whole and to deal with these common problems both analytically and in terms of policy alternatives, despite obvious structural diversities. This will be our task in Parts Two and Three.

For the present, however, we attempt to identify some basic criteria for distinguishing the most important structural **differences** among developing nations. Among many others these include:

- the size of the country (geographic, population and income);
- its historical evolution;
- its physical and human resource endowments;
- the relative importance of its public and private sectors;
- the nature of its industrial structure;
- its degree of dependence on external economic and political forces;
- the distribution of power and the institutional and political structure within the nation.

Let us briefly consider each, with specific reference to similarities and differences in Africa, Asia, the Middle East and Latin America.

Size and income levels

Obviously, the sheer physical size of a country, its population and its level of national income per head are important determinants of its economic potential and a major factor differentiating one Third World nation from another. Of the 143 developing countries, which are full members of the United Nations, 72 have less than 15 million people and 51 less than 5 million. Large and populous nations like Brazil, India, Egypt and Nigeria, exist side by side with small countries like Paraguay, Nepal and Jordan. Large size usually presents advantages of diverse resource endowment, large potential

[5] These countries are sometimes even referred to as the 'Fourth World' to underline their situation as 'the poorest of the poor' Third World countries and their special needs for international assistance. For a description and analysis, see H. C. Low and J. W. Howe, 'Focus on the Fourth World', in *Agenda for Action 1975*, published for the Overseas Development Council by Praeger, New York, 1975, pp. 35–54.

markets and less dependence on foreign sources of materials and products. But it also creates problems of administrative control, national cohesion and regional imbalance. As we shall see in Chapters 5 and 9, there does not appear to be any necessary or well defined relationship between a country's size, its level of national income per head and the degree of equality or inequality in its distribution of that income. Even excluding the wealthy OPEC oil states, India, with a population of over 680 million, had an annual income level of less than $240 a head in 1980, while nearby Singapore with less than 2.5 million people had an annual GNP of over $4 480 a head.

Historical background

Most African and Asian nations were at one time or another colonies of Western European countries – primarily Britain and France but also Belgium, the Netherlands, Germany, Portugal and Spain. Their economic structures, as well as their educational and social institutions have typically been modelled upon those of their former colonial rulers. Countries such as those in Africa which only recently gained their independence are therefore likely to be more concerned with consolidating and evolving their own national economic and political structures than simply with promoting rapid economic development, and their policies (for example, the rapid Africanisation of former colonial-held civil service jobs) may reflect a greater interest with political issues.

In Latin America and throughout most of the Arab Middle East a longer history of political independence plus a common heritage has meant that in spite of geographical and demographic diversity, the countries possess relatively similar economic, social and cultural institutions and face similar problems. In Asia, different colonial heritages and the diverse cultural traditions of the indigenous peoples have combined to create quite different institutional and social patterns in countries such as India (British) the Philippines (Spanish and American), Laos (French) and Indonesia (Dutch).

Physical and human resource endowments

A country's potential for economic growth is greatly influenced by its **physical** resource endowment (its land, minerals and other raw materials) and by its endowment of **human** resources (i.e. both numbers of people and their level of skills). The extreme case of the blessings of favourable physical resource endowments is, of course, the Arab Persian Gulf oil states. At the other extreme are countries like Togo, Laos, Haiti and Bangladesh, where endowments of raw materials and minerals as well as fertile land are relatively minimal.

In the realm of human resource endowments, not only are sheer numbers of people and their skill levels important but so also are their cultural outlooks, attitudes towards work and desire for self-improvement. Moreover, the level of administrative skills will often determine the ability of the public sector to alter the structure of production and the time in which such structural alteration can occur. Here one gets involved with the whole complex of interrelationships between culture, tradition, religion and ethnic or tribal fragmentation or cohesion. Thus the nature and character of a country's human resources are important determinants of its economic structure (see Chapters 17 and 18) and these clearly differ from one region to the next.

Relative importance of public and private sectors

We mentioned above that most developing countries have mixed economic systems, part private and usually a larger part public. The division between the two and their relative importance is mostly a function of historical and political circumstances. Thus, on the whole, Latin American nations have larger private sectors than do Asian and especially African nations. The degree of foreign ownership in the private sector is another important variable to consider when differentiating among LDCs. A large foreign-owned private sector usually creates economic and political opportunities as well as problems not found in countries where foreign investors are less prevalent. Often countries like those in Africa with severe shortages of skilled human resources tend to put greater emphasis on public sector activities on the assumption that their limited skilled manpower can be best used by co-ordinating rather than fragmenting economic activities.

Economic policies, for example those to promote more employment, will naturally be different for countries with large public sectors in comparison with those with sizable private sectors. In the former, direct government investment projects and large rural works programmes might be more desirable, while in the latter, public policies to influence private businessmen to employ more workers through special tax allowances might have a greater impact. Thus, although the problem (widespread unemployment) may be similar, the solution is likely to differ in countries with significant differences in the relative importance of their public and private sectors.

Industrial structure

The vast majority of Third World countries are agrarian societies in economic, social and cultural outlook. Agriculture, both subsistence and commercial, forms the principal economic activity in terms of the occupational distribution of the labour force, if not in terms of proportionate contributions to the gross national product. As we shall see in Chapter 15, farming is not only an occupation: it is a way of life for most people in Asia, Africa and Latin America. Nevertheless, the structure of agrarian systems and patterns of land ownership shows great differences between, say, Latin America and Africa, with Asian agrarian systems somewhat closer to those of Latin America in terms of patterns of land ownership. Nevertheless, there are substantial cultural differences which modify these similarities between Latin America and Asia.

It is in the relative importance of the manufacturing and service sectors that we find the widest variation among developing nations. Most Latin American countries, having a longer history of independence and, in general, higher levels of national income than African or Asian nations, possess more advanced industrial sectors. But in the 1960s and 1970s such countries as Taiwan, South Korea, Hong Kong, Brazil and Singapore greatly accelerated the growth of their manufacturing outputs and are rapidly becoming industrialised states. In terms of size India has one of the largest manufacturing sectors in the Third World, but this is nevertheless small in relation to its enormous rural population.

Table 2.2 provides information on the percentage distribution of labour force and GDP between agriculture and manufacturing in seventeen developing countries as well as in the US and UK. The contrast between the industrial structures of these countries is striking, especially in terms of the relative importance of agriculture.

In spite of common problems, therefore, Third World development strategies may vary from one country to the next depending on the nature, structure and degree of interdependence among its primary (agriculture, forestry and fishing), secondary (mostly manufacturing) and tertiary (commerce, transport and services) industrial sectors.

External dependence: economic, political and cultural

Related mostly to a country's size, resource endowment and political history will be its degree of dependence on foreign economic, social and political forces. For most Third World countries, this dependence is substantial. In some cases it touches on almost every facet of life. Most small nations are very dependent on the foreign trade that they conduct primarily with all the developed countries (see Chapter 19). Almost all are dependent on the importation of foreign and often inappropriate technologies of production. This fact alone exerts an extraordinary influence on the character of the growth process in these dependent nations.

But even beyond the strictly economic manifestations of dependence in the form of the international transfer of goods and technologies, is the international transmission of institutions (most notably systems of education and health), values, patterns of consumption, and attitudes towards life, work and self. Later chapters show that this transmission phenomenon brings very mixed blessings to most LDCs, especially to those with the greatest potential for self-reliance. A country's ability to chart its own economic and social destiny will depend to a great extent on its degree of dependence on these and other external forces.

Political structure, power and interest groups

In the final analysis, it is often not the correctness of economic policies alone that determines the outcome of national approaches to critical development problems. The political structure and the vested interests and allegiances of ruling elites (large landowners, urban industrialists, foreign manufacturers, bankers, trade unionists, etc.) will typically determine what strategies are possible and where the main blocks to effective economic and social change may lie.

The constellation of interests and power among different segments of the poulations of most developing countries will be the result of their economic, social and political histories and is likely to differ widely from one country to the next. Nevertheless, whatever the specific distribution of power among, say, the large landowners of Latin America, the politicians and high level civil servants in Africa, the oil sheikhs and financial moguls of the Middle East, or the landlords, moneylenders or wealthy industrialists of Asia, most developing countries are ruled directly or indirectly by small and powerful elites to a greater extent than even the developed nations.

Effective social and economic change, therefore, requires either that the support of elite groups be enlisted through persuasion or coercion, or that they be pushed aside by more powerful forces. Either way – and this point will be repeated often throughout this book – **economic and social development will be impossible without corresponding changes in the social, political and economic institutions of a nation** (e.g. land tenure system, educational structure, labour market functions, the distribution and control of physical and financial assets, laws of taxation and inheritance, provision of credit, etc.).

Economies as social systems: the need to go beyond simple economics

Up to this point we have confined our introductory

Table 2.2
Industrial structure in seventeen developing countries in comparison to USA and UK: 1979

	Percent of labour force in		Percent of gross domestic product	
	Agriculture	Manufacturing	Agriculture	Manufacturing
Africa				
Tanzania	83	6	54	9
Kenya	78	10	34	13
Nigeria	55	18	22	5
Uganda	83	6	55	6
Zaire	75	13	33	4
Asia				
Bangladesh	74	11	56	8
India	71	11	38	18
Indonesia	59	12	30	9
Philippines	47	17	24	24
Sri Lanka	54	14	27	21
South Korea	36	30	20	27
Latin America				
Mexico	37	26	10	29
Guatemala	56	21	—	—
Colombia	27	21	29	21
Brazil	40	22	11	28
Peru	38	20	10	26
Venezuela	19	27	6	16
USA	2	32	3	24
UK	2	42	2	25

Source: The International Bank for Reconstruction and Development, *World Development Report, 1981*, Oxford University Press, New York, 1981. Annex tables 3 and 19.

comments about economics largely to questions of output and incomes, prices and resource allocation, conditions of production, levels of living and the alternative economic systems in which these principal economic variables are determined. But, as we have just seen, an economic system needs to be viewed more broadly within the context of the overall social system of a country; in other words the interdependent relationships between so-called economic and non-economic factors. The latter include attitudes towards life, work and authority, public and private bureaucratic and administrative structures, patterns of kinship and religion, cultural traditions, systems of land tenure, the authority and integrity of government agencies, the degree of popular participation in development decisions and activities and the flexibility or rigidity of economic and social stratifications.

Throughout the course of this book we shall discover that the achievement of 'development' and the solution to development problems is a much more complicated task than some economists would lead us to believe. Increasing national production, raising levels of living and promoting widespread employment opportunities are as much a function of the values, incentives, attitudes and beliefs, and the institutional and power arrangements of a society, as they are the direct outcomes of the manipulation of strategic economic variables such as savings, investment and exports. Just as economists sometimes make the mistake of confusing their 'science' with universal practices, so they also often mistakenly dismiss these non-economic variables as non-quantifiable and, therefore, of dubious importance.

But, as we shall see in Parts Two, Three and Four, many of the failures of development policies in Third World nations arise precisely because these non-economic factors, for instance, the importance of land reform for rural development or the role of trade unions in influencing levels of urban unemployment, were intentionally or unintentionally excluded from the analysis. While the main focus of this book is on the nature of economics and its usefulness in understanding problems of development, we shall continually be reminding students of the manner in which values, attitudes and institutions play a crucial role in the development process.

Third World social systems as part of an interdependent international social system

We can extend the above analysis even further. Just as the economic life of developing nations is inevitably linked with its social, political and cultural life, so these domestic social systems are interconnected with the international social system: the organisation and rules of conduct of the global economy. An important aspect of this linkage is the phenomenon of the **dominance** and **dependence** that exists between many developed and less developed nations. Dominance and dependence relationships can indeed be pervasive. They are found in a wide range of international economic areas including foreign aid, private foreign investment, and the transfer of technology, where LDCs as a group often appear to be at the mercy of the global power of rich nations and their multinational corporations. But, as we have seen, dominance and dependence relationships may also exist in the political, intellectual and cultural sphere. Here many of the values, ideas, symbols, laws, attitudes and institutions of rich nations permeate, influence and shape the social systems of diverse Third World nations.

Conversely, there are many areas where the developed nations are beginning to recognise their own ultimate economic dependence on the less developed countries. This applies increasingly in respect of access to natural resources and raw materials, especially when dominant LDC suppliers are able to co-ordinate their activities. The prime example is the enormous destabilising impact which the quadrupling of international oil prices had first in 1974 and then again in 1979 and 1980 on the economies of all oil-importing nations (see Chapter 25).

But oil is not the only resource where formerly dependent economies can begin to exert influence on the rich, industrial nations. A substantial amount of the world's raw material resources are located in Third World countries. In many cases, however, their control and management may still rest primarily with powerful multinational corporations from developed countries. For example, Zambia, Chile, Peru and a few other Third World countries supply almost 80 per cent of the world's copper. Malaysia and Sri Lanka supply over 50 per cent of the world's natural rubber. Bolivia, Malaysia and Thailand account for 85 per cent of world trade in tin. Third World countries, including Jamaica, Surinam and Guyana, supply almost 90 per cent of developed nations' imports of bauxite. Other vital minerals of which Third World nations are major suppliers include manganese (Gabon, Brazil and Zaire), iron ore (Venezuela and India) and lead (Peru, Mexico and others).

In the area of commodity exports Brazil, Colombia, the Ivory Coast, Uganda and El Salvador produce almost the entire world supply of coffee, while Brazil and Ghana produce most of the world's cocoa. India, Sri Lanka, East Africa and China produce most of the world's tea while India, Pakistan, Bangladesh, Thailand and Nepal produce over two-thirds of the world's jute. As mentioned earlier, the Persian Gulf oil states alone control almost 60 per cent of the world's known petroleum reserves although they constitute less than one per cent of its population.

These statistics underline the now widely recognised fact that the economies of the world today are becoming highly economically interdependent and will grow even more so in the future. Nevertheless, Third World nations have always been and on balance remain greatly dependent on dominant rich country economic and political policies. It is impossible to talk about their development without dealing with this dependence phenomenon, even though, in recognition of this fact, many LDCs are attempting, either singularly or collectively, to pursue more self-reliant development strategies, while pressing demands for the creation of a new international economic order (see Chapter 25). As international political disputes moved away from the cold war politics of the 1950s and 1960s and began to focus more in the 1970s on the growing competition for increasingly scarce natural resources, many of which are located in Third World nations, the possibility of north–south (i.e. rich country–poor country) economic confrontation took on added importance. In the 1980s this international competition for dwindling natural resources is likely to assume even greater significance than it did in the 1970s. Energy and raw material scarcity is today a critical issue of worldwide significance. We discuss it further in Chapter 25.

Any study of Third World economics, therefore, which does not recognise and deal with the dual phenomena of persistent LDC economic, technological and institutional dependence on rich nations and the growing rich country dependence on Third World resource policies would be overlooking one of the most important elements in the long-run success or failure of diverse development efforts. Consequently, in the chapters that follow, and especially in Parts Two and Three, we shall constantly try to frame our discussions of critical development problems such as poverty, inequality and unemployment not only within the broad context of the economic and institutional characteristics of social systems in individual developing countries, but also within an international framework that views developing nations as part of an increasingly interdependent, but still highly unequal, global social system. We shall discover that many common forces are at work in this system and many curious economic paradoxes become clarified when problems of underdevelopment are viewed, as they should be, in both a domestic and a global context.

Summary

The central economic problems of all societies include traditional questions such as what, where, how, how much and for whom goods and services should be produced. But we need to broaden this set of questions to determine which groups actually make or influence economic decisions and for whose ultimate benefit these decisions are made. Finally, at the international level, the question of which nations and which powerful groups within particular nations exert the most influence with regard to the use and deployment of scarce global food and mineral resource supplies must also be considered.

After reviewing various definitions of national output and discussing the major types of economic systems and the diverse structural characteristics of Third World nations, we pointed out that any realistic analysis of development problems necessitates the supplementation of strictly economic variables like income, investment and employment with equally relevant non-economic factors. These may include the nature of land tenure arrangements, the influence of social and class stratifications, the structure of credit, education and health systems, the organisation and motivation of government bureaucracies, the machinery of public administration, the nature of popular attitudes towards work, leisure and self-improvement, and the values, roles and attitudes of political and economic elites. Economic development strategies which seek to raise agricultural output, create employment and eradicate poverty have often failed in the past because economists and other policy advisers neglected to view the economy as an interdependent social system where economic and non-economic variables are continually interacting, sometimes resulting in self-reinforcement and at other times in contradictory ways.

Finally, we concluded this second chapter by stressing the importance of viewing the internal social systems of less developed nations within the context of the international social system of all nations, rich and poor. Here, the phenomena of small but different power groups, mostly from rich nations, influencing global strategies and the corresponding vulnerability of Third World nations caught in a dominance and dependence situation *vis-à-vis* the industrial nations of both East and West is often emphasised. An analogous vulnerability and dominance/dependence relationship often also exists between the great masses of people and the relatively small but powerful elites in the underdeveloped nations themselves.

Nevertheless, the evolution of the world economy in the 1970s and 1980s and the emergence of global raw material and natural resource scarcities revealed, as no other event had previously, the increasing dependence of rich nations on poor ones and thus the growing *interdependence* of all nations and peoples within the international social system. What happens to life in Caracas, Cairo and Calcutta will in one way or another, have important implications for life in New York, London and Moscow. It was once said that 'when the United States sneezes, the world catches a cold'. A more fitting expression for the 1980s would perhaps be that 'the world is like the human body: if one part aches, the rest will feel it; if many parts hurt, the whole will suffer'.

Third World nations constitute these many parts of the global organism. The nature and character of their future development, therefore, should be a major concern of *all* nations, irrespective of their political, ideological or economic orientations. In the latter part of the twentieth century and in the twenty-first, there can no longer be 'two futures' – one for the few rich and the other for the many poor. In the words of a poet, 'there can be only one future, or none at all'.

Concepts for review

economic system
public sector
private sector
First World
Second World
Third World
gross domestic product (GDP)
gross national product (GNP)
national expenditure
consumption
capital stock
primary, secondary and tertiary industrial sectors
national income
social system
non-economic variables
interdependence
economic and social institutions
necessity goods
luxury goods
investment
price system and role of prices
market mechanism
pure market capitalism
advanced capitalism
perfect competition
invisible hand
market socialism
mixed systems
command socialism

Questions for discussion

1. Do you think that the concept of the 'Third World' is useful? Why or why not?
2. What are the central economic problems of all societies? Which do you think are the most important?
3. What is an economic system? Explain the essential differences between capitalist, socialist and mixed economies. Are these useful distinctions?
4. How would you describe the economic system of your own country? How did it evolve – by choice, accident or imposed from outside? Explain.
5. Explain the many ways in which developing countries may differ in their economic, social and political structures. They are linked together by a range of common problems. What are these common problems and how important do you think each is in your own country? Which do you think are the most important? Why?
6. Why is it important to view economies as 'social

systems' and to go beyond simple economic factors?

7. What do you think is meant by the expression 'interdependent international social systems'? In what ways are national economies becoming more interdependent as we approach the end of the twentieth century?

Further reading

On the central economic problems and economic systems, see GREGORY GROSSMAN, *Economic Systems*, Prentice-Hall, New Jersey, second edition, 1974; and GEORGE DALTON, *Economic Systems and Society: capitalism, communism and the Third World*, Penguin, 1974. On the diverse structure of Third World economies, see LESTER PEARSON (chairman), *Partners in Development: Report of the Commission on International Development*, Praeger, New York, 1969, Annex I.

Chapter 3 Important concepts and principles – I

> Teach a parrot to say 'supply and demand' and you will have a political economist.
> *Thomas Carlisle*

Introduction

To analyse the diversity of critical development problems, some basic understanding of general economic concepts and principles is needed. Unfortunately many of the fundamental economic concepts and principles found in 'Western' introductory textbooks, being derived from and relating to the special economic, institutional and structural characteristics of advanced capitalist nations, are neither relevant nor appropriate to the understanding or solving of the economic problems of Third World countries. Our purpose in this and the next chapter, therefore, is to distil from traditional economic theory those concepts and principles with particular relevance for an understanding of development problems. But first, let us review economic theory and briefly sketch the reasons why many of the so-called Western economic models and theories are inappropriate for the study of Third World development.

The nature of economic theory

Economic theory represents the way in which economists organise the interdependent facts of economic life, including production, consumption, incomes, prices, employment, exports, imports, savings and investment. While 'economics' as a discipline is concerned with the way in which scarce human and material resources are most efficiently employed for the social good, 'economic theory' consists of a generally accepted body of concepts and principles about economic behaviour which, if properly formulated and correctly arranged, can help us to understand and explain the workings of an economic system. The 'method' or thought process of economic theory is largely deductive: that is, on the basis of a known or assumed set of facts about the essential characteristics of an economy, an hypothesis is established and a model is set up. The model may be very simple or quite complex, but the essence of all models is that they are simplifications of reality. Conclusions about the functioning of an economy or an economic system can be logically deduced either from the characteristics of the model or from experiments within the model. To be worthwhile, however, models need to be constantly tested against reality through the use of statistics and statistical methods.

The first essential of any economic theory or model is that it should be capable of explaining the essential features of the economic process as it exists in the day-to-day realities of nations and regions. Any theory or set of principles must of necessity be based on simplifying assumptions and abstractions, but the type of assumptions or abstractions chosen cannot be decided in a vacuum. They must fit the realities and be appropriate to the characteristic features of economic life as recorded by observation and experience. Moreover, theories and principles which might be valid and appropriate for one type of economy in a given region or at a given moment may not be valid for other societies at the same or at different times. This brings us to an important point about economics and development, one which provides a principal rationale for the structure and design of this textbook.

The limited relevance of traditional 'Western' economic theory

Most development economists agree that what has come to be known as 'traditional' or 'Western' economic theory is of very limited relevance for understanding the characteristic features of the economies and economic processes in Third World nations. Perhaps the eminent Nobel-prize-winning Swedish economist Gunnar Myrdal best stated the case against the uncritical use of traditional economic concepts and theories in poor nations when he observed that:

> Economic theorists, more than any other social scientists, have long been disposed to arrive at general propositions and then postulate them as valid for every time, place and culture. There is a tendency in contemporary economic theory to follow this path to the extreme … when theories and concepts designed to fit the special conditions of the Western world – and thus containing the implicit assumptions about social reality by which this fitting was accomplished – are used in the study of underdeveloped countries, where they do *not* fit, the consequences are serious.[1]

Without going into specific detail at this stage of the extensive criticisms of Western economic models as guides to understanding and/or ameliorating conditions of underdevelopment in poor nations, a few general comments are needed.[2]

Economics, as taught in the developed nations and as generally transferred to and taught in the developing nations through the importation of Western textbooks, has traditionally been divided into three broad categories: **micro-economics, macro-economics** and **international economics.** Micro-economics focuses on the behaviour and activities of individual economic units, primarily producers and consumers. Macro-economics looks at the economy as a whole in terms of aggregate or 'macro' economic variables, such as consumption, savings, investment, the money supply, gross domestic product, employment and the overall price level. International economics examines the trading and monetary relationships between nation-states both as producers of exports and consumers of imports and thus represents a mixture of elements of micro- and macro-economic theory.

The conceptual framework and behavioural assumptions which unite each of these broad areas of traditional economic analysis are the threefold 'ideals' of consumer sovereignty, perfect competition and profit maximisation. Moreover, the institutional setting is always that of the 'pure' or idealised market economy. **Traditional economics is the economics of 'equilibrium' and stability in a developing world of disequilibrium and instability.** It is the economics of 'marginal' choice, of 'a little more or a little less' in a developing world where major, fundamental choices must be made to secure 'a lot more' in as short a time period as possible.

In traditional micro-economic theory, the basic questions of what and how much to produce are assumed to be determined by the aggregate preferences of all consumers as revealed by their market demand curves for different goods and services. Producers are assumed simply to respond to these 'sovereign' consumer preferences and, motivated by the desire to maximise profits, they will compete with each other **on equal terms** in the purchase of resources and the sale of their products. The economist's notion of perfect competition is central to this whole process. It assumes that all prices, wages, interest rates, etc., are determined by the free play of the forces of supply and demand (see p. 43 below) and that each of the millions of consumers and thousands of producers is so small in relation to total demand and supply that they cannot individually influence to any extent the market prices and quantities of goods, services and resources bought and sold. The ultimate rationale for the efficacy of this theory or model of economic activity is Adam Smith's famous notion of the invisible hand of capitalism. This postulates, as we learned in Chapter 2, that if each individual consumer, producer and supplier of resources pursues his or her own self-interest, they will, 'as if by an invisible hand', be promoting the overall interests of society as a whole.

Unfortunately, the facts of economic life in *both* the developed and the less developed nations of the

[1] Gunnar Myrdal, *Asian Drama: an inquiry into the poverty of nations*, Pantheon, New York, 1968, pp. 16–17.

[2] Do not be concerned if some of the terms and concepts discussed in the following few pages seem confusing. Their meaning will become clearer in the remainder of this and the next chapter.

world are such as to render much of traditional micro-economic theory of negligible importance either for analysis or policy. Consumers as a whole are rarely sovereign about anything, let alone with regard to questions of what goods and services are to be produced, in what quantities and for whom. Producers, whether private or public, have great power in determining market prices and quantities sold. The ideal of competition is typically just that: an 'ideal' with little relation to reality. Finally, the so-called invisible hand often acts not to promote the general welfare of all but to lift up those who are already well-off while pushing down that vast majority of the population which is striving to free itself from poverty, malnutrition and illiteracy.

Briefly, traditional macro-economic theory (sometimes known also as 'Keynesian theory' after the famous British economist, John Maynard Keynes, who was its principal architect in the 1930s) also views the economy and its institutions through competitive supply-and-demand spectacles. Here, however, one is dealing with the determinants of aggregate supply and demand for national output. The greater the level of aggregate demand, the higher the level of equilibrium employment and prices in the economy. Policy prescriptions for government intervention in the economy flow naturally from this theory. For example, in the Keynesian model unemployment is due to a deficiency of the aggregate demand for the potential output of a nation (goods and services which the nation as a whole could produce at maximum capacity). By increasing aggregate demand, therefore (e.g. by expanding government expenditures and/or lowering taxes so that people will have more money to spend) governments can accelerate economic activity and consequently induce higher levels of employment. Conversely, when aggregate demand exceeds the productive capacity (aggregate supply) of the economy so that inflation (rising prices) results, the role of government is to spend less and tax people more in order to reduce consumer demand and thus curtail general price increases.

Like micro-theory, traditional macro-theory reveals many inadequacies when applied to the realities of economic life in most Third World nations. This is particularly true in those developing economies with highly fragmented product, resource and financial markets. Such market fragmentation typically results from the co-existence of modern and traditional ways of doing things in both agriculture and industry. The problem is further compounded by inadequate and malfunctioning credit systems and a general LDC vulnerability to powerful foreign economic influences.

This general irrelevance of traditional Keynesian macro-economics for developing countries should not be surprising. The 'general' theory was in fact formulated in response to the employment problems which plagued the capitalist world during the depression of the 1930s. Much of this macro-theory is, indeed, considered to have limited relevance today, even in most Western developed nations where the problem is no longer simply economic stagnation and unemployment, but stagnation accompaned by inflation, a predicament which has come to be known as 'stagflation'. Manipulating aggregate supply and demand curves by general government economic policies thus appears no longer to be totally effective. As a result, traditional macro-models have lost much of their relevance.

If such a gap between macro-theory and economic reality exists in the industrial nations, how much more irrelevant it must seem for the underdeveloped countries whose institutions and economic systems don't even approximate to those of the developed nations, now or in the past! In fact as we shall see in Chapter 13, the traditional Keynesian or macro policy for alleviating industrial unemployment, i.e. the creation of more urban jobs through increased government expenditures may, under certain real world conditions in poor countries, actually increase the level of urban unemployment as a result of induced rural–urban migration. It may also worsen inflation. And, as we shall see in Part Two, this is not an isolated case of 'perverse' results occurring when standard theory is applied uncritically to the problems of Third World development. Many other phenomena which might at first appear to be theoretical paradoxes of development become less surprising when appropriate modifications of traditional theories are made in the light of the unique characteristics of developing nations.

Finally, in Chapter 20, we discover that much of the traditional theory of international trade, based as it is on the same competitive assumptions of micro-economics, offers only limited guidance for an understanding of the actual mechanics of international economic relations between rich and poor nations in the 1970s. Who benefits most from trade, how the gains are distributed and how international commodity prices are determined often bear little resemblance to the prescriptions of the traditional models of international trade and economic growth.

The common thought processes of economics

As students of development, we must therefore endeavour to identify only those economic concepts and principles that can help us to understand better and eventually solve the critical economic problems of Third World nations. In the remainder of this chapter and in Chapter 4, an attempt is made to describe and elucidate those economic concepts which appear to be particularly applicable to the diverse nations of Africa, Asia, the Middle East and Latin America. They are introduced at this early stage only to give you, the student, a broad feel for the common thought processes of economics even though the actual 'content' of the subject may differ in rich and poor countries. We apply these principles in greater depth to our discussions and analyses of some common development problems in Parts Two and Three. Moreover, many additional economic concepts and principles will be introduced in the problem-oriented chapters of Parts Two and Three where their special significance to the issue under investigation will be more obvious.

The distinction between common 'thought processes' as opposed to the diverse 'content' of economics is an important one which needs further clarification and emphasis. While we must recognise the limited applicability of many traditional Western economic concepts to problems of Third World development, we can at the same time claim a certain universality for the thought processes of economics: that is, the way economists go about analysing problems and reaching logical conclusions on the basis of explicit value judgments, realistic assumptions and reliable data. Although propositions may change and policy conclusions differ as a result of adjusting assumptions to fit the special economic and institutional characteristics of Third World nations, the methodology or thought process of economic analysis remains the same whether one is dealing with capitalist, socialist or Third World economies. It is this universality of economic thought processes and *not* the universality of specific theories that provides the intellectual linkage between economists and economics students in all nations. Common economic concepts and thought processes can transcend nation-states and ideological differences. On the other hand, so-called 'general' or 'universal' theories more often than not turn out to be 'special' cases of either the theory of advanced capitalism or that of 'scientific' socialism. Although disguised as universal truths, such theories when promulgated in developing countries can represent a subtle yet powerful form of 'intellectual imperialism'. As such, they need to be viewed with a healthy scepticism when applied uncritically to the unique economic, social and institutional circumstances of developing nations.

Some fundamental concepts and principles: scarcity, pricing, demand and supply

There are, however, certain concepts and principles of economics which are valid in varying degrees for all societies, be they rich or poor, capitalist, socialist or 'mixed'. But, as we have just discovered, there are many others which, though purporting to be general and widely applicable, are in reality specific to particular countries and cultures – that is, they apply only to certain types of nations (e.g. rich, industrial) with certain sets of values and traditions (e.g. free private enterprise, profit maximisation and consumer sovereignty). The following general economic concepts and principles are those which we believe to be particularly helpful for understanding the diverse economic problems and issues of developing nations. More will be presented in Chapter 4.

Scarcity and the role of prices

A commodity or resource is economically *scarce* when it is not free, that is, when in order to obtain it something of value (usually money or another scarce commodity or resource) has to be given up.[3] Scarcity, therefore, gives rise to *price*. This economic concept of scarcity must not be confused with the physical fact that resources such as water, land, even minerals and the beauties of nature are in limited supply. The water in the Indian Ocean is limited but it is not economically scarce; air in the atmosphere is limited but not scarce; before the need for energy, petroleum in the Persian Gulf was limited but it had no economic value and, therefore, was not scarce; and likewise in the nineteenth century land in certain parts of unpopulated Africa, North and South America and Asia was limited but not scarce (i.e. it was freely available and, in North America, people were even paid money to settle and cultivate the land).

In developing nations numerous resources are both very limited in supply and also very scarce. They therefore command a high price – more of something (money or some physical resource) must be given up in order to obtain a given quantity. Common examples include the most fertile land, skilled technical manpower, managerial abilities, foreign exchange, physical capital equipment, petroleum-based energy supplies and other industrial raw materials. In any economy it is the scarce resources that are the limiting factors or constraints on growth and development. It is these resources that have to be 'economised' – that is, utilised with great care. For example, in rich nations, both capitalist and socialist, capital goods such as machinery and equipment are in abundant supply while human labour is relatively scarce and therefore relatively more expensive than in most poor nations. As a result, rich countries attempt to 'economise' on labour by developing what are known as labour-saving machines such as computers, large tractors, fully automated food processing and textile equipment, heavy mechanical road-building equipment, and even automatic shoe-shining machines. According to the same logic, in most poor nations where unskilled human labour is more abundant and therefore relatively less scarce than capital, techniques of production should be adopted which are capital-saving or labour-intensive.

Scarce resources are used not only to produce *consumption* goods like food and clothing but also to maintain, improve, reproduce and multiply themselves so that even greater quantities of consumption goods can be produced in the future. This phenomenon of converting present into future goods is known as **investment.** It is a central factor in the acceleration of **economic growth** which leads to increasing amounts of consumption goods and services gradually being made available. It is important to note that investment consists not only of improving and adding to buildings, machinery and stocks of materials for production (the three principal components of **physical capital**), but also, through education and training, of improving the quality of people (**human capital**).

Scarce resources in almost all economies are bought and sold at a price. Economists view the price mechanism as an 'efficient' way of allocating scarce resources among alternative possible uses. Under certain conditions (discussed later) the price mechanism and the use of 'correct' prices for goods and resources (i.e. those which properly reflect their economic scarcity to society) is a very effective way of ensuring that these goods and resources are used to the maximum social advantage.

There are two essential characteristics which a price mechanism or system must possess if it is to function correctly in society's interest. First, the relative prices of final goods and services should reflect the relative benefit derived from the consumption of these final outputs by 'society'.[4] Secondly, and perhaps more important, the prices of

[3] Money may simply be defined as anything which is socially acceptable as a means of settling debts. A country's money supply normally consists of its notes and coins (currency) plus 'demand deposits' in commercial banks (i.e. checking accounts'). Sometimes, 'time deposits' (i.e. savings accounts) are also included. In traditional societies, many articles which possessed intrinsic value such as beads, cows, salt, cloth, etc., were used as means of payment. Economists typically regard money, which has no intrinsic value of its own, as fulfilling three basic functions: (1) it serves as a 'medium of exchange' in place of the more cumbersome and inefficient 'barter' system of traditional subsistence societies; (2) it serves as a 'unit of account' (e.g. shillings and cents, pesos, cruzeiros, Bhat, rupees, etc.) against which the monetary value of other scarce commodities and resources may be measured; and, finally (3) money serves as a 'store of value' which can be saved and used at a later date to yield future consumption.

[4] We use the word 'society' here in its broadest sense to reflect alternative political, social and economic regimes. These would include among others pure democracy, democratic socialism, centralised communism, benevolent and non-benevolent dictatorships, etc. But who decides what society wants, *for whom* these wants are met, and who benefits most is, as we saw in Chapter 2, a central question in every society. We say more about this important issue throughout the book.

goods and, especially, resources should reflect their relative scarcities. We discuss the concept of social benefits and costs as opposed to strictly private or individual benefits and costs in Chapter 4. Suffice it to say at this point that when the prices of resources like capital are a true reflection of their scarcity value (or 'social cost') to society as a whole, then both the quantities used and their allocation among alternative uses will be better (more 'efficient') than when actual prices do not adequately reflect economic scarcities. In many less developed nations, for a variety of institutional reasons, actual resource prices are a poor reflection of their economic scarcities. As we shall see in Chapter 13, the existence of these 'incorrect' prices and the consequent failure of many LDCs to allocate scarce resources in the most economically efficient manner is one, though perhaps not the most important, factor contributing to the widespread phenomenon of rising unemployment and underemployment in their rural and urban areas.

Demand and demand curves

Whether or not actual money prices are used (they did not exist, at least explicitly, in the early years of the centralised Soviet economy) to ration scarce physical and human resources, economic goods and social services, the concept of supply and demand and the associated price is fundamental to all of economics. In the idealised world of Western economics, it is the twin forces of demand and supply which determine the prices of commodities, the wages of workers and the interest rates charged to borrowers of money. Let us first examine the demand side of this relationship.

You have no doubt often recognised how people will hesitate to purchase a commodity or at least be inclined to buy less of it, when the price rises. Similarly, when the price falls either more will be purchased by the same people or new people who previously could not afford the product will now want to buy it. In general, therefore, both common sense and empirical observation tend to support the conclusion that there exists at any particular time a definite relationship between the prevailing price of a good (such as rice, corn, transistor radios, bicycles, petrol, etc.) and the quantity demanded. This 'negative' or 'inverse' relationship between price and quantity demanded – i.e. when prices rise (or fall) quantity demanded falls (or rises) – is known as the law of the downward sloping demand curve.

Table 3.1 gives an hypothetical illustration of a price–demand relationship for rice in, say, Kenya. At any price, for example, shs 3 per kg, there will be a certain quantity of rice that will be demanded by *all* Kenyan consumers. In row D of Table 3.1, we see that this quantity amounts to 8 million kg per month.

Table 3.1
An hypothetical price-quantity demand relationship for rice in Kenya

	Price (shs per Kg)	Quantity demanded (million Kg per month)
A	6	2
B	5	4
C	4	5
D	3	8
E	2	13
F	1	20

If the price were to fall to shs 2 per kg while all other prices and people's incomes remained unchanged, the total quantity demanded would increase from 8 to 13 million kg of rice per month (row E). However, if prices were to increase to, say, shs 4 per kg, we see from row C that the total quantity demanded would fall from 8 to 5 million kg.

Basically, there are two reasons why, when the price of a particular commodity falls (rises), people will purchase more (less) of it at any moment in time. First, a fall in price will bring in consumers who might previously have been eating greater quantities of maize meal and only a little rice per month; as rice becomes cheaper relative to maize meal, these consumers will tend to substitute some rice for maize meal. For a given level of monthly income they might purchase smaller amounts of maize meal but a good deal more rice. Alternatively, and this is the second principal reason for the inverse price–quantity demand relationship, there will be those consumers who were already consuming some rice but now, with the reduction in its price, can purchase more with their same monthly income without having to reduce their consumption of maize meal.

For example, suppose a Kenyan consumer has budgeted shs 50 per month for food purchases. For simplicity, let us assume that all this money will be spent on some combination of maize meal and rice. When the price of rice is shs 4 per kg, this consumer might be purchasing, say, 5 kg per month. With a total monthly rice expenditure of shs 20 (5 kg × shs 4 per kg = shs 20), he has shs 30 left to purchase say 10 kg of maize meal (at a price of shs 3 per kg). Now if the price of rice falls to shs 3 per kg, our consumer after purchasing 10 kg of maize meal will have shs 20 left over to purchase 6.67 kg of rice (20 ÷ 3 = 6.67) instead of the 5 kg which he was originally purchasing. Clearly, if he so desired, he could have purchased more of *both* maize meal and rice as a result of the fall in the price of rice. For example, he could have purchased 6 kg of rice at a cost of shs 18 and 10.67 kg of maize meal for the remaining shs 32. Thus a fall in the price of rice, other things (the price of maize meal and his monthly income) being equal, could lead not only to an increase in the quantity of rice demanded, but also a possible (though not necessary) increase in the quantity of maize meal purchased. The reason is straightforward. The one shilling fall in the price of a kg of rice means that our Kenyan consumer, who before the price drop was purchasing 5 kg per month at shs 4 per kg, now in effect has an additional income of shs 5 to spend on any goods: he can still purchase 5 kg but at a lower total cost of shs 15 instead of shs 20 when the price was shs 4.

This phenomenon is known as the 'income effect' of a price reduction. It arises because the one shilling fall in the price of rice is equivalent to a rise in our consumer's 'money' income by shs 5. And higher personal incomes are a major source of increased consumer demand. Suppose after the price reduction, our consumer still purchases 10 kg of maize meal (at shs 30) but increases his rice consumption from 5 to 6.67 kg per month (at a cost of $6\frac{2}{3}$ × shs 3 = shs 20). At the previous prices of shs 3 for maize meal and shs 4 for rice, in order to purchase the above 'basket' of goods – i.e. 10 kg of maize meal and 6.67 kg of rice – he would have needed a monthly income of 10 × shs 3 + 6.67 × shs 4 or shs 56.67 instead of what he actually has, namely shs 50. Had he been given an additional shs 6.67 per month while all prices remained unchanged, our Kenyan consumer would have been equally well off in both situations. Thus the fall in price is equivalent to a rise in personal income when the price reduction is measured in terms of real purchasing power.

A digression on the concept of 'real' as opposed to 'money' incomes

The above example illustrates a very important and often poorly understood concept in economics, namely the difference between **money income** and **real income**. Money income is simply the total number of dollars, pesos, shillings, cruzeiros, bhat, rupees, etc., that an individual earns per month. Real income is the quantity of physical goods and services he can purchase with his money income. Therefore, real income is simply money income adjusted for some general price level, normally the so-called consumer price index which is calculated as a weighted average of the prices of some 'typical' basket of goods and services purchased by the 'average' consumer (e.g. food, clothing, rents, restaurant meals, cinema prices, prices of durable goods such as automobiles, bicycles, etc.). It is real income which is the important concept in economic analysis since money itself has no intrinsic value apart from its dual function as a 'medium of exchange' and 'store of value' (through savings). During periods of rapidly rising prices, known as *inflation*, the distinction between money and real income increases becomes especially important.

To give the simplest illustration of the importance of distinguishing between real and money income, suppose we doubled the monthly *money* income of our Kenyan consumer from shs 50 to shs 100. At the same time, let us assume that the price of *both* maize meal and rice doubles from shs 3 and 4 respectively to shs 6 and 8. Assuming that these are the only two goods available for purchase, the question arises whether or not the consumer whose monthly salary has doubled is better off than before. Clearly, he is no better off because his *real* income has not changed even though his monthly salary or monthly income has doubled. A simultaneous doubling of all prices negates the income rise because no more goods and services can be purchased with the monthly income of shs 100 at a doubled general price level than with an income of shs 50 when the consumer price index was half of what it is now. Whether we are analysing wage negotiations between employers and employees, international commodity and resource price agreements, or internal relationships between the relative prices of agricultural (rural) and manufactured (urban) goods, we shall have many occasions throughout this book to draw attention to the important distinction between the monetary and real values of economic variables.

Price elasticity of demand

Returning now to our discussion of the general relationship between price and quantity demanded, we can plot the numbers in Table 3.1 on a simple two-dimensional graph to depict the principle of the downward sloping demand curve. Prices are measured on the vertical axis, and quantities demanded per unit time on the horizontal axis. Each combination of price-quantity numbers from Table 3.1 is plotted as points A to F in Figure 3.1 and a smooth curve passing through each point gives us a typical downward or (negative) sloping demand curve.

Figure 3.1
The downward-sloping demand curve

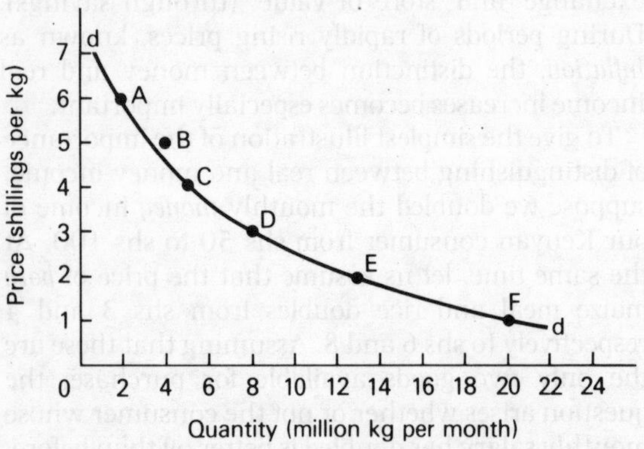

The location and especially the shape or slope of the demand curve provides important information about the nature of the commodity being demanded and the degree of responsiveness of consumers to price changes. Economists refer to this degree of responsiveness as the 'elasticity of demand'. It is defined as the percentage change in the quantity of any good demanded divided by (as a result of) its change in price; that is,

$$\text{elasticity of demand (Ed)} = -\frac{\text{percentage change in quantity demanded}}{\text{percentage change in price}}$$

The 'minus' sign is used to convert all elasticities to positive values – that is, Ed will range from zero to infinity – since the negative slope of demand curves would ordinarily yield negative elasticities (quantity rises when price falls).

Figure 3.2
Perfectly elastic and inelastic demand curves

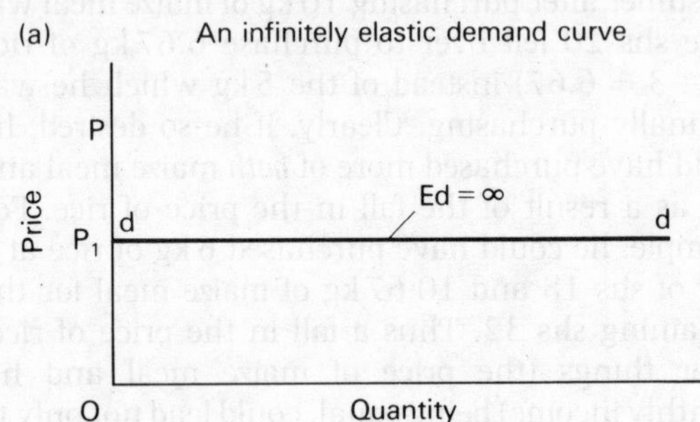

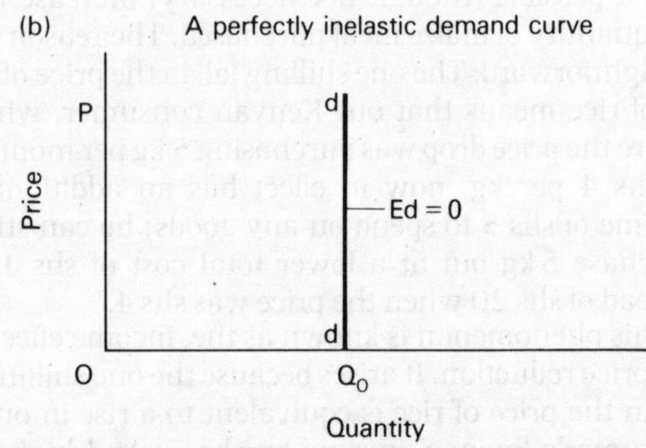

At two extremes we can have demand curves (note in a purely technical sense, the concept of a 'curve' includes the possibility that it is a straight line) which are either perfectly horizontal and parallel to the quantity axis or perfectly vertical and parallel to the price axis as depicted in Figure 3.2. In diagram (*a*) we have an illustration of a demand curve which shows that at or below a given price, P_1, consumers will purchase as much as is made available on the market. Such a demand curve is said to be **perfectly elastic** and its elasticity will be equal to infinity. At any price higher than P_1 nobody will demand any quantity of the item. Examples of horizontal demand curves over the entire range of quantities demanded are rare but one trivial illustration would be a central bank's demand for foreign currencies at some fixed exchange rate. For example, before 1971 the United States Government was prepared to purchase any quantitity of foreign gold supplies at $35 per ounce; at any higher price, it would purchase none. Commodities or resources which are very close substitutes like butter and margarine, two varieties of beer and different brands of petrol may exhibit perfect or near perfect elasticity over a narrow range of prices; for example if the price of one brand of petrol rises people may stop purchasing it and change to another brand.

In Figure 3.2(*b*) we have an illustration of a demand curve which is a vertical line, and the demand for this good is said to be **perfectly inelastic** (Ed = 0). It shows that no matter what the price, the quantity demanded will be Q_0 – no more, no less. A rise or fall in price will have no effect on quantity demanded. Perfectly vertical or inelastic demand curves over the entire range of prices are also rare, but for a more narrowly defined range of prices they can be quite common. Examples would include the demand for goods which are considered necessities and for which there are no satisfactory substitutes (e.g. rice and other good grains in South and South-east Asia, beans, groundnuts, yams, cassava and maize in Africa, and corn, wheat and manioc in most of Latin America). In each of these cases small to moderate changes in price will cause a negligible change, if any, in quantities demanded because these foods are necessary for subsistence and people's tastes and preferences are such that other types of food are not satisfactory substitutes.

Governments often can generate significant amounts of revenue by levying taxes and therefore raising the price to the consumer of non-essential goods which have relatively vertical or inelastic demand curves over a reasonable range of prices. Common examples include cigarettes, beer, petrol, cinema prices and hotel and restaurant services. More recently the major oil-producing states have demonstrated, to the chagrin of many nations both rich and poor, that when the international demand for crude oil is highly inelastic (i.e. there are no real substitutes and the commodity is essential to the workings of an industrial economy), it is possible arbitrarily to quadruple the price without any significant drop in quantities demanded.

We have so far used 'elasticity' only to describe the general nature of the demand curve for a particular good. We depicted in Figure 3.2 the limiting cases of infinite elasticity and perfect inelasticity. Various goods differ in the degree to which quantities demanded respond to changes in price. As we have seen, some commodities, for example subsistence foodstuffs and other less essential but greatly desired goods such as beer, petrol, cigarettes and crude oil, reveal little variation in quantities demanded, especially when prices rise but also when they fall. Other commodities, especially those for which there are good substitutes, show much greater quantity responsiveness to price changes.

Economists, however, use the term 'elasticity' more narrowly to denote the degree of responsiveness of quantities demanded to price changes *at any given price–quantity combination* on a particular commodity or resource demand curve. Technically, as we have seen, elasticity of demand is defined in terms of percentage changes in quantities demanded resulting from a given percentage change in price *when all other prices and consumer incomes remain unchanged.* If the price of rice falls by 10 per cent, will the total quantity demanded rise by a larger, an equal or a smaller percentage? When the total quantity demanded increases (or decreases) by a greater percentage than the price falls (or rises), then we say that the demand for that commodity is 'elastic' between the two price points. Its elasticity coefficient, Ed, is greater than one. When the percentage change in Q is *less* than the percentage change in P we have a case of an inelastic demand or of an elasticity of demand coefficient that is less than one at that price.

An alternative way of describing the concept of elasticity of demand is that when the elasticity is greater than, equal to, or less than unity, total revenue ($P \times Q$ = total revenue) will rise, remain the same, or fall when the price is reduced.[5] In cases

[5] For example, if the price of bicycles is reduced from 50 to 40 dollars (a 20 per cent reduction) and the total quantity demanded increases from 100 to 150 sold per month (a 50 per cent increase), the total revenue or sales generated from this price change will *increase* from 5 000 to 6 000 dollars. The elasticity of demand coefficient, Ed, will be approximately 2.5 ($50 \div 20$) and thus greater than unity. Consequently we see that in this case, where demand is elastic, total revenue will rise when prices fall. See if you can give numerical examples to illustrate the relationship between total revenue and unitary or inelastic demands.

where prices are raised, total revenue ($P \times Q$) will increase, remain the same, or decrease depending on whether the elasticity of demand is less than, equal to, or greater than unity.

Application of the price elasticity concept to domestic and international development policies

OPEC, energy and raw material prices

As an illustration of the importance of the elasticity concept and its relation to total revenue, consider the case of the international oil price increases of 1974. In that year 13 petroleum-producing nations acting as a group through the Organisation of Petroleum Exporting Countries (OPEC) unilaterally decided to increase the international price of crude oil by over 400 per cent.[6] The result was an extraordinary increase in the total revenue generated from OPEC's overseas sales. For example, between 1973 and 1974 total OPEC oil export earnings jumped from $24.2 billion to $100.7 billion even though the volume of exports showed a slight decline.

This tremendous revenue increase came about because the total quantity demanded declined by less than three per cent when prices rose by this unprecedented 400 per cent. The oil-producing nations thus knew that as a group they were being confronted by an international demand curve for crude oil which was highly *inelastic* at the going price (an elasticity coefficient in our example of 3 divided by 400 or approximately .007 which is almost an elasticity of zero). Once they could get together to adopt a uniform stance in international markets they could behave as **monopolists** (single sellers of a given product with no close substitutes), or more precisely as 'colluding' **oligopolists** (a few sellers of a given product). By agreeing to raise prices substantially and knowing that the international demand for crude oil was highly inelastic, they could act in the confidence of gaining substantial increases in revenue from overseas sales. The other nations of the world, and especially some of the LDCs who were the hardest hit, had little recourse but to succumb to this monopoly power. The importance of 'power' in economic affairs was never more evident than in OPEC's price-setting.

Similar but less blatant or visible actions are daily occurrences in the pricing policies of multinational corporations (giant private enterprises with subsidiaries and branch offices in many parts of the world). Their ability to control world markets by overt and covert collusion and unilaterally to set world prices within a wide range is common knowledge. We shall discuss the world energy shortage, multinational corporations and their impact on developing economies more fully in Parts Two and Three.

One might conclude that similar results to the oil producers' could be obtained by other less developed nations if those producing a similar commodity or resource were to band together and set their commodity and resource prices at artificially high levels. Third World sugar exporters led by Cuba were partially successful in jointly raising the price of sugar in 1974. Other examples might include tin, bauxite, iron ore, manganese, phosphates, coffee, cotton, cocoa, sisal and rubber producers. Unfortunately, with perhaps the exception of certain minerals, most primary and especially agricultural commodities are characterised by elastic international demand curves between existing and potentially higher world prices due to the availability of a wide range of substitute products. These include, for example, synthetic fibre substitutes for cotton and synthetic rubber substitutes for natural rubber. A price increase, therefore, would result in a loss of total revenue for nations exporting the primary products. Moreover, the high costs of production and the small current margin between prices and costs are such that a reduction in world prices of such commodities would not be feasible. Any increase in total revenue brought about by expanded levels of production would be more than offset by higher total costs. (We shall examine the nature of supply curves in the next section.) The net result would be smaller total profits (where profits are defined as the excess of total revenue over total costs) for the group as a whole, and worse still, for each individual nation and producer within the group. When we discuss international trade in Chapters 19 to 21 we examine further what measures Third World exporters of primary com-

[6] The 13 OPEC members are Saudi Arabia, Iran, Kuwait, Iraq, Nigeria, Algeria, Venezuela, Indonesia, Libya, Qatar, Ecuador, United Arab Emirates and Gabon.

modities might pursue to improve their trade positions, that is, to generate more export earnings.

The concept of consumer demand and price elasticity is, therefore, extremely important. It not only gives us an analytical framework for understanding some of the major problems of underdevelopment but also offers a conceptual and empirical methodology for formulating intelligent policies to promote economic and social progress. Included among the numerous applications of this concept for the real, day-to-day problems of developing nations are the following:

Farm price policies

Government pricing policies with regard to agricultural commodities produced and sold in domestic and international markets are a major component of development strategy. Many important issues arise, therefore, relating to agricultural pricing policies. For example, should governments subsidise farm prices (i.e. pay local farmers a higher price for their products than those in domestic or international markets)? Will higher food prices lead to more farm revenue and higher profits? But what about the higher price impact on the 'real' income levels of urban wage earners who have to purchase this food? What should be the relationship or ratio between the domestic prices of agricultural commodities compared to manufactured goods (a ratio often referred to as the 'terms of trade' between agricultural and manufactured goods)? Should the agricultural or industrial sector be encouraged to expand relative to the other through the provision of higher price incentives? These and many other related questions relevant to proper agricultural pricing policies require some knowledge of the domestic and international price elasticity of demand for different agricultural commodities (see Chapter 16).

Public wage policy

Should the government raise or lower wage rates in order to generate more employment? Just as there are demand curves for commodities, so too there are demand curves for different kinds of labour, relating wage rates to quantities of labour demanded. In general these demand curves also slope downward and to the right, as lowering wage rates for unskilled labour tends, other things being equal, to increase the quantity of labour demanded. At higher prices for labour (higher wage rates) the quantity demanded will generally decrease. The elasticity of demand for labour in this case would be the ratio between the percentage change in labour quantities demanded and the percentage change in wage rates. The demand for labour is said, therefore, to be elastic, unitary or inelastic according to whether this ratio exceeds, equals or is less than unity. Similarly, the demand for labour would be elastic (or inelastic) at any given wage rate if as a result of an increase in wages, the total wage bill (analogous to total revenue – i.e. $W \times Q_L$ where W is the wage rate and Q_L is the quantity of labour demanded) falls (or rises). Knowledge of the elasticity of labour demand thus becomes an essential ingredient in the formulation of enlightened government wage and employment policies. For example, if there is a high elasticity of demand for unskilled labour (and much unemployment), an increase in urban minimum wages, although politically appealing, may lead to lower levels of employment and, through induced rural–urban migration, higher levels of unemployment (see Chapter 14).

Excise taxes

Should the government levy excise taxes (i.e. a tax of a certain percentage on the final sale price) on certain consumer goods in order to generate more public revenue? If so, on which commodities should they be levied? In general, excise taxes of, say, 4 to 5 per cent are levied on commodities with relatively inelastic demands (cigarettes, beer, petrol, alcoholic beverages and restaurant bills). Since excise taxes raise the final price of the commodity to consumers, but, as we shall see below, not by the full amount of the tax except when the demand curve is 'perfectly' inelastic, those taxed goods with inelastic demands and which do not make great claims on individual consumer incomes will generate more total revenue (including tax revenue) than goods with highly elastic demands. But in cases such as this where excise taxes are levied on goods with inelastic demands, an additional question must be asked: On whom will the burden of the tax fall most heavily, the rich or the poor? *Ability to pay* thus becomes an important criterion, especially for governments concerned with problems of poverty and equity. For example, the demand for rice in South-east Asia or wheat in Latin America or maize meal in East Africa is highly price-*inelastic*. These are also the staple foods of the low-income classes. An excise tax which might, therefore, generate significant public revenues would hit the poor much more seriously than the rich. In most cases such a policy would be political suicide, even though economically sound from a revenue-raising point of view.

As a final example of excise taxes and demand elasticities, consider countries like Kenya, Mexico, Thailand and Brazil, with sizable foreign exchange (i.e. foreign currency) earnings from tourist industries. In Kenya, for example, where tourism is the second largest earner of foreign exchange, the government decided a few years ago to levy a 15 per cent hotel tax designed to generate an additional amount of foreign revenue to be used for development projects. One immediate result of the tax was to discourage local citizens and foreign residents living in Kenya from using the tourist facilities (i.e. game parks and coastal resorts). The demand was apparently highly price-elastic. Moreover, the excise tax, along with higher international air fares, raised the price of an all-inclusive holiday in Kenya to foreign tourists by an amount sufficient to cause many of them, especially Europeans, to take their holidays in southern Europe instead. The net effect of the tax may therefore have been an unchanged or low level of total government tax revenues to the extent that higher excise tax revenues were offset by lower total income tax revenues as a result of the fall in total income for the tourist industry as a whole. Again, this case illustrates the fact that some general knowledge of the value of the elasticity of demand becomes a major factor in the policy decision to initiate, increase, lower or abolish excise taxes.

School fees and educational demand

Should tuition and fees be charged for primary, secondary or higher educational facilities? Like any other good or service, there exists a demand for education which relates the quantity and quality demanded (number of years, vocational or academic, etc.) to the price (mainly tuition and related school fees). Clearly, the demand for education is much more than simply a function of its price, even after adjusting for different levels of personal income. Education is sought for a variety of reasons, not least as a vehicle for future higher incomes and economic and/or social mobility (see Chapters 17 and 18). Nevertheless, the question of tuition charges can have important implications for those who get educated and those who do not.

For example, one might speculate that the price elasticity of demand for, say, secondary academic education might be higher for families with low incomes than for families with high incomes. The former may have little or no money left over to spend on educating their children after payments for food, clothing, shelter and other basic necessities have been made. On the other hand, wealthier families whose expenditures on basic necessities may comprise only a small percentage of their monthly or annual incomes need not be concerned over the price of education, especially since they may view it as a necessity for their children's future welfare. It follows that charging high tuition at the secondary level (without any sort of grant or loan scheme for the poor) will tend to reduce the amount demanded among low income groups while having little adverse effect on the amount demanded by upper income groups. The net result would be that the poor are denied access to perhaps their only vehicle for economic advancement, while the rich have little trouble consolidating their position of economic dominance in the national economy.

For this reason many LDC governments have sought to lower the price of education to the poor by providing universal free primary education. However, many still charge sizable tuition fees at secondary level while providing free or even subsidised university education. The overall effects of these policies are to deny secondary education to the poor and to pay for and subsidise the university education of the upper middle classes and the rich out of public tax revenues generated in large part from the taxation of the lower and middle-income groups. Such a policy can hardly be said to be equitable, let alone economically sensible in terms of demand elasticities. An alternative policy of providing free or subsidised education for the poor (whose demand elasticities are higher) out of the public revenues generated from tuitions charged to the rich (whose demand elasticities are low) would not only equalise educational opportunities for all (the rich would still educate their children and the poor would not be denied it because of high prices) but it would also provide a more equitable mechanism for financing the educational system. We deal in greater detail with these and other issues relating education to development in Chapters 17 and 18.

Income elasticities of demand

Another important demand elasticity concept measures the ratio of the percentage increase in the quantity of a commodity or service demanded to the percentage increase in an individual's money income when the prices of that and all other goods and services are held constant. This ratio or coefficient is known as the income elasticity of demand since it measures the responsiveness of quantity demanded to income changes. However, unlike price elasticities where negative relationships between quantity and price prevail, income elasticities typically involve positive relationships: when an individual's income increases he usually demands more of a given commodity. But this positive relationship is neither a 'law' nor is it as generally applicable as the negative relationship between price and quantity. The possibility of negative income–demand relationships for certain commodities is particularly strong among low income groups in poor nations where the consumption of a single staple food, such as rice, corn or wheat, constitutes a large part or all of an individual or family's diet. In such situations, when the incomes of the poor rise, consumption of these goods may in fact go down as other previously more expensive foods like meat and fish now become financially attainable.

Goods which are demanded in smaller quantities when incomes rise are known as inferior goods as opposed to the more common **normal** goods, the consumption of which will rise when incomes increase. Note that 'inferiority' is not an intrinsic quality or attribute – it depends on individual tastes and the availability of alternative possibilities. Thus, for example, kidneys and intestines of goats and cows may be an inferior good in some societies and a luxury in others. Bananas, coconuts and pineapples may be inferior goods on a tropical island in the Pacific while being luxuries in Northern Europe.

Figure 3.3
Increasing incomes shift the demand curve to the right

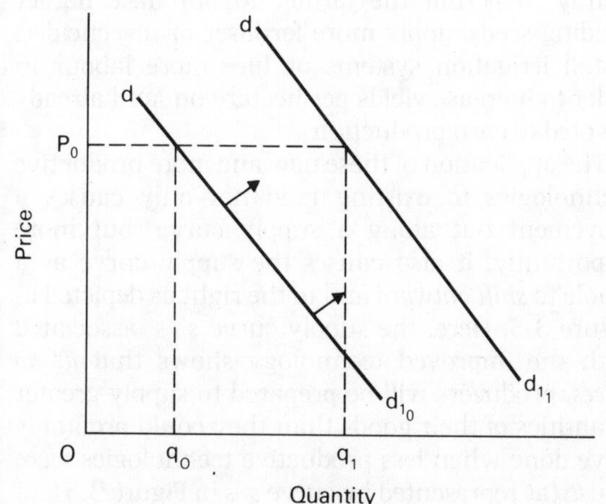

Since demand curves are derived by varying the price of a commodity while holding all other prices *and income* levels constant, we can portray the demand effects of higher income levels for normal goods by a rightward shift in the demand curve. This shift to the right is portrayed in Figure 3.3. At any price level (e.g. P_0) more of the commodity will be demanded (q_1) compared with q_0 on demand curve d_{1_0} when that curve shifts from d_{1_0} to d_{1_1}.

But by how much more will demand increase, and for which types of goods? Again we have a very important economic policy question for Third World governments. In an attempt to stimulate local production and employment, is it better to focus on raising income levels of the poor or the rich? Abstaining from value judgments about poverty, equality and the distribution of income, we know from empirical studies that lower income groups have higher income elasticities of demand for locally produced goods like processed foods, milk and dairy products, clothing and simple household goods and furnishings than upper income groups. Poor people tend to spend most, if not all, of any *additional* income on local products. This in turn will stimulate local production, provide more job opportunities and lead to higher income levels in the future.

On the other hand, the same studies show that upper income classes have relatively low income elasticities for local products but rather high elasticities for luxury goods imported from the more developed nations. They may spend sizable proportions of their increased income on imported items such as cars, television sets, household electrical appliances and special foods. In fact, locally produced goods as a whole might be 'inferior' goods in the demand and consumption habits of the rich. It follows that any increase in national income will have a greater expansionary effect on domestic production and employment if it accrues to the poor than if it were distributed to the rich. This conclusion has nothing to do with any value judgments about who is more deserving. It is simply due to the fact that the poor have a relatively higher income elasticity of demand for domestic as opposed to foreign goods.

The above example shows that some knowledge of the numerical magnitude of income elasticities of demand for different income groups in LDCs may be crucial in promoting economic development. Which industries to establish and/or promote; whether to have a highly progressive tax structure (i.e. one that taxes higher incomes at progressively higher rates) with redistribution programmes for the poor; and whether to focus development efforts in rural areas (where most of the poor live) or urban areas (where the majority of the rich live): these are some of the many important issues of economic development for which concepts such as income elasticities of demand are extremely relevant.

Supply curves and their elasticities

Just as demand curves relate quantities of goods, services and/or resources demanded by *purchasers* to alternative prices, so too supply curves show those quantities of these same goods, services and/or resources which *sellers* are willing to supply at various prices. Unlike the negative sloping demand curve, however, the supply curve normally has a *positive* slope, *upward* and to the right, indicating that at successively higher prices producers of commodities or sellers of services and resources are generally willing to provide successively greater quantities per unit time. Table 3.2 and the associated Figure 3.4 illustrate a simple hypothetical supply schedule and curve for corn.

Table 3.2
An hypothetical supply schedule for corn

	Possible prices ($ per kg)	Quantity sellers prepared to supply (kg per month)
A	10	30
B	8	25
C	6	19
D	4	12
E	2	4
F	1	0

Figure 3.4
A supply curve for corn

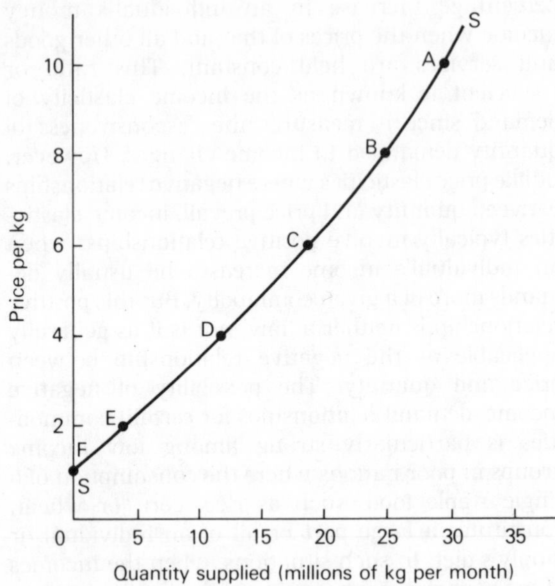

Given successively higher corn prices relative to the fixed prices of other farm products, farmers will try to increase their corn production. They may do this by devoting more land to corn crops either through expanding the total arable area or by converting existing arable land from some other commodity. Additionally, the higher prices received for corn might raise potential farm profits sufficiently to permit the farmer to purchase higher yielding seeds, apply more fertiliser or insecticides, install irrigation systems or hire more labour in order to increase yields per hectare on land already devoted to corn production.

The application of these new and more productive technologies to existing land not only causes a movement out along a supply curve, but more importantly, it also causes the supply curve as a whole to *shift outward* and to the right as depicted in Figure 3.5. Here, the supply curve *s′–s′* associated with the improved technology shows that *at all prices*, producers will be prepared to supply greater quantities of their goods than they could profitably have done when less productive technologies were in use (as represented by curve *s–s* in Figure 3.5).

Figure 3.5
Improved technologies shift supply curves to the right

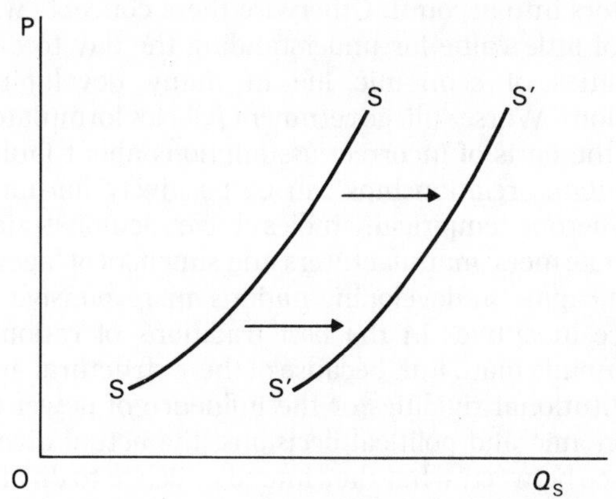

The elasticity concept which we explored with respect to demand curves applies to supply curves as well. In this case, however, the **elasticity of supply** measures the reponsiveness of quantities supplied to changing prices. More precisely, supply is said to be elastic, of unitary elasticity or inelastic when the ratio of the percentage change in quantity supplied to the percentage change in price is greater than, equal to, or less than one. Figure 3.6 illustrates the extreme cases of (*a*) a perfectly elastic supply curve, and (*b*) a perfectly inelastic (i.e. elasticity coefficient of zero) supply curve. In general, supply curves which approach the horizontal are more elastic over a relevant range of prices than supply curves which have a more vertical slope.[7]

Figure 3.6
Elastic and inelastic supply curves

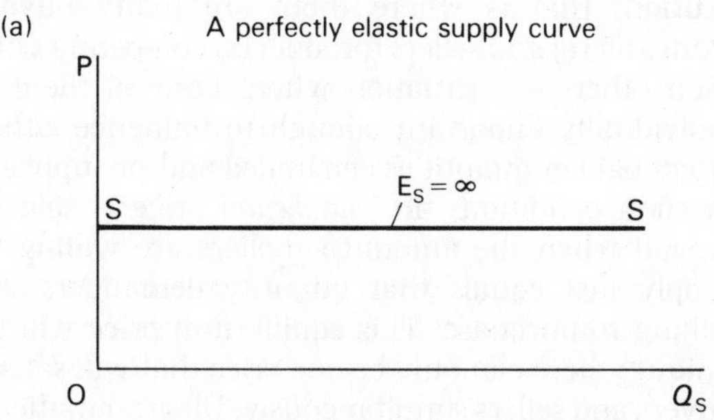

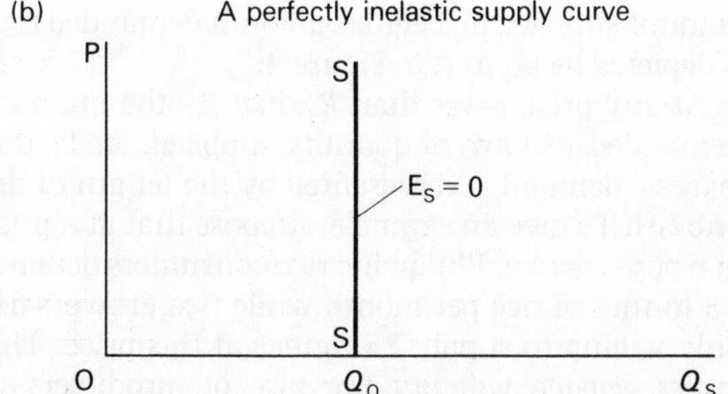

Supply elasticities, 'surplus' labour and structural rigidities in LDCs

The two extreme cases of infinitely elastic and zero elastic supply curves shown in Figure 3.6 each have an important history in the literature on economic development. We deal with these issues in considerably greater detail in later chapters but it may be helpful to the student to illustrate them briefly at this point.

In the case of infinitely elastic supply curves, much of the early theoretical and policy literature on the relationship between wages and urban employment in less developed nations was predicated on the assumption, first formulated by Sir W. Arthur Lewis, that poor countries were characterised by the existence of 'surplus' rural labour.[8] These rural workers were surplus to the extent that they added little to total agricultural output. They could, therefore, be transferred to the urban manufacturing sector with little or no loss of agricultural supply. Moreover, they were all assumed to be willing to work at a fixed urban wage rate which was slightly higher than their average real incomes in rural areas.

The concept of unlimited supplies of these surplus rural workers available for employment in the urban manufacturing sector at a fixed wage can be expressed diagrammatically by drawing a perfectly

[7] This statement is not as precise as it might appear since elasticities depend not only on the shape of a curve but also its position, the price at which it is being measured and the units chosen for the price and quantity axis. However, for our purposes, this broad generalisation is sufficient.

[8] Lewis's famous article 'Economic development with unlimited supplies of labour' first appeared in the journal *Manchester School* in 1954.

elastic supply curve of labour at the going wage, like that of Figure 3.6(*a*). (Note that in the case of labour supply curves, wage rates are measured on the vertical axis while quantities of labour supplied to urban industry are depicted on the horizontal axis.) This infinitely elastic labour supply at the fixed urban wage was a crucial component in Lewis's theory of economic development, which emphasised rapid industrialisation made possible through the transfer of cheap labour from lower productivity traditional agriculture to higher productivity modern manufacturing. We shall analyse the scope and limitations of this and similar theories of development in later chapters.

The case of perfectly inelastic (vertical) supply curves, as shown in Figure 3.6(*b*), has often been used to portray conditions of production in these developing economies where structural or institutional rigidities prevent producers from increasing output in response to rising prices. These rigidities may take the form of bottlenecks or 'constraints' in the availability of physical (machinery and equipment), human (managerial and entrepreneurial competence), and/or financial (access to credit) resource inputs necessary to expand production. For example, in the case of a rise in the price of corn, the small Mexican, Indian or Nigerian farmer may indeed *wish* to expand production as rapidly as possible in order to reap the benefits of higher prices. However, he may not *be able* to do so because, for example, he cannot obtain the credit he needs to purchase new seeds, fertiliser, mechanical equipment, etc. Alternatively, seeds, fertiliser, tubewells and mechanical equipment may simply not be available for purchase because of quotas and/or special privileges granted to other, more affluent farmers. Finally, due to an absence of well-trained agricultural extension officers whose job it is to acquaint farmers with new and more productive farming practices, he simply may not have the know-how necessary to increase his supply of corn to the market rapidly. Whatever the case may be, and this applies not only to agriculture but to many LDC manufacturing industries as well, the rise in price may fail to elicit a corresponding supply increase because of these non-economic institutional factors.

Structural and institutional rigidities and the resulting supply inelasticities are important factors contributing to the persistence of underdevelopment in Third World nations. It is essential, therefore, that traditional economic concepts such as the well behaved, gently upward sloping commodity or resource supply curve, be modified to take these factors into account. Otherwise these concepts will be of little value for understanding the day to day realities of economic life in many developing nations. Worse still, government policies formulated on the basis of incorrect assumptions about faulty economic relationships can be positively harmful. Numerous empirical studies have demonstrated that farmers, manufacturers and suppliers of labour and capital in developing nations *are* responsive to price incentives in the best traditions of rational economic man. But, because of these structural and institutional rigidities or the influence of power in economic and political decisions, the actual divergence between what they intend or desire to do and what is actually possible may be extremely large.

Demand, supply and price determination: theory and reality

Perhaps the most fundamental tenet in all Western economic theory is that which asserts that prices are determined by the interacting forces of demand and supply in markets characterised by **perfect competition**, that is where there are many buyers (consumers) and sellers (producers) competing with each other in a situation where none of them is individually important enough to influence either prices paid or quantities demanded and/or supplied. In such conditions an *equilibrium* price is said to prevail when the amount suppliers are willing to supply just equals that quantity demanders are willing to purchase. This equilibrium price will be unique; there can only be one price that will satisfy buyers and sellers simultaneously. Diagrammatically, the competitive equilibrium must occur at the point of intersection between demand and supply curves. Such an equilibrium price (P_1) where the amount supplied just equals amount demanded (Q_1) is depicted by point A in Figure 3.7.

At any price *lower* than P_1, like P_0, the quantity demanded will *exceed* quantity supplied. At P_0 this 'excess' demand is represented by the length of the line GH. To give an example, suppose that at a price of 6 pesos per kg, Philippine rice consumers demand 35 tonnes of rice per month while rice growers are only willing to supply 25 tonnes at this price. This *excess demand* will put pressure on producers to

Figure 3.7
Determination of equilibrium price and quantity in competitive markets

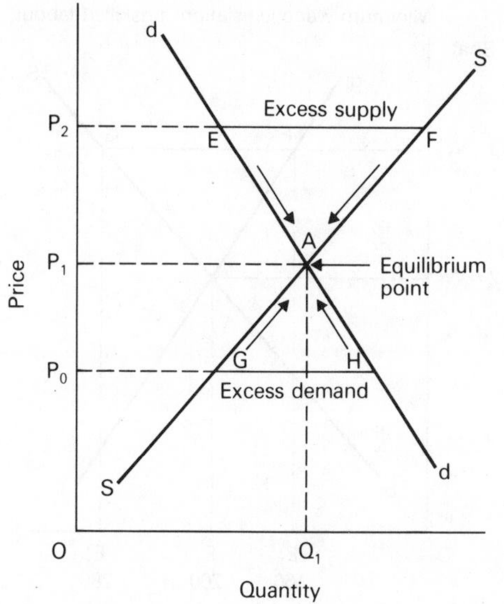

increase supplies. However, they are prepared to do this only at higher prices. Price will therefore be forced back up to P_1 as indicated by the arrows in Figure 3.7.

Conversely, at any price *higher* than P_1, e.g. P_2 in Figure 3.7, there will be *more* of the commodity offered on the market by suppliers than the amount demanders are willing to purchase. For example, suppose that at a price of 12 pesos per kg of rice, farmers might be willing to supply 40 tonnes per month while consumers are only demanding 27 tonnes at these higher prices. An *excess supply* equal to line EF will therefore exist and competition among sellers will tend to force the price back down to its equilibrium level at P_1. Only at the price quantity combination (P_1, Q_1) represented by point A will there be a balance or equilibrium between what producers are willing to supply and what consumers are willing to purchase.

Equilibrium prices will change only when there is a shift in either or both of the underlying demand and supply curves. See if you can show diagrammatically how an outward or rightward shift in the supply curve (for example, as a result of the use of improved technologies which permit farmers to produce greater quantities of rice for any given cost) will cause the equilibrium price to fall (demand remaining fixed). What about an outward shift in the demand curve resulting perhaps from an increase in consumer income levels? Will this tend to lead to a higher or lower equilibrium rice price when the supply curve remains stable?

The use of basic supply and demand analysis to describe and explain the determination of equilibrium price and quantity in market economies is fundamental to all of traditional economics. The forces of supply and demand are assumed to determine all domestic prices and wage rates, international commodity prices, domestic and international interest rates, foreign exchange rates and even the price of haircuts. And, in the idealised world of perfect competition (a world to which, for reasons soon to be explained, we shall not devote much attention), the theory that supply and demand determines all prices for goods, services and factors of production provides the Western economist with an intellectually appealing theoretical framework.

Unfortunately, however, the gap between theoretical elegance and mundane reality in domestic and international economic activities is often substantial. All too often students tend to forget (and their teachers frequently fail to remind them) that only under the most restrictive assumptions of a world of 'atomised' producers and consumers does the concept of competitive price determination prevail. In the real world the vast majority of prices are set by the relative power of a *few* powerful economic units. Giant domestic corporations have substantial price-setting and, through advertising and product manipulation, demand-creating power in both the developed and less developed nations. And, as we shall see in a later chapter, large multinational corporations with branch offices in many nations throughout the world have extraordinary international price-setting powers, especially when they co-ordinate their sales activities, or divide up world markets, which they often do. Trade unions exercise great power in wage determination in both developed and less developed nations. Often they are able to extract large wage increases from giant corporations only because the latter know that they can pass on these cost increases in the form of higher prices to the consumer. *Bargaining*, therefore, is an important factor in national and international price determination. Wealthy landowners and landlords can also exert great power on the agricultural input (e.g. machinery) and output (wheat, corn, beef, etc.)

pricing policies of Third World nations. Urban industrialists often have broad powers to control supplies and prices of domestically produced manufactured goods through their influence on trade legislations, for example, in the establishment of protective tariffs and physical quotas restricting the importation of lower cost competitive manufactured goods like textiles, shoes, simple home appliances, radios, etc., from foreign countries, both rich and poor. The list could go on indefinitely. However, for the present, our only purpose is to alert you at this early stage to the limitations of even this most cherished of economic principles.

In spite of some of its obvious limitations, however, traditional supply and demand analysis does provide us with a simple yet powerful conceptual tool for analysing a number of development issues. These include among others the employment effects of minimum wage legislation, the output effects of guaranteed agricultural prices, the distributive implications of wage subsidies, dual foreign exchange rates, non-competitive interest rates and capital depreciation allowances, the educational demand effects of raising school fees and the prices of other urban and rural social services, and, finally, the effects of tariffs and quotas on the demand for imports. Traditional supply and demand theory can indeed help us to analyse many of the economic problems and issues of developing nations. But its theoretical simplicity should not blind us to its very real limitations as a tool of description especially when it comes to analysing how prices and quantities are actually determined in domestic and international markets.

Institutional wage and price setting and the 'rationing' of jobs and food in imperfect Third World markets

As an illustration of a common outgrowth of 'non-competitive' pricing policies in the real world of developing economies, consider the case where the price of a commodity or resource is institutionally set above the level which would prevail if the idealised world of competitive markets really existed. Two such situations are depicted in Figure 3.8 – one where the price of unskilled labour is set *above* the competitive equilibrium wage rate (e.g. as a result of minimum wage legislation), and the other where the price of a staple commodity such as rice in the Philippines is set *below* its theoretical equilibrium level, e.g. in order to provide low-cost food for urban wage-earners.

Figure 3.8
Non-equilibrium pricing and the necessity of rationing

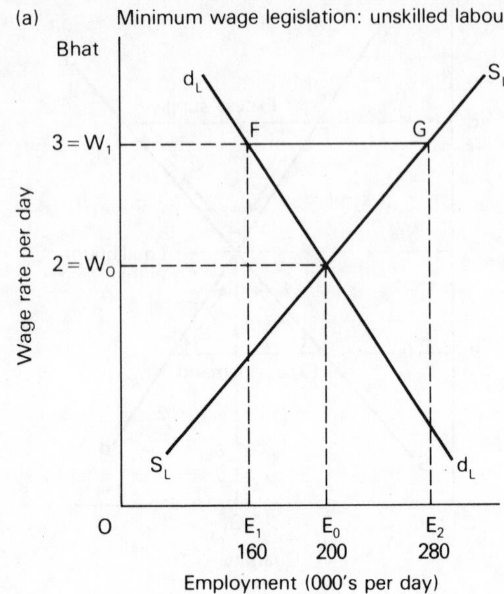

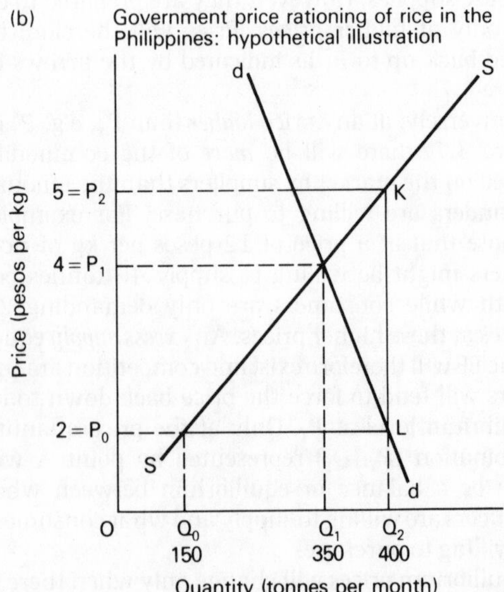

In Figure 3.8(*a*) we see that if perfectly competitive conditions prevailed, the twin forces of demand and supply would result in equilibrium wage rates being established at W_0 or \$2 per day with a corresponding level of employment of 200 000 workers as shown by point E_0. Only at this wage rate are the number of people *willing* to work just equal to the number of jobs available. Therefore, in a strictly technical sense of the number of job seekers being just equal to the number of job opportunities available at the going wage rate, there is full employment only at point E_0. However, competitive conditions do not prevail and either as a result of trade union pressures or government political vulnerability to the charge of perpetuating 'low' wages, the minimum wage is set at say W_1 or \$3 per day. We see that at this wage rate the number of job seekers as shown by point G on the labour supply curve will be at point E_2 or 280 000 workers on the employment axis. Point F on the labour demand curve reveals, however, that at the three-dollar wage, the number of job offerings will only be 160 000. The net result will be that E_1E_2 or 120 000 workers will be unemployed. Since these 120 000 additional workers are 'willing' to work at a wage rate of \$3 per day, some sort of rationing mechanism will be necessary to allocate 160 000 jobs among a total labour force of 280 000 job seekers.

Note that in competitive markets, price itself acts as the automatic rationing device, falling when there is an excess supply and rising when there is an excess demand (see Figure 3.7). As we shall see in Chapter 17, the rationing mechanism which is often used both explicitly and implicitly in underdeveloped nations with high rates of unemployment is the educational system itself. People are given preference for a limited number of jobs on the basis of the number of years of schooling completed, often irrespective of whether or not that additional schooling actually improves the individual's ability to do the job more effectively. However, as is usually the case with rationing, such an artificial and arbitrary employment screening device as the possession of certain educational credentials creates distorted incentives, forcing people to seek more years of schooling than they can either afford or utilise. This in turn leads to an excess demand (in terms of the number of available school places) for years of schooling and, consequently, the need to ration limited school places. A familiar 'vicious circle' is thus set in motion. But more on this employment–education phenomenon in Chapter 17.

In Figure 3.8(*b*) we have illustrated a hypothetical situation in which the government of a country in South-east Asia such as the Philippines where rice is a staple food decides that the domestic free market equilibrium price of rice, P_1 or 4 pesos per kg, would be too high for urban wage earners who, as a group, may possess considerable political power. Suppose that P_1 is also the world market price of rice, the price at which rice could be imported. The government therefore decides to set the price of rice in urban food markets at P_0 or 2 pesos per kg. For the moment assume that this is also the price paid to rice growers. At 2 pesos per kg QQ_0 or 150 tonnes of rice will be supplied by Philippine farmers while OQ_2 or 400 tonnes per month will be demanded by all consumers in Manila. There will therefore be an excess demand of 250 tonnes of rice per month.

Once again, some system of rationing rice such as limiting each consumer to, say, two kg per week will be necessary in order to distribute the limited supply to all Philippine consumers. In such instances where there is not enough of a staple food to satisfy popular demand, illegal transactions (black markets) are likely to proliferate and the rationing programme may turn out to be self-defeating. Those who can pay black market prices (which are likely to exceed the competitive equilibrium price of 4 pesos per kg) will get the rice while those (usually the very poor) who cannot pay will have little or no rice to eat.

An alternative approach to outright rationing and one usually adopted by LDC governments is to establish a dual, or two-price, system whereby producers are paid one price by the government for their rice (typically higher than the competitive equilibrium price) while consumers are charged another (lower) price. In Figure 3.8(*b*) we can verify that if the Philippine Government wishes to sell rice to urban consumers at a price of 2 pesos per kg as before they will need to provide 400 tonnes per month. But we can note from point K on the rice growers' total supply curve that 400 tonnes per month will be supplied *only* if the price which they receive is 5 pesos per kg (point P_2 on the price axis). The Philippine Government therefore, will need to pay rice growers a higher price of 5 pesos in order to sell the necessary 400 monthly tonnes of rice to Manila consumers for the much lower (subsidised) price of 2 pesos per kg.

The total cost of this hypothetical operation to the

Philippine Government will be $5 \times 900 \times 400 =$ 1 800 000 pesos (since there are approximately 900 kg in a ton) or the area represented by the rectangle OP_2KQ_2 in Figure 3.8(b). Consumers will purchase this rice at a total expenditure of $2 \times 900 \times 400 = 720\,000$ pesos, the area of OP_0LQ_2. The difference between government outlays to rice growers of 1 800 000 pesos and the amount it gets back (either through direct sales or through sales of private retail outlets) from consumers, 720 000 pesos, will be 1 080 000 pesos, or the area of the rectangle P_0P_2KL in the diagram. This 1 080 000 pesos in effect, would be the net loss, or net cost of the programme to the Philippine Government in its attempt to please both rural rice growers and urban wage-earning consumers through the establishment of a dual pricing system for rice.

Unfortunately, this very sizable net loss has to be covered from tax revenues extracted from either or both of these two groups (assuming for simplicity that they are the only two groups in the nation). Which group bears the greatest burden of this taxation will determine in the final analysis whether rural farmers or urban workers come out ahead on the overall deal. For example, if competitive markets had prevailed the equilibrium price–quantity combination would have been 350 tonnes selling at 4 pesos per kg (points Q_1 and P_1 in Figure 3.8(*b*)). Total consumer expenditures of $4 \times 900 \times 350 =$ 1 260 000 pesos would have just equalled the total receipts of Philippine rice farmers. The Philippine Government's dual price system in effect, therefore, represents an equal subsidy of approximately 540 000 pesos to both farmers (the difference between the amount they are paid under the government support programme, 1 800 000 pesos, and the amount they would have received had there been no such programme: 1 260 000 pesos) and to Manila consumers (p1 260 000 – p720 000 = p540 000). The total subsidy to both groups is 1 080 000 pesos which the government must raise from taxation. If each group pays the same amount of tax, p540 000 – then the subsidies and tax levies would cancel each other out and neither group will have been made better or worse off as a result of the dual price programme.

However, suppose the programme was financed by taxing rice growers 680 000 pesos and urban consumers 400 000 pesos. The programme in this instance would benefit Manila consumers at the expense of rural farmers. A net transfer payment or redistribution of income of 140 000 pesos from rural rice growers to urban wage labourers would thus have occurred.

As in many other cases, the actual outcome of this potential conflict between farmers and urban workers with regard to the distribution of costs and benefits of government food subsidy programmes will *not* be determined exclusively or sometimes even primarily by economic or equity criteria. On the contrary, it will often be influenced by non-economic forces, specifically by the relative political power of different groups who can therefore exert greater political pressure on governments to structure tax and other laws to their personal benefit. Although sound and sensible economic criteria should form the basis of all development policies, the role of politics and relative political power in influencing these policies should never be underestimated.

Concepts for review

- economic theory
- model
- traditional or Western economic theory
- consumer sovereignty
- profit maximisation
- micro-economics
- macro-economics
- scarcity
- prices and price mechanism or system
- economic constraint
- consumption
- investment
- human capital
- money
- demand curve
- income effect
- 'real' v. 'money' income
- price elasticity of demand
- relation between demand elasticity and total revenue
- income elasticity of demand
- inferior, superior and normal goods
- supply curve
- elasticity of supply
- 'surplus' labour
- equilibrium price
- institutional wages and prices
- dual price systems
- black market
- imperfect market
- rationing

Questions for discussion

1. What is economic theory about and what are its

essential characteristics? Why is it important for analysing development problems?

2. Why should we be sceptical about any claims of universal applicability of traditional theories? Explain.
3. To what extent is Western economic theory of limited relevance to understanding many of the economic problems of Third World countries? Give some specific examples.
4. What is the meaning of the assertion that although assumptions and propositions of economic theories may differ from one society to the next, the 'thought processes' of economics are similar – i.e. what do we mean by the notion of common economic thought processes?
5. What is the distinction between 'scarce' resources and 'limited' resources? What is the relationship between economic scarcity and prices?
6. What are the essential functions of a price system? Give some examples.
7. Why is it important to distinguish between real and money incomes? Give a specific illustration.
8. Why are the concepts of price and income elasticities of demand important for economic policies in less developed nations? Give two examples of their application to real world development issues.
9. Why might producers in less developed countries not be able to increase their supply when prices rise in accordance with the concept of a supply curve? What is the relationship between supply elasticities and producer responses to rising prices for their outputs?
10. Explain the concept of an equilibrium price and its determination by the forces of demand and supply. Why might such a demand–supply price determination theory not present a true picture of how international and domestic prices are determined in the real world? Give two examples.
11. Why is the concept of rationing important for understanding many of the day-to-day pricing and commodity allocation problems in Third World countries?
12. What is meant by a 'dual' price system? Why might it be established and how does it function? Give a specific example, say, with respect to the pricing of domestic staple foods like rice and maize.

Chapter 4 Important concepts and principles – II

> In the field of ideas, the Third World has frequently lived with concepts of development . . . which were often externally conceived and largely inappropriate.
> *Santiago Declaration of Third World Economists, 1973*

Introduction

In the previous chapter, we saw how many fundamental economic concepts, such as scarcity, demand and supply curves, competitive price determination and elasticities, can be applied to the problems of developing nations. We also saw, however, how some of even these most relevant of traditional economic concepts need to be modified to represent more accurately the structural and institutional realities of Third World nations.

In this chapter we concentrate on the theory of production, costs, revenue and profit maximisation, the choice of production techniques, questions of present versus future consumption, the welfare implications of trade-offs between the consumption of the rich and that of the poor, and the important distinction between social as opposed to private benefits and costs. These concepts are directly relevant to many of the problems and issues dealt with in Parts Two and Three.

Inputs, outputs and the 'laws' of production

The production function

Underlying supply curves is the whole concept of production theory, which deals with the determinants of costs, hence the amount a producer may be willing to supply at different prices. The present and future consumption of goods, services, leisure, beauty and so on, is the ultimate objective of all economic activity. But the mechanism by which these goods and services are produced either in response to consumer preferences as revealed by their aggregate demand curves (the phenomenon of 'consumer sovereignty') or as a result of the more centralised decisions of government or private corporate planners is important for the determination of what and how much of each will be available for consumption, now and in the future.

The transformation of physical and human inputs into final outputs of goods and services is described by the **theory of production.** Along with demand and supply analysis, it provides one of the central foundations for all traditional economics.

The concept of a **production function** is used by economists as a convenient shorthand way of expressing quantitatively the presumed existence of a **systematic, technical relationship** between the use of factors of production or resources (known as inputs) and the resulting maximum obtainable output. Thus the production function expresses a technological relationship between input and output: how much output of, say, cotton textile can be obtained if certain fixed amounts of human and physical inputs – labour, raw cotton and machinery – are combined and utilised in accordance with a known and fixed technique of production. At any time and for any given state of technology, therefore, the production function represents the *maximum* attainable output that can be produced for each and every combination of specified inputs.

Resources and factors of production

Until recently economists traditionally divided

productive inputs or resources into three broad categories: land, labour and capital. Land, or 'natural' resources, including water and minerals, was regarded as a gift of God or nature and in relatively fixed supply. Capital consisted of such things as buildings, roads, railways, communication facilities, machinery and equipment accumulated as a result of past savings and their investment. Labour, though it may accumulate as a result of population growth, was not originally conceived of as a resource whose quantity was subject to economic decisions.[1]

The problem with this strict threefold categorisation is that investment can be used not only to increase the stock of capital goods but also to educate human beings and improve the quality of land. Consequently, economists today define the resource capital in a much broader sense to include not only those things which are usually thought of as 'physical' capital (factories, machines, railroads, electric power generators, etc.) but also stocks of 'intermediate' goods (goods that are used in an intermediate stage for the production of other 'final' goods, e.g. fertiliser for wheat, oil for petrol and raw cotton for textiles) and 'human capital' to represent improved labour quality resulting from investment in formal academic or vocational education. For practical purposes, therefore, the resource or input 'labour' is often divided into specific sub-categories (e.g. unskilled, semi-skilled and skilled labour) to reflect differing qualities and levels of training.

Public and private investment in human beings through education and training serves to improve a very scarce human capital resource. In most cases such investment can be even more important for development than accumulating physical capital. The reason is simple. More capital goods cannot be used effectively if there are not enough people with the skill and training (including management) to know how to use them to the best advantage. With these qualifications about the nature of productive resources in mind (we shall discuss them in greater detail in later chapters) let us return now to the basic features of the theory of production.

[1] In Chapter 12, however, we discuss the new micro-economic theory of fertility behaviour in which family size decisions are presumed to be subject to economic calculations.

The case of one output and one variable input: total and marginal products

Let us start with the simplest case of production theory. Suppose we wish to analyse the production of coffee on a small privately owned commercial farm in Colombia, South America. It is a family farm of say, 10 hectares, producing nothing but coffee for export to North America. There is thus only one output, coffee. Let us assume further that there is only one *variable* input or factor of production: the labour of our Colombian farmer, plus that of his family and possibly some additional hired help. Labour is a 'variable' input in the sense that the farmer can choose to apply more or less (i.e. he can hire wage labour or just use the services of his family) depending on the amount of output he desires to produce. Land and, say, some simple farm tools are assumed to be the *fixed* inputs – that is, all ten hectares are covered with coffee plants and there is no additional land available for cultivation, nor can more tools be purchased.

Let us assume that coffee plants bud once every year during ordinary weather in Colombia. As the farmer goes about picking the beans which are ready, he has the choice of simply picking those most readily accessible or of taking more labour time to pick more exhaustively. The basic question of simple production theory then is the following: what is the *maximum* annual output that our Colombian coffee grower can produce if he employs one worker (himself), two workers (his wife and two older children part-time), three workers (his family plus one hired labourer), four workers, etc.?

Table 4.1
An hypothetical relationship between labour inputs and coffee output in Colombia

Number employed	Total (output) product (kg per year)	Marginal (output) product (kg per worker)
0	0	0
1	500	500
2	1200	700
3	2000	800
4	2600	600
5	3000	400
6	3200	200

The first two columns of Table 4.1 give an hypothetical numerical illustration of the output which can be obtained when different amounts of the variable labour input are applied to the fixed amount of land; it is the farmer's *production function* for coffee. We see that total output continues to increase as our coffee farmer utilises up to six labourers on his 10 hectares of land. Moreover, we may note from column (3) that after the application of the farmer's own labour which causes output to rise from zero to 500 kg of coffee per year, the addition of a second (his family) and third (hired worker) causes the extra or marginal output produced to increase by 700 and 800 kg respectively.

Economists call these successive increases in output the 'marginal product' of labour, and define it as the additional output produced by an extra worker when all other inputs (land and tools in this case) are held constant. More generally, *the marginal product of any factor of production is simply the change in total product resulting from the application of one additional unit of that variable input when all other inputs are fixed or held constant.*

Figure 4.1 provides a diagrammatic illustration of the total and marginal product information given in Table 4.1. In Figure 4.1(*a*) the total output (product) of coffee is read off the vertical axis while total labour inputs are shown on the horizontal axis. Similarly in Figure 4.1(*b*) marginal products are read off the vertical axis while corresponding labour inputs are once again plotted on the horizontal axis.

Figure 4.1
Total and marginal product curves

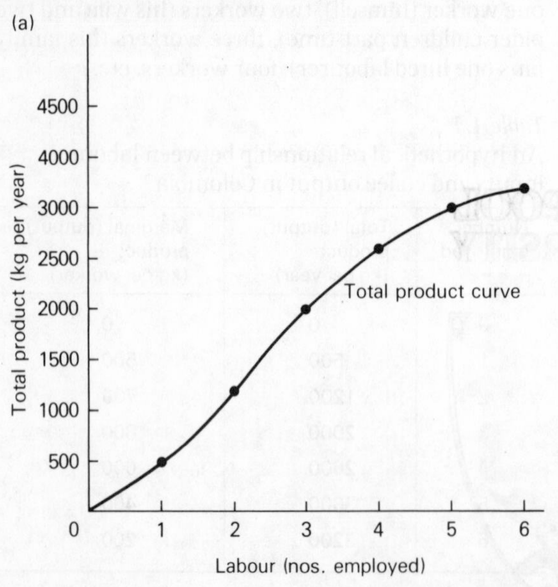

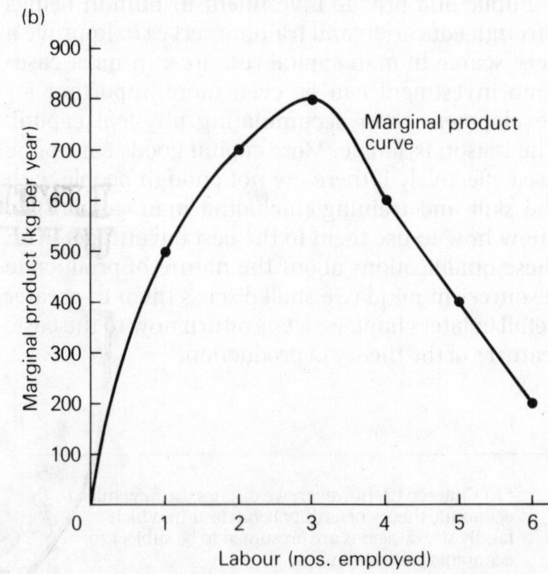

The principle of diminishing returns, rising costs, and profit maximisation

If you look again at Table 4.1, you will note that the addition of a fourth, fifth and sixth worker continues to cause total yearly coffee output to rise but at a slower pace. Increasing the total labour input from three to four workers, for example, raises total output from 2 000 to 2 600 kg per year. Yet the marginal product of this fourth worker (600 kg) is *less* than the marginal product of the third worker (800 kg per year). These successively smaller marginal labour products after the employment of three workers illustrates a very important principle of economics, the principle of diminishing returns. This states that beyond a certain number the application of *additional* quantities of one of the variable inputs of production – labour, land, materials, capital or management – will lead to progressively smaller *increments* of output (i.e. marginal products) *when all other inputs are held constant.* The more tools or machines a carpenter has to work with, the greater his output is likely to be; but after a point additional tools may be of no further help and may in fact complicate his work. The marginal product of the tools or machines will therefore fall. Similarly, in our case of the coffee farm in Colombia, the more workers who are hired to pick coffee beans the greater will be the total output of the land, but the less will be the added or marginal production of additional workers beyond three. Hiring more and more workers to pick coffee on a relatively small farm like this one will result in less work being done by each of them, since they will probably start to get in each other's way or develop lazy habits because there is not really enough work to keep everybody busy.

The principle of diminishing returns to a variable factor of production allows us to analyse the critical question of how many workers our Colombian coffee farmer should in fact hire if his goal is to maximise his profits from growing coffee – where profits are defined as the difference between total revenue and total costs. This is a valid behavioural assumption for cash crop production like coffee, cocoa, cotton, sugar and tea where the crop is being grown solely for commercial selling purposes. For staple, subsistence crops like rice, maize, sorghum or wheat, farmers may have non-commercial objectives such as meeting subsistence output needs rather than pure profit maximisation.

To determine optimal (i.e. profit maximising) output levels we require the following information in addition to that contained in Table 4.1: the fixed domestic selling price (and marginal revenue) for a kilo of coffee beans (e.g. 2 pesos per kg), the annual *fixed cost* of the farmer's coffee land and equipment and the wage rate (or *variable costs*) for farm labour (e.g. 800 pesos per crop year). With this information we can convert total product or output figures to total revenue measures ($TP \times P = TR$) and cost and marginal product information to total (and marginal) cost figures. The farmer should choose that output level and hire those workers that result in the greatest difference between total revenue and total costs. With the aid of Table 4.2, the mechanics of choosing optimal output levels for our hypothetical coffee grower should become clear.

In Table 4.2, columns 1, 2 and 5 are the same as in Table 4.1. Column 3 reflects the 2 peso per kg price of coffee that is being paid to Colombian coffee growers. Column 4 illustrates our grower's total revenue possibilities from the sale of his coffee and is simply column 2 multiplied by column 3. Column 6 shows a fixed cost of production of 1 000 pesos per year – where fixed costs are defined simply as those costs that must be paid by the grower *independent* of his output level (e.g. land taxes, fixed equipment depreciation etc.). Column 7 shows variable costs of production – those costs that vary with different output levels. In our case of only one variable input, labour, these represent the cost of hiring *x* workers at a going, fixed wage rate of 800 pesos per worker. Total cost in column 8 is then the sum of the fixed and variable costs of columns 6 and 7. Finally, column 9 shows *marginal costs* defined as the additional cost of producing one more unit of output. It is calculated in Table 4.2 as the change in total cost of adding one more labourer (800 pesos) divided by that worker's marginal product. Thus, for example, the first worker's marginal product is 500 kg of coffee. It costs the farmer 800 pesos to hire

Table 4.2
Choosing employment and output levels to maximise profits – elementary theory of the farm or firm

Number employed	Total product	Price of coffee (Peso per kg) = MR	Total revenue	Marginal product	Fixed cost (Peso)	Variable cost (p)	Total cost	Marginal cost
0	0	2	0	0	1000	0	1000	—
1	500	2	1000	500	1000	800	1800	1.62
2	1200	2	2400	700	1000	1600	2600	1.14
3	2000	2	4000	800	1000	2400	3400	1.00
4	2600	2	5200	600	1000	3200	4200	1.33
5	3000	2	6000	400	1000	4000	5000	2.00
6	3200	2	6400	200	1000	4800	5800	4.00

him. The marginal cost is therefore roughly 800/500 or 1.62 pesos per kilo. This is the first entry in column 9. The marginal cost to the farmer of the second worker is 800/700 or 1.14 pesos per kilo produced, while the fifth worker causes marginal cost to rise to 2 pesos per kilo. Note the important inverse relationship between columns 5 and 9 – *diminishing returns are what gives rise to increasing marginal costs and rising marginal costs provide the rationale for the upward sloping product supply curve of the firm or farm.* Only at higher product prices would a farm or firm be willing to supply more of its product because of rising costs of production.

It is clear from Table 4.2 that by hiring only, say, two workers, our coffee farmer will incur a loss of 200 pesos (compare column 8 with column 4 for row 3). If he hired six workers his profit would be 600 pesos. But he can *maximise* his profits at 1 000 pesos by hiring either four or five workers. Suppose he chooses to hire five workers so as to create more employment for the same profitable receipts. At an output level of 3 000 kg of coffee per year we note that *marginal cost* (2 pesos per kg) is just equal to *marginal revenue* (the change in total revenue from 5 200 to 6 000 pesos divided by the change in output from 2 600 to 3 000 kg, i.e. $8\,000 \div 4\,000 = 2$ pesos per kg). As long as marginal revenue exceeds marginal cost, a profit maximising firm will always be able to increase its profits by expanding its output. But eventually the principle of diminishing returns and rising marginal

Figure 4.2
Profit maximisation for a commercial farm

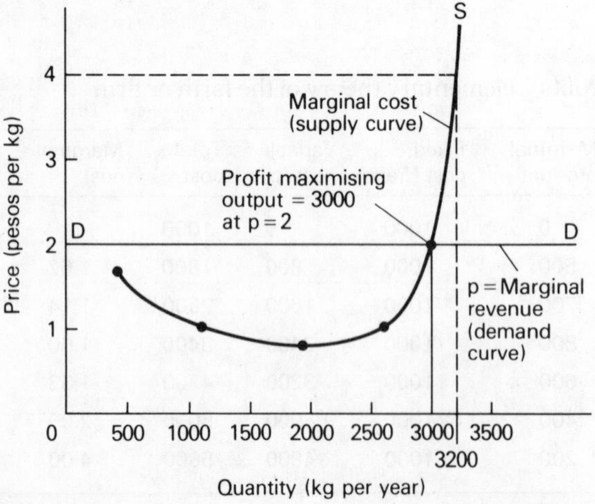

costs will dictate an output level at which any further expansion will result in lower profits. This is because the additional cost (marginal cost) of producing that extra output will exceed the additional revenue generated by the added production. It is what would happen if a sixth worker were hired by our coffee farmer.

The *basic rule for profit maximisation* for any profit motivated firm or farm, private or state owned, is thus the following: adjust output levels upward or downward until *marginal revenue equals marginal cost.* Where, however, enterprises, particularly those owned and operated by the state in developing nations, are motivated by other considerations such as employment generation subject say to a zero loss constraint, then the above well-known rule of Western economics will need to be modified and adapted to fit the institutional and policy circumstances of different societies.

Figure 4.2 portrays graphically the profit maximising output decision for our hypothetical Colombian coffee farmer. Suppose the price of coffee rose from 2 to 4 pesos per kg. What would be the new optimal output and employment level?

Another look at the 'surplus labour' concept

Recall now our discussion of the concept of rural 'surplus' labour in the previous chapter. Remember how this notion of unlimited potential supplies of labour for urban industry could be depicted graphically by an infinitely elastic urban labour supply curve at a fixed wage. Now the basic assumption underlying the supposed existence of widespread surplus rural labour in developing nations is none other than our principle of diminishing marginal products. Surplus labour arises, according to these development theories, because of the very high labour/land ratios in rural areas of poor nations. As a result of rapid rural population growth, increasing numbers of workers must be applied to fixed amounts of productive land. For example, in Colombia, for every 10-hectare coffee farm there may be 12 available workers whereas only, say, 9 can be used productively. In such situations the law of diminishing returns tells us that, unless new and better production technologies (use of irrigation, better seeds and fertiliser, etc.) are adopted to improve the quality and productivity of the land, the marginal productivities of the tenth, eleventh and twelfth coffee workers will be very low or even zero. Workers who add little or nothing to total agricultural output are therefore described as being economically 'surplus' and consequently a prime source of cheap labour for urban industrial growth. Whether or not the marginal product of labour in agriculture really is so low in poor nations is an issue which we take up in Chapter 16.

There are many other examples of the use of the concept of diminishing returns and the marginal product of a factor of production in development economics. It is therefore important for Third World economics students to understand this basic concept, if for no other reason than to be able to decide for themselves whether certain very influential theories like that of surplus labour and the policy guidelines which emanate from them or are not valid in their own particular countries and regions.

One output and two (or more) variable inputs: choosing the 'appropriate' technique of production

In most development situations, input-output production relationships will be considerably more complex than that pictured in Figures 4.1 and 4.2 for our Colombian coffee grower. At the very least, economists usually consider two variable inputs – labour and capital – as necessary to produce a given output. While most small-scale farming in tropical Africa, Asia and Latin America may essentially involve only one variable economic input (labour), larger producer operations (e.g. wheat and other cereal estates, sugar, cocoa and rubber plantations and, more importantly, most manufacturing enterprises) often involve choices about the use of machines (tractors, reapers, automatic textile looms, canning machines, etc.) as well as labour. In fact, as we shall see below, they typically involve choices (and, in some cases, non-choices) among a much wider range of economic and non-economic variable inputs than simply labour and capital. For present illustrative purposes, however, and as a basis for our later discussion of the phenomenon of technological transfer, appropriate technology, and unemployment we work with the notion of two-factor (labour and capital) production functions.

Suppose we take the case of a private local construction company which has just received a contract from the Indian Government to build a 100-kilometre road between a northern rural wheat-growing region and the nearest town. For simplicity, assume that there is only one available type of road-building machine designated *K* for capital and valued in units of 1 000 rupees per day – that is, the daily services of say four units of capital equipment, *K*, will cost the firm 4 000 rupees. All labour (*L*) is assumed to be unskilled and homogeneous (i.e. all road workers are of the same quality and, therefore, are potentially equally productive). A unit of labour (one worker) is paid 20 rupees per day. We shall assume finally that our road building company has a choice between two alternative methods of production, known as 'production processes' or 'technologies', for constructing roads in India. The first method requires a fixed combination of 4 units of capital equipment and 50 units of labour (i.e. 50 employees) in order to build 10 km of road per day. The second method for producing 10 km of road per day involves the combined use of 2 units of capital and 100 workers. Table 4.3 illustrates these two production processes and the cost per km for each.

We see that if technological Process 1 is used (combining 4 units of capital with every 50 units of

Table 4.3
Choosing the least-cost production for every 10 km of road-building in India

	Process 1			Process 2		
	Units needed ×	Cost per unit =	Total cost	Units needed ×	Cost per unit =	Total cost
K	4	R1,000	R4,000	2	R1,000	R2,000
L	50	R20	R1,000	100	R20	R2,000
		Total cost	R5,000		Total cost	R4,000
		Cost per km R500			Cost per km R400	

labour to produce 10 km of road) the total cost of constructing 10 km of road is 5 000 rupees, or an average cost of 500 rupees per km. The same 10 km of road can be produced by technological Process 2 for a total cost of 4 000 rupees or an average cost of 400 rupees per km. Since the required road length is 100 km, it could be built with Process 1 for a total cost of 50 000 rupees while Process 2 costs only 40 000 rupees.

In accordance with the principle of economy defined in Chapter 1, the optimal choice (the one which *minimises* the cost of producing a given level of output) is clearly Process 2. The reason the second production method turns out to be cheaper in this illustration is because it uses relatively more labour per unit of capital ($100 \div 2$ or a ratio of L to K of 50 to 1) than does Process 1 ($L/K = 12.5$) and labour is the cheaper (less 'scarce') factor of production. Process 2 is, therefore, said to be *relatively* more **labour-intensive** than Process 1 (i.e. it has a higher L/K ratio, 50 compared with 12.5). Conversely, Process 1 is said to be *relatively* **capital-intensive** – it has a higher K/L ratio; 0.08 compared with 0.02 for Process 2.

The above example of choosing the better (cheaper) of two alternative techniques of production illustrates another very important principle in economics and one which for a variety of institutional reasons is often violated in the actual day-to-day decisions of public and private enterprises in developing countries. This is the principle of 'optimisation' in the use of production inputs and it is a close relative of the principle of 'economy'. It states that when choosing among available techniques of production which are distinguished by different combinations of factor inputs (labour, capital, land, materials, management, etc.), the method of production which should be chosen should be that which, when factor prices are given, *minimises* the cost of producing a desired level of output or *maximises* the amount of output obtainable for any given cost. In most cases, the optimal or **appropriate technology** will be one which best economises on scarce resources (typically labour in rich industrial nations and capital and/or management in underdeveloped countries). In short, if input prices (wage rates for unskilled, skilled and managerial labour, rental and interest rates for physical and financial capital, and market prices for domestic and imported intermediate material inputs) correctly reflect their economic scarcity values, then in most Third World nations with a relative abundance of manpower the *appropriate* choice among various production techniques should be those technologies or production processes which are relatively labour-intensive.

Unfortunately the prices of labour and capital typically do not adequately reflect their true scarcity values in many less developed nations. This is due to a variety of economic and non-economic reasons. For example, powerful trade unions continually exert upward pressure on the level of urban wages. Wealthy local and foreign businessmen are often able to get LDC governments to lower imported machinery and equipment costs artificially (for example, by over-valuing foreign exchange rates).[2] They are often also granted special tax privileges related to domestic capital formation and given substantial capital depreciation allowances. Finally, large foreign and domestic corporations typically receive special access to import and export licences which only serve to reinforce their privileged economic and political positions.

All the above 'institutional' phenomena raise the market price of labour above its economic value while lowering the market price of capital far below what its domestic economic scarcity would imply. The result is that many inappropriate and costly capital-intensive techniques of production are adopted in both agricultural and manufacturing industries. If, on the other hand, factor prices truly reflected relative factor scarcities, there would be a greater incentive for private and public enterprises to adopt more labour-intensive production techniques. Numerous derivative problems, such as rising levels of urban unemployment and excessive losses of valuable foreign exchange, often follow in the wake of such inefficiencies (see Chapter 13).

Beyond the narrow economics of production functions: those untidy 'non-economic' factors

Theoretically, there exist production functions or 'states of the art' for every physical commodity and service produced and distributed in any economy.

[2] See Chapter 21 (p. 316), for an explanation of the meaning of implications of 'overvaluing' foreign exchange rates.

For example, there are the more common production functions for agricultural commodities like wheat, rice, corn, soyabeans, coffee and tea expressing the technical relationships between inputs such as land, labour, seed varieties, fertilisers, water and power and the corresponding output of the commodity. There are equally common though different production functions for manufactured goods such as textiles, radios, bicycles, furniture and soft drinks. These also show a systematic relationship between inputs or 'factors of production' and total output. Finally in the area of services, implicit though less common and easily definable production functions may operate between say, the inputs of an educational system (e.g. teacher quality, classroom size, availability of textbooks and quality of the curriculum) and its output (e.g. student performance in examinations or graduate contributions to national development).

If the production function relationships between input contributions and corresponding output levels are indeed fixed by engineering or technical factors for diverse commodities, one might expect to observe similar quantitative input–output relationships if the same commodity is produced with the same technical process in different societies. In fact, as we shall see in Chapter 19 this assumption of identical production functions for all nations is the basis of a very important theory of international trade. For example, if the production of 1 000 transistor radios per day requires say 15 electronic testing machines, 150 workers, 200 kilowatts of power and one supervisor in Japan or West Germany, why should not the same combination of factor inputs produce the same daily output of transistors in say, Sri Lanka, Sudan, Syria, Zambia or Peru? Again, why should a farmer with 20 hectares of land in Japan, using five full-time labourers, one small tractor, one tonne of fertiliser and four tubewells produce more tonnes of rice per hectare per year than his counterpart using the same production function in Indonesia, Thailand or the Philippines?

The fact is that production functions are *not* simply technical or engineering relationships applicable everywhere with similar results. This rather naïve assumption of the simple transferability of input–output relationships was one of the main reasons for the failure of many development strategies in the 1960s, especially where those strategies focused on the often indiscriminate establishment of import-substituting manufacturing industries (see Chapter 21). The basic drawback of the strictly economic production function analysis derives from its failure to give adequate attention to those institutional and structural aspects of social systems in developing nations which may turn out to be the most important determinants of how much output is obtainable from a given quantity or combination of economic inputs.

It is clear, for example, that an agricultural function (whether for wheat, rice, coffee, corn or soyabeans) in the majority of developing nations should take into account among its relevant inputs much more than simply land, labour, seed varieties, fertiliser, power and water. Even adjusting for qualitative differences in land and labour (i.e. better soil conditions and more educated farmers), factors such as the health and nutritional standards of farmers and farm workers, the degree of risk and uncertainty involved with alternative agricultural technologies (especially for subsistence farmers), access to credit at reasonable rates, availability of competent and concerned extension agents, systems of land tenure, distance from town and patterns of kinship and religion can be equally or more important inputs to the production process. Each of these variables is likely in many societies to be as systematically related to levels of agricultural production as labour and capital (see Chapters 15 and 16).

This is precisely where the economist's dilemma comes in. For, given its broadest interpretation, the production function could be said to include all these variables, both those which are economic (e.g. capital and credit) and those which are not (e.g. kinship patterns and land tenure systems). But it would then lose much of the appealing simplicity it possesses when expressed simply as a relationship between total output and total inputs of labour and capital. A choice must be made. Economists, being no different from other human beings, will usually choose the easy path and will often sacrifice relevance for convenience in describing the determinants of production in both developed and less developed nations. They are usually ready to grant the probable importance of variables other than labour and capital, including those which are strictly non-economic, in production analysis. But they then either forget all about these variables or avoid unnecessary complications by saying that they will leave it to some (usually non-existent) professional from another discipline to worry about them. This situation would be less damaging if such discussions remained within academic walls. Unfortunately, the problem of how to accelerate production in a variety of Third World industries will not go away.

Local academic and government economists, who like yourselves probably once took an introductory economics course, have in the past been and will continue in the future to be even more called upon by their governments for advice on methods of promoting agricultural and industrial expansion. The effectiveness of this advice will depend to a great extent on the degree to which they are able to transcend the restrictive assumptions of conventional economic models (like that of the simple production function or the determination of price by the purely competitive forces of supply and demand), and be bold and confident enough to supplement many of these admittedly valuable and relevant concepts in their analytical frameworks with necessary modifications for the prevailing and often unique attitudes and institutions extant in their societies. Such factors as land tenure systems, the availability of credit, the significance and pervasiveness of corruption at all levels of public and private activity, the power of class, caste or tribal interests, the distributive impact of taxes and tax loopholes, and the attitudes and objectives of trade unions, local manufacturing organisations, and foreign private enterprises may or may not be dominating factors in determining whether strictly economic approaches to promoting 'development' in general (we discuss the various meanings and ambiguities of this concept in Chapter 6), and increased production in particular, succeed or fail. But to deny their existence, or to recognise them and then casually to dismiss them when offering policy advice, would be, and in many instances in various LDCs has been, a major reason for the many failures of even the best-intentioned development strategies.

Savings, investment and the time dimension

We have seen that the concept of choice plays a central role in all economic analysis. But the dimensions of choice are much broader than simply the consumer's choice whether to eat rice or fish, or the producer's choice of how much output to produce or whether to employ labour-intensive or capital-intensive techniques of production. One extremely important dimension of choice concerns that between **present and future consumption** and between **production for current or future use.** Individual families, whether rich or poor, must decide how to divide their expenditures out of income in some proportion between present and future consumption. That part of income which is not consumed is called **savings**. Monetary savings can simply be stored for future use, but in most cases their 'real' value will probably decline due to inflation. Alternatively, savings can be deposited in a bank to earn **interest** so that their 'real' value may increase to the extent that the interest rate paid by the bank exceeds the rate of inflation.

For example, let us assume that there is only one commodity available for consumption, say bread, which sells today for 50 cents a loaf. An individual who earns 400 cents per week could therefore buy eight loaves. However, if he chooses instead to consume only 300 cents worth of bread per week (six loaves) and saves (deposits) the remaining 100 cents in a bank at an annual interest rate of 10 per cent, in one year's time that 100 cents will have grown to 110 cents. If in the meantime the price of bread increases by only 4 per cent from 50 to 52 cents a loaf, our consumer/saver will be able to purchase two loaves as before but will not have 6 cents left over. Therefore, after a year's time he could theoretically buy $2\frac{6}{52}$ or approximately 2.12 loaves of bread. His 'real' income – what he can actually buy with this money income (110 cents) – has increased as a result of his saving, by 6 per cent, the difference between the rate of interest (10 per cent) and the rate of inflation (4 per cent).

In general, then, we can define the change in the 'real' value of any monetary variable (income, savings, wages, interest, exports, consumption, investment, etc.) as the difference between the percentage change in the nominal or money value of the variable and the rate of inflation (i.e. the percentage change in some overall cost of living or price index). For example, if the average money wage increases by 10 per cent and the rate of inflation is 7 per cent, then the 'real' wage has increased by only 3 per cent.

Like consumers, private producers and governments must face a similar choice in deciding how to allocate existing resources between production for present consumption and production for future consumption. Resources devoted to expanding future income and consumption are known as **investments**. The allocation of these present 'real' resources (land, labour, capital, materials, management, etc.) to future production and consumption is the essence of the process of investment. Its major characteristic is the dominant role played by **time**. For example, the decision whether to allocate limited public funds in the form of price support subsidies to farmers to encourage them to expand their production of a staple commodity like corn or to devote these same resources to expanding educational opportunities is essentially a decision about present consumption (food now) as opposed to future consumption (food later as a result of a more educated and possibly therefore a more productive agricultural labour force). In addition to education, other types of public investment in Third World nations include roads, hospitals, rural sanitation and electrification programmes, and even early childhood nutrition, as well as the more common public and private investments in the form of new factories, machinery and equipment.

Such examples illustrate the rather thin line between the economist's traditional definitions of consumption and investment when these concepts are applied to real world situations of less developed nations. Is the provision of low cost food to the poor and early childhood nutrition programmes, for example, to be counted as consumption or investment? In rich nations where the incidence of malnutrition among the general population is relatively low, such activities can be classified as present consumption. In very poor nations where 40 to 60 per cent of the population, both young and old, may be suffering from some form of malnutrition, the above programmes would be not only of a present consumption nature but would also represent 'human capital' investments in the health and productivity of the labour force, both now and in the future.

The fact remains that investment in the form of expanding the nation's capital, both physical and 'human', has been and continues to be viewed by economists and politicians alike as a primary strategy for promoting social and economic development. But in order to devote the necessary resources to expand the stock of physical and human capital, **domestic saving** (individual, corporate and public) has to be increased to finance public and private investment. In other words, people have to be asked to consume less out of a given national income so that they and their descendants may consume more at a later time. We discuss the specific mechanism by which present saving and investment is translated into future economic growth in Chapter 6. For the present we simply consider the general implications for development strategy of choices between consumption now and consumption later.

Present and future consumption

Since the process of consumption occurs through time, how does one go about comparing the social value of consumption at different times? It is clear, for example, that a cruzeiro of consumption in Brazil or a rupee's worth in India in ten years' time may not be as valuable as a cruzeiro or rupee of consumption today, even if we assume that prices and, therefore, the 'real' value of a cruzeiro or rupee does not change. The reason is simply that we would normally expect that in ten years' time the average Brazilian and Indian consumer will have higher income levels[3] and therefore expenditure of a cruzeiro or rupee on, say, bread will not be as important as it is today.

Since governments in less developed countries have to be concerned with the 'time-path' of consumption (as well as public and private investment, private saving, taxation, etc.), consumption this year, next year, and in ten years' time compete with each other to a certain extent. How might one go about evaluating the relative importance of consumption at different periods? One widely used approach is to attach a number or 'weight' to consumption in each period to reflect the relative importance to society (however defined) of an additional or 'marginal' cruzeiro or rupee of

[3] As we shall discover in Chapter 9, this assumption of rising *real* per capita income levels over a ten year period, especially for the very poor, may not be borne out by the facts in countries such as Brazil, India and many others.

consumption in, say, period 3 as compared with, say, period 5. Consider the following illustration.

Suppose we write C_0, C_1, C_2, C_3, C_4 and C_5 as symbols representing the anticipated values at constant prices of total consumption (i.e. total 'real' consumption) in say Brazil, from year zero (today) to year 5. Dividing these values by the projected population, *P*, of Brazil over this period, we obtain a quantitative estimate of consumption per head, or 'per capita' (Latin for heads) consumption, over the five-year period, namely,

$$\frac{C_0}{P_0}, \frac{C_1}{P_1}, \frac{C_2}{P_2}, \frac{C_3}{P_3}, \frac{C_4}{P_4} \text{ and } \frac{C_5}{P_5}.$$

Let us assume that by following different economic policies, the Brazilian Government has the ability of raising one or more of the *C*s, but only at a cost of reducing one or more of the others. Economists call such a phenomenon a 'trade-off' between consumption in one period and another. Is there any basis for saying that an increase in C_1 at the expense of C_5 is any more important than an increase in C_5 at the expense of C_1? Not unless we assume that C_5/P_5 will be higher anyway than C_1/P_1. However, if such a growth assumption is made, and it usually is since one of the objectives of economic development is to increase the level of per capita consumption over time, then it follows that the urgency of raising consumption by one cruzeiro in year 5 is less than in year 1. The government might therefore give a lower weight to consumption in year 5 than year 1, to reflect the relatively lower importance attached to raising consumption per head in that later year. We could, therefore, rewrite our expression for per capita consumption in each period as

$$W_0\frac{C_0}{P_0}, W_1\frac{C_1}{P_1}, W_2\frac{C_2}{P_2}, W_3\frac{C_3}{P_3}, W_4\frac{C_4}{P_4} \text{ and } W_5\frac{C_5}{P_5}$$

where *W* is a numerical figure which indicates the relative 'qualitative' importance to be attached to increasing that particular *C*/*P* ratio by one cruzeiro.[4]

If consumption per capita in Brazil is expected to rise over time as a result of anticipated rapid overall economic growth, then there is a good case for arguing that the *W*s should fall over time – that W_1 be less than W_0, W_2 less than W_1 and so on with W_5 being the lowest of all. This is because the higher the real per capita consumption (e.g. we have assumed that say C_3/P_3 is greater than C_2/P_2), the less **relatively** important it becomes to increase it further. For example, W_0 can be set equal to unity (which means that present per capita consumption is used as the base number or measuring rod) so that the *W*s fall from unity and approach zero as we get further into the future (e.g. W_4 might be set at 0.40 and W_5 at 0.25). The rate at which the *W*s fall over time (e.g. 10 per cent per year) has been variously called by economists the **social discount rate** or the **consumption rate of interest**. For example, if the Brazilian Government were to decide that the social value of real per capita consumption in the distant future should be no different from today (note this is an intergenerational welfare or ethical question), then the consumption rate of interest would be calculated as that rate at which all future consumption will be discounted to make it equivalent to the value of present consumption. If *C*/*P* is expected to rise, then *W* must fall and the consumption rate of interest (the rate of fall in *W*) will be positive. The faster the expected rise in real per capita consumption, the higher the rate would be.

For example if $W_0 = 1$, $C_0/P_0 = 100$ and $C_1/P_1 = 125$, then solving for W_1 in the equation

$$W_0\frac{C_0}{P_0} = W_1\frac{C_1}{P_1}$$

we get,

$$W_1 = \frac{W_0(C_0/P_0)}{C_1/P_1} = \frac{100}{125} = 0.8$$

Therefore, W_1 should be chosen as 0.8 and the consumption interest rate, $r(= {}^1/w_1 - 1)$, would be 25 per cent. This means that an additional cruzeiro of consumption today is deemed to be 25 per cent more important than the same addition next year. Note that if C_1/P_1 were 150 instead of 125, W_1 would be 0.67 and the interest rate 50 per cent.

Finally, it is important to remember that the choice of weights for each period represents an ethical or value judgment about the importance of the welfare of different generations of Brazilians. People living now might be inclined to say 'let future generations take care of themselves' and therefore decide that welfare of future generations is not their

[4] Note that in our illustration we have attached importance *only* to increasing total consumption per head in any given year whereas the question of who gets the consumption is omitted. Clearly, distribution among people is just as important as distribution over time. We discuss this issue in the next section.

problem. Such an attitude would mean that future consumption should be given a weight of zero with the implication that only present consumption matters. This present-oriented attitude, though perhaps not in the extreme form which we have expressed it, is more understandable in very poor nations than in those which are relatively rich. It is in fact one of the main reasons why the 31 'least developed' countries find it so difficult to generate sufficient domestic savings to raise their rate of investment and thus accelerate rates of national economic growth.

Comparing internal consumption standards for different income groups

In the preceding discussion we indicated that a major reason for 'discounting' future consumption was the expectation that the ordinary process of economic growth would lead to higher levels of real per capita consumption in the future. But if a government attaches less weight to the consumption of an average citizen in five or ten years' time on the grounds that he will be richer, then it logically follows that relatively less weight should be attached to the consumption of a rich man today than to that of a poor man today.

Instead of simply taking the average real national consumption in a particular year as a broad measure of economic welfare, as we did in the previous section, we could have used some weighted average of the consumption of different population groups within the nation for each year. Theoretically, a separate 'weight' should be applied to each and every individual with a different consumption level. This is because the importance of each man's consumption may differ, just as the importance of consumption for whole populations may vary between different periods. Obviously, in reality it would not be practical or even possible to attach a weight to each and every individual's level of consumption. However, it is feasible instead to divide the population into, say, five different income groups and attach different weights to the consumption of individuals in each group.

For example, suppose we divided the Nigerian population into five income groups ranging from the bottom 20 per cent to the top 20 per cent: if, for example, there were 1 000 000 people we would take the 200 000 with the lowest income levels and place them in group P_1, the next 200 000 in group P_2, and so on up to group P_5. For each group, different weights W_1 to W_5, would have to be attached, with W_1 being the highest weight and W_5 the lowest. Clearly, the choice of actual weights to be assigned to each income group will be somewhat arbitrary since they will have to be chosen on the basis of normative value criteria about what is desirable. But such weights would at least be a better reflection of society's valuation of raising the consumption of different income groups according to relative need than not using any differential weights at all. This is precisely why countries try to structure their tax systems progressively with the rich paying higher average rates than the poor. To use equal weights on the other hand would imply that an additional Nigerian Naira of consumption which accrues to a very rich man would be deemed to have the same marginal social value as an additional Naira of consumption for a very poor man.

To illustrate the preceding discussion, take the case of the lowest and highest income-consumption groups (P_1 and P_5) in our example. Suppose the Nigerian Government attaches a weight, W_1 equal to 2.0 to the consumption level of the lowest income group and W_5 equal to 1.0 for the highest; that is,

$$W_1P_1 = 2.0P_1 \quad \text{and} \quad W_5P_5 = 1.0P_5.$$

It follows from these weights that the government considers programmes aimed at improving the conditions of the very poor to be twice as important as those leading to an equal monetary improvement for the very rich. Such an overall distributive weighting of consumption by differing income groups would also imply that of two possible government development projects with equal costs and equal returns, the one which raises income and consumption of the very poor by a greater amount will be chosen. Such a project, which benefits the poor disproportionately, is said to have a higher 'social' rate of return than another project which may yield the same overall financial return but whose benefits accrue primarily to the rich.

Note that there is nothing in economics or economic theory *per se* that dictates the relative importance of giving preference to the poor. In fact, much of the so-called 'welfare' economics of Western theory is based on the proposition that it is impossible to make 'interpersonal' comparisons. It is argued, therefore, that one cannot assign any greater social weight to the generation of income for the poor as oppposed to the rich since we cannot objectively or scientifically compare one man's welfare with that of another. But, as pointed out previously, LDC governments beset by widespread poverty and growing income disparities have to make such value decisions all the time when formulating a development strategy. This crucial issue of value choices as they relate to income distribution is discussed further in Chapter 10. We turn now to our final important economic concept: the distinction between social and private benefits and costs.

'Private' v. 'social' benefits and costs

Whenever a choice is made, individuals, whether they are conscious of it or not, are weighing the costs of the decision (both financial and perhaps psychological) against the probable benefits. When you purchase a radio, a new dress or a bottle of beer, your decision to part with a certain sum of money in return for the item indicates that you value what you are buying (the derived 'benefit' of the purchase) at least as high and probably higher than the price or 'cost' of the transaction. Your decision to enter the university implicitly involved a decision that the material benefits to be derived (the award of a university degree and the anticipated higher income-earning potential) were sufficiently greater in the long run than the costs (tuition, fees, books, earnings foregone from not being able to work full-time earlier, etc.). Diverse decisions, such as whether to attend a concert or a sporting event, to read a good book or just lie in the sun, and even to get married or stay single, involve implicit and sometimes explicit 'cost-benefit' calculations.

In economics, decisions by individual units (consumers, the family, the small farmer, the individual producer) involve a weighing of 'private' benefits and costs, that is, benefits and costs which affect only the individual or the isolated economic unit making the decision. The decision by our Colombian coffee farmer to hire an *additional* worker involved a comparison of the costs to him of this decision (the monthly wage of the worker) against his anticipated benefits (the market value of the extra or marginal product of this labourer). A consumer purchasing a bottle of beer will usually only weigh the cost to him (the price of beer) against his expected benefits (relief from thirst plus whatever benefits are derived from a little alcoholic stimulus).

In each of the above cases, it has been assumed that a 'correct' decision would occur so long as the individual consumer or producer making the decision could derive an excess of private benefit over private cost. In the theory of free enterprise or *laissez-faire* capitalism where it is conveniently assumed that each decision making unit (producer and consumer) is so small in relation to the overall market that it cannot affect the well-being of any other unit by its economic decisions, private benefit becomes synonymous with social benefit and private cost with social cost.[5] By social benefit and cost we mean the benefit which *society as a whole* may gain from any private or public decision and the cost which the whole society bears as a result of any individual or group decision.

External economies and diseconomies of production and consumption

Clearly, however, social benefits in excess of private benefits do occur, for instance when people with advanced education and training apply their skills for the betterment of less fortunate members of their society rather than simply using these acquired skills for their own personal financial benefit. Examples might include rural public health workers, dedicated agricultural extension agents, urban social workers, rural teachers and adult educational instructors. Similarly, when an individual firm provides on-the-job training for its

[5] Recall Adam Smith's theory of the 'invisible hand' of market capitalism.

unskilled labour, it is conferring a potential benefit to society as a whole in the form of a more highly skilled labour force, and particularly to other firms which might eventually hire this trained worker. These total direct and indirect social benefits may be greater than the direct private benefit (higher productivity) derived by the firm which does the training.

On the other hand, the social cost of a private decision is often greater than the private cost. Examples in consumption would include the individual who gets intoxicated, causing a disturbance and even injury to other people as a result of careless driving; the family which throws refuse and garbage into the road in front of its house, causing discomfort and perhaps sickness to neighbours; persons with infectious diseases who congregate in public places; and even the student who continues to play loud music in his dormitory room, preventing his room mate and other students from studying effectively.

In production, there are also many examples of situations in which individual decisions lead to social costs greatly in excess of private costs. The classic economic example is the pollution of the atmosphere or rivers caused by the effluent discharge of privately owned cement, paper and chemical factories. In these cases the costs of production to the firm (labour, rent, capital, materials, etc.) do not adequately reflect the costs to society as a whole in the form of polluted air and water and the associated aesthetic and physical discomforts. In developing countries more common examples would include overloaded and poorly maintained lorries and buses which spew forth noxious exhaust fumes on rural roads and urban streets, or the rapid erosion of agricultural land as a result of indiscriminate cutting down of trees for firewood and charcoal.

Economists have a particular name for the above phenomena where social and private benefits and cost diverge. They are known as **external effects** or **externalities** and they arise whenever the activities of an individual economic unit result in costs or benefits to other economic units or to society as a whole which have no correspondence to the actual (private) costs and benefits involved in and derived from the isolated decision of the economic unit in question. Benefits which accrue to society in excess of those which accrue to the decision-making unit itself are called **external economies** in production (e.g. on-the-job labour training programmes) and consumption (e.g. public health efforts, education, vocational training, nutritional supplementation programmes). Those costs which society as a whole or other individual decision-making units must bear as a result of the separate activities of another unit are known as **external diseconomies** in production (e.g. the pollution of air and water, the erosion of agricultural soil through improper use, and the higher risk of floods as a result of indiscriminate deforestation activities of public and private enterprises) and consumption (e.g. discarding private garbage in public streets, alcoholism, drug addiction, corruption, and prostitution).

Diverging private and social valuations: some implications

Whenever social costs and benefits differ from private cost and benefits (e.g. whenever external economies and diseconomies of production and consumption exist) decisions based purely on private calculations of benefits and costs lead to situations (in the case of diseconomies) where society as a whole can be made *worse off* as a result of some individual or group within that society being made *better off*. In such situations the 'correct' decision from a private point of view (e.g. rapid deforestation to supply timber for private paper mills) may be incorrect from a social viewpoint, and conversely in cases where social benefits exceed private benefits (e.g. rural health clinics, adult education and pre-school nutritional programmes).

The distinction between social and private benefits and costs of public and private decisions is an extremely important concept in our analysis and understanding of Third World economics. There are numerous situations in which the 'correct' benefit-cost calculations by private individuals (i.e., where the action leads to a net positive private benefit) can lead to situations in which a social benefit-cost calculation would have dictated against the decision (i.e., where there is a net loss to society as a whole). The decision by individual rural migrants, for example, to move to already overcrowded cities like Bombay, Caracas, Mexico City, Cairo and Lagos in search of relatively well-paid jobs in the face of heavy urban unemployment may be the correct one for the migrant attempting to maximise 'expected' income (see Chapter 14). However, as a result of this decision and, especially if the migrant remains unemployed for a long period of time, society incurs not only the cost of his lost agricultural output (sometimes referred to as his 'opportunity cost') but also the costs of housing and sheltering him, as well as the social, psychological and political costs of excessively high levels of urban unemployment.

Similarly, a 'correct' private decision by a family to increase its size (children are often important sources of old age security in poor nations) can, in an overpopulated, resource-poor nation, incur considerable economic costs to society as a whole (see Chapter 11). Government electrification or irrigation projects through the construction of dams like that at Aswan in Egypt can result in a sizable increase in the parasitic and debilitating disease known as schistosomiasis or bilharzia. Clearly, benefit-cost calculations of alternative investment projects which do not account for these external diseconomies to society as a whole may result in incorrect decisions, or at least in unforeseen complications.

But the concept of social v. private benefits and costs should not be constrained by national boundaries. Intellectual honesty requires us to view the world as a social system and to analyse the 'private' decisions of nation-states in terms of their social effects on the world as a whole. What may be in the best interests of one nation or group of nations (e.g. the rich industrial countries) may be positively harmful to the larger world population in developing countries. For example, the continual pervasive and uncontrolled depletion of the world's dwindling and non-renewable resources to meet the disproportionate consumption appetites of a minority of the world's population in North America, Europe, the Soviet Union and Japan, may make it that much more difficult for Third World nations to escape from the confines of abject poverty, low levels of living and rapid population growth.

One final point needs to be made before concluding this section. Almost all developing nations, regardless of ideology, make use of some type of price system as signals and incentives to allocate economic goods, services and resources among alternative uses in consumption and production. The price of borrowing money (the interest rate) is also often used to stimulate saving and investment for the growth of future production and consumption. The 'correctness' or 'non-correctness' of these product and resource prices (including wages and interest rates) can be important determinants of whether production, employment and investment decisions, both public and private, are taken in the best social interest. To the extent that overall factor and product prices, urban and rural wage rates, primary school fees and tuition charges for secondary and higher education and the relative prices of domestic and foreign goods do *not* reflect the true (i.e. scarcity) social costs of these goods, services and resources, any benefit–cost calculation based on these distorted prices will not only be incorrect from a strict economic point of view but also potentially very damaging to the long-run development aspirations of the society as a whole. There is probably no fundamental economic concept more relevant for understanding problems of Third World development than the crucial distinction between private and social benefits and costs.

Summary and conclusions

Economic theories and principles are the tools by which economists organise a variety of social and economic phenomena into simplified conceptual frameworks which enable them to understand and explain the workings of an economic system. The basic requirement of any economic theory or model is that it should be capable of explaining economic processes on the basis of *realistic* assumptions and abstractions appropriate to the characteristic features of diverse economies. Much of so-called 'traditional' or 'Western' economic theory is of limited relevance for understanding the characteristic features of the economic and social processes of developing nations. This is because it is based on assumptions and abstractions like the power of consumer sovereignty, the pervasive existence of competitive price determination, and the overriding motivational imperative of corporate profit maximisation, which may bear little resemblance to the factors affecting economic behaviour in poor nations. Moreover, such theories are often based on implicit assumptions about **attitudes** (e.g. the desire and ability to modernise, the exaltation of individual self-interest, the motivation for material advancement, the quest for efficiency, etc.) and **institutions** (e.g. effective tax and credit systems, well-functioning, efficient and incorruptible bureaucratic and administrative structures, functional and relevant educational systems, the legal and cultural sanctity of private property, close linkages between various economic sectors, etc.) which for the most part are missing or non-existent in many developing nations. It follows that a careful selection of appropriate economic concepts and principles adapted to the realities of these nations is not only desirable but essential to an adequate understanding of the way in which economics can contribute to Third World development.

A number of such broad concepts and principles, with illustrations of how they can be related to the real world problems of poor nations, were described in this and the preceding chapter. Concepts such as economic scarcity, the explicit and implicit role of prices, demand and supply curves, rationing, elasticities, 'real' versus monetary variables, production functions, cost curves and the concept of appropriate technologies, the role of 'non-economic' factors, trade-offs between present and future consumption, the welfare implications of income redistribution, and the vital distinction between social and private benefits and costs – these and other basic principles relevant for developing countries have been reviewed and analysed in these two chapters. We shall have many occasions to draw on them throughout the remaining chapters.

Concepts for review

production function
factors of production
fixed and variable inputs
marginal product
principle of diminishing productivity
production techniques or processes
intermediate goods
final goods
physical capital
human capital
labour-intensive technique
capital-intensive technique
principle of optimisation
'appropriate' technology
savings
present v. future consumption
interest and interest rates
social discount rate
private v. social valuations
private benefit
social benefit
private cost
social cost
external and internal economies
external and internal diseconomies

Questions for discussion

1. The production function is said to be an 'engineering' concept. What do we mean by this? Why do you think production functions might vary from one country to another or from one farm to another?
2. Explain the difference between quantity and quality of factors of production. Give examples of how the quality of different factors can be increased.
3. Why do you think the concept of a 'marginal product' is important? What is its relationship to the notion of surplus labour in LDCs?
4. Give a simple explanation of the principle of diminishing productivity with two examples. What are the essential assumptions about production that give rise to this concept?
5. What is meant by an 'appropriate' technology of production? Do you think that most developing countries should adopt labour-intensive or capital-intensive technologies? Why? How do resource prices influence techniques of production? What happens when resource prices (especially prices of capital and labour) do not reflect the true scarcity value of these resources to society?
6. What do we mean when we say that resources are misallocated? Do you think there is much misallocation in Third World countries? If so, why?
7. Traditional economic theory assumes that producers are able to adjust their production techniques quickly to changing factor prices. What are some of the difficulties with this assumption in the context of less developed nations?
8. What kinds of non-economic factors, especially attitudes and institutions, influence LDC production functions? Can you give some examples from your own country's experience?
9. What is the relationship between saving and investment? What is the essential ingredient of all investments? Why is investment so import-

ant to a country's economic wellbeing?

10. Why is present consumption typically valued higher than future consumption? How does the concept of a 'social' discount rate link present and future consumption? Do you think that this implicit social discount rate would be higher or lower in LDCs as compared with rich nations? Give your reasons why.
11. Do you think that a unit value (e.g. cruzeiro, shilling, rupee, bhat, peso, etc.) of extra consumption for a rich man should be given the same social weight as that for a poor man? If not, why? Is your answer based on a value premise or a scientific fact? Explain.
12. Why is it important to distinguish between 'social' and 'private' valuations of benefit and cost? Since most economic decisions are based on private valuations, there are likely to be important deviations between these private and the social calculations. Can you give some examples of such divergencies in developing economies?
13. Should economic policies be based on social or private valuations? Explain your answer.
14. Do you think 'externalities' are a pervasive phenomenon in Third World countries? Can you think of some external economies and diseconomies of production and consumption not mentioned in the text?

Chapter 5 Common characteristics of developing countries

> Of course there must be differences between developing countries ... [but] to maintain that no common ground exists is to make any discussion outside or across the frontiers of a single country meaningless.
> *Julian West, Oxford University*

> The Third World is important because of the massiveness of its poverty.
> *Padma Desai, Delhi School of Economics and Harvard University*

Introduction

While it is often risky to generalise about such diverse nations as those in Africa, Asia, the Middle East and Latin America (see Chapter 2 for a discussion of these differences) there are certain common characteristic economic features of developing countries which permit us to view them in broadly similar contexts. In this chapter we attempt to identify these similarities and provide illustrative data to demonstrate their existence. For convenience, we can classify these common characteristics into six broad categories:

1. Low levels of living
2. Low levels of productivity
3. High rates of population growth and dependency burdens
4. High and rising levels of unemployment and underemployment
5. Significant dependence on agricultural production and primary product exports
6. Dominance/dependence and vulnerability in international relations.

We shall deal with each of these categories in turn.

Low levels of living

In developing nations general levels of living tend to be very low for the vast majority of the people. This is true not only in relation to their counterparts in rich nations but often also in relation to small elite groups within their own societies. These low levels of living are manifested quantitatively and qualitatively in the form of low incomes (poverty), inadequate housing, poor health, limited or no education, high infant mortality, low life and work expectancy and sometimes a general sense of hopelessness. Let us look at some recent statistics comparing aspects of life in the underdeveloped countries with that of the more economically developed nations. Although these statistics are national aggregates, often have substantial errors of measurement and in some cases are not strictly comparable, they do provide at least a summary indication of levels of living in different nations.

Per capita national incomes

The Gross National Product (GNP) per head is often used as a summary index of the relative economic well-being of people in different nations. GNP itself is the most commonly used measure of the overall level of economic activity of a country. For example by the early 1980s, the total production of all the nations of the world was valued at more than 7 900 000 million US dollars, of which more than 6 500 000 million originated in the economically developed regions, while less than 1 400 000 million were generated in the less developed nations. When one takes into account the distribution of world population, this means that approximately 83 per cent of the world's total income is produced in the economically developed regions by less than one-fourth of the world's population. More than three-fourths of the world's population in Third

World nations is producing only 17 per cent of world output. More important, on the income side, the Third World, with almost 76 per cent of the world's population, subsists on less than 21 per cent of the world's income. The collective per capita incomes of the underdeveloped countries average less than one-eleventh of the per capita incomes of rich countries.

Figure 5.1
Per capita GNP in selected countries, US dollars, 1979

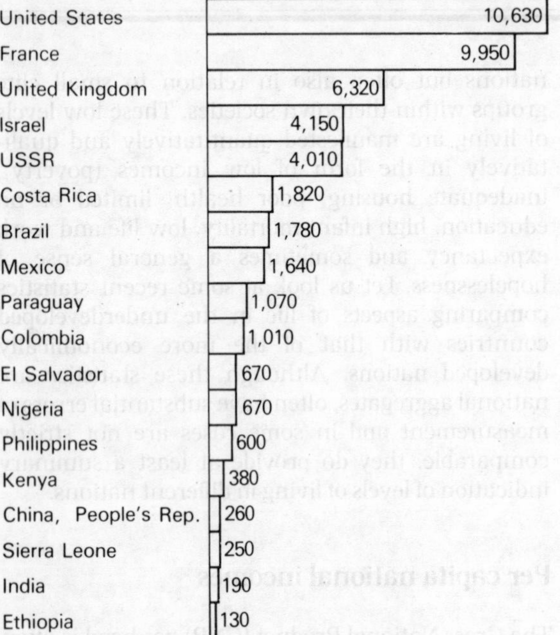

Source: *IBRD, World Development Report, 1981*, Annex Table I.

As an illustration of the per capita income gap between rich and poor nations, look at Figure 5.1. This shows that in 1979, the world's richest nation, the United States, had almost eighty times the per capita income of one of the world's poorest countries, Ethiopia, and over fifty times that of one of the world's largest nations, India. Appendix II to this chapter gives per capita income figures as well as other pertinent social and economic indicators of development for all nations of the world in the late 1970s.[1]

Relative growth rates of national (and per capita) incomes

In addition to having very much lower levels of per capita income, many Third World countries experienced slower GNP growth rates during the last decade than most of the developed nations. For example, in the 31 poorest countries, designated by the United Nations' classification system as 'least developed', average GNP growth rate amounted to only 3.4 per cent between 1960 and 1977. The remaining member nations classified by the UN as 'developing' showed an average growth rate of approximately 6.1 per cent during this same period. Taken all together, Third World nations showed an average annual GNP growth rate of approximately 5.5 per cent.

In contrast, the average annual growth rate among all developed countries during this period was approximately 4.9 per cent. This means that the income gap between rich and very poor nations narrowed at a rate of less than 1 per cent per year. However, when one takes account of the fact that the overall average annual rate of population growth in the developing countries is approximately 2.1 per cent while that of the developed world is only 0.6 per cent (see below), then the actual gap between per capita incomes in all developed and less developed countries widened at an annual rate of 0.9 per cent.[2] In money terms, during the 1960s and 1970s per capita incomes rose in the developed countries from $1,407 to $6,468 while those of the developing nations increased from $132 to $597. Thus the actual 'gap' widened by $4,596. And this occurred during the first two United Nations 'Development Decades'.

Table 5.1 provides recent data on comparative

[1] By the end of the 1974–5 oil price boom, countries like Kuwait, Qatar and the United Arab Emirates all had per capita incomes much higher than that of the United States. Yet in terms of total wealth (i.e. accumulated physical and financial assets) the United States is still far ahead of the rest of the world, even though by 1978, Sweden, Norway and Switzerland had also surpassed the USA in per capita terms.

[2] Recall that the rate of growth of per capita income is simply measured as the difference between GNP growth (4.9 per cent) and population growth (0.6 per cent) so that per capita incomes grew at 4.3 per cent in the DCs and only 3.4 per cent (5.5–2.1) in the LDCs.

trends in the growth of Gross National Product per capita between 1960 and 1979 for the same group of seventeen developing countries as in Table 2.2.

Table 5.1
Growth rates of GNP per capita, average annual growth (per cent), 1960–1979

Africa	
Tanzania	2.3
Kenya	2.7
Nigeria	3.7
Uganda	−0.2
Zaire	0.7
Asia	
Bangladesh	−0.1
India	1.4
Indonesia	4.1
Philippines	2.6
Sri Lanka	2.2
South Korea	7.1
Latin America	
Mexico	2.7
Guatemala	2.9
Colombia	3.0
Brazil	4.8
Peru	1.7
Venezuela	2.7

Source: *World Development Report 1981*, Annex Table 1.

The distribution of national income

The growing gap between per capita incomes in rich and poor nations is not the only manifestation of the widening economic disparities between the world's rich and poor. It is also necessary to look at the growing gap between rich and poor *within* individual less developed countries to appreciate the breadth and depth of Third World poverty. We discuss the question of income distribution and equity more fully in Chapters 9 and 10, but a few remarks at this point seem appropriate.

First, all nations of the world show some degree of inequality. One finds large disparities between incomes of the rich and poor in both developed and less developed countries. However, the gap between rich and poor is generally greater in the less developed countries than in the developed nations. For example, if we compare the share of national income accruing to the poorest 40 per cent of a country's population with that of the richest 20 per cent as an arbitrary measure of the degree of inequality, we find (see Table 5.2) that some countries, e.g. Brazil, Ecuador, Colombia, Peru, Mexico, Venezuela, Kenya, Sierra Leone, Philippines and Malaysia have substantial income inequality: others, e.g. India, Tanzania, Chile, France, Denmark and West Germany, have moderate inequality, while Taiwan, Libya, Israel, Yugoslavia, Canada, Japan, the United States and Czechoslovakia have relatively lesser inequalities in their overall income distribution. Moreover, it is also clear from Table 5.2 that there is no obvious relationship or correlation between levels of per capita income and the degree of income inequality. The Philippines, with the same *low* per capita income as Taiwan, has a much wider income disparity between the top 20 per cent and bottom 40 per cent of the population. Similarly, Venezuela, with almost the same *high* per capita income as Japan, had a much lower percentage of its income distributed to the bottom 40 per cent of its population. This phenomenon underlines the important point that **economic development cannot be measured solely in terms of the level and growth of overall income or income per capita; one must also look at how that income is distributed among the population** – that is, who benefits from development.

The extent of poverty

The magnitude and extent of poverty in any country depends upon two factors: (1) the average level of national income and (2) the degree of inequality in its distribution. Clearly, for any given level of national per capita income, the more unequal the distribution the greater will be the incidence of poverty. Similarly, for any given distribution, the lower the average income level, the greater will be the extent of poverty. But how is one to measure 'poverty' in any meaningful quantitative sense?

During the 1970s as interest in problems of poverty increased, development economists took the first step in measuring its magnitude within and across countries by attempting to establish a common poverty line. They went even further, however, and devised the now widely used concept of 'absolute poverty'. It is meant to represent a specific minimum level of subsistence income necessary to secure the 'basic physical needs' of food, clothing and shelter in order to assure 'continued survival'. A problem, however, arises

Table 5.2
Cross-classification of selected countries by per capita income level and inequality, constant 1971 $US

High Inequality[a]					High Inequality[a]				
	Per Capita GNP	Lowest 40%	Middle 40%	Top 20%		Per Capita GNP	Lowest 40%	Middle 40%	Top 20%
Per Capita GNP up to $300	($)	(percentages)			Per Capita GNP $300–$750	($)	(percentages)		
Kenya (1969)	136	10.0	22.0	68.0	Malaysia (1970)	330	11.6	32.4	56.0
Sierra Leone (1968)	159	9.6	22.4	68.0	Colombia (1970)	358	9.0	30.0	61.0
Iraq (1956)	200	6.8	25.2	68.0	Brazil (1970)	390	10.0	28.4	61.5
Philippines (1971)	239	11.6	34.6	53.8	Peru (1971)	480	6.5	33.5	60.0
Senegal (1960)	245	10.0	26.0	64.0	Gabon (1968)	497	8.8	23.7	67.5
Ivory Coast (1970)	247	10.8	32.1	57.1	Jamaica (1958)	510	8.2	30.3	61.5
Rhodesia (1968)	252	8.2	22.8	69.0	Costa Rica (1971)	521	11.5	30.0	58.5
Tunisia (1970)	255	11.4	53.6	55.0	Mexico (1969)	645	10.5	25.5	64.0
Honduras (1968)	265	6.5	28.5	65.0	South Africa (1965)	699	6.2	35.8	58.0
Ecuador (1970)	277	6.5	20.0	73.5	Panama (1969)	692	9.4	31.2	59.4
Moderate inequality[b]					Moderate Inequality[b]				
	Per Capita GNP	Lowest 40%	Middle 40%	Top 20%		Per Capita GNP	Lowest 40%	Middle 40%	Top 20%
Per Capita GNP up to $300	($)	(percentages)			Per Capita GNP $300–$750	($)	(percentages)		
Burma (1958)	82	16.5	38.7	44.8	Dominican Republic (1969)	323	12.2	30.3	57.5
Dahomey (1959)	87	15.5	34.5	50.0	Iran (1968)	332	12.5	33.0	54.5
Tanzania (1967)	89	13.0	26.0	61.0	Lebanon (1960)	508	13.0	26.0	61.0
India (1964)	99	16.0	32.0	52.0	Guyana (1956)	550	14.0	40.3	45.7
Malagasy Rep. (1960)	120	13.5	25.5	61.0	Uruguay (1968)	618	16.5	35.5	48.0
Zambia (1959)	230	14.5	28.5	57.0	Chile (1968)	744	13.0	30.2	56.8
Turkey (1968)	282	9.3	29.9	60.8					
El Salvador (1969)	295	11.2	36.4	52.4					
Low Inequality[c]					Low Inequality[c]				
	Per Capita GNP	Lowest 40%	Middle 40%	Top 20%		Per Capita GNP	Lowest 40%	Middle 40%	Top 20%
Per Capita GNP up to $300	($)	(percentages)			Per Capita GNP $300–$750	($)	(percentages)		
Chad (1958)	78	18.0	39.0	43.0	Surinam (1962)	394	21.7	35.7	42.6
Sri Lanka (1969)	95	17.0	37.0	46.0	Greece (1957)	500	21.0	29.5	49.5
Niger (1960)	97	18.0	40.0	42.0	Yugoslavia (1968)	529	18.5	40.0	41.5
Pakistan (1964)	100	17.5	37.5	30.0	Bulgaria (1962)	530	26.8	40.0	33.2
Uganda (1970)	126	17.1	35.8	47.1	Spain (1965)	750	17.6	36.7	45.7
Thailand (1970)	180	17.0	37.5	45.5					
Korea (1970)	235	18.0	37.0	45.0					
Taiwan (1964)	241	20.4	39.5	40.1					

when one recognises that minimum subsistence levels will vary from country to country and region to region reflecting different physiological as well as social and economic requirements. Economists have therefore tended to make conservative estimates of world poverty in order to avoid unsubstantiated

	High inequality[a]			
	Per Capita GNP	Lowest 40%	Middle 40%	Top 20%
Per Capita GNP above $750		($)	(percentages)	
Venezuela (1970)	1,004	7.9	27.1	65.0
Finland (1962)	1,599	11.1	39.6	49.3
France (1962)	1,913	9.5	36.8	53.7
	Moderate inequality[b]			
	Per Capita GNP	Lowest 40%	Middle 40%	Top 20%
Per Capita GNP above $750		($)	(percentages)	
Argentina (1970)	1,079	16.5	36.1	47.4
Puerto Rico (1968)	1,100	13.7	35.7	50.6
Netherlands (1967)	1,990	13.6	37.9	48.5
Norway (1968)	2,010	16.6	42.9	40.5
Germany, Fed. Rep. (1964)	2,144	15.4	31.7	52.9
Denmark (1968)	2,563	13.6	38.8	47.6
New Zealand (1969)	2,859	15.5	42.5	42.0
Sweden (1963)	2,949	14.0	42.0	44.0
	Low inequality[c]			
	Per Capita GNP	Lowest 40%	Middle 40%	Top 20%
Per Capita GNP above $750		($)	(percentages)	
Poland (1964)	750	23.4	40.6	36.0
Japan (1963)	950	20.7	39.3	40.0
Hungary (1969)	1,140	24.0	42.5	33.5
Czechoslovakia (1964)	1,150	27.6	41.4	31.0
United Kingdom (1968)	2,015	18.8	42.2	39.0
Australia (1968)	2,509	20.0	41.2	38.8
Canada (1965)	2,920	20.0	39.8	40.2
United States (1970)	4,850	19.7	41.5	38.8

[a]The share of the lowest 40 per cent is less than 12%.
[b]The share of the lowest 40 per cent is between 12% and 17%.
[c]The share of the lowest 40 per cent is 17% and above.
Source: Hollis Chenery et al., *Redistribution with Growth*, Oxford University Press for the World Bank and the Institute of Development Studies, University of Sussex, 1974, pp. 8–9.

exaggerations of the problem. One common methodology has been to establish an 'international poverty line' at, say, 75 constant US dollars (based, for example, on the value of the 1970 dollar) and then attempt to estimate the 'purchasing power equivalent' of that sum of money in terms of a developing country's local currency.

Table 5.3 presents some estimates of both the extent of absolute poverty (in terms of the proportion of a country's population with real incomes below the international poverty line) and its numerical magnitude (in terms of the actual number of people who can be classified as 'absolutely poor'). The data are drawn up for thirty-five developing countries from Latin America, Asia and Africa using 1979 population figures and 1975 poverty estimates from a well-known recent (1979) study by World Bank economists Ahluwalia, Carter and Chenery. Using conservative estimates, the authors concluded that almost forty per cent of Third World populations were attempting to survive at absolute poverty levels. The proportions are much higher in a number of heavily populated low income countries like Bangladesh (60 per cent), India (46 per cent) and Indonesia (62 per cent). In terms of total numbers, we see from Table 5.3 that over 418 million Asians, 60 million Latin Americans and 38 million Africans from our 35 country sample are barely achieving minimum subsistence incomes. If we then multiply the last figure in column 3 representing the average proportion of Third World populations below the poverty line (35 per cent) by the total population of developing countries in 1979 (3.15 billion), we arrive at the staggering figure of 1.1 billion people who may be classified as suffering from absolute poverty at the beginning of the 1980s! The actual figure, however, is more likely to be around 850 million if one accepts China's claims that it has been able to abolish poverty (see Chapter 15). This is also the most recent and reliable World Bank estimate. Nevertheless, it still represents almost twenty per cent of the total world population in 1979.

Finally, we can note once again from Table 5.3 that high per capita incomes do not necessarily preclude the existence of substantial absolute poverty. Since the actual share of national income that accrues to different population groups can vary widely among countries, the international poverty problem can be equally serious in countries with greatly divergent per capita income levels. For example, if we compare Peru with the Republic of Korea in Table 5.3, we discover that even though Peru had a higher per capita GNP in 1977, it still had two and one-half times the percentage of its population below the poverty line than did Korea (15 as compared with 6 per cent). Pakistan with approximately the same income level as Sri Lanka nevertheless had over three times the proportion of its population below the poverty line (34 compared with 10 per cent). Even adjusting for measurement errors, these results are quite striking.

Table 5.3
Population below the poverty line. 35 developing countries, 1979

	Per capita Gross National Product, 1977 ($)	Population, 1979 (millions)	Percentage of population in poverty (%)	Number of people in poverty (millions)
Latin America	**1240**	**315.4**	**19**	**59.9**
1. Argentina	1730	26.7	3	0.8
2. Brazil	1390	118.7	8	9.5
3. Chile	1170	11.0	9	1.0
4. Colombia	710	26.1	14	3.7
5. Guatemala	790	6.8	9	0.6
6. Mexico	1110	67.7	10	6.8
7. Peru	830	17.3	15	2.6
8. Venezuela	2820	13.5	5	0.7
Asia	**650**	**1045.4**	**40**	**418.4**
9. Bangladesh	90	87.1	60	52.3
10. Burma	140	32.9	56	18.4
11. India	150	660.9	46	304.0
12. Indonesia	300	140.9	62	87.4
13. Iran	2180	36.3	8	2.9
14. Korea, Rep. of	810	37.6	6	2.3
15. Malaysia	930	13.3	8	1.1
16. Pakistan	190	79.9	34	27.2
17. Philippines	450	46.2	29	13.4
18. Sri Lanka	200	14.5	10	1.5
19. Taiwan	1180	17.3	4	0.7
20. Thailand	410	46.2	23	10.6
21. Turkey	1110	44.3	11	4.9
Africa	**450**	**113.8**	**33**	**37.6**
22. Egypt	310	40.6	14	5.7
23. Ethiopia	110	31.8	62	19.7
24. Ghana	380	11.3	19	2.1
25. Ivory Coast	710	7.7	14	1.1
26. Kenya	270	15.4	48	7.4
27. Morocco	570	19.4	16	3.1
28. Nigeria	420	74.6	27	20.1
29. Senegal	420	5.5	29	1.6
30. Sudan	300	17.9	47	8.4
31. Tanzania	200	17.0	46	7.8
32. Tunisia	860	6.4	9	0.6
33. Uganda	260	13.2	45	5.9
34. Zaire	130	28.0	49	13.7
35. Zambia	450	5.6	7	0.4
Total	**761**	**147.6**	**35**	**516.1**

Note that the poverty percentages in column 3 are for 1975 as estimated by Ahluwalia *et al.* They are then applied to the 1979 population figures to calculate the 1979 poverty number estimates of col. 4.

Sources: Cols. 1 and 2: Population Reference Bureau, *1979 World Population Data Sheet*, Washington D.C., 1979.
Col. 3: M. S. Ahluwalia, N. Carter and H. Chenery, 'Growth and Poverty in Developing Countries,' *Journal of Development Economics*, Vol. 6, Sept. 1979, Tables 1 and 2.

Health

In addition to struggling on low income, many people in Third World nations fight a constant battle against malnutrition, disease and ill-health. Among the forty-two 'least developed' countries of the world, life expectancy in 1980 averaged approximately 50 years as compared with 60 years among other Third World countries and 74 years in developed nations. Infant mortality rates (that is, the number of children who die before their first birthday out of every 1 000 live births) average about 155 in the least developed countries compared with approximately 110 in other less developed countries and 27 in the developed countries. Some specific examples of countries are shown in Fig. 5.2.

Figure 5.2
Infant mortality rates in selected countries, 1981 (per thousand live births)

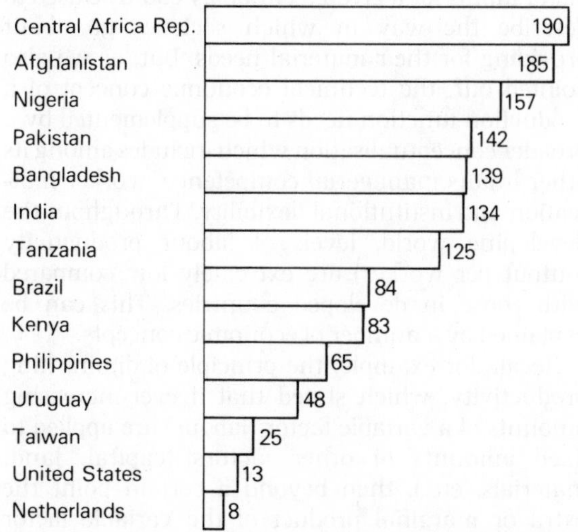

Source: Population Reference Bureau, *1981 World Population Data Sheet.*

Table 5.4 reveals even more. Over one billion people, half the population of the developing world (excluding China) in 1975, were living on diets that were deficient in essential calories. One third of them were children under two years of age. These people were concentrated in the poorest countries and, within these poor countries, in the lowest income groups. In both Asia and Africa, over 60 per cent of the population were barely meeting minimum caloric requirements necessary to maintain adequate health. Moreover, it has been estimated that this caloric deficit amounted to less than 2 per cent of world cereal production in 1975. This contradicts the widely held view that malnutrition is the inevitable result of an imbalance between world population and world food supplies. The more likely explanation can be found in the enormous imbalance in world income distribution. Thus, malnutrition and poor health in the developing world is as much, if not more, of a poverty problem than a food production problem – though the two are indirectly interrelated.

Table 5.4
Population with consumption below caloric requirements, 1975

Region	People (millions)	Per cent of population
Latin America	112	36
Asia	707	63
Middle East	61	33
Africa	193	61
Total	1,073	55

Source: S. Reutlinger and M. Selowsky, *Malnutrition and Poverty: Magnitude and Policy Options.* Johns Hopkins Press, Baltimore.

Another often-used measure of malnutrition is per capita daily protein consumption. It can vary from as high as 97 g per day in the United States to 63, 48 and 43 g per day in Brazil, India and Ghana respectively. In terms of world grain consumption, in the mid-1970s average annual consumption per person was approximately 650 kg in developed countries as contrasted with 180 kg in less developed countries.

Finally, medical care is an extremely scarce social service in many parts of the developing world. Recent data reveals that in the late 1970s the number of doctors per 100 000 people averaged only 9.7 in the least developed countries as compared to 158 in the developed countries. The ratio of hospital beds to population is similarly divergent between the two sets of nations. Moreover, when one realises that most of the medical facilities in developing nations are concentrated in urban areas where only 25 per cent of the populations reside, then the woefully inadequate provision of health care to the masses of poor people becomes strikingly clear. For example, in India 80 per cent of the doctors practice in urban areas where only 20 per cent of the population resides. In Kenya, the population to doctor ratio is 672 to 1 for the capital city of Nairobi and 20 000 to 1 in the rural countryside where 90 per cent of the Kenyan population actually lives.

Education

As a final illustration of the very low levels of living which permeate Third World nations, consider the spread of educational opportunities. The attempt to provide primary school educational opportunities has probably been the most significant of all LDC development efforts. In most countries education takes the largest share of the government budget. And, yet, in spite of some impressive quantitative advances in school enrolments, literacy levels remain strikingly low compared with the developed nations. For example, among the 31 least developed countries, literacy rates average only 34 per cent of the population (see Appendix II). The corresponding rates for other Third World nations and the developed countries are approximately 63 and 97 per cent respectively. Moreover, as we point out in Chapter 17, much of the education provided for those children who are able to attend school in the LDCs is ill-suited and often irrelevant to the needs of the nation.

Summarising our discussion so far, we can list the following common characteristics of developing countries:

(*a*) Low relative levels, and in many countries, slow growth rates of national income;
(*b*) Low levels and, in many countries, stagnating rates of income per capita growth;
(*c*) Highly skewed patterns of income distribution with the top 20 per cent of the population often receiving five to ten times as much income as the bottom 40 per cent.
(*d*) As a result of (*a*)–(*c*) above, great masses of Third World populations suffer from absolute poverty, with anywhere from 850 to 1 300 million people living on subsistence incomes of less than 100 US dollars per year.
(*e*) Large segments of the populations suffer from ill health, malnutrition and debilitating diseases, with infant mortality rates running as high as ten times the rate in developed nations;
(*f*) In education, low levels of literacy, significant school dropout rates, and inadequate and often irrelevant curricula and facilities.

Most importantly, it is the interaction of *all* these characteristics which tends to reinforce and perpetuate the pervasive problems of 'poverty, ignorance and disease' that restrict the lives of so many people in the Third World.

Low levels of productivity

In addition to low levels of living, developing countries are characterised by relatively low levels of labour productivity. We saw in Chapter 4 that the concept of a production function systematically relating outputs to the different combinations of factor inputs for a given technology could be used to describe the way in which societies go about providing for their material needs. But, as we also pointed out, the technical economic concept of a production function needs to be supplemented by a broader conceptualisation which includes among its other inputs managerial competence, worker motivation and institutional flexibility. Throughout the developing world, levels of labour productivity (output per worker) are extremely low compared with those in developed countries. This can be explained by a number of economic concepts.

Recall, for example, the principle of diminishing productivity, which stated that if ever-increasing amounts of a variable factor (labour) are applied to fixed amounts of other factors (capital, land, materials, etc.), then beyond a certain point the extra or marginal product of the variable factor declines. Low levels of labour productivity can therefore be explained by the absence or severe lack of complementary factor inputs such as physical capital and/or experienced management.

To raise productivity, according to this argument, domestic savings and foreign finance must be mobilised to generate investment in new physical capital goods (e.g. buildings and equipment), and also to build up the stock of 'human capital' (e.g. managerial skills) through investment in education and training. Institutional changes are also necessary to maximise the potential of this new physical and human investment. Such changes might include reform of land tenure, corporate tax, credit and banking structures, the creation or strengthening of an independent, honest and efficient administrative service; and the restructuring of educational and training programmes to make them more appropriate to the needs of developing societies. These and other non-economic inputs into the social production function must be taken into account if strategies to raise productivity are to succeed. An old proberb says that 'you can lead a horse to water, but you cannot make him drink'. In less developed nations it is equally true that you can create the economic opportunities for self-improvement, but without the proper institutional and structural arrangements you cannot succeed.

One must also take into account the impact of worker and management attitudes towards self-improvement, their degree of alertness, adaptability, ambition, and general willingness to innovate and experiment, and their attitudes towards manual work, discipline, authority, and possibly also exploitation. To these must be added the physical and mental capacity of the individual to do his or her job satisfactorily.

It is with regard to the state of a person's physical health that the close links between low levels of income and low levels of productivity in developing nations are most clearly revealed. It is well-known, for example, that poor nutrition in childhood can severely restrict the mental as well as the physical growth of individuals. Poor dietary habits, inadequate foods, and low standards of personal hygiene in later years can cause further deterioration in a worker's health and, therefore, can adversely influence his attitudes towards the job and the people around him. His low productivity may be due, not so much to a lack of complementary resources, but to his physical lethargy and inability, both physical and emotional, to withstand the daily pressures of competitive work. We may conclude, therefore, that **low levels of living and of productivity are self-reinforcing social and economic phenomena in Third World countries, and, as such, are the principal manifestations of their underdevelopment.**

High rates of population growth and dependency burdens

Of the total world population of approximately 4.5 billion in the early 1980s, more than three-fourths of the people live in the developing nations and less than one fourth in the developed countries. Birth and death rates are strikingly different: the birth rates of less developed countries are generally at very high levels, of 35–40 per thousand or more, while those of the developed countries are less than half that figure. Indeed, as shown in Table 5.5, the crude birth rate (the yearly number of live births per thousand population) is probably one of the most efficient ways of distinguishing the less developed

Table 5.5
Crude birth rates throughout the world (1980)

		Country
	50	Ethiopia, Mali, Kenya, Togo, Liberia, Zambia, Ivory Coast, Nigeria
	45	Bangladesh, Zaire, Sierra Leone, Uganda, Morocco, Sudan, Congo, Pakistan, Yemen, Saudi Arabia
	40	Lesotho, Paraguay, Iran, Ecuador, Peru, South Africa, Bolivia
	35	India, Indonesia, Egypt, Venezuela, Turkey, Burma
Crude birth rate	30	Colombia, Malaysia, Jamaica, Panama, Albania, Brazil, Dem. Rep. of Korea
	25	Israel, Rep. of Korea
	20	Poland, USSR, Cuba, China, Ireland, Spain, Uruguay
	15	Hungary, US, Canada, Australia, France, Japan, Greece
	10	Switzerland, Austria, Germany

Source: *World Development Report, 1981*, Annex table 18.

from the more developed countries. There are few less developed countries with a birth rate below 30 per thousand or developed nations with a birth rate above it.

Even though death rates in Third World countries are also higher than in the more developed countries, the difference in death rates, because of improved health conditions and the control of major infectious diseases, is substantially less than the difference in birth rates. As a result, the average rate of population growth is now about 2.1 per cent per year in Third World countries compared with only about 0.7 per cent in the developed world.

A major implication of high LDC birth rates is that the proportion of children under the age of 15 is almost half of the total population in these countries while in the developed countries the proportion is approximately a quarter of the total population. Thus the labour force in most developing countries has to support proportionally almost twice as many children as it does in richer countries. On the other hand, the proportion of older people over the age of 65 is much greater in the developed nations. Older people, as well as children, are often referred to as an economic 'dependency burden' in the sense that they are non-productive members of society and therefore must be supported financially by a country's labour force, (usually defined as those between the age of 15 to 64). The overall dependency burden (i.e. both young and old) represents only about one third of the populations of developed countries compared with half of the populations of the less developed nations. Moreover, in the latter countries, over 90 per cent of the dependants are children, whereas only 66 per cent are children in the richer nations.

We may conclude, therefore, that not only are Third World countries characterised by higher rates of population growth but they must also contend with greater dependency burdens than rich nations. The circumstances and conditions in which rapid population growth becomes a deterrent to economic development is, however, another question; one to be carefully examined in Chapters 11 and 12.

High and rising levels of unemployment and underemployment

One of the principal manifestations of, and factors contributing to, the low levels of living in developing nations is their relatively inadequate or inefficient utilisation of labour in comparison with the developed nations. Underutilisation of labour is manifested in two forms. First, it occurs as *underemployment* – those people, both rural and urban, who are working less than they would like, daily, weekly or seasonally. Underemployment includes also those who are nominally working full-time but whose productivity is so low that a reduction in hours would have a negligible impact on total output. The second form is *open unemployment* – those people

Table 5.6
Rates of unemployment in selected urban areas

Urban area	Ages 15–24	Ages 15 and over (total)
Ghana, large towns	21.9	11.6
Bogota, Colombia	23.1	13.6
Buenos Aires, Argentina	6.3	4.2
Chile, urban areas	12	6
Caracas, Venezuela	37.7	18.8
Bangkok, Thailand	7.7	3.4
Philippines, urban areas	20.6	11.6
Singapore	15.7	9.2

Source: Edgar O. Edwards, *Employment in Developing Countries*, Ford Foundation, August 1973, Table 2.

who are able and often eager to work but for whom no suitable jobs are available.[3]

Current rates of unemployment in the urban areas of developing countries average from 10 to 15 per cent of the urban labour force. But this is only part of the story. Unemployment among young people aged 15 to 24, many of whom have a substantial education, is typically almost twice the level as the overall average. Table 5.6 provides some rough estimates of unemployment by age for urban areas of selected Third World countries.

The figures in Table 5.6 represent, however, only a tiny fraction of labour underutilisation. When the underemployed are added to the openly unemployed **almost thirty per cent of the total urban and rural labour forces in Third World nations is underutilised.**

With LDC populations growing rapidly, their labour forces will also be increasing for some time to come. This means that jobs will have to be created at equivalent rates simply to keep pace with the growth of labour supply. Moreover, in urban areas where rural–urban migration is causing the labour force to 'explode' at annual rates of 5 to 7 per cent in many countries (especially those in Africa), the prospects for coping effectively with rising levels of unemployment and underemployment and with the frustrations and anxieties of an increasing vocal, educated but unemployed youth are, to say the least, frightening. The dimensions and implications of the unemployment problem in developing countries are discussed further in Chapters 13 and 14.

Substantial dependence on agricultural production and primary product exports

Small-scale agriculture in less developed nations

The vast majority of people in developing nations live and work in the rural areas. Almost 80 per cent of LDC populations are rurally based compared with less than 35 per cent in the economically developed countries. In terms of the proportions of their labour forces engaged in agriculture, the figure for less developed regions is 66 per cent compared with 21 per cent for developed nations. Moreover, agriculture contributes about 32 per cent of the gross national product of Third World nations while it amounts to only 8 per cent of the GNP of developed countries.

Table 5.7 provides a breakdown of population, labour force and agricultural production by region, of the developed and less developed world. Note in particular the striking difference between the proportionate size of the agricultural population in Africa and South Asia (70 and 65 per cent) in comparison with North America (5 per cent). In terms of actual numbers, there were almost 635 million agricultural labour force members in Asia and Africa producing an annual volume of output valued at US $166 million in 1977.[4] On the other hand in North America, less than one per cent of this total number of agricultural workers (4.5 million) produced over a quarter as much total output ($45 million). This means that the *average productivity of labour in agriculture is almost 35 times greater in North America than in Asia and Africa combined.* While international comparative figures such as these are often of extremely dubious quality both with regard to their precision and methods of measurement, they do nevertheless give us rough orders of magnitude. Even adjusting them for, say, undervaluing Third World agricultural output, the differences in agricultural labour productivity would still be very sizable.

The basic reason for the concentration of people and production in agricultural and other primary production activities in developing countries is the simple fact that at low incomes, the first priorities of any person are for food, clothing and shelter. Productivity is low not only because of the large numbers of people in relation to available land but also because LDC agriculture is often characterised by primitive technologies, poor organisation and

[3] See Chapter 13 for a more complete examination of the problem of underutilisation of labour in Third World nations.

[4] The total value of actual agricultural output was probably somewhat higher than this figure since much of the food output in LDCs is consumed directly by farm families, and therefore not always estimated in production figures.

Table 5.7
Population, labour force and production in 1981: developed and less developed regions

Region	Population (millions)	Urban (%)	Rural (%)	Labour force in agriculture (%)	Agricultural share of GNP (%)
World	4,492	39	61	47	—
Less Developed	3,348	33	67	60	26
Developed	1,144	74	26	7	4
Africa	486	25	71	70	28
South Asia	1,060	21	79	65	37
East Asia	1,548	31	69	54	23
Latin America	366	61	39	33	14
Europe	486	63	37	22	8
USSR	268	57	43	32	22
North America	254	74	26	5	3
Japan	118	72	28	21	7

Source: *World Development Report 1979,* Annex tables 3 and 19. Population Reference Bureau Inc., *1981 World Population Data Sheet.*

Table 5.8
Composition of world exports, 1977 (Percentages of manufactured and primary products)

Category	Developed	Less developed
Primary commodities		
Food, food products, and raw materials	18	24
Fuels	4	57
Manufactures		
Chemicals	9	2
Engineering products	36	2
Manufactures (non-metallic mineral and other)	31	14
Unspecified	2	1
Total	100	100

Source: Overseas Development Council, *Agenda for Action 1980*, Washington, 1980, p. 194.

limited physical and human capital inputs. The reason is that agriculture in Third World nations is predominantly non-commercial peasant agriculture. In many parts of the world, especially in Asia and Latin America, it is also characterised by land tenure arrangements whereby peasant proprietors usually rent rather than own their small plots of land. As we see in Chapter 16, such land tenure arrangements often take away much of the economic incentive for peasant output expansion.

Even where there is abundant land, primitive techniques and the use of hand ploughs, drag harrows and animals (oxen, buffalo, donkeys, etc.), or raw human power, necessitate that typical family holdings be not more than 5 to 8 hectares (12 to 20 acres). In fact, in many countries, average holdings can be as low as 1 to 3 hectares. The number of people this land must support both directly (through on the farm consumption) and indirectly (through production for urban and non-rural food consumption) often runs as high as 10 to 15 people per hectare. It is no wonder, therefore, that efforts to improve the efficiency of small farm production and to increase average yields per hectare of rice, wheat, maize, sorghum and millet are now and will continue to be top priority development objectives.

Dependence on exports

Since most economies of less developed countries are oriented towards the production of primary products, as opposed to secondary (manufacturing) and tertiary (service) activities, these primary commodities form their main exports to other nations (both developed and less developed). For example, Table 5.8 shows that in 1977, for all Third World countries, these primary products (food, raw materials, fuels and base metals) accounted for over 80 per cent of all exports. But, except for those few countries blessed with abundant supplies of petroleum and other valuable mineral resources, basic foodstuffs and raw materials alone account for most of the exports from the Third World.

As we shall see in Chapter 22, most poor countries need to obtain foreign exchange (foreign currencies) in addition to domestic savings in order to finance priority development projects. While private foreign investment flows plus foreign aid are a significant source of such foreign exchange, exports of primary products typically account for 60 to 75 per cent of the annual flow of total foreign currency earnings into developing countries.

Even though exports loom so important in many developing nations, over the past 20 years export growth (excluding oil exports) has not kept pace with that of the developed countries. Consequently, even in their best years, the developing nations have been losing ground in terms of their share of total world trade to the more developed countries. In 1950, for example, their share was nearly 33 per cent; it has fallen in almost every year since, and by 1980 had fallen to nearly 21 per cent. At the same time, the developed countries have increased their share of world trade (mostly by trading with each other) from 60 to 72 per cent. Moreover, the percentage of total Third World exports going to each other dropped from 28 per cent in 1960 to 25 per cent by 1980. Thus, the less developed countries have become even more dependent on the rich countries for outlets for their products while their overall share of world trade has been declining.

This growing LDC dependence on rich-country economies for foreign exchange brings us to the last major common characteristic of Third World nations – their dependence upon, and frequent dominance by, rich nations in the world economy.

Dominance, dependence and vulnerability in international relations

For many less developed countries, a significant factor contributing to the persistence of low levels of living, rising unemployment and growing income inequality is the highly unequal distribution of economic and political power between rich and poor nations. As we shall see later, these unequal strengths are manifested not only in the dominant power of rich nations to control the pattern of international trade but also in their ability often to dictate the terms in which technology, foreign aid and private capital are transferred to developing countries.

But there are other equally important aspects of the international transfer process which often serve to inhibit the development of poor nations. One subtle but nonetheless very significant factor contributing to the persistence of underdevelopment has been the transfer of First and Second World values, attitudes, institutions and standards of behaviour to Third World nations. Examples include the transfer of often inappropriate educational structures, curricula and school systems, the formation of Western style trade unions, the organisation of health services following the Western model, and finally the structure and operation of bureaucratic and administrative systems which may be out of tune with the priority needs and the available manpower of developing nations.

Of even greater potential significance, however, may be the influence of rich-country social and economic standards on developing-country salary scales, elite life styles and general attitudes towards the private accumulation of wealth. Such attitudes can breed corruption and economic plunder by a privileged minority. Finally, the penetration of rich-country attitudes, values and standards has contributed also to a problem widely recognised and referred to as the 'international brain drain' – i.e. the loss through emigration of highly educated and skilled personnel who may or may not have been trained in the local country.

The net effect of all these factors is to create a situation of 'vulnerability' among Third World nations in which forces largely outside their control can have decisive and dominating influences on their overall economic and social well-being. Many countries – most of the 45 least developed certainly – are 'small' and their economies 'dependent' with very little prospect for self-reliance. Their withdrawal from the world economy is virtually impossible. But, as we shall see in Chapters 21 and 22, hope can be found in their joining forces economically to increase local bargaining power and to scrutinise more carefully, and be more selective about, foreign investment and technical assistance.

For those few developing nations which possess greater assets and more bargaining power, the phenomenon of dominance becomes manifested more in the general tendency of the rich to get richer, often at the expense of the poor. But this is not simply a matter of rich *nations* growing at a faster pace than poor nations. It is also a matter of the rich and dominating sectors or groups *within* the LDC economy (e.g. the 'modern' industrial or agricultural sector; landlords, trade union leaders, industrialists, politicians, bureaucrats and civil servants in positions of power) growing richer, often at the expense of the much larger, but politically and economically less powerful, masses of poor people. This dual process of rich nations and powerful groups within poor nations simultaneously prospering while others stagnate is by no means an isolated phenomenon. We shall see that it is a rather common characteristic of international economic relations when we discuss the concept of 'dualism' and 'dual societies' in the next chapter.

Conclusion

The phenomenon of underdevelopment must be viewed in both a national and an international context. Economic and social forces, both internal and external, are responsible for the poverty, inequality and low productivity that characterise most developing nations. The successful pursuit of economic and social development will therefore require not only the formulation of appropriate strategies within the Third World but also a modification of the present international economic system to make it more responsive to the needs of developing nations. But first we must have a fairly clear idea about what we mean when we use the words 'development' and 'underdevelopment'. This will be our theme in the next chapter.

Concepts for review

dependency burden
per capita income
income gap
income inequality
absolute poverty
levels of living
infant mortality
malnutrition
literacy
labour productivity
crude birth rate
death rate
open unemployment
underemployment
exports
foreign exchange

Questions for discussion

1. Explain the distinction between low levels of living and low per capita incomes. Can low levels of living occur simultaneously with high levels of per capita income? Explain and give some examples.
2. What are some of the common characteristics of less developed countries? Can you think of others not mentioned in the text?
3. What are the advantages and disadvantages of using a concept such as an 'international poverty line'? Do you think that a real annual income of US $50 in, say, Mexico has the same meaning as in, say, Nigeria, Egypt or Thailand? Explain your answer.
4. Do you think that there is a strong relationship between health, labour productivity, and income levels? Explain.

5. What is meant by the statement that many Third World nations are subject to 'dominance, dependence and vulnerability' in their relation with rich nations? Can you give some examples?

Further reading

For a concise but very informative summary of the diverse structures and major economic characteristics of Third World nations, see LESTER PEARSON *et al., Partners in Development: Report of the Commission on International Development*, Praeger Paperbacks, New York, 1969, Annex I, pp. 231–353; also J. A. RAFFAELE, *The Economic Development of Nations*, Random House, New York, 1971. An excellent reference source for describing the structure of specific African nations can be found in the five-volume International Monetary Fund's *Survey of African Economies*, Washington, 1970, For Asia, see GUNNAR MYRDAL, *Asian Drama*, Pantheon, New York, 1968, vol. I. Part 3, while for Latin America CELSO FANTADOS' *Economic Development of Latin America*, Cambridge University Press, 1970, provides a good general introduction. Information on current economic trends within individual Third World countries and regions can best be obtained from the annual *World Development Report* published by the World Bank and from various United Nations publications including the annual *Statistical Yearbook* and the regular publications of the UN Economic Commission for Latin America (ECLA), for Africa (ECA) and for Asia and the Pacific (ESCAP). Concise statistical summaries can also be obtained from the annual *World Bank Atlas*. The World Bank (IBRD) and International Monetary Fund (IMF) also carry out studies of individual countries – see their current publications list for the most recent titles.

Appendix 1

Relative ranking of 15 Third World countries by various indices of development, 1979

	I Per capita income levels (highest to lowest)		II Per capita growth rates (highest to lowest)		III Income distribution: ratio bottom 40% to top 20% of population (highest to lowest)
1.	Taiwan	1.	Republic of Korea	1.	Republic of Korea
2.	Brazil	2.	Taiwan	2.	India
3.	Mexico	3.	Brazil	3.	Taiwan
4.	Republic of Korea	4.	Thailand	4.	Thailand, Philippines
5.	Colombia	5.	Nigeria	5.	Mexico
6.	Peru	6.	Colombia	6.	Colombia
7.	Nigeria	7.	Pakistan	7.	Peru
8.	Philippines	8.	Mexico	8.	Brazil
9.	Thailand	9.	Kenya	9.	N.A. – Kenya
10.	Zambia	10.	Philippines		Nigeria
11.	Ghana	11.	Peru		Ghana
12.	Kenya	12.	India		Bangladesh
13.	Pakistan	13.	Zambia		Pakistan
14.	India	14.	Bangladesh		Zambia
15.	Bangladesh	15.	Ghana		

	IV Literacy (% of population) (highest to lowest)		V Population growth rates (highest to lowest)		VI Infant mortality rates (lowest to highest)
1.	Republic of Korea	1.	Kenya	1.	Taiwan
2.	Taiwan	2.	Pakistan	2.	Republic of Korea
3.	Philippines	3.	Ghana, Bangladesh, Zambia	3.	Mexico
4.	Thailand	4.	Mexico	4.	Colombia, Philippines
5.	Mexico	5.	Peru	5.	Thailand
6.	Peru	6.	Philippines, Taiwan	6.	Peru
7.	Brazil	7.	Nigeria	7.	Kenya
8.	Kenya	8.	Thailand	8.	Brazil
9.	Zambia	9.	Colombia	9.	India
10.	India	10.	Brazil	10.	Bangladesh
11.	Pakistan	11.	India	11.	N.A. – Ghana
12.	N.A. – Ghana	12.	Republic of Korea		Zambia
	Bangladesh	13.	—		Pakistan
	Nigeria	14.	—		Nigeria
	Colombia	15.	—		

Sources: IBRD *World Development Report 1981*, Annex Tables 1, 21.
Population Reference Bureau, Inc., *1981 World Population Data Sheet*, Washington D.C.

Appendix II
Economic and social indicators of development

	Population, mid-1981 (mil.)	Per capita GNP 1980 ($)	Per capita GNP (real) growth rate 1970-79 (%)	Birth rate per 1,000	Death rate per 1,000	Life expectancy at birth (years)	Infant mortality per 1,000 live births	Literacy (%)	Per Capita public education expend's 1978 ($)	Per capita military expend's 1978 ($)	Total exports f.o.b. 1979 ($ mil.)
Low-Income (39) (p/c GNP<$400)	**2,188.6**	**255**	**0.7**	**30**	**12**	**59**	**101**	**49**	**9**	**15**	**31,632**
(excl. People's Rep. of China	**1,203.6**	**225**	**0.7**	**39**	**16**	**51**	**138**	**36**	**5**	**6**	**16,362**
Africa (25)	**180.5**	**228**	**−0.8**	**47**	**20**	**45**	**160**	**25**	**7**	**8**	**5,222**
*Benin	3.8	300	0.6	49	19	46	149	11	11	3	40
*Burundi	4.2	200	1.5	47	20	45	140	25	4	5	105
*Cape Verde	0.3	300	4.8	29	8	57	105	37	n/a	6	4
*Central African Rep.	2.4	300	0.9	42	19	46	190	7	8	4	85
*Chad	4.6	120	−2.4	44	21	44	190	15	3	8	58
*Comoros	0.4	300	−4.3	40	18	46	148	58	n/a	n/a	15
Equatorial Guinea	0.3	390	−4.2	42	19	46	165	20	10	25	n/a
*Ethiopia	33.5	140	0.3	50	25	39	178	15	3	5	423
*Gambia	0.6	250	0.4	48	23	41	217	10	11	0	58
*Guinea	5.1	290	0.6	46	21	44	220	20	9	4	280
*Guinea-Bissau	0.8	160	−0.6	41	23	41	211	5	n/a	10	14
*Lesotho	1.4	390	9.5	40	16	50	114	52	10	0	40
Madagascar	8.8	350	−2.5	45	19	46	102	50	13	6	410
*Malawi	6.2	230	3.0	52	20	46	142	25	5	4	233
*Mali	6.8	190	2.5	52	24	42	210	10	5	4	120
Mauritania	1.7	320	−0.7	50	22	42	187	17	16	30	148
Mozambique	10.7	270	−5.3	45	19	46	148	11	3	9	100
*Niger	5.7	330	−1.2	51	22	42	200	8	3	2	210
*Rwanda	5.3	200	1.6	50	19	46	127	23	4	3	90
Sierra Leone	3.6	270	−1.2	46	19	46	136	15	9	2	146
*Somalia	3.8	140	−0.8	48	20	43	177	60	7	12	110
*Tanzania, Unit. Rep.	19.2	260	0.8	46	16	50	125	66	12	10	600
*Uganda	14.1	280	−3.5	45	14	52	120	35	10	11	663
*Upper Volta	7.1	190	−1.2	48	22	42	182	5	4	14	70
Zaire	30.1	220	−2.6	46	19	46	171	15	6	10	1,200
Asia (13)	**2,002.1**	**257**	**1.0**	**28**	**11**	**60**	**96**	**52**	**10**	**16**	**26,210**
*Afghanistan	16.4	170	1.6	48	21	42	185	12	3	5	431
*Bangladesh	92.8	120	0.8	46	20	47	139	26	2	1	650
*Bhutan	1.3	80	−0.1	43	21	43	147	4	n/a	n/a	n/a
Burma	35.2	180	2.0	39	14	53	140	67	2	5	363
China, People's Rep.	985.0	290	n/a	18	6	68	56	66	15	26	15,270
India	688.6	240	1.6	36	15	52	134	36	5	5	6,440
Kampuchea, Dem. (Cambodia)	5.5	80	−9.5	33	15	45	150	36	n/a	n/a	10
*Lao People's Dem. Rep.	3.6	100	−9.0	44	20	42	175	28	2	10	20
*Maldives	0.2	260	−0.7	46	14	n/a	120	n/a	n/a	n/a	10
*Nepal	14.4	140	0.3	44	20	43	133	19	2	1	90
Pakistan	88.9	300	1.5	44	16	52	142	24	5	12	2,036
Sri Lanka	15.3	270	2.5	29	7	64	42	85	5	1	890
Vietnam	54.9	170	−7.0	37	9	62	115	87	4	18	n/a

Lower Middle-Income Countries

	Population mid-1981 (mil.)	Per capita GNP 1980 ($)	Per capita GNP (real) growth rate 1970-79 (%)	Birth rate per 1,000	Death rate per 1,000	Life expectancy at birth (years)	Infant mortality per 1,000 live births	Literacy (%)	Per capita public education expend's 1978 ($)	Per capita military expend's 1978 ($)	Total exports f.o.b. 1979 ($ mil.)
Latin America (1)	**6.0**	**270**	**1.8**	**42**	**16**	**51**	**130**	**23**	**2**	**2**	**200**
*Haiti	6.0	270	1.8	42	16	51	130	23	2	2	200
Lower Middle-Income (39) (p/c GNP $400-$999)	**454.5**	**566**	**3.3**	**38**	**14**	**53**	**98**	**57**	**15**	**24**	**47,216**
Africa (17)	**156.3**	**573**	**1.9**	**46**	**15**	**51**	**121**	**32**	**22**	**40**	**13,184**
Angola	6.7	470	−9.6	48	23	41	192	5	15	18	1,400
*Botswana	0.8	910	12.0	51	17	56	97	25	48	22	250
Cameroon	8.7	670	3.1	42	19	44	157	19	13	7	1,129
Congo, People's Rep.	1.6	730	−0.2	45	19	46	180	50	45	23	200
Djibouti	0.5	480	−4.9	49	22	n/a	n/a	5	n/a	n/a	20
Egypt	43.5	580	5.3	41	11	55	90	44	28	91	1,840
Ghana	12.0	420	−3.0	48	17	48	115	30	16	5	1,050
Kenya	16.5	420	2.6	53	14	53	83	45	17	12	1,162
Liberia	1.9	520	0.5	50	17	48	148	30	28	5	570
Morocco	21.8	860	3.5	43	14	55	133	28	41	42	1,872
São Tomé & Principe	0.1	490	−0.2	42	10	n/a	50	n/a	n/a	n/a	27
Senegal	5.8	450	0.1	48	22	44	160	10	12	10	320
*Sudan	19.6	470	1.5	48	18	46	141	20	4	14	700
Swaziland	0.6	680	4.4	47	19	46	168	50	38	2	160
Togo	2.6	410	1.2	49	19	46	121	18	21	8	210
Zambia	6.0	560	−1.9	49	17	48	144	39	24	41	1,120
Zimbabwe	7.6	630	−1.7	47	14	53	129	39	19	31	1,154
Asia (6)	**255.4**	**528**	**4.6**	**34**	**13**	**54**	**84**	**70**	**10**	**14**	**25,752**
†Indonesia	148.8	420	4.6	35	15	50	91	62	6	11	15,578
Mongolia	1.7	780	3.1	38	9	63	70	95	51	76	n/a
Philippines	48.9	720	3.9	34	10	61	65	88	11	11	4,601
Thailand	48.6	670	4.4	28	8	61	68	84	17	18	5,308
*Yemen Arab Rep.	5.4	460	10.8	48	25	40	160	13	10	52	15
*Yemen, People's Dem. Rep.	2.0	420	4.7	48	21	44	170	27	13	43	250
Latin America (10)	**36.1**	**766**	**0.6**	**41**	**12**	**57**	**100**	**74**	**21**	**25**	**7,229**
Bolivia	5.5	570	2.3	44	19	51	168	63	32	18	777
Dominica	0.1	620	−3.2	21	5	58	20	95	n/a	n/a	20
El Salvador	4.9	590	1.4	39	7	63	53	62	23	13	1,118
Grenada	0.1	690	−1.3	24	7	63	15	98	n/a	n/a	20
Guyana	0.8	690	0.0	28	7	69	46	91	46	10	291
Honduras	3.9	560	0.5	47	12	57	103	60	18	11	720
Nicaragua	2.5	720	−1.6	47	12	55	122	90	24	28	700
Peru	18.1	930	0.2	39	12	56	92	80	17	33	3,533
St. Lucia	0.1	850	2.8	32	7	67	33	85	n/a	n/a	35
St. Vincent	0.1	520	−1.7	35	7	67	38	76	n/a	n/a	15

Upper Middle-Income Countries

	Population mid-1981 (mil.)	Per capita GNP 1980 ($)	Per capita GNP (real) growth rate 1970-79 (%)	Birth rate per 1,000	Death rate per 1,000	Life expectancy at birth (years)	Infant mortality per 1,000 live births	Literacy (%)	Per capita public education expend's 1978 ($)	Per capita military expend's 1978 ($)	Total exports f.o.b. 1979 ($ mil.)
Oceania (5)	**3.9**	**761**	**0.5**	**43**	**15**	**51**	**116**	**39**	**42**	**8**	**1,051**
Pacific Is. Trust Terr.	0.1	950	1.5	31	5	n/a	31	n/a	n/a	n/a	n/a
Papua New Guinea	3.3	780	0.3	44	16	50	128	32	42	8	963
Solomon Islands	0.2	460	2.3	44	9	57	78	60	n/a	n/a	67
*Samoa	0.2	770	1.4	37	7	65	40	98	n/a	n/a	14
Tonga	0.1	520	1.1	13	2	n/a	21	100	n/a	n/a	7
Europe (1)	**2.8**	**840**	**4.2**	**29**	**7**	**69**	**87**	**72**	**31**	**60**	**n/a**
Albania	2.8	840	4.2	29	7	69	87	72	31	60	n/a
Upper Middle-Income (43) (p/c GNP $1,000-$3,499)	**712.4**	**1,800**	**4.5**	**34**	**10**	**62**	**83**	**67**	**60**	**57**	**204,591**
Africa (8)	**145.2**	**1,412**	**3.8**	**46**	**16**	**52**	**137**	**29**	**55**	**38**	**41,990**
†Algeria	19.3	1,920	2.8	46	14	56	127	35	115	36	9,255
Ivory Coast	8.5	1,150	1.3	50	19	46	138	20	64	11	2,516
Mauritius	1.0	1,060	6.4	28	7	67	34	80	64	2	400
Namibia	1.0	1,410	0.3	44	15	51	107	38	n/a	n/a	n/a
†Nigeria	79.7	1,010	5.3	50	18	48	157	15	34	28	16,800
Seychelles	0.1	1,770	3.8	28	7	65	27	58	n/a	n/a	3
South Africa	29.0	2,290	0.6	36	12	60	97	57	67	80	11,250
Tunisia	6.6	1,310	5.7	33	8	57	123	62	58	30	1,766
Asia (10)	**159.2**	**1,810**	**5.9**	**34**	**9**	**62**	**67**	**68**	**63**	**132**	**84,834**
†Iran	39.8	2,030	3.3	44	14	58	112	50	115	261	19,000
†Iraq	13.6	3,020	9.3	47	13	55	92	24	70	159	21,502
Jordan	3.3	1,420	6.0	46	13	56	97	70	31	87	402
Korea, Dem. People's Rep.	18.3	1,130	3.8	33	8	62	70	90	26	63	n/a
Korea, Rep.	38.9	1,520	8.1	23	6	66	37	93	32	75	15,055
Lebanon	3.2	1,740	4.9	34	8	65	45	68	n/a	58	600
Macao	0.3	2,020	15.0	28	8	n/a	22	79	n/a	n/a	387
Malaysia	14.3	1,670	5.4	31	8	61	44	60	71	45	10,148
Syrian Arab Rep.	9.3	1,340	4.6	42	9	62	81	53	55	147	1,637
Taiwan	18.2	2,160	7.2	25	5	72	25	82	55	106	16,103
Latin America (19)	**306.0**	**1,943**	**3.8**	**31**	**8**	**65**	**69**	**80**	**53**	**21**	**55,150**
Argentina	28.2	2,390	1.0	25	9	69	41	94	54	55	8,200
Bahamas	0.3	3,300	−4.7	22	5	69	28	90	n/a	n/a	2,800
Barbados	0.3	3,040	2.1	16	8	70	27	99	158	4	151
Belize	0.2	1,080	4.1	40	12	47	34	87	n/a	n/a	70
Brazil	121.4	2,050	6.1	32	8	64	84	76	55	18	15,250
Chile	11.2	2,160	0.8	22	7	67	38	88	50	73	3,766
Colombia	27.8	1,180	3.7	29	8	62	77	81	20	7	3,381

High-Income Countries

	Population mid-1981 (mil.)	Per capita GNP 1980 ($)	Per capita GNP (real) growth rate 1970-79 (%)	Birth rate per 1,000	Death rate per 1,000	Life expectancy at birth (years)	Infant mortality per 1,000 live births	Literacy (%)	Per capita public education expend's 1978 ($)	Per capita military expend's 1978 ($)	Total exports f.o.b. 1979 ($ mil.)
Costa Rica	2.3	1,730	3.2	32	4	70	22	90	99	11	923
Cuba	9.8	1,410	4.7	15	6	72	19	96	82	49	5,300
Dominican Rep.	5.6	1,140	3.7	37	9	60	96	67	18	17	869
†Ecuador	8.2	1,220	5.4	42	10	60	70	77	35	22	1,900
Guatemala	7.5	1,110	3.1	43	12	58	69	46	14	9	1,200
Jamaica	2.2	1,030	−3.7	27	6	70	16	86	79	9	790
Mexico	69.3	2,130	1.9	33	8	65	70	82	68	8	8,768
Panama	1.9	1,730	1.3	28	6	70	47	78	65	9	288
Paraguay	3.3	1,340	5.3	34	7	64	58	84	13	13	305
Puerto Rico	3.2	3,010	−0.3	22	6	74	18	88	n/a	n/a	n/a
Surinam	0.4	2,840	6.4	30	7	67	30	84	n/a	0	400
Uruguay	2.9	2,820	2.9	20	10	71	48	94	32	40	789
Oceania (1)	**0.6**	**1,850**	**3.0**	**28**	**4**	**71**	**41**	**64**	**82**	**12**	**249**
Fiji	0.6	1,850	3.0	28	4	71	41	64	82	12	249
Europe (5)	**101.4**	**1,908**	**5.1**	**24**	**9**	**66**	**75**	**75**	**80**	**71**	**22,368**
Malta	0.3	3,470	11.0	17	9	70	16	87	74	24	424
Portugal	10.0	2,350	1.1	15	8	70	39	70	73	64	3,468
Romania	22.4	1,900	9.6	18	10	70	30	98	103	56	9,724
Turkey	46.2	1,460	3.5	32	10	61	125	60	44	64	2,261
Yugoslavia	22.5	2,620	5.4	17	8	69	32	85	136	105	6,491
High-Income (51) (p/c GNP > $3,500)	**1,134.1**	**8,222**	**3.3**	**16**	**9**	**72**	**21**	**97**	**373**	**310**	**1,349,476**
Africa (3)	**4.3**	**7,397**	**−0.4**	**42**	**14**	**54**	**125**	**45**	**334**	**142**	**16,640**
†Gabon	0.7	4,440	5.2	33	22	43	78	12	100	78	1,700
†Libya	3.1	8,640	−1.6	47	13	55	130	50	387	156	14,800
Réunion	0.5	3,830	−0.9	25	6	65	21	63	n/a	n/a	140
Asia (11)	**143.6**	**9,802**	**4.3**	**18**	**7**	**73**	**18**	**90**	**474**	**191**	**238,505**
Bahrain	0.4	5,560	0.7	37	8	62	78	40	181	141	2,416
Brunei	0.2	11,890	4.6	28	4	66	20	64	239	642	2,649
Hong Kong	5.0	4,210	6.5	17	5	73	13	90	n/a	n/a	15,156
•Israel	3.9	4,500	1.6	25	7	74	16	88	303	839	4,553
•Japan	117.8	9,890	3.9	14	6	76	8	99	489	80	103,045
†Kuwait	1.4	22,840	1.4	41	5	70	39	60	454	613	17,499
Oman	0.9	4,380	3.8	49	19	47	142	20	94	914	2,284
†Qatar	0.2	26,080	−1.2	44	14	55	138	34	1,990	1,194	3,731
†Saudi Arabia	10.4	11,260	9.6	49	18	48	118	15	507	1,004	59,365
Singapore	2.4	4,480	6.7	17	5	71	13	75	84	186	14,233
†United Arab Emirates	1.0	30,070	2.4	37	9	60	65	56	277	836	13,574

High-Income Countries (continued)

	Population, mid-1981 (mil.)	Per capita GNP 1980 ($)	Per capita GNP (real) growth rate 1970-79 (%)	Birth rate per 1,000	Death rate per 1,000	Life expectancy at birth (years)	Infant mortality per 1,000 live births	Literacy (%)	Per capita public education expend's 1978 ($)	Per capita military expend's 1978 ($)	Total exports f.o.b. 1979 ($ mil.)
Latin America (5)	**17.6**	**3,713**	**2.9**	**35**	**6**	**66**	**43**	**83**	**148**	**42**	**18,933**
Guadeloupe	0.3	3,870	5.1	17	6	69	35	83	n/a	n/a	113
Martinique	0.3	4,640	4.3	16	7	69	15	88	n/a	n/a	133
Netherlands Antilles	0.3	4,290	0.9	28	7	62	25	93	n/a	n/a	3,100
Trinidad & Tobago	1.2	4,370	4.5	26	6	69	24	95	140	11	2,476
†Venezuela	15.5	3,630	2.7	36	6	66	45	82	149	44	13,111
Oceania (5)	**18.4**	**9,290**	**1.2**	**17**	**7**	**73**	**13**	**100**	**487**	**187**	**23,604**
•Australia	14.8	9,820	1.4	16	7	73	12	100	524	207	18,473
French Polynesia	0.2	6,780	3.1	34	7	58	38	95	n/a	n/a	35
Guam	0.1	7,010	5.2	26	4	n/a	16	n/a	n/a	n/a	25
New Caledonia	0.2	7,830	−4.2	26	7	64	30	91	n/a	n/a	377
•New Zealand	3.1	7,090	0.5	17	8	73	14	99	311	93	4,694
Europe (25)	**696.3**	**6,885**	**3.5**	**15**	**10**	**71**	**23**	**98**	**281**	**286**	**817,216**
•Austria	7.5	10,230	3.5	11	12	72	15	99	438	93	15,483
•Belgium	9.9	12,180	2.9	13	11	73	12	99	589	322	56,258
•Bulgaria	8.9	3,690	5.7	16	10	72	22	91	120	77	8,869
Channel Islands	0.1	6,780	1.1	11	12	n/a	19	n/a	n/a	n/a	n/a
Cyprus	0.6	3,560	4.3	21	8	73	16	76	75	39	456
•Czechoslovakia	15.4	5,290	4.3	18	12	70	19	95	144	143	13,198
•Denmark	5.1	12,950	2.1	12	11	74	9	99	752	259	14,506
•Finland	4.8	9,720	2.2	13	9	72	8	100	489	102	11,175
•France	53.9	11,730	3.0	14	10	73	10	99	512	350	98,059
•German Dem. Rep.	16.7	6,430	4.8	14	14	72	13	99	226	218	15,063
•Germany, Fed. Rep.	61.3	13,590	2.6	10	12	72	15	99	491	350	171,540
•Greece	9.6	4,520	4.1	16	9	73	19	84	74	220	3,855
•Hungary	10.7	3,850	5.1	15	13	70	24	98	142	79	7,938
•Iceland	0.2	11,330	2.8	19	6	76	11	99	397	0	781
•Ireland	3.4	4,880	2.3	20	10	73	15	98	232	59	7,180
•Italy	57.2	6,480	2.2	12	9	73	15	98	215	112	72,242
•Luxembourg	0.4	14,510	3.5	11	11	71	13	98	698	103	n/a
•Netherlands	14.2	11,470	2.2	12	8	75	8	99	730	304	63,667
•Norway	4.1	12,650	3.7	13	10	75	9	99	729	322	13,271
•Poland	36.0	3,830	5.9	20	9	71	22	98	101	99	16,233
•Spain	37.8	5,350	3.0	16	8	73	13	90	86	67	17,903
•Sweden	8.3	13,520	1.1	12	11	75	7	99	927	365	27,240
•Switzerland	6.3	16,440	0.2	12	9	75	9	99	710	280	26,507
•USSR	268.0	4,110	4.3	18	10	69	36	100	189	394	64,762
•United Kingdom	55.9	7,920	1.9	13	12	73	13	99	297	262	91,030
North America (2)	**253.9**	**11,243**	**2.3**	**16**	**9**	**74**	**13**	**99**	**577**	**468**	**234,578**
•Canada	24.1	10,130	2.9	15	7	74	12	99	688	174	56,000
•United States	229.8	11,360	2.2	16	9	74	13	99	565	499	178,578

Developing/Developed/World

	Population, mid-1981 (mil.)	Per capita GNP 1980 ($)	Per capita GNP (real) growth rate 1970-79 (%)	Birth rate per 1,000	Death rate per 1,000	Life expectancy at birth (years)	Infant mortality per 1,000 live births	Literacy (%)	Per capita public education expend's 1978 ($)	Per capita military expend's 1978 ($)	Total exports f.o.b. 1979 ($ mil.)
Developing Countries (143 countries)	3,400.5	711	2.4	32	12	59	96	54	24	29	450,812
Developed Countries (29 countries)	1,089.1	8,262	3.2	15	9	72	19	99	376	306	1,182,103
World (172 countries)	4,489.6	2,543	2.6	28	11	62	78	65	110	97	1,632,915

* Considered by the United Nations to be one of the 31 least developed countries.
† Member of the Organization of Petroleum Exporting Countries (OPEC).
• Considered by the ODC to be a developed country.

Source: Overseas Development Council, *US Foreign Policy and the Third World; Agenda 1982*, Praeger, New York, 1982, Annex B-4.

Chapter 6 The meaning of development

> It matters little how much information we possess about development if we have not grasped its inner meaning.
> *Denis Goulet, The Cruel Choice*

Introduction

Every nation strives after development; it is an objective that most people take for granted. While economic progress is an essential component of development, it is not the only one. This is because development is not purely an economic phenomenon. Ultimately it must encompass more than the material and financial side of people's lives. Development should therefore be perceived as a *multi-dimensional process* involving the reorganisation and reorientation of entire economic and social systems. In addition to improvements in incomes and output, it typically involves radical changes in institutional, social and administrative structures, as well as in popular attitudes and sometimes even customs and beliefs. Finally, although development is usually defined in a *national* context, its widespread realisation may necessitate fundamental modifications of the *international* economic and social system. But before analysing the complexities of development, we start by examining two major conceptual approaches to the study of economic development and then review the important notion of dualism and dual societies.

Two major approaches to the study of development –

Literature on economic development has been dominated by two major strands of thought: (1) the 'stages of economic growth' theories of the 1950s and early 1960s; (2) the 'structural-internationalist' theories of the late 1960s and the 1970s.

The thinking of the 1950s and early 1960s focused mainly on the concept of successive 'stages of economic growth' in which the process of development was seen as a series of successive stages through which all countries must pass. It was primarily an economic theory of development in which the right quantity and mixture of saving, investment and foreign aid were all that was necessary to enable Third World nations to proceed along an economic growth path which historically had been followed by the more developed countries. Development thus became synonymous with rapid economic growth.

This view has now been replaced to a great extent by what may be called the 'structural-internationalist' school of thought. This approach views underdevelopment in terms of international and domestic power relationships, institutional and structural economic rigidities, and the resulting proliferation of dual economies and dual societies both within and among the nations of the world. Structuralist theories tend to emphasise external and internal institutional constraints on economic development. Emphasis is placed on policies needed to eradicate poverty, to provide more diversified employment opportunities and to reduce income inequalities. These and other egalitarian objectives are to be achieved within the context of a growing economy but economic growth *per se* is not given the exalted status accorded to it by the linear stages model. Let us now look at each of the alternative approaches in greater detail.

The 'linear stages' model

When interest in the poor nations of the world began to materialise after the Second World War, economists in the industrialised nations were caught off guard. They had no readily available conceptual apparatus with which to analyse the process of economic growth in largely peasant, agrarian societies characterised by the virtual absence of 'modern' economic structures. But they did have the recent experience of the Marshall Plan, in which massive amounts of US financial and technical assistance enabled the war-torn countries of Europe to rebuild and modernise their economies in a matter of a few years. Moreover, was it not true that all modern industrial nations were once undeveloped peasant agrarian societies too? Surely, their historical experience in transforming their economies from poor agricultural subsistence societies to modern industrial and wealthy giants had important lessons for the 'backward' countries of Asia, Africa and Latin America. The logic and simplicity of these two strands of thoughts – the need for massive injections of capital investment and the historical pattern of the now developed countries – was too irresistible to be refuted by scholars, politicians and administrators in richer countries to whom people and ways of life in the Third World were often no more real than UN statistics or chapters in scattered anthropology books.

Out of this somewhat sterile intellectual environment and fuelled by the cold war politics of the 1950s and early 1960s and the resulting competition for the allegiance of newly independent nations, came the doctrine of the 'stages of economic growth'. Its most influential and outspoken advocate was the American economic historian, W. W. Rostow. According to the Rostow doctrine, the transition from underdevelopment to development can be described in terms of a series of steps or stages through which *all* countries must proceed. In the opening chapter of his book Professor Rostow wrote:

> This book presents an economic historian's way of generalizing the sweep of modern history. . . . It is possible to identify all societies, in their economic dimensions, as lying within one of five categories: the traditional society, the pre-conditions for take-off into self-sustaining growth, the drive to maturity, and the age of high mass consumption. . . . These stages are not merely descriptive. They are not merely a way of generalizing certain factual observations about the sequence of development of modern societies. They have an inner logic and continuity . . . they constitute, in the end, both a theory about economic growth and a more general, if still highly partial, theory about modern history as a whole.[1]

The advanced countries, it was argued, had at various times in history passed the stage of 'take-off into self-sustaining growth', and the underdeveloped countries, which were either still in the 'traditional society' or the 'preconditions' stage, had only to follow a certain set of rules or 'tricks' of development to 'take off' in turn into self-sustaining economic growth. One of the principal 'tricks' of development necessary for any take-off was the mobilisation of domestic and foreign savings in order to generate sufficient investment to accelerate economic growth. The economic processes by which more investment leads to more growth can be described in the following macro-economic terms.

Every economy must save (not consume) a certain proportion of its national income if only to replace worn out or impaired capital goods (buildings, equipment, materials). However, in order to grow, new investment representing net additions to the capital stock is necessary. If we assume that there is some direct economic relationship between the size of the total capital stock, K, and total GNP, Y, for example, if \$3 of capital are always necessary to produce a \$1 stream of GNP, it follows that any net additions to the capital stock in the form of new investment will bring about corresponding increases in the flow of national output (GNP).

Suppose this relationship, known in economics as the **capital–output ratio**, is 3 to 1. If we define this capital–output ratio as k and assume further that the national **saving ratio**, s, is a fixed proportion of national output (e.g. say 6 per cent) and that total new investment is determined by the level of total savings, then we can construct the following simple 'model' of economic growth:

1. Savings (S) is some proportion, s, of national income (Y) such that we have the simple equation

   (1) $S = s \cdot Y$

   [e.g. if $s = 0.06$ and $Y = \$100$m, then savings ($S$) will be \$6m]

[1] W. W. Rostow, *The Stages of Economic Growth, a non-communist manifesto*, Cambridge University Press, 1960, pp. 1, 3, 4 and 12.

2. Investment (I) is defined as the change (economists use the symbol Δ to express changes in variables) in the capital stock, K, and can be represented by ΔK such that
(2) $I = \Delta K$
But since the total capital stock, K, bears a direct relationship to total national income or output, Y, as expressed by the capital–output ratio, k, then it follows that
(2′) $K/Y = k$ or, $\Delta K/\Delta Y = k$
or, finally $\Delta K = k\Delta Y$.
3. Finally, since total national saving S must equal total investment, I, it follows that we can write this equality as
(3) $S = I$

But from equation (1) above we know that $S = s \cdot Y$ and from equations (2) and (2′) we know that $I = \Delta K = k\Delta Y$. It therefore follows that we can write the 'identity' of saving equalling investment shown by equation (3) as

(3′) $S = s \cdot Y = k\Delta Y = \Delta K = I$
or, simply as
(3″) $s \cdot Y = k\Delta Y$.

Now by dividing both sides of equation (3″) first by Y and then by k we obtain the following expression

(4) $\Delta Y/Y = s/k$.

Note that the lefthand side of equation (4), $\Delta Y/Y$ represents the rate of change or rate of growth of GNP (i.e. the percentage change in GNP).

Equation (4), which is famous in the theory of economic development,[2] states simply that the rate of growth of GNP ($\Delta Y/Y$) is determined jointly by the national saving ratio, s, and the national capital–output ratio, k. More specifically, it says that the growth rate of national income will be directly or positively related to the savings ratio (i.e. the more an economy is able to save – and invest – out of a given GNP, the greater will be the growth of that GNP) and inversely or negatively related to the economy's capital–output ratio (i.e. the higher is k, the lower will be the rate of GNP growth).

The economic logic of equation (4) is simple. In order to grow economies must save and invest a certain proportion of their GNP. The more they can save, and therefore invest, the faster they can grow. The actual rate at which they can grow for any level of saving and investment depends on how productive that investment is. The productivity of this investment – i.e. how much additional output can be had from an additional unit of investment – can be measured by the inverse of the capital–output ratio, k, since this inverse, $1/k$, is simply the output–capital or output–investment ratio. It follows that multiplying the *rate* of new investment, $s = I/Y$, by its productivity, $1/k$, will give us the rate by which national income or GNP will increase.[3]

Now, returning to the stages of growth theory, and using equation (4) of our simple growth model, we learn that one of the most fundamental 'tricks' of economic growth is simply to increase the proportion of national income which is saved (not consumed). If we can raise s in equation (4) then we can increase $\Delta Y/Y$, the rate of GNP growth. For example, if we assume that the national capital–output ratio in some less developed country, is say, 3 and the aggregate savings ratio is 6 per cent of GNP, then it follows from equation (4) that this country can grow at a rate of 2 per cent per year since

$$\frac{\Delta Y}{Y} = \frac{s}{k} = \frac{6\%}{3} = 2 \text{ per cent.}$$

Now if the national savings rate can somehow be increased from 6 to, say, 15 per cent (e.g. through increased taxes and/or general consumption sacrifices), then GNP growth can be increased from 2 to 5 per cent since now

$$\frac{\Delta Y}{Y} = \frac{s}{k} = \frac{15\%}{3} = 5 \text{ per cent.}$$

Rostow and others defined the take-off stage precisely in this way. Countries which were able to save 15 to 20 per cent of their GNP could grow ('develop') at a much faster rate than those who saved less. Moreover, this growth will then be self-sustaining. The 'tricks' of economic growth and development, therefore, are simply a matter of increasing savings and investment.

The main obstacle to or constraint on development according to this theory was the relatively low

[2] It is known as the 'Harrod–Domar' equation after two famous economists Sir Roy Harrod of England and Professor Evesey Domar of the United States who independently formulated a variant of the above model in the early 1950s.

[3] Since $s = I/Y$ and $1/k$ can be written as $1/(I/\Delta Y)$, it follows that

$$s \cdot \frac{1}{k} = \frac{I}{Y} \cdot \frac{\Delta Y}{I} = \frac{\Delta Y}{Y}.$$

level of new capital formation or investment in most poor countries. But if a country wanted to grow economically at, say, a rate of 7 per cent per year, and if it could *not* generate savings and investment at a rate of 21 per cent of national income (assuming that k, the capital–output ratio, is 3) but could only manage to save 15 per cent, then it could seek to fill this 'savings gap' of 6 per cent either through foreign aid or private foreign investment.

Thus, the capital constraint stages approach to growth and development became an intellectual and (in terms of cold war politics) 'opportunist' tool to justify the massive transfers of capital and technical assistance from the developed to the less developed nations. It was to be the Marshall Plan all over again, but this time for the underdeveloped nations of the Third World. Unfortunately, the 'tricks' of development embodied in the theory of stages of growth did not always work. This was not because more saving and investment is not a *necessary* condition of economic growth, but because it is not a *sufficient* condition.

Once again we are faced with an example of what we discussed extensively in Chapter 3: the inappropriateness and irrelevance of many of the implicit assumptions of Western economic theory for the actual conditions in Third World nations. The Marshall Plan worked for Europe because the European countries receiving aid possessed the necessary structural, institutional and attitudinal conditions (e.g. well-integrated commodity and money markets, highly developed transport facilities, well trained and educated manpower, the motivation to succeed, an efficient government bureaucracy, etc.) to convert new capital effectively into higher levels of output. The Rostow–Harrod-Domar models of economic growth and development implicitly assume the existence of these same attitudes and arrangements in less developed nations. But in many cases they are not present, nor are the complementary factors such as managerial experience, skilled labour, and the ability to plan and administer a wide variety of development projects, always present in sufficient quantities.[4]

But even at a more fundamental level, the 'stages' theory fails to take into account the crucial fact that contemporary Third World nations are part of a highly integrated and complex international system in which their best and most intelligent development strategies can be nullified by external forces beyond their control. One simply cannot claim, as many economists did in the 1950s and 1960s, that development is simply a matter of removing obstacles and supplying various 'missing components' like capital, foreign exchange, skills and management – a task in which the developed countries could theoretically play a major role. It was because of numerous failures and the growing disenchantment with this strictly economic theory of development that a more recent approach has emerged, one that attempts to combine economic and institutional factors into a social systems model of international development and underdevelopment.

The international-structuralist models

The second major approach to the study of underdevelopment has recently gained increasing support as a result of growing disenchantment with the earlier 'stages' and economic 'constraints' approach. This approach, which we have called the 'international-structuralist' model, essentially views Third World countries as being beset by a variety of institutional and structural economic rigidities and caught up in a dependence and dominance relationship to rich countries. There are two major streams of thought in the international-structuralist approach.

The 'neo-colonial' (neo-Marxist) dependence model

The first, which might be called the 'neo-colonial' dependence model, is an outgrowth of Marxist thinking. It attributes the existence and maintenance of Third World underdevelopment primarily to the historical evolution of a highly unequal international capitalist system of rich country–poor country relationships. Whether intentionally exploitive or unintentionally neglectful, the co-

[4] In Chapter 7 we examine the economic and non-economic determinants of growth in much greater detail.

existence of rich and poor nations in an international system dominated by such unequal power relationships between the 'centre' and the 'periphery' renders attempts by poor societies (the 'periphery') to be self-reliant and independent in their development efforts difficult and sometimes even impossible.[5] Certain groups in the developing countries (e.g. landlords, entrepreneurs, merchants, public officials and trade union leaders) who enjoy high incomes, social status and political power, constitute a small elite ruling class whose principal interest, whether knowingly or not, is in the perpetuation of the international capitalist system of inequality and conformity by which they are rewarded. Directly and indirectly, they serve (are dominated by) and are rewarded by (dependent upon) special interest power groups in the rich nations (e.g. multi-national corporations, national bilateral aid agencies, and multilateral donor organisations such as the World Bank and other specialised UN agencies). Their activities and viewpoints often serve to inhibit any genuine reform efforts which might benefit the wider population. In short, the neo-Marxist, neo-colonial, structural view of underdevelopment attributes a large part of the Third World's continuing poverty to the existence and policies of the industrial capitalist countries of the northern hemisphere, and their extensions in the form of small but powerful elite or 'comprador' groups in the less developed countries.[6]

One of the most forceful statements of the international dependence school of thought, especially as it applies to Latin America, is that of Theotonio Dos Santos who argues that:

> ... underdevelopment, far from constituting a state of backwardness prior to capitalism, is rather a consequence and particular form of capitalist development known as dependent capitalism ... dependence is a *conditioning* situation in which the economies of one group of countries are conditioned by the development and expansion of others. A relationship of interdependence between two or more economies or between such economies and the world trading system becomes a dependent relationship when some countries can expand through self-impulsion while others, being in a dependent position, can only expand as a reflection of the expansion of the dominant countries, which may have positive or negative effects on their immediate development. In either case, the basic situation of dependence causes these countries to be both backward and exploited. Dominant countries are endowed with technological, commercial, capital and socio-political predominance over dependent countries – the form of this predominance varying according to the particular historical moment – and can therefore exploit them, and extract part of the locally produced surplus. Dependence, then, is based upon an international division of labour which allows industrial development to take place in some countries while restricting it in others, whose growth is conditioned by and subjected to the power centres of the world.[7]

Various components of the neo-Marxist, dependence argument will be explored in greater detail when we discuss problems of poverty, income distribution, unemployment, international trade and foreign assistance in Parts Two and Three of the book. For those with a more active interest in the subject, Appendix III to this chapter provides a brief explanation of the central arguments of the neo-Marxist theory of underdevelopment.

The 'false paradigm' model

The second, less extreme and less doctrinaire international-structuralist approach to development, the 'false paradigm'[8] model, attributes Third World underdevelopment to primarily faulty and inappropriate advice provided by well-meaning but

[5] For one of the more comprehensive introductions to the neo-Marxist view of international development and underdevelopment, see Paul Baran, *The Political Economy of Growth*, Monthly Review Press, New York and London, 1962.

[6] Clearly such neo-colonial activities need not be limited solely to capitalist nations.

[7] T. Dos. Santos, 'The Crisis of Development Theory and the Problem of Dependence in Latin America', *Siglo*, Vol. 21, 1969. See also Benjamin J. Cohen, *The Question of Imperialism: The Political Economy of Dominance and Dependence*, New York, Basic Books, 1973.

[8] A paradigm is a pattern or an example which serves as a model for study and comparison.

often uninformed international 'expert' advisers from both developed-country assistance agencies and multi-national donor organisations such as the World Bank, UNESCO, ILO, UNDP and the International Monetary Fund. These 'experts' offer sophisticated concepts, elegant models and complex technical methods of economics and other social sciences (such as the stages–constraints approach) which can lead to inappropriate policies. Because of institutional and structural factors (such as the highly unequal ownership of land, disproportionate control over domestic and international financial assets and very unequal access to credit) these policies often merely serve the vested interests of existing power structures, both domestic and international.

In addition, according to this argument, leading university intellectuals, trade unionists, future high level government economists and other civil servants all get their training in developed-country institutions where they are unwittingly served an unhealthy dose of alien concepts and models camouflaged by excessive sophistication and esoteric irrelevance. Having little or no really useful knowledge to enable them to come to grips in an effective way with real development problems, they often tend to become unknowing or reluctant apologists for the existing system of elitist policies and institutional structures. In university economics courses, for example, this typically entails the perpetuation of the teaching of inappropriate or irrelevant Western concepts and models, while in government policy discussions too much emphasis is placed on the notion of capital–output ratios, savings and investment ratios and growth rates of GNP. As a result, desirable *institutional* and *structural* reforms, many of which we have mentioned in previous sections, are neglected or given only cursory attention.

Conclusions

Whatever their ideological and institutional differences of emphasis, both the neo-colonial exploitive and the false paradigm components of the international-structuralist theory of underdevelopment reject the exclusive emphasis on accelerating the growth of GNP as an index of development. Instead more emphasis is placed on needed structural and institutional reforms (both domestic and international) in order to eradicate absolute poverty, provide expanded employment opportunities, lessen income inequalities, and raise the general levels of living (including health, education and cultural enrichment) of the masses of people. While some structuralists would go so far as to say 'growth doesn't matter', the majority of thoughtful observers recognise that the most effective way to deal with these diverse social problems is to alter the *character* of the growth process itself, so that wider segments of Third World populations can participate in and benefit from its realisation.

Dualism and the concept of dual societies

Implicit in the international-structuralist view of the world, in both its neo-colonial and false paradigm aspects, is the notion of a world of **dual societies**: rich nations and poor nations internationally and pockets of wealth within broad areas of poverty in developing countries. **Dualism** is a concept widely discussed in Third World economics. It represents the existence and persistence of **increasing divergences** between rich and poor nations and peoples on various levels. Specifically, the concept of dualism embraces four key elements[9]:

1. **Different sets of conditions,** of which some are 'superior' and others 'inferior', can co-exist in a given space at the same time. For example, the co-existence of modern and traditional methods of production in urban and rural sectors, the co-existence of wealthy, highly educated elites with masses of illiterate poor people, and the co-existence of powerful and wealthy industrialised nations with weak, impoverished peasant societies in the international economy – these are all obvious manifestations of this first element of dualism.
2. **This co-existence is chronic** and not merely transitional. It is not due to a temporary

[9] See Hans Singer, 'Dualism Revisited: a new approach to the problems of dual society in developing countries', *Journal of Development Studies*, vii, 1, October 1970, pp. 60–61.

phenomenon which in time will eliminate the discrepancy between superior and inferior elements. In other words, the international co-existence of wealth and poverty is *not* simply a historical phenomenon which will be rectified in time. This is what the 'stages of growth' theory implicitly assumes but which the facts of growing international inequalities emphatically refute.

3. The degrees of superiority or inferiority not only fail to show any signs of rapidly diminishing, they even have an inherent tendency to increase. For example, the productivity gap between developed-country industry and its counterpart in the LDCs seems to widen with each passing year.

4. **The interrelations between 'superior' and 'inferior'** elements are such that the existence of the superior element does little or nothing to pull up the inferior. In fact, it may actually serve to push the latter down.

International dualism

These four components of dualism provide a near-perfect description of the contemporary situation in the international economic system. First, there are, as we have seen in Chapter 5, great differences in per capita incomes and levels of living currently co-existing between different countries, races, continents and climatic zones of the world. Second, these differences are clearly not short-term but chronic. The disparity between economic levels of living between, say, England and France on the one hand and India and sub-Saharan Africa on the other have persisted not for decades but for centuries. Third, these differences show signs of increasing rather than decreasing. We saw in the last chapter how growth rates of GNP and especially GNP per capita had widened in favour of the developed countries during the past decades. Fourth and finally, the interrelations between the rich and poor countries in the international economy, at least in the judgment of most members of the structuralist school of development thought, contain many elements which make the rapid growth of the former only marginally helpful and, in some cases, absolutely harmful to the development of the latter. These so-called international 'backwash' effects inhibiting the sustained development of Third World nations include, among others, the following forces of international dominance and dependence:

- the power of strong countries to control and manipulate world resource and commodity markets to their advantage;
- the spread of international capitalist domination of domestic LDC economies through the foreign investment activities of private multi-national corporations;
- the privileged access of rich nations to scarce raw materials;
- the export of unsuitable and inappropriate science and technology;
- the freedom for industrialised countries to 'impose' their products on fragile Third World markets;
- the transfer of outmoded and irrelevant systems of education to societies where education is perceived as a key component in the development process;
- the ability of rich countries to disrupt efforts at industrialisation by poor countries by 'dumping' cheap products in these controlled markets;
- harmful international trade theories and policies which lock developing countries into primary product exports with declining international revenues;
- harmful aid policies which often merely serve to perpetuate and exacerbate internal dualistic economic structures;
- the creation of elites in poor countries whose economic and ideological allegiance is to the external world both capitalist and socialist;
- the transfer of unsuitable methods of university training for unrealistic and often irrelevant international professional standards, for instance the externally conceived degree requirements for doctors, engineers, technicians and economists;
- the corresponding capacity of rich countries to lure trained personnel away from LDCs with attractive financial rewards (the international brain drain); and finally,
- the demoralising 'demonstration effect' of luxury consumption on the part of the wealthy both at home and abroad, as propagated, for example, in imported foreign movies and magazine advertisements.

As we pointed out in the previous section, it is easy and rather reassuring, but often unrealistic, to attempt to lay the blame for all the evils of underdevelopment at the international doorstep of rich nations. On the other hand, it is equally naive to believe that many of the serious problems of underdevelopment do not orginate abroad. Clearly, the continued economic growth of rich nations helps to make it possible for poor countries to maintain growth rates of output which are high by historical standards. At the same time, however, it is difficult to refute Professor Singer's observation that

> the very forces which are set in motion by the rapid growth of the richer countries – specifically the development of even more sophisticated, costly and capital-intensive technologies, and of mortality-reducing health improvements and disease controls – are such as to create forces within the poorer countries – specifically a population explosion, rising unemployment and inability to develop their own technological capacities, which may in fact assure that they will *not* have the time needed for the continued maintenance of current growth rates, let alone their acceleration, so as to result in acceptable levels of development.[10]

Domestic dualism

Our fourfold definition of dualism is equally descriptive of the internal economic structures of many developing countries. First, as we saw in Table 5.1, standards of living vary greatly between the top 20 per cent and bottom 40 per cent of the population with ratios as high as six and twelve to one being representative. The majority of those few with very high incomes live in urban areas, while the great clusters of mass poverty are generally to be found in rural regions. Even within most Third World urban areas one typically finds pockets of great wealth coexisting with spreading slums.

This initial element of dualism, the coexistence of 'superior' with 'inferior' phenomena, is not limited to the distribution of wealth, income and power. It exists also in the technological nature of Third World industrial production. Small enclaves of modern industries (mostly urban manufacturing) using modern imported capital-intensive production methods to produce sophisticated products in large quantities coexist with traditional labour-intensive, small-scale activities catering for limited local needs.

Second, the coexistence of small modern enclaves in the midst of traditional societies, and of a small group of progressive wealthy elites amid masses of poor, shows no sign of disappearing. The vast majority of Third World peoples seem today as untouched by development as they were, say, ten to fifteen years ago.

Third, the gap between the rich and poor and between modern and traditional methods of production shows signs of growing even wider, not only within individual LDCs but also among the Third World countries as a group. Countries such as Brazil, Panama, Costa Rica, Singapore, Taiwan, Thailand, Korea, Cyprus, Sierra Leone and Kenya have experienced relatively high rates of per capita income growth for a number of years now, while Bangladesh, Haiti, Mali, the Sudan, Ghana, India and Peru and many others have shown little or no per capita growth at all over the past decade. Within many nations, however, the gap between rich and poor seems to be widening. This is especially true in those Third World countries with markedly dualistic industrial structures, like Brazil, Mexico, the Philippines, Venezuela, Peru, Kenya, Zambia and India.

Finally, the 'spread effects' between the rising wealth of modern enclaves and improvement in living standards of the traditional society are less than obvious in most LDCs. In fact there seems to be little or no spread effect whatsoever. Many observers claim with some justification that it is the very growth of the stronger or 'superior' component of dualistic societies that keeps down, or at least is achieved at the expense of, the weaker or inferior element. We shall see precisely how this process has tended to be prolonged and intensified when we discuss the problems of poverty, income distribution, unemployment, rural development, education, trade, aid and technology in Parts Two and Three.

What do we mean by 'development'?

Let us now try to pull together many of the threads of previous sections of this chapter and, indeed, of

[10] Singer, *op cit.*, p. 62.

previous chapters in an attempt to define what we really mean by 'development'.

Traditional economic measures

In strictly economic terms, 'development' for the past two decades has meant the capacity of a national economy, whose initial economic condition has been more or less static for a long time, to *generate* and *sustain* an annual increase in its gross national product at rates of perhaps 5 to 7 per cent or more. For example, the 1960s and 1970s were dubbed the 'Development Decades' by a resolution of the United Nations, and development was conceived largely in terms of the attainment of a 6 per cent annual target growth rate of GNP. An alternative common economic index of development has been the use of rates of growth of per capita GNP, to take into account the ability of a nation to expand its output at a rate faster than the growth rate of its population. Levels and rates of growth of 'real' per capita GNP (i.e. monetary growth of GNP per capita *minus* the rate of price inflation) are typically used to measure in a broad sense the overall economic wellbeing of a population – that is, how many real goods and services are available for consumption and investment for the average citizen.

Economic development has in the past also been typically seen in terms of the planned alteration of the structure of production and employment so that agriculture's share of both declines, whereas that of the manufacturing and service industries increases. Development strategies, therefore, have usually focused on rapid urban industrialisation, often at the expense of agriculture and rural development. Finally, these principal economic measures of development were often supplemented by casual reference to and general acceptance of non-economic social indicators – gains in literacy, schooling, health conditions and services, provision of housing, for instance.

But on the whole, development in the 1950s and 1960s was nearly always seen as an economic phenomenon in which rapid gains in overall and per capita GNP growth would either 'trickle down' to the masses in the form of jobs and other economic opportunities, or create the necessary conditions for the wider distribution of the economic and social benefits of growth. Problems of poverty, unemployment and income distribution were of secondary importance to 'getting the growth job done'.

The new economic view of development

Unfortunately the experience of the 1950s and 1960s, when a large number of Third World nations *did* achieve the overall UN growth targets but the levels of living of the masses of people remained for the most part unchanged, signalled that something was very wrong with this narrow definition of development. A clamour was raised by an increasing number of economists and policy makers for the 'dethronement of GNP' and the promotion of direct attacks on widespread absolute poverty, increasingly inequitable income distributions and the spectre of rising unemployment. In short, **economic development was redefined in terms of the reduction or elimination of poverty, inequality and unemployment within the context of a growing economy.** 'Redistribution from growth' became a common slogan.

Professor Dudley Seers perhaps best posed the basic questions about the meaning of development when he asserted that:

> The questions to ask about a country's development are therefore: What has been happening to poverty? What has been happening to unemployment? What has been happening to inequality? If all three of these have declined from high levels, then beyond doubt this has been a period of development for the country concerned. If one or two of these central problems have been growing worse, especially if all three have, it would be strange to call the result 'development' even if per capita income doubled.[11]

The above assertion is not idle speculation, or the description of a hypothetical situation. There were, for example, a number of developing countries which experienced relatively high rates of growth of per capita income during the 1960s and 1970s but which simultaneously showed little or no improvement or witnessed an actual decline in employment,

[11] Dudley Seers, 'The Meaning of Development', *Eleventh World Conference of the Society for International Development*, New Delhi, 1969, p. 3.

equality and the real incomes of the bottom 40 per cent of their populations. By the earlier growth definition, these countries were developing. By the more recent poverty, equality and employment criteria, however, they were not.

Beyond narrow economic criteria

'Development' and 'underdevelopment' represent much more than economics and the simple quantitative measurement of incomes, employment and inequality. Underdevelopment is a real fact of life for over two billion people of the world – a state of mind as much as a state of national poverty. As Denis Goulet has so forcefully portrayed it:

> Underdevelopment is shocking: the squalor, disease, unnecessary deaths, and hopelessness of it all! No man understands if underdevelopment remains for him a mere statistic reflecting low income, poor housing, premature mortality or underemployment. The most empathetic observer can speak objectively about underdevelopment only after undergoing, personally or vicariously, the 'shock of underdevelopment'. This unique culture shock comes to one as he is initiated to the emotions which prevail in the 'culture of poverty'. The reverse shock is felt by those living in destitution when a new self-understanding reveals to them that their life is neither human nor inevitable. ... The prevalent emotion of underdevelopment is a sense of personal and societal impotence in the face of disease and death, of confusion and ignorance as one gropes to understand change, of servility toward men whose decisions govern the course of events, of hopelessness before hunger and natural catastrophe. Chronic poverty is a cruel kind of hell; and one cannot understand how cruel that hell is merely by gazing upon poverty as an object.[12]

The condition of underdevelopment is thus a consciously experienced state of deprivation rendered especially intolerable as more and more people acquire information about the development of other societies and realise that technical and institutional means for abolishing poverty, misery and disease do indeed exist.

Development must therefore be conceived of as a multi-dimensional process involving changes in structures, attitudes and institutions as well as the acceleration of economic growth, the reduction of inequality and eradication of absolute poverty. In essence, development must represent the entire gamut of changes by which an entire social system, tuned to the diverse basic needs and desires of individuals and social groups within that system, moves away from a condition of life widely perceived as unsatisfactory, and towards a situation or condition of life regarded as materially and spiritually 'better'.

Three core values of development

Is it possible to define broadly or conceptualise what we mean when we talk about development as the sustained elevation of an entire society and social system towards a better or 'more humane' life? The question 'What constitutes the good life?' is as old as philosophy and man himself. It is a timeless and perennial question which needs to be re-evaluated and freshly answered with the changing environment of world society. The appropriate answer for Third World nations in the last two decades of the twentieth century is not necessarily the same as it would have been in previous decades. But we believe, with Professor Goulet and others, that at least three basic components or core values should serve as a conceptual basis and practical guideline for understanding the inner meaning of development. These core values are **life-sustenance, self-esteem** and **freedom**, representing common goals sought by all individuals and societies.[13] They relate to fundamental human needs which find their expression in almost all societies and cultures at all times. Let us look at each in turn.

Life-sustenance: the ability to provide basic human needs

All people have certain basic human needs without which life would be impossible. These life-sustaining

[12] Denis Goulet, *The Cruel Choice: a new concept in the theory of development*, Atheneum, New York, 1971, p. 23.

[13] *Ibid.*, pp. 87–94.

needs include, indisputably, food, shelter, health and protection. When any of these is absent or in critically short supply we may state, without reservation, that a condition of 'absolute underdevelopment' exists. A basic function of all economic activity is to provide as many people as possible with the means of overcoming the helplessness and misery arising from a lack of food, shelter, health and protection. To this extent, we may claim that economic development is a necessary condition for the improvement in the quality of life which is 'development'. Without sustained and continuous economic progress at the individual as well as the societal level, the realisation of the human potential would not be possible. Clearly one has to 'have enough in order to be more'.[14] Rising per capita incomes, the elimination of absolute poverty, greater employment opportunities, and lessening income inequalities, therefore, constitute the necessary, but not the only, conditions for development.

Self-esteem: to be a person

A second universal component of the good life is self-esteem: a sense of worth and self-respect, of not being used as a tool by others for their own ends. All peoples and societes seek some form of self-esteem, although they may call it authenticity, identity, dignity, respect, honour or recognition. The nature and form of this self-esteem may vary from society to society and from one culture to another. However, with the proliferation of the modernising values of developed nations, many societies in Third World countries which may have possessed a profound sense of their own worth suffer from serious cultural confusion when they come in contact with economically and technologically advanced societies. This is because national prosperity has become an almost universal measure of worth. Because of the significance attached to material values in 'developed' nations, high value and esteem are nowadays increasingly conferred only on those countries who possess economic wealth and technological power – those who have 'developed'. Again, we may quote Professor Goulet:

> The relevant point is that underdevelopment is the lot of the majority of the world's population. As long as esteem or respect was dispensed on grounds other than material achievement, it was possible to resign oneself to poverty without feeling disdained. Conversely, once the prevailing image of the better life includes material welfare as one of its essential ingredients, it becomes difficult for the materially 'underdeveloped' to feel respected or esteemed ... nowadays the Third World seeks development in order to gain the esteem which is denied to societies living in a state of disgraceful 'underdevelopment'. ... Development is legitimised as a goal because it is an important, perhaps even an indispensable, way of gaining esteem.[15]

Freedom from servitude: to be able to choose

A third and final universal core value is the concept of freedom. Freedom here is not to be understood in the political or ideological sense (e.g. the 'free world'), but in the more fundamental sense of freedom or emancipation from alienating material conditions of life and freedom from the social servitudes of men to nature, ignorance, other men, misery, institutions and dogmatic beliefs. Freedom involves the expanded range of choices for societies and their members, together with the minimisation of external constraint in the pursuit of some social goal which we call 'development'. W. Arthur Lewis stressed the relationship between economic growth and freedom from servitude when he concluded that 'the advantage of economic growth is not that wealth increases happiness, but that it increases the range of human choice'.[16] Wealth can enable man to gain greater control over nature and his physical environment (e.g. through the production of food, clothing and shelter), than if he remained poor. It also gives him the freedom to choose greater leisure, to have more goods and services or to deny the importance of these material wants and live a life of spiritual contemplation.[17]

[14] *Ibid.*, p. 124.

[15] *Ibid.*, pp. 89, 90.

[16] W. Arthur Lewis, 'Is Economic Growth Desirable?' in *The Theory of Economic Growth*, Allen and Unwin, 1963, p. 420.

[17] It is not surprising that the so-called hippie 'counterculture' of the late 1960s grew up largely among young people from the upper middle and wealthy classes of 'developed' countries.

The three objectives of development

We may conclude that 'development' is both a physical reality and a state of mind in which society has, through some combination of social, economic and institutional processes, secured the means for obtaining a better life. Whatever the specific components of this better life, development in all societies must have at least the following three objectives:

- to increase the availability and widen the distribution of basic life-sustaining goods such as food, shelter, health and protection to all members of society;
- to raise levels of living, including, in addition to higher incomes, the provision of more jobs, better education and more attention to cultural and humanistic values. These all serve not only to enhance material well-being but also to generate greater individual and national self-esteem;
- to expand the range of economic and social choice to individuals and nations by freeing them from servitude and dependence not only in relation to other people and nation-states but also to the forces of ignorance and human misery.

We may, therefore, reformulate and broaden Professor Seers' questions about the meaning of development as follows:

1. Have general levels of living expanded within a nation to the extent that absolute poverty (i.e. deprivation of life-sustaining goods), the degree of inequality to income distribution, the level of employment and the nature and quality of educational, health and other social and cultural services have all improved?
2. Has economic progress enhanced individual and group esteem both internally *vis-à-vis* one another and externally *vis-à-vis* other nations and regions?
3. Finally, has economic progress expanded the range of human choice and freed people from external dependence and internal servitude to other men and institutions, or has it merely substituted one form of dependence (e.g. economic) for another (e.g. political or cultural)?

If the answer to each of the above three questions is 'yes', then clearly these phenomena constitute real development and a nation in which they are manifested can unquestionably be called developed. If only the first question (which is equivalent to Seers' three questions) can be answered affirmatively while the other two remain negative, such a country may properly be designated as 'economically more developed' even though it remains 'underdeveloped' in a more fundamental sense. In this sense, it is more proper to refer to the rich nations of the world as 'economically developed' and reserve judgment as to whether they are actually developed to a more thorough-going social, political and cultural analysis. To paraphrase Seers, if the second and third of these central questions for all societies evoke a negative response – i.e. if people feel less self-esteem, respect or dignity and if their freedom to choose has been constrained, then even if the provision of life-sustaining goods and improvements in levels of living are occurring, it would be misleading to call the result 'development'.

Underdevelopment and development: a multidimensional schematic summary

Figure 6.1 (page 100) represents a schematic attempt to portray and summarise the main economic and non-economic aspects of what we mean by underdevelopment. In it we have listed our three primary components of underdevelopment – low levels of living (life-sustenance), low self-esteem and limited freedom – as three rectangular boxes with arrows indicating general lines of causation. The left side of the chart, relating to the determinants of levels of living portrays the principal economic aspects of underdevelopment. The two boxes on the right side of the chart (self-esteem and freedom to choose) represent what are typically referred to as 'non-economic' aspects of development. In fact, economic phenomena and forces impinge on all three boxes while important non-economic forces like attitudes and institutions are also vital components of the determinants of levels of living. It is simply not possible to separate economic from non-economic phenomena when dealing with real world problems. But, in order fully to understand the concepts and processes portrayed in our schematic framework of underdevelopment, let us look briefly at how the three components are interrelated.

First, we see that low levels of living (insufficient life-sustaining goods and inadequate or nonexistent education, health and other social services) are all related in one form or another to low incomes. These low incomes result from the low average productivity of the *entire* labour force (not just those working) – i.e. total national output divided by the total labour force. Low labour force productivity can result from a variety of factors including, on the supply side, poor health, nutrition and work attitudes, high population growth and high unemployment and underemployment. On the demand side inadequate skills, poor managerial talents and overall low levels of worker education may, along with the importation from developed countries of labour-saving techniques of production, result in the substitution of capital for labour in domestic production. The combination of low labour demand and large supplies, therefore, results in the widespread underutilisation of labour. Moreover, low incomes lead to low savings and investment, thus also restricting the total number of employment opportunities. Finally, low incomes are also thought to be related to large family size and high fertility since children provide the major source of economic and social security in old age for poor families (see Chapter 11).

Note that the arrows in the upper left side of Figure 6.1 (the productivity-income relationship) form a series of continuous loops indicating that a process of circular causation or 'vicious circles' is in operation. For example, on the outer right loop we see that low incomes result in low savings which means low investment, limited labour demand, high unemployment, low productivity and therefore low incomes. On the inner right loop low incomes are shown as leading to restricted educational opportunities (both public and private) and inadequate managerial and high-level manpower training programmes. The result is that a relatively unskilled labour force produces at low levels of productivity which further perpetuates low incomes. The inner left loop shows low incomes leading to poor health and nutrition in the worker due to a lack of food, sanitation, etc., which in turn is a primary factor in the worker's poor performance and his attitudes towards promptness, discipline and self-improvement. Finally, the outer left loop shows the linkage between low incomes, high fertility, rapid population growth, high labour supply, high unemployment, low per capita labour productivity and, lastly, the perpetuation of chronically low incomes.

The important point to remember from all these loops and arrows is that **low productivity, low incomes and low levels of living are mutually reinforcing phenomena.** They constitute what Myrdal has called a process of 'circular cumulative causation' in which low incomes lead to low levels of living (income plus poor health, education, etc.) which keeps productivity low, which in turn perpetuates low incomes, and so on.

But low levels of living, broadly defined, do not by themselves define underdevelopment. They only reflect one, although we would argue the most crucial, component of the inner meaning of development and underdevelopment. Boxes (2) and (3) in Figure 6.1 – low self-esteem and limited freedom of choice and from external dependence and dominance – comprise the two other poles of the tripod of underdevelopment. Both are strongly influenced by low levels of living; both in turn contribute to these low levels. For example, there is nothing inherent in low levels of living to cause loss of esteem or dignity in the very poor *except* when their worth in their own and other people's eyes is largely determined by their material wellbeing. Thus the international transfer of material-oriented values from rich nations (through the cinema, television, newspaper, magazines, educational systems, foreign 'experts' and community 'developers', etc.) can and usually does alter the determinants of self-esteem so that low living levels cause individuals to feel a low sense of their real worth. Conversely, low self-respect can contribute to low levels of living as a result of poor attitudes towards life, work, cleanliness, punctuality and self-improvement. These phenomena are depicted by the arrows leading to and from boxes (1) and (2).

Low levels of living also influence and are influenced by limited freedom (box 3 and arrows between boxes 1 and 3). They make people and nations vulnerable to, dependent on, and often dominated by those who are materially better off, and greatly limit their range of choice regarding alternative national and personal life-styles. Conversely, limited freedom weakens nations and forces people to accept an international economic order in which the progress of the rich may have a chronic backwash effect perpetuating the low living levels of the poor.

Finally, note that boxes (2) and (3) are also

connected by arrows showing cause and effect. Limited freedom means that nations and individuals have little or no control over their own destinies. They are, therefore, likely to have a lower opinion of themselves and to lose some respect in the eyes of others. Conversely, nations and people with low self-esteem often do not have the economic, psychological or physical strength to resist domination and a loss of their freedom to choose.

Taken together, the three boxes in Figure 6.1 present a concise portrait of the nature and inner meaning of underdevelopment. While low levels of living, low self-esteem and limited freedom all work in a cumulative cause and effect process to perpetuate underdevelopment, it is clear that without improving the levels of living of people within a nation, the prospects for development would be non-existent. It follows that **the first priority** of moving from a chronic state of underdevelopment to one of development **must be the raising of people's levels of living.** For this reason economics must play a central role in the develop-

Figure 6.1
Underdevelopment: a multidimensional schematic framework

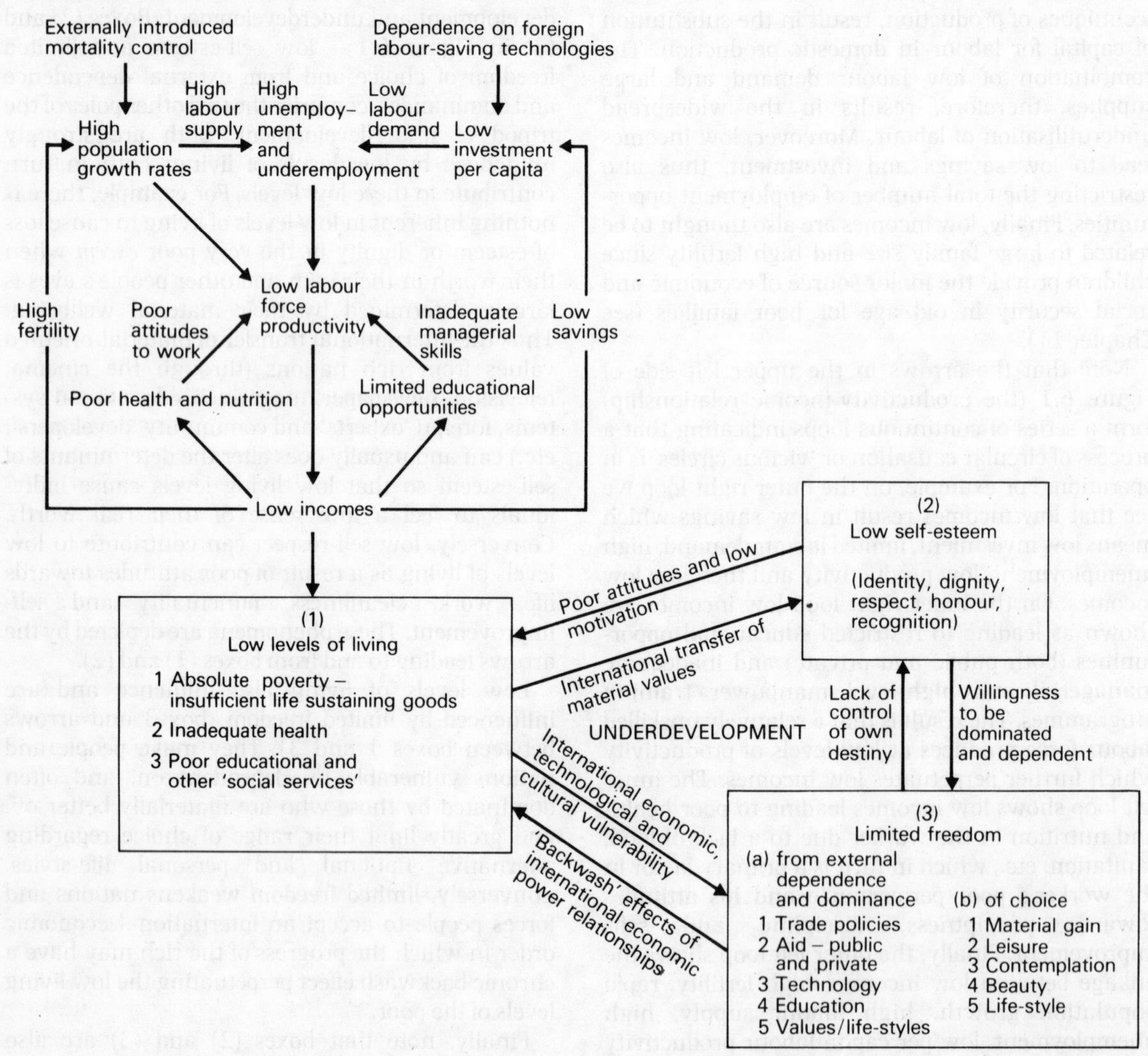

ment process. However, the impact of that role will be greatly diminished, even nullified, if at the same time the importance of attending to the determinants of national and personal esteem and of striving to broaden society's freedom to choose are not also afforded priority attention by Third World politicians and planners alike.

Concepts for review

development
underdevelopment
self-esteem
circular cumulative causation
spread effects
freedom to choose
dominance
dependence
vulnerability
'stages of growth' theory of development
capital–output ratio
capital stock
savings ratio
Harrod–Domar equation
necessary and sufficient conditions
structural theory of underdevelopment
neo-Marxist/neo-colonial model of underdevelopment
dualism
'false paradigm' model of underdevelopment
life-sustenance
vicious circle

Questions for discussion

1. Explain the essential distinction between the 'stages of growth' theory of underdevelopment and the 'international-structuralist' theories, both the 'neo-colonial' and 'false paradigm' models. Which do you think provides a better explanation of your own nation's situation? Explain.
2. Explain the meaning of dualism and dual societies. Do you think that the concept of dualism adequately portrays the development picture in most Third World countries? Explain.
3. Some people claim that international dualism and domestic dualism are merely manifestations of the same phenomenon. What do you think they mean by this and is it a valid conceptualisation? Explain.
4. Briefly describe the various definitions of the meaning of 'development' encountered in the text. What are the strengths and weaknesses of each approach? Do you think that there are other dimensions of development not mentioned in the text? If so, describe them. If not, explain why you believe that the textual description of the meaning of development is adequate.
5. Why is a strictly economic definition of development inadequate? What do you understand 'economic' development to mean? Can you give hypothetical or real examples of situations in which a country may be developing economically but still be 'underdeveloped'?
6. Why is an understanding of the meaning of development crucial to policy formulation in Third World nations? Do you think it is possible for a nation to agree on a rough definition of development and orient its strategies for achieving these objectives accordingly? What might be some of the roadblocks or constraints in realising these development objectives – both economic and non-economic?

Further reading

(*a*) On the complex question of what is the real meaning of 'development' and 'underdevelopment' see: DUDLEY SEERS, 'The Meaning of Development' in NANCY BASTOR, ed., *Measuring Development*, Cass, London, 1972; GUNNAR MYRDAL, *The Challenge of World Poverty*, Pantheon, New York, 1970, chs 1–4; CELSO FURTADO, *Development and Underdevelopment*, University of California Press, 1964, especially ch. 4; DENIS GOULET, *The Cruel Choice: a new concept in the theory of development*, Atheneum, New York, 1971, ch. 2; MAHBUB UL HAQ, 'Crisis in Development Strategies', *World Development*, i, 7, July 1973; IRMA ADELMAN, 'Development Economics: a reassessment of goals', *American Economic Review*, lxv, 2, May 1975; and the various readings in HENRY BERNSTEIN (ed.) *Underdevelopment and Development: the Third World today*, Penguin, 1973.

(*b*) For a survey of various theories of development see: EVERETT HAGEN, *The Economics of Development*, Irwin, 1968, chs 6 and 7; C. P. KINDLEBURGER, *Economic Development*, McGraw-Hill, 1965, Part One, and HOLLIS CHENERY, 'The Structuralist Approach to Development Policy', *American*

Economic Review, lxv, 2, May 1975. For an excellent summary statement of the concept of dualism and dual societies, see Hans Singer, 'Dualism Revisited: a new approach to the problems of dual society in developing countries', *Journal of Development Studies*, vii, 1, October 1970.

Appendix III: The neo-Marxist analysis of economic development problems[1]

In this Appendix we present a brief exposition of the neo-Marxists' views on economic development. Neo-Marxist theory rests on two foundations: the **theory of monopoly capitalism** and the **theory of imperialism.** Although in many ways the theory of imperialism follows from the theory of monopoly capital, the former does not entirely determine the latter. In other words, the specific forms that imperialism will take as a relationship of domination of the poor countries of the 'periphery' by the rich countries of the 'centre' cannot be fully anticipated. This 'indeterminacy' is enhanced in view of two factors: first, the predominance of **politics** over economics in international relations and the greater difficulty in predicting political decisions; and second, by the fact that neither the centre nor the periphery are homogeneous, so that there can be a multitude of types of domination and dependence. Thus, the neo-Marxist model only purports to show the *general* characteristics of this relationship, while at the same time allows enough room for a wide variety of specific situations.

The **fundamental thesis** of the neo-Marxists in the relationship between rich and poor countries is that the centre is actually inimical to the development of peripheral countries, and that a capitalist development of LDCs is *impossible* today. This is one of two major departures of the neo-Marxists from the writings of Marx, Engels, and the classical writers on imperialism. It can be explained, in very general terms, by means of the second major departure: namely, the need under monopoly capitalism for a system for external sources of demand and profitable outlets for investment, a need that is greater because of the operation of the Marxian law of the 'rising surplus' which makes monopoly capitalism more expansive and outwardly aggressive than its predecessor, competitive capitalism.

According to neo-Marxists, the relationship between the centre and periphery is, by virtue of the nature of the structural needs of the centre, necessarily one of **exploitation:** surplus (i.e. capitalist profits) is transferred, through various channels, from the periphery to the centre. This, in turn, aggravates the surplus-absorption difficulties of the centre and induces further outward expansion. Thus, the LDCs are caught in the explosive vicious spiral of the centre's surplus-absorption problem, while, at the same time, the **surplus drain** they are subjected to and **other factors** (which are explained below) make their economic development impossible.

There are, again, some important differences on this point: while some see this ever-present surplus drain as the decisive factor and a sufficient condition for the *impossibility* of LDC development, other neo-Marxists emphasise the 'other' factors that lead to the development of an inappropriate economic structure in the LDCs. They question the absolute validity of the **impossibility thesis**'. According to these neo-Marxists, a distinction must be made between the 'impossibility' and the 'inappropriate pattern' of LDC development.

This difference is crucial. Because of their emphasis on the surplus drain (which they assume to be of crippling magnitude), the early neo-Marxists saw imperialism as a system that creates a necessary *polarity* between an extremely poor periphery and a prospering centre. Poverty and wealth were seen as the two faces of the same coin. This view, which implies the impossibility of capitalist development of LDCs, is often unrealistic, dogmatic, and subject to damaging criticism. Quite arbitrarily, the early neo-Marxists assumed that: first, a very large part of the surplus is drained; and second, that the part of the surplus which is not drained is not utilised in a way conducive to local development. Thus, for them, even if the proportion of drained to not-drained is low, there is no growth.

By being more realistic on these two points, recent neo-Marxist writers like Samir Amin of Africa have tried to replace the dogmatic 'impossibility thesis' by

[1] The assitance of my student, Mr. George Yannacogeogos, in the preparation of this Appendix is much appreciated.

that of the **necessary inappropriateness of the pattern of LDC development.** Using Marx's terminology, Amin has called the surplus drain the 'continuing primitive accumulation' by the centre, but he allows both for a residue of surplus that is left in the hands of local LDC elites, and for the possibility of the rational utilisation of this surplus toward the development of LDCs. In this way, the neo-Marxist model's ability to fit the facts is thought to be greatly enhanced. The inappropriateness of the LDC's **pattern** of development is then seen as the necessary consequence of its inclusion in the periphery of the world capitalist system.

The neo-Marxists also reject the **vicious circle** arguments of the early, mainstream development literature. These theories, they claim, have served as ideological weapons for the creation of a climate of dependency, fatalism and resignation in poorer nations, and thus have helped perpetuate their poverty and their habit of looking for outside help for their development. Neo-Marxists argue that the real problem in LDCs is not the presence of the vicious circle itself – a phenomenon whose existence is acknowledged – but the lack of a significant stimulus to development which is aggravated by the surplus drain. Here, again, we have a *polar* view, in which the continuing 'primitive accumulation' by the centre implies a simultaneous *negative* primitive accumulation for the periphery. The centre's gain must of necessity be the periphery's loss. Surplus transfers, then, *create* and perpetuate underdevelopment in the LDCs, a phenomenon that Andre Gunder Frank has called 'the development of underdevelopment'.

Amin, too, adopts Frank's motto, but with an altered meaning. For him it means a 'dependent development', that is, an inappropriate pattern of growth imposed upon the country through its ties with the centre – literally, through its being included in the world capitalist system. This view in turn allows for the possibility of growth of aggregate income, an observed fact in many LDCs.

The crucial problem of how the available surplus is utilised in LDCs leads the neo-Marxists to the examination of **local elites.** They assert that no local development is to be expected from such elites. On the contrary, they are by their nature a factor contributing to underdevelopment. The analysis is based on the 'objective situation' in which these elites find themselves. Their economic behaviour – conspicuous consumption, investments in real estate and extreme risk-aversion, the export of their savings to be deposited with foreign banks for security, their avoidance of investments in industry – is, from the standpoint of private advantage, essentially a *rational* response to the circumstances in which they find themselves. Their fear of foreign competition – in case they undertook to invest in more productive activities – is seen as fully justified. Most elite members lack the amounts of capital required for the establishment of enterprises able to compete with giant foreign corporations. Also lacking are entrepreneurial skills and attitudes to work and innovation conducive to growth.

Amin offers the view that local elites are *not*, in fact, 'exploited' by the elites of the centre. What happens is simply that their field of independent activity and initiative is severely curtailed by these foreign elites. Anyway, many members of LDC elites profit, too, from foreign activities in their country.

The neo-Marxists do not deny that there is also a disheartening lack of **entrepreneurial and administrative talent** in the countries of the Third World. But they disagree with those who place this fact at the centre of their explanations of underdevelopment. They claim that entrepreneurial and administrative skills will be found or created as soon as the 'objective conditions' that will make possible and necessary their utilisation appear – conditions that cannot exist in an environment of dependence. This problem, they claim, is secondary; it is a consequence of the fundamental problem, which is the discouragement and systematic sabotaging of local development efforts by the centre.

From this view of the economic impotence of the elites at the periphery, the neo-Marxists are led to the conclusion that in LDCs only *the state* can mobilise the surplus in a way conducive to the country's development. This could be done in two ways: first, the state could itself become a capitalist and finance industrialisation with state-owned enterprises. Within the context of world capitalism, however, such a role for the state is necessarily limited. Second, the state could put sufficient funds in the hands of capable members of the local elite in the form of long-term loans. This common practice is behind the view of LDC states as **instruments of class creation.** Once the existence of a local industrial capitalist class is seen as a necessary precondition of growth, the state tries to create such a class out of an existing elite that is exclusively commercial, bureaucratic, and landed. But then the state is soon caught in a contradiction: an indigenous industrial capitalist class is likely to find itself pitted against more powerful foreign competitors – to whose needs the state typically caters in a servile manner – and also against the local commercial capitalist, bureaucratic and landed interests, who are as servile to the foreign interests as the state. Usually, then, the state invests in sectors not competing with the foreign interests such as infrastructural investments and tourism.

The relatively high investments in infrastructure, mainly **transport and communications**, that the neo-Marxists believe to be characteristics of LDCs are seen either as the result of the policies of Third World governments that had no other investment choices because of foreign competition, or as a 'natural' policy for 'comprador-type' regimes who thus aid by local means in the exploitation of the country by foreign capital. As proof of this last thesis it is asserted that roads are built in such a way as to serve the needs of foreign companies, not those of the indigenous population: access to trade centres, ports, and locations of multinational companies.

The second area of high local investment, **tourism**, is seen with wrathful scorn. This, neo-Marxists claim, is the direct result of dependence, an easy solution to chronic LDC problems. It brings in foreign exchange, creates employment, and raises the level of construction activities – construction being one of the few industries that are not usually taken over by foreigners. But the resulting ills are greater than the benefits: contact with foreign habits – often the habits of a wealthy class – disrupts the indigenous culture and creates consumption patterns and tastes locally that are likely to worsen the country's balance-of-payments and its saving ability. 'Demonstration effects' become very significant in LDCs: foreign consumption patterns are symbols of status.

Finally, some neo-Marxists also criticise the current **dualist** theories of development as somewhat misleading, because these theories neglect what, according to them, is the basic fact, the 'compulsive' and intentional transfer of surplus from the traditional to the modern sector within LDCs and from the periphery to the centre in the world economy. For them nothing short of political and social 'revolution' can alter the current state of affairs and bring about self-reliant development.

This completes our brief examination of the neo-Marxists' critique of contemporary economic development. At its core is a rigid ideology and an extremely demanding goal of economic development together with the brutal realisation of its necessity; a necessity, it is claimed, that grows out of the great moral and economic evils of dependence, even of 'dependent development', and because of the irrationality of the current international system that fosters these evils.

However, other less radical observers, while agreeing with much of the neo-Marxist analysis (though disputing fundamental propositions), would argue that change *can* be initiated from both within and outside the present system – and need not be 'revolutionary' in character. They point out that the neo-Marxists have no prescriptions beyond 'revolution' and note that revolutionary movements have a tendency to substitute one type of exploitation (political, religious and social) for another (economic).

But, whatever the relative merits of the dispute between neo-Marxist and other forms of 'structuralist' and 'traditionalist' theories, one can be sure that it will rage on in the coming years as the development debate intensifies.

Further reading

Samir Amin, *Accumulation on a World Scale: a critique of the theory of underdevelopment*, transl. Brian Pearce, Monthly Review Press, New York, 1974; Samir Amin, *Unequal Development: an essay on the social formations of peripheral capitalism*, transl. Brian Pearce, Monthly Review Press, New York, 1976; Paul Baran, *The Political Economy of Growth*, Monthly Review Press, New York, 1957; Andre Gunder Frank, 'The Development of Underdevelopment', *Monthly Review*, xviii, 14, 1966.

Chapter 7 Economic growth: causes and characteristics

> The advantage of economic growth is not that wealth increases happiness but that it increases the range of human choice.
> *W. Arthur Lewis*

Introduction: The growth game

'Economic growth is the name of the game' – so goes a common saying in modern economic discourse. But in fact the study of economic growth can be traced as far back as the very beginnings of the discipline itself. Most economists would ascribe this beginning to the year 1776 when Adam Smith first published his famous treatise, *The Wealth of Nations*, which could just as well have been called *The Economic Growth of Nations*. For the past two decades in particular, the primary focus of world economic attention has been on measures to accelerate the growth of national incomes. Economists and politicians alike, from all nations, rich and poor, capitalist, socialist and mixed, have worshipped at the shrine of economic growth. At the end of every year, statistics are compiled for all countries of the world showing their relative rates of GNP growth. 'Growthmanship' has become a way of life. Governments can rise or fall if their economic growth performance ranks high or low on this global score card. As we have seen, Third World development programmes are often assessed by the degree to which their national output and incomes are growing. In fact, for many years conventional wisdom equated 'development' with the rapidity of total output growth.

In view of the central role that this concept has assumed in world-wide assessment of relative national economic performance, it is important to understand the nature and causes of economic growth. In this chapter, therefore, we extend our earlier discussion of production theory to examine the concept of a national production function and the various components that determine the level, composition and growth of national output. After looking at the historical record of economic growth in contemporary rich nations, we then isolate six principal economic, structural and institutional components which appear to have characterised all growing economies. In the next chapter, we ask the question: Of what relevance is the historical growth experience of contemporary developed nations to the plans and strategies of present-day developing countries? We conclude these two chapters on economic growth with a discussion of the controversial but crucial question 'Are the benefits of growth worth the associated costs?' And what about the supposed conflict between rapid economic growth and a more equitable distribution of its benefits? This leads directly into Part Two where, in Chapters 9 and 10, we take up the important question of the determinants of the distribution of national income and the dilemma of Third World poverty and inequality.

The production possibilities of a society: extending our simple theory of production

In Chapter 4, we introduced the basic economic concept of a production function. Recall that a production function systematically relates various combinations of factor inputs such as land and labour to different levels of output for a given technology. We used the example of a Colombian coffee farmer to show how, with a given quantity of land (e.g. 10 hectares) and state of technology, total output would vary with different quantities of labour inputs. The specific nature of this input–output relationship was described by the principle of diminishing marginal productivity whereby the application of increasing amounts of a variable factor (labour) to a fixed factor (land) would after a point lead to a situation in which each additional worker would add smaller and smaller amounts of total output – that is to say, the marginal product of successive workers would decline.

If each worker were paid the same wage, then the cost per unit of output would increase as more workers picked coffee on a fixed amount of land. For example, if the fifth hired worker picked 20 kg of coffee beans per day while the sixth added (i.e. had a marginal product of) only 15 kg, then if both were paid 60 pesos per day the *unit cost* of the fifth worker would be 3 pesos per kg of output while the sixth worker would cost 4 pesos per kg. It is for this reason that the principle of diminishing returns has as its corollary on the cost side the principle of rising unit (average) and marginal costs. The phenomenon of rising marginal costs is what gives the supply curve of coffee and most other goods a positive slope: higher marginal costs of production mean that producers are unwilling to supply more of their product unless they are offered a higher price to compensate for the higher (marginal) cost of generating that additional output. Diagrammatically, the supply curve of a firm or farm is therefore respresented by the rising portion of its marginal cost curve – see Figure 4.2.

Suppose we now extend our basic concept of production from the case of one output (coffee) with two inputs (land and labour) to the case of two outputs (say rice and radios to represent broadly 'agricultural' and 'manufactured' goods) with two variable inputs, capital (machines, equipment, etc.) and labour. At the same time we hold the third input, land, constant. Let us further assume that these are the only two outputs the economy can produce. The question arises, how much rice and how many radios can this society produce? In other words, what are its 'production possibilities'?

Take rice first. If all available labour and capital are applied to a given amount of farmland in the country, it might be possible, given the current state of rice technology, to produce, say, 1 000 tonnes per month. But with all society's labour and capital used up in rice production, there will be no output of radios. At the other extreme, if all labour and capital in the country were to be devoted exclusively to the manufacture of radios, given the current state of technology, it might be possible to produce, say, 3 000 radios per month. Thus our society in question has two extreme production possibility combinations: 1 000 tonnes of rice and no radios per month or 3 000 radios and no rice per month. These two combinations are listed as possibilities A and F in Table 7.1.

Table 7.1
Alternative production possibilities of rice and radios: an hypothetical example

Possibility combination	Tonnes of rice (per month)	Quantities of radios (per month)
A	1,000	0
B	800	1,000
C	600	1,800
D	400	2,400
E	200	2,800
F	0	3,000

Between these extremes are other possible combinations of producing *both* rice and radios. But in order to have some of both rice and radios, it is not possible to have the extreme amount of either: to produce some radios, the production of some rice has to be given up, and vice versa. This is because labour and capital inputs are required in varying combinations to produce each product. If all the available labour and capital is being devoted to rice production, as shown by combination A in Table 7.1, then in order to begin to produce radios some of these resources will have to be reassigned from the agricultural to the manufacturing sector. This in turn means a reduction in total monthly rice output. **When resources are fully and efficiently employed, the production of some commodity has to be sacrificed in order that more of another can be produced.** In effect, the 'cost' of getting more radios produced is the amount of rice that must be sacrificed.

Another way of stating this important economic principle is that the 'opportunity cost' of producing radios is measured by that quantity of rice (and, indirectly, the real resources needed to produce that foregone rice output) which must be sacrificed in order to produce these additional radios.

We see, for example, from combination B in Table 7.1 that in order to produce 1 000 radios our economy must sacrifice 200 tonnes of rice per month. The opportunity cost of producing the first 1 000 radios is therefore 200 tonnes of rice, or one-fifth of a tonne per radio. If 800 more radios per month are to be manufactured, then an additional 200 tonnes of rice must be sacrificed (combination C). The opportunity cost per additional radio per month has risen from one-fifth to one-quarter of a tonne. Similarly, we can verify from combination D that the sacrifice of 200 more tonnes of rice will only result in an additional output of 600 radios, an opportunity cost of one-third of a tonne of rice per radio. Completing the table we have combination E where 200 tonnes of rice and 2 800 radios are produced.

Figure 7.1
A production possibility curve for rice and radios

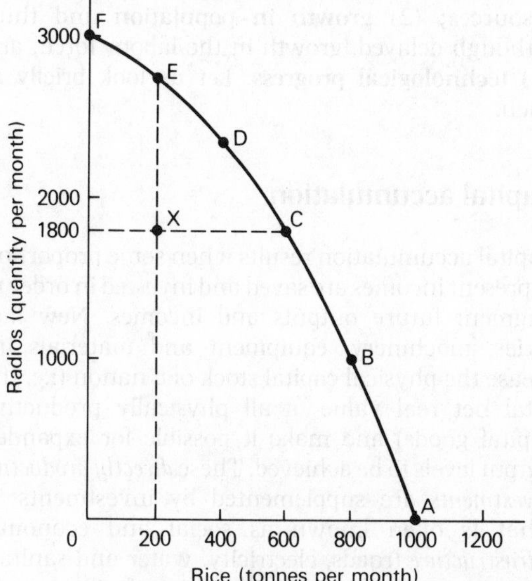

Table 7.1 illustrates two concepts fundamental to all economics. First, the six combinations of rice and radio production together constitute a locus of points known as the 'production possibilities' of this society. These combinations are plotted graphically in Figure 7.1 where tonnes of rice per month (or, alternatively, total agricultural output) are plotted on the horizontal axis and numbers of radios per month (or, more broadly, total manufacturing output) are listed on the vertical axis. The resulting 'bow-shaped' schedule of output combinations is known as the 'production possibility' curve. This curve portrays the *maximum* attainable output of radios against any given amount of rice produced *when all available resources are fully employed.* Conversely, the curve in Figure 7.1 shows the *maximum* output of rice for any given production of radios.

In short, the production possibility curve for an economy describes the maximum attainable combinations of any commodities which that society is capable of producing, in terms both of the prevailing state of technology and the quantity and quality of its productive resources (land, labour, capital, management, etc.). **The production possibility curve, therefore, only has meaning for a full-employment, maximum efficiency economy.** If there is widespread unemployment, or if resources are being used inefficiently, or if there is poor management, then the actual combination of, say, rice and radios which is being produced by a given society might be that shown by point X in Figure 7.1. At point X 200 tonnes of rice and 1 800 radios are being produced, whereas if there were no unemployment and/or there was a more efficient and effective management, the total output could be anywhere on the segment C–D–E on the production possibility frontier. For that matter, a lower level of unemployment and/or a slightly more efficient production process could result in a rice–radio combination at any point in the *area* of the triangular arc bounded by points X, C, D and E. Can you verify that at any point on or within this triangular arc, total output of *either* or *both* products will be higher than at point X?

The second fundamental economic concept depicted by the bow-shaped production possibility curve of Figure 7.1 is the notion that **in a full-employment economy or, better, an economy which is making full use of all its productive resources, the output of some product must be given up in order to get more of some other product.** This assumes that productive resources can be transferred from one commodity to another. We have described this sacrificed or foregone output as measuring the opportunity cost, or the cost to society of producing more of the given commodity, in this case how much rice must be sacrificed to produce more radios when all resources are fully employed. Moreover, we have seen in our numerical example that this opportunity cost *increases* as more and more of a given product is produced: as more radios are produced the number of tonnes of rice that have to be sacrificed per unit radio is constantly increasing, and vice versa.

The basic reason for this increasing social opportunity cost is that the technology of producing different commodities is typically very different. For example, the manufacture of radios may require a lot of capital and few labourers *relative to* the production of rice which requires a lot of labour and *relatively* few capital goods. In a fully employed economy, one operating on the 'frontier' of its production possibility curve, the sacrifice of say, a unit of radio output to produce more rice implies the release of the corresponding quantities of capital and labour which were required to produce this unit of radio output. This may amount to, say, 10 units of capital and 5 workers. But a unit of additional rice output may require 20 workers for every 10 units of capital. Therefore, more than one unit of radio has to be sacrificed to get an additional unit of rice. Moreover, the principle of diminishing returns dictates that ever increasing amounts of capital and labour will have to be released from the manufacture of radios (more radios have to be given up) in order to produce an additional unit of rice given the fixed availability of land. Thus, the opportunity cost of rice production will rise as more is produced. The same logic would apply in reverse to additional radio production and the sacrifice of ever increasing amounts of rice.

Note that all the preceding discussion of trade-offs between radios and rice in terms of rising opportunity costs was based on the assumption of a full-employment economy. Where labour is idle and/or other productive resources are under-utilised, as at point X in Figure 7.1, then more of *either* or *both* outputs can be produced without necessarily sacrificing any output of either radios or rice. In other words, **in an economy with unemployed resources, the social opportunity cost or the cost to society of additional output may be close to zero.**

When we discuss the problem of unemployment and underemployment in Chapters 13 and 14 we shall see that in most Third World nations, and increasingly so even in those developed nations with rising unemployment, it is more realistic to analyse development problems on the assumption that the combination of agricultural and manufactured goods actually produced lies well within the national production possibility boundary. As we shall see, this recognition can lead us to very different policy conclusions than would be reached if we were to assume that production automatically occurs on the possibility boundary.

In spite of these criticisms, however, we can conveniently apply the concept of a production possibility frontier to describe the essential analytical nature of the processes of economic growth in all countries.

The economics of growth: basic concepts and illustrations

The major factors in, or components of, economic growth in any society are: (1) **capital accumulation,** including all new investments in land and human resources; (2) **growth in population** and thus, although delayed, growth in the labour force; and (3) **technological progress.** Let us look briefly at each.

Capital accumulation

Capital accumulation results when some proportion of present incomes are saved and invested in order to augment future outputs and incomes. New factories, machinery, equipment and materials increase the physical capital stock of a nation (i.e. the total net real value of all physically productive capital goods) and make it possible for expanded output levels to be achieved. These *directly productive investments* are supplemented by investments in what is often known as social and economic *infrastructure* (roads, electricity, water and sanitation, communications, etc.) which facilitate and integrate economic activities. For example, investment by a farmer in a new tractor may increase the total output of the vegetables which he can produce, but without adequate transport facilities to get this extra product to local markets his investment may not add anything to actual national food production.

But there are other less direct ways to invest in a nation's resources. The installation of irrigation facilities may improve the quality of a nation's agricultural land by raising productivity per hectare. If, for example, 100 hectares of irrigated land can produce the same output as 200 hectares of non-irrigated land using the same other inputs, then the installation of such irrigation is the equivalent of doubling the quantity of unirrigated land. Use of chemical fertilisers and control of insects like locusts may have equally beneficial effects in raising the productivity of existing farmland. All these forms of investment are ways of improving the *quality* of existing land resources. Their effect in raising the total stock of productive land is, for all practical purposes, indistinguishable from the simple clearing of hitherto unused but usable land.

Similarly, investment in human resources can improve its quality and thereby have the same or even a more powerful effect on production as an increase in human numbers. Formal schools, vocational and on-the-job training programmes and adult and other types of informal education may all be made more effective in augmenting human skills and resources as a result of direct investment in buildings, equipment and materials (books, projectors, science equipment, vocational tools and machinery such as lathes and grinders). The advanced and relevant training of teachers as well as good introductory textbooks in economics may make an enormous difference in the quality, leadership and productivity of a given labour force. This concept of investment in human resources is therefore analogous to that of improving the quality and thus the productivity of existing land resources through strategic investments.

All the above phenomena and many others are forms of investment which lead to capital accumulation. Capital accumulation may add new resources (e.g. by the clearing of unused land) or upgrade the quality of existing resources (e.g. by irrigation, fertiliser, pesticides, etc.). But its essential feature is that it involves a *trade-off* between present and future consumption (see Chapter 4), giving up a little now so that more can be had later.

Population and labour force growth

Population growth (with the associated, although delayed, increase in the labour force) has traditionally been considered a positive factor in stimulating economic growth. A larger labour force means more productive manpower, while a larger overall population increases the potential size of domestic markets. However, it is questionable whether rapidly growing manpower supplies in labour-surplus developing countries exert a positive or negative influence on economic progress (see Chapter 11 for a discussion of the pros and cons of population growth for economic development). Obviously, it will depend on the ability of the economic system to absorb and productively employ these added workers, an ability largely associated with the rate and type of capital accumulation and the availability of other related factors, such as managerial and administrative skills.

Given some initial understanding of these first two fundamental components of economic growth (capital accumulation and land and labour growth, both quantitative and qualitative) and disregarding for a moment the third, technology, let us see how they interact via the production possibility curve analysis to expand society's potential total output of *all* goods. Recall from our earlier example that for a given technology and a given amount of physical and human resources, the production possibility curve portrayed the *maximum* attainable output combinations of rice and radios.

Suppose now that with unchanged technology the quantity of those physical and human resources were to double, either as a result of investments that improved the quality of the existing resources or investment in new resources: land, capital and, in the case of larger families, labour. Figure 7.2 shows that this doubling of total resources will cause the entire production possibility curve to shift uniformly outward along its whole range from P–P to P^1–P^1. More radios and more rice can now be produced. Since these are assumed to be the only two goods produced by this economy, it follows that the gross national product (the total value of all goods and services produced) will be higher than before. In other words, the process of economic growth is under way.

Note that even if the country in question is operating with underutilised physical and human resources as at point X in Figure 7.2, a growth of productive resources can result in a higher total output combination as at point X^1 even though there may still be widespread unemployment and underutilised or idle capital and land. But note also that there is nothing deterministic about the necessity of resource growth leading to higher

Figure 7.2
The effect of expanded physical and human resources on the position of society's production possibility frontier

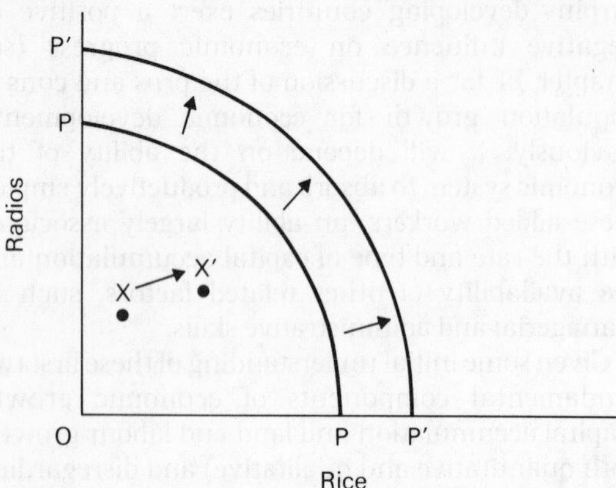

Figure 7.3
Non-symmetrical shifts in production possibility curves when (a) only the capital stock expands and (b) only land increases in quantity and/or quality

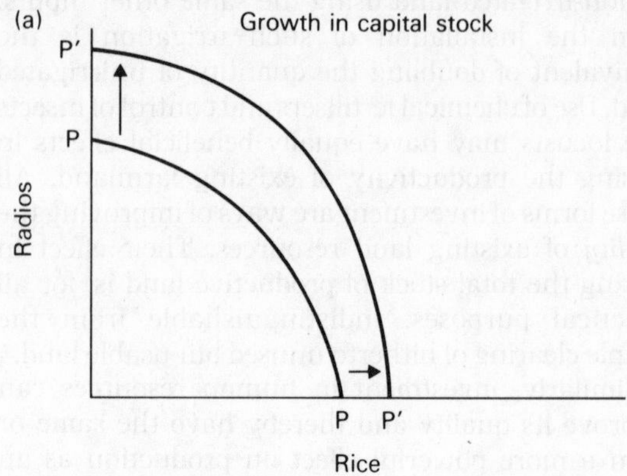

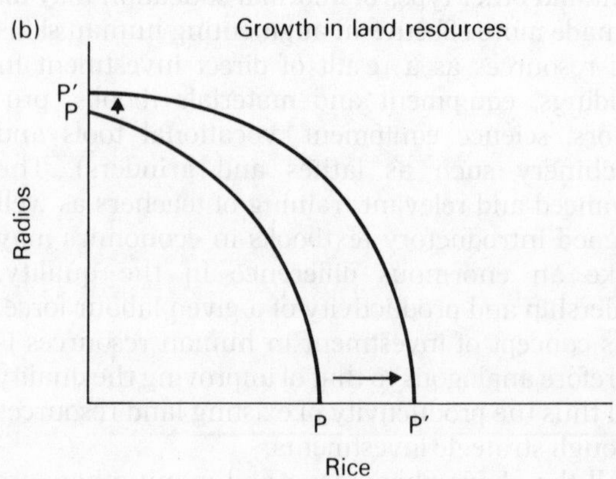

output growth. This is not an economic law and there are many contemporary Third World countries whose poor growth record bears witness to this phenomenon (see the statistical table in Appendix II of Chapter 5, for example). Nor is resource growth even a necessary condition for *short-run* economic growth since the better utilisation of existing idle resources can raise output levels substantially, as portrayed in the movement from point X to X¹ in Figure 7.2. Nevertheless, in the *long run*, the improvement and upgrading of the quality of existing resources as well as new investments designed to expand the quantity of these resources are a principal means of accelerating the growth of national output.

Now instead of assuming the proportionate growth of *all* factors of production, let us assume that say, only capital, or only land is increased in quality and quantity. Diagrams (*a*) and (*b*) of Figure 7.3 show that if radio manufacturing is a *relatively* larger user of capital equipment while rice production is a *relatively* land-intensive process, then the shifts in society's production possibility curve will be more pronounced for radios (Figure 7.3(*a*)) when capital grows rapidly and rice (Figure 7.3(*b*)) when land quantity or quality grow relatively faster. However, since under normal conditions both products will require the use of both factors as productive inputs, albeit in very different combinations, the production possibility curve still shifts slightly outward along the radio axis in (*a*), when capital is increased, and along the rice axis in (*b*), when only the quantity and/or quality of land resources are expanded.

Technological progress

It is now time to consider the third, and to many economists, the most important source of economic growth – technological progress. In its simplest form, technological progress can be said to result from new and improved ways of accomplishing traditional tasks such as growing maize, making clothing, or building a house. There are three basic classifications of technological progress: neutral, labour-saving and capital-saving.

Neutral technological progress is associated with higher output levels being achieved with the same quantity and combinations of factor inputs. Simple innovations like those that arise from the division of labour whereby instead of each individual trying to produce all his material needs there is specialisation, with one person performing only one task (e.g. constructing thatched roofs) while others focus on different jobs (e.g. growing maize). Such specialisation often results in higher total output levels and greater consumption quantities for all individuals. In terms of our production possibility analysis, a neutral technological change which, say, doubles total output is conceptually equivalent to a doubling of all productive inputs. The outward shifting production possibility curve of Figure 7.2, therefore, could also be a diagrammatic representation of neutral technological progress.

On the other hand, technological progress may be **labour-saving** or **capital-saving** – that is, higher levels of output can be achieved with the same quantity of labour (capital) inputs. The use of electronic computers, automated textile looms, high speed electric drills, tractors and mechanical ploughs – these and many other types of modern machinery and equipment can be classified as labour-saving. As we shall see in Part Two, the history of technological progress in the twentieth century has been largely one of rapid advances in labour-saving technologies of producing anything from beans to bicycles to bridges.

Capital-saving technological progress is a much rarer phenomenon, because almost all the world's scientific and technological research is conducted in the developed countries, where the mandate is to 'save labour', not capital. But in the labour-abundant (capital-scarce) countries of the Third World, capital-saving technological progress is what is most needed. Such progress results in more 'efficient' (i.e. lower cost) labour-intensive methods of production – for example, hand or rotary-powered weeders and threshers, foot-operated bellows pumps, back-mounted mechanical sprayers, etc., for small-scale agriculture. As we show in Chapter 13, the indigenous LDC development of low-cost, efficient, labour-intensive (capital-saving) techniques of production is one of the most essential ingredients in any long-run employment-oriented development strategy.

Technological progress may also be **labour or capital-augmenting.** Labour-augmenting technological progress occurs when the quality or skills of the labour force are upgraded, for example, by the use of videotapes, televisions and other electronic communications media for classroom instruction. Similarly, capital-augmenting technological progress results in the more productive use of existing types of capital goods as, for example, the substitution of steel for wooden ploughs in agricultural production.

Let us now look again at our production possibility curve for rice and radios to examine two very specific examples of recent technological progress as it relates to output growth in Third World countries. In the 1960s, agricultural scientists at the International Rice Research Institute in the Philippines developed a new and highly productive hybrid rice seed, known as IR-8 or 'miracle rice'. These new seeds along with later further scientific improvements enabled some rice farmers in parts of South-east Asia to double and triple their per hectare yields in a matter of a few years. In effect, this technological progress was 'embodied' in the new rice seeds (one could also say it was 'land-augmenting') which permitted higher output levels to be achieved with essentially the same complementary inputs (although more fertiliser and pesticides were recommended). In terms of our production possibility analysis, the higher yielding varieties of hybrid rice could be depicted as in Figure 7.4 by an outward shift of the curve along the rice axis with the intercept on the radio axis remaining essentially unchanged (e.g. the new rice seeds could not be used to increase radio production).

Figure 7.4
The new high-yielding rice varieties cause the P-P curve to shift outward along the 'rice' axis

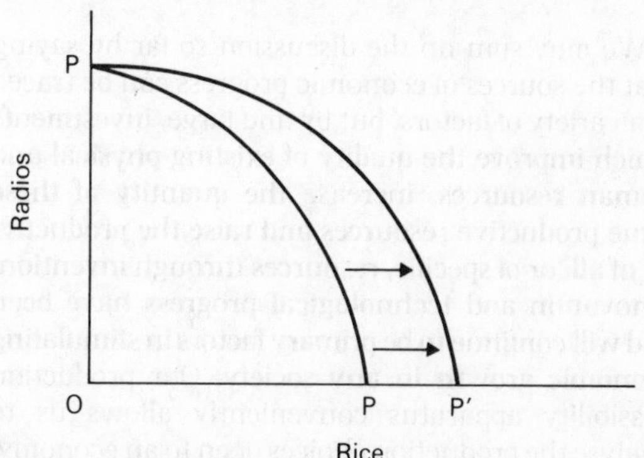

With regard to the technology of radio production, the invention of the transistor probably has had as significant an impact on communications as the invention of the steam engine did on transportation. Even in the remotest parts of Africa, Asia and Latin America the transistor radio has become a prized possession. Without the need for complicated, unwieldy and fragile tubes, radio production grew enormously with the introduction of the transistor. The production process became less complicated and workers were able to increase significantly their total productivity. Figure 7.5 shows that, as in the case of higher yielding rice seeds, the technology of the transistor can be said to have caused the production possibility curve to rotate outward along the vertical axis. For the most part the rice axis intercept remained unchanged (although perhaps the ability of rice paddy workers to listen to music on their transistor radio while working may have made them more productive).

Figure 7.5
The invention of the transistor causes the P-P curve to shift outward along the 'radio' axis

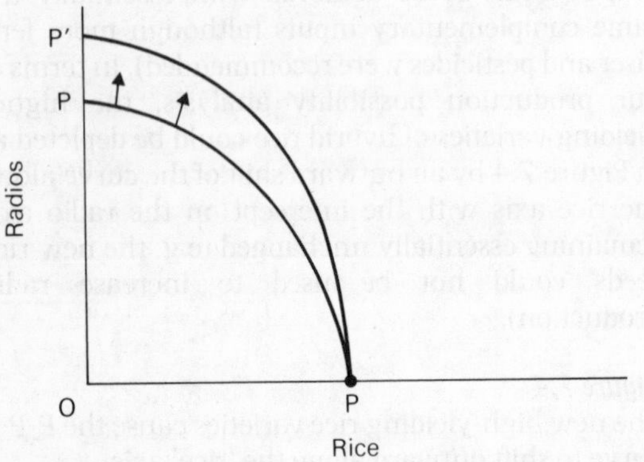

We may sum up the discussion so far by saying that the sources of economic progress can be traced to a variety of factors, but by and large, **investments which improve the quality of existing physical and human resources, increase the quantity of these same productive resources and raise the productivity of all, or of specific, resources through invention, innovation and technological progress have been and will continue to be primary factors in stimulating economic growth in any society.** Our production possibility apparatus conveniently allows us to analyse the production choices open to an economy, to understand the output and opportunity-cost implications of idle or underutilised resources, and to portray the effects on economic growth of increased resource supplies and improved technologies of production.

Having provided this introduction to the simple economics of growth, we can now look more carefully at the historical experience of economic growth in contemporary 'developed' nations in order to analyse in detail the nature of those economic and non-economic factors that are essential to long-term growth. We shall then see what relevance all this has for the growth prospects of developing countries.

The historical record: six characteristics of modern economic growth

Professor Simon Kuznets, who received the Nobel Prize in economics in 1971 for his pioneering work in the measurement and analysis of the historical growth of national incomes in developed nations, has defined a country's economic growth as 'a long-term rise in capacity to supply increasingly diverse economic goods to its population, this growing capacity based on advancing technology and the institutional and ideological adjustments that it demands'.[1] All three principal components of this definition are of great importance. (1) The **sustained rise in national output** is a manifestation of economic growth and the ability to provide a wide range of goods is a sign of economic maturity. (2) **Advancing technology** provides the basis or preconditions for continuous economic growth – a necessary but not sufficient condition. In order to realise the potential for growth inherent in new technology, however: (3) **institutional, attitudinal and ideological adjustments** must be made. Technological innovation without concomitant social innovation is like a light bulb without electricity: the

[1] Simon Kuznets, 'Modern Economic Growth: findings and reflections', Nobel lecture delivered in Stockholm, Sweden, December 1971. Much of the information and analysis in this section is based on Kuznets' work.

potential exists but without the complementary input nothing will happen.

In his exhaustive analysis of modern economic growth, Professor Kuznets has isolated six characteristic features of the growth process of almost every contemporary developed nation (e.g. North America, Western Europe, Japan and the Soviet Union). They include:

- **two aggregate economic variables**
  1. high rates of growth of per capita output and population;
  2. high rates of increase in total factor productivity, especially labour productivity;
- **two structural transformation variables**
  3. high rates of structural transformation of the economy;
  4. high rates of social and ideological transformation;
- **two factors affecting the international spread of growth**
  5. the propensity of economically developed countries to reach out to the rest of the world for markets and raw materials;
  6. the limited spread of this economic growth to only a third of the world's population.

Let us briefly examine each of these six characteristics.

High rates of per capita output and population growth

In the case of both per capita output and population growth, all contemporary developed countries have experienced large multiples of their previous historical rates during the epoch of modern economic growth, roughly from around 1770 to the present. For the non-Communist developed countries, these *annual* growth rates over the past 200 years averaged almost 2 per cent for per capita output, 1 per cent for population, and therefore 3 per cent for total output (i.e. real GNP). These rates (which imply a doubling time of roughly 35 years for per capita output, 70 for population and 24 for real GNP) were far greater than those experienced during the entire era before the start of the industrial revolution in the late eighteenth century. For example, per capita output during the last two centuries has been estimated to be at almost ten times that of the pre-modern era; population has grown at a multiple of four or five times the earlier period, and therefore the acceleration in the growth rate of total output or GNP is estimated to have been some forty or fifty times as large as that experienced before the nineteenth century.

High rates of productivity increase

The second aggregate economic characteristic of modern growth is the relatively high rate of rise in total factor productivity (i.e. output per unit of all inputs). In the case of the major productive factor (labour), rates of productivity increase have also been large multiples of the rates in the pre-modern era. For example, it has been estimated that rates of productivity increase account for anything from 50 to 75 per cent of the historical growth of per capita output in developed countries. In other words, **technological progress including the upgrading of existing physical and human resources accounts for most of the measured historical increases in per capita GNP.** We shall discuss the crucial role which technological advance played in generating and sustaining economic growth shortly.

High rates of economic structural transformation

The historical growth record of contemporary developed nations reveals a third important characteristic: the high rate of structural and sectoral change inherent in the growth process. Some of the major components of this structural change include the gradual shift away from agricultural to non-agricultural activities and, more recently, away from industry to services; a significant change in the scale or average size of productive units, away from small family and personal enterprises to the impersonal organisation of huge national and multi-national corporations; and finally, a corresponding shift in the spatial location and occupational status of the labour force away from rural, agricultural and related non-agricultural activities towards urban-oriented manufacturing and service pursuits. For example, in the United States, the proportion of the total labour force engaged in agricultural activities was 53.5 per cent in 1870. By 1960 this figure had declined to less than 7 per cent. Similarly, in an old European country like Belgium the agricultural labour force dropped from 51 per cent of the total in 1846 to 12.5 per cent in 1947 and less than 7 per cent by 1970. In view of the fact that it took many centuries for agricultural labour forces to drop to even 50 per cent of the total labour supply before the nineteenth century, a drop of 40 to 50 points in the last hundred years in countries such as the United States, Japan, Germany, Belgium and Great Britain, underlines the rapidity of this structural change.

High rates of social, political and ideological transformation

For a significant economic structural change to take place in any society, concomitant transformations in attitudes, institutions and ideologies are often necessary. Obvious examples of these social transformations include the general urbanisation process and the adoption of the ideals, attitudes and institutions of what has come to be known as 'modernisation'. Gunnar Myrdal has provided a lengthy list of these modernisation ideals in his seminal treatise on underdevelopment in Asia, *Asian Drama*.[2] They include the following characteristics:

Rationality
The substitution of modern methods of thinking, acting, producing, distributing and consuming for age-old and traditional practices. According to the first Indian Prime Minister, Jawaharlal Nehru, what underdeveloped nations need is 'a scientific and technological society. It employs new techniques whether it is on the farm, in the factory or in transport. ... Modern technique is not a matter of just getting a tool and using it. Modern technique follows modern thinking. You can't get hold of a modern tool and have an ancient mind. It won't work.'[3] The quest for rationality implies that opinions about economic strategies and policies should be logically valid inferences rooted as deeply as possible in knowledge of relevant facts.

[2] Gunnar Myrdal, *op. cit.*, pp. 57–69.

[3] Jawaharlal Nehru, 'Strategy of the Third Plan', in *Problems in the Third Plan: a critical miscellany*, Government of India, Ministry of Information and Broadcasting, 1961, p. 46.

Planning
The search for a rationally co-ordinated system of policy measures that can bring about and accelerate economic growth and development (see Chapter 23).

Social and economic equalisation
The promotion of more equality in status, opportunities, wealth, incomes and levels of living.

Improved institutions and attitudes
Such changes are envisaged as necessary in order to increase labour efficiency and diligence: promote effective competition, social and economic mobility and individual enterprise; permit greater equality of opportunities; make possible higher productivity; raise levels of living and promote development. Included among social institutions needing change are outmoded land tenure systems, social and economic monopolies, educational and religious structures, systems of administration and planning, etc. In the area of attitudes, the concept of 'modern man' embodies such ideals as efficiency, diligence, orderliness, punctuality, frugality, honesty, rationality, change-orientation, integrity and self-reliance, co-operation and willingness to take the long view.

In Part Two we look more carefully at some of these characteristics of modernization as they relate to contemporary Third World countries to see how they fit into a development-oriented economic strategy.

The international economic outreach

The last two characteristics of modern economic growth deal with the role of developed countries in the international arena. The first of these relates to the propensity of rich countries to reach out to the rest of the world for primary products and raw materials, cheap labour and lucrative markets for their manufactured products. Such outreach activities (some people might regard them as 'exploitation') are made possible economically by means of the increased power of modern technology, particularly in transport and communication. These had the effect of unifying the globe in ways that were not possible before the nineteenth century. They also created the possibilities for political and economic dominance of poor nations by their more powerful neighbours to the north. In the nineteenth and early twentieth centuries the establishment of colonies and the 'opening up' or 'partitioning' of previously inaccessible areas such as sub-Saharan Africa and parts of Asia and Latin America provided the expanding economies of the northern hemisphere with cheap raw materials and with export markets for their growing manufacturing industries.

The limited international spread of economic growth

In spite of the enormous increases in world output over the past two centuries, the spread of modern economic growth is largely still limited to less than one-third of the world's population. As we discovered in Chapter 5, this minority of the world's population enjoys almost 85 per cent of the world's income. Moreover, as we also saw later in that chapter, unequal international power relationships between developed and less developed countries have a tendency to exacerbate the gap between rich and poor. The further economic growth of the former is often achieved at the expense of the latter.

Conclusions: the interdependence of growth characteristics

The six characteristics of modern growth reviewed here are highly interrelated and mutually reinforcing. High rates of per capita output result from rapidly rising levels of labour productivity. High per capita incomes in turn generate high levels of per capita consumption, thus providing the incentive for changes in the structure of production, since as incomes rise the demand for manufactured goods and services rises at a much faster rate than the demand for agricultural products. Advancing technology required to achieve these output and structural changes causes the scale of production plants and the characteristics of economic enterprise units to change in both organisation and location. This in turn necessitates rapid changes in the location and structure of the labour force and in status relations among occupational groups (for example, the income shares of landlords and farmers decline while those of manufacturers and industrialists tend to rise). It also means changes in other aspects of society, including family size, urbanisation and the material determinants of self-esteem and dignity.

Finally, the inherent dynamism of modern economic growth, coupled with the revolution in the technology of transportation and communication, necessitates an international outreach on the part of those countries which developed first. But the poor countries affected by this international outreach may either, for institutional, ideological or political reasons, not be in a position to benefit from the process, or may simply be weak victims of rich-country policies designed to exploit them economically.

If the common ingredient and linkage in all these interrelated growth characteristics is, as Professor Kuznets suggests, the 'mass application of technological innovations', then the rapid growth which makes possible the economic surplus to finance further programmes in scientific research has a built-in tendency to be self-generating. In other words, **rapid economic growth makes possible basic scientific research which in turn leads to technological inventions and innovations which propel economic growth even further.**

We have an important hint here why the growth process seems to benefit the already rich nations disproportionately in relation to the poor ones: 95 per cent of all scientific research is undertaken in rich countries on rich-country problems. This research and the resulting technological progress which it engenders are of little direct benefit to poor nations whose resource and institutional conditions differ greatly from those of the developed nations. Wealthy nations can afford basic scientific research; poor ones cannot. Developed countries can therefore provide a continuous mechanism for self-sustaining technological and economic advance that is beyond the financial and technical capabilities of most developing countries. This is one of the major underlying economic reasons why the rich tend to get relatively richer while the poor get relatively poorer.

Concepts for review

production possibility curve
opportunity cost
average and marginal costs
diminishing returns and increasing (opportunity) costs
capital accumulation
technological progress
labour and capital-augmenting technological progress
labour and capital-saving technological progress
inventions v. innovations
economic growth
social and institutional innovations
economic structural transformation
modernisation ideals
rationality
resource endowment
economies of scale

Questions for discussion

1. Describe the nature and meaning of a production possibility curve. What are its crucial underlying assumptions?
2. Concave (or bow-shaped) production possibility curves are said to exhibit increasing opportunity costs. Explain what is meant by the concept of opportunity cost and why these costs might increase as one moves along a production possibility frontier.
3. Under what conditions would an economy be operating inside its P–P frontier? What determines the shape and position of a country's P–P frontier?
4. How would you describe the economic growth process in terms of the production possibility analysis? What are the principal sources of economic growth and how can they be illustrated using P–P frontier diagrams?
5. What does the historical record reveal about the nature of the growth process in the now developed nations? What were its principal ingredients?

Further reading

On the historical record of economic growth the classic study is that of the Nobel prize-winning Harvard economist, SIMON KUZNETS, whose life work is best revealed in two volumes: *Modern Economic Growth: rate, structure and spread,* Yale University Press, 1966; *Economic Growth of Nations: total output and production structure,* Harvard University Press, 1971. But the best and most concise summary of his findings can be found in SIMON KUZNETS, 'Modern Economic Growth: findings and reflections', *American Economic Review*, lxiii, 3, June 1973, pp. 257–258. See also, BARRY E. SUPPLE, ed., *The Experience of Economic Growth*, New York, Random House, 1963, especially Part II.

Chapter 8 Economic growth and development: lessons and controversies

> The growth position of the less developed countries today is significantly different, in many respects, from that of the presently developed countries on the eve of their entry into modern economic growth.
> *Simon Kuznets*

Introduction

Some lessons and implications of modern growth for developing countries

A basic question emerging from our discussion in Chapter 7 of the six characteristics of modern economic growth is, 'Why did the growth experience of the more developed nations not spread more rapidly to the less developed?' Two broad explanations come immediately to mind. The first relates to the internal conditions of most Third World countries and the other to the character of the international economic and political relationships between rich and poor nations.

Economic growth, as we have seen, results not only from the growth in quantity and quality of resources and improved technology but also from a social and political structure that is conducive to such change. Economic growth demands a stable but flexible social and political framework which is capable of accommodating and even encouraging rapid structural change. It also requires a social environment capable of resolving the inevitable interest group and sectoral conflicts that accompany such structural change, for example, the transition from a land-based rural agrarian society to a highly skilled, urban-oriented industrial and service economy. Shifts in relative power and influence from, say, the rural aristocracy to the new urban industrialists, or from a few large landlords to many smaller commercial farmers who own rather than lease their land, are examples of structural transitions involving potential conflicts of interest.

In short, unless local attitudes and institutional conditions exist which are amenable to structural change and, without holding back the growth-promoting groups in society, still provide opportunities for wider segments of the population to participate in the fruits of economic progress, efforts to stimulate growth through narrowly conceived economic policies are likely to fail. As we shall discover in many of the chapters in Part Two, the apparent failure of some developing countries to generate more rapid rates of economic growth in spite of heavy investments in human and physical resources and the importation of sophisticated technological practices can be traced largely to the inflexibility of their social and political institutions and the reactionary power of certain vested interest groups.

The second, and not unrelated, explanation for the limited spread effects of modern economic growth relates to the economic and political policies of the developed countries themselves *vis-à-vis* the developing nations. As we discovered in Chapter 5, the dominant power of rich nations collectively to influence and control the conditions of their international trading relationships with poor countries and to transfer their economic, social, political and cultural values and institutions as well as their technology to these societies in opportunist ways may have greatly inhibited the latter's economic progress, for three reasons. First, such wholesale transfers create and perpetuate dominance/dependence relationships between rich and poor in which the latter remain largely incapable of controlling their own economic destiny or evolving an ethos of self-reliance. Second, the transfers themselves may be largely inappropriate and counterproductive to the development aspirations of many Third World countries. Finally, it may simply not be in the private long-run economic and political interests for the one-fourth of the world's population who now control four-fifths of the world's production to share this abundance with the other three-fourths. A world of increasingly scarce resources and commodities may not be compatible with truly global economic progress, especially when the relative distribution of power is so unequal (see Chapter 25).

The analogy here between inflexible and reactionary domestic social structures and elite power groups inhibiting national economic growth and similar inflexibilities and reactionary policies among a small group of elite nations is obvious. Just as the economic growth of individual nations required flexible social and political institutions capable of resolving conflicts and promoting structural change, so too any realistic notion of 'world development' must accept that without an analogous flexibility at the international level (i.e. a genuine commitment on the part of developed nations to assist or, at least, not impede the economic progress of poor societies), global economic progress will probably never occur. Without such flexible global institutions (e.g. world trade and aid relationships) and an international rather than provincial outlook on the part of world leaders, it is not unreasonable to anticipate the emergence of growing conflict and perhaps even world-wide violence between the few who prosper and the many who do not. In the face of inflexible social and political structures, domestic civil wars have often broken out to resolve economic conflicts in the developed nations; the American Civil War in the 1860s is an example. Recently such violent conflicts related to struggles between small elites and the masses of poor, usually represented by other elites, have occurred with growing frequency in a number of developing countries (Sri Lanka, Pakistan, Algeria, Libya, Nigeria, Angola, Thailand, Chile, Haïti, Ethiopia, Veitnam, Cambodia, Sudan, Mozambique, and, most recently, Iran, Nicaragua and El Salvador). In the absence of a more equitable distribution of the fruits of world economic growth and more flexible international institutions, Third World nations may well grow impatient with the present international system and begin as a group to exercise their own potential power. The outcome may or may not be violent. But the underlying conditions for such potential violence seem to grow with each passing year.[1]

The limited value of the historical growth experience: differing initial conditions

One of the principal failures of development economics of the 1950s and early 1960s was its inability to recognise and take into account the *limited* value of the historical experience of economic growth in the West for charting the development path of contemporary Third World nations. Such theories as the 'stages of economic growth' and related models of rapid industrialisation gave too little emphasis to the very different and less favourable initial economic, social and political conditions of today's less developed countries. The fact is that the growth position of the less developed countries today is in many important ways significantly different from that of the present developed countries as they embarked on their era of modern economic growth.

We can identify, for example, at least *eight* significant differences in initial conditions between these two groups of countries, differences that require a much amended analysis of the growth prospects and requirements of present-day economic development:

1. resource endowments, both physical and human;
2. per capita incomes and levels of GNP in relation to the rest of the world;
3. climate;
4. population size, distribution and growth;
5. historical role of international migration;
6. international trade benefits;

[1] In Chapter 25 we examine the prospects for international co-operation or conflict in the context of the Third World's growing demands for a 'new international economic order'.

7. basic scientific and technological research and development capabilities;
8. stability and flexibility of political institutions.

Each of these conditions is discussed below with a view to formulating a more realistic set of requirements and priorities for generating and sustaining rapid economic growth.

Resource endowment, physical and human

Contemporary developing countries are on the whole often less well endowed with natural resources than the developed nations were when they began their modern growth. (We are not here talking about the present very depleted natural resources of many rich countries, but what they possessed on the eve of their development.) With the exception of those few (mostly Middle Eastern) Third World nations blessed with abundant supplies of petroleum and other minerals and raw materials in growing world demand, most less developed countries, especially those in Asia where almost one-third of the world's population live, are poorly endowed with natural resources. Moreover, in parts of Latin America and especially in Africa where natural resources are more plentiful, heavy investments of capital are needed to exploit them. Such finance is not easy to secure without sacrificing substantial autonomy and control to those powerful developed-country multi-national corporations who alone are at present capable of large-scale efficient resource exploitation.

The historical difference in skilled human resource endowments is even more pronounced. The ability of a country effectively to exploit natural resources is dependent on, among other things, the managerial and technical skills of its people. The populations of today's less developed countries are on the whole less educated, less experienced and less skilled than were their counterparts in the early periods of economic growth in the West, or, for that matter, the Soviet Union and Japan at the outset of their more recent growth processes.

Relative levels of per capita income and GNP

The two-thirds of the world's present population living in developing countries today have on average a much lower level of real per capita income than their counterparts had in nineteenth-century England, North America or France, or in early twentieth-century Russia and Japan. As we discovered in Chapter 5, well over three-quarters of the population of Third World countries is attempting to subsist at bare minimum levels. Obviously, the average standard of living in, say, early nineteenth-century England was nothing to envy or admire. But it was probably not as economically debilitating and precarious as it is today for many people in the Third World, especially those in the forty or so least developed countries.

Secondly, at the beginning of their modern growth era, today's developed nations were economically in advance of the rest of the world. They could therefore take advantage of their relatively strong financial positions to widen the income gap between themselves and other less fortunate countries. On the other hand, today's LDCs begin their growth process at the low end of the international per capita and GNP scale. Their relatively weak position in the world economy is analogous to that of a 1 500 metre race between a young athlete and an old man where the former is given a 1 000 metre start. Such backwardness is not only economically difficult to overcome or even reduce but, psychologically, it creates a sense of frustration and a desire to grow at any cost. This can in fact inhibit the long-run improvement in national levels of living.

Climatic differences

Almost all Third World countries are situated in tropical or sub-tropical climatic zones. It is an historical fact that almost every successful example of modern economic growth has occurred in a temperate zone country. Such a dichotomy cannot simply be attributed to coincidence: it must bear some relation to the special difficulties caused directly or indirectly by differing climatic conditions.

One obvious climatic factor directly affecting conditions of production is that in general the extremes of heat and humidity in most poor countries contribute to deteriorating soil qualities and the rapid depreciation of many natural goods. It also contributes to the low productivity of certain crops, the weakened regenerative growth of forests, and the poor health of animals. Finally, and perhaps most important, these extremes of heat and humidity not only cause discomfort to workers but also weaken their health, reduce their desire to engage in strenuous physical work, and generally lower their levels of productivity and efficiency.

Population size, distribution and growth

In Chapters 11 and 12 we discuss in detail some of the development problems and issues associated with rapid population growth. At this point, we merely point out that Third World population size, density and growth constitute another important difference between less developed and developed countries. Before and during their early growth years Western nations experienced a very slow secular trend in population growth. As industrialisation proceeded population growth rates increased, primarily as a result of falling death rates but also because of slowly rising birth rates. However, **at no time during their modern growth epoch did European and North American countries have natural population growth rates in excess of two per cent per annum.**

By contrast, the populations of most Third World countries have been increasing at annual rates in excess of 2.5 per cent over the past few decades and some are rising even faster today. Moreover, the concentration of these large and growing populations in a few areas means that most LDCs today start with considerably higher population–land ratios than European countries in their early growth years. Finally, in terms of comparative absolute size, it is a fact that, with the exception of the USSR, no country that embarked on a long-term period of economic growth approached the present-day population size of India, Egypt, Pakistan, Indonesia, Nigeria or Brazil. Nor, as we have just seen, were their rates of natural increase anything like those of present-day Mexico, Kenya, Algeria, Iran, Philippines, Bangladesh, Zaïre or Guatemala. In fact, many observers even doubt whether the industrial revolution and high long-term growth rates of per capita income of contemporary developed countries could have been achieved, or proceeded so fast and with such minimal setbacks and disturbances, especially for the very poor, had their populations been expanding so rapidly.

Table 8.1

Average annual overseas emigration from Europe, 1846–1939 (in thousands)

	Total European overseas emigration	Total	British Isles	(Ireland)	Germany	Norway Sweden Denmark	Switzer-land France Low Countries	Total	Italy	Austria Hungary Czecho-slovakia	Russia Poland Lithuania Finland	Spain Portugal	Balkans
1846–1850	256.6	254.3	199.1	(118.8)	35.5	4.3	14.4	2.3	.2	1.6	.1	.4	
1851–1855	342.3	331.3	231.7	(139.0)	74.9	6.9	17.8	11.0	.7	4.0	.2	6.1	
1856–1860	197.1	184.7	123.5	(43.7)	49.4	4.5	7.3	12.5	4.2	2.2	.2	5.9	
1861–1865	219.3	202.9	143.6	(39.1)	43.5	9.7	6.1	16.4	8.2	2.2	.3	5.9	
1866–1870	354.9	308.4	170.8	(47.8)	83.4	39.3	14.9	37.4	18.7	5.7	.6	12.4	
1871–1875	370.7	310.1	193.9	(59.0)	79.0	22.1	15.1	60.6	23.3	10.5	5.0	21.8	
1876–1880	258.0	192.8	114.9	(28.4)	46.2	23.2	8.5	65.2	28.9	11.8	7.2	17.3	
1881–1885	661.3	480.7	228.0	(67.1)	171.5	58.4	22.8	180.6	64.0	34.6	17.1	64.5	0.4
1886–1890	737.7	407.2	214.8	(62.0)	97.0	60.8	34.6	330.5	134.2	52.5	45.5	96.7	1.6
1891–1895	674.8	273.9	128.4	(45.5)	80.5	48.1	16.9	400.9	150.2	67.6	72.2	108.9	2.0
1896–1900	543.2	137.5	81.0	(30.2)	24.9	22.1	9.5	405.7	165.7	77.2	55.8	102.4	4.6
1901–1905	1,038.9	253.0	156.0	(36.8)	28.4	53.9	14.7	785.9	320.6	203.0	143.4	97.4	21.3
1906–1910	1,436.7	322.2	234.6	(31.0)	26.4	43.7	17.6	1114.3	402.4	265.4	211.6	185.4	49.5
1911–1915	1,365.3	325.6	265.7	(38.4)	15.8	28.6	15.5	1039.5	312.2	243.6	216.8	220.2	46.7
1916–1920	405.5	123.9	101.1	—	2.4	11.2	9.2	281.8	126.6	11.5	7.8	121.3	14.6
1921–1925	629.5	295.2	197.7	—	58.9	26.2	12.2	334.4	130.9	23.8	56.8	96.3	26.5
1926–1930	555.6	253.5	163.3	—	54.0	23.9	13.3	302.2	89.4	23.0	75.5	74.7	39.6
1931–1935	130.8	50.0	30.4	—	12.7	3.1	3.8	81.0	28.2	5.1	20.9	19.6	7.2
1936–1939	147.4	60.4	30.3	—	17.3	4.2	5.6	87.2	23.6	6.3	20.8	27.4	9.1

Sources: Dudley Kirk, *Europe's Population in the Interwar Years,* Princeton: League of Nations, 1946, p. 279, for Ireland, Brinley Thomas, *Migration and Economic Growth*, Cambridge University Press, 1954, p. 284.

The historical role of international migration

Of perhaps equal historical importance to the differing rates of natural population increase is the fact that in the nineteenth and early twentieth centuries there was a major outlet for excess rural populations in international migration. As Table 8.1 reveals, international migration was widespread and large in scale. In countries such as Italy, Germany and Ireland, periods of severe famine or pressure on the land often combined with limited economic opportunities in urban industry to 'push' unskilled rural workers towards the labour-scarce nations of North America, Australia and New Zealand. Thus, as Brinley Thomas argues in his treatise on migration and economic growth in the nineteenth century, the 'three outstanding contributions of European labour to the American economy – 1 187 000 Irish and 919 000 Germans between 1847 and 1855, 418 000 Scandinavians and 1 045 000 Germans between 1880 and 1885, and 1 754 000 Italians between 1898 and 1907 – had the character of evacuations'.[2]

Whereas the main thrust of international emigration up to the First World War was both over long distances and permanent, the period since the Second World War has witnessed a resurgence of international migration within Europe itself which is essentially over short distances and temporary in nature. However, the economic forces giving rise to this migration are basically the same, that is, surplus rural workers from southern Italy, Greece and Turkey have recently flocked into areas of labour shortages of which West Germany and Switzerland are the most notable. Table 8.2 gives an example of the magnitude and direction of Italian migration between 1960 and 1964.

The fact that this contemporary migration from regions of surplus labour in southern and south-eastern Europe is of a non-permanent nature provides a valuable dual benefit to the relatively poor areas from which these unskilled workers migrate. In addition to relieving the home governments of the costs of providing for people who in all probability would remain unemployed, the opportunity to earn money in nearby countries and send a large percentage of these earnings home provides a valuable and not insignificant source of foreign exchange to the country in which the worker is permanently domiciled.

In view of the above discussion, one might reasonably ask why the large numbers of impoverished peoples in Africa, Asia and Latin America do not follow the example of workers from south-eastern Europe and seek temporary or permanent jobs in areas of labour shortage. Historically, at least in the case of Africa, migrant

[2] Brinley Thomas, *Migration and Economic Growth*, Cambridge University Press, 1954, p. 118.

Table 8.2
Italian emigration (1960–1964)

Region	1960	1961	1962	1963	1964
European Economic community	170,580	175,266	158,900	107,578	113,200
Total Europe	309,876	329,597	313,400	235,134	236,600
North America	34,219	29,754	27,876	26,492	26,466
Central/South America	18,823	10,252	6,568	3,837	3,322
Australasia	19,629	16,379	14,411	11,539	10,890
Africa	1,283	1,022	706	589	1,128
Asia	78	119	255	20	178
Total	383,908	387,123	363,216	277,611	278,584

Source: 'Italian emigration: some aspects of migration in 1964' *International migration* iv, 2 1966, p. 122.

labour both within and between countries was rather common and did provide some relief for locally depressed areas. Even today, considerable benefits accrue, and numerous potential problems are avoided, by the fact that thousands of unskilled labourers in Upper Volta are able to find temporary work in neighbouring Ivory Coast. The same is true for Ghanains in Nigeria, Egyptians, Pakistanis and Indians in Kuwait and Saudi Arabia, Colombians in Venezuela and Mexicans in the United States. Nevertheless, the fact remains that **there is very little scope for reducing the pressures of overpopulation in Third World countries today through massive international emigration.**

The reasons for this relate not so much to a lack of local knowledge about opportunities in other countries but to the combined effects of geographical (and thus economic) distance and, more important, to the restrictive nature of immigration laws in developed countries. Moreover, the irony of international migration today is not merely that this historical outlet for surplus people has effectively been closed, but that a large percentage of those people who do migrate from poor to richer lands are the very ones whom the less developed countries cannot afford to lose: the highly educated and skilled. Since the great majority of these migrants move on a permanent basis, this perverse 'brain drain' not only represents loss of valuable human resources but, more importantly, loss of a productive factor which could prove to be a serious constraint on the future economic progress of the Third World. For example, during the 1960s and 1970s the emigration of high level professional and technical manpower from the developing to the developed countries of the United States, Canada and the United Kingdom alone amounted to over 400 000 skilled workers (see Table 18.2). So the fundamental point remains that the possibility of international migration of *unskilled* workers on a scale resembling that of the nineteenth and early twentieth centuries no longer exists to provide an effective safety valve for the contemporary surplus populations of Africa, Asia and Latin America.

The growth stimulus of international trade

International trade has often been referred to as the 'engine of growth' which propelled the development of the now economically advanced nations forward during the nineteenth and early twentieth centuries. Rapidly expanding export markets provided an additional stimulus to growing local demands for the establishment of large-scale manufacturing industries. Together with a relatively stable political structure and flexible social institutions, these increased export earnings enabled the newly developing country of the nineteenth century to borrow funds in the international capital market at very low interest rates. This capital accumulation in turn stimulated further production, made possible increased imports, and led to a more diversified industrial structure. All countries in the nineteenth century were able to participate in this dynamic growth of international exchange largely on the basis of relatively free trade, free capital movements and the unfettered international migration of unskilled surplus labour.

Today the situation is very different. **Third World countries without oil face formidable difficulties generating rapid economic growth on the basis of world trade.** While being a latecomer to the international economic system in the nineteenth century was often a real advantage, it has often been less advantageous in the twentieth century. Ever since the First World War, most developing countries have experienced a deteriorating trade position. Their exports have expanded, but not as fast as the exports of developed nations. Their terms of trade (the price they receive for their exports relative to the price they have to pay for imports) have declined steadily. Exports have had to grow faster just to earn the same amount of foreign currencies as in previous years. Moreover, the developed countries are so far ahead of the LDCs economically that they can afford through their advanced science and technology to remain more competitive, develop more new products (often synthetic substitutes for traditional LDC primary commodity exports), and obtain international finance on much better terms. Finally, where developing countries are lower cost producers of competitive products with the developed countries (e.g. textiles, clothing, shoes and some light manufactures) the latter have typically resorted to various forms of tariff and non-tariff barriers to trade, including import quotas, sanitary requirements and special licensing arrangements.

We discuss the economics of international trade and finance in detail in Chapters 19 to 21. For the present it is enough to point out that the so-called 'international engine of growth' that roared across the northern hemisphere in the nineteenth century has for the most part struggled and crawled for lack of sufficient fuel and need of repairs for most newcomers to the growth game in the twentieth century.

Basic scientific and technological research and development capabilities

A recurrent theme throughout this chapter has been the crucial role played by basic scientific research and technological development in the modern economic growth experience of contemporary developed countries. Their high rates of growth have been sustained by the interplay between mass applications of many new technological innovations based on a rapid advancement in the stock of scientific knowledge and further additions to that knowledge made possible by growing surplus wealth. But, as we discovered in an earlier chapter, even today the process of scientific and technological advance in all its stages, from basic research to product development, has been heavily concentrated in the rich nations. Almost 98 per cent of all world research and development expenditure originates in these countries. Moreover, research funds are spent on solving the economic and technological problems of concern to rich countries in accordance with their own economic priorities and resource endowments. Rich countries are mainly interested in the development of sophisticated products, large markets and technologically advanced production methods using large inputs of capital and high levels of skills and management while economising on their relatively scarce supplies of labour and raw materials. Poor countries, by contrast, are much more interested in simple products, simple designs, saving of capital, use of abundant labour and production for smaller markets. But they have neither the financial resources nor the scientific and technological know-how at present to undertake the kind of research and development that would be in their best long-term economic interests. Their dependence on inappropriate foreign technologies creates and perpetuates the internal economic dualism of which we spoke in Chapter 6.

We may conclude, therefore, that in the important area of scientific and technological research, contemporary Third World nations are in an extremely disadvantageous competitive position *vis-à-vis* the developed nations. In contrast, when the latter were embarking on their early growth process they were scientifically and technologically greatly in advance of the rest of the world. They could consequently focus their attention on staying ahead by designing and developing new technology at a pace dictated by their long-term economic growth requirements.

Stability and flexibility of political and social institutions

The final distinction between the historical experience of developed countries and the situation faced by contemporary Third World nations relates to the nature of social and political institutions. One very obvious difference between the now developed and the less developed nations is that well before their industrial revolutions the former were independent consolidated nation-states able to pursue national policies on the basis of a general consensus of popular opinions and attitudes towards 'modernisation'. As Professor Myrdal has correctly pointed out:

> They [the now developed countries] formed a small world of broadly similar cultures, within which people and ideas circulated rather freely. ... Modern scientific thought developed in these countries (long before their industrial revolutions) and a modernized technology began early to be introduced in their agriculture and their industries, which at that time were all small-scale.[3]

In contrast to those pre-industrial culturally homogeneous, materially oriented and politically unified societies with their emphasis on rationalism and modern scientific thought, many developing countries of today have only recently gained their political independence and have yet to become consolidated nation-states with an ability to formulate and pursue national development strategies effectively. Moreover, the modernisation ideals embodied in the notions of rationalism, scientific

---

[3] Gunnar Myrdal, *The Challenge of World Poverty*, Pantheon, New York, 1970, pp. 30–31.

thought, individualism, social and economic mobility, the work ethic and dedication to national material and cultural values are concepts largely alien to many contemporary Third World societies, except for their educated ruling elites. Until stable and flexible political institutions can be consolidated with broad public support, the present social and cultural fragmentation of many Third World countries is likely to inhibit their desires to accelerate national economic progress.

The desirability of growth: social benefits and costs

Throughout this and the previous chapter we have assumed that economic growth is desirable and that, given the choice between growth and no growth, all countries and peoples would prefer the former. Yet in recent years, especially in some Western nations, a cry to stop growth has been increasingly heard from both young and old (although, interestingly enough, not from both rich *and* poor). In Chapter 6 we showed that economic growth is desirable but that it should not be equated with 'development'; growth is a *necessary* but far from *sufficient* condition for the ultimate real development of Third World societies.

It seems appropriate, therefore, at this stage to be more explicit about the nature of the social costs as well as the social benefits of economic growth. For assistance in this discussion, we turn to the appendix, 'Is economic growth desirable?' in W. Arthur Lewis' Nobel prize winning classic book, *Theory of Economic Growth*, first published in 1955. Many of his observations are as relevant today as they were over two decades ago. He begins his discussion of the costs and benefits of economic growth by noting that:

> Like everything else, economic growth has its costs. If economic growth could be achieved without any disadvantages, everybody would be wholly in its favour. But since growth has real disadvantages, people differ in their attitude to growth according to the different assessment which they give to its advantages and disadvantages. They may dislike the kind of society which is associated with economic growth, preferring the attitudes and institutions which prevail in stable societies. Or, even if they are reconciled to the institutions of growing societies, they may dislike the transitional processes in the course of which stable societies are converted into growing societies; they may therefore conclude either that the benefits of growth are not worth the cost of the disturbance it involves, or also that growth should be introduced slowly, so that the society may have as long as possible to adjust itself to the changes which economic growth requires.[4]

Some benefits of growth

Lewis goes on to list what he sees as the principal benefits of economic growth. First and foremost is the notion that **economic growth benefits society** not because wealth necessarily increases happiness, but **because it increases the range of human choice.** This is what we listed as the third crucial component of our inner meaning of development: the freedom to choose (see pp. 97–8). The case for economic growth is that it gives man greater control over his physical and social environment and thereby increases his freedom. Economic growth enables him to escape from his bondage to famine, ill-health and disease, including such natural killers as cholera, smallpox, malaria, yellow fever, plague, leprosy and tuberculosis. Lewis comments ironically: 'If you think that it is better to die than to live, and best not to be born, you are not impressed by the fact that economic growth permits a reduction in death rates. But most of us are still primitive enough to take it as axiomatic that life is better than death.'[5] Of course all this assumes that the benefits of growth are widely distributed – a moot point to which we return in the next two chapters.

Among the other freedoms which economic growth makes possible, assuming for the present that its benefits are widely distributed, are the freedom to choose greater leisure as well as more goods; the availability of more services (hospitals,

[4] W. A. Lewis, *Theory of Economic Growth*, Allen and Unwin, 1963, p. 420.

[5] *Ibid.*, p. 421.

schools, theatres, etc.) as well as goods and leisure: the luxury to enjoy many of the higher cultural activities like music, art, drama and philosophy; and the chance for women to be 'liberated' from the drudgery of their traditional tasks and their seclusion in the household. Finally, economic growth makes possible the spread of humanitarianism in terms of the greater ability of rich societies to care for those who are weak and cannot help themselves: the blind, the crippled, the mentally deranged and the otherwise incapacitated.

The principal costs of growth

As in almost all activities that affect human welfare, economic growth not only confers benefits on society, mainly in the form of greater freedom, it also carries with it certain social costs. These can be classified broadly in two groups: (1) the negative effects of growth on conditions of living; (2) the undesirable nature of attitudes and institutions which are necessary for economic growth, i.e. the negative cultural aspects of the so-called 'modernisation' ideals.

In the first category is the rapid transformation of economic structure which is typical of the growth process. Most obvious among these costs is the phenomenon of urbanisation, brought about largely by migration from the rural countryside. Such migration carries with it the associated psychological costs involved in pulling up traditional roots, and the subsequent adjustment to the anonymity and higher costs of urban living. Traditional artisan and craftsman skills lose their value and are replaced by the dulling repetition of assembly line production. Slum towns (favellas, squatter settlements, etc.) spring up round the edges of modern cities and bring with them congested and unhealthy living conditions and the associated evils of violence, thieving, drunkenness and prostitution.

The major source of economic growth, technological innovations, which often require concomitant social innovations (new modes of production and life styles) inevitably lead to surprises and unanticipated costs. In fact the mass application of major inventions and innovations may produce unexpected negative social effects far beyond the initial imagination of the inventor or entrepreneur. To give an example, one can easily trace the sequence of events originating with the mass production and distribution of the automobile as a primary means of transportation in developed nations leading to the growth of suburbs, the exodus of the more affluent from the city centres, the concentration of the very poor in urban ghettoes and inner-city slums and, finally, to the proliferation of violence, drug abuse and criminal activities in many urban areas of countries like the United States. In addition, the concentration of millions of petrol-consuming and effluent-discharging motor cars in small urban areas has led to problems of environmental health and oil resource depletion that could hardly have been anticipated in the early 1920s when the passenger car was first being mass-produced.

The point is that rapid economic growth made possible by the rapid succession and mass diffusion of technological innovations through the mechanism of necessary social innovations will typically be accompanied by a relatively high incidence of direct and indirect negative effects. Some of these effects can be anticipated and dealt with at the outset. Others are unexpected and must be dealt with as they arise. But many of the most harmful side effects of rapid economic growth, such as environmental decay and resource depletion, are not necessarily inevitable results of economic progress. On the contrary, in many cases these negative effects were allowed to accumulate and become serious technological or social problems because the necessary social, political and institutional responses to alleviate their consequences were either deemed unimportant or were simply neglected. One may assume, or at least hope, that once an unexpected negative result of economic growth emerges and before it becomes too serious a threat to human welfare, new material and especially social technologies will be developed to lead to its reduction or removal.

The second broad area of the social costs of economic growth relates to the changes necessary in attitudes and institutions. Many people consider changes in what have been called modernisation ideals to be inimical to the overall wellbeing of people steeped in ancient and traditional, cultural and spiritual approaches to life. They would prefer that these traditional attitudes and institutions (such as the extended family, systems of land ownership, structures of authority, other-worldly spiritual and religious orientations, etc.) should never change, even if in the process economic growth rates are reduced or even eliminated.

Typically, five aspects of the so-called modernisation ideals have come under criticism: the economising spirit, the emphasis on individualism, the reliance on reason and rationality, the growth of scale and associated impersonal nature of production, and the supposed dependence of growth on increased inequality of incomes.

The **economising spirit** which seeks to maximise output (or utility) for a given cost (expenditure), or minimise the cost of achieving a desired level of output or satisfaction, is sometimes criticised as a rationalisation for the exploitation of the weak by the powerful (e.g. when large and wealthy corporations pay low wages). Alternatively, it is sometimes alleged that such economising is merely a disguised form of unfettered materialism which detracts from the human happiness derived from purely aesthetic or spiritual development. This latter criticism is directed not so much at the accumulation of unnecessary material goods but rather on the over-emphasis on material accumulation for its own sake that prevails in many economically developed nations.

Critics of economic growth often deplore the cult of **individuality** inherent in the pursuit of unbridled self-interest. Reliance on the 'invisible hand' to transform private benefits into social benefits may provide a theoretical justification for such individuality, but it cannot restore the human qualities of the extended family or the cohesiveness of traditional social systems which are destroyed in the process. Whether the trade-off between individual economic and social mobility and tribal or group identity is worth the effort is debatable. Most societies have concluded that it is, judging from the extent to which such transformations from group to individual behaviour have occurred throughout the world.

A third line of attack on growth derives from its association with the notion of **rationality** or 'rational economic man'. Economic growth depends on scientific and technological progress. This in turn develops from the methodology of scientific investigation, an inherently rational process. Reason and rationalism can be criticised because they rely too heavily on objectivity and the scientific 'facts' at the expense of 'gut' feelings, subjective judgments and emotional valuations. As we have repeatedly pointed out, value judgments and subjective beliefs *do* have an important role to play in economic analysis. But once such value judgments have been specified, reliance on reason, objective evaluation and factual information should assume a crucial role. While it cannot be definitely proved that emotive judgments about development policies are any less correct than scrupulous reliance on objective and scientific decision-making processes, it remains true that most intelligent people would rather base their decisions and policy judgments on carefully reasoned arguments than simply and exclusively on intuitive feelings. As we suggest in Parts Two and Three, our whole approach to the description and analysis of development problems must rely on a logical and rational operating procedure of problem definition and solution.

A fourth line of attack deplores the inexorable disappearance of the village craftsman, the traditional skills, the personal nature of production and the small family farm and firm under the onslaught of large impersonal corporations. **Economies of scale** (i.e. lower unit costs of production arising out of the larger scale of operation) are manifested in assembly line methods of production, division of labour, and the use of machinery. Critics of such modern methods of production focus on the dehumanising aspects of automation and division of labour. Individual workers lose their pride in producing something like a sturdy pair of shoes, a fine piece of furniture, or a solid agricultural tool from start to finish. Instead, division of labour requires them to focus on only one aspect of the production process (e.g. putting buttons on shirts) while others work on different aspects. Moreover, economies of scale mean growth in the size of bureaucratic and administrative units in corporations and public agencies. In the process men are separated from the ownership of their tools and lose all sense of decision-making. Tensions grow, authority replaces autonomy and the time-clock supersedes the freedom inherent in self-employment. Day after day, workers must awake at the same hour, start work at the same time, break from work to eat at pre-appointed hours, do the same things and leave for home at the same time. Life can easily become drab and monotonous and human beings can be reduced to the role of mechanical cogs in the impersonal wheel of giant industry.

There is much truth to the above arguments on the human level and they clearly reflect one of the major social costs of modernisation. But at the same time, economics of large-scale production create possibilities of many more wagepaying jobs and generate greater opportunities for individuals to raise their levels of living above what would be possible in traditional small-scale enterprises. Moreover, by lowering costs of production, economies of large-scale enterprise can bring a wider range of material goods and services into the economic reach of many middle and lower income workers.

A fifth and final criticism of modern economic growth focuses on a supposed necessity for wide **income disparities** to arise in order for saving and investment to be generated to sustain this growth. A large and increasingly criticised body of economic theory has been built up on the assumption that only the rich (the capitalists) save and invest while the poor spend all their income on life's necessities. Therefore, since increased saving and investment are essential inputs into the growth process, wide disparities are not only justified from a long-term perspective but are in fact an inherent and necessary manifestation and outgrowth of the early stages of economic growth. Proponents of this theory conclude by arguing that eventually much of this growth will trickle down to the masses, but that it is more important in the initial periods to maximise the size of the 'GNP pie' before worrying about how it is cut up among different groups of people.

Conclusions: the need for a balanced perspective

The debate between those who advocate growth at any cost and those who want to focus on distribution and equity is probably the most central issue in all development economics. In view of its importance, the next two chapters thoroughly examine this question. Here we simply note that much of the criticism of economic growth from the equity point of view is in reality a criticism of the social institutions that exacerbate and perpetuate these income differentials (e.g. inheritance of property, asset distribution, ownership of land, tax laws, educational opportunities, etc.). The supposed conflict between growth and distribution, as we shall see in the next chapter, is not necessarily a conflict at all. In fact, better distribution policies can *enhance* growth prospects even during its initial periods, while more rapid economic growth increases the possibilities of greater benefits for a wider population, both now and in the future. The recent experience of Taiwan and South Korea are often cited as prime examples of countries which have achieved rapid economic growth and a wide distribution of its benefits during the early stages of economic development.

Quoting Professor Lewis once again, we conclude our discussion of the costs and benefits of growth by noting that:

> First, some of the alleged costs of economic growth are not necessarily consequences of growth at all – the ugliness of towns or the impoverishment of the working classes, for instance. Second, some of the alleged evils are not in fact *intrinsically* evil – the growth of individualism, or of reasoning, or of towns, for example. As in all human life, such things can be taken to excess, but they are not intrinsically any less desirable than their opposites. From this it follows, however, thirdly, that the rate of economic growth can be too high for the health of a society. Economic growth is only one good thing among many, and we can take it to excess. Excessive growth may result in, or be the result of, excessive materialism, excessive individualism, excessive mobility of population, excessive inequality of income, or the like. Societies are not necessarily wise to choose to speed up their rate of growth above its current level – if they do, they will experience substantial costs, in social or in spiritual terms, and whether the potential gains exceed the potential losses must be assessed separately in each situation as best we may. It is because economic growth has both its gains and its losses that we are all almost without exception ambivalent in our attitudes towards economic growth. We demand the abolition of poverty, illiteracy and disease, but we cling desperately to the beliefs, habits and social arrangements which we like, even when these are the very cause of the poverty which we deplore.[6]

We now approach the hotly debated issue of possible conflicts and trade-offs between rapid economic growth and more equitable distributions

[6] *Ibid.*, p. 429–30.

of personal income. It is hoped that the present and previous chapters have provided an adequate foundation for this discussion by giving the student a broad yet balanced perspective on the true nature and meaning of economic growth, both historical and contemporary, as well as a realistic appraisal of some of its social benefits and costs. Although the relentless and often blind pursuit of rapid economic growth as the ultimate key to Third World development has been widely challenged, especially by those in Third World countries themselves, it remains true that without some form of sustained economic growth, few of the many development objectives are likely to be realised. It is the 'character' of economic growth (who benefits from growth and how it is achieved), not growth *per se*, that is the real issue.

Concepts for review

- resource endowment
- economies of scale
- trade as an engine of growth
- flexible v. rigid political and social institutions
- relation between basic science and technological innovation
- division of labour
- research and development (R and D)
- costs and benefits of growth
- indirect effects of technological inventions and innovations
- economising spirit
- assembly-line, mass production

Questions for discussion

1. Of what relevance is the historical record of modern economic growth for contemporary Third World nations? How important are differences in initial conditions? Give and describe some examples of the kinds of initial conditions in your own country that make it different from most contemporary developed nations at the beginning of their modern growth experience.
2. What is meant by the statement: 'Social and institutional innovations are as important for economic growth as technological and scientific inventions and innovations'? Explain your answer.
3. What do you think were the principal reasons why economic growth spread rapidly amongst the now developed nations during the nineteenth and early twentieth centuries but has failed to spread to an equal extent to contemporary less developed nations?
4. Outline some arguments for and against the pursuit of rapid economic growth. Do you agree or disagree with Professor W. Arthur Lewis' analysis of the desirability of economic growth? Explain your answer.
5. Some influential and perceptive observers of international development like the Nobel prize-winning Swedish economist Gunnar Myrdal, argue that 'modernisation ideals' are necessary for sustained economic growth. What are these so-called modernisation ideals? Do you agree or disagree with Professor Myrdal's position? Explain your answer with specific reference to your own nation.

Further reading

For the most comprehensive general statement of the nature of economic growth as applied to less developed countries, see W. ARTHUR LEWIS, *Theory of Economic Growth*, Allen and Unwin, London, 1955. An extensive critique of the historical growth record of developed nations as applied to Third World countries can be found also in GUNNAR MYRDAL, *The Challenge of World Poverty*, Pantheon, New York, ch. 2, and (by the same author) *Asian Drama*, Pantheon, 1968, ch. 14.

Part Two Problems and policies – domestic

Introduction To Parts Two and Three

A note to the student on the organisational structure and operating procedure for analysing diverse development problems in Parts Two and Three

In Part One, we examined the major characteristics of Third World nations, reviewed some basic economic concepts relevant to Third World problems and explored the nature and meaning of economic growth and development. In Parts Two and Three we focus on a number of crucial development problems which are top priority issues in almost all developing countries. Our task here is not only to describe the nature of these problems but also to demonstrate how economic analysis can contribute to their ultimate resolution. It is of little value to understand basic economic concepts and principles if one is not also able to apply them to real world development problems.

Accordingly, the problem chapters in Parts Two and Three are, in general, organised around a common five-stage operating procedure. We believe that this procedure provides a convenient methodology for analysing and solving any problem, whether in economics or any other field. The five stages of problem analysis are:

1. Problem statement and principal issues.
2. Importance of problem in diverse developing nations.
3. Possible goals and objectives.
4. Role of economics.
5. Policy alternatives and consequences.

Each of these problem areas analysed usually requires two chapters for discussion (e.g. poverty and inequality in Chapters 9 and 10, population in 11 and 12).

Statement of problem

Each discussion begins with an analysis of what it is we are trying to understand (e.g. population growth, unemployment, poverty, etc.). Basically, four questions are asked:

- What is the problem all about?
- Why is it a problem?
- How important is it?
- What are the principal issues?

The purpose of this first step is to clarify the nature and importance of the problem so that the student can recognise why so much attention is given to the issue in the newspapers, development plans, political speeches and international writings of scholars and journalists.

Significance and variations of problem in Third World countries

Here we attempt to provide a capsule statistical summary of the relative importance of the particular problem under review in diverse developing nations. How does it vary from one country to the next and what, if any, are the qualitative as well as quantitative differences in Africa, Asia, the Middle East and Latin America? It is clear, for example, that while rising unemployment and underemployment is a common phenomenon in developing nations, the nature, extent and significance of the problem may be quite different in sub-Saharan Africa as compared with, say, the Arab Middle East, Latin America or South Asia. Our purpose is not to overload the student with comparative Third World statistics. Rather, it is to give him a feeling for the ubiquitous nature of certain development problems while advising him that the significant principal manifestations of the problem may vary from country to country and region to region. As a result, the policy approaches designed to cope with the problem can, and often do, also differ in their scope and content.

Possible goals and objectives

Our next step is to set out the likely development goals and objectives as they relate to this particular problem. Here unavoidably we must deal with value judgments and priorities. For example, if greater equality is an overall objective of government policy, then factors such as the distribution of income, the spread of educational opportunities and the role of labour-intensive rural development projects take on a certain significance. However, if the objective is maximum growth of GNP irrespective of its distribution, then these same criteria may carry less weight. The point is that any attempt to deal with real world development problems must be based on explicit economic and social value premises about what is desirable and what are the priorities among different desirable goals. In fact, the very selection of specific problems to be discussed and analysed (e.g. poverty, inequality, unemployment, population growth, education, rural development, trade, aid, technology, etc.) reflects a value judgment on the part of the author, albeit one which is rooted in the consensus opinion of a great diversity of those who study and act on Third World development problems.

The role of economics and economic principles

After setting forth a possible set of goals and objectives related to a specific development problem, we ask the following pertinent questions:

- What are the economic components of the problem?
- How can economic concepts and principles help us to understand the problem better and possibly to solve it?
- Do the economic components dominate the problem and, if so or if not, how might they be related to the non-economic components?

At this stage we draw on many of the relevant economic concepts discussed in Part One. Also, as the occasion arises, we introduce new concepts especially relevant to the topic under discussion. For example, supply and demand analysis may be relevant to one set of problems (e.g. wage and employment determination) while not to others (e.g. agricultural pricing and international exchange). On the other hand, once the goals, objectives and value premises have been specified, our distinction between social and private benefits and costs will be revealed as a core concept for a wide range of development problems.

Policy alternatives and consequences

The final step in our problem-solving procedure is to suggest alternative economic policy approaches and to examine their possible consequences for the problem. Again, the nature of the policy options available to governments depends both on the specific goals and on the significance of the economic aspects of the overall problem. Each policy alternative needs to be evaluated in light of a variety of priority development goals. As a result, the possibility of trade-offs between goals must be always considered. For example, the goal of rapid GNP growth may or may not be incompatible with the elimination of unemployment or the eradication of rural poverty. Similarly, the encouragement of private foreign investment may not be compatible with the desire to be more self-reliant. In either case, when such a conflict of goals becomes apparent, choices have to be made on the basis of priorities and the socio-economic consequences of giving up or curtailing one objective in favour of another. It is at this final stage of evaluating the indirect consequences which a particular policy designed to eliminate one problem might have in the exacerbation of other problems, that the wisdom of the broad-gauged economist can be most important.

By following this five-step problem-solving procedure in Parts Two and Three we hope to help the student not only to a more comprehensive understanding of contemporary development issues, but also, and more important, to approach and reach independent judgments about any other economic problem that may arise in the future. We believe that in the long run the possible 'costs' of trying to cram all problems into a somewhat rigid five-step pattern rather than following a less tightly organised discussion will be greatly outweighed by the benefits. Providing students with a coherent and logical procedure for analysing diverse development problems will, in our opinion, yield significant results. Long after many of the specific economic concepts have been forgotten, the student who has learned how to deal rationally with diverse problems, be they of economics or of life, in the context of an organised and consistent conceptual approach will perhaps discover that something of lasting value has been retained from his first course in Third World economics.

Chapter 9 Growth, poverty and income distribution: theory and evidence

No society can surely be flourishing and happy, of which by far the greater part of the numbers are poor and miserable.
Adam Smith, 1776

The fact of poverty is not new: what *is* new is the suspicion that economic growth by itself may not solve or even alleviate the problem.
Montek S. Ahluwalia, Pakistan

Introduction

The growth controversy

The 1970s witnessed a remarkable change in public and private perceptions about the ultimate nature of economic activity. In both rich and poor countries, disillusionment grew about the relentless pursuit of growth as the principal economic objective of society. In the developed countries, the major emphasis seemed to shift away from growth towards more concern for the 'quality of life'. This concern was manifested principally in the environmental movement. There was an outcry against the onslaught of industrial growth and the consequent pollution of air and water, the depletion of natural resources and the destruction of many natural beauties. A major influential book entitled, *The Limits to Growth*,[1] appeared, which purported to document the fact, first expounded in the early nineteenth century by Ricardo and Malthus, that the earth's finite resources could not sustain a continuation of high growth rates without major economic and social catastrophes. It is a testimony to the mood of the period that in spite of obvious flaws in logic and many dubious assumptions, this book became widely publicised and acclaimed.

In the poor countries the main concern centred on the question of growth versus income distribution. Many Third World countries which had experienced relatively high rates of economic growth by historical standards in the 1960s, began to realise that such growth had brought few significant benefits to their poor. For those hundreds of millions of people in Africa, Asia, the Middle East and Latin America, levels of living seemed to stagnate and, in some countries, even to decline in real terms. Rates of rural and urban unemployment and underemployment were on the rise. The distribution of incomes between rich and poor seemed to get worse with each passing year. Many people felt that rapid economic growth had failed to eliminate or even reduce the widespread absolute poverty that remains a fact of economic life in all developing nations. In both the developing and the developed worlds, the call for the 'dethronement of GNP' as the major objective of economic activity was widely heard. In its place concern for the problems of poverty and equality became the major theme of the second development decade. Mahbub ul Haq of Pakistan seemed to speak for a great number of observers when he succinctly asserted that 'we were taught to take care of our GNP as this will take care of poverty. Let us reverse this and take care of poverty as this will take care of the GNP.'[2]

Since the elimination of widespread poverty and growing income inequalities is at the core of all development problems and, in fact, defines for many the principal objective of economic policy, we begin Part Two of this book by focusing on the nature of the poverty and inequality problem in Third World

[1] D. L. Meadows *et al.*, *The Limits to Growth*, Universe Books, New York 1972.

[2] Mahbub ul Haq, 'Employment and Income Distribution in the 1970s: a new perspective', *Development Digest*, October 1971, p. 7.

countries. Although our principal focus is on economic inequalities in the distribution of incomes and assets, the student should be aware that these are only a small part of the broader inequality problem in developing countries. Of parallel or even greater importance are inequalities of power, prestige, status, recognition, job satisfaction, conditions of work, degree of participation, freedom of choice and many other dimensions of the problem that relate more to our second and third components of the meaning of development: self-esteem and freedom to choose. But, as in most social relationships, one cannot really separate the economic from the non-economic manifestations of inequality. Each reinforces the other in a complex and often inter-related process of cause and effect.

Our basic problem-solving approach in this and the next chapter is as outlined in the Introduction to Parts Two and Three. First, in this chapter, we define the nature of the poverty and income distribution problem in developing countries and consider its quantitative significance in various Third World nations. In Chapter 10, we set forth possible goals and objectives, examine in what ways economic analysis can shed light on the poverty and inequality problem and, finally, explore alternative possible policy approaches directed at the elimination of poverty and the reduction of excessively wide disparities in Third World distributions of income. A thorough understanding of these two fundamental economic manifestations of underdevelopment provides the basis for analysis of more specific development problems, including population growth, unemployment, rural development, education, international trade and foreign assistance, in the succeeding chapters of these two Parts.

Problem statement and related issues: who gets how much of what?

A simple and convenient way to approach the twin problems of poverty and income distribution is to adopt once again our production-possibility framework. In this case, however, let us divide production in our hypothetical developing economy into two classes of goods. First, there are **necessities** such as basic foods, simple clothing, minimum shelter, etc. The second class of goods, **luxuries**, might include expensive cars, large houses, sophisticated consumer goods, fashionable clothes, gourmet foods, etc. Assuming for the present that production occurs on the possibility frontier (i.e. that all resources are fully and efficiently employed), the question arises as to what combination of economic necessities and luxuries will actually be chosen by the 'society' in question. Who will do the choosing and how?

Figure 9.1 illustrates the issue. On the vertical axis we have aggregated all luxury goods and on the horizontal axis are grouped all necessities. The production possibility curve, therefore, portrays the maximum combinations of both types of goods which this economy could produce by making efficient use of all available resources with the prevailing technological knowhow. But it does *not* tell us precisely which combination among the many possible ones will actually be chosen. For example, the same *real* GNP would be represented at points A and B in Figure 9.1. At point A many luxury goods and very few necessities are being produced, while at point B few luxuries and many necessities are being supplied to the population. One would normally expect the actual production combination in low-income countries to be somewhere in the vicinity of point B. But, with the exception of 'command' economies, where production and distribution decisions are centrally planned, the basic determinant of output combinations in market and mixed economies is the level of effective aggregate demand exerted by all consumers. Recall from Chapter 3 that the position and shape of society's aggregate demand curve for

Figure 9.1
Choosing what to produce: luxuries v. necessities

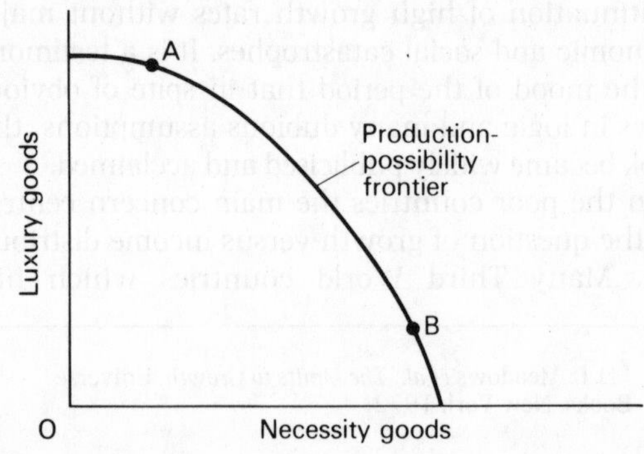

different products is determined primarily by the level and especially the distribution of national income.

Take, for example, the simple case of an economy consisting only of two consumers and two goods, luxuries and necessities. We know from both historical and cross-country expenditure studies that individuals or families with low incomes spend very high proportions of their incomes on basic necessities such as food, clothing and simple shelter. On the other hand, relatively rich people spend a low proportion of their income on these necessities and a relatively high proportion on what we have called luxury goods – 'luxurious' at least in the context of what poor societies can afford. For our illustration, let us suppose that a person is poor if he has 5 units or less of income per year. Such a person might spend 90 per cent of his income on 'necessities', that is, his 'propensity to consume' necessities will be 0.9 which when multiplied by his income level will show his total consumption or expenditure on necessities. The remaining 10 per cent will be spent on 'luxuries' – a propensity to consume of 0.1. On the other hand, a rich person (one who has more than say 5 units per year) will spend on the average only 20 per cent of his income on necessities (a propensity to consume of 0.2) and 80 per cent (or a propensity of 0.8) on luxuries. We are assuming, therefore, for simplicity that all income is expended on these two goods.

Now suppose that the total GNP or national income in our simple two-person, two-good economy is 8 units and that this income is divided **equally** into 4 units of personal income for each individual, where *Y* stands for the level of personal income. Table 9.1 shows that in such a situation each individual with a propensity to spend 90 per cent of his 4 units income on necessities will allocate 3.6 units of his income ($0.9 \times 4 = 3.6$) on these goods so that the total demand for necessity goods will be 7.2 units. On the other hand, each person will spend only 0.4 (i.e. 0.1×4) on luxuries so that a total of only 0.8 units of income will be spent on luxury goods. If this demand is translated into production, the point on the production possibility curve where this economy will be operating will be in the vicinity of point B in Figure 9.1.

Now assume that this same national income of 8 units is distributed **very unequally** with individual number 1 getting 7 units and individual number 2 only 1 unit. Table 9.2 shows that in this case of the coexistence of relative wealth and extreme poverty.

Table 9.1

Expenditure and production patterns for an hypothetical two-person, two-good economy with equal incomes

	Individual no. 1	Individual no. 2
Personal income (Y)	Y = 4	Y = 4
Propensity to consume and expenditure on:		
1. Necessities ($0.9 \times Y$ if $Y \leq 5$)* or ($0.2 \times Y$ if $Y > 5$)	3.6 ($= 0.9 \times 4$)	3.6
2. Luxuries ($0.1 \times Y$ if $Y \leq 5$) or ($0.8 \times Y$ if $Y > 5$)	0.4 ($= 0.1 \times 4$)	0.4

Total demand for necessities = 7.2 (= 3.6 + 3.6)
Total demand for luxuries = 0.8 (= 0.4 + 0.4)
Total expenditure (= Total GNP) (= 8.0 (per capita income = 4.0)

* Note the symbol ≤ means 'less than or equal to', and > means 'greater than'. Thus $0.9 \times Y$ if $Y \leq 5$ is read as the propensity to consume necessities is equal to 0.9 or 90 per cent of the level of personal income if that income (Y) is 'less than or equal to' (≤) 5 units. These symbols are convenient shorthand mathematical expressions.

total demand for necessity goods will amount to 2.3 units (i.e. the rich person will spend 1.4 and the poor person 0.9 units respectively) while the total demand for luxury goods is 5.7 units (5.6 for the rich individual and 0.1 for the poor one). Production will take place in the vicinity of point A in Figure 9.1. We see, therefore, that in spite of the relative poverty of the country as a whole, the very unequal distribution of income means that the rich individual can dictate the overall pattern of production since his demand preferences carry more weight in the consumer goods market than those of the poor person. In both examples GNP (8) and per capita income (4) were exactly the same but given the different distribution of this income, significant differences in production and consumption patterns ensued.

To drive home the point, suppose that our economy consists of five individuals and that it has the same 4 unit per capita income as in the previous 'two-individual' cases, so that total GNP equals 20 units. If this GNP were equally distributed among the five individuals who have the same preferences for luxuries and necessities as in the previous case, total demand for necessities would be 18 units and that for luxuries would be only 2 units. Production, therefore, would occur in the vicinity of point B in Figure 9.1. However, if instead we assume that 80 per cent of the income (16 units) goes to 20 per cent of the population (one individual) while the remaining 80 per cent of the population (the other four individuals) divide among themselves 20 per cent of the income (4 units), then as can be verified from Table 9.3 total output of luxury goods will amount to 13.2 units while only 6.8 units of necessities will be produced. Production would consequently take place in the vicinity of point A in Figure 9.1. Moreover, at the individual level the one rich person will be consuming 3.2 units of food and other necessities while each of the other four very poor people have only enough money to purchase 0.9 units each, an amount which may barely be enough for survival.

As a final example, let us assume that the economy portrayed in Table 9.3 *doubles* its real GNP from 20 to 40 units over a given period of time while the population increases by only 60 per cent from five to eight individuals. Per capita income will, therefore, have grown by 25 per cent over this period from 4 to 5 units per person. If this doubled national income of 40 units were distributed in equal shares to all eight people, each would be able to consume 4.5 units of necessities and 0.5 units of luxury goods. Their real levels of living will therefore also have increased by 25 per cent from the previous situation. Clearly, 'economic' development can be said to have occurred in this economy. Production would still occur in the vicinity of point A in Figure 9.1 although, as we saw in the previous chapter, the entire production possibility curve would have shifted outward to reflect the growth of GNP.

Note that a further doubling of real GNP from 40 to 80 units with similar 60 per cent increases in population (from 8 to approximately 13) and 25 per cent growths in per capita income (from 5 to approximately 6.3), will result in a shift in the pattern of demand and, therefore, production. This is because **the high growth of GNP and its equitable**

Table 9.2
Expenditure and production patterns for an hypothetical two-person, two-good economy with highly unequal incomes

Personal income (Y)		Individual no. 1 Y = 7	Individual no. 2 Y = 1
Propensity to consume and expenditure on:			
1. Necessities (0.9 if Y≤5) or (0.2 if Y>5		1.4 (= 0.2×7)	0.9 (= 0.9×1)
2. Luxuries (0.1 if Y≤5) or (0.8 if Y>5)		5.6 (=0.8×7)	0.1 (=0.1×1)
Total demand for necessities	=2.3 (=1.4+0.9)		
Total demand for luxuries	= 5.7 (= 5.6+0.1)		
Total expenditure (= Total GNP)	= 8.0 (per capita income = 4.0)		

Table 9.3
Expenditure and production patterns for an hypothetical five-person, two-commodity economy with a highly unequal distribution of income

Personal income (Y)		Individual no. 1 Y = 16	Individuals nos. 2–5 Y = 1 (×4 = 4)
Propensity to consume and expenditure on:			
1. Necessities	(0.9 if Y ≤ 5) or (0.2 if Y > 5)	3.2 (= 0.2 × 16)	0.9 (×4 = 3.6)
2. Luxuries	(0.1 if Y ≤ 5) or (0.8 if Y > 5)	12.8 (= 0.8 × 16)	0.1 (×4 = 0.4)
Total demand for necessities	= 6.8 (3.2 + 0.9 × 4)		
Total demand for luxuries	= 13.2 (12.8 + 0.1 × 4)		
Total expenditure (Total GNP)	= 20.0 (per capita income = 4.0)		

distribution have eliminated poverty in the sense that every member of the population now has a real personal income of 6.3 units which is above our arbitrary hypothetical poverty line of 5 units. As a result, the pattern of consumption will shift from a relative emphasis on necessities to more emphasis on what were formerly considered to be luxuries. In terms of our production possibility curve analysis, not only does the curve shift outward as a result of economic growth but the point on the curve at which production occurs will shift away from B and towards A in Figure 9.1. The numerical details of this shift are shown in Table 9.4.

Now take the other case where both GNP and per capita incomes grow as above, but instead of these incomes being equitably distributed, again assume that their distribution is highly skewed with the top 20 per cent getting 80 per cent of the income. In the case of GNP quadrupling from 20 to 80 units while per capita incomes grow by almost 60 per cent from 4 to 6.3, we see from Table 9.5 that two individuals (slightly less than 20 per cent of the population) have personal incomes of 64 units (i.e. each gets approximately 32 units) while the remaining eleven individuals receive only 16 units, or 1.5 units each. Again, production will be biased towards the region of point A in Figure 9.1.[3]

[3] The fact that under our assumption of a very unequal income distribution the demand for necessities is higher (Table 9.5) than with the equal distribution (Table 9.4) is due to our simplistic assumption that propensities to consume luxuries differ sharply as income levels rise from 5 to 6 units. We employed this assumption to illustrate our main point. In actuality, these propensities rise slowly with income growth.

Table 9.4
The effects of growing GNP and higher per capita incomes with equitable distribution on patterns of demand and production

Personal income (Y)		Each of 13 individuals 6.30 units (×13 = 81.9)
Propensity to consume and expenditure on:		
1. Necessities	(0.2 × Y since Y > 5.0)	1.26 (= 0.2 × 6.3) (×13 = 16.4)
2. Luxuries	(0.8 × Y since Y > 5.0)	5.04 (= 0.8 × 6.3) (×13 = 65.5)
Total demand for necessities	= 16.4 (= 1.26 × 13)	
Total demand for luxuries	= 65.5 (= 5.04 × 13)	
Total expenditure (= total GNP)	= 81.9 (per capita income = 6.3)	

The examples given in the preceding tables illustrate a number of critical points about economic growth, income distribution and poverty. First, we have seen that two countries with the same levels of GNP and per capita income may have entirely different production and consumption structures (i.e. they may be operating at different points on the same production possibility curve) depending on whether or not personal incomes are distributed equitably. **For a given low level of GNP and per capita income, the more unequal the distribution of income, the more aggregate demand will be influenced by the consumption habits of the rich.** In spite of the fact that they may constitute only a small proportion of the population, the rich can control a very disproportionately large share of national resources. Their dominant purchasing power can bias production towards manufactured luxury goods even while the masses of people are barely subsisting. This is an excellent example of a situation in which the traditional theory of consumer sovereignty as manifested in market demand curves represents in fact the sovereignty not of all consumers but of the very few rich ones who dominate the market and determine what goods should be produced. As a result of highly unequal income distributions, we find a number of low-income Third World countries devoting a sizable proportion of their financial, technical and administrative resources to the production of sophisticated consumption goods (television sets, stereophonic equipment, electronic components, etc.) to cater for the demands of a very small but economically powerful minority located mostly in urban areas. If incomes were more equitably distributed, the pattern of demand would be geared more towards the production of basic foods and other necessities which would further help to eliminate rural poverty and raise levels of living for broader segments of the population.

The second basic point illustrated by our numerical examples is that **high rates of economic growth and rising levels of per capita income do not necessarily imply economic development** in the sense of improved levels of living for the masses of people. Comparing Tables 9.3 and 9.5 for example, we find that although GNP has grown by 400 per cent and per capita incomes by over 55 per cent, the actual level of personal income received by the bottom 80 per cent of the population grew by 50 per cent while the top 20 per cent experienced an income growth of 100 per cent. Even more striking is the growth in the absolute income gap between rich and poor. Whereas the real incomes for the bottom 80 per cent grew by only 0.5 units over the period in question, that of the top 20 per cent grew by a total of 16 units, more than thirty times as fast in absolute terms as for the poor. The absolute gap thus widened from 15 to 30.5 units of income. In short, the quadrupling of GNP and the almost 60 per cent rise in per capita income had almost no tangible benefit in terms of raising the levels of living of 80

Table 9.5
The effects of growing GNP and higher per capita incomes with highly skewed income distribution on patterns of demand and production

Personal income (Y)	2 Individuals (top 20%) Y = 32 units (×2 = 64)	Each of 11 individuals (bottom 80%) Y = 1.5 units (×11 = 16)
Propensity to consume and expenditure on:		
1. Necessities (0.9 × Y if Y ≤ 5) or (0.2 × Y if Y > 5)	6.4 (×2 = 12.8)	1.35 (×11 = 14.8)
2. Luxuries (0.1 × Y if Y ≤ 5) or (0.8 × Y if Y > 5)	25.6 (×2 = 51.2)	0.15 (×11 = 1.6)
Total demand for necessities = 27.6 (= 12.8 + 14.8)		
Total demand for luxuries = 52.8 (= 51.2 + 1.6)		
Total expenditure (GNP) = 80 units* (per capita income = 6.3)		

* Note the numbers do not add up exactly due to rounding.

per cent of the population. In fact, over this period the numbers of the very poor *increased* from four to eleven, almost 200 per cent, as a result of population growth. Although this may appear to be an exaggerated and artificially contrived statistical example, it is in fact a quite close approximation to the actual experience of a number of Third World countries during the past two decades.

We are now in a better position to examine five basic questions about the relationship between economic growth, income distribution and poverty.

1. Are rapid economic growth and more equitable distributions of income compatible or conflicting objectives for low-income countries? Alternatively, is rapid growth achievable only at the expense of greater inequalities in the distribution of income or can a lessening of income disparities contribute to higher growth rates?
2. What deternines the character of economic growth – who benefits?
3. What is the extent of relative inequality in Third World countries and how is this related to the extent of absolute poverty?
4. Who are the poor and what are their economic characteristics?
5. What types of policies are required to reduce the magnitude and extent of absolute poverty?

We attempt to answer these questions in the remainder of this and the following chapter.

Inequality and world poverty: a summary of evidence

Basic concepts: size and functional distributions of income

We can get some idea of the answers to questions 3 and 4 relating to the extent and character of inequality and poverty in Third World countries by pulling together some recent evidence from a variety of sources. In this section, we shall define the dimensions of the income distribution and poverty problems and identify some similar elements which characterise the problem in many Third World nations. But first we should be clear about what we are measuring when we speak about the distribution of income.

Economists usually like to distinguish between two principal measures of income distribution both for analytical and quantitative purposes: (1) the 'personal' or 'size' distribution of income; (2) the 'functional' or 'distributive factor share' distribution of income.

1. Size distribution

The personal or size distribution of income is the measure most commonly used by economists. It simply deals with individual persons or households and the total incomes they receive. The way in which that income was received is not considered. What matters is how much each individual earns, irrespective of whether or not the income was derived solely from employment or from other sources such as interest, profits, rents, gifts, inheritance, etc. Moreover, the locational (urban or rural) and occupational sources of the income (e.g. agriculture, manufacturing, commerce, services, etc.) are neglected. If both Mr X and Mr Y receive the same annual personal income, they are classified together irrespective of the fact that Mr X may work 15 hours a day on his farm while Mr Y doesn't work at all but simply collects interest on his inheritance.

Economists and statisticians, therefore, like to arrange all individuals by ascending personal incomes and then divide the total population into distinct groups or 'sizes'. A common method is to divide the population into successive quintiles (five groups) or deciles (ten groups) according to ascending income levels and then determine what proportion of total national income is received by each income group. For example, Table 9.6 shows a hypothetical but fairly typical distribution of income for a Third World country. In this table twenty 'individuals' (households) representing the entire population of the country, are arranged in order of ascending annual personal incomes ranging from the individual with the lowest income (0.8 units) to the one with the highest (15 units). The total or national income of all individuals amounts to 100 units and is the sum of all entries in column 2. In column 3 the population is grouped in quintiles, or five groups of four individuals each. The first quintile represents the bottom 20 per cent of the population on the income scale. This group receives only 5 per cent (i.e. a total of 5 money units) of the total national income. The second quintile (individuals five to eight) receives 9 per cent of the total income.

Table 9.6
An hypothetical (but typical) size distribution of LDC personal income by income shares – quintiles and deciles

Individuals	Personal income (money units)	Percentage share in total income: Quintiles	Deciles
1	0.8		
2	1.0		1.8
3	1.4		
4	1.8	5	3.2
5	1.9		
6	2.0		3.9
7	2.4		
8	2.7	9	5.1
9	2.8		
10	3.0		5.8
11	3.4		
12	3.8	13	7.2
13	4.2		
14	4.8		9.0
15	5.9		
16	7.1	22	13.0
17	10.5		
18	12.0		22.5
19	13.5		
20	15.0	51	28.5
Total 20	Total national income 100.0	Total % 100	Total % 100

Measure of inequality; ratio of bottom 40% to top 20% = 14÷51 = 0.28

Alternatively, the bottom 40 per cent of the population (quintiles one and two) is receiving only 14 per cent of all the incomes received in this country. On the other hand, the fifth quintile or top 20 per cent of the population receives 51 per cent of the total income.

A common measure of income inequality which can be derived from column 3 is the ratio of the incomes received by the bottom 40 per cent compared with the top 20 per cent of the population. This ratio is often used as a measure of the degree of inequality between the two extremes of very poor and very rich in a country. In our example, this inequality ratio is equal to 14 divided by 51 or approximately 1 to 3.7, or 0.28.

To provide a more detailed breakdown of the size distribution of income, decile or 10 per cent shares are listed in column 4. We see for example, that the bottom 10 per cent of the population (the two poorest individuals) is receiving only 1.8 per cent of the total income while the top 10 per cent (the two richest individuals) receives 28.5 per cent. Finally, if we wanted to know what the top 5 per cent of the income distribution scale receives, we would divide the total population into twenty equal groups of individuals (in our example, this would simply be each of the twenty individuals) and calculate the percentage of total income received by the top group. In Table 9.6, we see that the top 5 per cent of the population (the twentieth individual) receives 15 per cent of the income, a higher share than the combined shares of the lowest 40 per cent of the population.

Lorenz curves. Another common way to analyse personal income statistics is to contruct what is known as a Lorenz curve, named after Conrad Lorenz, an American statistician who in 1905 devised this convenient and widely used diagram to show the relationship between population groups and their respective income shares. Figure 9.2 shows how it is done. On the horizontal axis the numbers of income recipients are plotted, not in absolute terms but in cumulative percentages. For example, at point 20 we have the lowest (poorest) 20 per cent of the population, at point 60, the bottom 60 per cent, and at the end of the axis all 100 per cent of the population has been accounted for. The vertical axis portrays the share of total income that is earned or received by each percentage of population. It also is cumulative up to 100 per cent so that both axes are equally long and the entire figure is then enclosed in a square. A diagonal line is drawn from the lower lefthand corner (the origin) of the square to the upper righthand corner. At every point on that diagonal, the percentage of income received is *exactly equal* to the percentage of income recipients; for example, the point halfway along the length of the diagonal represents 50 per cent of the income being distributed to exactly 50 per cent of the population. At the threequarter point on the diagonal, 75 per cent of the income would be distributed to 75 per cent of the population. In other words, the diagonal line in Figure 9.2 is representative of 'perfect equality' in the size distribution of income. Each percentage group of income recipients is receiving that same percentage of the total income; for example, the bottom 40 per cent receives 40 per cent of the income while the top 5 per cent receives only 5 per cent of the total income.

Now the Lorenz curve shows the *actual* quantitative relationship between the percentage of income recipients and the percentage of the total income which they did in fact receive during, say, a given year. In Figure 9.2 we have plotted this Lorenz curve using the decile data contained in

Figure 9.2
The Lorenz curve

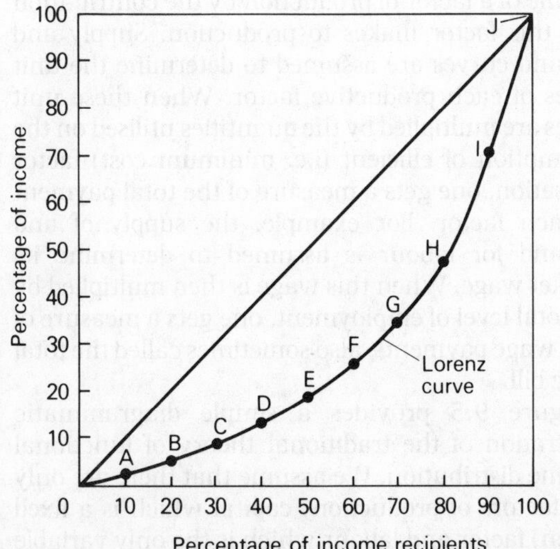

Table 9.6. In other words, we have divided both the horizontal and vertical axes into ten equal segments corresponding to each of the ten decile groups. Point A shows that the bottom 10 per cent of the population receives only 1.8 per cent of the total income. Point B shows that the bottom 20 per cent is receiving 5 per cent of the total income, and so on for

Figure 9.3
The greater the curvature of the Lorenz line, the greater the relative degree of inequality

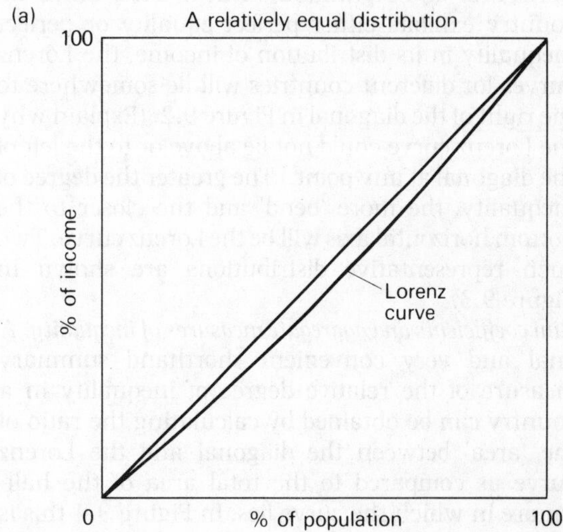

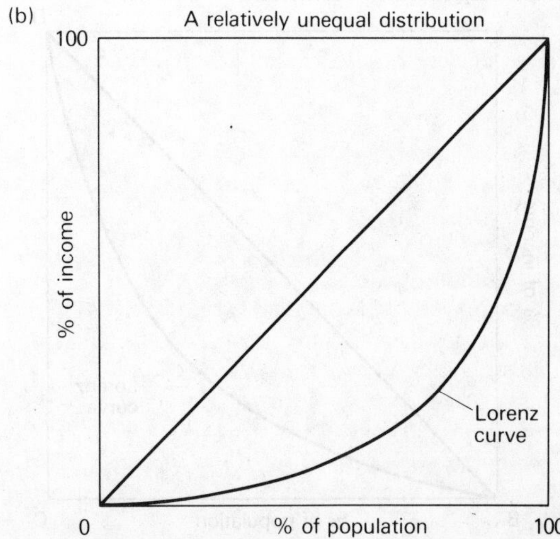

each of the other eight cumulative decile groups. Note that at the halfway point, E, 50 per cent of the population is in fact only receiving 19.8 per cent of the total income.

The more the Lorenz line curves away from the diagonal (perfect equality), the greater the degree of inequality represented. The extreme case of perfect inequality, a situation in which one person receives *all* the national income while everybody else receives nothing, would be represented by the coexistence of the Lorenz curve with the bottom horizontal and righthand vertical axes. Since no country exhibits either perfect equality or perfect inequality in its distribution of income, the Lorenz curves for different countries will lie somewhere to the right of the diagonal in Figure 9.2. (Explain why the Lorenz curve could not lie above or to the left of the diagonal at any point.) The greater the degree of inequality, the more 'bend' and the closer to the bottom horizontal axis will be the Lorenz curve. Two such representative distributions are shown in Figure 9.3.

Gini coefficients and aggregate measures of inequality. A final and very convenient shorthand summary measure of the relative degree of inequality in a country can be obtained by calculating the ratio of the 'area' between the diagonal and the Lorenz curve as compared to the total area of the half-square in which the curve lies. In Figure 9.4 this is the ratio of the shaded area A to the total area of the triangle BCD. This ratio is known as the 'Gini concentration ratio' or more simply, the **Gini coefficient**, named after the Italian statistician C. Gini who first formulated it in 1912. Gini coefficients are aggregate inequality measures and can vary anywhere from zero (perfect equality) to one (perfect inequality). In fact, as we shall soon discover, the Gini coefficient for countries with highly unequal income distributions typically lies between 0.5 and 0.7 while for countries with relatively equitable distributions it is of the order of 0.2 to 0.35. The coefficient for our hypothetical distribution of Table 9.6 and Figure 9.2 is approximately 0.61, a relatively unequal distribution.

Figure 9.4
Estimating the Gini coefficient

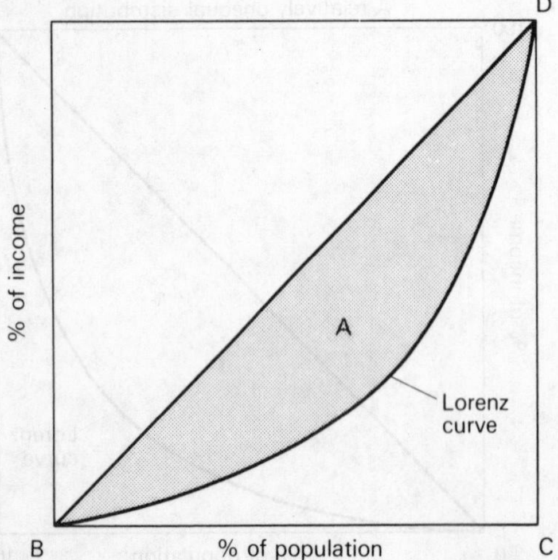

2. Functional distribution

The second common measure of income distribution used by economists, the 'functional' or 'factor share distribution', attempts to explain the share of total national income that each factor of production receives. Instead of looking at individuals as separate entities, the theory and measure of functional income distribution inquires into the percentage that labour receives as a whole and compares this with the percentages of total income distributed in the form of rent, interest and profit (i.e. the returns to land and financial and physical capital). Although specific individuals may receive income from all these sources, this is not a matter of concern for the functional approach.

A sizable body of theoretical economic literature has been built up around the concept of functional income distribution. It attempts to explain the income of a factor of production by the contribution that this factor makes to production. Supply and demand curves are assumed to determine the unit prices of each productive factor. When these unit prices are multiplied by the quantities utilised on the assumption of efficient (i.e. minimum cost) factor utilisation, one gets a measure of the total payment to each factor. For example, the supply of and demand for labour is assumed to determine its market wage. When this wage is then multiplied by the total level of employment, one gets a measure of total wage payments, also sometimes called the total wage bill.

Figure 9.5 provides a simple diagrammatic illustration of the traditional theory of functional income distribution. We assume that there are only two factors of production; capital which is a fixed (given) factor and labour which is the only variable

Figure 9.5
Functional income distribution in a market economy: an illustration

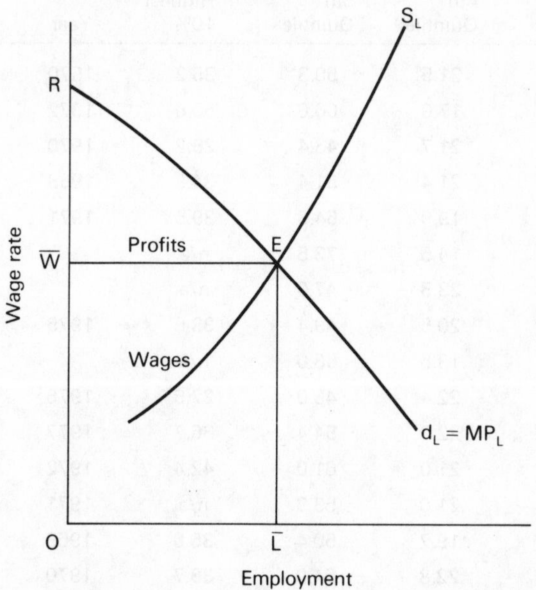

factor. Under competitive market assumptions, the demand for labour will be determined by labour's marginal product – i.e. additional workers will be hired up to the point where the value of their marginal product equals their real wage. But, in accordance with the principle of diminishing marginal products (see Chapter 4), this demand for labour will be a declining function of the numbers employed. Such a negatively sloped labour demand curve is shown by line d_L in Figure 9.5. With an upward sloping labour supply curve S_L the 'equilibrium' wage will be equal to OW and the equilibrium level of employment will be OL. Total national output (= total national income) will be represented by the area OREL.[4] This national income will be distributed in two shares – OWEL going to workers in the form of wages and WRE remaining as capitalist profits (i.e. the return to owners of capital). In a competitive market economy, therefore, factor prices are determined by factor supply and demand curves while factor shares always combine to exhaust the total national product. Income is distributed by 'function' – labourers receive 'wages', owners of land receive 'rents' and capitalists obtain 'profits'. It is all a very neat and logical theory since each and every factor gets paid only in accordance with what it contributes to national output – no more, no less.

Unfortunately, the relevance of the functional theory is greatly vitiated by its failure to take into account the important role and influence of 'non-market' forces such as 'power' in determining these factor prices – e.g. the role of collective bargaining between employers and trade unions in the setting of 'modern sector' wage rates and the power of capitalists and wealthy landowners to manipulate prices on capital, land and output to their own personal advantages. We shall have more to say about the relative strengths and weaknesses of the size versus the functional approach to analysing income distribution later in the chapter. But first we review some empirical data to get a more precise idea of the magnitude of the problems of inequality and poverty in a wide range of developing nations.

Inequality: variations among countries

As a first step in determining the significance of the income distribution and poverty problems in Third World countries, let us look at recent data collected from 15 countries on the percentage shares in total national income going to different percentile groups. This is done in Table 9.7. Though methods of collection, degree of coverage and specific definitions of personal income may vary from country to country, the figures recorded in Table 9.7 do give a concise picture of the magnitude of income inequalities in these Third World countries. For example, we see from the last row by averaging income shares for different percentile groups among all 15 countries, that on average the *poorest* 20 per cent of the population receives only 4.3 per cent of the income while the *highest* 10 and 20 percentile groups receive 36.3 and 54.4 per cent of total national income respectively.

Now consider the relationship, if any, between levels of per capita income and degree of inequality for a large sample of both developed and less developed countries. Table 9.8 presents a cross-classification of these countries into three groups. The groupings correspond to high, moderate and low degrees of inequality, as measured by specified ranges of the Gini coefficient, and high, middle and

[4] The summation of each worker's 'marginal' product will equal total national product (GNP) which will be distributed as the national income.

Table 9.7
Some income distribution estimates

	Lowest 20%	2nd Quintile	3rd Quintile	4th Quintile	5th Quintile	Highest 10%	Year
Argentina	4.4	9.7	14.1	21.5	50.3	35.2	1970
Brazil	2.0	5.0	9.4	17.0	66.6	50.6	1972
Sri Lanka	7.5	11.7	15.7	21.7	43.4	28.2	1970
Chile	4.4	9.0	13.8	21.4	51.4	34.8	1968
Costa Rica	3.3	8.7	13.3	19.9	54.8	39.5	1971
Ecuador	2.5	3.9	5.6	14.5	73.5	n/a	
Egypt	4.2	9.8	15.5	23.5	47.0	n/a	
India	7.0	9.2	13.9	20.5	49.4	33.6	1975
Kenya	3.8	6.2	8.5	13.5	68.0	n/a	
Rep. of Korea	5.7	11.2	15.4	22.4	45.0	27.5	1976
Mexico	2.9	7.4	13.2	22.0	54.4	36.7	1977
Peru	1.9	5.1	11.0	21.0	61.0	42.4	1972
Philippines	3.7	8.2	13.2	21.0	53.9	n/a	1971
Tanzania	5.8	10.2	13.9	19.7	50.4	35.6	1969
Venezuela	3.0	7.3	12.9	22.8	54.0	35.7	1970
Averages	4.3	8.3	12.8	20.2	54.4	36.3	

Source: *World Development Report, 1981*, Annex Table 24.

low income levels in accordance with specified ranges of real GNP per head. As an alternative inequality measure to the Gini coefficient, Table 9.8 provides a measure of the degree of concentration of incomes at the lowest and highest levels of the distribution scale by showing for each country the ratio of the income share of the lowest 40 per cent to the highest 20 per cent of the respective populations.

A number of specific and interesting conclusions emerge from a careful examination of Table 9.8.

1. All countries, whether capitalist, socialist or 'mixed', show some degree of inequality. This is important because we need to have some idea of what kinds of distributions are practical and feasible; in other words, to establish some reasonable 'benchmarks' or 'targets' towards which a country might strive rather than to attempt to achieve the idealised, impractical and perhaps undesirable, goal of perfect equality.
2. Socialist countries like Czechoslovakia, Hungary, Poland and Bulgaria have the highest degree of equality in their distribution of incomes (i.e. they have the lowest Gini coefficients).
3. Developed countries on the whole exhibit a relatively more equal distribution than *most* Third World countries. This is primarily because most economically advanced countries have been able to develop over the years effective mechanisms to transfer some proportion of their incomes from rich to poor. For example, progressively higher income tax rates combined with public expenditure, social security payments, unemployment compensation, and outright welfare payments to the very poor are methods used to temper the wide income disparities which might normally result in the course of private economic activity. Such income transfer mechanisms are still either largely non-existent or ineffectively administered in most underdeveloped countries.
4. Third World countries have a significant variation in their degree of inequality as shown by the wide range of their Gini coefficients.
5. Perhaps more importantly, there seems to be no

Table 9.8
Classification of countries by income levels and inequality

High Inequality Gini > .50				
Country	Year	Per Capita Income	Ratio	Gini
Income US $300				
Brazil*	(70)	231	6.5/66.7	.61
Colombia*	(70)	251	9.4/59.5	.54
Ecuador*	(70)	202	6.4/73.5	.66
Gabon*	(60)	261	6.0/71.0	.65
Honduras	(67–68)	224	7.3/67.5	.61
Iraq*	(56)	172	6.8/68.0	.61
Madagascar*	(60)	93	13.5/61.0	.52
Peru*	(70–71)	297	6.5/60.0	.57
Rhodesia*	(68)	214	8.2/69.0	.62
Senegal*	(60)	171	10.0/64.0	.56
Middle Income $500–$750				
Jamaica	(58)	388	8.2/61.5	.56
Lebanon	(55–60)	454	13.0/61.0	.52
Mexico	(68)	464	10.2/65.8	.58
Panama*	(69)	560	9.4/59.3	.54
South Africa*	(65)	530	6.2/58.0	.56
Venezuela	(62)	750	9.7/58.0	.52

Moderate Inequality Gini = .40–.50				
Country	Year	Per Capita Income	Ratio	Gini
Income US $300				
Dahomey*	(59)	65	15.5/50.0	.44
El Salvador*	(69)	248	12.7/52.0	.45
Guyana	(55–56)	272	14.0/45.7	.40
India	(61–64)	84	14.0/54.0	.46
Philippines	(65)	150	11.6/55.4	.50
Sudan	(63)	91	14.2/50.3	.43
Tanzania	(67)	70	14.0/57.0	.48
Thailand	(62)	92	12.9/57.7	.50
Tunisia*	(61)	156	10.5/55.0	.50
Zambia	(59)	150	14.6/57.0	.49
Middle Income $500–$750				
Argentina	(61)	681	17.3/52.0	.42
Chile	(68)	427	13.0/56.8	.49
Costa Rica	(71)	423	14.7/50.6	.43
Uruguay	(67)	460	14.3/47.4	.42
High Income > US $750				
Denmark*	(68)	1,838	13.6/47.6	.42
Finland*	(62)	1,193	11.1/49.3	.45
France	(62)	1,373	9.5/53.7	.50
Germany W.*	(64)	1,614	15.4/52.9	.45
Netherlands*	(67)	1,437	13.6/48.5	.43
Puerto Rico	(63)	988	13.7/50.6	.44

Low Inequality Gini < .40				
Country	Year	Per Capita Income	Ratio	Gini
Income US $300				
Ceylon	(69–70)	155	17.0/45.0	.37
Taiwan	(64)	201	20.4/40.1	.32
Chad*	(58)	63	18.0/43.0	.35
Ivory Coast	(59)	139	17.5/55.0	.43
Korea, South	(70)	180	18.0/45.0	.36
Libya	(62)	220	23.5/37.0	.26
Malaysia	(57–58)	203	17.7/43.9	.36
Niger*	(60)	73	18.0/42.0	.36
Pakistan (E & W)	(63–64)	83	17.5/45.0	.37
Uganda*	(70)	110	17.1/47.1	.38
Middle Income $500–$750				
Bulgaria*	(62)	407	26.8/33.2	.21
Greece*	(57)	341	21.0/49.5	.37
Israel*	(57)	686	20.2/39.4	.30
Poland*	(64)	649	23.4/36.0	.25
Spain	(64–65)	572	17.0/45.2	.38
Surinam	(62)	311	21.7/42.6	.31
Yugoslavia	(68)	451	18.5/41.5	.33
High Income* US $750				
Canada	(65)	2,057	20.0/40.2	.32
Czechoslovakia*	(64)	880	27.6/31.0	.18
Hungary*	(69)	870	24.0/33.5	.24
Japan	(63)	780	20.7/40.0	.31
New Zealand*	(68–69)	1,800	15.5/42.0	.37
Norway*	(63)	1,609	16.6/40.5	.35
Sweden*	(63)	2,220	14.0/44.0	.39
United Kingdom	(68)	1,599	18.8/39.0	.32
United States*	(70)	3,603	19.7/38.8	.31

The data on countries without the asterisk is based on household size distribution.
Per Capita Income is in 1964 US $ to the closest two years.
Ratios are ratio of bottom 40 per cent to top 20 per cent.
* The data is based on active workers' income distribution.
Source: Montak Ahluwalia, 'Dimensions of the Problem', in Chenery, Duloy and Jolly, (eds.), *Redistribution with growth: an approach to policy,* Washington 1973, p (2) 4.

apparent relationship between levels of per capita income and the degree of income concentration. Even within the group of very low income countries (those with per capita incomes of less than $300) we see from Table 9.8 that the share of income accruing to the bottom 40 per cent varies from 6.5 per cent (Brazil) to over 20 per cent (Taiwan).

'Absolute' poverty: its extent and magnitude

Now let us switch our attention from relative income shares of various percentile groups within a given population to the more significant question of the extent and magnitude of 'absolute poverty' in Third World countries. In Chapter 5, remember, we saw that the extent of 'absolute poverty' can be defined by the number of people living below a specified minimum level of income – an imaginary 'international poverty line'. Such a line knows no national boundaries and is independent of the level of national per capita income. Absolute poverty can and does exist, therefore, just as readily in New York city as it does in Calcutta, Cairo, Lagos or Bogota – although its magnitude is likely to be much lower in terms of total numbers or percentages of the total population. In a recent paper focused on the dimensions of Third World poverty and its relationship to economic growth, World Bank economists Ahluwalia, Carter and Chenery concluded that 'almost 40 per cent of the population of the developing countries live in absolute poverty defined in terms of income levels that are insufficient to provide adequate nutrition. The bulk of the poor are in the poorest countries: in South Asia, Indonesia and sub-Saharan Africa. These countries account for two-thirds of the total (world) population and well over three-fourths of the population in poverty. The incidence of poverty is 60 per cent or more in countries having the lowest level of real GNP'.[5]

Table 9.9 shows the authors' estimates of absolute poverty levels in 1975 with projections to the year 2000 for 36 Third World countries divided into 'low' (less than $150 per capita incomes measured in 1970 US dollars), 'medium' (between $150 and $325) and 'high' ($325 to $1 300) per capita income levels. Note that they project substantial declines in absolute poverty – though by no means an eradication of it – by the turn of the century. However, this projection is based on several optimistic assumptions regarding future trends in real economic growth and the distribution of its benefits. The year 2000 projections can be taken, therefore, as lying at the optimistic end of the spectrum of possibilities.

[5] M. S. Ahluwalia, N. Carter and H. Chenery, 'Growth and Poverty in Developing Countries', *Journal of Development Economics*, Vol. 6., Sept. 1979, p. 306.

One final point, analogous to conclusion 5 above regarding the apparent absence of any necessary relationship between levels of per capita income and the distribution of that income, needs to be mentioned. It is that **high per capita incomes** *per se* **do not guarantee the absence of significant numbers of absolute poor.** Since the share of income accruing to the lowest percentile of a population can vary widely from one country to another, it is possible for a country with a high per capita income to have a larger percentage of its population below an international poverty line than a country with a lower per capita income. Thus, for example, if we look again at Table 9.9 we see that Taiwan and Guatemala had approximately the same level of real per capita income in 1975 even though the proportion of Guatemala's population below the poverty line is more than twice as large as that of Taiwan. Similarly, Korea with 60 per cent of the per capita income level of Peru has a proportion of its low income people below the poverty line that is 40 per cent the size of Peru's (6 compared with 15 per cent of their respective populations). This simply shows that problems of poverty and highly unequal distributions of income are not just the result of natural economic growth processes. Rather, they depend on the *character* of that economic growth and the political and institutional arrangements according to which rising national incomes are distributed among the broad segments of a population.

Economic characteristics of poverty groups

So far we have painted a broad picture of the income distribution and poverty problem by showing how the magnitude of absolute poverty results from a combination of low per capita incomes and highly unequal distributions of that income in many Third World countries. Clearly, for any given distribution of income, the higher the level of per capita income the lower will be the numbers of the absolutely poor. But, as we have seen, higher levels of per capita income are no guarantee of lower levels of poverty. An understanding of the nature of the size distribution of income, therefore, is central to any analysis of the poverty problem in low income countries.

But painting a broad picture of Third World poverty is not enough. Before we can formulate

Table 9.9
Income growth and poverty in 36 developing countries, 1975 and 2000 (projected)

Country	1975 GNP per capita	GNP growth rates 1960–75	GNP growth rates 1975–2000	Share of lowest 40 per cent 1975 estimate	Share of lowest 40 per cent 2000 projection	Percentage of population in poverty, 1975	Number of people in poverty (millions) 1975 estimate	Number of people in poverty (millions) 2000 projection
Group A (under $150)								
1. Bangladesh	72	2.4	4.6	20.1	17.4	60	52	56
2. Ethiopia	81	4.3	4.1	16.8	15.0	62	19	25
3. Burma	88	3.2	2.5	15.7	15.2	56	20	29
4. Indonesia	90	5.2	5.5	16.1	12.7	62	76	30
5. Uganda	115	4.0	3.2	14.4	14.0	45	6	12
6. Zaire	105	4.3	4.8	14.6	12.7	49	11	13
7. Sudan	112	3.0	6.0	14.5	12.0	47	10	8
8. Tanzania	118	6.8	5.4	14.3	12.3	46	8	9
9. Pakistan	121	5.6	5.2	16.5	14.5	34	32	26
10 India	108	3.6	4.5	17.0	14.6	46	277	167
Subtotal	**99**	**3.8**	**4.7**	**16.7**	**13.9**	**49**	**510**	**375**
Group B ($150–$325)								
11. Kenya	168	7.0	5.9	8.9	7.7	48	7	11
12. Nigeria	176	7.1	5.2	13.0	11.8	27	27	30
13. Philippines	182	5.6	7.3	11.6	10.3	29	14	6
14. Sri Lanka	185	4.2	3.8	19.3	18.2	10	2	2
15. Senegal	227	1.5	4.0	9.6	8.9	29	1	2
16. Egypt	238	4.2	6.1	13.9	13.5	14	7	5
17. Thailand	237	7.5	6.7	11.5	10.9	23	13	4
18. Ghana	255	2.7	2.1	11.2	11.9	19	2	6
19. Morocco	266	4.4	6.2	13.3	10.9	16	4	2
20. Ivory Coast	325	7.7	5.8	10.4	10.4	14	1	1
Subtotal	**209**	**5.5**	**5.8**	**12.0**	**10.1**	**24**	**81**	**70**
Group C ($325–$1300)								
21. Korea	325	9.3	8.1	16.9	19.1	6	3	1
22. Chile	386	2.3	6.0	13.1	14.3	9	1	1
23. Zambia	363	3.4	4.9	13.0	12.9	7	0	1
24. Colombia	352	5.6	7.4	9.9	11.5	14	5	2
25. Turkey	379	6.4	6.3	9.3	10.4	11	6	4
26. Tunisia	425	6.1	7.5	11.1	13.3	9	1	0
27. Malaysia	471	6.7	6.7	11.1	13.3	8	1	1
28. Taiwan	499	9.1	6.2	22.3	24.4	4	1	0
29. Guatemala	497	6.1	6.0	11.3	12.4	9	1	1
30. Brazil	509	7.2	7.9	9.1	11.9	8	16	7
31. Peru	503	5.7	6.3	7.3	8.8	15	3	2
32. Iran	572	9.5	7.2	8.2	11.0	8	5	2
33. Mexico	758	6.8	6.8	8.2	10.8	10	8	6
34. Yugoslavia	828	5.8	6.1	18.8	23.9	4	1	0
35. Argentina	1,097	4.0	4.5	15.1	18.5	3	1	1
36. Venezuela	1,288	5.8	6.8	8.5	12.9	5	1	1
Subtotal	**577**	**6.4**	**6.9**	**9.9**	**10.0**	**8**	**54**	**30**
Total	**237**	**5.4**	**6.2**	**9.8**	**6.5**	**35**	**644**	**475**

Source: M. S. Ahluwalia *et al.*, 'Growth and Poverty in Developing Countries,' *Journal of Development Economics*, Vol. 6, Sept. 1979, Tables 1 and 2.

effective policies and programmes to attack poverty at its source, we need some specific knowledge of who these poverty groups are and what are their economic characteristics. As we show in the next chapter when we deal with alternative policies to combat poverty, it is *not* sufficient simply to focus on raising growth rates of GNP in the expectation or hope that this national income growth will 'trickle down' to improve living standards for the very poor. On the contrary, direct attacks on poverty by means of poverty-focused policies and plans appear to be more effective both in the short and longer runs. But one cannot attack poverty directly without detailed knowledge of its location, extent and characteristics.

Perhaps the most valid generalisation about the poor is that they are disproportionately located in the rural areas and that they are primarily engaged in agricultural and associated activities. Data from a broad cross-section of Third World nations support this generalisation. We find, for example, that about two-thirds of the very poor scratch out their livelihood from subsistence agriculture either as small farmers or low-paid farm workers. The remaining one-third are located partly in rural areas (engaged in petty services) and partly on the fringes and marginal areas of urban centres where they engage in various forms of self-employment such as street-hawking, trading, petty services and small-scale commerce. But, on average, we may conclude that **about 75 to 80 per cent of all target poverty groups are located in the rural areas of Africa and Asia and about 70 per cent in Latin America.**

It is interesting to note in light of the rural concentration of absolute poverty that the largest share of most LDC government expenditures over the past two decades has been directed towards the urban area and, within that area, towards the relatively affluent modern manufacturing and commercial sectors. Whether in the realm of directly productive economic investments or in the fields of education, health, housing and other social services, this urban modern sector bias in government expenditures is at the core of many of the development problems to be discussed in succeeding chapters. We need only point out here that, in view of the disproportionate numbers of the very poor who reside in rural areas, any policy designed to alleviate poverty must necessarily be directed to a large extent towards rural development in general and the agricultural sector in particular (see Chapters 15 and 16).

Economic growth and the extent of poverty

We mentioned in the previous section that exclusive reliance on the natural forces of economic growth significantly to reduce the extent of absolute poverty in most developing countries would probably be insufficient. This issue is so central to development theory that it warrants further examination. The basic question is: does the pursuit of economic growth along traditional GNP maximising lines tend to improve, worsen or have no perceptible effect on the distribution of income and the extent of poverty in newly developing countries? Unfortunately, economists do not at present possess any definitive knowledge of the specific factors that affect changes in the distribution of income over time for individual countries. Professor Kuznets, to whom we owe so much for his pioneering analysis of the historical growth patterns of contemporary developed countries, has suggested that in the early stages of economic growth the distribution of income will tend to worsen while at later stages it will improve. Although long-run data for Western nations seem to support Professor Kuznets's proposition, a look at recent data from Third World nations is less convincing.

In Figure 9.6 we have plotted rates of growth of GNP for 13 Third World countries on the horizontal axis and the growth rate of income of the lowest 40 per cent of their population along the vertical axis. The data are for two points in time, shown in parentheses after each country, and the figure is intended to reveal any obvious relationship between growth rates of GNP and improvement in income levels for the very poor. Each country's data, therefore, are plotted in the figure at a point reflecting its combination of GNP growth and the income growth of the lowest 40 per cent of its population. Countries above the 45° line are those countries where the distribution of income has improved (i.e. the incomes of the bottom 40 per cent grew faster than the overall GNP growth rate), while countries below the 45° line have experienced a worsening of their income distributions over the indicated period.

The scatter of points in Figure 9.6 does *not* reveal any strong or obvious relationship between GNP growth and the distribution of income. High growth rates do not necessarily worsen the distribution of income as some have suggested. Indeed, countries like Taiwan, Iran and Korea have experienced relatively high rates of GNP growth and had improved, or at least unchanged, distributions of income. Nevertheless, there are countries like Mexico and Panama which have grown just as fast but experienced a deterioration of their income distribution. On the other hand, there does not seem to be a necessary relationship between low GNP growth and improved income distribution. In several Third World countries like India, Peru and the Philippines low rates of GNP growth appear to have been accompanied by a deterioration of the relative income shares of the bottom 40 per cent. Yet, Sri Lanka, Colombia, Costa Rica and El Salvador with similarly low GNP growth rates managed to improve the relative economic well-being of their low income populations.

Although admittedly sketchy and limited to a short period of time, these data do suggest once again that it is the 'character' of economic growth (i.e. how it is achieved, who participates, which sectors are given priority, what institutional arrangements are designed and emphasised, etc.) that determines the degree to which that growth is or is not reflected in the improved living standards of the very poor. Clearly, it is not the mere fact of rapid growth *per se* that determines the nature of its distributional benefits.

This 'character of economic growth' argument is further reinforced by an extensive empirical study of forty-three developing nations in which the relationship between the shares of income accruing to the poorest 60 per cent of the population on one hand and a country's aggregate economic performance on the other were analysed.[6] It was found that the principal impact of economic development on income distribution has been, on average, to *decrease* both the absolute and the relative incomes of the poor. There was no evidence of any automatic 'trickle-down' of the benefits of economic growth to the very poor. On the contrary, the growth process experienced by these 43 LDCs has typically led to a 'trickle-up' in favour of the small middle class and especially the very rich. The authors, therefore, concluded that 'economic structure, not level or rate of economic growth, is the basic determinant of patterns of income distribution'.[7] We pursue this important issue further in Chapter 10.

Figure 9.6
A comparison of rates of GNP growth and income growth rates of the 'bottom 40 per cent' in selected LDCs

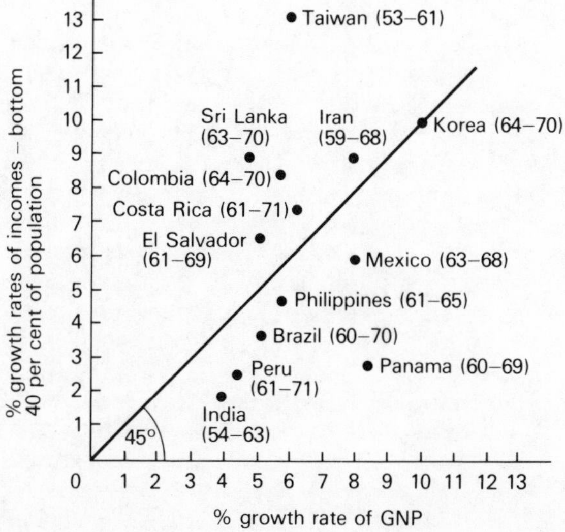

Concepts for review

propensity to consume	rent, interest and profits
luxury v. necessity goods	quintiles and deciles
aggregate consumer demand and income distribution	highly skewed distribution of income
personal income	income inequality
size distribution of income	Lorenz curve
	Gini coefficient
functional distribution of income	absolute poverty
	scatter diagram
factor shares and marginal productivity	

Questions for discussion

1. Most development economists now seem to agree that the level and rate of growth of GNP and per

[6] I. Adelman and C. T. Morris, *Economic Growth and Social Equity in Developing Countries*, Stanford University Press, 1973.

[7] *Ibid.*, p. 186.

capita income do not provide sufficient or even accurate measures of a country's 'development'. What is the essence of their argument? Give some examples.
2. Distinguish between size and functional distributions of income. Explain how each concept might be used to analyse income distribution in a nation. Which do you feel is the more appropriate concept? Explain.
3. What is meant by 'absolute' poverty? Why should we be concerned with the measurement of absolute poverty in Third World nations?
4. What are the principal economic characteristics of poverty groups? What do these characteristics tell us about the possible nature of a 'poverty focused' development strategy?
5. In the text, when we examined statistics from a wide range of Third World countries, we found *no* direct relationship (positive or negative) between a country's level of GNP, GNP per capita or rate of economic growth and its extent of absolute poverty, or the degree of equality in its distribution of income. Assuming that these data are indeed correct, what do they tell us about the importance of the character of a nation's growth process, and about its institutional structure?
6. What is the relationship between a Lorenz curve and a Gini coefficient? Give some examples of how Lorenz curves and Gini coefficients can be used as summary measures of equality and inequality in a nation's distribution of income.

Further reading

For the most comprehensive description of the various meanings and measures of income distribution see JAN PEN, *Income Distribution*, Penguin, 1971, chs 1–3. For the most up-to-date summary of the poverty and income distribution problem in LDCs using recent cross-country data with appropriate analysis and alternative policy strategies, see HOLLIS CHENERY, *et al.*, *Redistribution with Growth: an approach to policy*, Oxford University Press, 1974 and M. S. AHLUWALIA *et al.*, 'Growth and Poverty in Developing Nations', *Journal of Development Economics*, Vol. 6., Sept. 1979. Other useful readings include: GUNNAR MYRDAL, 'Equity and growth', *World Development*, i. 11, November 1973; FELIX PAUKERT, 'Income distribution at different levels of development: a survey of evidence', *International Labour Review*, August–September 1973; A. B. ATKINSON, 'On the measurement of inequality', *Journal of Economic Theory*, September 1970; I. ADELMAN and C. T. MORRIS, 'An anatomy of income distribution patterns in developing nations', *Development Digest*, October 1971; ARUN SHOURIE, 'Growth, poverty and inequalities', *Foreign Affairs*, li, 2, January 1973 and World Bank, *World Development Reports, 1978 and 1980*, Oxford, New York, 1978 and 1980.

Chapter 10 Attacking poverty and inequality: the policy options

The basic problem of development should be redefined as a selective attack on the worst forms of poverty. Development goals must be defined in terms of the progressive reduction and eventual elimination of malnutrition, disease, illiteracy, squalor, unemployment and inequalities.
Mahbub ul Haq[1]

A society that is not socially just and does not intend to be, puts its own future in danger.
Pope John Paul II, Brazil, 1980

Introduction

Redefining goals and objectives: growth with improved income distribution

The necessity of reorienting development priorities away from exclusive preoccupation with maximising rates of GNP growth and towards broader social objectives like the eradication of poverty and the reduction of excessive income disparities is now widely recognised throughout the Third World. The gap between problem redefinition and specific action, however, can be quite enormous. Abstracting from the serious political, institutional and power structure problems of a reorientation of development strategy towards greater concern for the very poor, economics itself has very little in the way of either a received theory or a set of agreed policies to eradicate poverty. Unlike theories of how economies grow and what types of investment strategies can maximise economic growth rates, there is relatively little consensus among economists on what strategies should be followed, and whether *any* strictly 'economic' strategy can eliminate or greatly reduce the incidence of poverty. This is not only because the problems of poverty and income distribution are largely political and institutional in origin, but also because the theoretical determinants of income distribution are poorly understood in the developed countries towards which the bulk of existing economic theory has been directed, let alone the underdeveloped countries, where much of this theory is irrelevant.

But the history of economics has been marked by the evolution of theories and concepts that have grown out of responses to specific real world economic problems and not merely as a natural organic process unrelated to the world at large. The Malthusian theory of population, the Marxist theory of the increasing misery of the masses, the neoclassical theory of maximising behaviour and atomistic competition, the Keynesian theory of income and employment determination, and the Harrod–Domar theories of economic growth all represent direct reponses to what were perceived to be the principal economic and social problems of the times. Given the current emphasis on problems of poverty and income distribution, therefore, it is not unreasonable to anticipate that as economists increasingly turn their attention away from exclusive concern with growth, new and better theories and policies will emerge to comprehend and cope with these very serious problems that are the daily scourge of hundreds of millions of people throughout the world.

Although rapid economic growth does not automatically provide the answer, it nevertheless remains an essential ingredient in any realistic poverty-focused programme of development. Nor are rapid economic growth and more equitable distributions of income incompatible as development objectives. The choice is not between more growth and more equality but concerns the *type* of economic growth Third World countries wish to

[1] Director of Policy Planning, World Bank, formerly Chief Economist, National Planning Commission of Pakistan.

pursue – one that principally benefits the very rich or one in which the benefits are more widely distributed. In the next section we present some of the economic arguments why growth and equality are not in conflict. For present purposes, however, we may conclude that **development strategy requires not only a concern with accelerating economic growth but also a direct concern with improving material standards of living for those very sizable segments of Third World populations who have been largely bypassed by the economic growth of the last two decades.**

A principal development objective, therefore, should be to generate a desired pattern of overall and broad-based income growth with special emphasis on accelerating the growth of incomes of target poverty groups. Such an aim requires a very different strategy from one which is simply oriented towards maximising the growth rate of GNP, irrespective of the distributional consequences.

The role of economic analysis: redistribution from growth

Growth v. equity: the non-existence of conflict

Although much of economic analysis has been strangely silent on the relationship between economic growth and the resulting distribution of income, some theorists believe that highly unequal distributions are *necessary* conditions for generating rapid growth. In fact, in the 1960s and 1970s, the explicit and implicit acceptance of this proposition by economists from both developed and less developed countries has tended to turn their individual and collective attentions away from problems of poverty and income distribution. If wide inequalities are a necessary condition of maximum growth and if in the long run maximum growth is a necessary condition of rising standards of living for all through the natural 'trickle down' processes of competitive and mixed economic systems, then it follows, according to this theory, that direct concern with the alleviation of poverty would be self-defeating. Needless to say, such a viewpoint, whether correct or not, provides a psychological, if not conscious, rationalisation for the accumulation of wealth by powerful elite groups.

The basic economic argument to justify large income inequalities was the assumption that high personal and corporate incomes were necessary conditions of **saving** which made possible **investment** and economic growth through a mechanism such as the Harrod–Domar model described in Chapter 6. *If* the rich save and invest significant proportions of their incomes while the poor spend all their income on consumption goods, and *if* GNP growth rates are directly related to the proportion of national income which is saved, then, apparently, an economy characterised by highly unequal distributions of income would save more and grow faster than one with a more equitable distribution of income. Eventually, it was assumed that national and per capita incomes would be high enough to make possible sizable redistributions of income via tax and subsidy programmes. But until such a time is reached, any attempt to redistribute incomes significantly would only serve to lower growth rates and delay the time when a larger income pie could be cut up into bigger slices for all population groups.

There are four general reasons why we believe this argument to be incorrect and why **greater equality in Third World countries may in fact be a condition for self-sustaining economic growth.**

First, common sense, supported by a wealth of recent empirical data, bears witness to the fact that, unlike the historical experience of the now developed countries, the rich in contemporary Third World countries are *not* noted for their frugality nor for their desire to save and invest substantial proportions of their incomes in the *local* economy. Instead, landlords, businessmen, politicians and other rich elites are known to squander much of their incomes on imported luxury goods, expensive houses, foreign travel and investment in gold, jewellery and foreign banking accounts. Such savings and investments do not add to the nation's productive resources. In fact, they represent substantial drains on these resources in that the income so dervied is often extracted from the sweat and toil of common, uneducated and unskilled labourers. In short, the rich do not necessarily save and invest significantly larger proportions of their incomes (in the real economic sense of 'productive' domestic saving and investment) than the poor. Therefore, a growth strategy based on sizable and growing income inequalities may in reality be nothing more than an opportunistic myth designed to perpetuate the vested interests and maintain the *status quo* of the economic and political elites of Third World nations, often at the expense of the great majority of the general population. Such strategies might better be called 'antidevelopmental'.[2]

Second, the low incomes and low levels of living for the poor which are manifested in poor health, nutrition and education can lower their economic productivity and thereby lead directly and indirectly to a slower-growing economy. Strategies to raise the incomes and living standard of, say, the bottom 40 per cent would, therefore, contribute not only to their material wellbeing but also to the productivity and income of the economy as a whole.

Third, raising the income levels of the poor will stimulate an overall increase in the demand for locally produced necessity products like food and clothing. On the other hand the rich tend to spend more of their additional incomes on imported luxury goods. Rising demands for local goods provide a greater stimulus to local production, local employment and local investment, and thus create the conditions for rapid economic growth and a broader popular participation in that growth.

Fourth and finally, a more equitable distribution of income achieved through the reduction of mass poverty can stimulate healthy economic expansion by acting as a powerful material and psychological incentive to widespread public participation in the development process. On the other hand, wide income disparities and substantial absolute poverty can act as a powerful material and psychological disincentive to economic progress. It may even create the conditions for its ultimate rejection by the masses of frustrated and politically explosive people, especially those with considerable education.

GNP as a biased index of national development and welfare

We have already criticised reliance on GNP and its growth rate as the principal indicator of development and economic wellbeing. Figures for GNP per capita give no indication of how national income is actually distributed and who is benefiting most from the growth of production. We have seen, for example, that a rising level of absolute and per capita GNP may camouflage the fact that the poor are no better off than before.

Many people (including some economists) are often unaware that **the calculation of GNP and especially its rate of growth is in reality largely a calculation of the rate of growth of the incomes of the upper twenty per cent of the population who receive a disproportionately large share of the national product.** GNP growth rates therefore, should *not* be used as an index of improved economic welfare for the general population. As an extreme example, suppose an economy consisted of only ten people, nine of whom had no income at all and the tenth received 100 units of income. The GNP for this economy would therefore be 100 and per capita GNP would be 10. Now suppose that everyone's income increases by 20 per cent so that GNP rises to 120 while per capita income grows to 12. For the nine individuals with no income before and still no income now (i.e. $1.2 \times 0 = 0$), such a rise in per capita income provides no cause for rejoicing. The one rich individual still has all the income. GNP, instead of being a welfare index of society as a whole, is merely measuring the welfare of a single individual!

The same thought processes apply to the more realistic situation where incomes are very unequally distributed, although not perfectly unequal as in the above example. Taking the figures from Table 9.6, where we divided the population into quintiles and showed that the bottom 20 per cent received only 5 per cent of the income while the remaining four quintile groups received 9, 13, 22 and 51 per cent income shares respectively, we find that together these income shares exhaust the total GNP of 100. If we now assume that income levels in each income class are a measure of their relative economic welfare and that the rate of income growth in each quintile is a measure of the economic welfare growth of that class, we can approximate the growth in total welfare of society as the simple weighted sum of the growth of income in each class. This in fact is what the rate of GNP growth measures, where the weights applied to each income class, however, are their respective shares of national income. To be specific, in the case of a

[2] For empirical support of this argument with regard to rural saving and investment, see Keith Griffin, 'Rural Development: the policy options', in E. O. Edwards (ed.) *Employment in Developing Nations*, Columbia Press, New York, 1974, pp. 190–91.

population divided into quintiles according to rising income levels, we would have[3]:

$$G = w_1g_1 + w_2g_2 + w_3g_3 + w_4g_4 + w_5g_5 \quad (1)$$

where

G = a weighted index of growth of social welfare,

g_i = the growth rate of income of the ith quintile (where the i quintiles are ordered 1, 2, 3, 4 and 5 in our example),

and

w_i = the 'welfare weight' of the ith quintile (i.e. in our example $w_1 = 0.05$, $w_2 = 0.09$, $w_3 = 0.13$, $w_4 = 0.22$ and $w_5 = 0.51$).

As long as the weights add up to unity and are non-negative, our overall measure of the growth of social welfare, G, must fall somewhere between the maximum and minimum income growth rates in the various quintiles. In the extreme case of all income accruing to one individual or one group of individuals in the highest quintile and where the 'welfare weights' are the income shares (as they are with GNP growth calculations), equation (1) would be written as:

$$G = 0g_1 + 0g_2 + 0g_3 + 0g_4 + 1g_5 = 1g_5 \quad (2)$$

The growth of 'social welfare' would, therefore, be associated exclusively with the growth of incomes of the top quintile of the population.

In the example derived from Table 9.6, the GNP income share weighted index of social welfare would be written as:

$$G = 0.05g_1 + 0.09g_2 + 0.13g_3 + 0.22g_4 + 0.51g_5 \quad (3)$$

Now suppose the income growth rate of the bottom 60 per cent of the population is zero (i.e. $g_1 = g_2 = g_3 = 0$) while that of the top 40 per cent is 10 per cent (i.e. $g_4 = g_5 = 0.10$). Equation (3) could therefore be written as:

$$G = 0.05(0) + 0.09(0) + 0.13(0) + 0.22(0.10) + 0.51(0.10) = 0.073$$

and the 'social' welfare index would rise by over 7 per cent, which is the rate of growth of GNP (i.e. GNP would rise from 100 in Table 9.6 to 107.3 if the incomes of the fourth and fifth quintiles grew by 10 per cent). Thus we have an illustration of a case where GNP rises by 7.3 per cent, implying that social wellbeing has increased by this proportionate amount even though 60 per cent of the population are no better off than before. These bottom 60 per cent still have only 5, 13 and 22 units of income respectively. Clearly, the distribution of income would be worsened (the relative shares of the bottom 60 per cent would fall) by such a respectable growth rate of GNP.

The numerical example given by equation (3) clearly illustrates our basic point. The use of the growth rate of GNP as an index of social welfare and as a method of comparing the 'development' performance of different countries can be very misleading, especially where countries have very different distributions of income. The welfare weights attached to the growth rates of different income groups are very unequal, with a heavy social 'premium' being placed on the income growth of the highest quintile groups. In the example of equation (3), a one per cent growth in the income of the top quintile carries over ten times the weight of a one per cent growth in the lowest quintile (i.e. 0.51 compared with 0.05) because it implies an absolute increment which is ten times larger. In other words, **using the measure of GNP growth as an index of improvements in social welfare and development accords to each income group a welfare valuation that corresponds to their respective income shares,** i.e. a one per cent increase in the income of the richest 20 per cent of the population is implicitly assumed to be over ten times as important to society as a one per cent increase in the income of the bottom 20 per cent! It follows that the best way to maximise social welfare is to maximise the rate of growth of the incomes of the rich while neglecting the poor! If ever there was a case for *not* equating GNP growth with 'development', the preceding example should provide a persuasive illustration.

Constructing a poverty-weighted index of social welfare

An alternative to using the simple rate of GNP growth or 'distributive share' index of social welfare would be to construct an 'equal weights' or even a 'poverty-weighted' index of social welfare. The latter

[3] This illustration is derived from Ahluwalia and Chenery, 'A Conceptual Framework for Economic Analysis', in Chenery, Duloy and Jolly, *op. cit.*, pp. (3)2–4.

two indices might be especially relevant for those countries which are concerned with the elimination of poverty as a major development objective. As the name implies, an equal weights index weighs the growth of income in each income class not by the proportion of total income in that class but by the proportion of the total population in each class; that is, all people are treated (weighted) equally. In an economy which is divided into quintiles such an index would give a weight of 0.2 to the growth of income in each quintile. Thus a 10 per cent increase in the income of the lowest 20 per cent of the population would have the same bearing on the overall measure of social welfare improvement as a 10 per cent increase in the top 20 per cent group or in any other quintile group even though the absolute increase in income for the bottom group will be much smaller than for the upper groups.

Using an equal weights index in our example of a 10 per cent income growth of the top two quintiles while the bottom three remain static, we would have

$$G = 0.20g_1 + 0.20g_2 + 0.20g_3 + 0.20g_4 + 0.20g_5 \qquad (4)$$

or, inserting growth rates for g_1 to g_5,

$$G = 0.2(0) + 0.2(0) + 0.2(0) + 0.2(0.1) + 0.2(0.1) = 0.04.$$

Social welfare will have increased by only 4 per cent using this equal weights index compared to the 7.3 per cent increase recorded by using the distributive shares or GNP growth rate index. Even though recorded GNP still grows by 7.3 per cent, this alternative welfare index of 'development' shows only a 4 per cent rise.

Finally, consider a developing country which is genuinely and solely concerned with improving the material wellbeing of, say, the poorest 40 per cent of its population. It might therefore, wish to construct a poverty-weighted index of development which places a subjective social value *only* on the income growth rates of the bottom 40 per cent. In other words, it might arbitrarily place a welfare weight on w_1 of, say 0.6 and w_2 of, say, 0.4 while w_3, w_4 and w_5 are given zero welfare weights. Using our same numerical example, the social welfare growth index for this country would be given by the expression:

$$G = 0.60g_1 + 0.40g_2 + 0g_3 + 0g_4 + 0g_5 \qquad (5)$$

which, when substituting $g_1 = g_2 = g_3 = 0$ and $g_4 = g_5 = 0.10$ becomes

$$G = 0.6(0) + 0.4(0) + 0(0) + 0(0.1) + 0(0.1) = 0.$$

The poverty-weighted index therefore records *no* improvement in social welfare (i.e. no development) even though recorded GNP has grown by 7.3 per cent!

Although the choice of welfare weights in any index of development is purely arbitrary, it does represent and reflect important social value judgments about goals and objectives for a given society. It would certainly be interesting to know, if this were possible, what are the *real* implicit welfare weights of the various development strategies of different Third World countries. The point is that, as long as the growth rate of GNP is explicitly or implicitly used to compare development performances, we know that a 'wealthy weights' index is actually being employed.

To put some real world flavour into the preceding discussion of alternative indices of improvements in economic welfare and to illustrate the usefulness of alternative weighted growth indices in evaluating the economic performance of different countries, consider the data in Table 10.1. The table shows the growth of income in 17 countries as measured first by the rate of growth of GNP, second by an equal weights index and thirdly by a poverty weights index where the actual weights assigned to income growth rates of the lowest 40 per cent, the middle 40 per cent and the top 20 per cent of the population are 0.6, 0.4 and 0.0 respectively. The countries represent both rich and poor nations from diverse regions. Some interesting conclusions emerge from a review of the last three columns of the table.

1. Economic performance as measured by equal and poverty-weighted indices is notably worse in some otherwise high GNP growth countries e.g. Brazil, Mexico and Panama. Since these countries all experienced a deterioration in their income distribution and a growing concentration of income growth in upper groups over this period, the equal and poverty weights indices naturally show a less impressive development performance than the simple GNP measure.
2. In four countries (Colombia, El Salvador, Sri Lanka and Taiwan) the weighted indices show a better performance than GNP growth. This is because the relative income growth of lower income groups proceeded more rapidly over the period in question in those four countries than

Table 10.1
Income distribution and growth

No.	Country	Period	I. Income growth Upper 20%	Middle 40%	Lowest 40%	II. Annual increase in welfare (A) GNP weights	(B) Equal weights	(C) Poverty weights
1.	Korea	64–70	12.4	9.5	11.0	11.0	10.7	10.5
2.	Panama	60–69	8.8	9.2	3.2	8.2	6.7	5.2
3.	Mexico	63–68	8.8	5.8	6.0	7.8	6.5	5.9
4.	Taiwan	53–61	4.5	9.1	12.1	6.8	9.4	11.1
5.	Costa Rica	61–71	4.5	9.3	7.0	6.3	7.4	7.8
6.	Canada	61–65	7.0	5.3	6.5	6.2	6.1	6.1
7.	Colombia	64–70	5.2	7.9	7.8	6.2	7.3	7.8
8.	El Salvador	61–69	3.5	9.5	6.4	5.7	7.1	7.4
9.	Philippines	61–65	5.0	6.7	4.4	5.5	5.4	5.2
10.	Brazil	60–70	6.7	3.1	3.7	5.2	4.1	3.5
11.	United States	60–66	5.6	5.2	4.1	5.2	4.8	4.5
12.	Finland	52–62	6.0	5.0	2.1	5.1	4.0	3.1
13.	Sri Lanka	63–70	3.1	6.3	8.3	5.0	6.5	7.6
14.	Yugoslavia	63–68	5.0	5.0	4.3	4.9	4.7	4.5
15.	France	56–62	5.6	4.5	1.4	4.8	3.5	2.4
16.	Peru	61–71	3.9	6.7	2.4	4.6	4.4	3.8
17.	India	54–63	5.3	3.5	2.0	4.2	3.3	2.5

Source: Ahluwalia and Chenery, 'A conceptual framework for economic analysis', *Redistribution with Growth: An Approach to Policy*, World Bank (3) 5.

that of the higher income groups.

3. In five countries (Costa Rica, Korea, Peru, Philippines and Yugoslavia) little change in income distribution during the period in question results in little variation between the GNP measure and the two alternative wighted indices of social welfare.

We may conclude, therefore, that **a useful summary measure of the degree to which economic growth is biased towards the relative improvement of high income or low income groups is the positive or negative divergence between a weighted (equal or poverty) social welfare index and the actual growth rate of GNP.**

Finally, our analysis leads us to conclude that the presumed trade-off between rapid economic growth and a more equitable distribution of income is in reality better expressed as a trade-off between income growth rates among different income groups. If a weighted welfare index is used to measure economic development, then it is not only possible but may even be desirable for a lower growth rate of GNP to be associated with a higher rate of economic development, at least in terms of the specific value judgments of a particular egalitarian society.

Combining the economics of growth and distribution

The reformulation of indices of development to take account of alternative social premiums for different income groups takes us a long way towards a better understanding of the relationship between economic growth and income distribution. For one thing, the use of such indices underlines the importance of focusing on the *direct* improvement in living standards for the lowest income groups rather than worrying about non-existent conflicts between growth and distribution or about the overall pattern of income distribution in Third World countries. On the other hand, the recognition that real development entails direct attacks on the sources of poverty within a country is useless without a thorough knowledge of what determines income levels and relative rates of growth within different income groups. Unfortunately economic theory offers us little guidance here since it has always been concerned not with the size distribution of income (i.e. who gets what) but rather with the determinants of the functional distribution of income (i.e. how much of the total GNP is attributable to the total productivity of labour, capital, land, etc.). Even if the traditional theory of the determinants of functional income distribution had relevance for understanding the economic processes of contemporary developing nations (which, as we saw in Chapter 9, it does not, due to unreal assumptions about factor pricing, competitive markets and the influence of power), knowledge of how incomes are functionally distributed would still not help us to understand how and why incomes tend to be concentrated in certain population groups. For this we need to know how income-earning factors of production are distributed among different groups of people. We know, for example, that personal income consists not only of income derived from the supply of an individual's labour but also, and primarily for upper income groups, from an individual's control over other income-earning assets such as land and capital (both physical and financial).

When we analyse the real determinants of highly unequal distributions of income, **it is the very unequal distribution of the ownership of 'productive assets' such as land and capital within different segments of Third World populations that largely accounts for the wide income divergence between rich and poor.** The concentration of physical and financial capital as well as land in the hands of small economic and political elites enables them to expand their stock of human capital through education, and thereby to control even greater shares of the national product. As in the international sphere, it is a case of the rich getting richer while the poor stagnate. Any attempt to improve the living standards of the poor significantly must therefore focus not only on increasing the economic returns to the limited factors they possess (i.e. raising the returns to their labour through more employment) but also on progressively altering the existing pattern of concentration of both physical and human capital towards low income groups. Such redistribution can probably best be achieved in a growing economy. This leads us directly into the subject of alternative policy approaches.

The range of policy options: some basic considerations

Those Third World countries which aim to reduce poverty and excessive inequalities in the distribution of income, need to know how best to achieve their aim. What kinds of economic and other policies might LDC governments adopt to reduce poverty and inequality while maintaining or even accelerating economic growth rates? Since we are concerned here with moderating the size distribution of incomes in general and raising the income levels of, say, the bottom 40 per cent of the population in particular, it is important to understand the various determinants of the distribution of income in an economy and see in what ways government intervention can alter or modify their effect.

Areas of intervention

We can identify four broad areas of possible government policy intervention which correspond to the following four major elements in the determination of Third World economy's distribution of income.

1. Functional income distribution: the returns to labour, land and capital as determined by factor prices, utilisation levels and the consequent shares of national income that accrue to the owners of each factor.
2. Size distribution: the functional income distribution of an economy can be translated into the size distribution by knowledge of how ownership and control over productive assets and labour skills are concentrated and distributed throughout the population, and with the growth of these assets over time. It is the distribution of these asset holdings and skill endowments that ultimately determines the distribution of personal income.
3. Moderating (reducing) the size distribution at the upper levels through progressive taxation of personal income and wealth. Such taxation increases government revenues and converts a market-determined level of personal income into a fiscally corrected 'disposable' personal income. It is an individual's or family's disposable or after-tax income which is the actual amount available for expenditure on goods and services and for saving.
4. Moderating (increasing) the size distribution at the lower levels through public expenditures of tax revenues to raise the incomes of the poor

either directly (e.g. by outright money transfers) or indirectly (e.g. through public employment creation, the provision of free or subsidised primary education, etc.). Such public policies raise the real income levels of the poor *above* their market-determined personal income levels.

Third World governments have many options and alternative possible policies to operate in the four broad areas of intervention outlined above. Let us briefly identify some of them.

Policy options

Altering the functional distribution of income through policies designed to change relative factor prices

This is the traditional economic approach. It is argued that, as a result of institutional constraints and faulty policies, the relative price of labour (basically, the wage rate) is higher than that which would be determined by the free interplay of the forces of supply and demand. For example, the power of trade unions to raise minimum wages to artificially high levels (e.g. higher than would result from supply and demand), even in the face of widespread unemployment, is often cited as an example of the 'distorted' price of labour. From this it is argued that measures designed to reduce the price of labour relative to capital (e.g. through lower public sector wages, public wage subsidies to employers, etc.) will cause employers to substitute labour for capital in their production activities. Such factor substitution increases the overall level of employment and ultimately raises the incomes of the poor, who typically possess only their labour services.

On the other hand, it is often correctly pointed out that the price of capital equipment is often institutionally set at artificially low levels (i.e. below what supply and demand would dictate) through various public policies such as investment incentives, tax allowances, subsidised interest rates, low tariffs on capital good imports such as tractors, automated equipment, etc. If these special privileges and capital subsidies were removed so that the price of capital would *rise* to its true scarcity level, then producers would have a further incentive to increase their utilisation of the abundant supply of labour and lower their uses of very scarce capital. Moreover, owners of capital (both physical and financial) would not receive the artificially high economic returns they now enjoy. Their personal incomes would thereby be reduced.

Since factor prices are assumed to function as the ultimate signals and incentives in any economy, 'getting these prices right' (i.e. lowering the relative price of labour and raising the relative price of capital) would not only increase productivity and efficiency but also reduce inequality by providing more wage-paying jobs for the currently unemployed or under-employed unskilled and semiskilled workers. It would also lower the artificially high incomes of owners of capital. Removal of such factor price distortions would therefore go a long way towards combining more growth, efficiently generated, with higher employment, less poverty and greater equality.

We deal more extensively with the important question of factor price distortions, employment generation and choice of appropriate production techniques in Chapter 13 when we discuss the employment problem in developing nations. For the present we may conclude that there is much merit to the traditional factor price distortion argument and that 'getting the prices right' should contribute to a reduction in poverty and an improved distribution of income. How much it actually contributes will depend on the degree to which firms and farms switch to more labour-intensive production methods as the relative price of labour falls and the relative price of capital rises. This is an important empirical question, the answer to which will vary from country to country (see Chapter 13). But some improvement can be expected.

Modifying the size distribution through the progressive redistribution of asset ownership

Given factor prices and utilisation levels for each type of productive factor (labour, land and capital), we can arrive at estimates for the total earnings of each asset. In order to translate this functional income into personal income, we need to know the **distribution** and **ownership concentration** of these assets among and within various segments of the population. Here we come to what is probably the most important fact about the determination of income distribution within an economy. **The**

ultimate cause of the very unequal distribution of personal income in most Third World countries is the very unequal and highly concentrated patterns of asset ownership within these countries. The principal reason why less than 20 per cent of their populations receive over 50 per cent of the national income is that this 20 per cent probably owns and controls well over 70 per cent of the productive resources, especially physical capital and land but also human capital in the form of better education. Correcting factor prices is certainly not sufficient to reduce income inequalities greatly nor to eliminate widespread poverty where the ownership of asset holdings and educated skills is highly concentrated.

It follows that **the second and perhaps most important line of policy to reduce poverty and inequality is to focus directly on reducing the concentrated control of assets, the unequal distribution of power, and the unequal access to educational and income-earning opportunities which characterise many developing countries.** A classic case of such redistribution as it relates to the rural poor, who comprise 70 to 80 per cent of the target poverty group, is land reform. The basic purpose of land reform is to transform tenant cultivators into smallholders who will then have an incentive to raise production and improve their incomes. But, as we shall see in Chapter 16, land reform may be a weak instrument of income redistribution if other institutional and price distortions in the economic system prevent small farm holders from securing access to much needed inputs such as credit, fertiliser, seeds, marketing facilities and agricultural education.

In addition to the redistribution of existing productive assets like land ownership, there are dynamic redistribution policies which could be gradually pursued. For example, Third World governments could transfer a certain proportion of annual savings and investments to low income groups so as to bring about a more gradual and perhaps politically more acceptable redistribution of *additional* assets as they accumulate over time. This is what we mean by the expression 'redistribution from growth'. Whether such a gradual redistribution from growth is any more possible than a redistribution of existing assets is a moot point, especially in the context of very unequal power structures. But some form of asset redistribution, whether static or dynamic, appears to be a necessary condition for any significant reduction of poverty and inequality in most Third World nations.

Human capital in the form of education and skills is another example of the unequal distribution of productive asset ownership. Public policy, therefore, should promote a wider access to educational opportunities as a means of increasing income-earning potential for more of the population. But, as in the case of land reform, the mere provision of greater access to education is no guarantee that the poor will be any better off unless complementary policies (for example, the provision of more productive employment opportunities for the educated) to capitalise on this increased human capital are adopted. The relationship between education, employment and development is discussed further in Chapter 18.

Modifying the size distribution at the upper levels through progressive income and wealth taxes

Any national policy designed to improve the living standards of the bottom 40 per cent must ensure sufficient financial resources are available to transform paper plans into programme realities. The major source of such development finance is the direct and progressive taxation of both income and wealth (see Chapter 24). Direct progressive income taxation focuses on personal and corporate incomes with the richer required to pay a progressively larger percentage of their total income than the poor. Taxation on wealth (i.e. the stock of accumulated income-earning assets) typically focuses on personal and corporate property taxes but may also include progressive inheritance taxes. In either case the burden of the tax is designed to fall most heavily on the upper income groups.

Unfortunately, in many less developed countries (and developed countries as well) the gap between what is supposed to be a progressive tax structure and what different income groups actually pay can be substantial. Progressive tax structures on paper often turn out to be *regressive* in practice, that is to say, the lower and middle income groups pay a proportionately larger share of their incomes in taxes than the upper income groups. This is largely because the poor are often taxed at the *source* of their incomes or expenditures (by withholding taxes from wages, general poll taxes or indirect taxes levied on goods such as cigarettes and beer). On the other hand, the rich derive by far the largest part of their incomes from the return on physical and financial assets which often go unreported. They often also have the power and ability to avoid paying taxes without fear of government reprisal. Policies to enforce progressive rates of direct taxation on income and wealth, especially at the highest levels, are what is most needed in this area of redistribution activity. (See Chapter 24 for further discussion of taxation for development.)

Modifying the size distribution at the lower levels through direct transfer payments and the public provision of goods and services

The direct provision of tax-financed public consumption goods and services to the very poor is another potentially very important instrument of a comprehensive policy designed to eradicate poverty. Examples include public health projects in rural villages and urban fringe areas, primary school lunch and preschool nutritional supplementation programmes, and the provision of clean water supplies and electrification to remote rural areas. Moreover, direct money transfers and subsidised food programmes for the urban and rural poor as well as direct government policies to keep the price of essential foodstuffs low represent additional forms of public consumption subsidies. All these policies have the effect of raising the real personal income levels of the very poor beyond their actual market-derived monetary incomes.

The role of technological research

A final but much broader policy approach which in addition to the distribution of assets and influence over institutions affects the whole character of subsequent economic development is the nature and orientation of technological research. As we discovered in previous chapters, almost 98 per cent of all current world technological research occurs in developed countries and focuses on developed country problems. The dependence of Third World countries on this foreign and often inappropriate technology, whether in agriculture or industry, or in public health and education, is a major inhibiting factor on any long-term programme of structural economic transformation oriented towards the reduction of poverty and inequality. In the absence of appropriate (i.e. more labour-intensive) technologies of small-scale food production, of low-cost housing, of health measures, of small-scale manufacturing and of low-cost training and education, attempts to 'get prices right' and even to redistribute assets can be rendered ineffective. The development of an active policy of promoting indigenous technological research and development on relevant problems affecting the levels of living of all people, but especially the poor, may be indispensable to any viable long-run programme of growth without poverty in developing countries.

Conclusion: the need for a package of policies

To summarise our discussion of alternative policy approaches to the problem of growth, poverty and inequality in Third World countries, the need is not for one or two isolated policies but for a package of complementary and supportive policies, including the following four elements:

1. A policy or set of policies designed to **correct factor price distortions** so as to ensure that market or institutionally established prices provide accurate (i.e. socially correct) signals and incentives to both producers and resource suppliers. Getting the price right should help to contribute to greater productive efficiency, more employment and less poverty.
2. A policy or set of policies designed to bring about far-reaching **structural changes in the distribution of assets**, power and access to education and associated income-earning opportunities. Such policies go beyond the narrow realm of economics and touch on the whole social, institutional, cultural and political fabric of diverse developing nations. But without such radical structural changes and asset redistributions, whether immediately effectuated (e.g. through popular revolutions) or gradually introduced over time (through established political processes), the chances of significantly improving the living conditions of the masses of rural and urban poor will be highly improbable, perhaps even impossible.
3. A policy or set of policies designed to **modify the size distribution of income** at the upper levels

through the enforcement of legislated progressive taxation on incomes and wealth and at the lower levels through the expanded provision of publicly provided consumption goods and services.

4. A policy or set of policies designed to **promote indigenous technological research and development** on relevant Third World problems where emphasis is placed on finding efficient (mostly, labour-intensive) methods of providing low-cost health, housing and training services, improving small-scale agriculture and expanding urban and rural employment opportunities.

The interaction between all these policies would provide a comprehensive agenda for any national attack on the pervasive problems of mass poverty and income inequality. Within the context of such a comprehensive four-pronged national policy, however, one needs to ask a final but far from trivial question: 'Can Third World countries actively pursue policies to reduce poverty and promote equality while remaining open to and dependent upon the public financial resources, private investment, imported products, and most importantly, the values, symbols, ideals, attitudes and institutions of advanced industrial countries?' In other words, can growth with equity be realistically pursued in isolation (as in the case of China); if not, can Third World countries collectively become more self-reliant masters of their own economic and social destinies while still actively participating in an increasingly interdependent, yet highly unequal, global system? It is a difficult and perplexing question, but one which every developing nation and every thoughtful individual within these nations needs to ponder. We raise it again and attempt to provide some possible answers in the concluding chapter of the book.

Concepts for review

character of economic growth
'trickle down' theory of development
propensity to save
welfare index
GNP index
equal weights index
poverty-weighted index
asset ownership
disposable income
factor-price distortions
redistribution policies
progressive income and wealth taxes
regressive tax
indirect tax
subsidy
package of policies

Questions for discussion

1. In the text it is asserted that the major determinant of a country's income distribution was its distribution of productive and income-earning assets. Explain the meaning of this statement giving examples of different kinds of productive and income earning assets.
2. Are rapid economic growth (either GNP or per capita GNP) and a more equitable distribution of personal income necessarily conflicting objectives? Summarise the arguments both for and against the presumed conflict of objectives and state and explain your own view.
3. GNP is said to be a biased index of national development and economic welfare. Explain the meaning of this statement giving a specific hypothetical or real example of such a bias.
4. What is the value of constructing an 'equal weights' or especially a 'poverty-weighted' index of social welfare? Under what conditions will these welfare indices differ from GNP? Explain your answer.
5. Economic growth is said to be a 'necessary but sufficient condition' to eradicate absolute poverty and reduce inequality. What is the reasoning behind this argument?
6. Outline the range of major policy options available to LDC governments to alter and modify the size distribution of their national incomes. Which policy or policies do you believe are absolutely essential and which are important but not crucial? Explain your answer.

Further reading

See reading list at the end of Chapter 9.

Chapter 11 The great population debate

The central issue of our time may well turn out to be how the world addresses the problem of ever expanding human numbers.
James Grant, Director-General, UNICEF

Consideration of population problems cannot be reduced to the analysis of population trends only.
World Population Plan of Action, Bucharest, August 1974

Introduction
Number and controversies

By January, 1982, the world's population had passed the 4.5 billion mark. Optimistic projections by the United Nations placed the figure at over 6.1 billion by the year 2000. Over four-fifths of that population will inhabit the developing world, and ninety per cent of the increase will occur in Third World nations. What will be the economic and social implications for levels of living, national and personal esteem, and freedom of choice – that is, for 'development' – if such quantitative projections are realised? Are such projections inevitable or will they depend on the success or failure of Third World development efforts? Finally, and more significantly, is rapid population growth *per se* as serious a problem as many in the developed world believe; or is it a manifestation of more fundamental problems of underdevelopment and the unequal utilisation of global resources between rich and poor nations, as many others (mostly in the developing world) believe?

These and other questions lie at the core of the current world-wide interest in and debate about world population growth and human welfare. The main elements of this debate were clearly evident at the first World Population Conference held in Bucharest in August 1974. This chapter, therefore, attempts to analyse the nature and context of the current population debate, both as it relates to the domestic concerns of many developing countries and in its world-wide context. In Chapter 12 we look more closely at the economics of population growth and examine various policy approaches, both in the developing and the developed world, to dealing with the causes and effects of global population growth.

The basic issue: population growth and the quality of life

Every year between 85 and 90 million people are being added to a world population of just over 4.5 billion. About 73 million of these additional people will be born each year in Third World countries. These increases are unprecedented in the history of mankind. But the problem of population growth is not simply a problem of numbers. It is a problem of human welfare and of 'development' as defined in Chapter 6. Rapid population growth has serious potential consequences for the well-being of mankind throughout the world. If 'development' entails the improvement in peoples' levels of living – their incomes, health, education and general well-being – and if it also encompasses their self-esteem, respect, dignity and freedom to choose, then the really important question about population growth is: **How does the contemporary population situation in many Third World countries contribute to or detract from their chances of realising the goals of development, not only for the current generation but also for future generations?** Conversely, how does 'development' affect population growth?

Among the major issues relating to these basic questions are the following:

- Will Third World countries be capable of improving the **levels of living** for their people with the current and anticipated levels of population growth? To what extent does rapid population increase make it more difficult to provide essential social services like housing, transport, sanitation and social security?
- How will the developing countries be able to cope with the vast increases in their labour forces over the coming decades? Will **employment opportun-**

ities be plentiful or will it be a major achievement just to keep unemployment levels from rising?

- What are the implications of higher population growth rates among the world's poor for their chances of overcoming the human misery of **absolute poverty?** Will **world food supply** and its distribution be sufficient not only to feed the anticipated population increase in the coming decades but also to improve nutritional levels to the point where all humans can have an adequate diet?
- Will Third World countries be able to extend the coverage and improve the quality of their **health and educational systems** so that everyone can at least have the chance to secure adequate health care and primary education?
- To what extent are low levels of living an important factor in limiting the **freedom of parents to choose family size?** Is there a relationship between poverty and family size?
- To what extent is the **growing affluence** and the desire to grow further among the economically more developed nations an important factor in preventing poor nations from accommodating their growing populations? Is the pursuit of increasing affluence among the rich an even more detrimental force to rising living standards among the poor than the absolute increase in their numbers?

In view of the above questions, it becomes essential to frame the population question not simply in terms of numbers, or densities, or rates, or movements but, as Bernard Berelson, former President of the Population Council, has said, with full consideration of

> the qualities of human life: prosperity in place of poverty, education in place of ignorance, health in place of ignorance and death, environmental beauty in place of deterioration, full opportunities for the next generations of children in place of current limitations. Population trends, if favorable, open man's options and enlarge his choices. Thus, population policy is not an end, but only a means – a means to a better life. That is what the concern about population is about, or ought to be.[1]

[1] Bernard Berelson, *World Population: Status Report 1974*, New York, The Population Council, 1974, p. 47. The information in the following section is primarily derived from pp. 3–20 of this *Report*.

The significance of the problem: population growth – past, present and prospective

World population growth through history

Throughout most of the two million years of man's existence on earth his numbers have been few. When he first started to cultivate food through agriculture some 12 000 years ago, the estimated world population was no more than five million, less than the number of people living today in Mexico City, Buenos Aires or Bangkok (see Table 11.1). At the beginning of the Christian era nearly 2 000 years ago, world population had grown to nearly 250 million, less than half the population of India today. From the year AD 1 to the beginning of the industrial revolution around 1750, it almost trebled, to 728 million people, less than the total number of those living in China today. During the next two hundred years (1750–1950), an additional 1.7 billion people were added to the earth's numbers. But in the last 30 years (1950–1980) world population has almost doubled again, bringing the total figure at the end of 1980 to almost 4.4 billion people. If this trend were to continue to the year 2000, the world's population would then be almost 6.2 billion people.

Turning from absolute numbers to percentage growth rates, we can see from Table 11.2 that for almost the whole of man's existence on earth until approximately 300 years ago, the human population grew at an annual rate not much greater than

Table 11.1
Estimated world population growth through history

Year	Estimated population (millions)
10,000 BC	5
AD 1	250
1650	545
1750	728
1800	906
1850	1,171
1900	1,608
1950	2,486
1970	3,632
1980	4,390

Source: Berelson, *op cit.*, p. 3

zero – i.e. 0.002 per cent or 2 per thousand. Naturally, this overall rate has not been steady since there have been many ups and downs in the earth's numbers as a result of natural catastrophes and variations in growth rates among regions. By 1750 the population growth rate had accelerated by 150 times from 0.002 per cent to 0.3 per cent per year. By the 1950s, the rate had again accelerated, this time by threefold to about 1.0 per cent per year. Today, only 30 years later, the world's population growth rate has almost doubled to a remarkable 1.8 per cent per year.

The relationship between annual percentage increases and the time it takes for a population to double in size is shown in the last column of Table 11.2. We see that before 1650 it took nearly 35 000 years, or about 1 400 generations, for world population to double. Today, in less than 40 years, little more than one generation, world population will double.[2] Moreover, whereas it took almost 1 750 years to add 480 million people to the world's population between AD 1 and the onset of the industrial revolution, at current growth rates 480 million people are being added to the earth's numbers every six years!

The reason for the sudden change in overall population trends is that for almost all man's recorded history the rate of population change, whether up or down, has been strongly influenced by the combined effects of famine, disease, malnutrition, plague and war, conditions that resulted in high and fluctuating death rates. Now, in the twentieth century, such conditions are coming increasingly under man's technological and economic control. As a result, human mortality (the death rate) is lower than at any other point in man's existence. It is this decline in mortality resulting from rapid technological advances in modern medicine and the spread of public health measures throughout the world, particularly in the last 30 years, that has resulted in the unprecedented increases in population growth, especially in Third World countries. For example, death rates in Africa, Asia and Latin America have fallen by as much as

Table 11.2
World population growth rates and doubling times: an historical review

Period	Approximate growth rate %	Doubling time (years)
Appearance of man to early historical times	0.002	35,000
1650–1750	0.3	240
1850–1900	0.6	115
1930–1940	1.0	70
Present (1980s)	1.8	40

Source: Berelson, *op cit.*, p. 3

50 per cent during the last 20 to 30 years while birth rates have remained relatively high.

In short, **population growth today is primarily the result of a rapid transition from a long historical era characterised by high birth and death rates to one in which death rates have fallen sharply while birth rates, especially in developing countries, have remained at or near their historical high levels.**

The structure of the world's population

The world's population is very unevenly distributed by geographic region, by fertility and mortality levels, and by age structures.

1. Geographical region

Of the world's total population in 1982, more than three-fourths live in developing countries and less than one-fourth in the economically developed nations. Figure 11.1 shows the regional distribution of the world's population as it existed in 1980 and as it is projected for the year 2000.

Given current population growth rates in different parts of the world (significantly higher in the LDCs), the regional distribution of the world's population will inevitably change by the year 2000. By that time it is likely there will be almost 4 billion more people on the earth than in 1950. However, over 60 per cent or 2.5 billion of the added people will be in Asia where overall population size should have increased by some 300 per cent during the 50-year period. The corresponding increases in Africa and Latin America are estimated at almost 400 per cent

[2] For those interested, a convenient shorthand method of calculating doubling times is simply to divide any growth rate into the number 72. For example, something (an asset, population, GNP, etc.) growing at 2 per cent per year will double its value in *approximately* 35 to 36 years.

Figure 11.1
World population by region: 1980 and 2000 (projected)

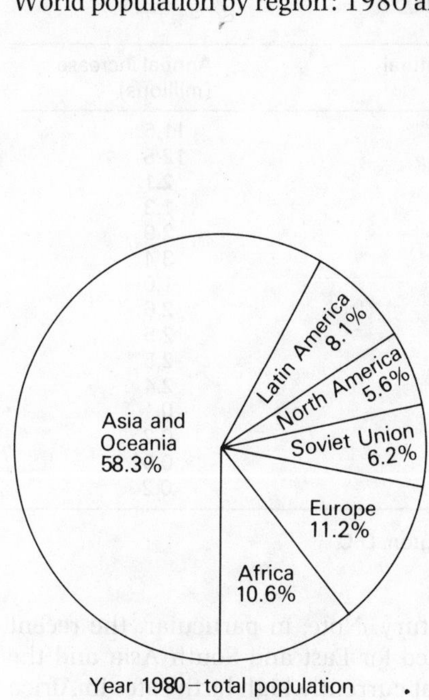

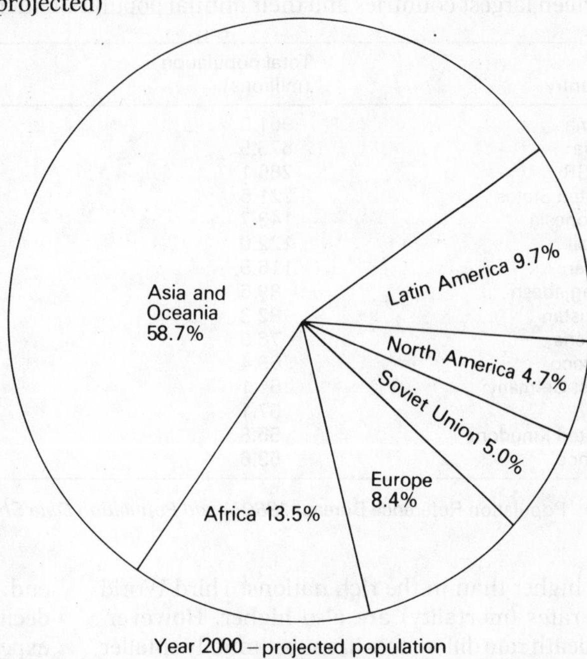

with an addition of almost 1 billion people. Together these three Third World continents will probably constitute over 80 per cent of the world's population by the year 2000 as contrasted with 70 per cent in 1950. Correspondingly, the proportion of the world's population living in Europe, the Soviet Union and North America will have fallen from 30 to less than 20 per cent of the total.

Consider finally the distribution of national populations. Table 11.3 lists the fifteen largest countries in the world in the 1980s. Together they account for about 70 per cent of the world's population. While these countries come from all the continents and from both developed and underdeveloped regions, it is instructive to note that in terms of annual increases in world population, countries such as India, Indonesia, Brazil, Bangladesh, Pakistan, Nigeria and Mexico all add more to the world's annual population increase than most of the economically more developed countries. For example, Mexico, ranked eleventh in size, adds much more to the absolute growth of the world's population than does the United States, ranked as the fourth largest country. Similarly, Brazil, ranked sixth, adds more people annually than does the Soviet Union, and so too Nigeria compared with Japan.

2. Fertility and mortality trends

The rate of population increase is quantitatively measured as the percentage yearly net relative increase (or decrease, in which event it is negative) in population size due to natural increase and net international migration. Natural increase simply measures the excess of births over deaths or, in more technical terms, the difference between **fertility** and **mortality**. Net international migration, while still negligible, is increasing in importance today as it was in the nineteenth and early twentieth centuries when it was a source of population increase in North America, Australia and New Zealand and corresponding decrease in Western Europe. Population increase in Third World countries, therefore, depends almost entirely on the difference between their birth and death rates.

The difference between developing and developed nations in terms of their rates of population growth can be explained simply by the fact that birth rates (fertility) in developing countries are generally

Table 11.3
The fifteen largest countries and their annual population increases, 1980

Country	Total population (millions)	Rate of natural increase	Annual increase (millions)
China	961.0	1.2	11.5
India	673.5	1.9	12.8
USSR	266.1	0.8	2.1
United States	221.6	0.6	1.3
Indonesia	143.7	2.0	2.9
Brazil	122.0	2.8	3.4
Japan	116.9	0.9	1.0
Bangladesh	89.6	2.9	2.6
Pakistan	82.3	3.0	2.5
Nigeria	76.9	3.2	2.5
Mexico	69.4	3.4	2.4
West Germany	61.1	−0.2	−0.1
Italy	57.1	0.4	0.2
United Kingdom	55.8	0.0	0.0
France	53.6	0.4	0.2

Source: Population Reference Bureau, *1980 World Population Data Sheet*, Washington, D.C.

much higher than in the rich nations. Third World death rates (mortality) are also higher. However, these death rate differences are substantially smaller than the differences in birth rates. As a result, the average rate of population growth in the developing countries is now about 2.1 per cent per year whereas most of the economically developed countries have annual growth rates of only about 0.6 per cent (see column 2 of Table 11.3). Let us look briefly at contrasting fertility and mortality trends in these two sets of nations.

As just noted, the major source of difference in population growth rates between the less developed and the more developed countries is the sizable difference in birth or fertility rates between the former and the latter. Recall from Chapter 5 that almost all Third World nations have birth rates ranging from 30 to 50 per thousand. By contrast, in almost all developed countries the rate is less than 20 per thousand (see Table 5.5). Moreover, LDC birth rates today are substantially higher than they were in pre-industrial western Europe. This is largely because of early and almost universal marriage in contemporary Third World countries. But there are signs of the beginnings of a substantial decline in LDC fertility, especially in countries such as Taiwan, South Korea, Singapore and Hong Kong where rapid economic and social development have taken place. Table 11.4 records the recent and projected declines in Third World birth rates to the end of the century. Note, in particular, the recent declines reported for East and South Asia and the expectation that currently high birth rates in Africa will persist at least until the 1990s.

On the other hand, there has been a narrowing of the gap in mortality rates between developed and less developed countries. The primary reason is undoubtedly the rapid improvement in health conditions throughout the Third World. Modern vaccination campaigns against malaria, smallpox, yellow fever and cholera, as well as the proliferation of public health facilities, clean water supplies, improved nutrition and public education have all worked together over the past 25 years to lower death rates by as much as 50 per cent in parts of Asia and Latin America and by over 30 per cent in much of Africa and the Middle East. Nevertheless, the average duration of life remains almost 20 years greater in the developed countries. But even this gap has been sharply reduced in the last 25 years. In 1950 life expectancy at birth for people in Third World countries averaged 35–40 years compared with 62–65 years in the developed world. By 1980 the difference had fallen to 16 years as life expectancy in the LDCs increased to 56 years (a gain of 42 per cent), while in the industrial nations it had risen to 72 years (an increase of 13 per cent). Today, because of still relatively high infant mortality rates, Africa has the lowest life expectancy, 46 years, while the most favourable region is Europe, where life expectancy at birth now averages about 72 years. Table 11.5 shows the rapid decline in Third World death rates between 1950 and 1980.

3. Age structure and dependency burdens

World population today is very youthful. Children under the age of 15 constitute just under half the total population of Third World countries while they make up only a quarter of the populations of developed nations. For example, 46 and 49 per cent of the population of Nigeria and Kenya respectively were below 15 years in 1980; for Brazil the comparable figure was 42 per cent and for Indonesia, India and the Philippines it was 42, 43 and 46 per cent respectively. In countries with such an age structure, the youth dependency ratio – that is the proportion of youths (below 15 years) to economically active adults (ages 15–64) – is very high. Thus the working force in developing countries must support almost twice as many children as they do in the wealthier countries. For example, in Sweden and the Soviet Union the working force age group (15–64) amounts to almost 65 per cent of the total population. This work force has to support only 21 and 27 per cent of the population who are its youthful dependents. By contrast, in countries like Pakistan and Ghana the economically active work forces and the child dependants both approach 50 per cent of the total population. In general, the more rapid the population growth rate, the greater will be the proportion of dependent children in the total population and the more difficult it becomes for those who are working to support those who are not.

Birth rates in relation to income levels, GNP growth rates and income distribution

Whatever the line of causality, high birth rates are generally associated with national poverty.

Table 11.4
Crude birth rates, 1950–2000 (per 1,000 population)

	1950–1955	1960–1965	1970–1975	1980–1985	1990–1995	1995–2000
World Total	35.6	34.0	30.3	28.1	25.4	23.8
Developed Countries	22.7	20.3	16.7	15.9	15.2	14.9
Developing Countries	41.8	40.0	35.5	32.1	28.3	26.2
Africa	48.1	47.6	46.1	45.0	40.1	36.9
Middle East	47.9	48.0	46.3	44.2	40.0	36.9
Latin America	41.4	39.9	36.3	34.4	31.3	29.6
China	39.8	33.8	26.0	20.1	18.0	17.4
East Asia	36.6	38.3	30.1	26.1	22.4	20.3
South Asia	43.2	44.1	40.5	36.9	31.0	27.8

Source: UN, *World Population Trends and Prospects, 1950–2000*, 1979, New York, Tables 2–A and 2–B.

Table 11.5
Crude death rates, 1950–2000 (per 1,000 population)

	1950–1955	1960–1965	1970–1975	1980–1985	1990–1995	1995–2000
World Total	18.3	14.4	12.0	10.6	9.2	8.7
Developed Countries	10.1	9.0	9.2	9.7	10.1	10.1
Developing Countries	22.2	16.8	13.2	10.9	9.0	8.3
Africa	26.9	22.4	18.8	15.4	12.0	10.6
Middle East	25.3	20.9	16.6	13.4	10.4	9.2
Latin America	14.5	11.5	9.3	7.7	6.5	6.0
China	20.1	13.6	9.4	8.3	7.8	7.7
East Africa	30.0	11.8	8.7	7.4	6.7	6.6
South Asia	24.6	19.8	15.8	12.5	9.9	8.8

Source: UN, *World Population Trends and Prospects, 1950–2000*, 1979, New York, Tables 2–A and 2–B.

Table 11.6
The relationship between national per capita incomes, growth rates, income distribution, and birth rates: selected Third World countries

Country	Birth rate 1979 (per 1000)	Per capita GNP 1979 ($)	Per capita GNP growth rate 1960–1979 (%)	Income distribution ratio of top 20% to bottom 40%
Brazil	29	1780	4.8	9.5
Colombia	30	1010	3.0	6.8
Costa Rica	29	1820	3.4	4.6
India	34	190	1.4	3.0
Mexico	36	1640	2.7	5.0
Peru	38	730	1.7	8.7
Philippines	34	600	2.6	4.5
Senegal	48	430	−0.2	6.4
South Korea	25	1480	7.1	2.7
Sri Lanka	28	230	2.2	2.3
Taiwan	19	3760	7.0	3.8
Thailand	31	590	4.6	4.5

Source: *World Development Report, 1981*, Annex Tables 1, 18, 25.

However, it would be a mistake to claim simply that, since high birth rates are generally associated with countries having low per capita incomes (the less developed nations), while low birth rates generally are found in countries with high per capita incomes (the more developed nations), it follows that raising per capita levels of income will lead to low birth rates.

Consider, for example, Table 11.6, where 12 Third World countries are listed according to their 1979 per capita income levels, their per capita GNP growth rates from 1960 to 1970, their income distribution ratios measuring the income multiple of the top 20 to the bottom 40 per cent of the income scale, and the magnitude of their crude birth rates.

The three diagrams in Figure 11.2 graphically portray the relationship, or non-relationship as the case may be, between each of the three major income variables and the birth rate as shown in Table 11.6. For example, in Figure 11.2(*a*) we have plotted the birth rate for each country against its level of per capita income to test the widely held hypothesis that there exists a close *negative* association between birth rates and per capita incomes. In Figure 11.2(*b*) these same birth rates are plotted against growth rates in per capita incomes to see if more rapid rates of income growth are closely associated with lower fertility levels. Finally, in Figure 11.2(*c*) birth rates are plotted against income distribution ratios to see if lower ratios (i.e. more equal distributions of income) are associated with lower birth rates.

Taking Figure 11.2(*a*) first, it is immediately evident that there is no apparent direct or inverse relationship between levels of per capita income and birth rates, at least for the 12 countries under consideration. Countries with similar relatively high birth rates like Colombia, the Philippines, Peru and Thailand have widely varying levels of per capita income. Similarly, countries with close but relatively low birth rates like Sri Lanka, South Korea, Taiwan and Costa Rica have national incomes varying from US $230 to $3760 per capita. So we can reject the simple hypothesis that higher per capita incomes are necessarily associated with higher or lower birth rates, at least over the range of incomes represented by the 12 LDCs in our sample.

Looking now at Figure 11.2(*b*) we see that there appears to be a negative relationship between growth rates of GNP per capita and birth levels. Again countries like Peru, India, the Philippines, Mexico and Brazil, which have a variation of only four points in their birth rates (i.e. from 34 to 38 per thousand), have wide variations in their income growth performances (ranging from a rate of 1.4 per cent per annum in India to 4.8 per cent in Brazil). On the other hand, countries with the same relatively low birth rates, such as Sri Lanka and South Korea, have variations of over 300 per cent in their respective GNP growth rates (2.2 per cent for Sri

Lanka compared with 7.1 per cent for South Korea).[3]

Finally, if we compare relative country birth rates with their relative degree of income inequality as in Figure 11.2(*c*), we discover that there *does* appear to be some relationship between lower (higher) birth rates and less (more) inequality in the distribution of income. Our 12 countries seem to fall roughly into two distinct groups: those with relatively low inequality ratios and relatively low birth rates (Taiwan, Sri Lanka, South Korea and Costa Rica), and the others with moderate to high inequality ratios and relatively higher birth rates (India, Thailand, Philippines, Senegal, Mexico, Colombia, Peru and Brazil).

We may tentatively conclude, therefore, that **countries which strive to lessen the inequality in their distribution of income or, alternatively, attempt to spread the benefits of their economic growth to a wider segment of the population may be better able to begin to lower their birth rates than countries where the benefits of growth are more unevenly shared,** even though these latter countries may have both higher levels and faster growth rates of per capita income. However, given a development policy oriented towards a more equitable pattern of income distribution, higher rates of GNP growth are likely to result in even greater reductions in fertility; contrast, for example, South Korea and Taiwan with, say, Brazil and Thailand.

Basically the reason why direct attacks on poverty and low levels of living are probably more effective measures to lower birth rates than simple growth maximisation is that higher levels of living provide the necessary motivations for families to *choose* to limit their size. Widespread poverty tends to sustain high birth rates for the obvious reason that families living without adequate incomes, employment, health, education and social services have little security for the future other than reliance on their children. They are caught in an 'underdevelopment trap' *vis-à-vis* their family size not only because their levels of living are low but also because their self-esteem and dignity may thereby be questioned and their freedom to choose a desired family size, however large, is constrained by their poverty and economic uncertainty. Further discussion of the meaning of development related to desired family size follows in the next chapter.

The hidden momentum of population growth

Perhaps the least understood aspect of population growth is its tendency to continue even after birth rates may have declined substantially. Population growth has a built-in tendency to continue, a powerful momentum which, like a speeding motor car when the brakes are applied, has a tendency to continue for some time before coming to a stop. In the case of population growth this momentum can persist for decades after birth rates drop.

There are two basic reasons for this hidden momentum. First, high birth rates in contemporary Third World countries obviously cannot be substantially altered overnight. The social, economic and institutional forces which have influenced fertility rates over the course of centuries do not simply disappear, even at the urging of national leaders. We know from the experience of European nations that such reductions in birth rates can take many decades. Consequently, even if developing countries decide to give the limitation of population growth top priority it will still take many years to lower national fertility to desired levels.

The second and less obvious reason for the hidden momentum of population growth has to do with the age structure of LDC populations. We saw in the previous section that underdeveloped nations with high birth rates have large proportions of children and adolescents in their population (sometimes as high as 50 per cent). In such a high fertility population, young people greatly outnumber their parents and when their generation reaches adulthood the number of potential parents will inevitably be much larger than at present. It follows that even if these new parents have only enough children to replace themselves (say two per couple as compared with their parents who may have had four children) the fact that the total number of couples having two children is much greater than the number of couples who previously had four

[3] For further statistical evidence on the non-relationship between rates of population growth and rates of GNP per capita growth for a sample of 79 Third World nations, see: Derek T. Healey, 'Population Growth and Real Output Growth in Developing Countries: a survey and analysis', Department of Economics, University of Adelaide, South Australia (mimeo), 1974.

Figure 11.2
The relationship between incomes and birth rates in twelve Third World countries

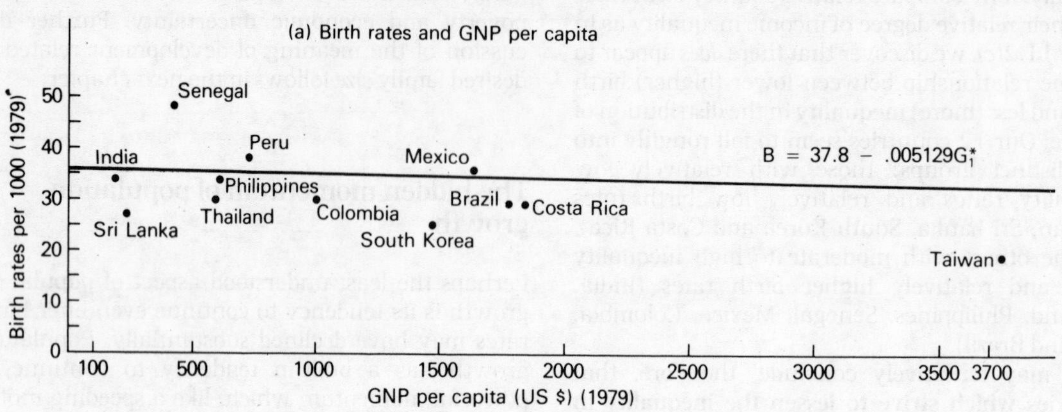

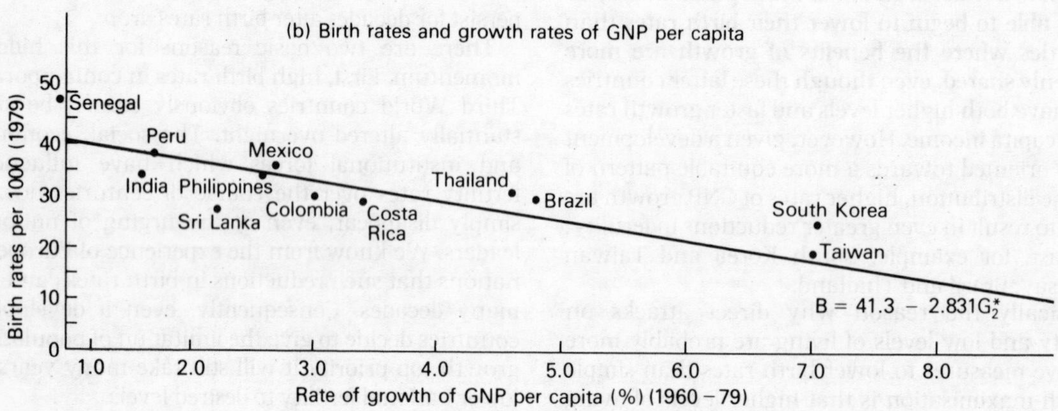

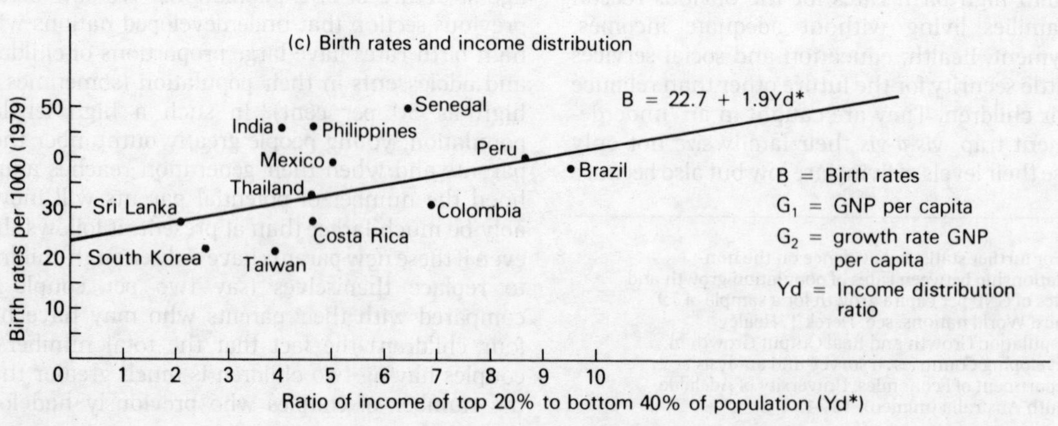

children means that the total population will still increase substantially before levelling off.

To give an example, suppose for simplicity we assume that country X has a total population of 600 consisting only of 100 married couples, each of which has four children (two girls and two boys). When these 400 children grow up, suppose they all marry, forming 200 new couples of childbearing age. Assume now that instead of four children per family, these new couples have only two children each (one boy and one girl). Assuming the death of the first generation of parents, the total population of country X will have grown from 600 to 800 people (i.e. 200 families of four people in each family). Now when the children of these two-child families grow up and get married, if they too have only two children per couple, then there will again be 200 families with four people in each for a total population of 800 people. Country X will, therefore, have been able to stabilise its population size *only* after two generations or approximately 50 years! This is why it takes many years to curtail population growth in high fertility countries. Too often politicians, planners, and even economists, are unaware of this basic arithmetic of population momentum. They assume incorrectly that growth rates can be manipulated in the short run with the same ease as the manipulation of, say, saving and investment rates or the levels and rates of taxation.

Suppose now that we make the extremely optimistic and unreal assumption that by the period 1980–1985 fertility rates in all developing countries will have declined to the replacement levels now characteristic of most developed countries (roughly two children per family). Even given such unrealistically optimistic assumptions, the population of the Third World would still continue to grow for many decades. In fact, it would not level off until it had reached a size fully 88 per cent greater than its 1970 level, an increase of more than 2.2 billion people. And those heavily populated countries like Mexico, India, Bangladesh, Indonesia, Nigeria and others would all also experience very substantial increases as a result of the momentum which is *already* built into the age structure of their current populations.

If we take a less optimistic but somewhat more realistic assumption that LDC fertility declines to replacement levels not by 1980–1985 but instead by the years 2000–2005, 20 years later, we obtain a different set of figures. In this case the population of the Third World would not level off until its built-in momentum had resulted in an overall increase of 158 per cent and an additional 4 billion people had been born. This would be more than the total world population in 1975. These figures emphasise dramatically the importance to eventual population size of the date at which countries are able to lower their fertility levels. In the above example, a mere 20 years meant an additional 1.8 billion people, almost two-thirds of the present population of the entire Third World.

Table 11.7 strikingly illustrates the arithmetic of population momentum using actual data and projections for a number of developing countries. We see that countries like Bangladesh, Mexico, the Philippines and Nigeria with high current birth rates have the highest built-in momentum of population growth. Note also that even though a country like India has approximately the same percentage growth momentum as Egypt, its current size means that it stands to gain almost 750 million more people than Egypt even if both achieve replacement birth rates by the year 2000.

These illustrations vividly demonstrate the extent to which most Third World countries are *already* virtually assured of substantial population increases, whatever happens to fertility levels. As they set goals for desirable future population sizes, they may as well assume that increases of the order of 80 to 125 per cent are coming, irrespective of any policy strategies. But this should not be a cause for despair or a diminished commitment on the part of those countries which genuinely believe that slowing down population growth is in their best national interest. For, as we have seen from the above example, every year that passes without a reduction in fertility means a larger multiple of the present total population size before it can eventually level off.

Goals and objectives: some conflicting opinions

Before discussing specific goals and objectives it must be recognised that there is a wide divergence of opinion, especially within the developing world itself, about whether population growth is in fact as

Table 11.7
Population 'momentum' and projected population increases of selected Third World countries under alternative optimistic fertility assumptions

Country	Population circa 1970 (millions)	Eventual population size in 2005 (millions): Replacement by 1980–85	Eventual population size in 2005 (millions): Replacement by 2000–05	Percentage increase from 1970 level: Replacement by 1980–85	Percentage increase from 1970 level: Replacement by 2000–05
India	534	1,002	1,366	+ 88%	+156%
Brazil	94	192	266	+104	+183
Bangladesh	69	155	240	+125	+248
Nigeria	65	135	198	+108	+205
Pakistan	57	112	160	+ 96	+181
Mexico	51	111	168	+118	+229
Philippines	38	79	119	+108	+213
Egypt	34	64	92	+ 88	+171
All LDCs	2,530	4,763	6,525	+ 88	+158
All Developed Countries	1,122	1,482	1,610	+ 32	+ 44
World	3,652	6,245	8,135	+ 71	+123

Source: Tomas Frejka, Reference Tables to *The Future of Population Growth,* New York; The Population Council, 1973.

serious a problem as some believe. On the one hand, one must recognise that population growth is not the only, or even the primary, source of low levels of living, eroding self-esteem and limited freedom in Third World nations. On the other hand, it would be equally naïve to argue that rapid population growth in many countries and regions is *not* a serious intensifier of our three integral components of underdevelopment, especially the first and third. The following summary of some of the main arguments for and against the idea that rapid population growth is a serious development problem, forms the basis for discussion of whether a consensus of opinion can be identified from which specific goals and objectives can be postulated.[4]

Population growth is not a real problem

We can identify three general lines of argument on the part of those individuals, primarily from Third World countries, who assert (1) that the problem is not population growth but some other issue; (2) that population growth is a false issue deliberately created by dominant rich-country agencies and institutions to keep LDCs in their underdeveloped 'dependent' conditions, or (3) that for many countries and regions of the Third World population growth is, in fact, desirable.

1. 'Some other issue'

Many knowledgeable people from rich as well as poor nations argue that the real problem is not population growth *per se* but:

(*a*) *Underdevelopment.* If correct strategies are pursued which lead to higher levels of living, greater esteem and expanded freedom, then population will take care of itself. Eventually, it will disappear as a problem as it has in all the present-day economically advanced nations. According to this argument, underdevelopment is the real problem and development should be the only goal. Economic progress and social mechanisms will more or less automatically regulate population growth and distribution. As long as the vast majority of people in Third World countries remain impoverished, uneducated and physically and psychologically weak, the large family will constitute the only real source of social security (i.e. parents will continue to be denied the

[4] For a more detailed discussion of these divergent opinions, see Michael Teitelbaum, 'Population and Development: is a consensus possible?', *Foreign Affairs,* July 1974, pp. 749–57.

freedom to choose a small family, if they so desire). Proponents of the underdevelopment argument then conclude that birth control programmes will surely fail, as they have in the past, where there is no *motivation* on the part of poor families to want to limit their size.

(*b*) *World resource depletion* primarily by the developed nations. Population can only be an economic problem in relation to the availability and utilisation of scarce natural and material resources. The fact is that the developed countries, with only one-third of the world's population, consume almost 80 per cent of the world's resources. For example, the average North American or European consumer uses up, directly and indirectly, almost 16 times as much of the world's food, energy and material resources as his counterpart in Third World countries. In terms of depletion of the world's limited resources, therefore, the addition of another child in the developed countries is as significant as the birth of 16 additional children in the underdeveloped countries. According to this argument, the *developed* nations should curtail or cut back on their excessively high consumption standards, rather than the less developed nations restrict their population growth. The latter's high fertility is really due to their low levels of living which in turn are largely the result of the over-consumption of the world's scarce resources by rich nations. It is this combination of rising affluence and extravagant, selfish consumption habits in rich countries and among rich people in poor countries which should be the major world concern, *not* population growth.

(*c*) *Population distribution.* According to this third line of argument, it is not numbers of people *per se* which are causing population problems but their distribution in space. Many regions of the world (e.g. sub-Saharan Africa) and many regions within countries (e.g. the north-east and Amazon regions of Brazil) are in fact *underpopulated* in terms of available or potential resources. Others simply have too many people concentrated in too small an area (e.g. central Java or most urban concentrations in LDCs). What is needed, therefore, instead of moderating the quantitative rate of population growth is governmental efforts to reduce rural–urban migration and to bring about a more rational spatial distribution of the population in terms of available land and other productive resources.

2. 'A deliberately contrived false issue'

The second main line of argument denying the significance of population growth as a major development problem is closely allied to the neo-colonial dependence theory of underdevelopment discussed in Chapter 6. Basically, it is argued that the frenetic overconcern in the rich nations with the population growth of poor nations is in reality an attempt by the former to hold down the development of the latter in order to maintain the *status quo* for their own self-interest. Rich countries are pressuring poor nations to adopt aggressive population control programmes even though they themselves went through a period of sizable population increase which accelerated their own development processes.

An extreme version of this argument views population control efforts by rich countries and their allied international agencies as racist or genocidal attempts to reduce the relative or absolute size of those poor, largely non-white populations of the world who may some day pose a serious threat to the welfare of the rich, predominantly white, populations. Worldwide birth control campaigns are seen, therefore, as manifestations of the fears of the developed world in the face of a possible radical challenge to the international order by the people who are its first victims, i.e. those in Third World countries.

3. 'Growth is desirable'

A more conventional economic argument is that population growth in many Third World countries or regions is in fact desirable to stimulate economic development.[5] Larger populations provide the needed consumer demand to generate favourable economies of scale in production, to lower production costs and to provide a sufficient and low-cost labour supply to achieve higher output levels. Moreover, it is argued that many rural regions in the Third World are in reality *underpopulated* in the sense that there is much unused but arable land that could yield large increases in agricultural output if only more people were available to cultivate it. Many regions of tropical Africa and Latin America and

[5] See for example, Colin Clark, 'The "population explosion" myth', *Bulletin of the Institute of Development Studies*, Sussex, May 1969.

even parts of Asia are said to be so situated.

In Africa, for example, it has even been argued that there are many regions which had *larger* populations in the remote past than today.[6] Their rural depopulation resulted not only from the slave trade, but also from compulsory military service, confinement to 'reservations' and the forced labour policies of former colonial governments. For example, the sixteenth-century Congo Kingdom is said to have had a population of approximately 2 million. But by the time of the colonial conquest and after 300 years of slave trade, the population of the region had fallen to less than one-third of that figure. Today's Zaïre has barely caught up to that sixteenth-century figure.[7] Other regions of west and eastern Africa provide similar examples, at least to those who advocate rapid population growth in Africa.

In terms of ratios of population to arable land (i.e. land under cultivation, fallow land, pastures and forests), Africa south of the Sahara is said by the supporters of population expansion to have a total of 1 400 million hectares. Land actually being cultivated, however, amounts to only 170 million hectares or about one hectare per rural inhabitant. Thus, only 12 per cent of all potential arable land is under cultivation and this very low rural population density is therefore viewed as a serious drawback to raising agricultural output.[8] Similar arguments have been expounded with regard to such Latin American countries as Brazil and Argentina.

Three other non-economic arguments, each found to some degree in a wide range of developing countries, complete the 'population-growth-is-desirable' viewpoint. First, many countries claim a need for population growth to protect currently underpopulated border regions against any expansionist intentions of neighbouring nations. Second, there are many ethnic, racial and religious groups within less developed countries whose differential attitudes towards family size have to be protected both for moral and political reasons. Finally, military and political power are often seen as dependent on a large and youthful population.

Many of these arguments have a certain realism about them if not in fact, then at least in the perceptions of vocal and influential individuals in developing countries. Clearly, some of the arguments have greater validity for some Third World countries than others. The important point is that they represent a considerable range of opinions and viewpoints within the Third World and therefore need to be seriously weighed against the counter arguments of those, mostly in the developed world, who believe that rapid population growth is indeed a real and important problem for underdeveloped countries. Let us now look at some of these counter arguments.

Population growth is a real problem

Positions supporting the need to curtail population growth through special programmes and policies are typically based on one or more of four arguments[9]:

1. The population 'hawk' argument

The extreme version of the population-as-a-serious-problem position attempts to attribute almost all the world's economic and social evils to excessive population growth. Unrestrained population increase is seen as the major crisis facing mankind today. It is claimed to be the principal cause of poverty, low levels of living, malnutrition and ill-health, environmental degradation, and a wide array of other social problems. Value-laden and incendiary words such as the 'population bomb' or 'population explosion' are tossed around at will. Indeed, dire predictions of world food catastrophes and ecological disaster are attributed almost entirely to the growth in numbers. Such an extreme position leads some of its advocates to assert that 'world' (i.e. LDC) population stabilisation or even decline is the most urgent contemporary task even if it requires severe and coercive measures to 'control' family size in Third World countries.

[6] See Samir Amin, 'Underpopulated Africa', paper given at the *African Population Conference*, Accra, December, 1971.

[7] *Ibid.*, fn. 2.

[8] *Ibid.*, p. 3.

[9] Teitelbaum, *op. cit.*, pp. 752–753.

2. Provision of family planning services

A much less extreme and draconian anti-population-growth argument asserts that there are many families in Third World countries who would *like* to limit their size, if only they had the *means* to do so. Hence, the main problem is to provide modern birth control devices such as the pill, the inter-uterine device (IUD), and increasingly, 'voluntary' sterilisation through male vasectomy. Family planning programmes with clinics throughout the country therefore need to be established both to 'educate' people about modern methods of fertility control and to provide them with cheap and safe means to practise it.

3. Human rights

At a United Nations convention held in Teheran, in 1968 a resolution was adopted asserting that 'it is a fundamental human right for each person to be able to determine the size of his or her own family'. A more contemporary version of this position, at least in the more affluent societies, asserts that every woman has the fundamental right to the control of her own bodily reproductive processes, including the right to legal abortion as well as contraception. Since maternal and child health are also related to the ability of parents to space their children at greater intervals, the human rights position bases its 'freedom to choose' advocacy of family planning on health as well as family size grounds.

4. 'Development' plus population programme

This is by far the principal argument advanced by a majority of those who hold that too rapid population growth should be a real concern of Third World countries. Its basic proposition is that population growth intensifies and exacerbates the economic, social and psychological problems associated with the condition of 'underdevelopment', especially since it retards the prospects for a better life for those already born. It also severely draws down limited government revenues simply to provide the most rudimentary economic, health and social services to the additional people. This in turn prevents an improvement in the levels of living of the existing generation.

As we have seen, widespread absolute poverty and low levels of living are major causes of large family size due in part to parental desires for increased economic security in old age. It follows that economic and social 'development' are *necessary* conditions for bringing about an eventual slowing down or cessation of population growth at low levels of fertility and mortality. But, according to this argument, it is not a *sufficient* condition – that is, 'development' provides people with the incentives and motivations to limit their family size, but family planning programmes are needed to provide them with the technological means to avoid unwanted pregnancies. Even though countries like France, Japan, the United States, Great Britain and, more recently, Taiwan and South Korea, were able to reduce their population growth rates without widespread family planning clinics, it is argued by advocates of the development-plus-population-programme position that the provision of these services will enable other countries desiring to control excessive population growth to do so more *rapidly* than if these family planning services were not available.

Goals and objectives: towards a consensus

In spite of what at first sight may appear to be diametrically opposed arguments between those for and against population growth, there does appear to be a common ground, an intermediate position on which both sides can agree (that is, with the possible exception of those who advance the extreme versions of the population 'hawk' or the pro-natalist positions). The ethical values which provide the basis for this consensus are rooted in what we have called in Chapter 6 the inner meaning of 'development' in conjunction with the United Nations' human rights declaration of 1968 referred to in the previous section. The following four propositions constitute the essential components of this intermediate or consensus opinion.

1. **Population growth is *not* the primary or even a significant cause of low levels of living, gross inequalities or the limited freedom of choice which characterises much of the Third World.** The fundamental causes of these problems must be sought rather in the dualistic nature of the

domestic and international economic and social order.

2. **The problem of population is not simply one of numbers but of the qualities of human life** and its material well-being. Thus, LDC population size must be viewed in conjunction with developed country affluence in relation to the quantity, distribution and utilisation of world resources – not just in relation to indigenous resources of the LDCs themselves.
3. **But rapid population growth does serve to intensify problems of 'underdevelopment'** and make prospects for 'development' that much more remote. As we have seen, the momentum of growth means that, barring catastrophe, the population of Third World countries will increase dramatically over the coming decades, no matter what fertility control measures are adopted. It follows that high population growth rates, while not the principal cause of underdevelopment, are nevertheless contributing factors in specific countries and regions of the world.
4. **Many of the real problems of population arise not from its overall size but its concentration,** especially in urban areas, as a result of accelerated rural–urban migration (see Chapter 14). A more rational and efficient spatial *distribution* of national populations thus becomes a viable alternative, in some countries, to the mere slowdown of overall population numbers.

In view of the above propositions and the development and human rights value premises implicit in them, we may conclude that the following goals and objectives might be included in any realistic approach to the issue of population growth in many developing countries.

1. In those countries or regions where the population size, distribution and growth is viewed as an existing and/or potential problem, the primary objective of any strategy to limit its further growth must deal, not only with the population variable *per se*, but, more importantly, with the underlying social and economic conditions of underdevelopment. Goals such as the elimination of absolute poverty, gross inequality, widespread unemployment especially among females, limited female access to education, malnutrition and poor health facilities need to be given high priority both as necessary concomitants of development and as the fundamental motivational basis for the expanded freedom of the individual to choose an optimal and, in many cases, smaller than present family size.
2. In order to maximise the achievement of smaller families through development-induced motivations, family planning programmes providing both the education and the technological means to regulate fertility *for those who wish to regulate it* need to be established.
3. Developed countries need to assist Third World countries to achieve their lowered fertility and mortality objectives not only by providing contraceptives and funding family planning clinics but, more importantly, (*a*) by curtailing their own excessive depletion of resources through programmes to lower the unnecessary consumption of scarce materials and non-renewable resources; (*b*) by making genuine commitments to eradicating poverty, illiteracy, disease and malnutrition in Third World countries as well as their own; and (*c*) by recognising in both their rhetoric and their international economic dealings that development is the real issue, not simply population control.

With these observations in mind, we can now turn to a more specific analysis of the economics of population growth in Chapter 12.

Concepts for review

general fertility rate	life expectancy at birth
doubling time	dependency ratio
infant mortality rate	age structure of population
rate of population increase	hidden momentum of population growth
rate of natural increase	replacement fertility
crude birth rate	population distribution
crude death rate	

Questions for discussion

1. Population growth in Third World nations has proceeded at unprecedented rates over the past few decades. Compare and contrast the present rate of population growth in less developed countries with that of the modern developed nations during their early growth years. What has been the major factor contributing to rapid Third World population growth since World War II? Explain.

2. What is the relationship between the age structure of a population and its dependency burden? Is the so-called dependency burden higher or lower in Third World countries? Why?
3. Does there appear to be any distinctive statistical relationship between Third World birth rates and (*a*) levels of per capita GNP; (*b*) rates of per capita GNP growth and/or (*c*) degree of equality or inequality in income distributions? If so, explain why you think such a relationship between birth rates and one or more of the above variables might exist.
4. Explain the meaning of the notion of the 'hidden momentum' of population growth. Why is this an important concept for projecting future population trends in different Third World nations?
5. Outline and comment briefly on some of the arguments *against* the idea that population growth is a serious problem in Third World nations.
6. Outline and comment briefly on some of the arguments *in favour* of the idea that population growth is a serious problem in Third World nations.

Further reading

(*a*) For a concise quantitative review of the world population picture in the 1970s, see B. Berelson, W. P. Mauldin and S. Segal, 'Population: current status and policy options', Center For Policy Studies, *Working Paper No. 44*, The Population Council, May 1979.

(*b*) An excellent survey article on the various interrelationships between population and economic development can be found in R. H. Cassen, 'Population and Development: a survey', World Development, iv, No. 10–11, October 1976. Two additional volumes of readings on the subject are Ronald Ridker (ed.), *Population and Development: the search for selective interventions*, Baltimore, Johns Hopkins University Press, 1976 and Richard Easterlin (ed.), *Population and Economic Change in Developing Countries*, University of Chicago Press, for the National Bureau of Economic Research, Chicago 1980.

(*c*) For a concise and informative summary of the debate on population and development, both 'for' and 'against', see Michael S. Teitelbaum, 'Population and Development: is a consensus possible?', *Foreign Affairs*, July 1974.

Chapter 12 Economics of population and development

The basis for an effective solution of population problems is, above all, socio-economic transformation.
World Population Plan of Action, Bucharest, August 1974

We hereby reaffirm that the principal aim of social, economic and cultural development . . . is to improve levels of living and enrich the quality of life of the people. And we reiterate the necessity of linking population programs with development plans.
Colombo Declaration of Third World Parliamentarians, Sri Lanka, September 1979

Introduction

Development and fertility

In recent years economists have begun to focus increasing attention on the relationship between economic development and population growth. The most difficult problem for such an analysis is to be able somehow to separate cause from effect. Does economic development accelerate or retard population growth rates; or does rapid population growth contribute to or retard economic development? What are the linkages, how strong are they, and in what direction do they operate? In this chapter we examine three major approaches to the economics of population analysis: the theory of demographic transitions, the Malthusian 'population trap' and the new micro-economics of fertility. Our aim is to assess the degree to which these approaches do or do not shed light on the main goals and objectives enumerated in the previous chapter.

The theory of the demographic transition

The theory of the 'demographic transition' attempts to explain why all contemporary developed nations have more or less passed through the same three stages of modern population history. Before their economic modernisation, these countries for centuries had stable or very slow growing populations as a result of a combination of high birth rates and almost equally high death rates. This was **Stage I. Stage II** began to occur when modernisation, associated with improved public health methods, better diets, higher incomes, etc., led to a marked reduction in mortality which gradually raised life expectancy from under 40 to over 60 years. However, the decline in death rates was not immediately accompanied by a decline in fertility. As a result, the growing divergence between high birth rates and falling death rates led to sharp increases in population growth compared to past centuries. Stage II thus marks the beginning of the demographic transition – the transition from stable or slow-growing populations to rapidly increasing numbers. Finally, **Stage III** occurs when the forces and influences of modernisation and development

Figure 12.1
The demographic transition in western Europe

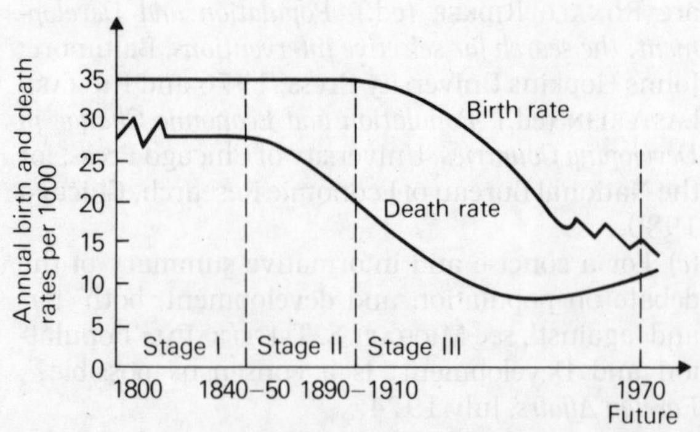

cause fertility to begin to decline so that eventually falling birth rates converge with lower death rates, leaving little or no population growth.

Figure 12.1 roughly depicts the three historical stages of the demographic transition in Western Europe.

Before the early nineteenth century, birth rates hovered around 35 per thousand. This resulted in population growth rates of around 5 per thousand or less than one-half of one per cent per year (i.e. $\frac{5}{1000} = 0.005$). Stage II, the beginning of western Europe's demographic transition, was initiated around the first quarter of the nineteenth century by slowly falling death rates as a result of improving economic conditions and the gradual development of disease and death control through modern medical and public health technologies. The decline in birth rates (Stage III) did not really begin until late in the nineteenth century with most of the reduction concentrated in the current century, many decades after modern economic growth had begun and long after death rates began their descent. But since the initial level of birth rates was generally low in western Europe as a result of late marriage and celibacy, overall rates of population growth seldom exceeded the one per cent level, even at their peak. By the end of western Europe's demographic transition in the second half of the twentieth century, the relationship between birth and death rates which marked the early 1800s had reversed, with birth rates fluctuating and death rates remaining fairly stable or slightly rising. This latter phenomenon is simply due to the older age distributions of contemporary European populations.

Figure 12.2
The beginning of a demographic transition in Third World countries

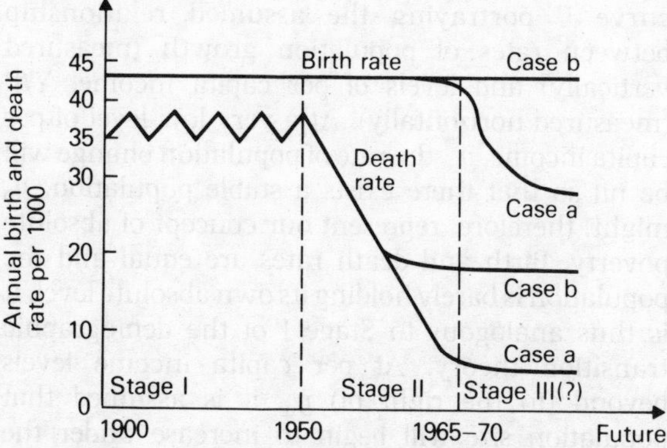

Source: Berelson, *World Population: Status Report 1974*, p. 6.

Figure 12.2 shows the contrasting population histories of contemporary Third World countries.

Birth rates in underdeveloped countries today are considerably higher than they were in pre-industrial western Europe. This is because most women in LDCs marry at an earlier age than in pre-industrialised Europe. As a result, there are more families for a given population size and also many more years in which to have children. Beginning in the 1940s and especially in the 1950s and 1960s Stage II of the demographic transition occurred throughout most of the Third World. The application of highly effective imported modern medical and public health technologies caused LDC death rates to fall much more rapidly than in nineteenth-century Europe. Given their historically high birth rates at over 40 per thousand in many countries, this has meant that Stage II of the LDC demographic transition has been characterised by population growth rates well in excess of 2 to 2.5 per cent per annum.

With regard to Stage III, we can distinguish between two broad classes of developing countries. In case A in Figure 12.2, modern methods of death control combined with rapid and widely distributed rises in levels of living have resulted in death rates falling as low as 10 per thousand and birth rates also falling rapidly to levels between 25 and 30 per thousand. These countries, most notably Taiwan, South Korea, Costa Rica, Chile and Sri Lanka, have thus entered Stage III of their demographic transition and have experienced rapidly falling rates of overall population growth. In the late 1970s several other countries including China, Colombia, Indonesia, the Dominican Republic, Thailand and the Philippines appeared to be entering a period of sustained fertility decline consistent with case A.

On the other hand, most Third World countries fall into the category of Case B in the chart. After an initial period of rapid decline, the further decline of death rates has not occurred, largely because of the persistence of widespread absolute poverty and low levels of living, Moreover, the persistence of high birth rates as a result of these low levels of living causes overall population growth rates to remain relatively high. These countries (most in south and south-east Asia, the Middle East and Africa) are still in Stage II of their demographic transition.

The important question, therefore, is when and under what conditions are Third World nations likely to experience falling birth rates and a slower expansion of population? On this issue many of both the traditional and modern economic theories of population and development have been constructed. Two of the best-known are the traditional Malthusian 'population trap' model and the more recent 'micro-economic' theory of fertility.

The Malthusian 'population trap'

The basic model

More than 180 years ago, the Reverend Thomas Malthus put forward a theory of the relationship between population growth and economic development which still survives today. Writing in 1798 in his *Essay on the Principle of Population*, and drawing on the concept of diminishing returns, Malthus postulated a universal tendency for the population of a country, unless checked by dwindling food supplies, to grow at a *geometric* rate, doubling every 30 to 40 years.[1] At the same time, because of diminishing returns to the fixed factor, land, food supplies could only expand roughly at an *arithmetical* rate. In fact, with each member of the population having less land to work with, his marginal contribution to food production would actually start to decline. Since the growth in food supplies could not keep pace with the burgeoning population, per capita incomes (defined in an agrarian society simply as per capita food production) would have a tendency to fall so low as to lead to a stable population barely existing at or slightly above the subsistence level. Malthus, therefore, contended that the only way to avoid this condition of chronic low levels of living or 'absolute poverty' was for people to engage in 'moral restraint' and limit the numbers of their progeny. Thus, one might regard Malthus as the 'father' of the modern birth control movement.

Modern economists have given a name to the Malthusian idea of a population being inexorably forced to live at subsistence levels of income. They have called it the 'low level-equilibrium population trap' or, more simply, the Malthusian 'population trap'. Diagrammatically, the basic Malthusian model can be illustrated by comparing the shape and position of curves representing population growth rates and aggregate income growth rates when these two curves are each plotted against levels of per capita income. This is done in Figure 12.3.

Figure 12.3
The Malthusian 'population trap'

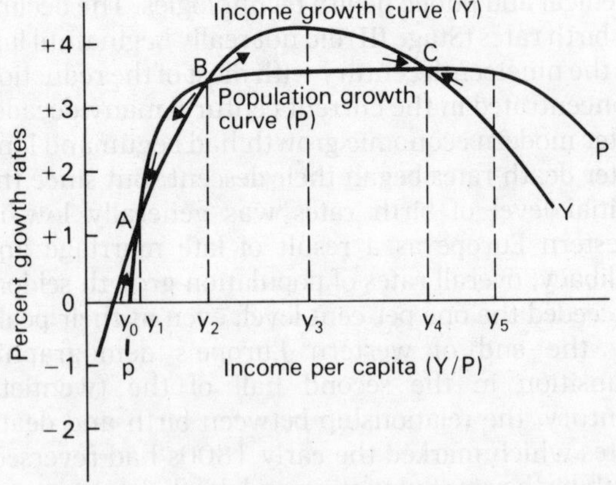

On the vertical axis we plot numerical percentage changes, both positive and negative, in the two principal variables under consideration: total population and aggregate income. On the horizontal axis are levels of per capita income. Look first at the curve P portraying the assumed relationship between rates of population growth (measured vertically) and levels of per capita income, Y/P (measured horizontally). At a very low level of per capita income, y_0, the rate of population change will be nil so that there exists a stable population. y_0 might, therefore, represent our concept of absolute poverty. Birth and death rates are equal and the population is barely holding its own absolute level. It is thus analogous to Stage I of the demographic transition theory. At per capita income levels beyond (to the right of) y_0, it is assumed that population size will begin to increase under the pressure of falling death rates. Higher incomes mean less starvation and disease. And, with birth rates

[1] A geometric progression is simply a doubling or some other multiple of each previous number, like 1, 2, 4, 8, 16, 32, 64, 128, 256, 512, 1 024 . . ., etc. Like compound interest, geometric progressions have a way of attaining large numbers very rapidly.

always assumed to be at the biological maximum, falling death rates provide the impetus for an expanding population (Stage II). In Figure 12.3, population growth achieves its maximum rate, roughly 3.3 per cent, at a per capita income level of y_2. It is assumed to remain at that level until much higher per capita income levels are realised. Thereafter (i.e. beyond y_5), in accordance with Stage III of the demographic transition, birth rates will begin to decline and the population growth rate curve becomes negatively sloped and once again approaches the horizontal axis.

The other part of the Malthusian theory requires us to plot a relationship between the growth rate of aggregate income (in the absence of population growth) and levels of per capita income. We can then compare the two rates, aggregate income and total population. If aggregate income (total product) is rising faster, per capita income by definition must be increasing; if total population is growing faster than total income, per capita income must be falling. In Figure 12.3 the rate of aggregate income growth (also measured vertically) is assumed at first to be positively related to levels of per capita income, that is, the higher the level of per capita income, the higher the rate of increase in aggregate income. The economic reason for this positive relationship is the assumption that savings vary positively with per capita income. Countries with higher per capita incomes are assumed to be capable of generating higher savings rates and thus more investment. Given a Harrod–Domar type model of economic growth (see Chapter 6, pp. 88–89), higher savings rates mean higher rates of aggregate income (GNP) growth. Beyond a certain per capita income point (y_3), however, the income growth rate curve is assumed to level off and then begin to decline as new investments and more people are required to work with fixed quantities of land and natural resources. This is the point of diminishing returns in the Malthusian model. (Note that the possibility of technological progress is not considered.) The aggregate income growth curve therefore is conceptually analogous to the total product curve in our simple theory of production described in Chapter 4.

Observe that in Figure 12.3 the curves are drawn so that they intersect at three points, A, B and C. Point A represents the point at which the Malthusian population trap level of per capita income (y_1) is attained. It is known as a *stable* equilibrium point in the sense that any small movement of per capita income to the left or right of point A will cause the per capita income equilibrium point to return to y_1. For example, as per capita income rises from y_1 towards y_2, the rate of population increase will exceed the rate of aggregate income growth, i.e. the P curve is vertically higher than the Y curve. We know that whenever population is growing faster than income, per capita income must fall. The arrow pointing in the direction of A from the right, therefore, shows that per capita income must fall back to its very low level at y_1 for all points between y_1 and y_2. Similarly, to the left of point A incomes grow faster than population causing the equilibrium per capita income level to rise to y_1.

According to Malthus and the neo-Malthusians, poor nations will never be able to rise much above their subsistence levels of per capita income unless they initiate *preventive* checks (birth control) on their population growth. In the absence of such preventive checks, *positive* checks (starvation, disease, wars) on population growth will inevitably provide the restraining force.

Completing our description of the population trap model portrayed in Figure 12.3, we see that point B is an *unstable* equilibrium point. If per capita income can somehow jump rapidly from y_1 to y_2 (e.g. as a result of a 'big push' investment and industrialisation programme) before Malthusian positive checks take their toll, it will continue to grow until the other stable equilibrium point C at per capita income level y_4 is reached. Point B is an unstable equilibrium point in the sense that any movement to the left or right will continue until either point A or C is reached. See if you can explain why point B is an unstable per capita income equilibrium point given the shape and position of the population and income growth curves while point C is a stable per capita equilibrium point.

Criticisms of the model

The Malthusian 'population trap' model provides a simple and in many ways appealing theory of the relationship between population growth and economic development. Unfortunately it is based on a number of simplistic assumptions and hypotheses that do not stand up to the test of empirical verification. We can criticise the population trap theory on two major grounds.

First, and most importantly, the model (and, indeed, Malthus) assumes away or does not take into account the enormous impact of technological progress in offsetting the inhibiting forces of rapid population growth. As we discovered in Chapter 7, the history of modern economic growth has been most closely associated with rapid technological progress in the form of a continuous series of scientific, technological and social inventions and innovations. 'Increasing' rather than 'decreasing' returns to scale has been a distinguishing feature of the modern growth epoch. While Malthus was basically correct in assuming a limited supply of land, he did not (and, in fairness, could not at that time) anticipate the manner in which technological progress could augment the availability of land by raising its quality (i.e. productivity) even though its quantity might remain roughly the same.

In terms of the population trap diagram, rapid and continuous technological progress can be represented by an upward shift of the income growth (total product) curve so that *at all levels of per capita income* it is vertically higher than the population growth curve. This is shown in Figure 12.4. As a result, per capita income will grow steadily over time. All countries, therefore, have the potential of escaping the Malthusian population trap.

A second basic criticism of the trap model is its assumption that national rates of population increase are directly (positively) related to the level of national per capita income. At relatively low levels of per capita income, therefore, we should expect to find that population growth rates increase with increasing per capita incomes. However, as we discovered in Chapters 2 and, especially, 11, there appears to be *no* clear correlation between population growth rates and levels of per capita income among Third World nations. As a result of modern medicine and public health programmes, death rates have fallen rapidly and have become independent of the level of per capita income in most Third World nations. On the other hand, as we discovered in Figure 11.2(*a*), birth rates seem to show no definable relationship with per capita income levels. Our conclusion, therefore, is that it is not so much the **aggregate** level of per capita income that matters for population growth but, rather, how that income is **distributed.** The social and economic institutions of a nation and its philosophy of development are

Figure 12.4
Technological (and social) progress allows nations to avoid the population trap

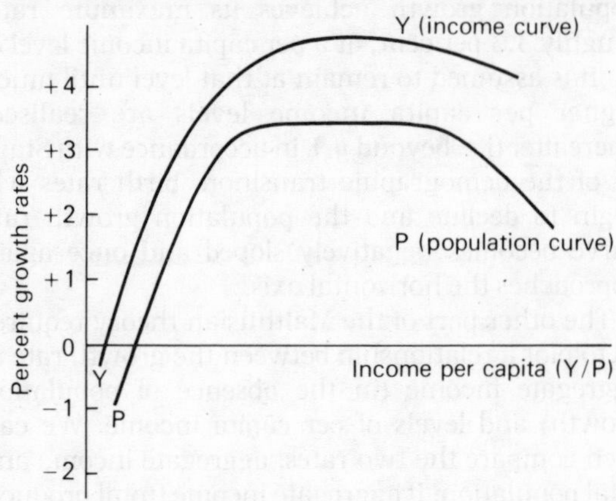

probably greater determinants of population growth rates than are aggregate economic variables and simplistic macro models of economic growth.

We can thus largely reject the Malthusian and neo-Malthusian theories as applied to contemporary Third World nations on the grounds that (1) they do not take adequate account of the role and impact of technological progress; (2) they are based on an hypothesis about a macro relationship between population growth and levels of per capita income which does not stand up to empirical testing; and (3) they focus on the *wrong* variable, per capita income, as the principal determinant of population growth rates. A much better and more valid approach centres on micro-economics, in which individual, and not aggregate, levels of living become the principal determinant of a family's decision to have more or fewer children. We now turn to this more recent micro approach to the economics of population and development.

The theory of consumer behaviour and the household economics of fertility

Consumer choice and the demand for goods

In recent years economists have begun to look more

closely at the micro-economic determinants of family fertility in an attempt to provide a better theoretical and empirical explanation of the observed falling birth rates associated with Stage III of the demographic transition. In doing this, they have drawn upon the traditional neo-classical theory of household or consumer behaviour for their basic analytical model and utilised the principles of economy and optimisation to explain family size decisions. Families with a given money income and a fixed set of tastes or preferences for various goods and services are assumed to confront an array of relative prices for these goods and services. They then determine how best to divide their total expenditure among these items on the behavioural assumption that they will attempt to maximise the total satisfaction or utility which they can expect to derive from the consumption of these goods. For example, if a rupee, peso or shilling spent on a bottle of beer yields greater psychological satisfaction (more 'utility') to a consumer than the same marginal expenditure on any other good or service, then the principles of economy and optimisation dictate that he should use this money to purchase the beer. A consumer's decisions are deemed rational as long as each last unit of expenditure on all goods and services yields the same marginal or additional utility.[2]

The negatively sloped demand curve can then be derived from this model of rational consumer or household choice since a relative fall in the price of a good causes the derived marginal utility per unit of expenditure to rise – i.e. the same satisfaction can be derived at a lower total cost so that satisfaction per unit of expenditure on this particular good must rise. Rational consumers, therefore, will shift their expenditures away from other goods and towards this good until the relative marginal utilities per rupee, peso or shilling of expenditure on *all* goods and services were once again equalised. Such an eventual equalisation of marginal utilities is brought about by the important behavioural assumption of traditional demand theory that as more of any commodity or service is consumed per unit time, the additional or marginal utility derived by the consumer will fall – i.e. the fifth bottle of cola will yield less marginal satisfaction to a thirsty consumer than the second, third or fourth bottle. The basic principle of diminishing marginal utility in consumption is thus conceptually analogous to the principle of diminishing marginal productivity in the traditional theory of production which we discussed in Chapter 4. The net result is our basic demand concept that a fall in the price of any good or service will ordinarily lead to an increase in quantities demanded when all other relevant consumer variables (i.e. incomes and the prices of other goods and services) are held constant. The demand curve for that good or service will, therefore, be negatively sloped as in Figure 3.1.

Work and leisure

This basic neo-classical theory of household choice can be extended to cover decisions between work and leisure. If a person works, he can earn a wage which at its hourly, daily or weekly level will yield an income which can be applied to derive satisfaction or 'utility' from the goods and services which this income can acquire. Alternatively, leisure itself can be considered an economic good to the extent that its 'consumption' also yields a certain satisfaction. But the price of leisure is the opportunity cost, or the foregone income of not working: the wage. Rational consumers, therefore, are assumed to divide their available time (24 hours a day) between work and leisure (including, say, eight hours' sleep) on the same conceptual basis that determines their choice among different commodities – that is, they attempt to equalise or attain an equilibrium between the relative marginal utilities of work (the utility of money income) and leisure. Now, if the price or opportunity cost of leisure increases (i.e. the wage rate rises), our theory postulates once again that less of this item will be demanded. Alternatively, the quantity of hours of wage labour supplied for work will be increased. This inverse relationship between wage rates and the utility of leisure provides the theoretical basis for the upward sloping labour supply curve discussed in Chapter 3.

[2] This 'rational' choice process in traditional consumption theory is thus entirely analogous to that of production theory whereby a cost-minimising or profit-maximising producer is assumed to allocate his expenditure on factor inputs such that each last unit of expenditure on every factor yields the same 'marginal product' – no more, no less.

The demand for children

The same basic theoretical apparatus of individual consumer or family choice for goods, services and leisure has recently been extended to include the choice of whether or not to have an additional child, on the assumption that fertility behaviour also has a strong component of economic rationality. This micro-economic theory of fertility assumes that in many ways children are consumption and investment goods like any other. It follows therefore, that the demand for children at the household level can also be influenced by family preferences for, say, a certain number of surviving (usually male) children (i.e. in regions of high mortality, parents may produce more children than they actually desire in the expectation that some will not survive), by the cost of rearing these children and by levels of family income. Children, especially in poor societies, are seen partially as economic investment goods to the extent that there is an 'expected return' in the form of child labour and the provision of financial support for parents in old age when these children reach adulthood and earn a living. As Professor Kuznets has noted in a recent exhaustive empirical study:

> They [the LDCs] are prolific because under their economic and social conditions large proportions of the population see their economic and social interests in more children as a supply of family labour, as a pool for a genetic lottery, and as a matter of economic and social security in a weakly organized, non-protecting, society.[3]

On the other hand, it is recognised that there is a strong *intrinsic* satisfaction from family formation, so that children, especially the first two or three, can also be viewed as alternative 'consumer goods' in their parents' decision-making process.

The economic choice mechanism in this theory of fertility is assumed to exist primarily with regard to the *additional* or *marginal* children who are considered as investments, it being assumed that the demand for the first few children is relatively fixed and determined largely by cultural or psychological consumption factors. In deciding whether or not to have additional children, therefore, parents are assumed to weigh economic benefits against costs, where the principal benefits are, as we have seen, the expected income from child labour, usually on the farm, and their later financial support for elderly parents. Balanced against these benefits are the two principal elements of cost: (1) the opportunity cost of the mother's time, i.e. the income she could earn if she were not at home caring for her children; and (2) the cost of educating children, i.e. the 'trade-off' between having fewer (high quality) educated children versus more 'low quality' uneducated children.

Using the same thought processes as in the traditional theory of consumer behaviour, the micro-economics of family fertility leads to the conclusion that when the 'price' or 'cost' of children rises as a result, say, of increased educational and employment opportunities for women, or a rise in school fees, or the establishment of minimum age child labour laws, or the provision of publically financed old age social security schemes and so on, then parents will demand *fewer* additional children, substituting perhaps quality for quantity or a mother's employment income for her child-rearing activities. It follows that one way to induce families to desire fewer children is to raise the 'price' of child rearing by, say, providing greater educational opportunities and a wider range of higher paying jobs for young women.

Some empirical evidence

Statistical studies in countries like Chile, the Philippines, Taiwan and Thailand have given some preliminary credence to the economic theory of fertility. For example, it has been found that high female employment opportunities outside the home and greater female and male school attendance especially in the primary and early years of secondary schooling were associated with lower levels of fertility.[4] As women become better educated, they tend to earn a larger share of

[3] Simon Kuznets, *Fertility Differentials Between Less Developed and Developed Regions: components and implications.* Economic Growth Center, Yale University, Discussion Paper No. 217, November 1974, pp. 87–88.

[4] See, T. Paul Schultz, 'Fertility Determinants: a theory, evidence and application to policy evaluation', *Rand Corporation*, Santa Monica, California, January 1974.

household income and to produce fewer children. Moreover, these studies have confirmed the strong association between decline in child mortality and the subsequent decline in fertility. Assuming that households desire a *target* number of surviving children, increased incomes and levels of living can decrease child mortality and therefore increase the chances that the firstborn will survive. As a result, fewer births are desired to attain the same number of surviving children. This fact alone underlines the importance of improved public health and child nutrition programmes in ultimately reducing Third World fertility levels.

Finally, while increased income may enable the family to support more children, the evidence seems to show that with higher incomes parents will tend to substitute child quality for quantity by investing in fewer, more educated children whose eventual earning capacity will be much higher. Additionally, it is argued that more income also will tend to lower fertility because the status effect of increased incomes raises the relative desire for material goods, especially among low income groups who previously had no opportunity to purchase these goods.

The implications for 'development' and 'fertility'

All the above can be summarised by saying that **the effect of social and economic progress in lowering fertility in developing countries will be greatest where the majority of the population and especially the very poor share in its benefits.** Specifically, birth rates among the very poor are likely to fall where there is:

- an increase in the education of women and a consequent change in their role and status;
- an increase in female non-agricultural wage employment opportunities which raises the price or 'cost' of their traditional child-rearing activities;
- a rise in family income levels through the increased direct employment and earnings of husband and wife and/or through the redistribution of income and assets from rich to poor;
- a reduction in infant mortality through expanded public health programmes and better nutritional status for both parent and child;
- development of old age and other social security systems outside the extended family network to reduce the economic dependence of parents on their offspring.

In short, expanded efforts to make jobs, education and health more broadly available to poverty groups in Third World countries will not only contribute to their economic and psychological well-being (i.e. to their development) but it can also contribute substantially to their *motivation* for smaller families (i.e. their freedom to choose) which is vital to reducing population growth rates in poor nations. The provision of well-executed family planning programmes can then give effect to these desires for smaller families by maximising their realisation in the shortest possible time.

Some policy approaches

In the light of the above analysis and in terms of the broad goals and objectives discussed in Chapter 11, what kinds of economic and social policies might the governments of developing and developed countries and international assistance agencies consider to bring about a reduction in the overall rates of world population growth? There are three areas of policy which can have important direct and indirect influences on the wellbeing of present and future world populations:

- those general and specific policies which **developing-country** governments can initiate to influence and perhaps even control their population growth and distribution;
- those general and specific policies which **developed-country** governments can initiate in their own countries to lessen their disproportionate consumption of limited world resources and to promote a more equitable distribution of the benefits of global economic progress;
- those specific ways in which developed-country governments and international assistance agencies can assist developing countries to achieve their population policy objectives, whatever they may be, in shorter periods of time.

Let us deal with each of these in turn.

What developing countries can do

As we have seen from both the cross-country data given in Chapter 11 and the analytical and empirical content of the micro-economic theory of fertility, the principal variables influencing the demand for children at the family level are those which are most closely associated with the concept of 'development' as defined in Part One. Thus, certain development policies are crucial influences on the transition from a high growth to a low growth population. These policies aim at eliminating absolute poverty, lessening income inequalities, expanding educational opportunities, especially for women, providing increased job opportunities for both men and women, bringing the benefits of modern preventive medicine and public health programmes (especially the provision of clean water and sanitation) to the rural and urban poor, improving maternal and child health through more food, better diets, and improved nutrition so as to lower infant mortality, and, finally, creating a more equitable provision of other social services to wider segments of the population. Again, it is neither numbers nor parental irrationality that is at the root of the Third World population problem. Rather it is the pervasiveness of abject poverty and low levels of living that provides the economic rationale for large families and burgeoning populations.

While such broad long-run development policies are essential to ultimate population stabilisation, there are some specific policies that LDC governments might try to lower birth rates in the short run. Basically, governments can attempt to control fertility in five ways:

1. They can try to persuade people to have smaller families through the **communications media** and the **educational process,** both formal (school system) and informal (adult education).
2. They can establish **family planning programmes** to provide health and contraceptive services in order to encourage the desired behaviour. Such publicly sponsored or officially supported programmes now exist in over 75 Third World countries covering almost 87 per cent of LDC populations. Today only a few large countries such as Brazil, Burma, Ethiopia and Peru do not have such programmes.
3. They can deliberately **manipulate economic incentives and disincentives** to have children, for example through the elimination or reduction of maternity leaves and benefits, the reduction or elimination and/or the imposition of financial penalties for having children beyond a certain number, the establishment of old age social security provisions and minimum age child labour laws, the raising of school fees and the elimination of heavy public subsidies for secondary and higher education, and finally, the subsidising of smaller families through direct money payments. Singapore, India, Korea, Taiwan and China are all currently conducting social experiments to influence family size through alternative incentive/disincentive policies. For example, Singapore is assigning scarce public housing without giving preference to family size. It is also limiting paid maternity leave to a maximum of two children, scaling the delivery fee according to child numbers, and reducing income tax relief from five to three children. In India, a tea estate has experimented with financial deposits into individual worker savings accounts to women during their periods of non-pregnancy. The deposits are scaled according to the number of children and the whole account can be cancelled if a woman bears too many children. These accumulated savings are then paid out when the woman reaches the age of 45, as a form of social security in the place of children. In Taiwan there is an experiment in a rural township in which the local government is depositing funds into bank accounts for young couples to cover the costs of educating their first two children. However, if the couple has a third child, part of this money is forfeited and it is all forfeited at the birth of the fourth child. The programme is thus expressly designed to encourage families to have fewer but more educated children. In 1980 China initiated a tough new drive on births with a goal of lowering the annual birth rate to 1 per cent during the decade. Among other measures a financial disincentive programme was started which included a provision that salaries of those workers who have a third child are reduced by 10 per cent until that child reaches the age of 14. The child is also denied free education and medical care. Women are not permitted to marry before the age of 23 while the minimum age of marriage for men was raised to 26. Additional incentives include housing priorities for couples with no more than

two children, job preference for the children of small families, the allocation of private garden plots to those with small families and, finally, increased pension benefits scaled inversely to the number of children a retired person has had. Early results indicated that both the India and Taiwan experiments seem to be achieving their goals. For a while in the mid-1970s India also had a major vasectomy programme under way in which men were given a direct cash payment, transistor radios or even free tickets to championship football matches if they agreed to undergo 'voluntary' sterilisation. But the programme was both ineffective and politically damaging (see 5 below). The results of the new Chinese incentive programmes, however, will be interesting to observe.

4. They can attempt **to redirect the distribution of their populations** away from the rapidly growing urban areas as a result of massive rural–urban internal migration by eliminating the current imbalance in economic and social opportunities in urban as compared to rural areas. As we shall see in Chapter 16 rural development programmes are increasingly being emphasised in contemporary Third World development strategies, in part to stem the rising tide of rural–urban population movements and thus to promote a more geographically balanced distribution of the population.
5. Finally, governments can attempt **directly to coerce people** into having smaller families through the power of state legislation and penalties. For obvious reasons, few governments would attempt to engage in such coercion, especially since it is not only morally questionable and often politically unacceptable but also because it is almost always very difficult to administer. The defeat of Mrs. Indira Gandhi's government in the Indian elections of 1977 was largely due to the popular backlash against the government's forced sterilisation programme. Her return to power in 1980 was accompanied by a commitment *not* to reintroduce coercive birth control policies.

What the developed nations can do in their own countries

When we view the problems of population in terms of a global perspective, as we should, the question of the relationship between population size and distribution and the depletion of many non-renewable resources in developed and under-developed countries assumes major importance. In a world where 6 per cent of the people in one country, the United States, account for 40 per cent of annual world resource use and where slightly over 30 per cent of the world's population accounts for 80 per cent of its annual resource utilisation, then clearly we are not dealing only, or even primarily, with a problem of numbers. We must also be concerned with the impact of rising affluence and the very worldwide distribution of incomes on the depletion of many non-renewable resources such as petroleum, certain basic metals and other raw materials essential for economic growth.

In terms of food consumption, basic grains like wheat, corn, rice, etc., are by far the most important source of man's *direct* food energy supply (52 per cent). Consumed *indirectly* (e.g. grain fed to livestock which are then consumed as beef, poultry, pork and lamb or indirectly as milk, cheese and eggs) it makes up a significant share of the remainder. In resource terms, more than 70 per cent of the world's cropland goes into grain production. And yet, the average North American directly and indirectly consumes five times as much grain and the corresponding agricultural resources – land, fertiliser, water, etc. – as his counterpart in India, Nigeria or Colombia. With regard to energy, probably the second most essential resource to modern society, consumption of energy fuels (fossil-oil and coal – nuclear and hydro-electric) by the average American in 1971 was 25 times the average Brazilian, 60 times the average Indian, 191 times the average Nigerian and 351 times the average Ethiopian consumption level! The use of this energy to power private automobiles, operate home and office air-conditioners and activate electric toothbrushes in the developed nations means that there is potentially that much less to, say, fertilise small family farms in the less developed nations. Alternatively, it means that poor families will have to pay more to obtain these valuable resource inputs.

Many similar examples could be given of the gross inequalities in resource use. Perhaps more importantly, one could cite innumerable instances of the unnecessary and costly wastage of many scarce and non-renewable resources by the affluent developed nations. The point, therefore, is that **any world-wide**

programme designed to engender a better balance between resources and people by limiting Third World population growth through social intervention and family planning must also include the responsibility of rich nations systematically to simplify their own currently profligate life styles. Only then will needed resources be freed which could be used by poor nations to generate the social and economic development essential to slower population growth.

For example, a 10 per cent reduction in beef consumption by North Americans (which on the whole would probably be healthy for them) would free many million tons of grain to feed the hungry in poor nations. At the very least such a demand reduction would alleviate the upward pressure on world grain prices. More hopefully, massive food aid programmes to the 'least developed' nations could become more feasible. A similar reduction in energy consumption would greatly reduce current pressures on world petroleum supplies. This would make it easier for nations in Asia and Africa to obtain more cheaply the necessary supplies of energy and fertilisers to expand their agricultural output. It is difficult and somewhat ironic for rich nations to preach moderation in family size to poor countries when they themselves refuse to moderate their disproportionate and wasteful use of world food and energy resources.[5]

In addition to simplifying life styles and consumption habits, one other very positive but unlikely internal policy which rich nations could adopt to mitigate current world population problems would be to liberalise the legal conditions for the international emigration of poor, unskilled workers and their families from Africa, Asia and Latin America to North America, Europe and Australia. The international migration of peasants from western and southern Europe to North America, Australia and New Zealand in the nineteenth and early twentieth centuries was a major factor in moderating the problems of underdevelopment and population pressure in European countries. No such 'safety valve' or outlet exists today for Third World countries. But, clearly, there are many underpopulated regions of the world and many labour-scarce societies which could benefit economically from international migration.

How developed countries can assist developing countries in their various population programmes

There are also a number of ways in which rich-country governments and multilateral donor agencies can assist developing-country governments to achieve their population policy objectives in shorter periods of time. The most important of these concerns the willingness of rich countries (including now the wealthy Arab oil states) to be of genuine assistance to poor countries in their development efforts. Such genuine support would consist not only of expanded public and private financial assistance but also of improved trade relations, more appropriate technological transfers, assistance in developing indigenous scientific research capacities, better international commodity pricing policies, and a more equitable sharing of the world's scarce natural resources.[6]

There are two other activities more directly related to fertility moderation where rich-country governments and international donor agencies can help. The first of these is the whole area of research into the technology of fertility control: the contraceptive pill, modern interuterine devices (IUDs), voluntary sterilisation procedures, etc. Research has been going on in this area for a number of years, almost all of it financed by international donor organisations, private foundations and developed-country aid agencies. Further efforts to improve the effectiveness of this contraceptive technology while minimising the health risks need to be encouraged.

The second area includes financial assistance from developed countries for family planning programmes, public education and national population research activities in the developing countries. This has been the main traditional area of developed-country assistance in the field of population. Total resources devoted to these activities have

[5] Of course, there is the counter-argument that curtailing consumption in rich nations will have short-run harmful effects on poor nation economic growth as a result of an immediate decline in the latter's exports of raw materials. It is for this reason that a cutback in excessive rich-country consumption needs to be accompanied by a large scale increase in resource transfers to developing nations.

[6] These and other areas of international economic relations between rich and poor countries will be examined in Parts Three and Four.

risen dramatically from around \$2 million in 1960 to almost \$3 000 million by the mid 1970s. It is a moot point, however, whether such resources might not have been more effectively used to achieve their fertility goals had they instead been devoted directly to assisting LDCs to raise the levels of living of their poorest peoples. As we have seen, it is of little value to have sophisticated family planning programmes where the people are not motivated to reduce family size.

Conflicts, trade-offs and choices among alternative policies and competing objectives

Our discussion of possible policy options for curtailing population growth in Third World countries and freeing scarce world resources for development activities on the part of rich countries was intended principally to illustrate the range of alternatives which might be followed in light of stated objectives. However, diverse policies need to be weighed against alternative and often conflicting goals. For example, two common population objectives are the lowering of fertility in order to slow down overall population growth and the reduction of rural–urban migration to avoid excessive urban concentrations and to improve the spatial distribution of a given population. It turns out, however, as we show in Chapter 14, that one of the principal strategies for lowering fertility – more education, especially for women – happens to be an important factor stimulating the movement of people from rural to urban areas. Thus, while more education might decrease family size, it might also increase rural–urban migration and urban population congestion with its attendant social, physical and psychological problems. In such a situation a simultaneous policy to develop rural areas would be needed. This would provide expanded rural job opportunities in addition to improved health, cultural and social amenities so that the more educated will remain in rural areas adding to total production and having fewer children as their levels of living increase.

In addition to analysing possible goal conflicts and trade-offs, policy-makers in developing countries, even more than in developed nations, are faced with severe budgetary constraints. They therefore have to choose among alternative policies in terms of some social benefit/cost framework. Would an extra rupee, bhat, or shilling of expenditure be more effective in lowering fertility if it went towards family planning programmes, nutritional supplementation projects, educational expansion, employment creation or direct incentive and disincentive schemes? Unfortunately, the problem does not end here, for there are many *other* goals and objectives of development which may take precedence over fertility reduction. Choices always have to be made, not only on the basis of fundamental economic concepts such as the principle of economy and optimisation, but also in terms of explicit value judgments about what is desirable and what are the priorities among alternative goals.

While it might be an important objective in certain densely populated Third World nations, we believe that direct attempts to reduce population growth need not be a *primary* objective. A decrease in population growth is more likely to be the natural consequence of policies directly designed to raise levels of living among the now poverty-stricken masses of Asia, Africa and Latin America. True development will normally motivate people to have fewer children. Well-conceived and well-executed family planning and other direct population education programmes can then play an important and useful role. But their widespread success can *only* occur within the context of a *successful* poverty-focused national strategy of development. This seems to be the basic conclusion and consensus of opinion among the majority of those economists who have studied the population problem in a wide spectrum of developing nations. It also represents the *unanimous* position of the hundred-plus nations which took part in the first World Population Conference at Bucharest in 1974.

Concepts for review

family planning programmes	opportunity cost of a woman's time
demographic transition	economic incentives and disincentives for fertility reduction
'macro' population–development relationship	private v. social benefits and costs
marginal utility	

micro-economic theory of fertility reduction
Malthusian 'population trap'
education and fertility relationship
investment in children
LDC–DC population policies

Questions for discussion

1. Describe briefly the theory of demographic transition. At what stage in this transition does your country seem to be? Explain.
2. How does the so-called household or micro-economics of fertility relate to the theory of consumer choice? Do you think that on the level of individual families, economic incentives and disincentives do influence family size decisions? Explain your answer giving some specific examples of such incentives and disincentives.
3. 'The world population problem is not just a matter of expanding numbers but also one of rising affluence and limited resources. It is as much a problem caused by developed nations as it is one deriving from Third World countries.' Comment on this statement.
4. Outline and comment briefly on the various policy options available to Third World governments in their attempt to modify or limit the rate of population growth.
5. Is population growth perceived as a real problem in your nation? If so, what would you suggest might be the best strategy for reducing population growth rates? If not, explain why it is not seen as a real problem and why you do or do not agree with this appraisal of the present situation.

Further reading

On the general relationship between population growth and economic development broadly defined see: RICHARD A. EASTERLIN (ed.), *Population and Economic Change in Developing Countries*, University of Chicago, 1980 and LÉON TABAH (ed.), *Population Growth and Economic Development in the Third World*, Ordina, Belgium, 1976.

On the new 'micro-economics' of fertility, see: HARVEY LEIBENSTEIN, 'An Interpretation of the Economic Theory of Fertility: promising path or blind alley?', *Journal of Economic Literature*, 12, No. 2, 1974; T. PAUL SCHULTZ, 'Fertility Determinants: a theory, evidence, and an application to policy evaluation', *Rand Corporation Monograph R-106*, Jan 1974; RICHARD A. EASTERLIN, 'An Economic Framework for Fertility Analysis', *Studies in Family Planning*, The Population Council, March 1975; MARC NERLOVE, 'Household and Economy: towards a new theory of population and economic growth', *Journal of Political Economy*, 82, No. 2, Pt 2, 1974; SUSAN H. COCHRANE, 'A Review of some Micro-economic Models of Fertility', *Population Studies*, 29, No. 3, 1975.

Finally, an excellent comprehensive survey of population policies in developing countries can be found in TIMOTHY KING *et al.*, *Population Policies and Economic Development*, Johns Hopkins U.P., Baltimore and London, 1974.

Chapter 13 Unemployment: dimensions of a global problem

> The cities are filling up and urban unemployment steadily grows . . . the 'marginal men', the wretched strugglers for survival on the fringes of farm and city, may already number more than half a billion. By 1980, they will surpass a billion, by 1990 two billion. Can we imagine any human order surviving with so gross a mass of misery piling up at its base?
> *Robert McNamara, Former President of the World Bank*

Introduction

The employment problem – some basic issues

Historically, the economic development of western Europe and North America has often been described in terms of the continuous transfer of economic activity and people from rural to urban areas. As urban industries expanded, new employment opportunities were created while labour-saving technological progress in agriculture reduced rural manpower needs. The combination of these two phenomena made it possible for Western nations to undergo an orderly and effective rural to urban transfer of their human resources. Many economists concluded that economic development in the Third World, too, necessitated a concerted effort to promote rapid urban industrial growth. They tended to view cities, therefore, as the 'growth centres' and focal points of an expanding economy. Unfortunately this strategy of rapid industrialisation has, in most instances, failed to bring about the desired results predicted by historical experience.

In fact, many Third World countries today are plagued by an historically unique combination of massive rural to urban population movements, stagnating agricultural productivities and growing urban unemployment and underemployment. Substantial urban unemployment in LDC economies is probably one of the most striking symptoms of their inadequate development. In a wide spectrum of poor countries, open unemployment in urban areas now affects 10 to 20 per cent of their labour forces. The incidence of unemployment is much higher among the young and increasingly more educated in the 15 to 24 year age bracket. Even larger fractions of *both* urban and rural labour forces are underemployed. They neither have the complementary resources (if they are working full-time) nor the opportunities (if they work only part-time) for increasing their very low incomes to levels comparable with those in the modern manufacturing, commerce and service sectors. It is because of its relationship to the problem of Third World poverty, therefore, that the employment issue occupies such a central place in the study of underdevelopment.

But the dimensions of the employment problem in Third World countries go beyond the simple shortage of work opportunities or the underutilisation and low productivity of those who do work long hours. It also includes the growing divergence between inflated attitudes and job expectations, especially among the educated youth, and the actual jobs available in urban and rural areas. In particular, the growing aversion to manual and agricultural work fostered in urban and white-collar oriented educational systems creates severe strains for poor societies attempting to accelerate national development.

The employment problem in Third World countries therefore has a number of facets that make it historically unique and thus subject to a variety of unconventional economic analyses. There are three major reasons for this:

1. Unemployment regularly and chronically affects much larger proportions of labour forces in a variety of different ways than did open unemployment in the industrialised countries, even during the worst years of the Great Depression.
2. The causes of Third World employment problems are much more complex than those in the developed countries. They therefore require a variety of policy approaches rather than say simple Keynesian type policies to expand aggregate demand as in Western societies. In many cases such approaches go beyond narrow economic policies to touch on the social, institutional and attitudinal character of these societies.
3. It is important to bear in mind that whatever the dimensions and the causes of unemployment in Third World nations, the human circumstances of abject poverty and low levels of living associated with this lack of productive work are such as have rarely been experienced in the now developed countries. There is an urgent need, therefore, for concerted policy action by both the less developed and the more developed nations. As we shall see, the LDCs need to readjust domestic policies to include employment creation as a major social and economic objective while the developed countries need to review and readjust their traditional economic policies *vis-à-vis* the Third World, especially in the area of trade and technology transfer.

Since it is impossible to do justice to the many complexities and nuances of employment problems in diverse Third World countries, our focus in this chapter and the next is on two major questions that face almost all LDCs.

- Why has rapid industrial growth failed to generate substantial new urban employment opportunities in many underdeveloped countries?
- Why do masses of people continue to migrate from diverse rural areas into the crowded and congested cities in spite of high and rising levels of urban unemployment?

In investigating these two issues, we show why the urbanisation process in less developed countries has differed so markedly from the historical experience of the now developed countries, and why growing unemployment and underemployment are not inevitable in the early economic growth process. Rather they will be seen as symptoms of farther-reaching economic and social disturbances both within LDCs and in their relationship with developed countries.

Although our overall purpose in these two chapters is to examine the nature and dimensions of the employment problem in Third World countries, we focus primarily on *urban* unemployment and underemployment, especially as related to the pervasive phenomenon of rural–urban migration. In Chapters 15 and 16 we look more closely at problems of agricultural unemployment and underemployment within the broad framework of rural development strategies. This chapter begins, therefore, with a quantitative profile of trends in employment, unemployment, urbanisation and labour force growth in a large sample of developing countries. We then discuss the nature and dimensions of urban unemployment and the linkages between unemployment, poverty and income distribution. Urban unemployment principally results from two fundamental economic factors: a slow growing *demand* for urban labour in the modern, industrial sector combined with a rapidly growing supply of urban labour from rural areas. An analysis of the urban unemployment phenomenon, therefore, necessitiates an examination of the economic causes and determinants of migration from rural to urban areas (in Chapter 14). We then consider alternative development strategies designed to reduce excessive rural–urban population flows while still generating more urban (and rural) employment opportunities.

Dimensions of the employment problem in Third World nations

First let us look at some of the quantitative dimensions of the employment and unemployment problem in diverse Third World nations.

Employment and unemployment: trends and projections

During the 1970s, increased interest in the widespread and growing problem of Third World unemployment and underemployment among individual development economists, national planning authorities and international assistance agencies led to a much broader and more precise picture of the quantitative dimensions of the problem than was available only a decade before. In particular, the International Labour Organization (ILO) launched its ambitious 'World Employment Programme' at the beginning of the 1970s with a series of detailed case studies of the employment problem in a wide range of countries including Colombia, Kenya, Sri Lanka, Iran and the Philippines. These and similar studies in other countries documented the seriousness of the existing problem and the likelihood that it would worsen over the coming years.

Table 13.1 provides a summary picture of employment and unemployment trends since 1960 with projections to the year 1990 for 'all developing countries' as well as for Africa, Asia and Latin America. We see first that unemployment grew from approximately 36.5 million in 1960 to over 54 million workers in 1973, an increase of 46 per cent. This averages out to an annual rate of increase of 3 per cent which is higher than the annual rate of employment growth during this same period. Thus, unemployment was growing faster than employment in the developing world as a whole.

When we also consider that the 'underemployed' in 1973 comprised approximately an additional 250 million people, then the combined unemployment and underemployment rate reaches a staggering 29 per cent for all developing countries, with Africa experiencing a labour underutilisation rate of 38 per cent. Moreover, with rapid labour force growth (see below), the marginal unemployment rate (that is, the proportion of new labour force entrants unable to find regular jobs) is likely to be even higher than the average figures shown in Table

Table 13.1
Employment and unemployment in developing countries, 1960–1990

Indicator	1960	1970	1973	1980	1990
All developing countries*					
Employment (000)†	507,416	617,244	658,000	773,110	991,600
Unemployment (000)	36,466	48,798	54,130	65,620	88,693
Unemployment rate (%)	6.7	7.4	7.6	7.8	8.2
Combined unemployment and underemployment rate (%)‡	25	27	29		
Africa	31	39	38		
Asia	24	26	28		
Latin America	18	20	25		
All Africa					
Employment (000)†	100,412	119,633	127,490	149,390	191,180
Unemployment (000)	8,416	12,831	13,890	15,973	21,105
Unemployment rate (%)	7.7	9.6	9.8	9.8	9.9
All Asia*					
Employment (000)†	340,211	413,991	441,330	516,800	660,300
Unemployment (000)	24,792	31,440	34,420	43,029	59,485
Unemployment rate (%)	6.8	7.1	7.2	7.7	8.3
All Latin America					
Employment (000)†	66,793	83,620	89,180	106,920	140,120
Unemployment (000)	3,258	4,527	5,820	6,618	8,103
Unemployment rate (%)	4.7	5.1	6.1	5.8	5.5

* Excluding China.
† Including underemployment.
‡ Not calculated for 1980 and 1990.

Source: Yves Sabolo, 'Employment and unemployment, 1960–90', *International Labour Review,* 112, No. 6 (1975), Table 3 and Appendix.

13.1. Although the extent of labour underutilisation is lower in Asia and Latin America, the quantitative and qualitative dimensions of the problem are just as serious as in Africa. For example, even though Asia may have a lower rate of unemployment than Africa, the absolute numbers involved are many times larger (34.4 million in 1973 compared with 13.9 million for Africa).

Projections to 1990 indicate that the rate of Third World unemployment will rise steadily and that the total numbers unemployed would have reached 65 million by 1980 and are expected to be almost 90 million by 1990. Adding projections for the underemployed could give a figure as high as 500 million workers in the 1980s who are either unemployed, employed part-time or whose productivity is very low. Although these figures are only rough estimates, they do strikingly underline the seriousness of the problem particularly in the context of the rapid growth of urban populations.

Urbanisation and urban population growth: people on the move

The cities of the developing world are growing at an extremely rapid pace. Millions of people are migrating each year from rural to urban areas, even though many of the largest cities have, for all practical purposes, given up trying to provide more than minimal sanitation, health, housing and transportation services to their dense populations. Industrial production has expanded, but so too has urban unemployment and underemployment. In the countryside the poorest people are scarcely better off now than they were 15 years ago, and in some areas their situation has worsened.

As large as these cities are today, many are destined to become substantially larger in the years to come. For example, Figure 13.1 shows that in 1950 about 38 per cent of city dwellers lived in the developing world. By 1975, however, about the same number of developing world people – 750 million – lived in cities as those in the developed world. By the year 2000, more than two and a half times that number will populate the urban areas of the developing countries, while the cities of the industrialised world will have increased by less than 50 per cent. Whereas only 16 developing-world cities had a population in excess of 4 million in 1975, by the year 2000 there will be 61. The cities of Africa are expected to grow by 336 per cent, to almost 250 million population; South Asia by 298 per cent, to almost 800 million; Latin America by 235 per cent, to more than 450 million; and East Asia by 225 per cent, to over 500 million.

Figure 13.1
Total urban population: developed and developing countries, 1950, 1975, 2000 (projected)

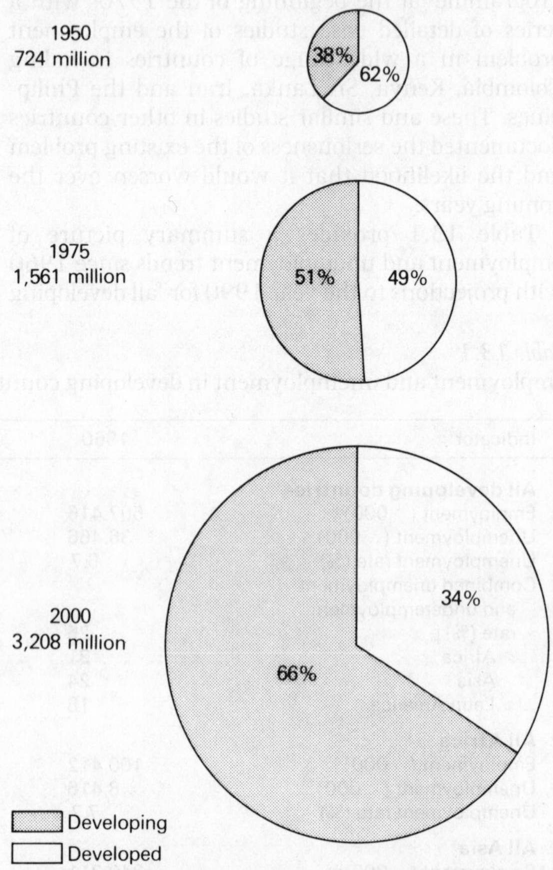

In 1950, 11 of world's largest cities were in the industrialised countries; in 1980 only seven were; by the year 2000, only three will be (see Figure 13.2). Metropolitan Mexico City will be the largest urban area in the year 2000, with about 31 million people, followed by São Paulo, Brazil, with 26 million, Tokyo-Yokohama with more than 24 million, New York with almost 23 million, and Shanghai with a slightly smaller population. Of more significance and alarm, however, are prospects for cities such as Bombay (17.1 million),

Calcutta (16.7 million), Jakarta (16.6 million), Cairo (13.1 million), Madras (12.9 million), and Manila (12.3 million) where both urban services and new employment opportunities have already fallen far behind population increases.

Figure 13.2
The 15 largest metropolitan areas (UN estimates for 1980 and 2000, in millions)

1980		2000	
New York	20.4	31.0	Mexico City
Tokyo	20.0	25.8	Sao Paulo
Mexico City	15.0	24.2	Tokyo
Sao Paulo	13.5	22.7	New York
Shanghai	13.4	22.8	Shanghai
Los Angeles	11.7	19.9	Peking
Peking	10.7	19.0	Rio de Janeiro
Rio de Janeiro	10.7	17.1	Bombay
London	10.3	16.7	Calcutta
Buenos Aires	10.1	16.6	Jakarta
Paris	9.9	14.2	Seoul
Osaka	9.5	14.2	Los Angeles
Düsseldorf	9.3	13.1	Cairo
Calcutta	8.8	12.9	Madras
Seoul	8.5	12.3	Manila

Source: United Nations, *Patterns of Urban and Rural Growth*, Population Studies No. 68, Department of Economic and Social Affairs (New York: United Nations, 1980), ST/ESA/Series A.68.

As a specific illustration of developing-world urban population growth, consider Mexico City. In 1940 the population of Mexico City was slightly in excess of a million and a half inhabitants. This represented only 8 per cent of the total Mexican population. Over the next 40 years, however, the situation changed dramatically. Between 1940 and 1950 Mexico City's population almost doubled. Significantly, over 70 per cent of this increase – 850,000 people – was due to internal rural-to-urban migration (with minor boundary reclassification) and only 30 per cent to natural increase. In the 1950s, the city gained over 1 930 000 new inhabitants, about half of whom were migrants. In the 1960s, the population swelled to over 8.3 million as almost one and a half million new migrants arrived, twice the number of the previous decade. The massive migration into Mexico City during the period 1940–70 also provided the base for the current high level of natural population increase. More than half of the city's growth during this period resulted directly or indirectly from heavy internal migration. Demographers estimate that the present Mexico City population is almost 14 million and that by the year 2000 it will reach 31 million. Although the numbers may be larger than other developing country cities, as shown in Figure 13.2, Mexico City's phenomenal growth pattern is shared by a sizable proportion of Asian urban areas, with some of the most rapid growth processes only now gathering momentum in Africa.[1]

Table 13.2
Internal migration as a source of urban growth: selected developing countries

Country	Annual urban growth (%)	Share of growth due to migration (%)
Argentina	2.0	35
Brazil	4.5	36
Colombia	4.9	43
India	3.8	45
Indonesia	4.7	49
Nigeria	7.0	64
Philippines	4.8	42
Sri Lanka	4.3	61
Tanzania	7.5	64
Thailand	5.3	45

Source: K. Newland, *City Limits: Emerging Constraints on Urban Growth*, Worldwatch Paper no. 38, Washington, D.C., August 1980, p. 10.

Rural-to-urban migration is therefore a major contributor to the rapid growth of developing world cities. For example, it is estimated that net migration now accounts for between one-third and three-fourths of the urban population growth in developing countries. Table 13.2 provides some recent data on the share of urban growth due to migration for a representative group of developing countries. Directly and indirectly, then, the phenomenal growth of most developing-world cities has largely

[1] For a more detailed examination of the urbanisation problem in developing countries, see Michael P. Todaro with Jerry Stilkind, *City Bias and Rural Neglect: The dilemma of urban development*, The Population Council, New York City, 1981.

been the result of migration on a historically vast scale. Let us look, therefore, at the question of labour supply.

Labour force: present and projected

The number of people searching for work in a less developed country depends primarily on the size and age composition of its population. Among the numerous processes relating trends in overall population growth to the growth of indigenous labour forces two are of particular interest. First, whatever the overall magnitude of the population growth rate, its fertility and mortality components have a *separate* significance. A 3 per cent (or 30 per 1 000) natural growth rate when crude birth and death rates are 50 and 20 has different labour force implications from a birth and death rate combination of 40 and 10. This is because the age structure of the population will be different for a high birth and death rate economy than for a low birth and death rate one, even though the natural rate of increase is the same for both. Since birth rates obviously affect only the numbers of newly born while death rates affect (although unevenly) all age groups, a high birth and death rate economy will have a greater percentage of the total population in the dependent age group (i.e. 1–15 years) than will a low birth–death rate economy. The rapid reductions in death rates recently experienced by most LDCs have therefore expanded the size of their present labour forces while continuous high birth rates create high present dependency ratios and rapidly expanding future labour forces.

Second, the impact of fertility decline on labour force size and age structures operates only after very long lags, even when the decline is rapid. The resason is the phenomenon of population momentum described in Chapter 11. For example, a 50 per cent fall in LDC fertility rates by the late 1970s would have reduced the male labour force by only 13 per cent by the end of the century, a reduction from about 1.27 billion to 1.11 billion workers. This is certainly not a trivial reduction and its long-run impact would be substantial. Nevertheless, the essential fact remains that over the next 15 years those who enter the labour force have *already been born* while the size of the labour force over the next two decades is fairly well determined by current fertility and mortality rates.

Table 13.3
Growth of the labour force, 1970–2000

	Average Annual Percentage Growth Rate		
	1970–80	1980–90	1990–2000
Developing Countries	2.2	2.2	2.1
Developed Countries	1.2	0.7	0.5
Asia and Pacific	2.6	2.3	2.0
Latin America	2.7	3.0	2.7
Middle East and North Africa	2.6	2.9	2.2
Sub-Saharan Africa	2.2	2.5	2.6

Source: *World Development Report, 1979, op cit.*, Table 27.

Present labour force projections suggest annual increases of the order of 2.2 per cent for all less developed regions during the present decade and approximately 2.1 per cent for the 1990s (see Table 13.3). But within the Third World, Latin American countries are likely to experience the greatest rates of labour force growth over the next 20 years, while Asian and African countries follow close behind. In terms of actual numbers, however, which demonstrate the prospective magnitude of the LDC employment problem more dramatically than percentage rates of growth, reasonable projections for the year 2000 indicate that there will be over 920 million more job seekers than in 1970 with over 46 per cent of these concentrated in South Asia and 31 per cent in East Asia (see Table 13.4).

The magnitude and age structure of urban unemployment

Given rapid rates of urban labour force growth in the range of 4 to 7 per cent per annum and the relatively slower growth of urban employment opportunities (averaging about 2.5 per cent – see below), the problem of urban unemployment has attained very serious and, in some some cases, crisis proportions in many Third World nations. Current rates of open unemployment (people without any regular or part-time job) in the cities of Africa, Asia, the Middle East and Latin America average about 13 per cent of the urban labour force or approximately 45 million people. But the problem is considerably more serious for those between the ages of 15 and

Table 13.4
Labour force projections 1970–2000

	Labour force in millions (and % of total)			
	1970	1980	1990	2000
Developed countries	498.3(33)	554.7(30)	593(28)	649(25)
Less developed countries	1013.5(67)	2180.9(70)	1547(72)	1933(75)
Regions				
South Asia	430.1(43)	549 (43)	691(45)	886(46)
East Asia	379.6(37)	467.3(37)	519(33)	602(31)
Africa	125.8(12)	160.3(12)	212(14)	277(14)
Latin America	76.2 (8)	102 (8)	129(8)	172 (9)

Source: Based on data from International Labour Office, Statistical Branch, as reported in ODC *Agenda 1979*, Table A–13, p. 179.

24, many of whom have had significant amounts of schooling. Table 13.5 shows that in almost all LDC urban centres, rates of unemployment in this age bracket are almost double the rates of recorded unemployment for the urban labour force as a whole.

Rates of open urban unemployment, however, only reveal the visible aspects of the employment problem in Third World nations. The actual underutilisation of labour takes many other forms, including various manifestations of underemployment and hidden unemployment. Although data on the various forms of underemployment in LDC cities are scarce, recent studies of countries like Colombia, Kenya, Sri Lanka and the Philippines indicate that as many as 30 per cent, or over 100 million people, in Third World urban areas may be counted as being heavily underutilised.

Dimensions of labour underutilisation: some definitional distinctions

To get a full understanding of the significance of the urban unemployment problem we must also take into account, in addition to the openly unemployed, those larger numbers of others who may be visibly active, but in an economic sense, are grossly underutilised. As Professor Edgar O. Edwards has correctly pointed out in his comprehensive survey of employment problems in developing countries:

> In addition to the numbers of people unemployed, many of whom may receive minimal incomes through the extended family system, it is also necessary to consider the dimensions of (1) time (many of those employed would like to work more hours per day, per week or per year), (2) intensity of work (which brings in considerations of health and nutrition), and (3) productivity (lack of which can often be attributed to inadequate, complementary resources with which to work). Even these are only the most obvious dimensions of effective work, and factors such as motivation, attitudes, and cultural inhibitions (as against women, for example) must also be considered.[2]

Edwards therefore distinguishes among the following five forms of underutilisation of labour[3]:

1. **Open unemployment.** Both voluntary (people who exclude from consideration some jobs for which they could qualify, implying some means of support other than employment) and involuntary.
2. **Underemployment.** Those working less (daily, weekly, or seasonally) than they would like to work.
3. **The visibly active but underutilised.** Those who would not normally be classified as either unemployed or underemployed by the above definitions, but who in fact have found alternative means of 'marking time', including:
   (*a*) **Disguised underemployment.** Many

[2] Edgar O. Edwards, *Employment in Developing Countries: Report on a Ford Foundation study*, Columbia University Press, 1974, p. 10.

[3] *Ibid.*, pp. 10–11.

Table 13.5
Rates of urban unemployment by age

	15–24	15 and over
Ghana, 1960 large towns	21.9	11.6
Bogota, Colombia, 1968	23.1	13.6
Buenos Aires, Argentina, 1965	6.3	4.2
Chile, 1968 urban areas	12.0	6.0
Caracas, 1966	37.7	18.8
Panama, 1963/64 urban areas	17.9	10.4
Uruguay, 1963 mainly urban	18.5	11.8
Venezuela, 1969 urban areas	14.8	7.9
Bangkok, Thailand, 1966	7.7	3.4
Ceylon, 1968 urban areas	39.0	15.0
India, 1961/62 urban areas	8.0	3.2
Korea, 1966	23.6	12.6
Malaya, 1965 urban areas	21.0	9.8
Philippines, 1965 urban areas	20.6	11.6
Singapore, 1966	15.7	9.2
Teheran	9.4	4.6

Source: David Turnham and Ian Jaeger, *The Employment Problem in Less Developed Countries*, OECD, 1970.

people seem occupied on farms or employed in government on a full-time basis even though the services they render may actually require much less than full time. Social pressures on private industry may result also in substantial amounts of disguised under-employment. If available work is openly shared among those employed, the disguise disappears and under-employment becomes explicit.

(*b*) **Hidden unemployment.** Those who are engaged in 'second choice' non-employment activities, perhaps notably education and household chores, primarily because job opportunities are not available (a) at the levels of education already attained, or (b) for women, given social mores. Thus, educational institutions and households become 'employers of last resort'. Moreover, many of those enrolled for further education may be among the less able as indicated by their inability to compete successfully for jobs before pursuing further education.

(*c*) **The prematurely retired.** This phenomenon is especially apparent, and steadily growing, in the civil service. In many countries, retirement ages are falling at the same time that longevity is increasing. Premature retirement serves as a means of creating promotion opportunities for some of the large numbers pressing up from below.

4. **The impaired.** Those who may work full time but whose intensity of effort is seriously impaired through malnutrition or lack of common preventive medicine.
5. **The unproductive.** Those who can provide the human resources necessary for productive work but who struggle long hours with inadequate complementary resources to make their inputs yield even the essentials of life.

Although all the above manifestations of the underutilisation of labour in LDCs are highly interrelated, and each in its own way is of considerable significance, we limit our discussion throughout the remainder of this chapter to the specific problem of urban unemployment and underemployment.

Linkages between unemployment, poverty and income distribution

There is a close relationship between high levels of unemployment and under-employment on the one hand and widespread poverty and unequal distributions of income on the other. Those without regular employment or with only scattered part-time employment are usually also among the very poor. Those with regular paid employment in the public or private sector are typically among the middle- to upper-income groups. But it would be wrong to assume that everyone who does not have a job is necessarily poor while those who work full-time are relatively well off. This is because there may be many unemployed urban workers who are 'voluntarily' unemployed in the sense that they are searching for a specific type of job, perhaps because of high expectations based on their presumed educational or skill qualifications. They refuse to accept jobs which they feel to be inferior and are able to do this because they have outside sources of financial support (e.g. relatives, friends or local money-lenders). Such people are unemployed by definition, but they may not be poor.

Similarly, there are many individuals who may work full-time in terms of hours per day but may nevertheless earn very little income. Many self-employed workers in the so-called urban 'informal' sector (e.g. traders, hawkers, petty service providers, workers in repair shops, etc.) may be so classified. Such people are by definition fully employed but often they are still very poor.

In spite of the above reservations about a too literal linkage between unemployment and poverty, it remains true that one of the major mechanisms for reducing poverty and inequality in less developed nations is the provision of adequately paid, productive employment opportunities for the very poor. As we have seen in Chapter 10, the creation of more employment opportunities should not be regarded as the sole solution to the poverty problem. Much farther-reaching economic and social measures are needed. But the provision of more work and the wider sharing of the work available would certainly go a long way towards solving the problem. Employment, therefore, must be an essential ingredient in any poverty-focused development strategy.

The lag between industrial output and employment growth: the misplaced emphasis of the 1950s and 1960s

If we were asked to identify the most important and pervasive economic policy pursued by the vast majority of Third World nations during the postwar period, the quest for rapid industrialisation would no doubt be chosen. In fact, during the 1950s and early 1960s it almost became a dogma of development literature that successful economic development could be realised only through the twin forces of capital accumulation and industrial growth. By concentrating their efforts on the development of a modern industrial sector to serve the domestic market and to facilitate the absorption of 'redundant' or 'surplus' rural labourers in the urban economy, less developed countries, it was argued, could proceed most rapidly towards the achievement of considerable economic self-sufficiency. A natural consequence has been the extraordinary growth of urban centres resulting from an accelerated influx of rural, unskilled workers in search of scarce urban jobs.

Unfortunately, optimistic predictions about the ability of the modern industrial sector to absorb these migrants have not been realised. In fact, the failure of modern urban industries to generate a significant number of employment opportunities is one of the most obvious failures of the development effort over the past two decades. Throughout Africa, Asia and Latin America, we consistently hear of widespread and rising urban unemployment. Roughly estimated unemployment rates of 10 to 25 per cent in the modern sector are to be found not only in so-called labour surplus countries such as Pakistan, the Philippines, India and Egypt, where rapid rates of population growth sometimes appear to preclude any possibility of significantly reducing unemployment, but also in many African countries such as Ghana, Zaïre, Kenya, Tanzania and Zambia, where at present the population problem is not so visible. Even in those countries with the most rapidly growing industrial sectors, such as Venezuela and Brazil, urban unemployment rates have continued to hover around 15 per cent for over a decade.

In essence, the basically similar phenomenon common to these otherwise structurally diverse countries is that of either stagnating or slowly growing urban employment opportunities in the midst of a rather rapid pace of industrialisation and an ever increasing flow of unskilled rural workers into urban areas. It is not uncommon to find manufacturing output growing at a rate of 6 to 10 per cent and above, while employment grows at a meagre 1 to 3 per cent per annum, if at all (see Table 13.6). Certainly, the ensuing employment problem with its attendant social and political implications is much more blatant in those countries already faced with severe population pressures in rural areas. However, a point to be emphasised (easily overlooked when historical examples of Western economic growth are followed as prototypes for contemporary developing countries) is that there seems to be today an inherent structural imbalance between the manpower demands of a highly capital-intensive internationally mobile industrial technology and the manpower supplies of individual less developed nations. In nineteenth-century England or Germany, a large proportion of the unskilled labourers released from rural areas could find productive employment in labour-intensive industries whose output was competitive in growing world markets. Neither the limited size of domestic markets nor the keenly competitive or, in other cases, well-protected markets of the twentieth-century industrial leaders seem to give sufficient scope to the anticipated employment-creating powers of many of these same manufacturing industries in Third World countries.

Table 13.6
Industrialisation and employment in developing countries

Region/ Countries	Manufacturing annual output growth (1963–69)	Manufacturing employment growth (1963–69)
Africa		
Ethiopia	12.8	6.4
Kenya	6.4	4.3
Nigeria	14.1	5.3
Egypt (UAR)	11.2	0.7
Asia		
India	5.9	5.3
Pakistan	12.3	2.6
Philippines	6.1	4.8
Thailand	10.7	−12.0
Latin America		
Brazil	6.5	1.1
Colombia	5.9	2.8
Costa Rica	8.9	2.8
Dominican Republic	1.7	−3.3
Ecuador	11.4	6.0
Panama	12.9	7.4

Source: David Morawetz, 'Employment implications of industrialization in developing countries', *Economic Journal*, 84 September 1974.

However, an even more important reason why too much emphasis cannot be placed on the expansion of the modern industrial sector to solve the urban employment problem is the simple fact that in most developing countries this sector employs only 10 to 20 per cent of the total labour force. For example, if the manufacturing sector employs, say, 20 per cent of the country's labour force, it would need to increase employment by 15 per cent per year just to absorb the increase in a total work force growing at 3 per cent per year (i.e. $0.2 \times 0.15 = 0.03$). None of the countries in Table 13.6 have been able to achieve such a high rate of employment growth in their manufacturing sectors. In fact, such industrial employment growth is virtually impossible to achieve in any economy.

Again the contrast between the present urban situation in LDCs and the historical situation in the now more developed countries is worth noting. In nineteenth-century western Europe, the pace of industrialisation was much faster than that of urbanisation. The percentage of the working force in industry was always higher than that of the population living in cities. For example, in France in 1856 only 10 per cent of the total population lived in cities of 20 000 inhabitants and over, while 29 per cent of the working force was engaged in manufacturing. In Germany in 1870 the comparative figures were 12 per cent urbanisation and 30 per cent engaged in manufacturing. Since the labour forces of both France and Germany were growing at no more than one per cent per annum over this period, the manufacturing sector needed to grow at a rate of only 3.3 per cent to absorb the *total* yearly labour force increases.

By contrast, the pace of industrialisation in less developed countries has been much slower than that of urbanisation. In almost all Third World countries the percentage of populations living in cities greatly *exceeds* the proportion engaged in manufacturing. For example, in 1980 Brazil had over 50 per cent of its population living in urban areas of 20 000 or more while only 18 per cent were engaged in manufacturing; Colombia had an urbanisation rate of almost 48 per cent with only 12.5 per cent engaged in manufacturing. Given these very different demographic and structural economic circumstances, it would be totally unrealistic to rely on accelerated industrial growth to solve the problems of growing unemployment, even if such growth could have a substantial labour-using bias, which it usually does not.

Some economic approaches to the employment problem

Over the years economists have formulated a

number of economic models of employment determination. The majority of these models have focused on, or been derived from, the social, economic and institutional circumstances of the developed nations. They have, nevertheless, often been uncritically and inappropriately applied to the unique circumstances of employment problems in developing countries. In recent years, however, more relevant and realistic economic models of employment and development have been constructed. In some cases, they lead to policy conclusions diametrically opposed to those of the traditional theories.

We now review four major economic models of employment determination. The first two, the 'classical' and 'Keynesian' models, are those traditionally taught in introductory economics textbooks. Neither of these theories has much relevance to the employment problems of developing countries. The third and fourth models, like the Keynesian model, grow out of the more recent 'neo-classical' tradition of economics. The first of these centres on the relationship between capital accumulation, industrial output growth and employment generation, while the second considers the impact of distorted factor prices on resource (especially labour) utilisation. Both models, again like the Keynesian model, concentrate exclusively on the demand side of the employment equation; that is, on policies to increase labour demand.

A fifth model or group of models, which we may designate the 'two-sector labour transfer' or rural–urban migration models, focus on the determinants of both labour demand and labour supply. These are the subject of Chapter 14. Even more than the neo-classical models (although still in the same tradition), the labour transfer migration models seek to take purposeful account of the institutional and economic realities of underdeveloped nations.

We conclude this chapter, therefore, by examining the first four models of employment determination, and then devote considerable space in Chapter 14 to the fifth.

The traditional free market competitive model:

Flexible wages and full employment

In the world of traditional Western economics, characterised by consumer sovereignty, individual utility and profit maximisation, perfect competition and economic efficiency with very many atomistic producers and consumers, none of whom is large enough to influence prices or wages, the level of employment and the wage rate are determined simultaneously with all other prices and factor uses in the economy by the forces of demand and supply. Producers would demand more workers as long as the value of the marginal product produced by that worker (i.e. his physical marginal product multiplied by the market price of the product he produces) exceeds his cost (i.e. the wage rate). Since the law of diminishing marginal product is assumed to apply, and since product prices are fixed by the market, the value of labour's marginal product and thus the demand curve for labour will be negatively sloped as in Figure 13.3. More workers will be hired only at successively lower wage rates.

Figure 13.3
Wage and employment determination by demand and supply: the traditional approach

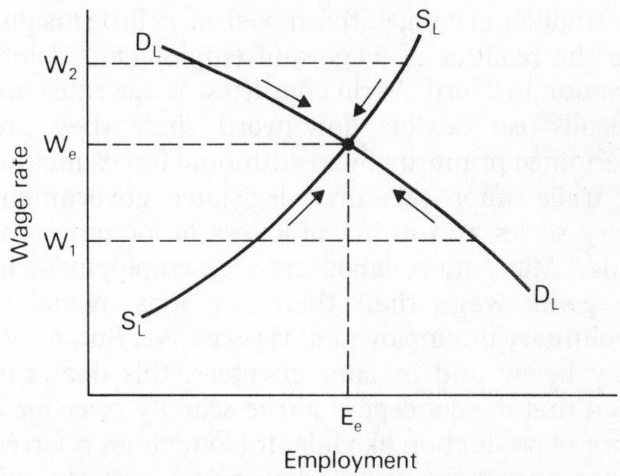

On the supply side, individuals are assumed to operate on the principle of utility maximisation. They will therefore divide their time between work and leisure in accordance with the relative marginal utility of each. A rise in wage rates is equivalent to an increase in the price (or opportunity cost) of leisure. When the price of any item rises, in general its demand will decrease and other items will be substituted. It follows that more labour services will be supplied at successively higher wage rates so that the aggregate supply curve of labour will be positively sloped. This supply curve is also depicted in Figure 13.3.

We see from Figure 13.3 that only at one point, the equilibrium wage rate W_e, will the amount of work that individuals are *willing* to supply just equal the amount that employers will demand. At any higher wage, e.g. W_2, the supply of labour will exceed demand and competitive pressures among workers will force the wage rate down to W_e. At any lower price, e.g. W_1, the labour quantity demanded will exceed the quantity supplied and competition among producers will drive the wage rate up until it reaches its equilibrium level at W_e. At W_e total employment will be depicted by point E_e on the horizontal axis. **By definition, this will be full employment**, i.e. at the equilibrium wage, and only at this wage will all those willing to work be able to obtain jobs so that there is no 'involuntary' unemployment. In other words, in the idealised flexible wages world of classical economics, there can never be unemployment.

Limitations of the competitive model for developing countries

The traditional competitive model offers little insight into the realities of wage and employment determination in Third World countries. Wage rates are typically *not* flexible downward since they are determined primarily by institutional forces including trade union pressures, legislated government salary scales and hiring practices of foreign companies. Many more labourers seek employment at the going wage than there are jobs available. Involuntary unemployment is pervasive. But, as we show below and in later chapters, this does not mean that the concept of a true scarcity price for a factor of production like labour (sometimes referred to by economists as its 'shadow' price), even though it may differ from the actual price of that factor, does not have important analytical and policy content for Third World nations. On the contrary, as noted in Part One, the 'thought processes' of traditional economics as well as certain concepts, can have general validity in a great diversity of economies. The concept of a hypothetical market-determined equilibrium wage is one of these concepts that can serve as a useful analytical policy guideline (see pp. 206–7 below).

The Keynesian model

Insufficient effective demand and unemployment

The 1930s ushered in a Great Depression in the Western world, the like of which had not been experienced by the developed countries during their entire modern growth era. Widespread and seemingly chronic unemployment and low levels of national output shook economists out of the complacency of their idealised classical world. Clearly there was something very inadequate about the traditional theory of wage and employment determination.

Two major theoretical responses emerged to explain what apparently was going on. At the micro level, the theory of 'imperfect competition' associated with Professors Joan Robinson of England and Edward H. Chamberlain of the United States, was developed to explain the nature and implications of markets which were dominated by one (monopoly) or a few (oligopoly) sellers of products or by one or more purchasers of resources (monopsony and oligopsony). In each of these cases of imperfect competition, it was demonstrated that resources (including labour) would be underutilised and total production would be less than what would occur if product and resource markets were characterised by perfect competition. Such market failures often provided the theoretical justification and economic rationale for increased government intervention in the economic system to offset the negative output and employment effects of monopoly and other forms of concentrated selling power. In Chapter 23 we discuss in more detail the market failure argument, among others, as a basis for development planning in Third World nations.

The other and by far the more influential theory which emerged in response to the harsh economic realities of the Great Depression was macro oriented, that is, it focused on aggregate economic variables. This is the famous Keynesian theory of national income and employment determination named after John Maynard Keynes who developed it in his now classic treatise *The General Theory of Employment, Interest and Money*, published in 1936. What may have appeared to be a 'general theory' of employment at the time, however, has now been recognised, especially in the less developed countries, as a 'special theory' of unemployment for the developed countries.

Basically, the Keynesian theory views the determination of national output and employment in terms of the level of *aggregate demand* for the goods and services which an economy has the *potential* to produce, given its resources and technology. Aggregate demand in its simplest form for a 'closed economy' (i.e. one without any foreign trade) consists of three fundamental components: (1) the total demand for all goods and services by private consumers (denoted by C for consumption); (2) the total demand for investment goods by private industry (denoted simply I for investment); and (3) the demand for goods and services, both consumption and investment, by the government (denoted G for government). The level of national income or GNP (denoted as Y) is then defined simply as:

$$\text{National income } (Y) = \text{Consumption } (C) + \text{Investment } (I) + \text{Government expenditure } (G)$$

or, simply

$$Y = C+I+G \quad (1)$$

For an 'open economy' with foreign trade, one would need to add expressions for exports (X) and imports (M), the difference constituting a 'surplus' balance of trade (i.e. $X-M>0$) and thus an additional positive component of aggregate demand, or a 'deficit' trade balance ($X-M<0$) which would lower national income. Thus, for an open economy, equation (1) would be written as:

$$Y = C+I+G+(X-M).^{4} \quad (2)$$

Finally, since governments need to collect taxes (T) to finance some or all of their expenditures, the net economic impact of government activity is $G-T$(if G is greater than T, the government is operating at a deficit; T greater than G would imply a surplus). Equation (2) therefore becomes:

$$Y = C+I+(G-T)+(X-M). \quad (3)$$

For illustrative purposes, however, let us use only equation (1). National income and/or expenditure (Y) is determined by the level of aggregate demand ($C+I+G$). This level of national output is assumed to be uniquely associated with a level of national employment (N), via the concept of a 'national production function'. Such a national production function is in concept entirely analogous to the simple one-product (in this case, aggregate national output), three-factor (i.e. land, capital and labour) production function described in Chapter 4. For any given technology and stock of fixed land and capital, total national output (real GNP) will be uniquely and positively associated with different levels of employment: i.e. higher levels of national output (Y) are associated with higher levels of employment (N). But since for any given society total employment is limited by the size of the labour force, there will be some unique level of **maximum national output** which can be achieved only at full employment. This full employment level of national income, sometimes called **potential output**, may be denoted Y_F.

The main contention of the Keynesian theory, and the factor which distinguished it from the classical model, was that there was nothing inherent in a market economy to *guarantee* that the *actual* level of national income (Y) would be exactly equal to its *potential*, full-employment level (Y_F). It all depends on the level of total aggregate demand (i.e. on $C+I+G$). If the combined sums of C plus I plus G yields a level of national output (Y) that is *less* than the potential full employment output level (Y_F), then by definition and logic there will be a certain level of unemployment represented by the size of the output gap between Y and Y_F. It follows, therefore, that if consumption and investment are already determined by the existing level of national income, the only way that aggregate demand can be increased is for the government to increase its level of total expenditure (i.e. raise G). Government deficit expenditure ($G-T>0$) thus becomes necessary to fill in the gap between actual and potential GNP so as to increase the level of national output and consequently eliminate unemployment.

In short, the Keynesian prescription for reducing or eradicating unemployment is simple: increase aggregate total demand through direct increases in government expenditure or by government policies that indirectly encourage more private investment (e.g. low interest rates on business loans, tax allowances, investment subsidies, etc.). As long as there is unemployment and slack in the economy, the supply of goods and services will respond automatically to this higher demand and create the

[4] Recall that equation (2) was used for accounting purposes to show the expenditure breakdown of GDP for ten Third World nations in Table 2.1 (p. 00).

conditions for more income and higher levels of employment.

Limitations of the Keynesian model in developing countries

The Keynesian model as applied to Third World economies has two major deficiencies. First, being derived from advanced-country economies, it is implicitly based on the institutional and structural assumption of well functioning product, factor and money markets that characterise these countries. Specifically, it is based on the assumption, correct for developed nations but not for LDCs, that firms and farms can respond quickly and effectively to increases in the demand for their products by rapidly expanding output and employment. But in most Third World countries the major bottleneck to higher output and employment levels is not insufficient aggregate demand but structural and institutional constraints on the supply side. Shortages of capital, raw materials, intermediate products, skilled and managerial human resources, combined with poorly functioning and insufficiently organised commodity and loan markets, poor transport and communications, shortages of foreign exchange and import-dominated consumption patterns among the rich – all these, and many other structural and institutional factors, militate against the simple notion that expanded government and private demand will be effective measures to solve employment (and poverty) problems in most Third World countries. In fact, under conditions of severe constraints on the supply side (i.e. where the aggregate supply curve of national output is price inelastic), expanding aggregate demand through deficit-financed government expenditure may merely result in higher prices and chronic inflation. This was the common experience of many Latin American countries during the 1950s and 1960s. The world-wide inflation of the 1970s can also be attributed largely to supply contraints, especially in raw materials, energy resources and food products.

The second major limitation of the Keynesian model for most LDCs is also related to conditions of supply in Third World countries, this time the supply of labour to the urban industrial sector. As we show in Chapter 14 when we discuss the economics of rural–urban migration, the creation of additional modern sector urban jobs by increasing aggregate demand is likely to attract many more additional migrants from rural areas. Since urban wages are typically much higher than average rural incomes, every urban job created may induce three or four new job seekers to migrate from the countryside. The net result may be that the creation of additional urban jobs through traditional Keynesian policies designed to reduce unemployment may in fact cause urban unemployment to rise! Moreover, since many of the rural migrants were productive farmers or low-paid farm workers, **the overall level of national employment and output may be reduced by Keynesian policies designed to increase employment and output.**

We may conclude that for many reasons, but especially because of structural and institutional supply constraints and the phenomenon of induced rural–urban migration, the Keynesian macro model of employment determination has little analytical relevance, and its policy prescriptions can be counterproductive for those less developed nations beset by unemployment problems.

Models of output and employment growth: the fallacy of conflicting objectives

A natural extension of the Keynesian model which dominated many theories of development in the 1950s and 1960s focused on policies to increase the levels of national output rapidly through accelerated capital formation. Since the 'static' Keynesian model associated levels of employment uniquely with levels of GNP, it followed that by maximising the rate of growth of GNP, Third World countries could also maximise their rate of labour absorption. The principal theoretical tool used to describe the growth process was the simple Harrod–Domar model described in Chapter 6. Although many sophisticated variants of this model appeared later, the basic idea remained the same.

Economic growth is explained as the combined result of the rate of saving and the resultant physical capital accumulation on the one hand, and the capital/output ratio (i.e. the physical productivity of new investment) on the other (see pp. 88–89). For a given aggregate capital/output ratio, therefore, the rate of national output and employment growth could be maximised by maximising the rate of saving and investment. A natural and inevitable outgrowth of this neo-Keynesian model was the emphasis on generating domestic savings and foreign exchange to make possible heavy capital investments in the growing urban industrial sector. The 'big push' for rapid industrialisation became the code word for development and growth, especially in the 1950s and early 1960s.

But as we saw in Table 13.6, in spite of relatively impressive rates of industrial output growth in many less developed countries, the rate of employment growth has lagged significantly behind, in some cases even stagnated. Why has rapid industrial output growth failed to generate correspondingly rapid rates of employment growth?

Basically, the reason is the growth in labour productivity. By definition, the rate of growth in output less the rate of growth in labour productivity approximately equals the rate of growth of employment. Suppose total output equalled 100 units and total employment 20. Total labour productivity (output per unit of labour), therefore, would equal 100 divided by 20, or 5 units per worker. Now if output increased to 150 units while employment expanded to 25 units, labour productivity would rise from 5 to 6 units (e.g. $150 \div 25 = 6$). In terms of percentage changes, output will have grown by 50 per cent, employment by 25 per cent and labour productivity by 20 per cent. Although the difference between output growth and labour productivity growth (30 per cent) is not exactly equal to employment growth (25 per cent), their difference becomes very small for small output changes. Thus, the formula 'output growth equals labour productivity growth plus employment growth' can be used for dividing output growth approximately into its productivity and employment components.

It follows from the above illustration that if output is growing at 8 per cent per year while employment is expanding by only 3 per cent, the difference is due to the rise in labour productivity which is growing at approximately 5 per cent per year. The original Harrod–Domar model did not specifically incorporate technological change, though later modifications did. It was what is known as a 'fixed coefficient' model (i.e. it assumed a fixed relationship between changes in output levels and changes in capital stock). This constant capital/output ratio was then paralleled in early versions of the model by a constant output/labour ratio (i.e. a fixed productivity of labour coefficient). It follows from this constant labour productivity assumption that a 10 per cent increase in national output (GNP) will always be accompanied by a 10 per cent increase in employment. But, if labour productivity is rising so that fewer workers are required to produce any given level of total output, a 10 per cent output growth may bring only a 3 per cent increase in employment.

In general, increases in labour productivity are desirable. But what is really desirable are increases in 'total' factor productivity: output per unit of *all* resources. The productivity of labour can increase for a variety of reasons, however, some good and some not so good. Improved education, better training and better management are all good. But increases in labour productivity as a result of the substitution of capital for labour in production processes or as a result of the importation of sophisticated and expensive labour-saving machinery and equipment (tractors, power tools, automated textile machinery, heavy construction equipment, etc.) may be less satisfactory in heavily populated nations. Not only can such capital accumulation waste valuable domestic financial resources and foreign exchange, it can also curtail the growth of new employment opportunities. Moreover, the importation of inappropriate and expensive labour-saving capital equipment may, in fact, *reduce* total factor productivity and thereby *increase* average costs of production even though it increases labour productivity. In other words, the average total costs of production may rise, even though average labour costs fall, as a result of the underutilised productive capacity that often ensues when expensive mechanical equipment designed for large-scale production in developed countries is imported into less developed countries where the local market is too small for the efficient utilisation of such sophisticated equipment.

Our conclusion, therefore, is that typical Harrod–Domar type economic models of capital accumulation and growth and the types of economic policies which they imply often lead to rapid output growth but lagging job creation. If the overriding development objective is to maximise the rate of GNP growth, this approach may be the right one. But if it is equally or more important to create jobs, then different policies (e.g. focusing on the promotion of labour-intensive industries such as small-scale agriculture and manufacturing) may be better.

One final point: for many years, economists and development planners, blinded by the appealing simplicity of the Harrod–Domar type growth models and preoccupied with the pursuit of economic growth at almost any cost, took it for granted that there was a conflict between the two objectives of maximum GNP growth and maximum employment creation. It almost became a dogma of development literature that the pursuit of maximum labour absorption would curtail overall rates of GNP growth. But just as the conventional wisdom which assumed that GNP growth and more equitable income distribution were mutually exclusive objectives has recently been reversed, so too are most economists now convinced that an employment-oriented (and, therefore, indirectly a poverty-oriented) development strategy is likely also to be one which *accelerates* rather than retards overall economic progress. This is especially true with regard to the growth and development of the rural and small-scale urban sectors. More employment means more income for the poor, which in turn implies a greater demand for locally produced basic consumption goods. Since these products tend to be more labour-intensive than many of those produced by large-scale industry, both domestic and foreign, which cater primarily for the luxury demands of the rich, it follows that more jobs and higher incomes can become self-reinforcing phenomena. They ultimately lead to higher growth rates of *both* national output and aggregate employment. But in order to achieve this dual objective, a complementary policy of removing factor price distortions may be required. This leads us to our fourth model of employment determination.

Factor price distortions and appropriate technology: the price incentive model

We briefly discussed the question of factor price distortions and their impact on poverty and employment in Chapter 9 and at other points in earlier chapters, especially Chapter 4. However, since the 'neo-classical price incentive' school of thought has occupied such a prominent place in the debate about employment problems in developing countries, it is important to recall it here.

The basic proposition of the price incentive model is quite simple and in the best tradition of neo-classical economic analysis. Following the principle of economy, producers (firms and farms) are assumed to face a given set of relative factor prices (e.g. of capital and labour) and to utilise that combination of capital and labour which minimises the cost of producing a desired level of output. They are further assumed to be capable of producing that output with a variety of technological production processes ranging from highly labour-intensive to highly capital-intensive methods. Thus, if the price of capital is very expensive relative to the price of labour, a relatively labour-intensive process will be chosen. On the other hand, if labour is relatively expensive, our economising firm or farm will utilise a more capital-intensive method of production (i.e. it will economise on the use of labour).

Given that most countries in the Third World are endowed with abundant supplies of labour but possess very little capital, either financial or physical, one would naturally expect production methods to be relatively labour-intensive. But in fact one often finds production techniques in *both* agriculture and industry to be heavily mechanised and capital-intensive. Large tractors and combines dot the rural landscape of Asia, Africa and Latin America while people watch idly by. Gleaming new factories with the most modern and sophisticated automated machinery and equipment are a common feature of urban industries while idle workers congregate outside the factory gates. Surely this phenomenon could not be the result of a lesser degree of economic rationality on the part of Third World farmers and manufacturers.

The explanation, according to the price incentive school, is simple. Because of a variety of structural, institutional and political factors, the actual market prices of labour and capital are higher and lower respectively than their true scarcity or 'shadow' values (i.e. the prices which would result from the free play of competitive supply and demand). Market wage structures are relatively high because of trade union pressure, politically inspired minimim wage laws, growing employee fringe benefits and the high wage policies of foreign companies. In former colonial nations high wage structures are often relics of expatriate remuneration scales based on European levels of living and 'hardship' premiums. On the other hand, the price of scarce capital is kept artificially low by government policies that subsidise capital formation by means of various investment incentives, e.g. accelerated depreciation allowances, tax rebates and duty-free capital imports.

The net result of these distorted factor prices is the encouragement of unnecessary and inappropriate capital-intensive methods of production in both agriculture and manufacturing industries. Note, that from the point of view of minimising private costs of firms and farms, the choice of a capital-intensive technique is correct. Producers are only rationally responding to the existing structure of factor price incentives, even if these prices are distorted. However, from the point of view of society as a whole, the *social* cost of under-utilised capital and especially labour is very substantial. Government policies to 'get the prices right', therefore, would by lowering the relative price of labour contribute not only to more employment but also to a better overall utilisation of scarce capital resources as the result of adopting more 'appropriate' techniques of production.

The actual employment impact of removing factor price distortions will depend on the degree to which labour can be substituted for capital in the production process of various industries. Economists refer to this as the 'elasticity of substitution' and define it roughly as the ratio of the percentage change in the proportion of labour used relative to capital (i.e. the labour–capital or L/K ratio) compared with a given percentage change in the price of capital relative to labour (i.e. P_K/P_L). For example, if the relative price of capital rises by one per cent in the manufacturing sector and the labour/capital ratio rises as a result by say, 1.5 per cent, then the elasticity of substitution in the manufacturing industry will be equal to 1.5. If P_K/P_L falls by say 10 per cent while L/K falls by only 6 per cent, then the elasticity of substitution for that industry would be 0.6. Relatively high elasticities of substitution (e.g. ratios greater than say 0.7) are indicative that factor price adjustments can have a substantial impact on levels and combinations of factor utilisation. In such cases factor price modifications may be an important means of generating more employment opportunities.

In general, most empirical studies of the elasticity of substitution for manufacturing industries in less developed countries reveal coefficients in the range of 0.5 to 1.0.[5] These results indicate that for most Third World nations a *relative* reduction in wages (either directly or by holding wages constant while letting the price of capital rise) of say 10 per cent will lead to a 5 to 10 per cent increase in employment. But, given the fact that the organised wage and manufacturing sector employs only a small proportion of the total labour force, the *total* impact of even a 10 per cent increase in industrial employment will not be sufficient to solve the employment problem. Nevertheless it can make a contribution to the ultimate solution. Therefore, policies to eliminate factor price distortions *do* have an important role in any overall employment-oriented development strategy.

[5] For a useful summary of evidence on this issue, see David Morawetz. 'Employment Implications of Industrialisation in Developing countries', *Economic Journal*, September 1974.

Concepts for review

complementary resources
urbanisation
labour force
underutilisation of labour
open unemployment
underemployment
disguised under-employment
hidden unemployment
voluntary unemployment
'informal' sector
industrialisation
employment gap
'total' factor productivity
small scale industry
neo-classical price incentive model
output–employment lag
classical model
equilibrium wage rate
flexible wages
'shadow' price
Keynesian model
imperfect competition
monopoly and oligopoly
aggregate demand
full employment
potential output
deficit expenditure
fixed input coefficients
'big push' theory of development
elasticity of (factor) substitution
closed economy
'appropriate' technology

Questions for discussion

1. Discuss the nature of the 'employment problem' in Third World countries. Include in your discussion a review of the various manifestations of the underutilisation of labour.
2. Why should we be so concerned with unemployment and underemployment? Why is it a serious development problem?

3. Compare and contrast the contemporary urbanisation process in Third World countries with the historical experience of western Europe and North America. What are the major differences and how did they arise?
4. What is the relationship, if any, between unemployment (and underemployment) and the problems of poverty and inequality?
5. What are the principal economic reasons for the widespread failure of rapid LDC industrial growth to generate equally rapid employment growth? Is such a large output–employment lag an inevitable result of the process of modern industrial growth? Explain your answer.
6. Briefly describe the 'classical' flexible wages model of employment determination. In what sense can one say that in such a model there can never be unemployment?
7. Briefly describe the main assumptions and features of the Keynesian model of income and employment determination. How does unemployment arise in this model and how can governments promote full employment?
8. The Keynesian model of employment determination seems to offer some simple policy prescriptions for generating full employment which, by and large, have proved successful over the past 25 years in the industrially developed countries. What are the principal limitations of using this same approach for solving Third World employment problems? Is it possible that Keynesian policy prescriptions could actually *worsen* the problem of urban unemployment? Explain the meaning behind your answer.
9. What is the relationship between factor-price distortions, 'appropriate' technology and LDC employment problems?

Further reading

The literature on Third World employment problems has grown to voluminous proportions over the past few years. Out of many excellent surveys, the following are perhaps the best: EDGAR O. EDWARDS, ed., *Employment in Developing Nations*, Columbia University Press, 1974; DAVID TURNHAM and IAN JAEGER, *The Employment Problem in Less Developed Countries*, OECD, Paris, June 1970; RICHARD JOLLY *et al.*, *Third World Employment: Problems and Strategy*, Penguin Modern Economics Readings, 1973; INTERNATIONAL LABOUR OFFICE, *Employment in Africa: some critical issues*, Geneva, 1974; PAUL BAIROCH, *Urban Unemployment in Developing Countries*, ILO, Geneva, 1973.

For comparative and comprehensive studies of Colombia, Kenya, Ceylon and the Philippines, see the various ILO expert mission reports available from the International Labour Office in Geneva and its various UN distributional outlets in Africa, Asia and Latin America.

Chapter 14 Rural to urban migration: theory and policy

> We are firmly persuaded that the most fundamental and promising attack on employment problems in developing countries is in efforts to redress the present urban bias in development strategies.
> *Edgar O. Edwards, Report on Employment in Developing Countries*

Introduction

In this chapter we focus on one of the most perplexing dilemmas of the development experience. This is the phenomenon of massive and historically unprecedented movements of people from the rural countryside to the burgeoning cities of Africa, Asia and Latin America. Two major theoretical approaches to the problem of rural–urban labour transfer will be discussed in the first part of the chapter. We will then conclude by examining a range of alternative public policies designed to curtail the excessive flow of migration and to deal with the serious urban unemployment problems that continue to plague the vast majority of Third World countries.

The economics of labour transfer and rural-urban migration: two approaches

The Lewis-Fei-Ranis model of development

Perhaps the best known of all employment models relating specifically to the developing countries is that originally formulated in 1954 by Nobel Laureate W. Arthur Lewis, and formalised in 1961 by Professors Gustav Ranis and John Fei. In the Lewis–Fei–Ranis model the underdeveloped economy consists of two sectors: (1) a traditional, **agricultural subsistence sector** characterised by zero or very low productivity 'surplus' labour, and (2) a high productivity modern **urban industrial sector** into which labour from the subsistence sector is gradually transferred. The primary focus of the model is on both the process of labour transfer and the growth of employment in the modern sector. Both labour transfer and urban employment growth are brought about by output expansion in the modern sector. The speed with which they occur is given by the rate of investment or capital accumulation in the modern sector. Such investment is made possible by the excess of modern sector profits over wages where it is assumed that 'capitalists' always reinvest all of their profits. Finally, the level of wages in the industrial sector is assumed to be constant and determined as a fixed premium over the subsistence level of wages in the traditional agricultural sector. (Lewis assumed that urban wages would have to be at least 30 per cent higher than average rural income to induce workers to migrate from their home areas.) However, at this constant urban wage, the supply of rural labour is considered to be perfectly elastic.

The following provides a simple illustration of the Lewis–Fei–Ranis model. We have depicted the process of modern sector growth in Figure 14.1. On the vertical axis we have the real wage (equal in a competitive economy to the marginal product of labour) and on the horizontal axis the quantity of labour.

OA represents the average level of real subsistence income in the traditional rural sector. *OW*, therefore, is the real wage in the capitalist sector. At this wage, the supply of rural labour is assumed to be 'unlimited' or perfectly elastic, as shown by the horizontal labour supply curve *WS*. Given a fixed supply of capital, K_1, in the initial stage of modern sector growth, the demand curve for labour is determined by labour's declining marginal product and is shown by curve $D_1(K_1)$. Since profit-maximising modern sector employers are assumed to hire labourers up to the point where their marginal product is equal to the real wage (i.e. the point *F* of intersection between the labour demand and supply curves), total modern sector employment will be equal to OL_1. Total modern sector output would be given by the area bounded by points OD_1FL_1. The share of this total output which is paid to workers in the form of wages would be equal to the wage, *OW*, multiplied by the level of employment, OL_1. This wage bill would be equal, therefore, to the area of the rectangle $OWFL_1$ in Figure 14.1.

The surplus output shown by the area WD_1F would be the total profits that accrue to the capitalists. Since it is assumed that all these profits are reinvested, the total capital stock in the modern sector will rise from K_1 to K_2. This larger capital stock causes the total product curve of the modern sector to rise which in turn induces a rise in the marginal product or demand curve for labour. This outward shift in the labour demand curve is shown by line $D_2(K_2)$ in the figure. A new equilibrium employment level will be established at point *G* with

Figure 14.1
The Lewis model of growth and employment in a dual labour surplus economy

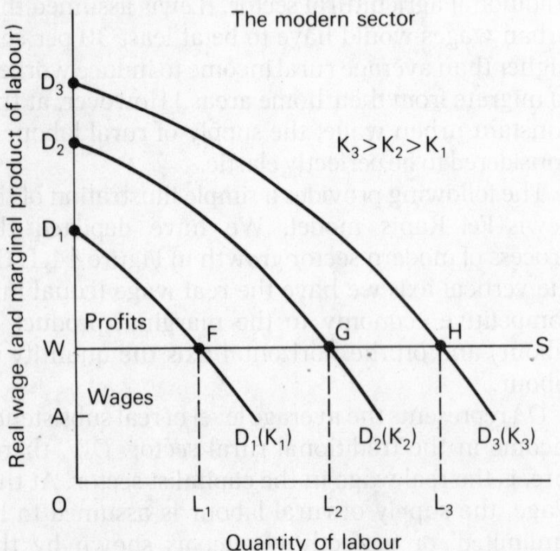

OL_2 workers now employed. Total output rises to OD_2GL_2 while total wages and profits increase to $OWGL_2$ and WD_2G respectively. Once again, these larger profits (WD_2G) are re-invested, increasing the total capital stock to K_3, shifting the labour demand curve to $D_3(K_3)$ and raising the level of modern sector employment to L_3.

The process of modern sector growth and employment expansion is assumed to continue until all 'surplus' rural labour is absorbed in the urban industrial sector. Thereafter the labour supply curve becomes positively sloped and both urban wages and employment will continue to grow. The structural transformation of the economy will have taken place and the process of industrial modernisation will increasingly dominate overall economic activity.

Although the Lewis–Fei–Ranis model of development is both simple and roughly in conformity with the historical experience of economic growth in the West (see Chapter 7), it has three key assumptions which are sharply at variance with the realities of underdevelopment in most Third World countries.

First, the model implicitly assumes that the rate of labour transfer and employment creation is proportional to the rate of capital accumulation. The faster the rate of capital accumulation, the higher the growth rate of the modern sector and the faster the rate of new job creation. This has a certain Harrod–Domar flavour to it. But what if surplus capitalist profits are reinvested in more sophisticated labour-saving capital equipment rather than just duplicating the existing capital as is implicitly assumed in the Lewis model? Figure 14.2 reproduces the basic Lewis–Fei–Ranis model. Only this time the labour demand curves do not shift uniformly outward but, in fact, cross. Demand curve $D_2(K_2)$ has a greater negative slope than $D_1(K_1)$ to reflect the fact that the additional capital stock K_2-K_1 is of a more labour-saving variety than K_1.

We see that even though total output has grown substantially (i.e. OD_2EL_1 is significantly greater than OD_1EL_1), total wages ($OWEL_1$) and employment (OL_1) remain unchanged. All the extra output accrues to capitalists in the form of excess profits. Figure 14.2, therefore, provides an illustration of what we might call 'anti-developmental' economic growth: *all* the extra income and output growth is distributed to the few owners of capital while income levels of the masses of workers remain unchanged. Although total GNP would rise, a poverty-weighted

Figure 14.2
Labour-saving capital accumulation modifies the employment implications of the Lewis model

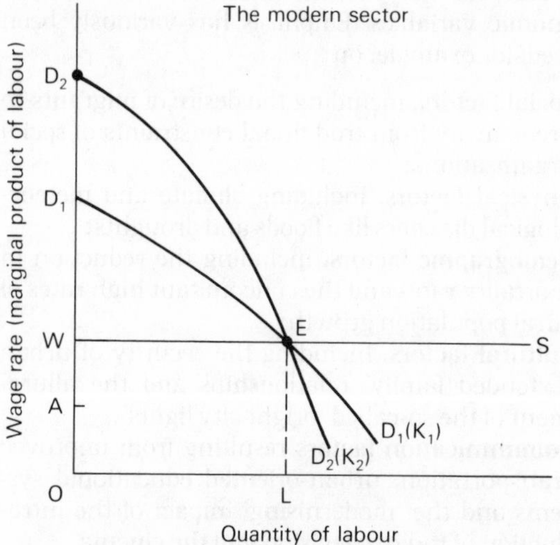

index of development like that described in Chapter 10 would show no improvement in social welfare.

Second, the model assumes that 'surplus' labour exists in rural areas while there is full employment in the urban areas. Most contemporary research indicates that almost exactly the reverse is true in many Third World countries: there is substantial open unemployment in urban areas but almost no general surplus labour in rural locations. There are both seasonal and geographic exceptions to this rule (e.g. parts of the Asian subcontinent and isolated regions of Latin America where land ownership is very unequal) but by and large it is empirically more correct than the Lewis–Fei–Ranis assumption.

The third key assumption at variance with reality is the notion of the continued existence of constant real urban wages until the supply of rural surplus labour is exhausted. One of the most striking features of the urban wage situation in almost all developing countries, however, has been the tendency for these wages to rise substantially, both in absolute terms and relative to average rural incomes, even in the presence of rising levels of open unemployment.

Taking into account the labour-saving bias of modern technological transfer, the widespread non-existence of rural surplus labour, the prevalence of 'urban surplus' labour, and the tendency for urban wages to rise rapidly even where substantial urban open unemployment exists, we conclude that the Lewis–Fei–Ranis model offers little analytical and policy guidance for solving Third World employment problems.

Nevertheless the model has some analytical value in that it emphasises two major elements of the employment problem: the structural and economic differences between the rural and the urban sectors, and the central importance of the process of labour transfer between them. With these two elements in mind, we now turn to the more widely utilised 'expected income' models of rural–urban migration and urban unemployment in less developed countries.

An 'expected income' model of rural-urban migration

Until recently research on rural–urban migration in less developed countries has been largely dominated by the work of geographers, demographers and sociologists. For the most part, economists have preferred to ignore migration while operating within the confines of their traditional Lewis-type 'two-sector' models. In a closed economy, these sectors usually consisted of the agricultural and the industrial with the implicit understanding that one could substitute 'rural' for 'agricultural' and 'urban' for 'industrial'. Emphasis has been placed on traditional economic variables, such as output growth rates, savings and investment, and relative productive efficiency. The efficient allocation of human resources between sectors, if discussed at all, has been assumed to be a natural outgrowth of a self-adjusting competitive mechanism which functioned to equate sectoral wage rates and productivities. Rural–urban migration was portrayed as a manifestation of this self-adjusting mechanism (with its implicit full employment assumptions) and, as such, was not deemed of sufficient intrinsic importance to warrant detailed theoretical and empirical investigation.

The discouraging record of the 1960s in relation to rapid urbanisation and growing levels of urban unemployment in developing nations, however, has shown that it is not enough to regard migration as of secondary importance. It has shaken development economists out of their complacent faith in the long-run allocative efficiency of the competitive market mechanism. Moreover, it has forced them to question the applicability of their traditional economic models to the realities of the social, economic and institutional environments of contemporary Third World nations.

The evidence is clear. Urban areas have grown extremely rapidly, often at rates unprecedented in history. Between 1960 and 1970, for example, the population of urban areas is estimated to have grown by 60 per cent in Africa, 52 per cent in Latin America, and 51 per cent in South Asia, while rural areas grew by only 16 per cent in the same decade. Simultaneously, urban unemployment and underemployment emerged as a problem of utmost importance and concern to politicians, planners and researchers alike. Without question, the phenomenon of accelerated rural–urban labour migration has been the principal cause of both the high rates of urban population growth and the rising levels of urban unemployment. In many African cities in particular, urban growth rates of 7 to 10 per cent per annum are not uncommon, and they are unlikely to diminish in the coming decade.

Thus an understanding of the causes and determinants of rural–urban migration and the relationship between migration and relative economic opportunities in urban and rural areas is central to any analysis of Third World employment problems. Since migrants comprise the majority of the urban labour force in developing nations, the magnitude of rural–urban migration has been, and will continue to be, the principal determinant of the supply of new job seekers. And if migration is the key determinant of the urban labour supply, then the migration process must be understood before the nature and causes of urban unemployment (which, in essence represents an excess of job seekers over job opportunities), can be understood in its turn. Government policies to ameliorate the urban unemployment problem must be based in the first instance on knowledge of who comes to town and why.

The migration process

The factors influencing the decision to migrate are varied and complex. Since migration is a *selective* process affecting individuals with certain economic, social, educational and demographic characteristics, the relative influence of economic and non-economic factors may vary not only between nations and regions but also within defined geographic areas and populations. Much of the early research on migration tended to focus on social, cultural and psychological factors while recognising but not carefully evaluating the importance of economic variables. Emphasis has variously been placed, for example, on:

- **social factors,** including the desire of migrants to break away from traditional constraints of social organisations;
- **physical factors,** including climate and meteorological disasters like floods and droughts;
- **demographic factors,** including the reduction in mortality rates and the concomitant high rates of rural population growth;
- **cultural factors,** including the security of urban 'extended family' relationships and the allurement of the so-called 'bright city lights';
- **communication factors** resulting from improved transportation, urban-oriented educational systems and the 'modernising' impact of the introduction of radio, television and the cinema.

All these 'non-economic' factors are of course relevant. However, there now seems to be widespread agreement among economists and non-economists alike that rural–urban migration can be explained primarily by the influence of economic factors. These include not only the standard 'push' from subsistence agriculture and 'pull' of relatively high urban wages, but also the potential 'push-back' of high urban unemployment.

Migrant characteristics

It is convenient to divide the main characteristics of migrants into three broad categories; demographic, educational and economic.

Demographic characteristics

Urban migrants in developing countries tend to be young men and women between the ages of 15 and 24. Various studies in Africa and Asia have provided quantitative evidence of this phenomenon in countries such as Kenya, Tanzania, Ghana, Nigeria, India, Thailand, Korea and the Philippines. In many countries the proportion of migrating women seems to be on the increase as their educational opportunities expand. In Latin America a review of rural–urban migration indicated that women now constitute the majority in the migration stream, probably as a result of Latin America's relatively advanced state of urbanisation compared with other developing continents.

Educational characteristics

One of the most consistent findings of rural–urban migration studies is the positive correlation between educational attainment and migration. There seems to be a clear association between the level of completed education and the propensity to migrate: those with more years of schooling, everything else being equal, are more likely to migrate than those with less. In a recent study of Tanzania, for example, the relationship between education and migration is clearly documented, especially in terms of the impact of declining urban employment opportunities on the educational characteristics of migrants. Tanzanian secondary school leavers were found to constitute a rising proportion of the migration stream. The explanation is that limited urban employment opportunities are rationed by educational levels and only those workers with some secondary education have a chance of finding a job. Those with only some primary school education find it very difficult to secure employment. Their proportionate numbers in the migrant stream therefore, have apparently begun to decline.

Economic characteristics

For many years the largest percentage of urban migrants were those poor, landless, unskilled individuals whose rural opportunities were for the most part non-existent. In colonial Africa, seasonal migration was predominant, with migrants from various income levels seeking short-term urban jobs. Recently, however, with the emergence of a stabilised, modern industrial sector in most urban areas of the less developed countries, the financial assets of migrants from rural areas have become important only to the extent that individuals with larger financial resources can survive longer while searching for the elusive urban job. In short, migrants seem to come from all socio-economic strata, with the majority being very poor only because most rural inhabitants *are* poor.

Towards a generalised theory of the economics of rural–urban migration

As we discovered in Chapter 7, the historical economic development of Western Europe and the United States was closely associated with, and in fact often defined in terms of, the movement of labour from rural to urban areas. For the most part, with a rural sector dominated by agricultural activities and an urban sector concentrating on industrialisation, the overall economic development was characterised by the gradual reallocation of labour out of agriculture and into industry through rural–urban migration, both internal and international.

Urbanisation and industrialisation, therefore, became synonymous. This historical model served as a blueprint for the development of Third World nations, as evidenced, for example, by the Lewis–Fei–Ranis theory of labour transfer.

But the overwhelming evidence of the 1960s and 70s, when Third World nations witnessed a massive migration of rural populations into urban areas in spite of rising levels of urban unemployment and underemployment largely negates the validity of the Lewis–Fei–Ranis models of development. In a series of articles, the present author has sought to develop a theory of rural–urban migration to explain the apparently paradoxical relationship (at least to economists) of accelerated rural–urban migration in the context of rising urban unemployment.[1]

The basic nature of the Todaro migration model

Starting from the assumption that migration is primarily an economic phenomenon which for the individual migrant can be a quite rational decision, despite the existence of urban unemployment, the Todaro model postulates that migration proceeds in response to urban–rural differences in **expected rather than actual earnings.** The fundamental premise is that migrants consider the various labour market opportunities available to them, as between the rural and urban sectors, and choose the one which maximises their 'expected' gains from migration. Expected gains are measured by (1) **the difference in real incomes between rural and urban work** and (2) **the probability of a new migrant obtaining an urban job.** A schematic framework

[1] See for example, Michael P. Todaro, 'An Analysis of Industrialisation, Employment and Unemployment in LDCs', *Yale Economic Essays*, Vol. 8, No. 2 (1968), pp. 329–492; and 'A Model of Labour Migration and Urban Unemployment in Less Developed Countries', *American Economic Review*, Vol. 59, No. 1 (1969), pp. 138–48.

showing how the various factors affecting the migration decision interact is portrayed in Figure 14.3

In essence, the Todaro theory assumes that members of the labour force, both actual and potential, compare their expected incomes for a given time horizon in the urban sector (i.e. the difference between returns and costs of migration) with prevailing average rural incomes, and migrate if the former exceeds the latter.

Consider the following illustration. Suppose the average unskilled or semi-skilled rural worker has a choice between being a farm labourer (or working his own land) for an annual average real income of, say, 50 units, or migrating to the city where a worker with his skill or educational background can obtain wage employment yielding an annual real income of 100 units. The more commonly used economic models of migration, which place exclusive emphasis on the income differential factor as the determinant of the decision to migrate, would indicate a clear choice in this situation. The worker should seek the higher-paid urban job. It is important to recognise, however, that these migration models were developed largely in the context of advanced industrial economies and, as such, implicitly assumed the existence of full or near-full employment. In a full employment environment the decision to migrate can be predicated solely on securing the highest-paid job wherever it becomes

Figure 14.3
A schematic framework for the analysis of the migration decision

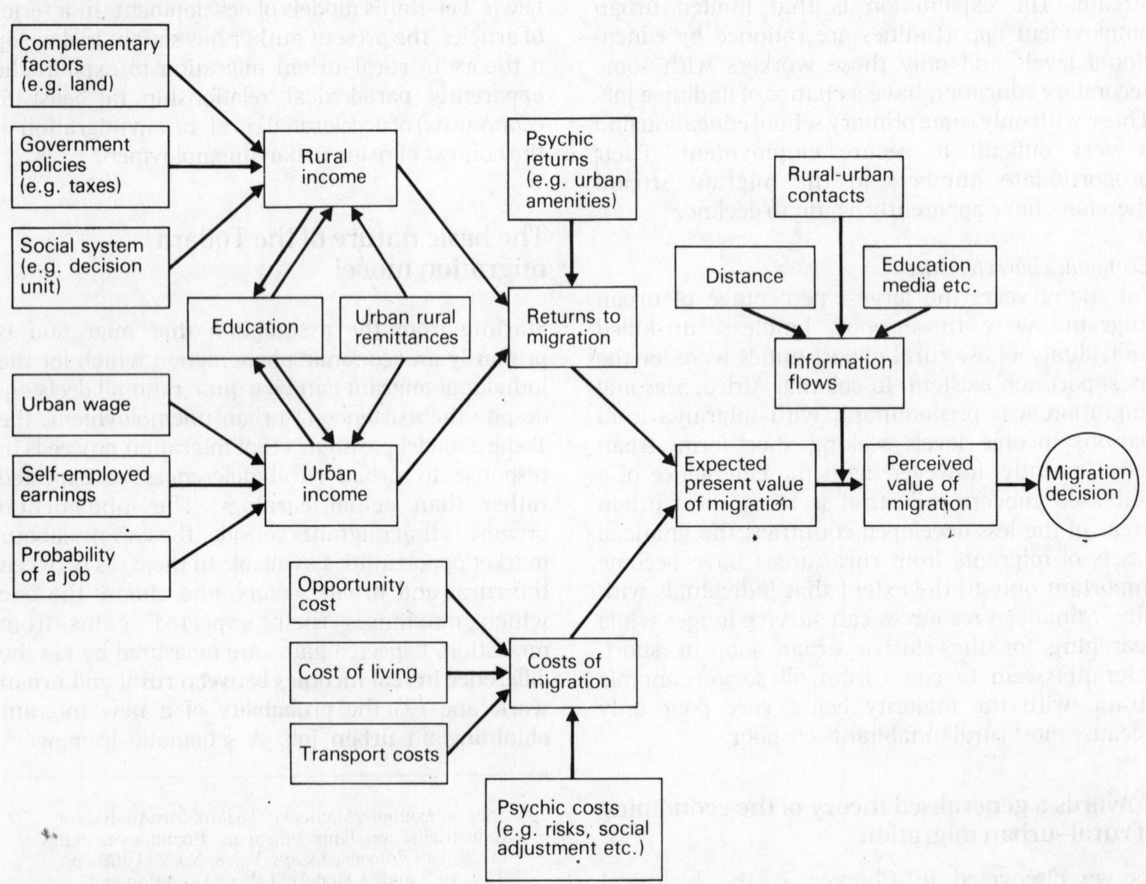

Source: D. Byerlee, 'Rural Urban Migration in Africa', *International Migration Review*, Winter 1974, p. 553.

available. Simple economic theory would then indicate that such migration should lead to a reduction in wage differentials through the interaction of the forces of supply and demand, both in areas of emigration and in points of immigration.

Unfortunately such an analysis is not realistic in the context of the institutional and economic framework of most Third World nations. First of all, these countries are beset by a chronic and serious unemployment problem, with the result that a typical migrant cannot expect to secure a highly paid urban job immediately. It is much more likely, therefore, that on entering the urban labour market the migrant will either become totally unemployed or will seek casual and part-time employment in the urban 'traditional' sector. In making his decision to migrate, the individual must balance the probabilities and risks of being unemployed or underemployed for a considerable period of time against the positive urban–rural real income differential. The fact that a typical migrant can expect to earn twice the annual real income in an urban area than in a rural environment may be of little consequence if the actual likelihood of his securing the higher-paying job within, say, a one-year period is one chance in five. Thus, the probability of his being successful in securing the higher-paid urban job is 20 per cent, and therefore his 'expected' urban income for the one-year period is in fact 20 units (i.e. $0.20 \times 100 = 20$) and not the 100 units that an urban worker in a full-employment environment would expect to receive. With a one-period time horizon and a probability of success of 20 per cent it would be irrational for this migrant to seek an urban job, even though the differential between his urban and rural earnings capacity is 100 per cent. On the other hand, if the probability of success were, say, 60 per cent so that the expected urban income is 60 units, it would be entirely rational for our migrant with his one-period time horizon to try his luck in the urban area, even though unemployment may be extremely high.

If we now approach the situation more realistically by assuming a considerably longer time horizon, especially in view of the fact that the vast majority of migrants are between the ages of 15 and 24 years, then the decision to migrate should be represented on the basis of a longer-term, more 'permanent' income calculation. If the migrant anticipates a relatively low probability of finding regular wage employment in the initial period but expects this probability to increase over time as he is able to broaden his urban contacts, it would still be rational for him to migrate, even though expected urban income during the initial period or periods might be lower than expected rural income. As long as the 'present value' of the net stream of expected urban incomes over the migrant's planning horizon exceeds that of the expected rural income, the decision to migrate is justifiable.[2] This, in essence, is the process portrayed in Figure 14.3.

Rather than equalising urban and rural wage rates as in a perfectly competitive labour market model, rural–urban migration in our model acts as an equilibrating force which equates rural and urban *expected* incomes. For example, if average rural income is 60 and urban income is 120, then a 50 per cent urban unemployment rate would be necessary before further migration would no longer be profitable. Since expected incomes are defined in terms of *both* wages and employment probabilities, it is possible to have continued migration in spite of the existence of sizable rates of urban unemployment. In the above numerical example, migration would continue even if the urban unemployment rate were 30 or 40 per cent.

To sum up, the Todaro migration model has four basic characteristics:

1. **Migration is stimulated primarily by rational economic considerations** of relative benefits and costs, mostly financial but also psychological.
2. **The decision to migrate depends on 'expected' rather than actual urban–rural real wage differentials** where the 'expected' differential is determined by the interaction of two variables, the actual urban–rural wage differential *and* the probability of success in obtaining employment in the urban sector.
3. **The probability of obtaining an urban job is inversely related to the urban unemployment rate.**
4. **Migration rates in excess of urban job opportunity growth rates are not only possible but rational** and even likely in the face of wide urban–rural *expected* income differentials. High rates of urban unemployment are, therefore, inevitable outcomes of the serious imbalance in economic

[2] Recall our discussion of 'present values' in Chapter 4 in the context of the 'time dimension' concept.

opportunities between the urban and rural areas of less developed countries.

Some policy implications

While such a theory might at first seem to devalue the critical importance of rural–urban migration by portraying it as an adjustment mechanism by which workers allocate themselves between rural and urban labour markets, it does have important policy implications for development strategy with regard to wages and incomes, rural development and industrialisation. These implications include:

Imbalances in urban–rural employment opportunities

Since migrants are assumed to respond to differentials in expected incomes it is vitally important that *imbalances between economic opportunities in rural and urban sectors be minimised.* Specifically, if we define the urban 'expected' wage as the real wage, W_u, multiplied by the probability of obtaining an urban job, P_u, (where P_u is defined as the number of urban jobs, E_u, divided by the urban labour force L_u), so that the urban–rural expected income differential is $W_u \cdot (E_u/L_u) - W_r$, then the *larger* the differential between real urban and rural wages, $W_u - W_r$, the *lower* must be the urban employment rate, E_u/L_u, to bring about equality between expected incomes. Alternatively, this specification indicates that the larger the gap between urban and rural real wages, the higher must be the urban *unemployment* rate, $1 - E_u/L_u$, before migration in excess of job opportunities ceases. It follows that permitting urban wage rates to grow at a greater pace than average rural incomes will stimulate further rural–urban migration in spite of rising levels of urban unemployment. This heavy influx of people into urban areas not only gives rise to socio-economic problems in the cities, but it may also eventually create problems of labour shortages in rural areas, especially during the busy seasons.

Urban job creation

Urban job creation is an insufficient solution for the urban unemployment problem. The traditional (Keynesian) economic solution to urban unemployment (i.e. the creation of more urban jobs) without simultaneous attempts to improve rural incomes and employment opportunities, can lead to the paradoxical situation where *more urban employment leads to higher levels of urban and rural unemployment.* Once again, the imbalance in 'expected' earning opportunities is the crucial concept. Since migration rates are assumed to respond positively to *both* higher urban wages and higher urban employment opportunities (or probabilities), it follows that for any given positive urban–rural wage differential (in most LDCs urban wages are typically three to four times as large as rural wages), higher urban employment rates will widen the expected differential and induce even higher rates of rural–urban migration. For every new job created, two or three migrants who were productively occupied in rural areas may come to the city. Thus, if 100 new jobs are created, there may be as many as 300 new migrants and, therefore, 200 more urban unemployed. A policy designed to reduce urban unemployment, therefore, may lead not only to the higher levels of urban unemployment but also to lower levels of agricultural output and employment.

Educational expansion

Indiscriminate and costly educational expansion will lead to further migration and unemployment. Our basic migration model also has important policy implications for curtailing investment in educational expansion, especially at the higher levels. The heavy influx of rural migrants into urban areas at rates much in excess of new employment opportunities has necessitated a rationing device in the selection of new employees. Although within each educational group such selection may be largely random, many observers have noted that employers tend to use educational attainment or number of years of completed schooling as the typical rationing device. For the same wage, they will hire those with more education in preference to those with less, even though extra education may not contribute to better job performance. Jobs which could formerly be filled by those with primary education (sweepers, messengers, filing clerks, etc.) now require secondary training; those formerly requiring a secondary certificate (clerks, typists, bookkeepers, etc.) now necessitate a degree. It follows that for any given urban wage, if the probability of success in securing a modern sector job is higher for those with more education, their expected income differential will also be higher and the more likely they will be to migrate to the cities. Our basic model, therefore, provides an economic rationale for the observed fact in most LDCs that rural inhabitants with more education are more likely to migrate than those with less.

From the viewpoint of educational policy, it is safe to predict that as job opportunities become scarce in relation to the number of applicants, students will experience increasing pressure to proceed further up the educational ladder. The private demand for education, which in many ways is a 'derived demand' for urban jobs, will continue to exert tremendous pressure on governments to invest in post-primary school facilities. But for many of these students the spectre of joining the ranks of the 'educated unemployed' becomes more of a reality with each passing year. Government over-investment in post-primary educational facilities often turns out to be an investment in idle human resources. This is not only bad economics: in the long run it is likely also to be bad politics if the student uprisings in Sri Lanka, Bangladesh (when it was East Pakistan) and Ethiopia are at all instructive. Chapters 17 and 18 deal with this and other issues related to the economics of education in greater detail.

Wages and prices

Wage subsidies and traditional scarcity factor pricing can be counterproductive. As we have seen in Chapter 13, a standard economic policy for generating urban employment opportunities is to eliminate factor-price distortions by using 'correct' prices. Since actual urban wages generally exceed the market or 'correct' wage as a result of a variety of institutional factors, including minimum wage legislation, it is often correctly argued that the elimination of wage distortions through price adjustments or a subsidy system will encourage more labour-intensive modes of production. While such policies can effectively generate more urban employment opportunities, they can also lead to higher levels of unemployment in accordance with our argument above about induced migration. The overall welfare impact of a relative wage reduction policy when both the rural and urban sectors are taken into account is not immediately clear. Much will depend on the level of urban unemployment, the size of the urban–rural expected income differential, and the magnitude of induced migration as more urban jobs are created.

Rural development

Programmes of integrated rural development should be encouraged. Policies which operate only on the demand side of the urban employment picture, such as wage subsidies, direct government hiring, elimination of factor price distortions, and employer tax incentives, are probably far less effective in the long run in alleviating the *unemployment* problem than are policies designed directly to regulate (i.e. slow down) the supply of labour to urban areas. Clearly, however, some combination of both policies is most desirable.

Many informed observers of Third World development agree on the crucial importance of rural and agricultural development if the urban unemployment problem is to be solved (see Chapters 15 and 16). Most of the proposals call for the restoration of a proper balance between rural and urban incomes, and the moderation of government policies which give development programmes a marked bias towards the urban industrial sector (e.g. in the provision of health, educational and other social services).

Given the political difficulties of reducing urban wage rates, the need continuously to expand urban employment opportunities through judicious investments in small- and medium-scale labour-intensive industries, and the inevitable growth of the urban industrial sector, every effort must be made to broaden the economic base of the rural economy at the same time. The present unnecessary economic incentives for rural–urban migration need to be minimised through creative and well-designed programmes of integrated rural development. These should focus on income generation, both farm and non-farm, employment growth, health delivery, educational improvement, infrastructure development (electricity, water, roads, etc.) and the provision of other rural amenities. Successful rural development programmes adapted to the socio-economic and environmental needs of particular countries and regions are the only viable long-run solution to the problem of excessive rural–urban migration.

To assert, however, that there is an urgent need for policies designed to curb the excessive influx of rural migrants is not to imply an attempt to reverse what some have called 'inevitable historical trends'. Rather, the implication of the Todaro migration model is that there is a growing need for a *policy package* that does not exacerbate these historical trends towards urbanisation by *artificially* creating serious imbalances in economic opportunities between urban and rural areas.

Conclusions: the shape of a comprehensive employment strategy

At various points throughout this and the previous chapter, we have mentioned possible policy approaches designed to improve the very serious employment situation in many less developed countries. We conclude by summarising the consensus opinion of most economists on the shape of a **comprehensive employment strategy**. This strategy has five key elements.

Creating an appropriate rural–urban economic balance

A more appropriate balance between rural and urban economic opportunities appears to be indispensable to ameliorating urban unemployment problems in most developing countries. The main thrust of this activity should be in the integrated development of the rural sector, the spread of small-scale industries throughout the countryside and the reorientation of economic activity and social investments towards raising incomes in the rural areas.

Expansion of small-scale, labour-intensive industries

The composition or 'product mix' of output has obvious effects on the magnitude of employment, since some products (often basic consumer goods) require more labour per unit of output and per unit of capital than others. Efforts to expand these mostly small-scale, labour-intensive industries can be accomplished in two ways: *directly* through government investment and incentives, and *indirectly* through income redistribution (either directly or from future growth) to the poor whose structure of consumer demand is both less import-intensive and more labour-intensive than the rich.

Elimination of factor-price distortions

There is ample evidence to demonstrate that correcting factor-price distortions primarily through the elimination of various capital subsidies and curtailing the growth of urban wages would undoubtedly increase employment opportunities and make better use of scarce capital resources. But by how much and how quickly these policies would work is not clear. Surely correct pricing policies by themselves are insufficient to alter significantly the present employment situation, for the reasons described in Chapter 13.

Choosing appropriate labour-intensive technologies of production

One of the principal inhibiting factors to the success of any long-run programme of employment creation both in urban industry and rural agriculture is the almost complete technological dependence of Third World nations on imported (typically labour-saving) machinery and equipment from the developed countries. Both domestic and international efforts must be made to reduce this dependence by developing indigenous technological research and adaptation capacities in the developing countries themselves. Such efforts might first be linked to the development of small-scale, labour-intensive rural and urban enterprises. They could also focus on the development of low-cost, labour-intensive methods of providing rural infrastructure needs, including roads, irrigation and drainage systems, and essential health and educational services. Clearly, this is an area where scientific and technological assistance from the developed countries could be most fruitful.

Modifying the direct linkage between education and employment

The emergence of the phenomenon of the educated unemployed in many developing countries is calling into question the appropriateness of massive quantitative expansion of educational systems, especially at the higher levels. Formal education has become the rationing tunnel through which all prospective job-holders must pass. As modern sector jobs multiply more slowly than the numbers leaving the educational tunnel, it becomes necessary to extend the length of the tunnel and to narrow its exit. While a full discussion of educational problems and policies must await Chapters 17 and 18, we may point out that one way to moderate the excessive demand for additional years of schooling (which in reality is a demand for modern sector jobs) would be for governments, often the largest employers, to base their hiring practices and their wage structures on other criteria. Moreover, by creating attractive economic opportunities in rural areas, it will become easier to redirect educational systems towards the needs of rural development. It is ironic that many Third World educational systems, being offshoots of Western systems, are oriented towards preparing students to function in a small modern sector employing at the most 20 to 30 per cent of the labour force. Many of the skills necessary for development, especially rural development, remain largely neglected.

A final comment on population

There can be little doubt that reducing population growth rates is a principal means of ameliorating the employment problem in the long run for the simple reason that it would reduce the future number of job seekers. We know that in the short to medium run (e.g. the next 25 years) for all practical purposes the size of the labour force is already determined. This does not negate the need to lower fertility rates, especially in heavily populated Third World nations, as soon as possible. The reason why we have not included the need for an active, government-supported or sponsored family planning programme among our five priority policy areas is simply that, as stressed in Chapter 12, each of the five policies suggested above will contribute indirectly to lowering levels of fertility by raising levels of living for the very poor, especially in rural areas. For example, the provision of expanded job opportunities for women in developing countries may be a most effective strategy not only for raising levels of rural and urban living but also for causing the birth rate to fall.

Concepts for review

two-sector models
modern sector
labour-saving capital accumulation
rural–urban migration
'push' and 'pull' migration factors
job probabilities
migrant time horizon
'institutional' urban wage
educated unemployed
wage subsidy
unlimited supplies of labour
demand curve for labour
extended family system
'expected' income
present values
income differentials
urban–rural economic imbalances
induced migration
school leaver problem
economic and social infrastructure

Questions for discussion

1. Describe briefly the essential assumptions and features of the Lewis–Fei–Ranis surplus labour model of development. What are the major strengths and weaknesses of this two-sector model for analysing the actual process of rural–urban labour transfer in most Third World countries?
2. Describe briefly the essential assumptions and major features of the Todaro model of rural–urban migration. One of the most significant implications of this model is the paradoxical conclusion that government policies designed to create more urban employment may in fact lead to more urban unemployment. Explain the reasons why such a paradoxical result might be forthcoming.

3. 'The key to solving the serious problem of excessive rural–urban migration and rising urban unemployment and underemployment in Third World countries is to restore a proper balance between urban and rural economic and social opportunities.' Discuss the reasoning behind this statement and give a few specific examples of government policies which will promote a better balance between urban and rural economic and social opportunities.
4. For many years the 'conventional wisdom' of development economics assumed that there existed an inherent conflict between the objective of maximising output growth and promoting rapid industrial employment growth. Why might these two objectives be mutually supportive rather than conflicting? Explain.
5. What is meant by the expression 'getting prices right'? Under what conditions will eliminating factor-price distortions generate substantial new employment opportunities? Be sure to include in your discussion a brief definition of what is meant by 'factor-price distortions'.

Further reading

The Lewis–Fei–Ranis models of development in labour-surplus economies are best described in the following original papers by these well-known development economists: W. A. Lewis, 'Economic Development with Unlimited Supplies of Labour', *Manchester School,* 1954; J. C. H. Fei and G. Ranis, 'A Theory of Economic Development', *American Economic Review*, 1961.

Among the many readings on the critical problem of rural–urban migration in developing countries, the following are perhaps the most comprehensive: D. Byerlee, 'Rural-Urban Migration in Africa: theory, policy and research implications', *International Migration Review*, 1974; J. R. Harris and M. P. Todaro, 'Migration, Unemployment and Development: a two-sector analysis', *American Economic Review*, March 1970; M. P. Todaro, *Internal Migration and Economic Development: a review of theory, evidence, methodology and research priorities'*, International Labour Organisation, Geneva, 1976; and Sally Findlay, *Planning for Internal Migration*, US Dept. of Commerce, ISRD–4, Washington D.C., 1977.

Chapter 15 Agricultural stagnation and agrarian structures

It is in the agricultural sector that the battle for long term economic development will be won or lost.
Gunnar Myrdal

The main burden of development and employment creation will have to be borne by the part of the economy in which agriculture is the predominant activity: that is, the rural sector.
Francis Blanchard, Director General of the International Labour Organisation, 1975.[1]

Introduction

The imperative of rural development

If migration to the cities of Africa, Asia and Latin America is proceeding at historically unprecedented rates, a large part of the explanation can be found in the economic stagnation of the outlying rural areas. This is where the people are. Over 1.8 billion people in the Third World grind out a meagre and often inadequate existence in agricultural pursuits. Over 2.5 billion people lived in rural areas in the early 1980s. Estimates indicate that this figure will rise to almost 3.1 billion by the year 2000. People living in the countryside of Latin America and Asia comprise considerably more than half the total populations of such diverse nations as Brazil, Peru, India, Indonesia, Burma, Bolivia, Sri Lanka, Pakistan and the Philippines. In Africa the ratios are much higher, with almost every country having rural dwellers in excess of three-quarters of the total population. In spite of the massive migration to the cities, however, the absolute population increase in rural areas of most developing nations will continue to be greater than that of urban areas for at least the next decade.

Of greater importance than sheer numbers is the fact that the vast majority (almost 70 per cent) of the world's poorest people are also located in rural areas and engaged primarily in subsistence agriculture. Their basic concern is survival. These are the many hundreds of millions of people who have been bypassed by whatever economic 'progress' has been attained. In their daily struggle to subsist, their behaviour may appear irrational to some Western economists, who have little comprehension of the precarious nature of subsistence living. If 'development' is to take place and become self-sustaining, it will have to start in the rural areas in general and the agricultural sector in particular. There can be no national development without rural development. **The core problems of widespread poverty, growing inequality, rapid population growth and rising unemployment all find their origins in the stagnation and often retrogression of economic life in rural areas.**

Five main questions need to be asked about Third World agriculture and rural development.

1. How can total agricultural output and productivity per capita be substantially increased in a manner that will directly benefit the average small farmer and landless rural dweller?
2. What is the process by which traditional low productivity subsistence farms are transformed into high productivity commercial enterprises?
3. Do traditional small farmers and peasant cultivators stubbornly resist change or are they acting rationally within the context of their particular environment?
4. Are economic incentives sufficient to elicit output increases among peasant agriculturalists or are institutional and structural changes in rural farming systems also required?
5. Is raising agricultural productivity sufficient to improve rural life or must there be concomitant improvements in educational, medical and other social services? In other words, what do we mean

[1] 'Time for Transition – a Mid-Term Review of the Second United Nations Development Decade', ILO, Geneva, 1975.

by 'rural development' and how can it be achieved?

Our approach in this chapter and the next starts with a brief factual account of the relative stagnation of the agricultural sector in most Third World nations over the past two decades. We conclude this chapter by describing and analysing the basic characteristics of agrarian systems in Latin America, Asia and Africa to see if we can identify some important similarities and differences. Chapter 16 starts with an analysis of the economics of subsistence agriculture and a discussion of the stages of transition from subsistence to commercial farming in developing nations. Our focus is not only on the economic factors but on the social, institutional and structional requirements of small-farm modernisation. We then discuss the meaning of 'rural development' and review alternative policies designed to raise levels of living, esteem and freedom in Third World rural areas. A brief look at the Chinese experience with rural development and the lessons, if any, which this experience offers to other Third World nations concludes these two chapters on agriculture and rural development.

Agricultural stagnation in the development decade

As we have seen in previous chapters, many developing countries experienced respectable rates of GNP growth during the 1960s and 1970s. The greatest proportionate share of this overall growth, however, occurred in the manufacturing and commerce sectors where recorded rates of annual output growth often exceeded 10 per cent. In contrast, agricultural output growth for most developing regions remained stagnant during these decades, so that the share of agricultural output in total GNP declined. Table 15.1 reveals that although the agricultural sector accounts for most of the employment in Third World countries, it accounts for a much lower share of the output. In no Third World region does agricultural production constitute half of the total national product. This is in marked contrast to the historical experience of advanced countries where agricultural output in their early stages of growth always contributed at least as much to total output as the share of the labour force engaged in these activities. The fact that contemporary Third World agricultural *employment* is typically twice as large in proportion to the total as agricultural *output* simply reflects the relatively low levels of agricultural labour productivity compared with that in manufacturing and commerce.

Table 15.1
Output and employment in Third World agriculture, 1978

Third World regions	% of labour force in agriculture	Output of agriculture, forestry and fishing as % of GNP
South Asia	71	25
East Asia	55	20
Latin America	40	25
Africa	65	40

Source: *World Development Report, 1980*, Annex tables 6, 19.

The data in Table 15.1, and especially in Chapter 9 where we discussed the sectorial location of absolute poverty, strongly suggest that a direct attack on rural poverty through accelerated agricultural development is necessary to raise rural living standards. Mere concern with maximising GNP growth is not enough. Unfortunately the record of the past two decades offers little encouragement, as can be seen from Table 15.2.

Over the two decades which ended in 1970, per capita food production and per capita agricultural production (which includes not only food but also non-edible agricultural products like cotton, sisal, rubber, etc.) each increased less than one per cent per year in the Third World as a whole. Moreover, Table 15.2 shows that the rates of growth of both these measures of agricultural performance were much slower in the 1960s than in the 1950s. In fact the agricultural sector in LDCs completely stagnated in the 1960s. People on the whole were little or no better off in terms of the per capita availability of food at the end of the decade than they were at the beginning. In constrast, in the more developed countries, per capita food production continued to rise at an annual rate nine times higher.

Looking at each major region within the Third World, we can also see from Table 15.2 that the

Table 15.2
The growth (and stagnation) of per capita food and agricultural output in Third World regions

	Per capita food production		Per capita agricultural production	
Region	1948/52–70	1960–70	1948/52–70	1960–70
Latin America	0.4	0.6	0.2	0.0
Far East (excl. Japan)	0.8	0.3	0.7	0.3
Near East (excl. Israel)	0.7	0.0	0.8	0.0
Africa (excl. South Africa)	0.0	0.7	0.3	0.5
All underdeveloped countries	0.6	0.1	0.6	0.0
Developed capitalist countries	1.1	0.9	1.0	0.6

Source: K. Griffin, 'Agrarian policy: the political and economic context,' *World Development*, Vol. I, II, November 1973, p. 3.

same broad tendencies were at work. In Latin America there was some increase in the growth of per capita food production, but agricultural production as a whole showed no such increase. The picture for Africa is even more dismal. Per capita food *and* agricultural production declined sharply in the 1960s. This suggests that the average African suffered a fall in his level of food consumption during the decade. Since food consumption constitutes by far the largest component in a typical African's standard of living, the total decline of almost 10 per cent in per capita food consumption indicates that the region as a whole may have been becoming even less developed during the 1960s.

The agricultural performance in Asia was only slightly better. In the Near East there was a decline in the rate of growth compared with the pre-1960 period. During the 1960–1970 decade both per capita food and agricultural production tended to stagnate. Rates of growth also fell in the Far East, although production per capita did increase at about 0.3 per cent per annum.

We may conclude that in spite of some impressive rates of per capita GNP growth recorded in Third World regions during the 1960s, the agricultural sector not only showed negligible progress as a whole but even showed a sharp decline when compared with the previous decade. Since the vast majority of people in developing countries seek their livelihoods in this sector, Table 15.2 confirms what we discovered in Chapter 9, that the magnitude and extent of Third World poverty has probably worsened over the past 10 to 15 years. This is especially so when one realises once again that *per capita* aggregates for food consumption mask the inherently unequal distribution of that consumption just as per capita GNP figures fail to give any indication of the magnitude of absolute poverty. If the distribution of limited food supplies is at all analogous to the highly unequal distribution of income in many LDCs, then the food situation for millions of people was even worse in the 1960s than the data in Table 15.2 reveal.

Finally, if we take a look at the experience of the 1970s as shown in Figure 15.1, the per capita food production picture for the Third World shows a very negligible improvement in 1980 when compared with the 1961–1965 period. Even though total food production increased by 54 per cent between 1961–1965 and 1980, rapid population growth in the LDCs meant that *per capita* food production rose by only 6 per cent. Compounding this production problem along with the persistence of severe droughts and famines in many parts of central Africa and South Asia was the unprecedented rise in world food prices during the first half of the 1970s. The combination of growing populations, increased resource scarcities and rapidly rising food prices has undoubtedly meant a marked deterioration in levels of living for that sizable segment of mankind that spends 80 per cent of its income on food. A doubling in the price of wheat, maize or rice (as occurred in the early 1970s) cannot possibly be offset by increased expenditures for these already impoverished people. It can only drive a subsistence diet below the subsistence and survival level.

Figure 15.1
Indexes of total food production and per capita food production in developing countries, 1955–1980 (1961–1965 = 100)

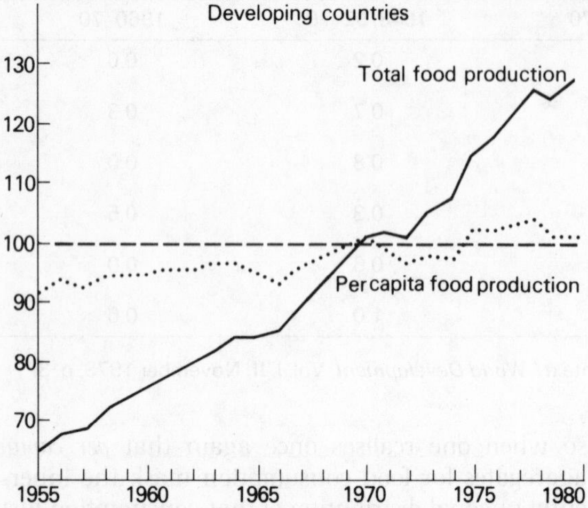

Source: Overseas Development Council, *The United States and World Development Agenda* (1980), p. 177.

A major reason for the relatively poor performance of Third World agriculture has been the relative neglect of this sector in the development priorities of the 1950s and 1960s. This neglect of agriculture and the accompanying bias towards investment in the urban industrial sector in turn can be traced largely to the misplaced emphasis on rapid industrialisation which permeated development thinking and strategy during these past two decades. For example, during the 1950s and throughout most of the 1960s the share of total national investment allocated towards the agricultural sector in a sample of 18 LDCs was approximately 12 per cent, even though agricultural output in these countries constituted almost 30 per cent of their GNPs and more than 60 per cent of their total employment.[2]

As a result of the disappointing experience of the past two decades and the realisation that the future of most less developed countries will depend to a large extent on what happens to their agriculture, there has been a marked shift in development thinking and policy-making. This shift has been away from the almost exclusive emphasis on rapid industrialisation and towards a more realistic appreciation of the overwhelming importance of agricultural and rural development for the ultimate realisation of national development. A necessary first essential towards understanding what is needed for agricultural and rural development, however, must be an understanding of the nature of agricultural systems in Third World regions in general and the economic aspects of the transition from subsistence to commercial agriculture in particular.

The structure of Third World agrarian systems

Two kinds of world agriculture

When we look at the state of contemporary agriculture in most poor countries, we realise the enormity of the task that lies ahead. A brief comparison between agricultural productivity in the developed nations with that of the less developed nations makes this clear.[3] World agriculture, in fact, comprises two very distinct types of farming: (1) the **highly efficient agriculture of the developed countries** where substantial productive capacity and high output per worker permits a very small number of farmers to feed entire nations; and (2) the **inefficient and low productivity agriculture** of **developing countries**, where in many instances the agricultural sector can barely sustain the farm population, let alone the burgeoning urban population, even at a minimum level of subsistence.

The gap between the two kinds of agriculture is immense. This is best illustrated by the disparities in labour productivity, shown in Table 15.3. In 1960 the agricultural population of the developed nations totalled about 115 million people. They produced a total output amounting to $78 billion, or about $680 per capita of their agricultural population. In contrast, we see from Table 15.3 that the per capita product of the agricultural population in the

[2] E. F. Szczepanik, 'Agricultural capital formation in selected developing countries', *Agricultural Planning Studies*, No. 11, FAO, 1970.

[3] See Raanan Weitz, *From Peasant to Farmer: a revolutionary strategy for development*, Columbia University Press, 1971, pp. 6–9. Much of the following analysis is drawn from this informative and thoughtful book.

Table 15.3
Agricultural population and production in developed and less developed countries, 1960, 1980 and 2000

	1960		1980		2000	
	Developed nations	LDCs	Developed nations	LDCs	Developed nations	LDCs
Agricultural population (millions)	115	850	75	1,230	50	1,480
Agricultural production total (billions)	$78	$43	$125	$77	$186	$135
Per capita (Agricultural population)	$680	$52	$1,660	$63	$3,720	$91

Source: Weitz, *op cit.*, p. 7.

underdeveloped countries in 1960 was only $52. In other words, agricultural labour productivity in developed countries was more than 13 times as large as that in the less developed countries. Projections for the end of the century (year 2000), show this productivity gap widening eventually to 40 to 1.

In the developed countries the steady growth of agriculture has been occurring since the mid-eighteenth century. It has benefited primarily from technological and biological improvements that have resulted in ever higher levels of labour and land productivity. This growth rate accelerated after World War I and particularly after World War II. As a result, fewer farmers have been able to produce more food. This is especially the case in the United States where less than 6 per cent of the total work force is agricultural compared with more than 70 per cent in the early nineteenth century. For example, in 1820 the American farmer could produce only four times his own consumption. One hundred years later, in 1920, his productivity had doubled and he could provide enough for eight people. It took only another 32 years for this productivity to double again and then only 12 more years for it to double once more. By 1980 a single American farmer could provide enough food to feed almost 75 people. Moreover, during the entire period average farm incomes in North America were steadily rising.[4]

The picture is entirely different when we turn to the agricultural production experience of Third World nations. In many poor countries agricultural production methods have changed relatively slowly over time. In Chapter 16 we discover that much of this technological stagnation can be traced to the special circumstances of subsistence agriculture with its high risks and uncertain rewards. Rapid rural population growth has compounded the problem by causing great pressure to be exerted on existing resources. Where fertile land is scarce, especially throughout South and Southeast Asia but also in many parts of Latin America and Africa, rapid population growth has led to an increase in the number of people living on each unit of land. Given the same farming technology and the use of traditional non-labour inputs (e.g. simple tools, animal power, traditional seeds, etc.), we know from our principle of diminishing returns that as more and more people are forced to work on a given piece of land, their marginal (and average) productivity will decline. The net result is a continuous deterioration in real living standards for rural peasants.

As an extreme example of this situation, consider the case of India. At the end of the nineteenth century, food consumption was only slightly above the minimum regarded as necessary for survival. Today many believe that it is below that standard, with many hundreds of thousands of people on the verge of starvation. In recent years the volume of production has been expanding, but not fast enough to keep up with the rapid increase in human numbers. As a result farm labour productivity hardly changed during the 1960s and 1970s. The experience of most other developing countries has been similar.

In order to avert massive starvation and to raise levels of living for the average rural dweller, agricultural production and the productivity of both labour and land must be rapidly increased throughout Asia, Africa and Latin America. Third World

[4] Weitz, *op. cit*, pp. 7–8.

nations need to become more self-sufficient in their food production. But unless some major economic, institutional and structural changes are made, their dependence, especially on North American food supplies, will increase in the 1980s and 1990s.

Peasant agriculture in Latin America, Asia and Africa

In many developing countries, various historical circumstances have led to a concentration of large areas of land in the possession of a small class of powerful land owners. This is especially true in Latin America and parts of the Asian subcontinent. In Africa, both historical circumstances and the availability of relatively more unused land has resulted in a different pattern and structure of agricultural activity, although in terms of levels of farm productivity, there is little to distinguish among the three regions.

A common characteristic of agriculture in all three regions, and for that matter in many developed countries as well, is the position of the family farm as the basic unit of production. As Professor Weitz points out:

> For the vast number of farm families, whose members constitute the main agricultural work force, agriculture is not merely an occupation or a source of income; it is a way of life. This is particularly evident in traditional societies, where farmers are closely attached to their land and devote long, arduous days to its cultivation. Any change in farming methods perforce brings with it changes in the farmer's way of life. The introduction of biological and technical innovations must therefore be adapted not only to the natural and economic conditions, but perhaps even more to the attitudes, values and abilities of the mass of producers, who must understand the suggested changes, must be willing to accept them, and must be capable of carrying them out.[5]

In spite of the very obvious differences between agricultural systems in Asia, Latin America and Africa, and among individual nations within each region, certain broad similarities enable us to make some generalisations and comparisons. In particular, agrarian systems in many parts of Asia and Latin America show more structural and institutional similarities than differences, while African subsistence farmers exhibit many economic behaviour patterns similar to those of their counterparts in the other two regions. We examine first the major features of agricultural systems in Latin America and Asia.

Latin America and Asia

Although the heritage and culture in these two regions are quite distinct, they have some characteristics of peasant life in common. Francis Foland has succinctly described these as follows:

> Both the Latin American and Asian peasant is a rural cultivator whose prime concern is survival. Subsistence defines his concept of life. He may strive to obtain his and his family's minimal needs by tilling an inadequate piece of land which is his own or, more often, which is rented from or pawned to a landlord or money lender, or by selling his labour for substandard wages to a commercial agricultural enterprise. Profits which might come to him through the fortunes of weather or market are windfalls, not preconceived goals. Debt rather than profit is his normal fate, and, therefore, his farming techniques are rationally scaled to his level of disposable capital; human and animal power rather than mechanized equipment; excrement rather than chemical fertilisers; traditional crops and seeds rather than experimental cultivations.
>
> No effective social security, unemployment insurance, or minimum-wage law ease his plight. His every decision and act impinge directly upon his struggle for physical survival. In countries with a high proportion of peasantry, traditional food crops which a rural family can itself convert readily into the daily fare for its grain – or tuber-based diet dominate the agriculture; corn in Mexico, rice in Indonesia, mandioca in Brazil, soyabeans in China. India's is typical of peasant agriculture with seventy-five per cent of the cropped land devoted to food grains such as rice, wheat, millet, barley and lentils. When these fail, as in Maharashtra in

[5] *Ibid.*, p. 9.

Table 15.4
Minifundios and latifundios in the agrarian structure of selected Latin American countries

	Minifundios		Latifundios	
	% of farms	% of occupied land	% of farms	% of occupied land
Argentina	43.2	3.4	0.8	36.9
Brazil	22.5	0.5	4.7	59.5
Colombia	64.0	4.9	1.3	49.5
Chile	36.9	0.2	6.9	81.3
Ecuador	89.9	16.6	0.4	45.1
Guatemala	88.4	14.3	0.1	40.8
Peru	88.0	7.4	1.1	82.4

Source: Furtado, *op cit.*, p. 54.

1972, a peasant is reduced to trading his bullocks for a few bananas.[6]

Although the day-to-day struggle for survival permeates the lives and attitudes of peasants in both Latin America and Asia (and, also, Africa although the rural structure and institutions are considerably different), the structural nature of their agrarian existence differs markedly. In Latin America, the peasant's plague is the **latifundio-minifundio** system. In Asia, it is the fragmented and heavily congested dwarf parcels of land.

The latifundio-minifundio pattern and underutilisation of resources in Latin America

In Latin America, as indeed in Asia and Africa, agrarian structures are not only part of the production system but also a basic feature of the entire social and political organisation of rural life. The type of agrarian structure which has prevailed in Latin America since colonial times and which provides much of the region with its social organisation is the pattern of agricultural dualism known as 'latifundio-minifundio'. Basically, **latifundios** are very large landholdings and are defined in Latin America as farms large enough to provide employment for more than 12 people. In contrast **minifundios** are the smallest farms and are defined as those farms which are too small to provide employment for a single family (two workers) with the typical incomes, markets and level of technology and capital prevailing in each country or region.

According to the United Nations' Food and Agricultural Organisation (FAO), *1.3 per cent of landowners in Latin America hold 71.6 per cent of the entire area of land under cultivation.* If we exclude those countries that have carried out drastic land reforms during the last 60 years (Mexico, Bolivia and Cuba), Latin America's agrarian structure seems to follow a uniform pattern. This pattern is basically one in which a small number of latifundios control a very large proportion of the agricultural land while a vast number of minifundios must scratch a survival existence on a meagre fraction of the occupied land. Moreover, they must be ready to provide unpaid seasonal labour to the latifundios.

Table 15.4 provides a dramatic picture of this very unequal distribution of landholdings in seven Latin American countries. In no case do minifundios, which comprise up to 90 per cent of the total farms, occupy more than 17 per cent of the total agricultural land. In those countries with very dense indigenous populations like Ecuador, Guatemala and Peru, minifundios are much more widespread. The latifundios on the other hand comprise less than 7 per cent of the total farms in these countries; yet they occupy as much as 82 per cent of the agricultural land. The average size of the latifundios in Argentina is 270 times that of the minifundios; in Guatemala, the latifundio is often as much as 1 732 times the size of the minifundio. Countries like Guatemala with large and rapidly growing indigenous populations crowded on to shrinking areas of poor land have even evolved what has come to be known as 'microfundios' as a major form of landholding. For example, there are at present over 75 000 microfundios in Guatemala yielding an average income that is less than one-third of that

[6] F. M. Foland, 'Agrarian unrest in Asia and Latin America', *World Development*, ii, 4 and 5, April–May 1974, p. 56.

provided by its minifundios and about one-thousandth of the average incomes realised on its latifundios.[7] Microfundio peasants cannot even meet their subsistence requirements; they are forced to sell their labour at pitiable wages to secure a minimum diet for their families.

But latifundios and minifundios do not constitute the entire gamut of Latin American agricultural landholdings. A considerable amount of production is also earned on what are known as 'family' farms and 'medium-sized' farms. The former provide work for two to four people (recall the minifundio could only provide work for less than two people) while the latter, also sometimes known as 'multi-family' farms, employ four to twelve workers (just below the latifundio). We see from Table 15.5 that in Argentina, Brazil and Colombia, these intermediate forms of farm organisation account for over 60 per cent of total agricultural output and employ similar proportions of agricultural labour.

The fact of heavy land concentration in the hands of a very few large landowners is compounded by the relative economic *inefficiency* of latifundios in comparison with other types of Latin American farm organisation. Economists normally assume that large farms (or firms) use productive resources more efficiently than small ones, on the grounds that large enterprises can take advantage of economies of large-scale production and thereby lower costs. In terms of agriculture, the efficient utilisation of large tractors and combine harvesters requires large tracts of land, otherwise, this capital equipment will be grossly underutilised. The evidence from a wide range of Third World countries, however, indicates that small farms are more efficient (lower-cost) producers of most agricultural commodities. For example, minifundios in Argentina, Brazil and Chile yield more than twice the value of output per hectare under cultivation than do the latifundios and more than ten times the value per hectare of total farmland.[8] This finding does not contradict the theory, since most large farms in developed countries are lower cost producers compared with small family farms. Rather, the reason is to be found in the poor utilisation of productive farm resources in Third World nations, especially land resources on latifundios in Latin America. In terms of farm yields per unit of land actually under cultivation, the latifundios of Argentina, Brazil, Colombia, Chile and Guatemala are all below not only the minifundios but also the medium-sized family farms.[9] Moreover, in Brazil it was discovered that the latifundios with an average area 31.6 times larger than that of the family farm, invested only eleven times as much. Much of the arable latifundio land was left idle. The net result was that total factor productivity on family farms was twice as high (and, therefore, unit costs twice as low) as on the large latifundio tracts of land. It follows that a redistribution of these large unused arable lands to family farms would probably raise national agricultural output and productivity. In terms of simple economic efficiency, the above argument is persuasive. However, the pattern of landownership and control in Latin America is based on much more than economic criteria. It touches the whole social and political fabric of Latin American societies.

Such a concentrated distribution of land ownership is typically accompanied in Latin America, as it is in many parts of Asia, by a feudal-type social system in which the masses of small producers are dependent on the benevolence and goodwill of the large landowner. He has the power backed by local social and political institutions to permit them to make a meagre living off his land or to deny them even this opportunity, in which case they have no means of subsistence. The small producers pay for this privilege either by giving up to the landowner large proportions of their output (sometimes as much as 80 per cent) or by working his land for nothing at different times of the year. In some cases, these tenant farmers must provide both output *and* free labour to the patron. Under such a system, land ownership provides not only economic benefits but also, and often more importantly, social status and political power.

In short, a major explanation for the relative economic inefficiency and misuse of fertile land on the latifundios in Latin America is simply that the landowners often value these holdings not for their potential contributions to national agricultural

[7] Celso Furtado, *Economic Development in Latin America*, Cambridge University Press, 1970, p. 54.

[8] *Ibid.*, pp. 56, 58.

[9] *Ibid.*, pp. 57–58.

Table 15.5
Agrarian structure indicators in selected Latin American countries (percentages)

	Minifundios	Family farms	Medium sized farms	Latifundios
Argentina				
% of total farmland	3	46	15	36
% value of agricultural product	12	47	26	15
% of labour employed	30	49	15	6
Brazil				
% of total farmland		6	34	60
% value of agricultural product	3	18	43	36
% of labour employed	11	26	42	21
Chile				
% of total farmland	—	8	13	79
% value of agricultural product	4	16	23	57
% of labour employed	13	28	21	38
Colombia				
% of total farmland	5	25	25	45
% value of agricultural product	21	45	19	15
% of labour employed	58	31	7	4
Guatemala				
% of total farmland	14	13	32	41
% value of agricultural product	30	13	36	21
% of labour employed	68	13	12	7

Source: Furtado, *op cit.*, p. 55.

output but rather because of the considerable power and prestige that are conferred by large landownership in many Latin American regions.

It follows, and we discuss this further in Chapter 16, that raising agricultural production and improving the efficiency of Latin American agrarian systems will require much more than direct economic policies that lead to the provision of better seeds, more fertiliser, less distorted factor prices, higher output prices and improved marketing facilities. It will also require a reorganisation of rural social and institutional structures to provide the Latin American peasant, who now constitutes almost 70 per cent of the total rural population, with a real opportunity to rise out of his present state of economic subsistence and social subservience.

The fragmentation and subdivision of peasant lands in Asia

If the major agrarian problem of Latin America can be identified as too much land under the control of too few people, the basic problem in Asia is one of too many people crowded on too little land. For example, the per capita availability of arable land in India is 0.295 hectares while in the People's Republic of China and Japan the figures are 0.202 and 0.068 hectares respectively. Central Java in Indonesia exemplifies the pressure of population on limited land that characterises the Asian agrarian scene. It has the dubious distinction of possessing the world's record population density – over 1 500 persons per square km.[10]

Throughout the twentieth century rural conditions in Asia have deteriorated significantly. Professor Myrdal identified three major and interrelated forces which have moulded the traditional pattern of land ownership into its present fragmented condition. They were (1) the intervention of European rule; (2) the progressive introduction of monetised transactions and the rise in power of the moneylender; and (3) the rapid growth of Asian populations.[11]

Briefly, the traditional Asian agrarian structure before European colonisation was organised around

[10] Foland, *op. cit.*, p. 57.
[11] Myrdal, *Asian Drama*, pp. 1033–52.

the village community. Local chiefs and peasant families each provided goods and services: produce and labour from the peasants to the chief in return for protection, rights to use community land and the provision of public services from the chiefs to the peasants. Decisions on the allocation, disposition and use of the village's most valuable resource, land, belonged to the tribe or village community, either as a body or through its chief. Land could be redistributed among village members either as a result of population increase or natural calamities like droughts, floods, famines, war or disease. Within the community, families had a basic right to cultivate land for their own use and they could be evicted from their land only after a decision by the entire village community.

With the arrival of the Europeans, mainly in the form of British, French and Dutch colonists, major changes in the traditional agrarian structure occurred (some of which had already begun). As Myrdal points out, 'colonial rule acted as an important catalyst to change, both directly through its effects on property rights and indirectly through its effects on the pace of monetisation on the indigenous economy and on the growth of population'.[12] In the area of property rights, European land tenure systems of private property ownership were both encouraged and reinforced by law. One of the major social consequences of the imposition of European private property land tenure systems was the

> breakdown of much of the earlier cohesion of village life with its often elaborate, though informal, structure of rights and obligations. The landlord was given unrestricted rights to dispose of the land and to raise the tribute from its customary level to whatever amount he was able to extract. He was usually relieved of the obligation to supply security and public amenities because these functions were taken over by the government. Thus his status was transformed from that of a tribute receiver with responsibilities to the community to that of an absolute owner unencumbered by obligations towards the peasants and the public, other than the payment of land taxes.[13]

Contemporary landlords in India and Pakistan are able to avoid much of the taxation on income derived from their ownership of land. Today the typical landlord in South Asia is an absentee owner who lives in the town and turns over the working of the land to sharecroppers and tenant farmers. In many respects, therefore, his position of power in the economic, political and social structure of the rural community is analogous to that of the Latin American patron, the only difference being that the former is an absentee owner while the latter often lives on his latifundio.

The creation of individual titles to land enabled another dubious agent of change in Asian rural socio-economic structures to rise to power: the moneylender. Once private property came into effect, land became a negotiable asset that could be offered by peasants as security for loans, and in the case of default could be forfeited and transferred to the often unscrupulous moneylender. At the same time Asian agriculture was being transformed from a subsistence to a commercial orientation, in response both to rising local demand in new towns and, more importantly, to external food demands of colonial European countries.

With the transition from subsistence to commercial production, the role of the moneylender changed drastically. In the subsistence economy his activities were restricted to supplying the peasant with money to tide him over a crop failure or to cover extraordinary ceremonial expenditures such as family weddings or funerals. Most of these loans were paid in kind (i.e. in the form of food) at very high rates of interest. With the development of commercial farming, however, the peasant's cash needs grew significantly. Money was needed for seeds, fertilisers and other inputs. It was also needed to cover his food requirements if he shifted to the production of cash crops such as tea, rubber or jute. Often moneylenders were more interested in acquiring peasant lands as a result of loan defaults than they were in extracting high rates of interest. By charging exorbitant interest rates or inducing peasants to secure larger credits than they could manage, moneylenders were able to drive the peasants off their land. They could then reap the profits of land speculation by selling this farmland to rich and acquisitive landlords. Alternatively, they often became powerful landlords themselves. At any rate, as a consequence of the moneylenders' influence, the economic status of Asian peasant cultivators has steadily deteriorated.

[12] *Ibid.*, p. 1035.
[13] *Ibid.*, p. 1035.

The final major force altering the traditional agrarian structure in Asia has been the rapid rate of population growth especially over the past 30 years. Myrdal notes in reference to the population phenomenon that

> When and where expansion in the cultivated area was not a feasible alternative – whether for physical, technical, social, economic or institutional reasons – population growth was reflected, in the first instance, in the cumulative subdivision and fragmentation of the acreages already under cultivation. Later this process, in combination with the emergence of private property and the rise of commercial agriculture and moneylending, often contributed to the rise of large landowners, the demise of small peasant proprietors, and the increase of the landless.[14]

The ultimate impoverishment of the peasantry was the inevitable consequence of this process of fragmentation, economic vulnerability and loss of land to rich and powerful landlords.

To give a dramatic example of the deterioration of rural conditions during this century, consider the cases of India, Indonesia and the Philippines. In 1901 there were 286 million Indians. Now there are more than twice that number. The Indonesian population grew from 28.4 million in 1900 to its present level of over 145 million. The population of Central Luzon in the Philippines has increased almost fivefold from its level of one million in 1903. In each case severe fragmentation of landholdings inevitably followed so that the average peasant holding in many areas of these countries today is less than two acres.

As these holdings shrink even further, production falls below the subsistence level and chronic poverty becomes a way of life. Peasants are forced to borrow even more from the moneylender at interest rates of 50 to 200 per cent. Most cannot repay these loans. They are compelled to sell their land and become tenants with large debts. Since land is scarce they are forced to pay high rents. If they are sharecroppers, they typically have to give the landlord 50 to 80 per cent of their crop. Since labour is abundant, wages are extremely low. Peasants therefore have no source of external income. They are trapped in a vice of chronic poverty from which there is no escape short of major rural reconstruction and reform. They thus share a common experience with their Latin American counterparts in the sense that both are gradually but inexorably being transformed from small proprietors to tenant farmers and share croppers, then landless rural labourers, then jobless vagrants and finally migrant slum-dwellers on the fringes of modern urban areas. Not only have their levels of living deteriorated but their sense of self-esteem and freedom from exploitation, which may have been relatively high in spite of low incomes in the past, have also vanished. These many hundreds of millions of people in Asia and Latin America are thus caught in a downward spiral of underdevelopment instead of an upward thrust towards real economic development and social progress.

[14] *Ibid.*, p. 1048.

Subsistence agriculture and extensive cultivation in Africa

As in Asia and Latin America, subsistence agriculture on small plots of land is the way of life for the vast majority of African people. However, the organisation and structure of African agricultural systems differ markedly from those found in contemporary Asia or Latin America. Except in former colonial settlement areas like the White Highlands of Kenya and some of the large sugar, cocoa and coffee plantations of East and West Africa, the great majority of farm families in tropical Africa still plan their output primarily for their own subsistence. Since the basic variable input in African agriculture is farm family and village labour, African agricultural systems are dominated by three major characteristics: (1) the importance of subsistence farming in the village economy; (2) the existence of land in excess of immediate requirements which permits a general practice of *shifting cultivation* and diminishes the value of landownership as an instrument of economic and political power; and (3) the rights of each family (both nuclear and extended) in a village to have access to land and water in the immediate territorial vicinity, excluding from such access those families who do not 'belong' to the community even though they may be of the same tribe.

Low productivity subsistence farming characteristic of most traditional types of African agriculture results from a combination of three forces restricting the growth of output:

1. In spite of the existence of some unused and potentially cultivable land, only small areas can be planted and weeded by the farm family at a time, using traditional tools such as the short-handled hoe, the axe and the long-handled knife or panga. Prevented in some countries from using animals by the notorious tsetse fly or by lack of fodder in the long dry seasons, traditional African farming practices must rely to a greater extent on the application of human labour to small parcels of land.
2. Given this limited amount of land that a farm family can cultivate in the context of a traditional technology and the use of primitive tools, these small areas tend to be intensively cultivated. As a result they are subject to rapidly diminishing returns to increased labour inputs. In such conditions, *shifting cultivation* is the most economic method of using limited supplies of labour on extensive tracts of land. Under shifting cultivation, once the minerals are drawn out of the soil as a result of numerous croppings, new land is cleared and the process of planting and weeding is repeated. In the meantime, the fertility is restored to formerly cropped land until eventually it can be used again. Under such a process, manure and chemical fertilisers are unnecessary, although in most African villages some form of manure (mostly animal waste) is applied to nearby plots that are intensively cultivated in order to extend their period of fertility.
3. The third major factor curtailing output increases in traditional African agriculture is the scarcity of labour available during the busiest part of the growing season, namely for planting and weeding. At other times much of the labour is underemployed. Since the time of planting is determined by the onset of the rains, and since much of Africa experiences only one extended rainy season, the demand for workers at times of planting and weeding during the early weeks of the rainy season usually exceeds all available rural labour supplies.

The net result of these three forces has been a relatively constant level of total agricultural output and labour productivity throughout much of Africa. As long as population size remained relatively stable, however, the pattern of low productivity shifting cultivation enabled most African tribes to meet their subsistence food requirements (with the obvious exception of climatic uncertainties in the form of severe and prolonged droughts such as that experienced in much of the Sahelian region of Africa during the early 1970s). But the feasibility of shifting cultivation breaks down as population densities increase, as they have during the past two decades. It tends to be replaced by sedentary cultivation on small owner-occupied plots of land. As a result, the need for other non-human productive inputs grows, especially in the more densely populated agricultural regions of Kenya, Nigeria, Ghana and Uganda. Moreover,with the growth of towns, the penetration of the monetary economy and the introduction of land taxes, purely subsistence agricultural practices are no longer viable. Mixed and exclusively commercial farming begins to appear.

Conclusion

We conclude our analysis by noting that although resource endowments, especially abundant land, and traditional African communal social systems differ markedly from those agrarian structures prevalent throughout much of Asia and Latin America, the contemporary economic status of the small farmer is not very different among the three regions. **Achieving subsistence is still the major objective of Third World peasant agriculture**. Even though the small African farmer may appear to have more room to manoeuvre than his typical Asian or Latin American counterpart, the rapid growth of rural populations in countries like Nigeria, Kenya and Uganda threatens to create mounting pressures for the further fragmentation of smallholder agriculture. Unless low productivity peasant agriculture can be transformed rapidly into higher productivity farming in Asia and Latin America (primarily through judicious land reform accompanied by structural changes in socio-economic institutions), and in Africa (basically through improved farming practices), the masses of impoverished rural dwellers face an even more precarious existence in the years immediately ahead.

Concepts for review

per capita food production
staple foods
agricultural labour productivity
the productivity gap
farm yields
agrarian system
latifundio
minifundio
microfundio
small farmer (family farm)
landlord
tenant farmer
sharecropper
moneylender
land tenure systems
shifting cultivation

Questions for discussion

1. Why should any analysis of Third World development problems place heavy emphasis on the study of agricultural systems, especially peasant agriculture, and the rural sector?
2. What were the principal reasons for the relative stagnation of Third World agriculture during the so-called Development Decade of the 1960s? How can this disappointing performance be improved on in the future? Explain.
3. It is sometimes said that the world consists of two kinds of agriculture. What is meant by this statement and how might it be illustrated both between and within countries?
4. Compare and contrast the nature of peasant or small-scale agriculture in Asia, Africa and Latin America. How do overall agricultural systems differ in these three regions? What are the common characteristics?
5. Explain the meaning of Professor Myrdal's statement at the beginning of this chapter: 'It is in the agricultural sector that the battle for long-term economic development will be won or lost'. Do you agree or disagree with this statement in the context of your own nation? Why?

Further reading

For specific studies of agriculture and agrarian systems in Third World regions, see especially: For Africa: P. Robson and D. A. Lury, eds, *The Economies of Africa*, Allen and Unwin, London, 1969. For Asia: Gunnar Myrdal, *Asian drama*, Pantheon, New York, 1968, chs 22, 23 and 26. For Latin America: Rodolfo Stavenhagen, ed., *Agrarian Problems and Peasant Movements in Latin America*, Doubleday, New York, 1970; Celso Furtado, *Economic Development in Latin America*, Cambridge University Press, 1970, chs 7 and 14; and, especially, Solon Barraclough, *Agrarian Structure in Latin America*, Lexington Books, 1973.

Three outstanding comparative studies of Third World agrarian systems are: Guy Hunter, *Modernizing Peasant Societies: a comparative study of Asia and Africa*, Oxford University Press, 1969; Keith Griffin, *The Political Economy of Agrarian Change*, Macmillan, 1974; and Dharam Ghai, *et al.* (eds.), *Agrarian Systems and Rural Development*, Holmes and Meier, New York, 1979.

Chapter 16 Subsistence agriculture and rural development

> The problem of rural poverty ... goes beyond the increase in farm yields. It cannot be resolved without a basic transformation of property relations in rural areas through land reforms.
> *Padma Desai (reflecting opinions of Third World social scientists at their meeting in Santiago, April 1973)*

Introduction

In this chapter, we continue our discussions of the rural sector in developing nations by looking specifically at the economics of small-scale agriculture. We show that any realistic analysis of subsistence farming in underdeveloped countries needs to go beyond the traditional micro theory of the individual firm or farm and give proper attention to basic Third World factors such as the relationship between the imperative of survival and the avoidance of risk, and the linkage between land tenure and the willingness of small farmers to innovate. After examining the economic processes by which subsistence farms are gradually transformed into commercial enterprises, we summarise some of the major strategy options for promoting what has come to be known as 'integrated' or 'comprehensive' rural development. A brief look at the Chinese experience with rural development provides a thought-provoking conclusion to our exploration of Third World agriculture.

The economics of small-scale agricultural development: the transition from subsistence to specialised farming

There are three major stages in the evolution of agricultural production.[1] The first and most primitive is the pure, low productivity subsistence farm. The second stage might be called 'diversified' or 'mixed' agriculture, where part of the produce is grown for self-consumption and part for sale to the commercial sector. Finally, the third stage represents the 'modern' farm which is exclusively engaged in high productivity, specialised agriculture catering entirely for the commercial market.

Agricultural modernisation in mixed market economies like those prevalent in the Third World may be described in terms of the gradual but sustained transition from subsistence to specialised production. But such a transition involves much more than reorganising the structure of the farm economy or the application of new agricultural technologies. We have seen that in most traditional societies agriculture is not just an economic activity; it is a way of life. Any government attempting to transform this traditional agriculture must recognise that in addition to adapting the farm structure to meet the demand for increased agricultural production, profound changes affecting the entire social, political and institutional structure of rural societies will often be necessary. Without such changes agricultural development will either never get started or, more likely, simply widen the already sizable gap between the few wealthy large landholders and the masses of impoverished tenant farmers, smallholders and landless labourers.

Before analysing the economics of agricultural and rural development, therefore, we need to understand the evolutionary process by which traditional subsistence farms are transformed into

[1] See Weitz, *op. cit.*, pp. 15–28.

modern specialised commercial farms both through the farm family's own efforts and also through supporting activities of governments and local institutions. The three stages of this process are outlined below.

Stage I
Subsistence farming: risk, uncertainty and survival

In the traditional subsistence farm, output and consumption are identical and one or two staple crops (usually wheat, barley, sorghum, rice or maize) are the chief sources of food intake. Output and productivity are low and only the simplest tools are used. Capital investment is minimal, while land and labour are the principal factors of production. The law of diminishing returns to the application of more labour to shrinking or shifting parcels of land is in operation. The failure of the rains, the appropriation of his land or the appearance of the debt-collecting moneylender are the bane of the peasant's existence and the source of fear for his survival. Labour is underemployed for most of the year, although workers may be fully occupied at seasonal peak periods such as planting and harvesting. The peasant usually cultivates only as much land as his family can manage without the need for hired labour; although many peasant farmers do employ one or two landless labourers. The environment is harsh and static. Technological limitations, rigid social institutions and fragmented markets and communication networks between rural areas and urban centres tend to discourage higher levels of production.

Throughout much of the Third World agriculture is still in this subsistence stage. But in spite of the relative backwardness of production technologies and the misguided convictions of some foreigners who attribute the peasant's resistance to change as a sign of incompetence or irrationality, the fact remains that given the static nature of the peasant's environment, the uncertainties which surround him, the need to meet minimum survival levels of output and the rigid social institutions into which he is locked, most peasants behave in an economically rational manner when confronted with alternative opportunities. As one informed observer has noted about peasant agricultural systems:

> Despite the almost infinite variety of village-level institutions and processes to be found around the world, they have three common characteristics which are pertinent to change: (1) they have historically proven to be successful, i.e. the members have survived; (2) they are relatively static, at least the general pace of change is below that which is considered desirable today; and (3) attempts at change are frequently resisted, both because these institutions and processes have proven dependable and because the various elements constitute something akin to an ecological unity in the human realm.[2]

Our discussion in Chapter 4 of the simple theory of farm production when labour is the only variable input (i.e. land, technology and management are fixed), offers important insights into the economics of subsistence agriculture. Specifically, it provides an economic rationale for the observed low productivity of traditional agriculture; the phenomenon of diminishing returns or diminishing marginal productivity.

Unfortunately, however, the standard economic theory of production does not satisfactorily explain why peasant agriculturalists are often very resistant to technological innovation in farming techniques or to the introduction of new seeds or different cash crops. According to the standard theory, a rational income or profit maximising farm or firm will always choose a method of production which will increase output for a given cost (in this case, the available labour time) or lower costs for a given output level (recall the principle of economy from Chapter 1). But the theory is based on the crucial assumption that farmers possess 'perfect knowledge' of all input–output relationships in the form of a technological production function for their crop. This is the point at which the theory loses its validity when applied to the environment of subsistence agriculture in much of Asia, Africa and Latin America.

Subsistence agriculture is a highly risky and uncertain venture. It is made even more so by the fact that human lives are at stake. In regions where farms are extremely small and cultivation is

[2] Clifton R. Wharton, Jr. 'Risk, Uncertainty and the Subsistence Farmer', *Development Digest*, vii, 2, April 1969, p. 3.

dependent on the uncertainties of a highly variable rainfall, average output will be low and in poor years the peasant and his family will be exposed to the very real danger of starvation. In such circumstances the main motivating force in the peasant's life may be the maximisation not of income but rather of his family's chances of survival. Accordingly, when risk and uncertainty are high, a small farmer may be very reluctant to shift from a traditional technology and crop pattern which over the years he has come to know and understand to a new one which promises higher yields but may entail greater risks of crop failure. When sheer survival is at stake it is more important to avoid a bad year (i.e. total crop failure) than it is to maximise the output in better years. In the jargon of economic statistics, risk-avoiding peasant farmers are likely to prefer a technology of food production which combines a low *mean* per-acre yield with low *variance* (i.e. less fluctuations around the average) to alternative technologies and crops which may promise a higher mean yield but also present the risk of greater variance.

Figure 16.1 provides a simple illustration of how attitudes towards risk among small farmers may militate against apparently economically justified innovations.[3]

In Figure 16.1 we measure levels of output and consumption on the vertical axis and time on the horizontal axis. We then draw two straight lines. The lower horizontal line measures the minimum physiological consumption requirements (MCR) necessary for the farm family's physical survival. This may be taken as the starvation minimum fixed by nature: any output below this level would be catastrophic for the peasant and his family. The upper positively sloped straight line represents the minimum level of food consumption that would be desirable (MDCL) in terms of the prevailing cultural factors affecting village consumption standards. It is assumed that MDCL rises over time to reflect rising expectations as traditional societies are opened up to external influences. The producer's attitude towards risk will be largely conditioned by his historical output performance relative to these two standards of reference.

[3] See Marvin P. Miracle, 'Subsistence Agriculture: analytical problems and alternative concepts', *American Journal of Agricultural Economics*, May 1968, pp. 292–310.

Figure 16.1
Small farmer attitudes toward risk: why it is sometimes rational to resist innovation and change

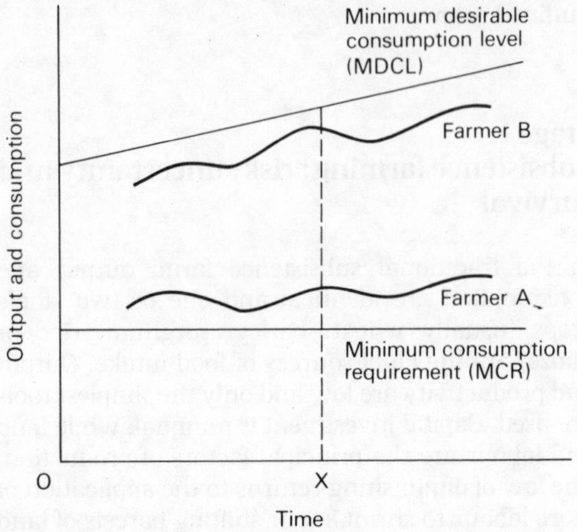

Looking at Figure 16.1, we see that at the moment of time X, Farmer A's output levels over the past few years have been very close to the minimum consumption requirement (MCR). He is barely getting by and cannot take a chance of falling below MCR. He will therefore have a greater incentive to minimise risk than will Farmer B, whose output performance over recent years has been well above the minimum subsistence level and is close to the culturally determined desirable consumption standard (MDCL). Farmer B will therefore be more likely to innovate and change than will Farmer A.

Many programmes to raise agricultural productivity among small farmers have foundered because of failure to provide adequate insurance (both financial credit and physical buffer stocks) against the risks of crop shortfalls, whether these risks are real or imagined in the peasant's mind. An understanding of the major role which risk and uncertainty play in the economics of subsistence agriculture would have prevented early and unfortunate characterisations of subsistence or traditional farmers as technologically backward, irrational cultivators with limited aspirations or just plain 'lazy natives' as in the colonial stereotype. Moreover, in many parts of Asia and Latin America, a closer examination of why peasant farmers have apparently not responded to an 'obvious' economic opportunity will often reveal that: (1) the landlord secured all the gain; or (2) the moneylender captured all the profits; or (3) the government 'guaranteed' price was never paid; or (4) complementary inputs (fertiliser, pesticides, supplies of water, adequate non-usurious credit, etc.) were never made available to the small farmer.

We may conclude that peasant farmers do act rationally and are responsive to economic incentives and opportunities. Where innovation and change fail to occur, we should not assume that peasants are stupid, irrational or conservative; instead we should examine carefully the environment in which the small farmer operates for the particular institutional or commercial obstacles which may be blocking or frustrating constructive change. As Professor Griffin has pointed out:

> If peasants sometimes appear to be unresponsive or hostile to proposed technical changes it is probably because the risks are high, the returns to the cultivator are low – for example, because of local custom or land tenure conditions, or because credit facilities and marketing outlets are inadequate and the necessary inputs – including knowledge – are missing.[4]

Efforts to minimise risk and remove commercial and institutional obstacles to small-farmer innovation are therefore essential requirements of agricultural and rural development.

Stage II
The transition to mixed and diversified farming

It is unrealistic to think in terms of instantly transforming a traditional agrarian system which has prevailed for many generations into a highly specialised commercial system. Attempts to introduce cash crops indiscriminately in subsistence farms have more often than not resulted in the peasant's loss of land to moneylenders or landlords. Subsistence living is merely substituted for subsistence production. Exclusive reliance on cash crops for small farmers can be more precarious than pure subsistence agriculture since risks of price fluctuations are added to the uncertainty of nature.

Diversified or mixed farming, therefore, represents a logical first step in the transition from subsistence to specialised production. In this stage the staple crop no longer dominates farm output since new cash crops such as fruits, vegetables, coffee, tea, pyrethrum, etc. are established, together with simple animal husbandry. These new activities can take up the normal slack in farm workloads during times of the year when disguised unemployment is prevalent. This is especially desirable in most Third World nations where rural labour is abundantly available for better and more efficient utilisation.

For example, if the staple crop occupies the land during only parts of the year, new crops can be introduced in the slack season to take advantage of both idle land and family labour. Alternatively, in many parts of Africa where labour is in short supply during peak planting seasons, simple labour-saving devices (such as small tractors, mechanical seeders, or animal-operated steel ploughs) can be introduced to free labour for other farm activities. Finally, the use of better seeds, fertilisers and simple irrigation to increase yields of staple crops like wheat, maize and rice can free part of the land for cash crop cultivation while still assuring an adequate supply of the staple food. The farm operator can thus have a marketable surplus which he can sell to raise his family's consumption standards and/or invest in farm improvements. Diversified farming can also minimise the impact of staple crop failure and provide a security of income previously unavailable.

The success or failure of such efforts to transform traditional agriculture will depend not only on the farmer's ability and skill in raising his productivity but even more importantly on the social, commercial and institutional conditions under which he must function. Specifically, if he can secure a reasonable and reliable access to credit, fertilisers, water, crop information, marketing facilities, etc., *and* if he can feel secure that he and his family will be the primary beneficiaries of any improvements, then there is no reason to assume that traditional farmers will not respond to economic incentives and new opportunities to improve their standard of living. On the contrary, evidence from such diverse countries as Colombia, Mexico, Nigeria, Ghana, Kenya, India, Pakistan, Thailand and the Philippines supports the notion that under proper conditions small farmers are responsive to incentives and opportunities and will make radical changes in what and how they

[4] Griffin, *op. cit.*, p. 6.

produce. Lack of innovation in agriculture, as we have seen, is usually due not to poor motivation or fear of change *per se*, but to inadequate or unprofitable opportunities.

Stage III
From divergence to specialisation: modern commercial farming

The specialised farm represents the final and most advanced stage of individual holding in a mixed market economy. It is the most prevalent type of farming in advanced industrial nations. It has evolved in response to and parallel with the overall development in other areas of the national economy. General rises in living standards, biological and technical progress and the expansion of national and international markets have provided the main impetus for its emergence and growth.

On specialised farms, the provision of food for the family with some marketable surplus no longer provides the basic motivational objective. Pure commercial profit becomes the criterion of success and maximum per acre yields derived from man-made (irrigation, fertiliser, pesticides, hybrid seeds, etc.) and natural resources become the object of farm activity. Production is entirely for the market and economic concepts such as fixed and variable costs, saving, investment and rates of return, optimal factor combinations, maximum production possibilities, market prices and price supports, etc. take on quantitative and qualitative significance. The emphasis in resource utilisation is no longer on land, water and labour as in subsistence and, often, mixed farming. Instead, capital formation, technological progress, and scientific research and development play a major role in stimulating higher levels of output and productivity.

Specialised farms may vary in both size and function. They may range from intensively cultivated fruit and vegetable farms to the vast wheat and corn fields of North America. In most cases sophisticated labour-saving mechanical equipment ranging from huge tractors and combine harvesters to airborne spraying techniques permit a single family to cultivate many thousands of acres of land.

The common feature of all specialised farms, therefore, is the emphasis on the cultivation of one particular crop, the size of capital-intensive and in many cases labour-saving techniques of production and the reliance on economies of scale to reduce unit costs and maximise profits. For all practical purposes, specialised farming is not different in concept or operation from large industrial enterprises. In fact some of the largest specialised farming operations in both the developed and, especially, the less developed nations, are owned and managed by large 'agribusiness' multinational corporate enterprises.

Stages of farm evolution: a summary

Table 16.1 summarises the basic characteristics of the three stages of farm evolution, subsistence, mixed and specialised, that parallel the broad stages of national economic growth. Most Third World nations are in the process of transition from subsistence to mixed farming (excluding, of course, the scattered enclaves of large and often foreign-owned specialised plantation agriculture). The further transition from mixed to widespread specialised farming may or may not be an ultimate national goal, especially in view of the serious nature of rural and urban unemployment problems. Moreover, the predominance of specialised farming in developing nations is a very tentative future aspiration. Its ultimate emergence depends on the solution of many other short- and intermediate-term problems. The improvement of small-scale, mixed farming practices that will not only raise farm incomes and average yields but also effectively absorb underutilised rural labour through the adoption of effective labour-intensive farming practices offers the major immediate avenue towards the achievement of a real people-oriented rural development.

In the following section we try to identify the main ingredients and policy alternatives for such a people-oriented, labour-intensive strategy of agricultural and rural development.

Towards a strategy of agricultural and rural development: some main requirements

If agricultural and rural development aims at a progressive improvement in levels of living achieved primarily through increases in small-farm incomes, output and productivity, then it is important to identify the major sources of agricultural progress and the basic conditions essential to its achievement. These are necessarily interrelated. But for purposes of description we may separate each into three components.

Sources of small-scale agricultural progress	*Conditions of general rural advancement*
1. Technical change and innovation	1. Modernising farm structures to meet rising food demands
2. Appropriate government economic policies	2. Creating an effective supporting system
3. Supportive social institutions	3. Changing the rural environment to improve levels of living

Each of these six interrelated components of agricultural and rural development is discussed in turn.

Improving small-scale agriculture

Technology and innovation

In most developing countries new agricultural technologies and innovations in farm practices are preconditions for sustained improvements in levels of output and productivity. In many parts of Africa and Latin America, however, increased output has been achieved without the need for new technology, simply by extending cultivation into unused but potentially productive lands. Most of these have by now been exploited and there is not much scope for further significant improvement.

Two major sources of technological innovation can increase farm yields. Unfortunately they have very different implications for Third World agricultural devlopment.

The first of these innovations is the introduction of mechanised agriculture to replace human labour. The introduction of *labour-saving* machinery (e.g. large tractors) can have a dramatic effect on the volume of output per worker, especially where land is extensively cultivated and labour is scarce. For example, one man operating a huge combine-havester can accomplish in a single hour the

Table 16.1
Distinguishing characteristics of the three stages of farm evolution

	Stages of farm evolution		
Characteristic	Subsistence	Mixed	Specialised
Composition of output	One dominant staple crop and auxiliary crops	diversified	one dominant cash crop and auxiliary crops
Purpose of production	domestic supply	domestic and market supply	market only
Work schedule	seasonal	balance	seasonal
Capital investment	low	medium	high
Income	low	medium	high
Income security	low	high	medium (price fluctuations)
Ratio of income to value of output	high	approximately half	low
Farmer's professional know-how	specialised	diverse	specialised
Dependence on a supporting system	none	partial	full

Source: Weitz, *op cit.*, p. 20.

equivalent output of a hundred workers using traditional methods.

But in the rural areas of most developing nations where land parcels are small, capital is scarce and labour is abundant, the introduction of heavily mechanised techniques is not only often ill-suited to the physical environment but, more importantly, often has the effect of creating more rural unemployment without necessarily lowering per unit costs of food production. The importance of such machinery can therefore be 'anti-developmental', since its efficient deployment requires large tracts of land (and thus the expropriation of small holdings by landlords and moneylenders), and it tends to exacerbate the already serious problems of rural poverty and unemployment.

By contrast, the second kind of innovations, which use biological (hybrid seeds) and chemical (fertiliser, pesticides, insecticides, etc.) methods, are *land-augmenting*, that is to say, they improve the quality of existing land and raise yields per unit of land. Only indirectly do they increase output per worker. Improved seeds, advanced techniques of irrigation and crop rotation, the increasing use of fertilisers, pesticides and herbicides, and new developments in veterinary medicine and animal nutrition represent major scientific advances in modern agriculture. These measures are technologically 'scale neutral', that is, theoretically they can be applied equally effectively on large and small farms. They do not necessarily require large capital inputs or mechanised equipment. They are therefore particularly well suited for tropical and subtropical regions and offer an enormous potential for raising agricultural output in Third World nations.

Policies and institutions

Unfortunately, although the new hybrid seed varieties of wheat, corn and rice (often collectively referred to as the 'miracle seeds' or the basis of the Green Revolution) are scale-neutral and thus offer the potential for small-farm progress, the *institutions* and *government policies* that accompany their introduction into the rural economy often are not.

On the contrary, all too frequently they merely serve the needs and vested interests of the wealthy landowner. Since the new hybrid seeds need access to complementary inputs like irrigation, fertilisers, insecticides, credit and agricultural extension services, if these are provided only to a small minority of large landowners, then the effective impact of the Green Revolution can be, and has been in parts of South Asia and Mexico, the further impoverishment of the masses of rural peasants. Large landowners with their disproportionate access to these complementary inputs and support services are able to gain a competitive advantage over smallholders and eventually drive them out of the market. Large-scale farmers obtain low-interest government credit while smallholders are forced to turn to the moneylender.

The inevitable though not intentional result is the further widening of the gap between rich and poor and the increased consolidation of agricultural land in the hands of a very few so-called progressive farmers. A developmental innovation with great potential for alleviating rural poverty and raising agricultural output thus becomes a further instrument for the impoverishment of the rural peasant class. What was designed to be developmental can thus turn out to be anti-developmental if public policies and social institutions (e.g. land tenure and rural credit arrangements) militate against the active participation of the smaller farmer in the evolving agrarian structure.

Three conditions for rural development

Let us now collect what has been said in the form of three propositions which constitute the necessary conditions for a people-oriented agricultural and rural development process.

Land reform

Proposition I. **Farm structures and land tenure patterns need to be adapted to the dual objectives of increasing food production and promoting a wider distribution of the benefits of agrarian progress.**

Agricultural and rural development which benefits the masses of people can only succeed in most Third World nations through a joint effort by the government and *all* the farmers (not just the large farmers). A first step in any such effort, especially in Latin America but also in parts of Asia, is the provision of secured tenure rights to the individual farmer. A small farmer's attachment to his land is very profound. It is closely bound up with his innermost feelings of self-esteem and freedom from coercion. When he is driven off his land or gradually impoverished through accumulated debts, not only is his material well-being damaged but, more importantly, his sense of self-esteem and his desire for self and family improvement can be permanently destroyed.

It is for these human reasons as well as for reasons of greater agricultural output that land reform is often proposed as a necessary first condition for agricultural development in many LDCs. **In most countries the highly unequal structure of land-ownership is probably the single most important determinant of the existing highly inequitable distribution of rural income and wealth.** It is also the basis for the character of agricultural development. When land is very unevenly distributed, as in many parts of Latin America and Asia (and increasingly so in parts of Africa as well), rural peasants can have little hope for economic advancement.

Land reform usually entails a redistribution of the rights of ownership and/or use of land away from large landowners and in favour of cultivators with very limited or no landholdings. Land reform can take many forms: the transfer of ownership to tenants who already work the land (as in Cuba, Ethiopia, Japan and Taiwan); transfer of land from large estates to small farms (as in Mexico); the appropriation of large estates for new settlement (as in Kenya); and the improvement or irrigation and subsequent development of large private or state-owned lands into farmer co-operatives (as in China and Tanzania). All these actions go under the heading of land reform and are designed to fulfil one central function: **the transfer of land ownership or control directly or indirectly to those who actually work the land.**

There is widespread agreement among economists and other development specialists on the need for land reform. To Myrdal, land reform holds the key to agricultural development in Asia. The Economic Commission for Latin America (ECLA) has repeatedly identified land reform as a necessary precondition for agricultural and rural progress. A 1970s Food and Agricultural Organisation (FAO) report concluded that in many Third World regions land reform remains a prerequisite for development. The report argued that such reform was more urgent today than ever before, primarily because: (1) income inequalities and unemployment in rural areas have worsened; (2) rapid population growth threatens further to worsen existing inequalities; and (3) recent and potential technological breakthroughs in agriculture (the Green Revolution) will be exploited primarily by large and powerful rural landholders and, as a consequence of the already highly unequal agrarian structure, will result in the increase in their power, wealth and capacity to resist future reform.

If programmes of land reform can be legislated and effectively implemented by the government (a crucial drawback of many such efforts in Asia and Latin America) then the basis for the transition from subsistence to mixed farming with improved output levels and higher standards of living for rural peasants will be established. But the mere enactment and enforcement of an egalitarian land reform programme is no guarantee of agricultural and rural development if it is not accompanied by complementary government programmes to transform the potentiality for improvement into actuality. This leads to our second proposition.

Supportive policies

Proposition II. **The full benefits of small-scale agricultural development cannot be realised unless government support systems are created which provide the necessary incentives, economic opportunities and access to needed inputs to enable small cultivators to expand their output and raise their productivity.**

While land reform is essential in many parts of Asia and Latin America, it is likely to be ineffective and perhaps even counterproductive unless there is a corresponding change in the *rural institutions* that control production (e.g. banks, moneylenders, seed and fertiliser distributors, etc.) *supporting government services* (technical and educational extension services, public credit agencies, storage and marketing facilities, rural transport and feeder roads, etc.) and *government pricing policies* with regard to both inputs (factor prices) and outputs. Even where land reform is not necessary but where productivity and incomes are low (as in the whole of Africa and much of South-east Asia), this broad network of external support services along with appropriate governmental pricing policies is an essential condition of sustained agricultural progress.

Integrated development objectives

Proposition III. **Rural development, while dependent primarily on small-farmer agricultural progress, implies much more. It encompasses (1) improvement in levels of living, including income, employment, education, health and nutrition, housing and a variety of social services; (2) decreasing inequality in the distribution of rural incomes and in urban–rural imbalances in incomes and economic opportunities; and (3) the capacity of the rural sector to sustain and accelerate the pace of these improvements.**

The proposition is self-explanatory. We need only add that the achievement of its three objectives is vital to national development. This is not only because the majority of Third World populations are located in rural areas but because, as we discovered in a previous chapter, the burgeoning problems of urban unemployment and population congestion must find their ultimate solution in the improvement of the rural environment. By restoring a proper balance between urban and rural economic opportunities and by creating the conditions for the broad popular participation in national development efforts and rewards, Third World nations will have taken a giant step towards the realisation of the true meaning of 'development'.

Rural development in China: an unique approach[5]

Since the opening of the People's Republic of China to foreign visitors in the early 1970s there has been widespread interest in and considerable debate about the Chinese model of rural development. The question most often asked is: of what relevance is it to other Third World nations in their attempt to eliminate mass poverty and build a unified and largely self-sufficient social and economic system? We can only hint at the range of possible answers in this brief section, but according to a well-known specialist on China, 'the Chinese experiment in rural development has already thrown up some very important truths and principles which every policy-maker or social scientist concerned with rural development should at least begin to think about'.[6]

The people's commune

Rural development in China is based on the 'people's commune', a 'multi-purpose political, administrative and organisational unit covering the full range of economic, social and administrative activities necessary and feasible in a rural community'.[7] The contemporary people's commune introduced in 1958 represents the fourth stage in the evolution of China's programme of agrarian reform. The first stage was characterised by China's traditional feudal system of land tenure in which 10 per cent of the rural population (landlords and rich peasants) owned 70 to 75 per cent of the land. This land was confiscated during the revolution of 1949 and distributed to the poor and landless peasants. But they found it difficult to cultivate the land economically on an individual basis without supporting commercial and social services. As a result, 'mutual aid teams' were formed during the second stage of agrarian reform between 1949 and 1952. These groups were still too small to be effective both in terms of their purchase of inputs and their efficiency in producing outputs. Thus, the third stage appeared in 1955–1956. It was characterised by the formation of Agricultural Producers' Co-operatives and then by Advanced Co-operatives ranging from 100 to 500 hectares. Such co-operatives were able to pool their resources effectively and consequently to raise agricultural yields. But they were not equipped to carry out the diverse economic, political and administrative functions required for sustained progress. As a result, in 1958

[5] Given the author's lack of first-hand familiarity with the economy of China, much of the information in this section is derived from Sartaj Aziz, 'The Chinese approach to rural development', *World Development*, ii, 2, February 1974, pp. 87–91.

[6] *Ibid.*, p. 87.

[7] *Ibid.*, p. 88.

the fourth and final stage of agrarian reform was introduced 'by converting and regrouping all the Advanced Co-operatives into People's Agricultural Communes and abolishing whatever individual ownership of land still existed in favour of communal ownership'.[8] Communal ownership includes all land in rural communities, all means of agricultural production and commune-owned industries.

Organisationally, each commune is divided into production 'brigades' and each brigade into a number of basic units known as 'work teams'. Each work team is equal to a village of about 25 to 30 families. It produces both to meet its own needs and to meet quotas allotted to it by the commune. The total land and population in a commune can vary anywhere from 3 000 to 12 000 hectares and from 9 000 to 50 000 people. There are reported to be about 26 000 communes in present-day China.

Poverty, employment and income distribution

Apparently, China has been able to reduce poverty by providing minimum levels of living for all its people, to eliminate rural unemployment by mobilising all available human resources into production brigades and work teams and greatly to narrow disparities in the distribution of personal income and wealth through the abolition of private assets and the introduction of a system of fixed wages and prices. Average real income levels of Chinese farmers appear to be two or three times those in India and Pakistan, and 50 to 100 per cent higher than in Thailand, Indonesia and the Philippines. More significantly, this average is relatively evenly distributed, with the highest income levels said to be only twice as large as the lowest. As we have seen, average income levels in other Third World countries often mask great differences between wealthy landowners and poor subsistence farmers. But, at an even more basic level, Chinese officials are quick to assert that 'the days in which the Chinese were without food and clothing are gone forever. There is no Chinese man or woman today whose basic needs of food, clothing, shelter, education and medical facilities are not met.'[9] Even though this statement is probably a substantial exaggeration, there are few other countries in the Third World which can make a similar claim.

How the Chinese system works: six important factors

The Chinese Commune system has six central attributes. The first and historically most important factor in the system was its ability to **mobilise the unemployed labour force** for land improvements, building dams and dykes, digging irrigation channels, constructing roads and cultivating existing land more intensively. As a result, average Chinese farm yields are twice those in India and Pakistan. Chinese food grain production increased from 108 million tons in 1949 to 246 million tons in the early 1970s. China is now, and has been for several years, more than self-sufficeint in food production in spite of its enormous population of over 950 million.

The second important factor about the Chinese commune has been its ability to **diversify its rural economic activity** from agriculture to forestry, fisheries and finally small industries. This was done only after a satisfactory base had been established within the agricultural sector itself. According to Aziz, 'this continuing diversification in economic activities can be regarded as the most important factor in tackling the problem of rural employment by absorbing the internal additions to the labour force and workers rendered potentially surplus by increasing productivity in agriculture.'[10]

The third major element of the system is its ability to **generate rural capital formation and industrialisation** through a system of transfers of 15 to 20 per cent of total commune revenue into an accumulation fund. These funds are then used to invest in productive improvements in commune industries, especially in the form of capital construction but increasingly also in mechanised farm equipment. Of perhaps even greater importance from the viewpoint of economic incentives has been the Chinese Government's deliberate attempts to improve rural standards of living by consciously raising the price of

[8] *Ibid.*, p. 88.

[9] As quoted in Aziz, *op. cit.*, p. 88.

[10] *Ibid.*, p. 89.

Table 16.2
Terms of trade between agriculture and industry, People's Republic of China, 1950–1970.

	(1) Agricultural Purchase Price Index	(2) Industrial Retail Prices in Rural Areas Index	(3) Ratio of (1) to (2)
1950	100.0	100.0	100.0
1951	119.6	110.2	108.5
1952	121.6	109.7	110.8
1953	132.5	108.2	122.4
1954	136.7	110.3	123.9
1955	135.1	111.9	120.7
1956	139.2	110.8	125.6
1957	146.2	112.1	130.4
1958	149.5	111.2	134.4
1970	n/a	n/a	166.7

Source: John G. Gurley, 'Rural Development in China, 1949–1972 and the Lessons to be Learned from It,' in E. O. Edwards (ed.) *Employment in Developing Nations*, Columbia University Press, 1974, p. 396.

agricultural goods relative to that of industrial goods (i.e. the 'terms of trade' between agriculture and industry). As Table 16.2 reveals, between 1950 and 1970 the quantity of industrial goods that a *given* amount of agricultural produce could purchase increased by almost 67 per cent.

A fourth significant aspect is the commune's role in **providing essential social services to all rural people**, particularly in the fields of education and health. Schools and hospitals are provided out of the commune's own savings. The people are therefore able to realise the direct social benefits of their labour.

The unique system of Chinese **decentralised rural planning** with its emphasis on the maximum exploitation of local resources to meet local needs is the fifth strategic aspect of the commune system. Chinese planning differs from that of most other countries by its emphasis on mass participation in the planning process rather than production targets and industrial or regional preferences being decided in the urban offices of some out of touch central planners.

Sixth, and probably most important, is the strategic position of the commune in the **political** and **ideological system** of China. Again, we may quote Dr Aziz:

> The most important factor in the system of the Chinese Commune is its place in the ideological and political system of China. The main objective of the Chinese society is not the most rapid material progress or the creation of a consumer society but the evolution of a classless society in which social inequalities are reduced to the minimum, and where there is a high level of political and ideological consciousness and a pronounced concern for the well-being of every citizen. These goals are radically different from the implicit or expressed objectives of many other developing countries, where in the name of economic growth or economic development the main pursuits are essentially material in nature and the end result is generally the enrichment of a privileged minority or 'a consumer society but without anything to consume'. Pecuniary incentives are not absent in China – they have sought to meet everyone's basic needs and provide for a steady increase in real income – but the desire for a larger monetary reward is not the prime mover of the system: it is ideology plus organisation.[11]

Implications for rural development in other Third World nations

Since their formation in 1958 the Chinese rural communes have apparently made remarkable economic and social strides among which the following are most significant:

1. The transformation of an impoverished and

[11] *Ibid.*, p. 90.

stratified rural society into viable production units capable of meeting the food and basic material needs of the world's largest population.

2. The transformation of the rural economy into a diversified economic system with labour-intensive small-scale industry functioning in conjunction with labour-intensive agriculture.
3. The creation of a social system founded on principles of equality and social justice.
4. The development of a decentralised administrative and planning system that is close to the people and based on their perceived needs and requirements.

Scholars who first visited China in the early 1970s often claimed that in the short period since the 1949 Chinese revolution, China, which effectively isolated itself from the rest of the world, had 'already abolished absolute poverty; there is no unemployment in China and no inflation – the three problems which most other developing countries of Asia, Africa and Latin America have failed to solve so far'.[12] Information now available casts some doubt on these earlier 'official' versions of the successes of the agricultural system.[13]

But questions still remain. Of what relevance is the Chinese experience (assuming that those who have visited and write about China *are* accurately reflecting the prevailing situation) for other Third World nations? Specifically, without the powerful and massively supported political and ideological basis of Chinese society, can other LDCs develop effective rural co-operative efforts on a basis other than private property? Can they eliminate wide disparities in the distribution of wealth and income? Can they content the majority of their populations with only basic necessities such as food, clothing and shelter plus a few minor luxuries such as bicycles, radios and clocks, when both their leaders and their people are continually exposed to the 'demonstration effects' of mass consumption items like cars, fashionable clothes, TV sets, refrigerators and other luxury goods of developed countries? Is it possible for resource-deficient small countries like most of those in Asia, Africa and Latin America to shut themselves off from the rest of the world and become totally self-reliant? Finally, can the sense of security and prestige derived from private land-ownership – a sense so central to the societies of Asia and Latin America and increasingly so in Africa – be replaced by a sense of communal commitment and motivation based on a political ideology of equality and social justice? Is it feasible or even desirable?

These are not easy questions to answer without reference to particular nations and societies. Moreover, the real material benefit which the average Chinese rural dweller has obtained over the past quarter of a century is not without its price: his limited private freedom to choose a way of life that may not be in tune with the prevailing ideology. Freedom of choice may be relatively unimportant when sheer survival is the major concern, but it tends to assume increasing importance as basic material needs become satisfied. In other words, how long will the present ideological and economic system in China be able to be sustained as it opens itself and its people to outside influences? In 1981 and 1982, for example, the new Chinese leaders sought to modernise the economy by encouraging more private ownership and initiative, especially in the cities where the problem of growing urban unemployment started to become serious.

Even if for most underdeveloped countries the answer to many of the above questions would be negative, there is still much to be learned from the Chinese experience. Perhaps most important is the lesson it provides about agricultural output and promoting rural industries through small-scale labour-intensive activities supported by publicly provided economic and social services. While the Chinese model may not provide a blueprint for other less well endowed or culturally homogeneous Third World nations, it does provide a rough sketch of how it can be done. Perhaps, more importantly, it shows that it *can* be done, even for a country with over 950 million people.

[12] *Ibid.*, p. 91.

[13] John Wong, 'Some Aspects of China's Agricultural Development Experience: implications for developing countries in Asia,' in C. Wilber (ed.), *The Political Economy of Development and Underdevelopment* (2nd edition), Random House, New York, 1979, pp. 241–57.

Concepts for review

integrated rural development
subsistence farming
'mixed' commercial farming
'scale-netural' technological progress
agricultural extension services
Green Revolution

specialised farming
mechanisation
demonstration effects
population density
land reform
hybrid seeds
farmer co-operatives
government support systems
Chinese people's commune
risk and uncertainty
cash crops

Questions for discussion

1. It is sometimes asserted that small peasant farmers are backward and ignorant because they seem to resist agricultural innovations that could raise farm yields substantially. Is this resistance due to an inherent 'irrationality' on their part or might it be due to some other factors often overlooked by Western economists? Explain your answer.
2. In the chapter we described three stages in the transition from subsistence to 'modern' agriculture. What are the principal characteristics of these stages and how important is each of them in your own nation?
3. There appears to be widespread agreement that in those regions where the distribution of land ownership is highly unequal (e.g. mainly Latin America but also parts of Asia), land reform is a *necessary* but not *sufficient* condition for promoting and improving small-scale agriculture. What is meant by this statement and by the concept of land reform? Will the mere redistribution of land guarantee rural economic and social progress or are other policy measures necessary? Explain, giving specific examples of such supportive policies.
4. What is meant by comprehensive or 'integrated' rural development? What criteria would you use to decide whether or not such integrated rural development was or was not taking place? Would these criteria seem to be being met in your own country? Explain your answer.
5. The People's Republic of China has apparently evolved a unique approach to promoting rural development. What are the main characteristics of this approach and what have been its supposed achievements?
6. A crucial issue in the debate on development is whether or not the Chinese experiment in rural development offers any lessons or strategies that can be adopted in other Third World nations. Taking the case of your own country, do you think the Chinese experience has any relevance? Why, or why not?

Further reading

For a general introduction to problems of agriculture and rural development in Third World countries see: ERIK THORBECKE, ed., *The Role of Agriculture in Economic Development*, Columbia University Press, 1969; RAANAN WEITZ, *From Peasant to Farmer: a revolutionary strategy for development*, Columbia University Press, 1971; BRUCE F. JOHNSTON, 'Agriculture and Structural Transformation in Developing Countries: a survey of research', *Journal of Economic Literature*, viii, 2, June 1970; JOHN MELLOR, *The Economics of Agricultural Development*, Cornell University Press, 1966; A. T. MOSHER, *Creating a Progressive Rural Structure*, Agricultural Development Council, New York, 1969; T. W. SCHULTZ, *Transforming Traditional Agriculture*, Yale University Press, 1964; ROBERT SHAW, *Jobs and Agricultural Development*, Overseas Development Council, Washington, 1970; KEITH GRIFFIN, *The Political Economy of Agrarian Change*, Macmillan, 1974.

In addition to the Aziz article in *World Development*, February 1974, another survey article on Chinese rural development is that of JOHN G. GURLEY, 'Rural Development in China, 1949–1972 and the lessons to be learned from it' in E. O. EDWARDS, ed., *Employment in Developing Nations*, Colombia University Press, 1974, pp. 383–403. See also: CARL RISKIN, 'Small Industry and the Chinese Model of Development', *The China Quarterly*, April–June 1971, pp. 245–273; KEITH BUCHANAN, *The Transformation of the Chinese Earth*, Praeger, 1970; LLOYD G. REYNOLDS, 'China as a Less Developed Economy', *American Economic Review*, lxv, 3, June 1975, pp. 418–428; and, especially, John Wong, 'Some Aspects of China's Agricultural Development: implications for developing countries in Asia,' in Charles Wilber (ed.), *The Political Economy of Development and Underdevelopment*, Random House, New York, 1979.

Chapter 17 The economics of education

> The school in many underdeveloped countries is a reflection and a fruit of the surrounding underdevelopment, from which arises its deficiency, its quantitative and qualitative poverty. But little by little, and there lies the really serious risk, the school in these underdeveloped countries risks becoming in turn a factor of underdevelopment.
>
> *Joseph Kizerbo*[1]

Introduction

Most economists would probably agree that it is the human resources of a nation, not its capital nor its material resources, that ultimately determine the character and pace of its economic and social development. A somewhat extreme version of this position, especially in view of the financial windfalls of OPEC oil nations, has been expounded by Professor Harbison who in 1973 argued that:

> human resources ... constitute the ultimate basis for the wealth of nations. Capital and natural resources are passive factors of production; human beings are the active agents who accumulate capital, exploit natural resources, build social, economic and political organizations, and carry forward national development. Clearly, a country which is unable to develop the skills and knowledge of its people and to utilize them effectively in the national economy will be unable to develop anything else.[2]

The principal institutional mechanism for developing human skills and knowledge is the formal educational system. Most developing nations have been led to believe or have wanted to believe that it is the rapid *quantitative* expansion of educational opportunities which holds the basic key to national development. The more education, the more rapid the anticipated development. All countries have committed themselves, therefore, to the goal of universal primary education in the shortest possible time. This quest has become a politically very sensitive but often economically costly 'sacred cow'. Until recently few politicians, statesmen, economists or educational planners inside or outside the Third World would have dared publicly to challenge the cult of formal education.

Nevertheless, the challenge is gathering momentum, and it comes from many sources. It can be found most clearly in the character and results of the development process itself. After almost three decades of rapidly expanding enrolments and hundreds of billions of dollars of educational expenditure, the plight of the average citizen of Asia, Africa and Latin America seems little improved. Absolute poverty is chronic and pervasive. Economic disparities between rich and poor widen with each passing year. Unemployment and underemployment have reached staggering proportions, with the 'educated' increasingly swelling the ranks of those without jobs.

It would be foolish and naïve to blame these problems exclusively on the failures of the formal educational system. At the same time, one must recognise that many of the early claims made on behalf of the unfettered quantitative expansion of educational opportunities – that it would accelerate economic growth; that it would raise levels of living especially for the poor; that it would generate widespread and equal employment opportunities for all; that it would acculturate diverse ethnic or tribal groups; and that it would encourage

[1] Former Minister of Education, Upper Volta.

[2] Frederick H. Harbison, *Human Resources as the Wealth of Nations*, Oxford University Press, 1973, p. 3.

'modern' attitudes – have been shown to be greatly exaggerated and, in many instances, simply false.

As a result there has been a growing awareness in many developing nations that the expansion of formal schooling is not always to be equated with the spread of learning; that the student's and teacher's exclusive concern with the acquisition of school certificates and higher degrees should not necessarily be associated with the former's improved ability to undertake productive work; that education which is almost entirely oriented towards preparation for work in the urban modern sector can greatly distort student aspirations; and that too much investment in formal schooling, especially at the secondary and higher levels, can divert scarce resources from more socially productive activities (e.g. direct employment creation) and thus be a drag rather than a stimulus to national development.

The educational systems of Third World nations strongly influence and are influenced by the whole nature, magnitude and character of their development process. Formal education not only attempts to impart knowledge and skills to individuals to enable them to function as agents of economic change in their societies. It also imparts values, ideas, attitudes and aspirations which may or may not be in the nation's best developmental interests. Education absorbs the greatest share of LDCs' recurrent government expenditures, occupies the time and activities of the greatest number of adults and children (almost 30 per cent of Third World populations) and carries the greatest psychological burden of development aspirations. We must therefore examine its fundamental economic basis in less developed countries; and also its social and institutional ramifications.

The economics of education is a vital yet somewhat amorphous component of the economics of development. It is a young subject, having emerged as a separate branch of economics only in the 1960s. Yet when we recognise the principal motivation or demand for education in Third World countries as a desire for economic improvement by means of better access to highly paid jobs, we must understand the economic processes through which such aspirations are either realised or frustrated.

Our purpose in this chapter and the next is to explore the relationship (both positive and negative) between quantitative and qualitative educational expansion and development in terms of six basic issues that grow directly out of the discussions of previous chapters:

1. How does education influence the rate, structure and character of economic growth? Conversely, how does the rate, structure and character of economic growth influence the nature of the educational system?
2. Does education in general, and the structure of Third World educational systems in particular, contribute to or retard the growth of domestic inequality and poverty?
3. What is the relationship between education and fertility?
4. What is the relationship between education, rural–urban migration and urban unemployment? Are rising levels of the 'educated unemployed' temporary or chronic phenomena?
5. Do contemporary Third World formal educational systems tend to promote or retard agricultural and rural development?
6. What is the relationship, if any, between Third World educational systems, developed-country educational systems and the international migration of highly educated professional manpower from the less developed to the more developed nations?

We begin this chapter with a brief statistical profile of the status of education in developing countries. First we focus on public expenditure levels, enrolment ratios, literacy levels, dropout rates, costs and earnings differentials. After discussing the principal economic and environmental factors affecting the ability to learn, we review some basic concepts in the economics of education, the determinants of the demand for and supply of school places and the distinction between private and social benefits and costs of investment in education. Chapter 18 begins with a detailed examination of the six issues outlined above to see if any definite conclusions about the relationship between education and various key components of the development process can be reached, and concludes with a review of alternative policy options open to Third World governments in their attempt to evolve education and educational systems which will serve more effectively the needs and aspirations of all their people.

A statistical profile of education in Third World regions

Public educational expenditure

In most developing countries, formal education is the largest 'industry' and the greatest consumer of public revenues. Poor nations have invested huge sums of money in education. Literate farmers with at least a primary education are thought to be more productive and more responsive to new agricultural technologies than illiterate farmers. Specially trained craftsmen and mechanics who can read and write are assumed to be better able to keep up to date with changing products and materials. Secondary school leavers with arithmetical and clerical skills are needed to perform technical and administrative functions in a growing public and private bureaucracy. In former colonial countries many of them were also needed to replace departing expatriates. University graduates with advanced professional and general training were needed to provide essential professional (medical, engineering, architectural, etc.) and managerial (economics and commerce) skills necessary for modernised public and private sectors.

In addition to these obvious manpower planning needs, the people themselves, both rich and poor, have exerted tremendous political pressure for the expansion of school places in Third World countries. Parents quickly realised that in an era of scarce skilled manpower the more schooling and certificates their children could accumulate the better would be their chances of getting secure and well-paid jobs. For the poor especially, more years of schooling were perceived to be the only avenue of hope for their children to escape from poverty.

As a result of these forces on both demand and supply, there has been a tremendous acceleration in public expenditures on education in the LDCs during the last two decades. Both the proportion of national income and of national budgets spent on education has increased rapidly. In Asia total public expenditure tripled during the 1960s. In Africa and Latin America, public educational expenditure more than doubled. In fact the increase in public expenditure on education during the 1960s and 1970s was more pronounced than for any other sector of the economy. By the 1980s educational budgets in many Third World nations were absorbing anywhere from 20 to 35 per cent of total government recurrent expenditures.

Enrolment

Between 1960 and 1980 the total number of persons enrolled in the three main levels of education in Africa, Asia, the Middle East and Latin America rose from 163 million to 385 million, an average annual increase of 5 per cent. Although the largest part of this increase has been in primary education, it is in the second and third levels that the greatest proportionate increases have occurred: 12.7 and 14.5 per cent per annum respectively compared with approximately 8 per cent per annum for primary enrolment. Nevertheless, primary enrolment still accounted for nearly 80 per cent of the total LDC school enrolment in the 1970s. Table 17.1 shows comparative data on enrolment ratios at the primary, secondary and higher education levels for a selected group of low and middle income developing countries in 1960 and 1978. The remarkable increases in enrolments at both the primary and secondary levels is strikingly evident from this table.

Dropouts

One of the major problems of Third World education is the very high percentage of students who drop out before completing a particular educational cycle. For example, it has been estimated that in Latin America 60 out of every 100 students who enter primary school drop out before completion. In some Latin American countries, the primary school dropout rate is as high as 75 per cent. In Africa and Asia the median dropout rates are approximately 54 and 20 per cent respectively. But here too the variation among countries has been very wide with dropout rates as high as 81 and 64 per cent respectively in certain African and Asian nations.

At the secondary level median dropout rates for those entering in 1975 were 38 per cent in Africa and 18 per cent in Latin America and Asia. In Europe the rate was approximately 11.4 per cent. One consequence of the disproportionately high median rate for Africa is the serious and growing problem of the secondary school leaver who joins the ranks of the educated unemployed.

Table 17.1
Enrolment ratios in selected developing countries: primary, secondary and higher education, 1960 and 1978

	Numbers enrolled as a percentage of age group					
	Primary		Secondary		Higher	
	1960	1978	1960	1978	1960	1978
Low income LDCs						
Bangladesh	47	72	8	22	1	3
Ethiopia	7	38	1	9	(—)	(—)
India	61	79	20	28	3	8
Tanzania	25	70	2	4	(—)	(—)
Sri Lanka	95	94	27	52	1	1
Indonesia	71	94	3	16	(—)	2
Middle income LDCs						
Thailand	83	82	13	28	2	5
Philippines	95	100	26	56	13	24
Colombia	77	100	12	43	2	10
Korea, Rep. of	94	100	27	63	5	10
Brazil	95	88	11	24	2	13
Mexico	80	100	11	39	3	11
Developed Countries	100	100	58	82	16	34

Source: IBRD, *World Development Report, 1981*, Annex Table 23.

Literacy

The percentage throughout the world of adults (persons aged 15 and over) who are illiterate, fell in the two decades between 1960 and 1980 from 60 to 51 per cent. However, due to rapid population growth, the actual number of adult illiterates rose by nearly 70 million to an estimated total of 850 million in 1980. The highest illiteracy rates are found in Africa (73.7) and the Arab States (73) followed by Asia (46.8) and Latin America (23.6). In North America and Europe illiteracy rates have fallen to 1.0 and 2.5 per cent respectively. Information on literacy rates for particular countries can be obtained from Appendix II to chapter 5.

Costs per student and relative earnings by education

Criticism has intensified in recent years of the very serious disproportionate costs per pupil of education at various levels in the LDCs. This is especially true when one compares secondary and higher educational cost with primary level costs. While much of this criticism in the past had been based on scattered *ad hoc* empirical and interpretive information, a recently published international comparative study provides detailed data on the magnitude of these cost divergences.

Table 17.2 compares the ratio of total costs per student year by educational level for a selected group of developed and less developed countries. The data reveal that whereas in the three developed countries shown the ratio of total per pupil costs of secondary to primary education is 6.6 to 1 and that of higher to primary education is 17.6 to 1, in the seven LDCs shown these relative costs are 11.9 and 87.9 to 1 respectively. Another way of interpreting the 87.9 relative cost figure of higher to primary education is that for the equivalent cost of educating one university student for one year, 88 primary school children could be educated for one year in these seven developing countries. In some African countries like Sierra Leone, Malaŵi, Kenya and Tanzania cost ratios per pupil between higher and primary education range as high as 283 to 1. Since in over half the world's underdeveloped countries the ratio of pupils in primary schools to students in higher education is above 100 to 1 as compared, for example, to ratios of less than 10 to 1 in the developed countries, it follows that LDCs tend to

Table 17.2
Ratios of total costs by educational level per student year (primary = 1)

Groups of countries	Relative cost Secondary/Primary	Higher/Primary
USA, Great Britain, New Zealand,	6.6	17.6
Malaysia, Ghana, South Korea, Kenya, Uganda, Nigeria, India	11.9	87.9

Source: G. Psacharopoulos, *The Returns to Education: an international comparison*, Elseview 1972, Table 8.2.

spend large proportions of their educational budgets on the very small proportion of their students who are enrolled in their universities and professional schools.

If one then compares the data in Table 17.3, showing the relative average earnings of individuals by education level, with those on costs, it becomes clear that the differences in the relative earnings of people with different levels of education between the developed and the less developed nations are much less than the differences in the unit educational costs. For example, looking again at the figures for LDCs in the second columns of Tables 17.2 and 17.3 we see that while a university student costs 87.9 times as much as a primary pupil to educate for one year, the university student on average earned only 6.4 times as much as the typical primary pupil – a very high differential, but not as high as the cost differential. To the extent that average relative earnings reflect average relative productivity, the wide disparity between relative earnings and relative costs of higher versus primary education implies that in the past LDC governments may have unwisely invested too much in higher education. These funds might have been more productively invested in primary school expansion. This does not necessarily imply that in future the relative cost/benefit ratios will continue to favour primary school expansion; much depends on the relative employment prospects of the various educational groups.

Table 17.3
Ratios of average annual earnings of labour by educational level

Country Group	Relative earnings Secondary/Primary	Higher/Primary
USA, Canada, Great Britain	1.4	2.4
Malaysia, Ghana, South Korea, Kenya, Uganda, Nigeria, India	2.4	6.4

Source: G. Psacharopoulos, *op cit.*, Table 8.4.

Some basic problems of primary and secondary education

Inertia and inefficiency

While the foregoing statistics provide a useful summary of enrolments, dropouts, literacy, costs per student and returns to education in the form of deferred labour earnings, there are other underlying but less quantifiable problems of education in the Third World, problems sometimes serious in industrialised nations also. These are broadly referred to as the **inefficiencies and inertia of educational systems.**

One might start with the outdated content and dubious quality of education at all levels. As stated by a former Deputy Director-General of UNESCO:

> The learning techniques ... remain the same:

> the rote method, the technique of cramming, and, once the examination menace is passed, of forgetting all these useless impedimenta. The examination system is not an evaluation of a student's personality and intellectual equipment, his powers of thinking for himself, reflection, and reasoning. It is a challenge to resourceful deception and display of superficial cleverness. ... Looked at as a business enterprise, the school and college present a woebegone spectacle. We find in education antediluvian technology which would not survive for an instant in any other economic sector. The teaching methods and learning techniques ... are rusty, cranky and antiquated.

Deficiencies of learning methods and curricula are closely related to inadequate competence and motivations of most teachers who are usually underpaid and without incentive or opportunity to learn any more themselves than they took in at their start. The situation is hardly better among educational administrators.

Poor management and distorted incentives

Indeed problems seem most acute and difficult to remedy in the realm of educational management, its direction, organisation and programming. Here are the immediate causes of perpetuating old and dysfunctional patterns. Rigidity persists along with a lack of requisite information of the society's needs, conditions and developmental possibilities, and a lack of practically oriented research, experimentation and evaluation.

These problems of education result in part because socially perceived needs within the educational system vastly exceed available funds and other resources. But they also result from demands, pricing and financial and non-financial incentives in the society at large, *outside* the educational system. What society and individuals want of education are often impossible dreams, demands frequently out of line with priorities of national development, indeed, often running against those priorities.

These demands sometimes also take the form of political interference in the educational system and distortion of its governing policies. Political pressures intrude at all levels in education, forcing the system to respond, but these pressures may have little to do with primary goals of national development or with real changing needs in the society as a whole.

Maladjustment to social needs at the primary level

Nowhere is the maladjustment of the educational system to national development needs more evident than in the rural primary schools. Primary education receives the lion's share of Third World educational expenditure. More than 50 per cent of all educational expenditure and almost 10 per cent of governmental recurrent expenditure is allocated to primary education. Primary education received approximately 3.8 per cent of the total GNP of less developed countries in 1980: over 60 billion dollars.

Given the tremendous importance of primary education for national development and the distinctive economic, social and cultural conditions of less developed nations, one must seriously question the advisability and utility of a system which for all practical purposes is no different in structure and content from its counterpart in the advanced nations.

The basic problems of rural primary education and the reasons why it is often out of tune with the real needs of poor societies can best be summarised as follows:

1. Over 70 per cent of the children in LDCs live and attend school in rural areas.
2. Over 80 per cent of these children are likely to spend their lives earning a living either directly from the land or from unskilled paid employment in rural areas. Yet primary schools spend very little time giving these students the knowledge, skills, and new ideas necessary to function efficiently in their rural environment (e.g. farming practices and management, hygiene, nutrition, community development, etc.).
3. Primary schools typically attempt to prepare students for secondary school with training in literacy, numeracy and foreign languages receiving highest priority. The training, moreover, usually consists of recitation, repetition and drill-learning rather than thinking and problem-solving.
4. In those developed nations in which the vast majority of primary school entrants proceed to secondary school which in turn tends to concen-

trate on college preparatory education, the heavy emphasis on literacy, numeracy and foreign languages is less questionable. But it has been estimated that it takes approximately five years (depending on age of entry) for a child to achieve literacy and even longer to master numeracy and foreign languages (even if the latter were really relevant).

5. The problem with this approach to primary and secondary education (i.e. structuring the primary school curriculum solely as a preparation for secondary school) in the LDCs is that:
   (*a*) For a variety of economic and social reasons, over 15 per cent of the children who enter primary school will drop out after the first year, with an additional 10 per cent dropping out the following year.
   (*b*) Approximately 50 per cent of those who enter the first class of primary school are unlikely to complete four years.
   (*c*) Less than 10 per cent of those who enter primary school are likely to succeed in reaching secondary school even though 25 to 30 per cent of the original entrants might complete the primary cycle.
   (*d*) Of those who do get to secondary school less than 60 per cent are likely to complete the course (the ratio is much lower in Africa) and only about 20 per cent will proceed to a university.
   (*e*) For those who stay right through secondary school but do not obtain a place in a university, the probability of their finding a job in the modern sector (towards which their secondary education has been oriented) is estimated at approximately one in three in Latin America and lower in parts of Asia and Africa.

Clearly something is seriously wrong with a primary and secondary educational system modelled upon its counterpart in economically advanced societies and transferred to an environment to which it has little if any relevance (we shall deal with the problems of university education in the next section). But to document these problems is not to answer them. What is urgently needed are detailed studies and well conceived experiments to answer such crucial questions as the following[3]:

1. At what age should a child, who is going to have only a few years of primary education, enter school?
2. Should primary education in a rural community in a developing country be full-time or part-time?
3. Given some type of formal education for children, do literacy and numeracy constitute the highest priority areas of instruction for those destined to spend their lives in a rural zone?
4. Given that the medium of instruction in higher and secondary education is in a language other than the mother tongue, is it necessary to teach this language in primary school?
5. Given that for financial reasons it is not possible to lengthen the training of teachers (salaries are usually directly related to length of training), can the type of training given to teachers be changed and the curriculum and inspection system altered, so that the teacher becomes more effective?
6. If children are given certain ideas which they forget because they have no possibility of practising them, are they more or less likely to accept and practise these ideas again when they are reintroduced later in adult life?
7. Have the children who drop out of primary school after one, two or three years gained much, if anything? If not, can a curriculum be designed so that they would benefit more?
8. Are the highest priority areas of instruction the same for (*a*) those children proceeding to secondary education; (*b*) those children getting paid employment in the modern sector; (*c*) those children remaining in the rural areas? If not, is it possible to structure the system in such a way as to provide both some equality of opportunity, and the fulfilment of differing requirements?
9. Related to 8 above, is it possible to design a reasonably just and incorruptible selection procedure which does not over-influence what is taught in the schools?
10. Should the school and community be integrated? Should adult and child education be integrated? Should mass education (or community development) be designed to solve

[3] Nicholas Bennet, 'Primary Education in Rural Communities: an investment in ignorance', Paris, International Institute for Planning (mimeo), 1972, pp. 5–6.

particular developmental problems? If so, how should these things be achieved?

These and other questions of great significance to the nation-building aspirations of diverse Third World countries need to be answered if their primary (and secondary) educational systems are going to make maximum contributions to economic development.

Problems of higher education

President Julius Nyerere of Tanzania perhaps best summed up the role of universities in developing societies when he said:

> The University in a developing society must put the emphasis of its work on subjects of immediate moment to the nation in which it exists, and it must be committed to the people of that nation and their humanistic goals. . . . We in poor societies can only justify expenditure on a University – of any type – if it promotes real development of our people. . . . The role of a University in a developing nation is to contribute; to give ideas, manpower, and service for the furtherance of human equality, human dignity and human development.[4]

Higher education (tertiary level) in the LDCs is a very much smaller world than that of the primary and secondary levels. The proportion of enrolled students in higher education is less than 5 per cent of all students compared with over 95 per cent in the primary and secondary levels. The proportion of the number of teachers in higher education is correspondingly less than 8 per cent of the total.

While there is a considerable variety of institutions in higher education (e.g. colleges and professional schools), the university is generally identified as the most important and apex institution. Yet Third World universities have been found by practically all informed observers to be as maladjusted and out of step with the real needs of development as the educational institutions in lower levels. Many of the problems basic to primary and secondary education already discussed recur in more or less aggravated form in universities: annual increases in the order of 15 to 20 per cent in student enrolments, rising costs, declining pupil–teacher ratios, deficient facilities, inappropriate curricula, administrative inertia and ever more serious problems of unemployment or malemployment for university graduates.

The basic causes of university defects have been examined in what is now a substantial literature, and are generally agreed on. Most Third World universities have been modelled in structure and function upon the older institutions in the industrialised societies. In the last 20 years many national programmes of university development have resulted (even where it was not the primary intention) in patterning university additions and changes in LDCs to resemble practices established in the United States, France, Great Britain and other developed countries. By long and powerful tradition the universities of the Western world are structured by professional disciplines, as they have been since medieval times. This structure, departments (discipline) and their grouping (faculty) was exported on a large scale to universities in the LDCs. Little thought or effort was given to questions of how this mode of academic organisation would serve existing Third World conditions. 'Excellence' continued to be measured in terms of international academic standards rather than contributions to national development. But the pressures of expanding enrolments, tight budgets and, most important, student demands for relevant and meaningful curricula have recently caused many Third World university leaders to rethink their role and mission and to begin to heed the perceptive advice of thoughtful statesmen like President Nyerere of Tanzania.

Factors affecting the ability to learn: causes and consequences

Recent evidence from a wide range of countries, both developed and less developed, has conclusively demonstrated that early factors in the life of a child –

[4] Julius Nyerere, 'The University's Role in the Development of New Countries', World University Service Assembly, Dar es Salaam, Tanzania, 27 June 1966

the health and feeding habits of his mother during her pregnancy, the child's own health and nutritional status during his or her first few years of life, the family's income and living conditions, etc. – can determine whether or not the child will perform well in school and in later life. Figure 17.1 portrays the influence of these early factors (individual, family and non-family environment) not only on school performance ('later factors') but also on individual capacities for behavioural change and the private and social benefits that are derived from such change mainly in the form of wage or self-employment.

For example, we see from Figure 17.1 that early malnutrition and disease can not only adversely affect a child's ability to read, write, perform arithmetic operations and think clearly and logically in school (his cognitive abilities). It can also adversely affect his chances of obtaining and/or holding a job (employment status) and lower his productivity and general performance in that job. Thus family and child health are important determinants of both school performance and the physical and mental ability of an individual to function effectively in later life.

Children from poor families with low levels of living are therefore often placed at a competitive disadvantage *vis-à-vis* the economically better off child in school activities. For example, most studies of school performance reveal that the four most important factors in the determination of a child's capacity to learn are:

1. **family environment**, including income levels, parents' education, housing conditions, number of children in household, etc.;
2. **peer group interactions**, i.e. the type of children with whom an individual child associates;
3. **personality**. i.e. the child's inherited intelligence and abilities;
4. **early nutrition and health**

If a child enters school deficient in all four factors, as many very poor children do, the educational process may have little effect on his capacity for self-improvement and economic advancement. In fact,

Figure 17.1
The learning system: causes, consequences and interaction

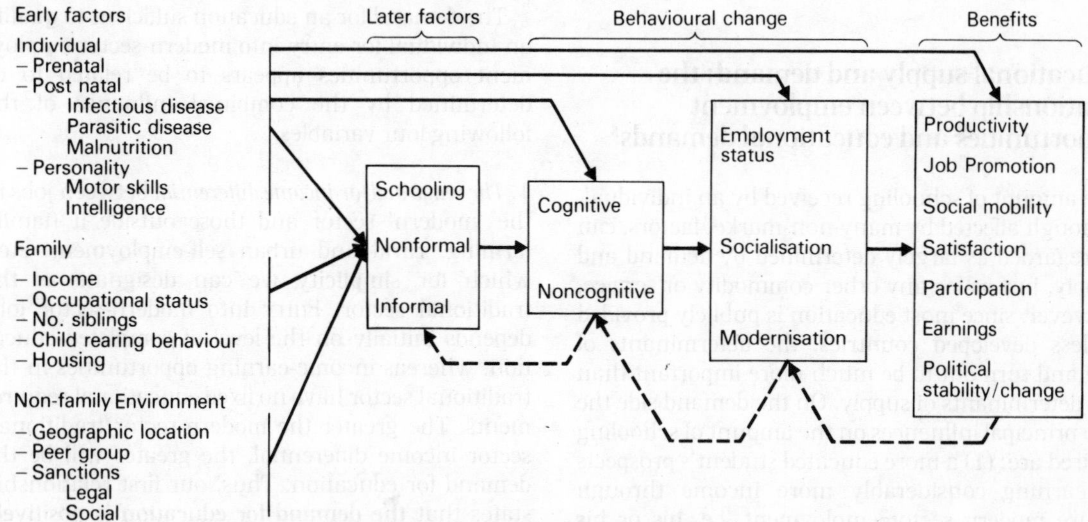

Source: John Simmons, 'Investment in Education for Developing Countries: national strategy options', Washington World Bank (mimeo), October 1973, p. 181.

he is very likely to be among the 50 per cent of primary school students who drop out before completing four years. Equality of educational opportunity – a social goal professed by all nations – can thus have little meaning in societies where children come from very unequal backgrounds.

The economics of education: some central concepts

Much of the literature and public discussion about the economics of education in Third World nations revolves around two central concepts introduced in Chapter 3, namely (1) the interaction of economically determined **demands** with politically responsive **supplies** in the determinants of how many school places are provided, what kind of instruction is promoted, and who gets access to these places; and (2) the important distinction between 'social' versus 'private' **benefits** and **costs** of different levels of education and the implications of these differentials for educational investment strategy.

Educational supply and demand: the relationship between employment opportunities and educational demands[5]

The amount of schooling received by an individual, although affected by many non-market factors, can be regarded as largely determined by demand and supply, just as for any other commodity or service. However, since most education is publicly provided in less developed countries, the determinants of demand turn out to be much more important than the determinants of supply. On the demand side the two principal influences on the amount of schooling desired are: (1) a more educated student's prospects of earning considerably more income through future modern sector employment, i.e. his or his family's 'private benefits' of education; and (2) the educational costs both direct and indirect which a student and/or his family must bear. The demand for education is thus in reality a 'derived demand' for high wage employment opportunities in the modern sector. This is because access to such jobs is largely determined by an individual's education. Most people (especially the poor) in less developed nations do not demand education for its intrinsic benefits but simply because it is the only way to get highly paid employment. These derived benefits must in turn be weighed against the costs of education.

On the supply side, the quantity of school places at the primary, secondary and university levels is determined largely by political processes, often unrelated to economic criteria. Because of mounting political pressure for greater numbers of school places throughout Third World nations, we can for convenience assume that the public supply of these places is fixed by the level of government educational expenditure. This in turn is influenced by the level of aggregate private demand.

Since it is the demand for education, therefore, which largely determines the supply (within the limits of government financial feasibility) let us look more closely at the economic (employment-oriented) determinants of this derived demand.

The demand for an education sufficient to qualify an individual for entry into modern-sector employment opportunities appears to be related to or determined by the combined influence of the following four variables.

1. *The wage and/or income differential* between jobs in the 'modern' sector and those outside it (family farming, rural and urban self-employment, etc.) which for simplicity we can designate as the traditional sector. Entry into modern-sector jobs depends initially on the level of completed education, whereas income-earning opportunities in the traditional sector have no fixed educational requirements. The greater the modern-sector/traditional-sector income differential, the greater will be the demand for education. Thus, our first relationship states that **the demand for education is positively related to the modern-traditional sector wage differential**. Since we know from empirical studies that these differentials can be considerable in most developing nations, we would expect the demand for education to be greater than if differentials were smaller.

[5] Much of the material in this section is drawn from the author's joint paper with E. O. Edwards, 'Educational Demand and Supply in the Context of Growing Unemployment in Less Developed Countries', *World Development*, i, 1973.

2. *The probability of success in finding modern sector employment.* An individual who successfully completes the necessary schooling for entry into the modern-sector labour market will in fact probably get that highly-paid urban job. Clearly, if urban unemployment rates among the educated are growing and/or if the supply of, say, secondary school graduates continually exceeds the number of new job openings for which a secondary graduate can qualify, then we need to modify the 'actual' wage differential and instead speak about an 'expected' income differential, that is, the wage differential modified by the probability or likelihood that a school graduate will be successful in securing the modern-sector job. Since the probability of success is inversely related to the unemployment rate, that is, the more people with appropriate qualifications who seek a particular job the lower will be the probability that any one of them will be successful, we can argue that **the demand for education through, say, the secondary level will be inversely related to the current unemployment rate among secondary school graduates.**[6]

3. *The direct private costs of education.* We refer here to the current out-of-pocket expenses of financing a child's education. These expenses include school fees, books, clothing and related costs. We would expect **the demand for education to be inversely related to these direct costs**, that is, the higher the school fees and associated costs, the lower would be the private demand for education, everything else being equal.

4. *The indirect or 'opportunity costs' of education.* An investment in a child's education involves more than just the direct out-of-pocket costs of that education, especially when the child passes the age at which he can make a productive contribution to family income, whether in kind or in money. For example, by continuing his education at secondary school, a child who has completed his primary schooling is in effect forgoing the money income which he could expect to earn or the output he could produce for the family farm during the years he spends receiving a secondary education. These opportunity costs must also be included as a variable affecting the demand for education. The relationship would again be inverse, that is, **the greater the opportunity costs, the lower will be the demand for education.**

Although several other important variables, many of which are non-economic, including cultural traditions, social status, education of parents and size of family certainly influence the demand for education, we believe that by concentrating on the four variables described above, important new insights can be gained on the relationship between the demand for education and the supply of employment opportunities.

To give an example, suppose we have a situation in LD Country X where the following conditions typically prevail:

(*a*) The modern–traditional or urban–rural wage gap is of the magnitude of, say, 100 per cent for primary versus non-primary school graduates.

(*b*) The rate of increase in wage employment opportunities for primary-school leavers is slower than the rate at which new primary school leavers enter the labour force. The same may be true at the secondary level and even the university level in countries such as India, Mexico, Egypt, Pakistan and more recently Ghana, Nigeria and Kenya.

(*c*) Employers, faced with an excess of applicants, tend to select by level of education. They will choose candidates with secondary rather than primary education even though satisfactory job performance may require no more than a primary education.

(*d*) Trade unions, supported by the political pressure of the educated, tend to bind the going wage to the level of educational attainment of job-holders rather than to the minimum educational qualification required for the job.

(*e*) School fees are often nominal or even non-existent. Moreover, in many cases, the state bears a larger portion of the student's costs at successively higher levels.

Under the above conditions, which conform closely to the realities of the employment and education situation in many Third World nations, we would expect the demand for education to be substantial. This is because the anticipated 'private'

[6] In fact, since most expectations for the future tend to be based on a 'static' picture of the employment situation that now prevails, we might anticipate that with a worsening employment picture individuals will tend to overestimate their expected incomes and demand even more education than is justified in terms of 'correct' private calculations of benefits and costs.

benefits of more schooling would be large compared to the alternative of little or no schooling while the direct and indirect private educational **costs** are so low. Over time, as job opportunities for the uneducated diminish, individuals must safeguard their position by acquiring a complete primary education. This may suffice for a while but the internal dynamics of the employment demand/supply process eventually leads to a situation in which job prospects for those with only primary education begin to decline. This in turn creates a growing demand for secondary education. But the demand for primary education must increase concurrently since some who were previously content with no education are now being 'squeezed' out of the labour market.

The irony is that *the more unprofitable a given level of education becomes as a terminal point, the more demand for it increases as an intermediate stage or precondition to the next level of education*! This puts great pressure on the government to expand educational facilities at *all* levels to meet the growing demand. If they cannot respond fast enough, the people may do so on their own, as evidenced, for example, by the Harambee school self-help movement in Kenya where private secondary schools were built throughout the country, to be taken over later by the government.

The upshot of all this is the chronic tendency for developing nations to expand their educational facilities at a rate which is extremely difficult to justify either socially or financially in terms of optimal resource allocation. Each worsening of the employment situation calls forth an increased demand for (and supply of) more formal education at all levels. Initially the uneducated swell the ranks of the unemployed. However, over time there is an inexorable tendency for the average educational level among the unemployed to rise as the supply of school graduates continues to exceed the demand for middle and high level manpower. The better educated must, after varying periods of unemployment during which aspirations are scaled downward, take jobs requiring lower levels of education. The diploma and degree thus become requirements for employment, not the education they were intended to signify.

Governments and private employers in many LDCs tend to strengthen the trend by continuously upgrading formal educational entry requirements for jobs which were previously filled by those less educated. Excess educational qualification becomes formalised and may resist downward adjustment. Moreover, to the extent that trade unions succeed in binding going wages to the educational attainments of job holders, the going wage for each job will tend to rise (even though worker productivity in that job has not significantly increased). Existing distortions in wage differentials will be magnified, stimulating the demand for education even further.

As a result of this 'educational displacement phenomenon', those who for some reason (mostly their poverty) are unable to continue their education will fall by the wayside as unemployed school leavers. At the same time the more affluent continue to overqualify themselves through more years of education. In the extreme case one gets a situation like that of contemporary India, where the higher education system is in effect an 'absorber of last resort' for the great numbers of educated unemployed. This is a terribly expensive form of unemployment compensation. Moreover, since people cannot remain students until they retire, these great masses will eventually have to emerge from behind the walls of academe into a world of tight labour markets. The result will be more visible unemployment among those who are both highly educated and highly articulate.

Finally, it should be pointed out that many individuals tend to resist what they see as a downgrading of their job qualifications. Consequently, even though on the demand-for-labour side employers will attempt to substitute the more educated for the less educated for a given job, on the supply side there will be many job seekers whose expectations exceed the realities of the labour market. They might prefer to remain unemployed for some time rather than accept a job they feel is beneath them. It follows that as a result of these frictional effects and lags in adjustment on the supply side, unemployment will exist at all levels of education, even though it is concentrated at lower levels and, in general, is inversely related to educational attainment.

Social versus private benefits and costs

The inexorable attraction of ever higher levels of education is even more costly than this simple picture suggests. Typically in developing countries, the 'social' cost of education (i.e. the opportunity cost to society as a whole resulting from the need to finance costly educational expansion at higher levels when these limited funds might be more productively used in other sectors of the economy) increases rapidly as students climb the educational ladder. The private costs (those borne by the student himself) increase more slowly or indeed may decline.

This widening gap between social and private costs provides an even greater stimulus to the demand for higher education than it does for lower levels. Educational demand therefore becomes increasingly exaggerated at the higher (post secondary) levels. But educational opportunities can be accommodated to these distorted demands only at full social cost. As demands are generated progressively through the system, the social cost of accommodation grows much more rapidly than the places provided. More and more resources may therefore be misallocated to educational expansion in terms of the social costs, and the potential for creating new jobs will consequently diminish for lack of public financial resources.

Figure 17.2 provides an illustration of this divergence between private versus social benefits and costs. It also demonstrates how this divergence can lead to a misallocation of resources when private interests supersede social investment criteria. In Figure 17.2(a) expected private returns to years of completed schooling are plotted against actual private costs. As a student completes more and more years of schooling his expected private returns grow at a much faster rate than his private costs for reasons explained earlier. In order to maximise the difference between expected benefits and costs (and thereby the private 'rate of return' to investment in education), the optimal strategy for a student would be to secure as much schooling as possible.

Consider now Figure 17.2(b) where social returns and social costs are plotted against years of schooling. The social benefits curve rises sharply at first, reflecting the improved levels of productivity of, say, small farmers and the self-employed that result from receipt of a 'basic education' and the attainment of literacy, numeracy and elementary vocational skills. Thereafter, the 'marginal' social benefit of additional years of schooling increases but at a decreasing rate – thus the reason for the declining slope of the social returns curve. On the other hand, the social cost curve shows a slow rate of growth for early years of schooling (basic education) and then a

Figure 17.2
Private versus social benefits and costs of education: An illustration

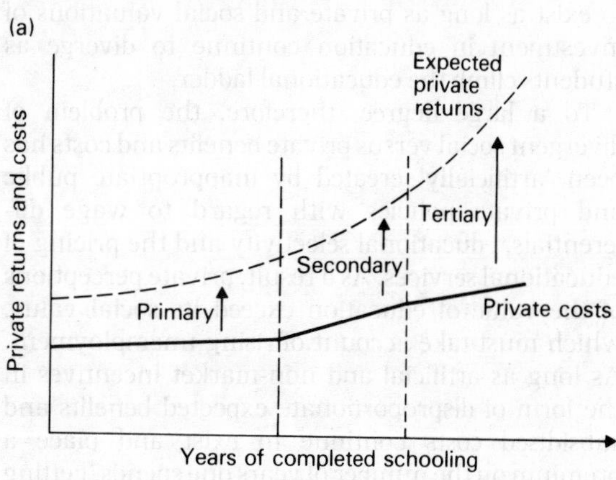

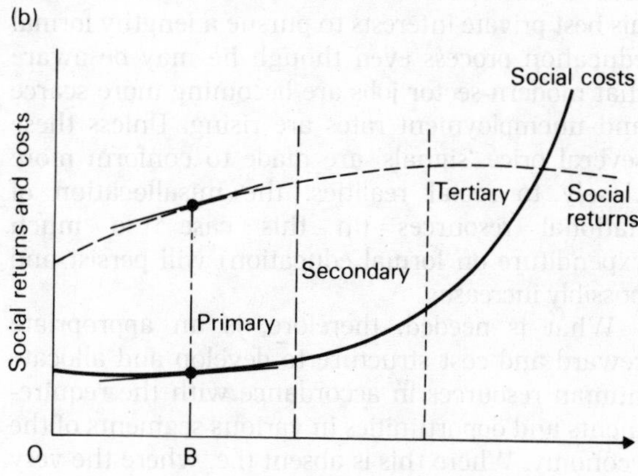

much more rapid growth for higher levels of education. This rapid increase in the marginal social costs of post primary education is due both to the much more expensive capital and recurrent costs of higher education (i.e. buildings and equipment) and, more important, to the fact that much post primary education in developing countries is heavily subsidised.

It follows from Figure 17.2(b) that the *optimal* strategy from a social viewpoint, i.e. the one that maximises the 'social' rate of return to educational investment, would be one that focuses on providing all students with at least OB years of schooling. Beyond OB years marginal social costs exceed marginal social benefits so that additional educational investment will yield a negative social rate of return. Figure 17.2, therefore, illustrates the inherent conflict between optimal private and social investment strategies – a conflict that will continue to exist as long as private and social valuations of investment in education continue to diverge as students climb the educational ladder.

To a large degree, therefore, the problem of divergent social versus private benefits and costs has been 'artificially' created by inappropriate public and private policies with regard to wage differentials, educational selectivity and the pricing of educational services. As a result, private perceptions of the value of education exceed its social value, which must take account of rising unemployment. As long as artificial and non-market incentives in the form of disproportionate expected benefits and subsidised costs continue to exist and place a premium on the number of years one spends 'getting an education', the individual will decide that it is in his best private interests to pursue a lengthy formal education process even though he may be aware that modern-sector jobs are becoming more scarce and unemployment rates are rising. Unless these several price 'signals' are made to conform more closely to social realities, the misallocation of national resources (in this case too much expenditure on formal education) will persist and possibly increase.

What is needed, therefore, is an appropriate reward and cost structure to develop and allocate human resources in accordance with the requirements and opportunities in various segments of the economy. Where this is absent (i.e. where the very high wage premiums paid to workers in the modern urban sector are complemented by the allocation of scarce jobs on the basis of ever increasing educational 'credentials') it can lead directly to two obvious misuses of human resources.

First, the output of the educational system being greatly in excess of that which the economy can absorb, many emerge from it seeking jobs for which they may be educationally qualified but which have been pre-empted by others with even more education. They become temporarily unemployed for as long as it takes for their aspirations and status requirements, partly perhaps instilled in them by the educational system itself, to adjust to the stinging realities of employment in the modern sector.

Second, those who adjust their sights downward and secure modern-sector employment normally have to take jobs for which they are over-educated in terms of the number of years spent on their education. Those who fail to get modern-sector jobs at all swell the ranks of the permanently unemployed or become self-employed in the traditional sector. They are thus denied the opportunity to contribute productively to the society which invested so heavily in their education. The combined effect of the overpaid and, in many cases, overeducated employed and the impoverished and unproductive educated unemployed reflects a serious misallocation of scarce national resources. The resources that were allocated to the expansion of the educational system might alternatively have been spent on rural public works projects. Such investment would provide emergency employment opportunities for school leavers as well as for those with less education.

Educational supply and demand: some policy approaches

Manipulating the supply of educational opportunities as a policy variable

In the preceding section we have assumed that the supply of educational opportunities accommodates itself to the aggregate demand for them. Indeed, the rapid expansion of educational facilities at post-compulsory levels during the 1970s alongside the growing number of educated unemployed suggests that the satiation of demand was the principal objective of education, even though it was not usually fully realised in practice.

The reasons for this pattern of government behaviour are essentially self-evident and in the circumstances practically irresistible. Given heavily subsidised or free education on the one hand and unrealistic income differentials between the modern and traditional sectors on the other, a substantial gap between the demand for education and the supply of employment opportunities is inevitable. Manipulating (i.e. restricting) the supply of educational opportunities within these limits is not likely to close the gap, though for reasons we have given its accommodation to demand is likely to widen it.

Instead, the manipulation of educational supply

changes the *visible* nature of the problem confronting governments without altering materially its basic dimensions or underlying causes. If governments opt for educational policies which seek to satisfy demand, as apparently they do, they will later face the problem of rationing job opportunities in the modern sector among the many who are educationally qualified. So far this problem has seemed to be politically tractable. However, as the average educational level among the unemployed rises and as their numbers grow (an almost certain prospect with present policies) the size of the resulting employment problem may overwhelm the rationing mechanism commonly employed.

That rationing mechanism is, as we have seen, the educational system itself. Jobs in the modern sector typically are allocated to those with higher levels of educational attainment. This rationing device has the appealing political merit of being apparently objective, relatively untainted by obvious favour, and patently dependent for its operation on many private as well as public decisions. But its operation does not relieve unemployment or improve the allocation of resources beyond ensuring that the most educated are indeed employed. So the magnitude of the problem is left to grow and an apparently fair rationing mechanism is unlikely to provide continuing political cover for an increasingly explosive situation.

But the need to ration employment still seems to be preferred in many developing countries to a scarcity of school places and the consequent need to ration educational opportunities. Politically it is most expedient to yield to current pressures rather than to anticipate future problems. As a result, educational supply increases, rapidly swelling enrolments and proliferating instructional activities. The pressures for expansion which stem directly from the burgeoning demand for education would in the extreme lead towards universal formal education at all levels. This undoubtedly has merits in advanced countries with full employment and incomes high enough to justify on social grounds the demand for education as a consumption good. It tends to equalise opportunities and to eliminate private and political favour as criteria for educational advancement. But the social cost of such efforts in poor countries with inadequate job opportunities, low incomes and essentially free education as privately perceived, is enormous. The future political costs may be even more enormous if widespread unemployment grows worse as a consequence.

Does this dismal picture of growing unemployment and overblown educational systems suggest that another built on an educational supply closely adjusted to prospective employment opportunities would be substantially happier? Probably not, in the extreme, though in such circumstances educational overqualification for limited jobs would diminish and more jobs could indeed be created with the funds saved on education. So long as education remains essentially privately free and modern-sector jobs are relatively lucrative, the demand for education must be excessive. The problem of severely rationing limited educational places would be gigantic. Even if it could be and were accomplished objectively, such a rationing mechanism would still be open to charges of favouritism. Moreover, the demands of those locked out of the educational system at every stage beyond literacy would be likely to be politically influential, even if the limitation of supply were economically advantageous.

Clearly the unsettling conditions associated with either extreme of educational supply policy when it is the *only* policy variable give cause for alarm. Within these extremes, however, and compared with the educational supply policies most governments appear to be pursuing, a greater reluctance to expand formal education in response to demand is admissible and would have a number of beneficial effects. Such a policy would narrow the gap between educational supply and job opportunities by reducing the former and releasing some resources for the expansion of the latter, slowing the rates of increase in the degree of overeducation for jobs and the numbers of educated unemployed. The widening gap between the demand for and supply of educational places would bring pressures on governments to reconsider their rationing devices and also to increase the share of educational costs which must be borne privately, particularly by those seeking education at higher levels. It should be recognised, however, that giving greater weight to prospective employment opportunities in planning educational expansion can only be a partial solution. It still does not solve the basic issue whereby the demand for education continues to outrun opportunities for productive employment.

Curtailing demand through gradual elimination of artificial incentives towards overeducation

No solution to the imbalance between educational demand and productive job opportunities can be found in the manipulation of educational supply alone. The pressures must build until policy attention is turned to the more fundamental issues of tempering demand to more realistic proportions and generating more urban and rural employment opportunities.

To temper the demand for education towards more realistic levels, Third World governments could strive to bring the private calculations of the benefits and costs associated with education closer to the social benefits and costs by:

1. **Making the beneficiary (as opposed to his family or society as a whole) bear a larger and rising proportion of his educational costs as he proceeds through the system (with appropriate subsidies for the able poor at low levels of education and through loan programmes at higher levels of education.).**

There are three principles in this policy recommendation. First, the share of educational costs borne privately should be substantially larger than they typically are in developing countries today. This would reduce demand for education beyond literacy. Second, the rate of educational subsidy should decline as an individual advances in the educational system. Thus the private demand for education would be curtailed more at high levels where it is socially most expensive and where most of the overeducation in terms of educational requirements for jobs takes place. A policy of declining subsidies would also respond to the valid criticism that current programmes involving rising subsidies are anti-egalitarian and in fact represent a subsidy to the rich by the poor. Third, the private share of educational cost should, so far as possible, fall on the beneficiary, not on his family or friends. It is his future earnings which will be increased, although his extended family is likely to share in the benefits. Ideally, he should pay for his education out of those future earnings. This suggests, of course, that private educational costs should be financed directly out of a student's own resources or indirectly through loans repaid either by financial levies against his future income or by social contributions of his expertise, such as service in rural areas. Such arrangements appear especially desirable and feasible at all levels of education beyond secondary. Below those levels the burden of private costs would probably continue to fall on the family, and would necessitate a system of subsidising the able poor.

2. **Reducing income differentials between the modern and traditional sectors and within the modern sector to ensure a more realistic appraisal of the prospective benefits of education.**

It would carry us too far from the field of education to consider means in detail here. We note only that these means are much more extensive than direct, sharp and unrealistic cuts in modern-sector money wages. They include more time-consuming processes of holding the line on average and minimum wages in the modern sector while rural productivity and prices are adjusted upward.

3. **Ensuring that minimum job specifications do not overvalue education.**

Students should not be encouraged to seek levels of education which over-qualify them for the jobs they can realistically expect to obtain. It is essential that the economic system should not exaggerate educational requirements to employment. Governments can take direct action on this matter by eliminating allocation of jobs by credentials within the civil service where a large share of modern-sector employment is to be found.

4. **Ensuring that wages are related to jobs and not to educational attainments.**

If the other policies are effective, this becomes essentially an interim measure. So long as over-education is increasing and those from the system must accept jobs which realistically require progressively lower educational qualifications, the tendency, particularly in teaching and the civil service, to tie salaries to levels of education simply increases rates of overpayment. This eventually induces even more students to follow the same socially misguided path.

To increase the supply of urban and rural job opportunities we have suggested in previous chapters that governments should:

1. Reduce factor-price distortions to the extent that these enter into employment decisions in both the public and private sectors.
2. Give more careful consideration to improving rural infrastructure and to the possible location of new modern sector activities in areas where wages have not yet reached the distorted levels

typical of established urban centres.

3. Allocate a larger share of public budgets to productive employment-creating activities and less to educational expansion than has been the pattern in the last decade.

This is not to say that funds spent on education do not create employment: they do. Our point is only that some of the funds so spent in the past might have been more usefully allocated to other more productive, labour-intensive activities, including the provision of complementary resources for the productive employment of the already educated. Education beyond literacy should compete for funds on these social benefit/cost criteria, not on the notion that it is a privileged activity exempt from such social and economic considerations.

Concepts for review

human resources
schooling
formal educational system
non-formal education
manpower planning
universal education
enrolment ratios
dropout (or wastage) rates
literacy
cognitive skills
derived demand
educational 'rates of return'
opportunity costs of education
educational certification
educational job displacement phenomenon
private v. social benefits of education
private v. social costs of education
overeducation
job rationing by education
on-the-job training
high-level manpower
pre-school environmental effects on ability to learn

Questions for discussion

1. What reasons would you give for the rather sizable school dropout rates in Third World countries? What might be done to lower these wastage rates?
2. What are the differences between 'formal' and 'non-formal' education? Give some examples of each.
3. It is often asserted that Third World educational systems especially in rural areas are dysfunctional – that is, they are not suited to the real social and economic needs of development. Do you agree or disagree with this statement? Explain your reasoning.
4. How would you explain the fact that relative costs of and 'returns' to higher education are so much higher in LDCs than in developed countries?
5. What is the supposed rationale for subsidising higher education in many Third World countries? Do you think that it is a legitimate rationale from an economic viewpoint? Explain.
6. 'Pre-school' environmental factors are said to be important determinants of school performance. What are some of these pre-school factors, how important do you think they are and what might be done to minimise their incidence among the population?
7. What do we mean by 'the economics of education'? To what extent do you think educational planning and policy decisions ought to be guided by economic considerations? Explain, giving hypothetical or actual examples.
8. What is meant by the statement 'the demand for education is a "derived demand" for highly paid modern sector job opportunities'? Many educational specialists claim that families and children in LDCs demand education not so much as an 'investment' good but as a 'consumption' good. What do you think is the meaning of this statement and what do you think is the relative importance of the consumption demand for education in your own country?
9. What are the linkages between educational systems, labour markets and employment determination in many Third World countries? Describe the process of 'educational job displacement'. Is it an important phenomenon in your own country? Explain.
10. Distinguish carefully between 'private' and 'social' benefits and costs of education. What economic factors give rise to the wide divergence between private and social benefit/cost valuations in most developing countries? Should governments attempt through their educational and economic policies to narrow the gap between private and social valuations? Explain.

Further reading

For an informative, general approach to the study of education and human resource development, see FREDERICK H. HARBISON, *Human Resources as the Wealth of Nations*, Oxford University Press, New York, 1973.

An excellent survey of current economic issues relating education to development can be found in: JOHN SIMMONS, 'Education for Development – Reconsidered', *World Development*, 7, 1979; M. BLAUG, *An Introduction to the Economics of Education*, Penguin, 1970.

For a broad analysis of how education can promote rural development, see PHILIP H. COOMBS and MANZOOR AHMED, *Attacking Rural Poverty: how non-formal education can help*, Johns Hopkins University Press, Baltimore, 1974.

A challenging and critical view of the role of education in society can be found in: IVAN ILLICH, *Deschooling Society*, Harper & Row, World Perspective, New York, 1970 and RONALD DORE, *The Diploma Disease: Education, Qualification and Development*, University of California Press, Berkeley 1976.

A good summary of the issues involved in the question of education and inequality can be obtained from: JAGDISH BHAGWATI, 'Education, class structure and income equality', *World Development*, i, 5, May 1973.

Chapter 18 Education and development: issues and options

> Virtually every serious commentator agrees that major reform within third world education is long overdue.
> *Richard Jolly*[1]

Introduction

Education and society

We have seen in the preceding chapter how the link between educational demands and the structure of labour markets in less developed countries can lead to an excessive quantitative explosion in the demand for school places. Such enormous demands and the ensuing political pressures for increased supply may be right out of proportion to the financial capabilities and state of development of a particular nation. As long as educational curricula are oriented towards preparation for white-collar urban jobs; as long as disproportionately highly paid but very limited modern-sector employment opportunities are rationed solely by educational level; and as long as governments subsidise the costs of education in increasing proportions as one moves from primary to secondary and from secondary to university level, then the expected private 'benefits' of even more years of schooling will continue to exceed private costs. On the other hand, the social costs (including, in addition to funds allocated to public education, the social costs of lost output involved in widespread unemployment and underemployment) may greatly exceed the net social benefits (e.g. higher national output levels). In such cases, and expecially where scarce public revenues used to finance quantitative educational expansion might find more socially productive outlets in, say, rural development projects, it might justly be claimed that there is too much formal schooling, especially at the higher levels.

It is no use discussing the relationship between education and development without explicitly linking the structure of the educational system to the economic and social character of the Third World society in which it is contained. Educational systems, more often than not, reflect the essential characteristics of that society. For example, if the society is very inegalitarian in economic and social structure, the educational system will probably reflect that bias in terms of who is able to proceed through the system. At the same time education *can* influence the future shape and direction of society in a number of ways, probably as a result of student pressures for both social and educational reform. Thus, the linkage between education and development is a two-way process. By reflecting the socio-economic structures of the societies in which they function (whether egalitarian or not), educational systems tend to perpetuate, reinforce and reproduce that economic and social structure. On the other hand, educational reform, whether introduced from within or outside the system, has great potential for inducing corresponding social and economic reform in the nation as a whole.

With these general observations in mind, let us look at six specific economic components of the 'development' question – growth, inequality and poverty, population and fertility, urban unemployment and internal migration, rural development and international migration – to see in what way they influence or are influenced by the educational systems of most Third World nations. Such an examination will demonstrate the important two-way relationships between education and development. It will also provide an even broader under-

[1] Former Director, Institute of Development Studies, University of Sussex, England.

standing of the principal problems and issues which have been discussed in previous chapters.

Education and economic growth

For many years the proposition that educational expansion promoted, or even determined, the rate of overall GNP growth remained unquestioned. The logic seemed fairly straightforward. Third World nations were very deficient in their supply of middle and high-level skilled manpower. Without such manpower, which it was assumed could be created only through the formal educational system, development leadership in both the public and private sectors would be lacking. In the absence of such leadership to plan, manage and run the economy, economic growth would be retarded, if not totally curtailed.

Impressive statistics and numerous quantitative studies of the 'sources of economic growth' in the West were paraded to demonstrate that it was not the growth of physical capital but that of 'human capital' which was the principal source of economic progress in the developed nations. Clearly, in the recently independent nations of Africa and Asia, there was an immediate need to rapidly build up the human as well as physical capital infrastructure in order to provide indigenous leadership for the myriad tasks of development. Rapid quantitative expansion of enrolments, therefore, appeared justified in light of the substantial manpower scarcities of the 1950s and 1960s. And, although it is extremely difficult to document statistically, it seems clear that the expansion of educational opportunities at all levels *has* contributed to aggregate economic growth by (1) creating a more productive labour force and endowing it with increased knowledge and skills; (2) providing widespread employment and income earning opportunities for teachers, school workers, builders, textbook and paper printers, school uniform manufacturers, etc.; (3) creating a class of educated leaders to fill vacancies left by departing expatriates or otherwise vacant positions in governmental services, public corporations, private businesses and the professions; and (4) presumably providing the kind of training and education that would promote literacy, numeracy and basic skills while encouraging 'modern' attitudes on the part of diverse segments of the population. Whether a social benefit-cost comparison of alternative investments in the economy would have generated even more economic growth, even if such calculations could be made, would not detract from the important contributions, non-economic as well as economic, which education can make and has made to aggregate economic growth. That an educated and skilled labour force is a necessary condition of sustained economic growth cannot be denied.

On the other hand, however, an investigation of education's role in the process of economic growth should not be confined to the latter's overall rate in the form of a single statistic. One must also consider the *structure* and *pattern* of that growth and its distributional implications; in other words, who benefits?

Education, inequality and poverty

Until recently most of the work on the economics of education in both the developed and the less developed nations centred on the linkages between education, labour productivity and output growth. This is not surprising since, as we have seen, the principal objective of development during the 1950s and 1960s was the maximisation of aggregate rates of output growth. As a result, the impact of education on the distribution of income and the elimination of absolute poverty was largely neglected. However, recent studies have demonstrated that rather than being a general force for equality, **the educational systems of most developing nations act to increase rather than to decrease income inequalities.**

The basic reason for this perverse effect of formal education on income distribution is the positive correlation between a person's education and his lifetime earnings. This is especially true for those who are able to complete secondary and university education, where income differentials over workers who have only completed part or all of their primary education can be of the order of 300 to 800 per cent. Since levels of earned income are so clearly dependent on years of completed schooling, it follows that large income inequalities will be reinforced and the magnitude of poverty perpetuated if students from middle and upper income brackets are represented disproportionately in secondary and university school enrolments. If for financial and/or other reasons the poor are effectively denied access to secondary and higher educational opportunities, then the educational system can actually perpetuate and even increase inequality in Third World nations.

Economist, John Simmons, for example, gives the following sketch of how the poor are beginning to regard education:

> Schooling, the poor quickly learn, in most countries, is an escape from poverty for only a few. The poor are the first to drop out because they need to work, the first to be pushed out because they fall asleep in class as one result of malnourishment, and the first to fail their French or English tests because upper income children have had better opportunities at home. The hope brought to village parents by the construction of the primary school soon fades. Enough schooling to secure a steady, even menial job for their son, let alone for their daughter, seems just beyond their grasp. Before . . . any schooling would have done to achieve their aspiration. Now a primary school certificate is needed, and some are saying that even students with some secondary schooling cannot get a steady job; and they could never afford to send their son away to town for secondary schooling.[2]

There are two fundamental economic reasons why one might suspect that many LDC educational systems are inherently inegalitarian in the sense that poor students have less chance of completing any given educational cycle than relatively rich students. First, the private **costs** of primary education, especially the 'opportunity cost' of a child's labour to poor families, is higher for poor students than for rich students. Second, the expected **benefits** of primary education are lower for poor students than for rich students. Together the high costs and lower expected benefits of education for the poor means that a family's rate of return from investment in a child's education is lower for the relatively poor than for the relatively rich. The poor are, therefore, more likely to drop out during early years of schooling. Let us briefly examine why 'costs' might be relatively higher and 'benefits' relatively lower for a poor child.

First, the higher opportunity cost of labour to poor families means that if the first few years of education are free for their children, they are not without cost to the family. Children of primary school age are needed to work on family farms, usually at the same time they are required to be at school. If a child cannot work because he is at school the family will either suffer a loss of valuable subsistence output or be required to hire paid labour to replace the absent child. In any case there is a real cost to a poor family of having an able-bodied child attend school when there is productive work to be done on the farm, a cost which is not reflected in school fees and one which is of much less significance to higher income families, many of whom may live in the urban areas anyway.

As a result of these higher opportunity costs, school attendance, and therefore school performance, tend to be much lower for children of poor families than for those from relatively higher income backgrounds. Thus in spite of the existence of free and universal primary education in many LDCs (which even when it exists typically covers only the first few years of schooling), children of the poor, especially in rural areas, are seldom able to proceed beyond the first few years of their education. Their relatively poor school performance may have nothing to do with a lack of cognitive abilities. On the contrary, it may merely reflect their disadvantaged economic circumstances.

This financial process of eliminating the relatively poor during their first few years of schooling is often compounded by the substantial school fees charged at the secondary level. In many Third World countries these yearly fees may be the equivalent of the average level of per capita income for the country as a whole and, therefore, be prohibitive to lower-income families. This in effect amounts to a system of educational advancement and selection based not on any criteria of merit but strictly on the basis of family income levels. It thus leads to a concentration of income in the succeeding generations within the same population groups which receive disproportionately high incomes in the present generation. It also eventually leads to a concentration of earned income among that group

[2] Simmons, *Investment in Education*, p. 206.

which already possesses the bulk of 'unearned' income and wealth, those whose physical and financial assets already place them in the upper deciles of the income distribution scale.

The inegalitarian nature of many Third World educational systems is compounded even further at the university level where the government may pay the full cost of tuition and fees as well as provide university students with income grants in the form of bursaries. Since most university students already come from upper income brackets (and were so selected at the secondary level), university education, highly subsidised from public funds which are often extracted from taxation of the poor, can represent a subsidy or transfer payment from the poor to the wealthy in the name of 'free' higher education.

On the benefit side, the poor are also at a disadvantage *vis-à-vis* the rich. Even if they are able to complete their primary education, the poor typically have more difficulty competing for rural and urban jobs with the relatively rich because of the latter's greater range of contacts and influences. In other words, for any given level of completed education (except perhaps university level education) the poor student will tend to be less likely to be selected for a job requiring that educational certification than the rich student. Even in the area of agriculture one could argue that although education may raise farm labour productivity the benefits of this will accrue disproportionately to those farm families that own their land and also have the complementary financial resources to modernise their agricultural techniques (i.e. the well-to-do large farmer). In the extreme case of landless rural labourers the greatest proportion of the benefits of their education and higher productivity may accrue largely to the rich landlord on whose farm they work.

It follows that in Third World countries characterised by highly unequal distributions of personal income, sizable secondary school fees and subsidised higher education, the educational system, especially at the secondary and higher levels, probably operates to increase inequality and perpetuate poverty. It should be stressed, however, that this outcome is not inherently the result of the educational system *per se*, but the institutional and social structure within which that system must function. Specifically, as long as wage differentials between different educational categories are artificially kept so wide in spite of rising levels of educated unemployment; as long as access to jobs is predicated almost exclusively on educational credentials irrespective of the relationship between years of schooling and job performance; and as long as a family's income serves as the basic criterion of who is able to proceed up the educational ladder to highly-paid jobs, then publicly supported educational systems will merely serve to reproduce the inegalitarian social and economic structure that, at least in theory, they were devised to combat. **Equality of educational opportunity can have little meaning if financial assets and income-earning opportunities are highly unequally distributed.**

Finally, we should point out that even if all the above cost and benefit distributions in favour of the rich were removed (by taxing higher earned incomes, subsidising the education of the poor, broadening employment opportunities for the poor, making the rich bear the full costs of their education, etc.) so as to make progress in the educational system strictly a function of merit and school performance, the poor would nevertheless still be at a competitive disadvantage. As we saw in Chapter 17, an early childhood characterised by poor nutrition and a congested and illiterate home environment has adverse mental effects.

We are therefore compelled to conclude that, like the problem of population where family planning programmes could be effective only in the context of an economic motivation for smaller families based on improved living standards, the solutions to the problems of inequality and poverty depend ultimately on direct measures to eliminate them (outlined in Chapter 10) and only partially on indirect measures such as more formal education. As long as the institutional, social and economic structures of Third World nations are organised to cater primarily for the needs and desires of upper income groups, an educational system which in principle at least is open to all classes, tribes and castes and which is considered socially progressive, a matter of national pride and an instrument of egalitarianism, can in reality merely provide a political cover for the further widening of the gap between rich and poor. But with rising unemployment, greater inequality and the chronic persistence of absolute poverty the political cover provided by thinly disguised inegalitarian systems of Third World education becomes ever more difficult to maintain. Ironically, it is typically the middle- and upper-income students themselves, especially at university level, who are often in the vanguard of economic and social reform. Examples include the economic and social reforms that have arisen out of student-led movements in Thailand, Ethiopia, Sri Lanka, Colombia, Pakistan and the Philippines, to name just a few.

Education, migration and fertility

Education appears to be an important factor influencing both rural–urban migration and levels of fertility. The relationship between education and migration, however, appears to be more powerful than that between education and fertility. Moreover, existing empirical evidence reveals that education influences labour mobility even more directly (i.e. through its impact on higher income expectations) than fertility.

Numerous studies of migration in the various Third World countries have documented the positive relationship between the educational attainment of an individual and his propensity to migrate from rural to urban areas. Basically, individuals with higher levels of education face wider urban–rural real income differentials and higher probabilities of obtaining modern-sector jobs than those with lower levels of education (see Chapter 14 for an explanation of how income differentials and job probabilities interact to determine migration patterns). The probability variable in particular accounts for the growing proportion of the more educated rural migrants in the face of rising levels of urban unemployment among the less educated.

With regard to the education and fertility relationship, the evidence is less clear. While most studies reveal an inverse relationship between the education of women and their size of family, particularly at lower levels of education, the mechanism through which education *per se* influences decisions regarding family size is still subject to considerable speculation.

Assuming that lower levels of urban unemployment (especially among the educated) and lower levels of fertility are important policy objectives for Third World governments, the basic issue is whether or not the continued rapid quantitative expansion of the formal educational system (and the resource allocation decisions implicit therein) will ameliorate or exacerbate the twin problems of rising urban unemployment and rapid population growth. The evidence (as well as the theory) seems to indicate once again that, given limited government resources, the further excessive quantitative expansion of school places beyond perhaps basic education is both undesirable and unwise. There are two main reasons for this contention.

First, as we discovered in Chapter 17, any rapid expansion of the formal primary system creates inexorable pressures on the demand for the expansion of secondary and tertiary school places. The net result is the widespread phenomenon of excessive expansion of school places in terms of real resource needs in many LDCs and the associated dilemma of rising levels of urban unemployment among a cadre of increasingly more educated and more politically vocal migrants.

Secondly, if, as many have argued, the education of women does affect their fertility behaviour primarily through raising the opportunity cost of their time in child-rearing activities, it follows that, unless sufficient employment opportunities for women (as well as for men) can be created, the reliance on educational expansion as a policy instrument for lowering fertility will be weak, if not totally ineffective.

We turn now to consider the economic relationships between education and migration and education and fertility separately and in more detail.

Education and migration

We have seen that the accelerated influx of rural migrants into urban centres is a phenemenon common to almost every Third World nation. The extraordinary growth of urban populations during the past decade can be attributed primarily to the large and, in many cases, growing scale of rural–urban migration. Many factors influence the decision to migrate but economic factors predominate, as almost all informed observers, regardless of their disciplinary training, agree. Sample surveys in Africa, Asia and Latin America invariably reveal that the overwhelming reason why people migrate is because wider opportunities for highly paid jobs exist in urban areas. Furthermore, individual country surveys consistently show that people living in rural areas who have been to school are far more likely to migrate than those with little or no formal education. In fact there seems to be a consistent positive correlation between an individual's level of education and his propensity to migrate.

In Chapter 14 we attempted to provide a theoretical framework for understanding the phenomenon of high, and in some cases, accelerating rates of rural–urban migration in the face of rising levels of urban unemployment. By focusing on expected income differentials, encompassing both the absolute urban–rural differential and the probability of obtaining an urban job, this framework can facilitate a better and more accurate analysis of the dynamics of rural–urban migration. This is especially so when analysing differential rates of migration by educational levels. Individuals with higher levels of educational certification tend to have a higher propensity to migrate than those with less education because: (1) the income disparity between what they can earn in urban areas compared with their rural opportunity costs is larger; and (2) they are more likely to obtain a lucrative modern-sector job.

The reason why the more educated are in an advantageous position and have a better chance of finding better paid urban jobs than the less educated is due not so much to their superior training as to the widespread 'filtering down' or 'occupational displacement' phenomenon which pervades the labour markets of LDCs (see Chapter 17). Faced with more applicants than job openings, governments and private employers tend to select individuals on the basis of their level of educational certification. As the urban labour supply continues to outpace demand, two forces are set in motion. On the demand side, jobs which were formerly filled by, say, those with primary schooling now require a secondary school certificate. On the supply side, job aspirants now need to get some extra years of further education in order to 'qualify' for jobs which only a few years earlier were being filled by those with less education.

The net result of these two forces is, as we have seen, the burgeoning of private demand for ever higher levels of formal education in order to meet more stringent job requirements (and the consequent explosive demand for primary education as a necessary first stage), the emergence of rising levels of unemployment and underemployment among the more educated, the growing proportion of the more highly educated among the migrant populations, the subsequent lowering of rural labour productivity, and the gradual drying-up of employment opportunities for those with limited education. Finally, given the strong political pressures for governments to try to satisfy the aggregate private demand for education (even though the social returns on such investment are likely to be considerably lower than net private benefits), there is an inexorable tendency to expand formal educational facilities often beyond the point where such investment can be said to be economically justified.

In order to break this vicious circle of excessive education and rising unemployment, immediate steps by LDC governments are needed to change the prevailing system of distorted labour market economic incentives which place an unduly high premium on the completion of more and more years of schooling. Restructuring educational systems to minimise the inherent (and, in many cases, inherited) urban bias, and to orient the curriculum more towards the real development needs of the nation (e.g. towards rural development), will have limited success in either curtailing rural–urban migration or changing students' attitudes unless there are also fundamental changes in incentives *outside* the educational system.

Education and fertility

Educational attainment is thought to influence many forms of behaviour, including, in the case of women's education, fertility behaviour. On the one hand, there is the direct relation between a woman's educational attainment and her propensity to enter the labour force. On the other, there is growing evidence of an inverse relationship between a woman's education and her fertility (i.e. more educated women tend to have fewer children). The apparent empirical linkages between educational attainment, labour force participation and fertility have been widely interpreted by economists to be the consequence of a causal mechanism in which education increases the opportunity cost of a woman's time through a positive effect on her earning opportunities in the labour force. Since it is assumed that child-rearing represents a time-intensive activity for the mother compared with other goods, it follows that the 'price' of children relative to that of other goods moves in line with the price of a woman's time. By linking fertility decisions within the framework of recent reformulations of the micro-theory of household behaviour (see Chapter 12), the conclusion is drawn that the rise in the price of a woman's time (or, alternatively, the opportunity cost of children) causes her to reallocate her time from non-market activities and leisure (i.e. being a housewife) to market labour force activities. Her desired and actual completed fertility will therefore decline. In short, education's effect on raising the 'price' of a woman's time is thought to account for the widely observed inverse empirical association between her educational attainment and her fertility behaviour.

There are reasons, however, why we should be somewhat cautious about this education–fertility hypothesis. First, if the expansion of women's employment opportunities is in fact the means through which education affects fertility, it may be important to identify the relative contribution of investment in job creating activities as compared with the simple expansion of educational facilities. Money allocated towards expanded female employment opportunities will probably affect fertility levels more directly than if the same funds were used to broaden women's access to education by expanding school facilities. Furthermore, it is one thing to find that educated women have fewer children than their less educated contemporaries. It is another thing to expect that this difference will predict how much a *general* increase over time in women's education in a country will diminish *overall fertility*. Clearly, the second effect will be weaker than the first, especially in countries plagued by high levels of unemployment.

Second, the education–labour-market–fertility hypothesis implies that investments in women's education may be less effective in reducing their fertility in rural areas where few women find jobs, regardless of their educational attainment. If reductions in fertility are to be viewed as an important social benefit of educating women, we must know more about how this change in behaviour is influenced by education and how it interacts with other economic and social forces in rural areas.

Finally, since educated women comprise a growing proportion of the urban migrant stream, the filtering down and occupational displacement phenomena described earlier and in the preceding chapter will apply equally to them, perhaps, even more so, in determining their probability of successfully securing wage employment in highly competitive urban labour markets. Women with limited education will have little or no chance of competing successfully for scarce urban jobs. They will therefore have to stay at school for many more years before fertility reduction via higher female employment becomes a reality. This may be a very costly way to curtail population growth.

We may note, in conclusion, that the social value and importance of an intentional expansion of educational opportunities for women is likely to be significant for a variety of economic and non-economic reasons. However, the rationale for such a differential expansion from the narrow perspective of potential fertility reduction is, compared with the alternatives, simply not convincing. Moreover, if education, especially at the higher levels, does have such a strong effect on the propensity to migrate from rural to urban areas, there may be an inherent conflict of goals in expanding formal educational opportunities beyond a basic education for all. In the absence of changes in labour market economic signals and incentives (wage levels, educational certification for jobs, etc.), ever higher levels of education for both men *and* women may merely lead to higher levels of urban unemployment, lower levels of agricultural output, and unchanged levels of fertility. In such economic circumstances, which in fact characterise many Third World nations, the further quantitative expansion without qualitative improvement (see next section) of formal educational opportunities may satisfy neither the objective of diminished rural–urban migration nor lower levels of fertility. In fact, both may be exacerbated.

Education and rural development

We argued in Chapter 16 that if national development is to become a reality in Third World nations there needs to be a better balance and integration between rural and urban development. Since most of the priority projects of the 1950s and 1960s focused on the modernisation and development of the urban sector, much more emphasis needs to be placed in future on expanding economic and social opportunities in rural areas. While agricultural development represents the main component of any successful rural development programme, simply because 80 per cent of Third World rural populations are engaged directly or indirectly in agricultural activities, rural development nevertheless must be viewed in a broader perspective.

First and foremost, it needs to be viewed in the context of far-reaching transformations of economic and social structures, institutions, relationships and processes in rural areas. The goals of rural development cannot simply be restricted to agricultural and economic growth. Rather, they must be viewed in terms of a balanced economic and social development with emphasis on the *equitable distribution* as well as the rapid generation of the benefits of higher levels of living. Among these broader goals, therefore, are the creation of more employment opportunities both on and off the farm; more equitable access to arable land; more equitable distribution of rural income; broadly distributed improvements in health, nutrition and housing; and, finally, a broadened access to the kind of formal (in school) and non-formal (out of school) education for adults as well as children that will have *direct relevance* to the needs and aspirations of rural dwellers.

How do present Third World systems of education fit into this holistic view of the meaning of rural development? Basically, not very well. In most Third World nations the formal primary school system is, with minor modifications, a direct transplant of the system in most developed countries. Emphasis is placed exclusively on literacy, numeracy and the learning of a foreign language (usually English or French). The method of instruction places emphasis on recitation, repetition and memorisation. The overriding goal is to prepare children to pass standard qualifying examinations for secondary schools and the curricula have a very strong urban bias. The priority needs of the greatest proportion of students – those who are destined to spend their lives living and working in rural areas – are given minimal attention. Major groups with important rural training needs such as out-of-school children and youth, women and small subsistence farmers are largely neglected by organised education programmes, both formal and informal. As a result, much of the primary education in the rural communities of developing nations contributes little to improving levels of agricultural productivity or towards assisting the student to function more effectively in his or her rural community.

What then might be the real and lasting educational needs for rural development? Philip H. Coombs, a noted educational economist, has provided one very appealing typology.[3] He groups these educational needs for both young people and adults, male and female, under four main headings:

1. *General or basic education.* Literacy, numeracy and elementary understanding of science and one's environment, etc. – what most primary and general secondary schools now seek to achieve.
2. *Family improvement education*, designed primarily to impart knowledge, skills and attitudes, useful in improving the quality of family life, on such subjects as health and nutrition, homemaking and child care, home repairs and improvements, family planning and so on.
3. *Community improvement education*, designed to strengthen local and national institutions and processes through instruction in such matters as local and national government, co-operatives, community projects and the like.
4. *Occupational education*, designed to develop particular knowledge and skills associated with various economic activities and useful in making a living.

For the most part only category 1 has been emphasised in most underdeveloped countries. But the types of learning needs required for the three main occupational subgroups of rural areas – farmers and farm workers, persons engaged in non-farm rural enterprises, and rural general services personnel – are likely to be very different from what is currently provided by most formal educational curricula. Table 18.1 shows how these learning needs vary from group to group within the rural environment. Effective and well-designed educational programmes catering for *each* of these three diverse occupational groups are needed if education is to make an important contribution to rural development.

[3] Philip H. Coombs with Manzoor Ahmed, *Attacking Rural Poverty: how nonformal education can help*, Johns Hopkins University Press, 1974, p. 15.

Table 18.1
Illustrative rural occupational groups and their learning needs

Groups	**Types of Learning needs** (at varying levels of sophistication and specialisation)
A. Persons directly engaged in agriculture 1. Commercial farmers 2. Small subsistence and semi-subsistence farm families 3. Landless farm workers	Farm planning and management; rational decision-making; record keeping; cost and revenue computations; use of credit Application of new inputs, varieties, improved farm practices Storage, processing, food preservation Supplementary skills for farm maintenance and improvement, and sideline jobs for extra income Knowledge of government services, policies, programmes, targets Knowledge and skills for family improvement (e.g., health, nutrition, home economics, child care, family planning) Civic skills (e.g., knowledge of how co-operatives, local government, national government function)
B. Persons engaged in off-farm commercial activities 1. Retailers and wholesalers of farm supplies and equipment, consumer goods and other items 2. Suppliers of repair and maintenance services 3. Processors, storers and shippers of agricultural commodities 4. Suppliers of banking and credit services 5. Construction and other artisans 6. Suppliers of general transport services 7. Small manufacturers	New and improved technical skills applicable to particular goods and services Quality control Technical knowledge of goods handled sufficient to advise customers on their use, maintenance, etc. Management skills (business planning; record keeping and cost accounting; procurement and inventory control; market analysis and sales methods; customer and employee relations; knowledge of government services, regulations, taxes; use of credit)
C. General services personnel: rural administrators, planners, technical experts 1. General public administrators, broad-gauged analysts and planners at subnational levels 2. Managers, planners, technicians, and trainers for specific public services (e.g., agriculture, transport, irrigation, health, small industry, education, family services, local government, etc.) 3. Managers of cooperatives and other farmer associations 4. Managers and other personnel of credit services	General skills for administration, planning, implementation, information flows, promotional activities Technical and management skills applying to particular specialities Leadership skills for generating community enthusiasm and collective action, staff team work and support from higher echelons

Source: Coombs, *op cit.*, p. 17.

Education and international migration: intellectual dependence and the 'brain drain'

In addition to the transfer of production and consumption technology, a major aspect of the international transfer of institutional technology lies in the area of transplanted formal educational systems. As has already been pointed out, Third World educational systems are, with minor modifications, almost identical to those of the developed nations – mainly former colonial countries such as France, England, Spain, Portugal, Belgium, Netherlands and the United States. Just as the international transfer of techniques of production may be ill-suited to the factor endowments and output priorities of less developed nations, so too the human resource needs of agrarian societies attempting to modernise may be and usually are quite different from those catered for by the formal educational systems of highly industrialised, highly urbanised and technologically sophisticated nations of the

Table 18.2
Gross immigration of professional and technical personnel from less developed countries into the United States, Canada, and United Kingdom, 1962–1977

Year	United States	Canada	United Kingdom	3-country sum
1962	9,024	1,381	—	—
1963	11,029	1,525	4,600	17,154
1964	11,418	1,873		
1965	11,001	3,707	3,230	17,938
1966	13,986	5,548	—	—
1967	23,361	7,897	2,900	34,158
1968	28,511	6,930	2,420	37,861
1969	27,536	7,585	1,720	36,841
1970	33,796	6,118	1,000	40,914
1971	38,647	5,184	1,270	45,101
1972	39,106	5,360	377	44,843
1973	31,939	—	—	—
1974	27,709	—	—	—
1975	29,856	7,531	—	37,387
1976	31,308	5,331	—	36,639
1977	34,510	3,626	—	38,136

Source: Edwin P. Reubens, 'International Migration in North-South Relations', in Edwin P. Reubens (ed.), *The Challenge of the New International Economic Order,* Westview Press, Colorado, 1981, p. 218.

West. The highly dysfunctional nature of such systems of formal education for Third World rural areas was portrayed in the previous section.

But in addition to rich-country dominance in the international development and transfer of physical and intellectual technology which tends to contribute to the widening income gap between developed and less developed nations, there is the problem of the international migration of high-level educated manpower – the so-called 'brain drain' – from poor to rich countries. Thousands of scientists, engineers, academics and doctors have been trained in home country institutions at considerable social cost only to reap the benefits from and contribute to the further economic growth of the already affluent nations. Table 18.2 reveals the annual magnitude of the professional and technical brain drain from the developing nations to North America and the United Kingdom for the period 1962 to 1977.

The international brain drain deserves mention, however, not only because of its effects on the rate and structure of LDC economic growth but also because of its impact on the style and approach of Third World educational systems. Thus, the brain drain has not merely reduced the supply of vital professional people available within the underdeveloped countries. Perhaps even more seriously, it has diverted the attention of *local* scientists, doctors, architects, engineers and academics away from important domestic problems. These include the development of appropriate technology, the promotion of low-cost preventive health care, the construction of low-cost housing, hospitals, schools and other service facilities, the design and building of functional yet inexpensive, labour-intensive roads, bridges and machinery, and the development of relevant university teaching materials such as appropriate introductory economics texts and the promotion of problem-oriented research on vital domestic development issues.

Instead, dominated by rich-country ideas as to what represents true international and professional 'excellence', those highly educated and highly skilled Third World professionals who do not physically migrate to the developed nations sometimes migrate 'intellectually' in terms of the orientation of their activities. This 'internal' brain drain can be much more serious than the external one. For example, one constantly finds doctors in less developed nations specialising in diseases of the heart while preventive tropical medicine is considered a second-rate speciality. Architects are concerned with the design of national monuments and 'modern' public buildings while low-cost housing, schools and clinics remain an area of remote concern. Engineers and scientists concentrate on the newest and most modern electronic equipment while simple machine tools, hand or animal-operated farm equipment, basic sanitation and water purifying systems, and labour-intensive mechanical processes are relegated to the attention of 'foreign experts'. Finally, academic LDC economists teach and research on irrelevant, 'sophisticated' mathematical models of non-existent competitive economies, while problems of poverty, unemployment, rural development and education are considered less intellectually 'interesting'.

In all these activities, criteria are based not on contributions to national development but rather on praise from the international community (i.e. professional mentors in the developed nations) as evidenced, for example, in the acceptance of an LDC scholar's publication in international professional journals or invitations for them to attend professional meetings in London, Paris, New York or Moscow.

The antidevelopmental effects of such professional attitudes and orientations in Third World nations (especially in former colonial countries) for a time tended to permeate the whole educational and intellectual establishment. While difficult to quantify in terms of rates of economic growth and levels of poverty, the combined brain drain and 'outward-looking' orientation of many LDC professionals has no doubt been an important contributing factor to the perpetuation of conditions of underdevelopment in the Third World. Recent student and faculty calls for more relevant curricula, teaching materials and research activities, however, attest to the emergence of a new spirit of nationalism and self-reliance which appears to be gathering momentum among Third World intellectuals. If a good university is to be more than 'just a collection of books' as the philosopher Thomas Carlyle once remarked, then Third World universities and professional schools have a vital role to play in making higher education more tuned to the real needs of social and economic development. Perhaps in ten years a section on 'intellectual dependence and the brain drain' will no longer be necessary. Let us hope so.

Major educational policy options[4]

Third World nations are confronted with two basic alternatives in their policy approaches to education. They can continue as in the past to expand formal systems quantitatively, with minor modifications in curricula, teaching methods and examinations, while retaining the same institutional labour market structures and educational costing policies. Or they can attempt to reform the overall educational system within the context of a people-oriented national development strategy which modifies both the conditions of demand for and the supply of educational opportunities in accordance with the real resource needs of the nation. In the author's view, the first alternative can only exacerbate the problems of unemployment, poverty, inequality, rural stagnation and international intellectual dominance that now define the very conditions of underdevelopment in much of Africa, Asia and Latin America. The second alternative is therefore preferable.

Since educational systems largely reflect and reproduce, rather than alter, the economic and social structures of the societies in which they exist, any programme or set of policies designed to make education more relevant for development needs must operate simultaneously on two levels:

1. modifying the economic and social signals and incentives *outside* the educational system which largely determine the magnitude, structure and orientation of the aggregate private demand for education and consequently the political response in the form of the public supply of school places;
2. modifying the *internal* effectiveness and equity of educational systems by appropriate changes in course content especially for rural areas, structures of public versus private financing, methods of selection and promotion, and procedures for occupational certification by educational level.

Only by policies designed *simultaneously* to achieve these two objectives can the positive links between education and development be successfully forged. We conclude, therefore, with a brief review of what these external and internal policies might specifically comprise.

[4] As in the preceding chapters, the policies put forward here are designed primarily to stimulate group discussion and individual analysis.

Policies external to educational systems: imbalances, signals and incentives

1. Minimising imbalances, incentive distortions and socio-political constraints

Policies which tend to remedy major economic imbalances and incentive distortions (e.g. in income and wage differentials) and to alleviate social and political constraints on upward mobility can have the multiple beneficial effect of increasing job opportunities, modifying the accelerated rate of rural–urban migration, and facilitating development-related modifications of educational systems.

2. Modification of job-rationing by educational certification

In order to break the vicious circle in which overstated job specifications make overeducation necessary for employment, policies are needed which will induce or require both public and private employers to seek realistic qualifications even though the task of job rationing may be made somewhat more difficult as a result. Basic to this procedure would be the elimination of school certificates for many of the jobs, especially in the public sector (janitors, messengers, filing clerks, etc.) which tends to set the pattern for the whole private sector.

3. Curbing the brain drain

Controlling or taxing the international migration of indigenously trained high-level professional manpower is a very sensitive area since it can potentially infringe on the basic human right and freedom to choose both the nature and the location of one's work. In a repressive regime that greatly limits human freedom, such a restrictive policy can be morally repugnant. On the other hand, however, when a nation invests scarce public financial resources in the education and training of its people only then to forgo the social returns on that investment as a result of international migration, it seems both economically and morally justifiable to seek either to restrict that movement in the national interest, or better, to tax if possible the overseas earnings of professional migrants and reinvest these revenues in programmes of national development. Such a tax on overseas earnings would act as an economic disincentive to migrate. Its implementation, however, would require the co-operation and assistance of the governments of countries to which these professionals migrate.

Policies internal to educational systems: efficiency, cost-effectiveness and relevance

1. Educational budgets

Where politically feasible, educational budgets should grow more slowly and be more oriented towards rural primary education.

In the light of growing unemployment among the educated, educational budgets of many Third World nations should grow more slowly than in the past to permit more funds to be used for the creation of employment opportunities. Moreover, a larger share of educational budgets should be allocated to the development of primary, as opposed to secondary and higher, education as a basis for self-education and rural work-related learning experiences.

2. Subsidies

Subsidies for the higher levels of education should be reduced. As a means of overcoming distortions in the aggregate private demand for education induced by excessive subsidies to education, especially at higher levels, policies should be promoted by which the beneficiary of education (as opposed to his family or society as a whole) would bear a larger and rising proportion of his educational costs as he proceeded through the system. This could be done either directly, through loan repayments, or by service in rural areas. At the same time low income groups should be provided with sufficient subsidies to permit them to overcome the sizable private costs (including 'opportunity costs') of schooling.

3. Primary school curricula in relation to rural needs

In order to maximise the productivity of rural human resources, primary school curricula as well as 'non-formal' educational opportunities for school dropouts and adults need to be directed more towards the occupational requirements of rural inhabitants whether in small-farm agriculture, artisan and entrepreneurial activities, or rural public and commercial services. Such curricula and task-related reorientations of rural learning systems, however, will not be effective in eliciting popular support unless **rural economic opportunities** are created through which small farmers, artisans and entrepreneurs can take advantage of their vocational knowledge and training. Without these incentives, people will justifiably view such formal and non-formal occupational training programmes with considerable scepticism. They would probably rather pursue the formal school certificate and take their chances in the urban job lottery.

4. Quotas

To compensate for the inequality effects of most existing formal school systems, some form of quotas may be required to ensure that the proportion of low-income students at secondary or higher educational levels at least approximates to their proportions in the overall population. Under present systems indirect quotas by income status often determine which students proceed through the educational system. Replacing this *de facto* quota system by an alternative which ensures that capable low-income students will be able to improve their own and their family's wellbeing by overcoming the financial barriers to educational advancement would go a long way to making educational systems true vehicles of economic and social equality. The nature of such quota systems will obviously vary from country to country. But there is no *a priori* basis for assuming that such a quota-by-income-level system will be any less efficient or socially productive for both growth and equity than the present system, which tends to perpetuate poverty and inequality while having a dubious impact on the overall rate of economic growth.

Conclusion: making education serve development

We conclude by reiterating a proposition with which we began the previous chapter; that it is the human resources of a nation that are largely responsible for its overall economic and social development. To make maximum effective use of these resources Third World nations need to orient their educational systems towards the real requirements and aspirations of all their people. We have seen that educational systems cannot make such an effective contribution if the economic and social structures in which they operate are inimical to the maximum participation of all people in both the work and the rewards of nation-building.

We have reviewed in these two chapters a range of economic, social and institutional factors *outside* the educational system which tend to create conditions of quantitative overexpansion of places in formal education. The widespread phenomena of rising levels of educated unemployment and the migration of the best and the brightest of rural youngsters into crowded urban slums attest to the validity of this assertion. Moreover, educational systems themselves, as now structured in many less developed countries, have a tendency to reinforce economic inequalities by promoting and then subsidising the education and hence the lifetime earning capacities of the already better-off segments of their populations. We have proposed a number of policy alternatives to combat this inherent, although in many cases largely unintentional, inegalitarian tendency of Third World educational systems.

We close with an admonition already expressed several times; that in the final analysis it will not be the imagination and perceptiveness of educational planners or economic policy advisors *alone* that will make education's contribution to national development a real and lasting one. It will also, perhaps more importantly, depend on the political will and the proven ability of Third World leaders to dedicate themselves and their policies to what President Julius Nyerere of Tanzania (a former schoolteacher) has called the 'furtherance of human equality, human dignity and human development'.

Concepts for review

basic education
family improvement education
international brain drain
socio-political constraints on educational mobility
economic 'signals' and incentives
equal educational opportunity
modern sector or urban bias of educational systems
internal effectiveness of educational systems
community improvement education
'functional' education
internal brain drain
educational subsidies
quota systems

Questions for discussion

1. Describe and comment on each of the following education-development relationships:
   (*a*) Education and economic growth: does education promote growth? How?
   (*b*) Education, inequality and poverty: do educational systems typical of most LDCs tend to reduce, exacerbate or have no effect on inequality and poverty? Explain with specific reference to your own country.
   (*c*) Education and migration: does education stimulate rural–urban migration? If so, why?
   (*d*) Education and fertility: does the education of women tend to reduce their fertility? If so, why and how?
   (*e*) Education and rural development: do most LDC formal educational systems contribute substantially to the promotion of rural development? Explain.
   (*f*) Education and the brain drain: what factors cause the international migration of high level educated manpower from LDCs to developed countries? What do we mean by the 'internal' brain drain? Explain, giving examples.
2. Governments can influence the character, quality and content of their educational systems by manipulating important economic and non-economic factors or variables both outside of and within educational systems. What are some of these external and internal factors and how can government policies make education more relevant to the real meaning of development?

Further reading

World Bank Education Sector Working Paper, Washington, December 1974, pp. 3–48; F. Champion Ward, ed., *Education and Development Reconsidered*, Praeger, New York, 1974.

See also Chapter 17.

Part Three Problems and policies – international

Chapter 19 International trade and economic development: the traditional view

The opening of a foreign trade . . . sometimes works a sort of industrial revolution in a country whose resources were previously underdeveloped.
John Stuart Mill, 1846

For unto everyone that hath shall be given, and he shall have abundance; but for him that hath not shall be taken away, even that which he hath.
Matthew 25:29; cf. 13:12

Introduction

The importance of international trade and finance

International trade has often played a crucial, though not necessarily a benign, role in the historical development of the Third World. Throughout Africa, Asia, the Middle East and Latin America primary product exports have traditionally accounted for a sizable proportion of individual gross national products. In some of the smaller countries, almost 25 to 30 per cent of the monetary GNP is derived from the overseas sale of agricultural commodities like coffee, tea, cotton, cocoa and sugar. In the special circumstances of the Persian Gulf oil-producing nations, the sale of unrefined and refined petroleum products to countries throughout the world accounts for almost 80 per cent of their national incomes. But, unlike the oil-producing states, most less developed countries must depend on *non*-mineral primary product exports for the vast majority of their foreign exchange earnings. Since the markets for these exports are often very unstable, primary product export dependence carries with it a degree of risk and uncertainty which few nations desire.

In addition to their export dependence, many developing countries rely even more on the importation of raw materials, machinery, capital goods, intermediate producer goods and consumer products both to fuel their industrial expansion and to satisfy the rising consumption aspirations of their people. For most non-petroleum-rich developing nations, import demands have exceeded the capacity to generate sufficient revenues from the sale of exports. This has led to chronic deficits on their balance of payments position *vis-à-vis* the rest of the world. While such deficits on the *current account* (i.e. an excess of import payments over export receipts for goods and services) were often more than compensated for by a surplus on the *capital account* of their balance of payments table (i.e. a receipt of foreign private and public lending and investment in excess of repayment of principal and interest on former loans and investments), in recent years the debt burden of repaying these earlier international loans and investments has become increasingly acute. In a number of LDCs severe deficits on both current and capital accounts, therefore, have led to a rapid depletion of their international monetary reserves. We explain the precise meaning of these and other concepts of international economics later in this chapter and in the next. Now we merely point out that a chronic excess of foreign expenditures over receipts (which incidentally may have nothing to do with an LDC's inability to handle its financial affairs but may, rather, be related to its vulnerability to global economic disturbances) can not only retard development efforts, it can also greatly limit a poor nation's ability to determine and pursue its most desirable development strategies.

But international trade and finance must be understood in a much broader perspective than simply the intercountry flow of commodities and financial resources. By opening their economies and societies to world trade and commerce and by looking outward to the rest of the world, Third World countries invite not only the intenational transfer of goods, services and financial resources, but also the developmental or antidevelopmental influences of the transfer of production technologies, consumption patterns, institutional and organisational arrangements, educational, health and social systems, and the more general values, ideals and life styles of the developed nations of the world, both capitalist and socialist. The impact of such technological, economic, social and cultural transfers on the character of the development process can be either benign or malevolent. Much depends on the nature of the political, social and institutional structure of the recipient country and its development priorities. Whether it is best for LDCs to look outward as the free traders and cultural internationalists advocate, or to look inward as the protectionists and cultural nationalists propose, or to be both simultaneously and strategically outward- *and* inward-looking in their international economic policies, as suggested by many middle-of-the-road economists, developing nations need to appraise their present and prospective situation in the world community realistically in the light of their specific development objectives. Only thus can they judge how much to expose themselves, if at all, to both the obvious benefits and the many dangers of international commerce.

Unfortunately, many small and very poor countries (and these constitute over half of all Third World nations) may have little choice whether to opt out or not. Even in these extreme cases the choice might not be simply of looking outward to the developed world for assistance or turning inward in an attempt to become more self-reliant. As we shall see, a more promising strategy, especially for the smaller LDCs, may be to look *both* outward but in a different direction (towards co-operation with other LDCs) and inward towards each other as members of a group of nations trying to integrate their economies and co-ordinate their joint development strategies.

The study of foreign trade and the international finance is among the oldest and most controversial branches of the discipline of economics. It dates back to the sixteenth century and Europe's mercantilist passion for Spanish gold. It flowered in the eighteenth and nineteenth centuries as modern economic growth was fuelled and propelled by the 'engine' of international trade. The greatest minds in economics – Adam Smith, David Ricardo and John Stuart Mill – provided the basic concepts and insights which to this day still endure. A deep and abiding concern with global international relations flourishes even more today, not only because of the still bitter controversies between those who champion more trade and those who advocate less, especially in the context of development, but also because modern transport and communications are rapidly shrinking the world to the point where some even refer to it as a 'global village'. It is for these and other reasons briefly mentioned above that we now begin our study of this very important and still very controversial field of economic analyses and policy.

Five basic questions about trade and development

In order to give our discussion contemporary relevance, our objective in this chapter is to analyse the main traditional theoretical approaches to the subject in the context of five basic questions of particular importance to Third World nations, individually and as a group.

1. How does international trade affect the rate, structure and character of LDC economic growth? This is the traditional 'trade as an engine of growth' controversy but set in terms of contemporary development aspirations.
2. How does trade alter the distribution of income and wealth within a country and among different countries or groups of countries? Is trade a force for international and domestic equality or inequality? In other words, how are the gains and losses distributed and who benefits?
3. Under what conditions can trade help LDCs to achieve their development objectives?
4. Can LDCs by their own actions determine how much they trade?
5. In light of past experience and prospective judgment, should LDCs adopt an outward-looking (freer trade, expanded flows of capital and human resources, ideas and technology, etc.) or an inward-looking (protectionism in the interest of greater self-reliance) policy or should they pursue some combination of both, for example in the form of regional economic co-operation? What are the arguments for and against these alternative trade strategies for development?

Clearly, the answers or suggested answers to these five central questions about trade and development will not be uniform throughout the diverse economies of the Third World. The whole economic basis for international trade is predicated on the fact that *countries do differ* in their resource endowments, their economic and social institutions, and their capacities for growth and development. Third World countries are no exception to this rule. Some are very populous yet deficient in natural resources and human skills. Others are sparsely populated yet endowed with abundant mineral and raw material resources. Still others (the majority) are small and economically weak, having at present neither the human nor the material resources on which to base a sustained and largely self-sufficient strategy of economic and social development. Yet, with the notable exception of the now very wealthy oil nations of the Middle East and a few other countries rich in internationally demanded mineral resources, most Third World nations face similar issues and choices in their international relations both with the developed countries and with each other. Consequently, while we shall try to place our generalisations about LDC trade prospects and policy alternatives in the context of a broad typology of Third World nations, our attempt to be catholic in coverage will necessitate a number of sweeping generalisations, many of which may not hold for a particular country at a particular time. On balance, however, we feel that the social benefits of this broad Third World perspective outweigh the social costs of our having to make some analytical and policy generalisations. Since the reader now possesses the economic tools for such a cost/benefit analysis, we leave it to his or her judgment to decide whether our approach has been fruitful or not.

Accordingly, we begin with a statistical summary of recent Third World trade performance and patterns. A simplified presentation follows of the classical and more recent theories of international trade and its effects on efficiency, equity, stability and growth (four basic economic concepts related to the central questions outlined above). Chapter 20 presents an extensive critique of free trade theories in light of both historical experience and the contemporary conditions and strategies of economic and social development. In succeeding chapters, some alternative trade and commercial policies for development are surveyed and the controversies surrounding each summarised.

The role of trade in development: a statistical review

Commodity exports

The export of commodities, of which primary products (food, food products, raw materials, oil, fuels) constitute over three-quarters of the total, provides by far the most important source of foreign exchange earnings for Third World nations. We see from Table 19.1, for example, that over the period from 1960 to 1978, receipts from commodity exports amounted to over 80 per cent of the total balance of payments receipts of the developing countries. They were more than twelve times as large as the value of official capital flows (foreign aid) to these countries in 1978. In other words, over the period from 1960 to 1978 the sale of commodities in foreign markets provided steadily greater amounts

Table 19.1
Major components of the balance of payments of Third World nations as a whole, 1960–1978 (in US $ billions)

Receipts or sources of funds	1960	1970	1978
Commodity exports	26.0	63.0	298.4
Official flows (gross)	4.8	9.9	49.1
Private investment	3.3	8.2	8.6
Private transfer payment (gross)	0.6	2.2	2.7
Allocation of Special Drawing Rights*	—	0.8	0.1
Total sources	34.7	84.1	358.9
Use of funds			
Commodity imports	29.5	64.8	271.1
Debt service	2.0	5.4	32.8
Other investment payments	3.0	7.6	3.9
Changes in reserves	−0.1	+3.0	15.2
Miscellaneous	0.3	3.3	35.9
Total uses	34.7	84.1	358.9

* See Chapter 21 for an explanation of the nature and function of Special Drawing Rights (SDRS).

Source: UNCTAD, *Handbook of International Trade and Development Statistics*, Supplement 1977, New York, 1978, Table 5.1, p. 178.
UNCTAD, *Handbook of International Trade and Development Statistics*, Supplement 1980, New York, 1981, Table 5.1, p. 250.

of foreign exchange than bilateral grants and loans (those provided by one government to another) and multilateral grants and loans (those from a variety of countries channelled through international organisations like the World Bank, the International Monetary Fund and the various regional development banks) combined.

Table 19.1, however, conceals the fact that for most LDCs the value of commodity exports over this period did not expand as fast as commodity imports, as it includes the export earnings of major oil producing countries. In 1979, for example, exports from developing countries amounted to $408.7 billion – 24.3 per cent of total world exports. However, the OPEC countries alone accounted for over half (219.0 billion) of this amount. In fact, the

Figure 19.1
Current account balances, by groups of countries, 1973–79 ($ billions)

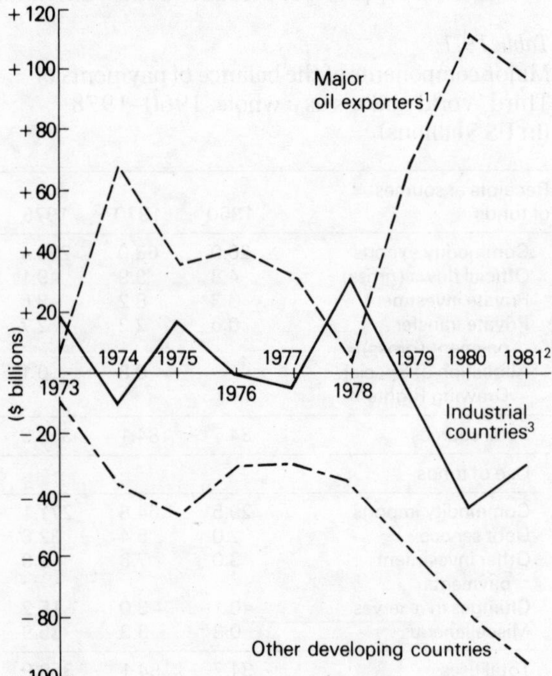

[1]Fund staff projections
[2]Australia, Finland, Greece, Iceland, Ireland, Malta, New Zealand, Portugal, Romania, South Africa, Spain, Turkey and Yugoslavia

Note: Centrally planned economies are not included.

Source: Overseas Development Council, *Agenda 1980*, Table E-1, p. 217, *UNCTAD Handbook of International Trade and Development Statistics Supplement*, 1980.

OPEC share of total world exports nearly doubled between 1960 and 1979, going from 6.7 per cent to 13.1 per cent. As a result and as shown in Figure 19.1, OPEC's excess of export earnings over import expenditures – its current account surplus – rose dramatically from slightly over $3 billion in 1973 to a high of $67 billion in 1974 (when oil prices quadrupled). Following 1974, the current account surplus hovered around $40 billion until 1978 when it plummeted to $12 billion as the OPEC governments made major investments in their economies that required enormous expenditures on imports. By 1980, however, the current account surplus peaked at $117 billion as oil prices were raised. In 1981–82, oil prices declined and so did OPEC's surplus. By contrast, the aggregate current account deficit of the non-oil exporting developing countries rose from an annual level of $11 billion in 1973 to $98 billion in 1980. This increased trade deficit alone exceeded the *total* annual flow of private foreign investments and public development assistance to *all* developing nations of the same period! Export and current account prospects for the non-oil, primary producers of the Third World look bleak for the first half of the 1980s.

If we look specifically now at the annual growth rate in the value of exports for the world as a whole and for its three sub-components (the 'First World' of developed market economies, the 'Second World' of developed socialist economies and the 'Third World' of developing countries) over the period 1950 to 1977, we find that between 1950 and 1970 First, Second and Third World exports grew at 7.0, 8.0 and 4.5 per cent annually. During the 1970 to 1977 period, however, the rates were 7.8, 10.4, and 3.0 respectively. These data are shown in Table 19.2.

As a result of the more rapid growth rates in the value of developed country (both capitalist and socialist) exports, their share of total world trade rose from 68.8 per cent in 1950 to 76 per cent in 1977. Again, if we exclude the major oil-exporting countries from Third World figures, we discover that the remaining less developed countries have been *losing ground* in terms of their proportionate share of total world trade in *every year* from 1950 to the end of the 1970s. For example, between 1960 and 1979 non-OPEC developing country exports fell from 14.8 per cent of total world exports to 12.4 per cent. This is an important indicator of their relatively weakened international trade position. The main

Table 19.2
Annual average growth rates of the value of exports

	1950–1960	1960–1970	1970–1977
World	7.0	7.1	7.3
Developed 'Market' countries	7.6	7.6	7.8
Developed 'Socialist' countries	8.0	8.0	10.4
Less developed countries	4.0	5.0	3.0

Source: *World Development Report, 1978*, Annex Table 6.

reason for this deteriorating position is that developed nations have been able to increase their share of world trade by annually exporting more to each other and to the Third World than the Third World countries have been able to export either to the developed nations or to themselves. Export trends for all LDCs appear favourable in Figure 19.2; however, if OPEC were excluded the value indices of LDC and DC exports would be reversed.

Moreover, during the past decade and a half the developing countries have been doing proportionately less trade with each other. The percentage of total exports going to each other remained roughly constant at 23 per cent between 1960 and 1979. In other words, Third World countries were

Figure 19.2
Unit value indices of exports from developed and developing countries (including OPEC), 1960–1979 (1970 = 100)

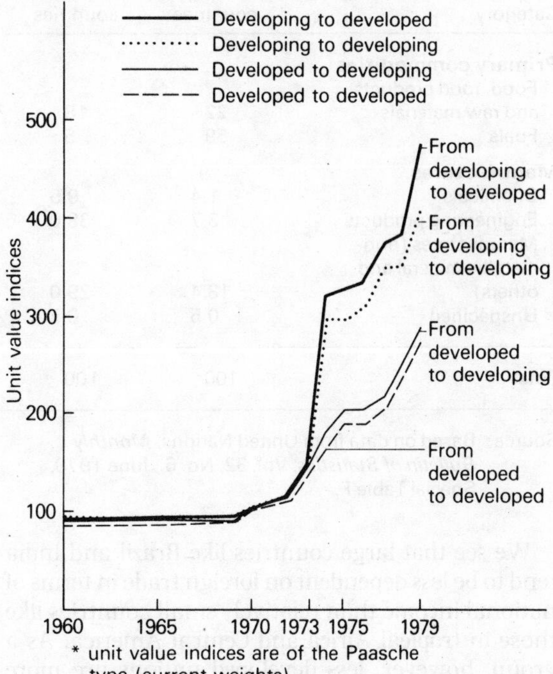

Source: *UN Monthly Bulletin of Statistics*, Vol. 35, No. 7, July 1981, Special Table E.

still as highly dependent as ever on rich countries for the sale of their products, while their own share of world trade was stagnating.

Table 19.3
Export earnings as a percentage of GNP in selected Third World countries, 1979

Country	Ratio of total exports to GNP
Ghana	24.2
Kenya	19.0
India	5.6
Sri Lanka	29.4
Zaire	18.5
Brazil	7.3
Colombia	15.4
Nicaragua	45.1
Philippines	16.4
Hong Kong	80.6
Nigeria	31.3
USA	7.5
USSR	6.0
France	18.4

Source: *World Development Report, 1981*, Annex tables 1,8.

Importance of exports in different Third World nations

While overall Third World figures for export growth rates and shares of total world exports are important indicators of patterns of trade for the group as a whole, the varying importance of exports and imports to the economic wellbeing of individual nations is masked by these aggregate statistics. In order, therefore, to provide a capsule picture of the relative importance of commodity export earnings to various Third World nations of different sizes and in different regions, Table 19.3 has been compiled. Comparisons with key developed countries are given at the bottom of the table.

Table 19.4
Commodity composition of exports, 1976

Category	Less developed countries	Developed countries
Primary commodities		
Food, food products and raw materials	22	18
Fuels	59	5
Manufactures		
Chemicals	1.4	9.5
Engineering products	3.7	38.0
Manufactures (non-metallic mineral and others)	13.4	29.0
Unspecified	0.5	0.5
Total	100	100

Source: Based on data from United Nations, *Monthly Bulletin of Statistics*, Vol. 32, No. 6, June 1978, Special Table F.

We see that large countries like Brazil and India tend to be less dependent on foreign trade in terms of national income than relatively small countries like those in tropical Africa and Central America. As a group, however, less developed nations are more dependent on foreign trade in terms of its share of national income than the highly developed countries. This is shown clearly in the USA and USSR, both of whose exports amount to less than 8 per cent of their respective GNP.

The composition of trade

Another critical dimension of the trade characteristics of Third World countries can be gleaned from analysis of the commodity composition of their exports and imports. As Table 19.4 shows, the LDCs depend heavily on their exports of raw materials and primary products while the developed nations export primarily manufactured goods.

We have an important clue here to why LDC export performance has been relatively weak compared with the export performance of rich countries. It all has to do with our elasticity of demand concept, introduced in Chapter 3. Most statistical studies of world demand patterns for different commodity groups tend to demonstrate that in the case of primary products the income elasticity of demand is relatively low. On the other hand for fuels, certain raw materials, and manufactured goods, the income elasticity is relatively high. For example, it has been estimated that a one per cent increase in developed country incomes will normally raise their import of foodstuffs from less developed countries by 0.6 per cent, agricultural raw materials like rubber and vegetable oils by 0.5 per cent, petroleum products and other fuels by 2.4 per cent and manufactures by about 1.9 per cent. Consequently, when incomes rise in rich countries their demand for food, food products and raw materials from the Third World nations goes up relatively slowly while the worldwide demand for manufactures, the production of which is dominated by the developed countries, goes up very rapidly.

Finally, the concentration of export production on a relatively few major primary commodities such as cocoa, tea, sugar and coffee renders certain LDCs very vulnerable to market fluctuations in specific products. For example, nearly half the Third World countries earn over 50 per cent of their export receipts from a single primary commodity, such as coffee, cocoa or bananas. Moreover, about 75 per cent of these nations earn 60 per cent or more of their foreign exchange receipts from no more than three primary products. Significant price variations, therefore, for these commodities can render development strategies highly uncertain. It is for this reason that international commodity agreements (such as those for coffee, cocoa and sugar) among primary producing nations exporting the same commodity have come into being in recent years.

The terms of trade

The question of changing relative price levels for different commodities brings us to another important quantitative dimension of the trade problems historically faced by Third World nations. The total value of export earnings depends not only on the **volume** of these exports sold abroad but also on the **price** paid for them. If export prices decline, a greater volume of exports will have to be sold merely to keep total earnings constant. Similarly, on the import side, the total foreign exchange expended depends on both the quantity and price of imports.

Clearly, if the price of a country's exports is falling *relative* to the prices of the products it imports, it will have to sell that much more of its export product and

Table 19.5
Terms of trade index numbers:* developed and developing countries 1960–1979 (1970 = 100)

Regions, countries and territories	1960	1963	1964	1965	1966	1967	1968	1969	1970	1971	1972	1973	1974	1975	1976	1977	1978	1979
Developed countries	107	107	110	109	107	109	109	109	111	110	111	110	97	100	99	98	100	97
Major oil exporters	33	30	30	30	29	29	29	29	30	33	34	36	99	100	106	107	94	114
Other developing countries	108	100	102	105	107	102	109	109	113	106	106	109	109	100	99	105	98	90

* Unit value index of exports divided by unit value index of imports.

Source: UNCTAD, *Handbook of International Trade and Development Statistics: Supplement 1980.* New York, 1981, Table 2.5.

enlist so much more of its productive factors merely to secure the same level of imported goods that it purchased in previous years. In other words, the real or social opportunity costs of a unit of imports will rise for a country when its export prices decline relative to its import prices.

Economists have a special name for the relationship or ratio between the price of a typical unit of exports and the price of a typical unit of imports. It is called the *commodity terms of trade* and it is expressed as P_x/P_m where P_x and P_m represent export and import price indices calculated on the same base period (e.g. 1970 = 100). The terms of trade are said to 'deteriorate' for a country if P_x/P_m falls, that is, if export prices decline relative to import prices, even though both may rise. Historically, the prices of primary commodities (the exports of most LDCs) have declined relative to manufactured goods (the principal exports of developed nations). As a result, the terms of trade of the non-oil exporting developing countries have on the average tended to worsen over time while they showed a relative improvement for the developed countries (see Table 19.5). For example, Table 19.5 shows that between 1960 and 1979 the terms of trade for developed countries slightly decreased while that of the Third World fell by almost 20 per cent (from 108 to 90). The LDCs therefore had to sell greater quantities of their primary products (the international demand for which, as we have seen, is relatively 'income inelastic') in order to purchase a given quantity of manufactured imports. One estimate has placed the extra costs of deteriorating terms of trade for the LDCs at over \$2.5 billion per year during the last decade. By contrast, oil exporting nations realized an extraordinary improvement in their terms of trade from an average of 33 in 1960 to 114 by 1979 (Table 19.5) and much higher by the end of 1981.

Much of the argument against primary product export expansion and in favour of diversification into manufactured exports for Third World countries during the 1950s and 1960s was based on this secular deterioration of their commodity terms of trade. But since past commodity price trends are no indication of what future prices will be (witness the dramatic rise and then fall in world food grain and other primary commodity prices during the 1973–1977 international economic period) and since the vulnerability of Third World nations is not confined solely to adverse movements in commodity terms of trade (how are these prices determined anyway?), it is important to understand both the basic theory and practice of international economics lest we lose sight of the forest by focusing on a single tree.

The traditional theory of international trade

Specialisation and the principle of comparative advantage: the classical labour-cost model

The phenomenon of transaction and exchange is

basic to human relationships throughout the world. Even in the remotest villages of Africa people regularly meet in the village market to exchange goods, sometimes for money but mostly for other goods through simple barter transactions. A transaction is an exchange of two things: something is given up in return for something else. In an African village women may barter food like cassava for cloth or simple jewellery for clay pots. Implicit in all transactions is a price. For example, if 20 cassavas are traded for say a metre of bark cloth, then the implicit price (or 'terms of trade') of the bark cloth is 20 cassavas. If in turn 20 cassavas can be exchanged in the same market for one small clay pot then it follows that clay pots and pieces of bark cloth can be exchanged on a one to one basis. A price system is already in the making.

Why do people trade? Basically, because it is profitable to do so. People possess different abilities and resources and may want to consume goods in different proportions. Different preferences as well as different physical and financial endowments open up the possibility of profitable trade. People usually find it profitable to trade the things they possess in large quantities (relative to their tastes or needs) in return for things they want more urgently. Since it is virtually impossible for each individual or family to provide itself with all the consumption requirements of even the simplest life, they usually find it profitable to engage in those activities for which they are best suited or have a 'comparative advantage' in terms of their natural abilities and/or resource endowments. They can then exchange any surplus of these home-produced commodities for products which others may be relatively more suited to produce. The phenomenon of specialisation based on comparative advantage arises, therefore, to some extent in even the most primitive of subsistence societies.

The same principles of specialisation and comparative advantage have long been applied by economists to the exchange of goods between individual nations in the form of international trade. In answer to the questions of what determines which goods are traded and why some countries produce some things while others produce different things, economists since the time of Adam Smith have sought the answer in terms of *international differences in costs of production and prices of different products.* Countries, like people, specialise in a limited range of production activities because it is to their advantage to do so. They specialise in those activities where the gains from specialisation are the largest.

But why, in the case of international trade, should costs differ from country to country? For example, how can Germany produce cameras, sewing machines and cars more cheaply than, say, Kenya and exchange these manufactured goods for Kenya's relatively cheaper agricultural produce (fruits, vegetables, coffee and tea)? Again, the answer is to be found in international differences in the structure of costs and prices. Some things (basically manufactured goods) are relatively cheaper to produce in Germany and can profitably be exported to other countries like Kenya; other things (like agricultural goods) can be produced in Kenya at a lower relative cost and are therefore imported into Germany in exchange for its manufactures.

The concept of *relative* cost and price differences is basic to the theory of foreign trade. It is known as the 'principle of comparative advantage'. It asserts that a country will specialise in the export of those products which it can produce at the lowest relative cost. To use our example, Germany may be able to produce cameras, cars *and* fruits and vegetables at lower *absolute* unit costs than Kenya, but since the commodity cost differences between countries are greater for the manufactured goods than for agricultural products, it will be to the advantage of Germany to specialise in the production of manufactured goods and exchange them for Kenya's agricultural produce. Thus, while Germany may have an absolute cost advantage in both commodities, its *comparative* cost advantages lies in manufactured goods. Conversely, Kenya may be at an absolute disadvantage *vis-à-vis* Germany in both manufacturing and agriculture in that its absolute unit costs of production are higher for both types of products. It can nevertheless still engage in profitable trade because it has a 'comparative' advantage in agricultural specialisation (or, alternatively, because its absolute cost disadvantage is less in agriculture). It is this phenomenon of differences in comparative advantage, therefore, that gives rise to profitable trade even among the most unequal of trading partners. In the following paragraphs we provide a simple numerical and graphical example of this fundamental principle.

Perhaps the best way to demonstrate the theoretical advantages of trade is to consider what would happen to a nation's production and consumption levels in its absence. Let us for simplicity and convenience divide the world into two groups: the Third World and the rest of the world. For the moment think of 'Third World' as a single country. Suppose Third World is endowed with 100 units of labour. It is capable of producing two types of goods, agricultural and manufactured goods. A unit of manufacturing output requires 5 units of labour while a unit of agricultural output may require only 1 labour unit. If these input–output relationships (i.e. 5 labour input units per unit of manufacturing output and 1 labour input unit per unit of agricultural output) are *fixed* by the prevailing technology, then if the entire labour supply were in manufacturing production, a total of 20 units could be produced. Alternatively, if all Third World labour were to engage in agriculture, a total of 100 units of output could be produced. Finally, if Third World wished to produce some of each of these two categories of goods, it could do so by transferring labour from one to the other in a **constant proportion** of five to one, i.e. for every additional unit of manufacturing output desired 5 units of labour and, therefore, 5 units of agricultural output will have to be sacrificed. In other words, if Third World were producing 100 units of agricultural output by applying all its labour to this sector and if it wanted to produce 10 units of manufactured goods, it would have to reduce its food output by 50 units (50 labourers). It therefore has the choice of producing any of the three options: 20 manufacturing and zero agriculture, zero manufacturing and 100 agriculture, or 10 manufacturing and 50 agriculture. In fact, it could theoretically produce any number of combinations along its 'production possibility' line BPA in Figure 19.3. Note that in this simple labour–cost model the production possibility line is straight because labour is the only variable factor of production and it is used in *fixed proportions* (constant quantities) for each unit of output. We revert to the typical bow-shaped production possibility curve in the next section.

Line BPA therefore represents *both* the production and the consumption possibilities of Third World, that is, if there are no unemployed resources its people could produce and consume any combination of manufactured and agricultural goods represented by line BPA. Moreover, the relative costs and prices of agriculture in terms of manufactured goods are reflected in the slope of line BPA, where the slope is measured by the vertical distance OB

Figure 19.3
Third World's production-possibility frontier

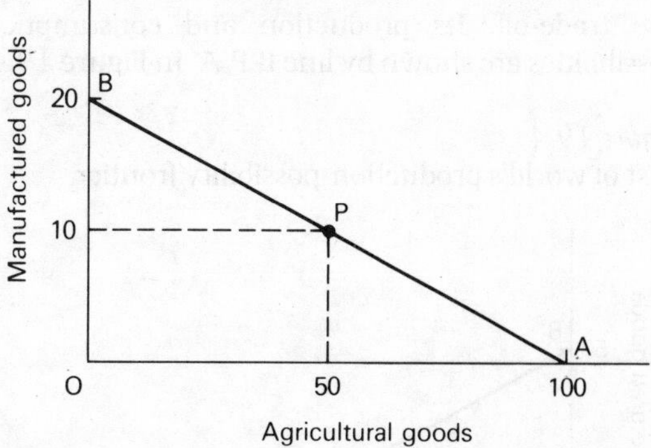

divided by the horizontal distance OA or, simply, OB/OA. This price ratio P_a/P_m is thus equal to $\frac{1}{5}$ (or 20/100 = OB/OA). A unit of manufactured goods costs five times as much as a unit of agricultural output because it requires five times as much labour and labour is the only scarce factor of production. In other words, in order to produce 5 more units of agricultural output, 1 unit of manufactured output will *always* have to be sacrificed. The actual production and consumption point in Third World's closed economy will be determined by domestic demand or consumer preference patterns which as we saw in Chapters 9 and 10 are greatly influenced by the domestic distribution of income. Let's assume that point P represents this final combination – i.e. 10 units of manufactured goods and 50 units of food are being produced and consumed in Third World's closed economy.

Now let us open up the possibility of trade by introducing another country which we shall call 'Rest of the World'. For simplicity, assume that in Rest of the World everything is the same as in Third World, including the same availability of 100 labour units. The only difference is that instead of requiring 5 units of labour as in Third World to produce one unit of manufactured output, Rest of World requires only two labour input units. Rest of World is thus a more efficient (lower cost) producer of manufactured goods than is Third World. Assume agriculture requires the same one labour input per unit of output as in Third World. Both 'countries', therefore, are equally efficient in food production (i.e. they have the same real labour costs per unit of output). If Rest of World's labour resources are fully employed, it is capable of producing 50 units of manufacturing output and no agriculture or 100 agriculture and no manufacturing; or any combination between these two extremes with a two-to-one trade-off. Its production and consumption possibilities are shown by line B′P′A′ in Figure 19.4.

Figure 19.4
Rest of world's production-possibility frontier

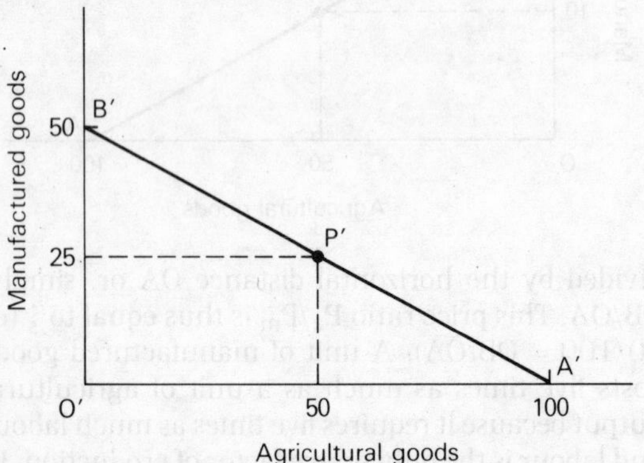

Note once again that the slope of this production possibility line will depict the relative costs and prices of Rest of World's agriculture in terms of its manufactured goods, (P_a/P_m). This slope will be equal to $\frac{1}{2}$ – i.e. $O'B'/O'A' = \frac{1}{2}$. For each unit of manufacturing output sacrificed, two units of agricultural output can be produced. Assume that Rest of World's domestic demand structure results in point P′ being the effective production and consumption combination, i.e. 50 units of food and 25 manufactured goods are produced and consumed.

Now if we allow Third World to trade with Rest of World, their differing cost and price structures create the possibility of profitable exchange for both. Even though Rest of World is just as efficient as Third World in agriculture (i.e. both require 1 unit of labour per unit of output), it is much more efficient in manufacturing, where it requires only two-fifths as much labour to produce a unit of output. Rest of World, therefore, has a comparative advantage and should specialise in the production of manufactured goods. Conversely, even though Third World does not have an absolute productivity and cost advantage in either commodity *vis-à-vis* Rest of World, it does have a comparative advantage in agricultural production. It should therefore specialise in food production and export the excess

Figure 19.5 The theoretical benefits of free trade between Third World and rest of world

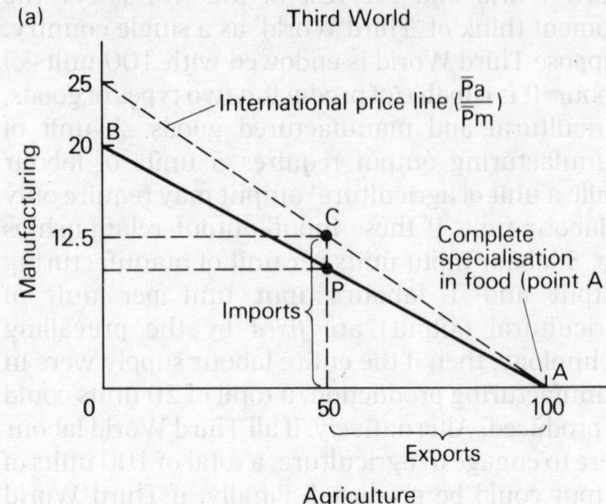

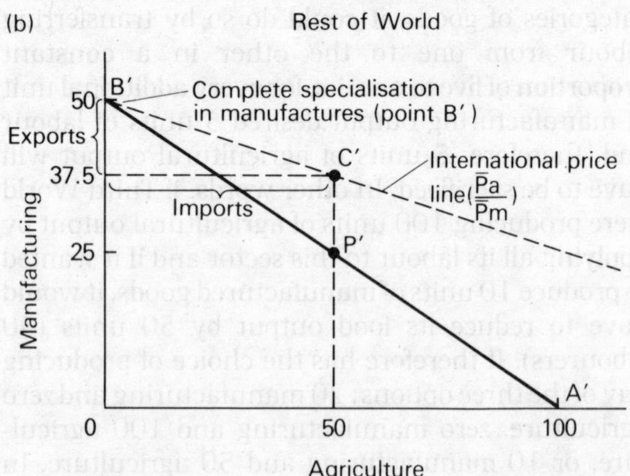

over its domestic consumption requirements in exchange for Rest of World's manufactured goods.

The opportunity for free trade between Third World and Rest of World will in theory create one worldwide market for goods with a single common price ratio. This world price ratio $(\bar{P}_a/\bar{P}_m)$ will depend on relative demand conditions in both regions for both commodities. It will have to settle somewhere between the two extremes of 1:5 and 1:2 in Third World and Rest of World in order for profitable trade to occur for both. Suppose it settled at 1:4 – i.e. a unit of manufactured goods trades for four units or, is four times as expensive as a unit of agriculture in 'world' commodity markets. Third World, therefore, could *completely specialise* in food production by producing 100 units. At the international price of one to four, it could then exchange, say, 50 units of its food for 12.5 units of Rest of World's manufactured goods. Third World's final (after trade) consumption combination, therefore, would be 50 units of food and 12.5 units of manufactured goods. This combination is shown by point C in Figure 19.5(*a*).

Similarly, Rest of World could specialise completely in the production of manufactures by producing 50 units of manufactured goods and trading 12.5 of these to Third World in return for 50 units of food products. Its consumption combination, therefore, would be 37.5 units of manufactured goods and 50 units of agricultural goods as shown by point C′ in Figure 19.5(*b*).

Figure 19.5 can now be used to show the two major theoretical benefits of free trade. The first is that **trade enables all countries to escape from the confines of their resource endowments and consume commodities in combinations that lie outside their production possibility frontiers.** This is clearly shown in both (*a*) and (*b*). By specialising in food production and engaging in trade, Third World is able to consume the same amount of food as before trade (i.e. 50 units) but 25 per cent more manufactured goods (i.e. 12.5 compared with 10). It is therefore clearly better off as a nation in terms of the total availability of goods. How these goods are distributed and who benefits is another question, and one which we take up later. Similarly, Rest of World by specialising completely in the production of manufactured goods and trading these at international prices with Third World is able to consume the same quantity of food as before (50 units) but 50 per cent more of its own manufactured goods (37.5 compared with 25) as shown by point C′ in diagram (*b*). It clearly is also better off. Note that both countries could have wound up consuming more of *both* commodities if they so desired. Thus, the important conclusion is drawn that **free international trade will benefit all nations of the world**, even though the benefits may be disproportionately distributed depending on world demand conditions and cost differences for different commodities in different countries.

The second major implication of the classical theory of international trade is that **free trade will maximise global output** by permitting every country to specialise in what it does best, i.e. by concentrating on the production of those goods in which it has a comparative advantage. We see from Figure 19.4 that without trade total world production and consumption of food and manufactured goods would equal 100 and 35 units respectively (points P + P′). As a result of specialisation and trade, total world output of food stayed the same while world manufacturing output increased by over 40 per cent, from 35 to 50 units. Clearly, using other labour input coefficients we could demonstrate that specialisation and trade can lead to world output increases for *all* traded commodities. Finally, note that commodity trade is balanced in the sense that the value of exports equals the value of imports in both regions. This is an important assumption of classical trade theory.

Relative factor endowments and international specialisation: the neo-classical model

The two-country, two-product, classical theory of free trade just presented is a static model based strictly on a one variable factor labour cost, complete specialisation approach to demonstrating the gains from trade. This nineteenth-century free trade model primarily associated with David Ricardo and John Stuart Mill was modified and refined in the twentieth century by two Swedish economists, Eli Hecksher and Bertil Ohlin, to take into account differences in factor supplies (mainly land, labour and capital) on international specialisation. The Hecksher–Ohlin neo-classical (i.e. variable proportions) factor endowment approach also enables one to describe analytically the impact of economic growth on trade patterns and the impact of trade on the structure of national economies and on the differential returns or payments to various factors of production.

Unlike the classical labour cost model, however, where trade arises because of fixed but differing labour productivities for different commodities in different countries, the factor endowment model assumes away inherent differences in relative labour productivity by postulating that **all countries have access to the same technological possibilities for all commodities.** If domestic factor prices were the same, all countries would use identical methods of production and therefore have the same relative domestic product price ratios and factor productivities. The basis for trade arises, therefore, not because of inherent technological differences in labour productivity for different commodities between different countries but because **countries are endowed with different factor supplies**. Given different factor supplies, relative factor prices will differ (e.g. labour will be relatively cheap in labour-abundant countries) and so too will domestic commodity price ratios and factor combinations. Countries with cheap labour will have a relative cost and price advantage over countries with relatively expensive labour in those commodities which make abundant use of labour (e.g. primary products). They should therefore focus on the production of these labour-intensive products and export the surplus in return for imports of capital-intensive goods.

On the other hand, countries well endowed with capital will have a relative cost and price advantage in the production of manufactured goods which tend to require relatively large inputs of capital compared with labour. They can then benefit from specialisation and export of their capital-intensive manufactures in return for imports of labour-intensive products from labour-abundant countries. Trade therefore serves as a vehicle for a nation to capitalise on its abundant resources through more intensive production and export of those commodities that require large inputs of those resources, while relieving its factor shortage through the importation of commodities that utilise large amounts of its relatively scarce resources.

To sum up, the factor endowment theory is based on two crucial propositions:

1. **Different products require productive factors in different relative proportions**. For example, agricultural products generally require relatively greater proportions of labour per unit of capital than manufactured goods which require more machine time (capital) per worker than most primary products. The proportions in which factors are actually used to produce different goods will depend on their relative prices. But, no matter what factor prices may be, the factor endowments model assumes that certain products will always be relatively more capital-intensive while others will be relatively more labour-intensive. These relative factor intensities will be no different in India from those in the United States; primary products will be the relatively labour-intensive commodities compared with, say, secondary manufactured goods in both India and the United States.
2. **Countries have different endowments of factors of production**. Some countries like the United States have large amounts of capital per worker and are thus designated as 'capital-abundant' countries while others like India, Egypt or Colombia have little capital and much labour. They are thus designated as 'labour-abundant' nations. In general, developed countries are assumed to be relatively capital-abundant (one could also add that they are well endowed with skilled labour) while, for the most part, Third World countries have little capital and much unskilled labour, i.e. they are labour-abundant countries.

The factor endowments theory goes on to argue that capital-abundant countries will tend to specialise in such products as motor cars, aircraft, sophisticated electronic communication goods, computers, etc., which utilise capital intensively in their technology of production. They will export some of these capital-intensive products in exchange for those labour- or land-intensive products like food, raw materials and minerals which can best be produced by those countries that are relatively well endowed with labour and/or land.

This theory, described in much of the early literature on trade and development, encouraged Third World countries to focus on their labour- and land-intensive primary product exports. It was argued that by trading these primary commodities for the manufactured goods that developed countries were 'best suited' to produce, Third World nations could best realise the enormous benefits from free trade with the richer nations of the world. This free trade doctrine also served the political interests of colonising nations searching for raw materials to feed their industrial expansion and for market outlets for their manufactured goods.

The mechanism through which the benefits of trade are transmitted across national boundaries under the factor endowments approach is analogous to that of the classical labour-cost approach. Only in the factor endowment case with the possibility of differing factor combinations for producing different commodities, nations are assumed to be operating initially at some point on their concave (or increasing opportunity cost) production-possibility frontier determined by domestic demand conditions. Point A on Third World production-possibility frontier P–P in Figure 19.6(*a*) provides an example. With full employment of all resources and under perfectly competitive assumptions, Third World will be producing and consuming at point A where the relative price ratio, P_a/P_m, will be given the slope of the dotted line $([P_a/P_m]T)$ at point A.[1] Similarly, Rest of World may be producing and consuming at point A′ in Figure 19.6(*b*) with a domestic price ratio $([P_a/P_m]R)$ which differs (i.e. agricultural goods are relatively dearer or, conversely, manufactured goods relatively cheaper) from that of Third World. Note, with a closed economy both countries will be producing *both* commodities. However, Third World, being poorer, will produce a greater proportion of food products in its (smaller) total output.

The relative differences in costs of production and prices at points A and A′ (i.e. their different slopes) gives rise once again to the possibilities of profitable trade. As in the previous labour-cost model, the international free trade price ratio $(\bar{P}_a/\bar{P}_m)$ will settle somewhere between $([P_a/P_m]T)$ and $([P_a/P_m]R)$ the domestic price ratios of Third World and Rest of World respectively. The lines $(\bar{P}_a/\bar{P}_m)$ in Figure 19.6(*a*) and (*b*) denote the common world price ratio. For Third World, this steeper slope of $(\bar{P}_a/\bar{P}_m)$ means that it can get more manufactured goods for a unit of agriculture than in the absence of trade, that is the world price of agricultural goods in terms of manufactures is higher than Third World's domestic price ratio. It will therefore reallocate resources away from its costly capital-intensive manufacturing sector and specialise more on labour-intensive agricultural production. Under perfectly competitive assumptions it will produce at point B on its production frontier where its relative production (opportunity) costs are just equal to relative world prices. It can then trade along $(\bar{P}_a/\bar{P}_m)$, the prevailing international price line, exporting BD agricultural products in return for DC manufactured imports and arrive at a final consumption point C with more of *both* goods than before trade. To give a numerical example, suppose the free trade international price ratio, $(\bar{P}_a/\bar{P}_m)$ were

Figure 19.6
Trade with variable factor proportions and different factor endowments

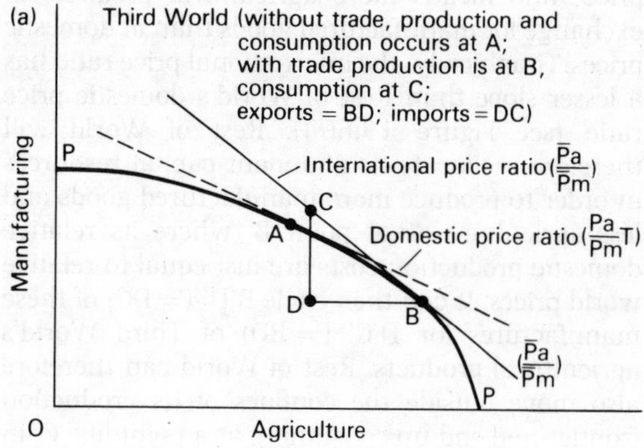

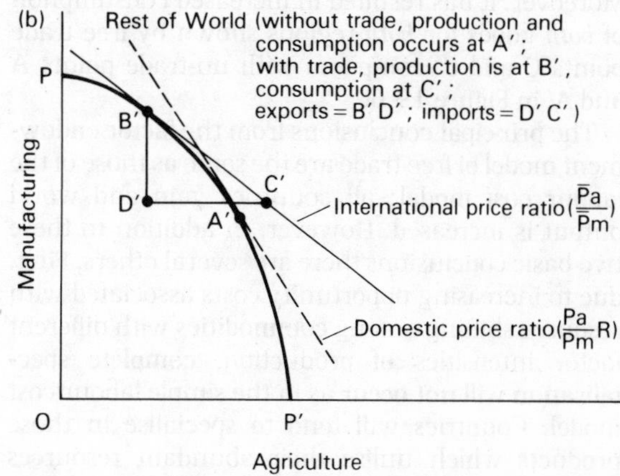

2 to 1; i.e. that a unit of agricultural goods sells at a price twice that of a unit of manufactured goods. This means that for every unit of agriculture which Third World exports to Rest of World, it can import *two* units of manufactured goods. The slope of the international price line graphically portrays this trading ratio or terms of trade. Therefore, if Third

[1] Recall from Chapter 7 that the slope of a line tangent to any point on the concave production possibility frontier will show the opportunity or real costs of reducing the output of one commodity in order to produce more of the other at that point on the curve. In a world of perfect competition these relative costs would also equal relative market prices. Therefore, the slope of the dotted line tangent to point A also shows relative commodity prices. The steeper the slope the higher would be the price of 'a' relative to 'm'. As we move from left to right, e.g. from point A to point B in Figure 19.6(*a*), the slope of the tangent line becomes progressively steeper, indicating the increasing opportunity costs of producing more food. Similarly a right to left movement along the production frontier (from B to A) would represent increasing opportunity cost of producing more manufactured goods in terms of forgone food output.

World exports BD agriculture (e.g. 30 units), it will receive DC manufactures (60 units) in return.

Similarly, for Rest of World the new international price ratio means more agricultural products in exchange for manufactured goods than at domestic prices. Graphically, the international price ratio has a lesser slope than Rest of World's domestic price ratio (see Figure 19.6(*b*)). Rest of World will therefore reallocate its abundant capital resources in order to produce more manufactured goods and less agriculture as at point B′ where its relative domestic production costs are just equal to relative world prices. It can then trade B′D′ (= DC) of these manufactures for D′C′ (= BD) of Third World's agricultural products. Rest of World can therefore also move outside the confines of its production frontier and end up consuming at a point like C′ in Figure 19.6(*b*). Trade is balanced: the value of exports equals the value of imports for both regions. Moreover, it has resulted in increased consumption of *both* goods for *both* regions shown by free trade points C and C′ compared with no-trade points A and A′ in Figure 19.6.

The principal conclusions from the factor endowment model of free trade are the same as those of the labour cost model: all countries gain and world output is increased. However, in addition to these two basic conclusions there are several others. First, due to increasing opportunity costs associated with resource shifting among commodities with different factor intensities of production, **complete specialisation will not occur** as in the simple labour cost model. Countries will tend to specialise in those products which utilise their abundant resources intensively. They will compensate for their scarce resources by importing those products which utilise these scarce resources most intensively. But rising domestic costs and, therefore, prices in excess of world prices will prevent complete specialisation from occurring.

Second, given identical technologies of production throughout the world, the equalisation of domestic product price ratios with the international free trade price ratio **will tend to equalise factor prices across trading countries.** Wage rates, for example, will rise in the labour-abundant Third World as a result of the more intensive use of human resources in the production of additional agricultural output. On the other hand, the price of scarce capital will decline due to the diminished production of manufactured goods which are heavy users of capital. In Rest of the World, the price of its abundant capital will rise relative to its scarce labour as more emphasis is placed on the production of capital-intensive manufactured goods and less on labour-intensive agriculture.

The factor endowment, variable factor proportions theory, therefore, makes the important prediction that **international real wage rates and capital costs will gradually tend towards equalisation.** This is also one of its greatest defects since we know that in the real world just the opposite is happening; that international income inequalities are increasing with each passing year. We shall see below how the restrictive and unreal assumptions of both the labour cost and factor endowment theories can often lead to erroneous conclusions about the actual structure of world trade and the distribution of its benefits.

Third, within countries the factor endowment theory of trade predicts that the **economic return to owners of the abundant resources will rise in relation to owners of scarce resources** as the abundant factor is more intensively utilised. In Third World countries this in general would mean a rise in the share of national income going to labour. In the absence of trade labour's share might be smaller. Thus **trade tends to promote more equality in domestic income distributions.**

Finally, by enabling countries to move outside their production possibility frontiers and secure capital as well as consumption goods from other parts of the world, **trade is assumed to stimulate, or be an 'engine' of, economic growth.** It also enables a nation to obtain those domestically expensive raw materials and other products (as well as knowledge, ideas, new technologies, etc.) with which it is relatively less well endowed at lower world market prices. It can thus create the conditions for a more broadly based and self-sustaining growth of a nation's industrial output.

Trade theory and development: the traditional arguments

The classical labour cost and the more recent neoclassical factor endowment theories of international trade provide the following theoretical answers to our five basic questions about trade and development.

1. **Trade is an important stimulator of economic**

growth. It enlarges a country's consumption capacities, increases world output and provides access to scarce resources and worldwide markets for products without which poor countries would be unable to grow.
2. **Trade tends to promote international and domestic equality** of factor returns and raise the real income of trading countries by making efficient use of each nation's and the world's resource endowments – e.g. raising relative wages in labour-abundant countries and lowering them in labour-scarce nations.
3. **Trade helps countries to achieve development** by promoting and rewarding those sectors of the economy where individual countries possess a comparative advantage whether in terms of labour efficiency or factor endowments.
4. In a world of free trade, **international prices and costs of production determine how much a country should trade** in order to maximise its national welfare. Countries should follow the dictates of the principle of comparative advantage and not try to interfere with the 'free' workings of the market.
5. Finally, in order to promote growth and development, **an outward looking internationalist policy is required.** In all cases, self-reliance and autarky based on isolation are asserted to be economically inferior to participation in a world of free and unlimited trade.

Such are the main contents and conclusions of the traditional theory of international trade. In the next chapter, we focus on a number of the theoretical and empirical arguments *against* this maximal free trade position in the context of Third World development. We then consider whether some kind of realistic balance can be struck in view of the realities of the contemporary world economy and the goals and aspirations of developing nations.

Concepts for review

export dependence
intermediate producer goods
primary products
commodity composition of trade
export concentration
commodity terms of trade
comparative advantage
absolute advantage
barter transactions
specialisation
foreign exchange earnings
commercial policy
consumption possibility line
foreign reserves
closed v. open economy
domestic v. international price ratios
free trade
gains from trade
labour theory of value
resource endowments
factor endowment trade theory
variable proportions production possibilities
labour-abundant v. capital-abundant nations
factor price equalisation
factor mobility

Questions for discussion

1. The effects of international trade on a country's development are often related to four basic economic concepts: efficiency, growth, equity and stability. Briefly explain what is meant by each of these concepts as they relate to the theory of international trade.
2. Compare and contrast the classical labour cost theory of comparative advantage with the neo-classical factor endowments theory of international trade. Be sure to include an analysis of assumptions and conclusions as well as diagrammatic illustrations.
3. Briefly summarise the major conclusions of the traditional theory of free trade with regard to its theoretical effects on world and domestic efficiency, world and domestic economic growth, world and domestic income distribution, and the pattern of world production and consumption.
4. Proponents of free trade, primarily developed country economists, argue that the liberalisation of trade relationships between rich and poor countries (i.e. the removal of tariff and non-tariff barriers) would work towards the long-run benefit of *all* countries. Under what conditions might the removal of all tariffs and other impediments to trade work to the best advantage of Third World countries? Explain.

Further reading

For an explication of the traditional classical and neo-classical theories of free trade, see: Peter Kenen, *International Economics*, 2nd Edition, Prentice-Hall. New Jersey, 1967; Gerald M. Meier, *The International Economics of Development: Theory and Policy*, Harper & Row, New York, 1968, ch. 2.

Chapter 20 Trade and development: theory and reality

> One of the dominant features of the presentday world order is the unequal relationship between the developed and the developing countries. The developing countries are poor and weak and, in any international bargaining, they are conveniently ignored or easily squeezed.
> *Statement of Third World Social Scientists, Santiago, 1973*

Introduction

Having presented the main features of the two major traditional theories of free trade, the classical labour cost and neo-classical factor endowment theories, we now scrutinise these theories carefully and ascertain to what extent their assumptions and conclusions fit the reality of contemporary international economic relations. Accordingly we begin this chapter by examining the relevance of traditional free trade theories in the light of Third World experience. Many Third World economists have been extremely critical of the trading relationships between developed and less developed nations. We examine this criticism and see how it alters our conclusions about the five questions posed at the beginning of Chapter 19. The chapter ends with an attempt to see whether any middle ground can be found between advocates and opponents of outward-looking international economic policies for Third World countries.

Some criticisms of traditional free trade theories in the context of Third World experience

Both the classical labour cost and the more recent (neo-classical) factor endowment theories of international trade are based on a number of explicit and implicit assumptions which in many ways are contrary to the reality of contemporary international economic relations. These theories therefore often lead to conclusions foreign to both the historical and contemporary trade experience of many Third World nations. This is not to deny the potential benefits of free trade, but rather to recognise that free trade exists mostly in the diagrams and models of economists, whereas the real world is beset by all varieties of national protection and international non-competitive pricing policies.

What are the major and crucial assumptions of the traditional theories of international trade, and how are these assumptions violated in the real world? What are the implications for Third World trade and international financial prospects of a more realistic assessment of the actual mechanism of international economic and political relations?

There are six basic assumptions of the classical and neo-classical trade models.

1. All productive resources are fixed in quantity and constant in quality across nations. They are fully employed and there are no movements (or mobility) of productive factors between countries.
2. The technology of production is fixed (classical model) or similar and freely available (factor endowment model) to all nations. The spread of such technology works to the benefit of every nation. Consumer tastes are also fixed and independent of the influence of producers: international 'consumer sovereignty' prevails.
3. Within nations, factors of production are per-

fectly mobile between different production activities and the economy as a whole is characterised by the existence of 'perfect competition'. There are no risks and uncertainties.
4. The national government plays no role in international economic relations, so that trade is strictly carried out among many atomistic and anonymous producers seeking to minimise costs and maximise profits. International prices are therefore set by the forces of supply and demand.
5. Trade is balanced for each country at any moment of time and all economies are readily able to adjust to changes in international prices with a minimum of dislocation.
6. The gains from trade that accrue to any country benefit the nationals of that country.

We can now take a critical look at each of these assumptions in the context of the contemporary position of Third World countries in the international economic system.

Fixed resources, full employment and the international immobility of capital and skilled labour

Trade and resource growth

This initial assumption about the static nature of international exchange, i.e. that resources are fixed, fully utilised and internationally mobile is central to the whole traditional theory of trade and finance. In reality, the world economy is characterised by rapid change while factors of production are fixed neither in quantity nor quality. Not only do capital accumulation and human resource development take place all the time, but trade has always been and will continue to be one of the main determinants of the unequal growth of productive resources in different nations. This is especially true with respect to those resources most crucial to growth and development such as physical capital, entrepreneural abilities, scientific capacities, the ability to carry out technological research and development and the upgrading of technical skills in the labour force.

It follows, therefore, that relative factor endowments and comparative costs are *not* given, but are in a state of constant change. Moreover, they are often determined by, rather than determining, the nature and character of international specialisation. In the context of unequal trade between rich and poor nations, this means that **any initial state of unequal resource endowments will tend to be reinforced and exacerbated by the very trade which these differing resource endowments were supposed to justify**. Specifically, if rich nations as a result of historical forces are relatively well endowed with the vital resources of capital, entrepreneurial ability and skilled labour, their continued specialisation in products and processes which intensively utilise these resources will create the necessary conditions for their further growth. On the other hand, Third World countries endowed with abundant supplies of unskilled labour, by specialising in products which intensively employ unskilled labour, and whose world demand prospects and terms of trade may be very unfavourable, may find themselves 'locked in' to a stagnant situation which perpetuates their 'comparative advantage' in unskilled productive activities. This in turn may inhibit the domestic growth of needed capital, entrepreneurship and technical skills.

A cumulative process is therefore set in motion in which trade exacerbates already unequal trading relationships, distributes the benefits largely to those who already have, and perpetuates the physical and human resource underdevelopment that characterises Third World nations. No country likes to think of itself specialising in unskilled labour activities while letting foreigners reap the rewards of higher skills, technology and capital. By pursuing the theoretical dictates of their factor endowments, less developed countries may lock themselves into a domestic economic structure that reinforces such relatively poor endowments and is inimical to their long-run development aspirations.

Unemployment, resource underutilisation and the 'vent for surplus' theory of trade

The assumption of full employment in traditional trade models, like that of the standard perfectly competitive equilibrium model of micro-economic theory, violates the reality of unemployment and underemployment in Third World nations. Two conclusions may be drawn from the recognition of widespread unemployment in the LDCs. First, underutilised human resources create the opportunity to expand productive capacity and GNP at little or no real cost by producing for export markets those products which are not in demand locally. This process is known as the 'vent for surplus' theory of international trade. It was first formulated by Adam Smith but more recently it has been applied to Third World nations by the Burmese economist Hla Myint.

According to this theory, the opening of world markets to remote agrarian societies creates opportunities not to reallocate fully employed resources as in the traditional models but, rather, to make use of formerly *underemployed* land and labour resources to produce greater output for export to foreign markets. The colonial system of plantation agriculture as well as the commercialisation of small-scale subsistence agriculture were made possible, according to this view, by the availability of unemployed and underemployed land and human resources. In terms of our production possibility analyses, the vent for surplus argument can be represented by a shift in production from point V to point B in Figure 20.1 with trade enlarging final domestic consumption from point V to point C.

We can see from Figure 20.1 that before trade, the resources of this closed Third World economy were grossly underutilised, with production occurring at point V, well within the confines of the production possibility frontier. OX primary products and OY manufactures were being produced and consumed. The opening up of the nation to foreign markets (probably as a result of colonisation) provides the economic impetus to utilise these idle resources (mostly excess land and labour) and expand primary product exportable production from OX to OX′ at point B on the production frontier. Given the international price ratio, ($\overline{P}_a/\overline{P}_m$), XX′ (equal to VB) primary products can now be exported in exchange for YY′ (equal to VC) manufactures with the result that the final consumption point, C, is attained with the same primary products (= OX) being consumed as before but Y′Y more imported manufactures now available.

The vent for surplus argument does provide a more realistic analytical scenario of the historical trading experience of many LDCs than either the classical or neo-classical models. However, it is a moot point whether LDC nationals as opposed to the colonial and expatriate entrepreneurs actually benefited from this process in the short run. In the long run, the heavy structural orientation of the LDC economy towards primary product exports in many cases created an export 'enclave' situation and thus inhibited the much-needed structural transformation towards a more diversified and self-reliant economy.

Figure 20.1
The 'vent for surplus' theory of trade in LDCs

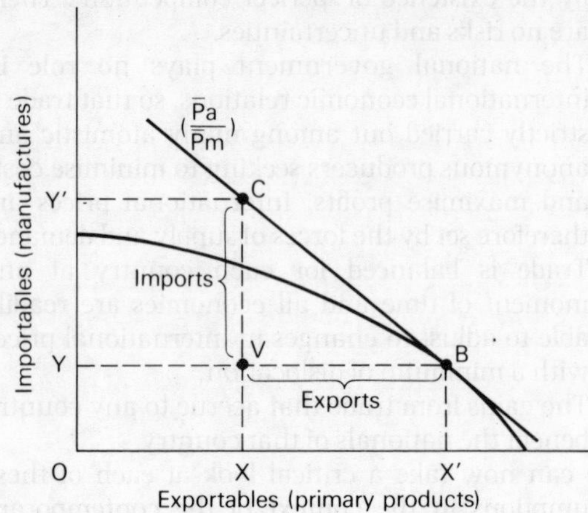

Initial production and consumption situation before trade is shown by point V.
With opening of trade, production of primary products (exportables) shifts from V to B.
At international price ratio ($\overline{P}_a/\overline{P}_m$), VB primary products can be exported for VC manufactured imports.
Final (after trade) consumption situation shown by point C. Same primary products being consumed (OX) as before but Y′Y more manufactures available as result of trade – i.e. consumption is OY′ instead of OY manufactures.

The second conclusion to be drawn from the recognition of widespread unemployment in the Third World is that the only way to create sufficient local job opportunities is to protect domestic industries (both manufacturing and agriculture) against low-cost foreign competition. This protection is accomplished through the erection of various trade barriers such as tariffs or quotas. Although we discuss the pros and cons of commercial policy in the next chapter, the point is that those LDCs which place priority on employment creation may wish to pursue a protectionist policy to build up local rural and urban industries so as to absorb their surplus labour.

International factor mobility and multinational corporations

The third component of the crucial first assumption of traditional trade theory (the international immobility of productive factors) is, after the assumption of perfect competition, the most unrealistic of all premises of classical and neo-classical trade theory. Capital and skilled labour have always moved between nations. The nineteenth-century growth experience of Western nations can largely be explained in terms of the impact of international capital movements. Perhaps the most powerful force in international economic relations during the past two decades has been the spectacular rise in power and influence of the giant multi-national corporations. These international carriers of capital, technology and skilled labour, with their diverse productive operations throughout the Third World, greatly complicate the simple theory of international trade, especially in the context of the distribution of its benefits. Companies like IBM, Ford Motor, Exxon, Philips, Mitsubishi, British Petroleum, Renault, Volkswagen, Coca-Cola, etc., have so internationalised their production process that calculation of the distribution of the benefits of international production between foreigners and nationals becomes exceedingly difficult. We return to this important issue in the next chapter when we examine the pros and cons of private foreign investment. For the present let us recognise that enormous international movements of capital and skills play a crucial role in contemporary world economic relations. To assume away their existence and their impacts on the economies and economic structures of Third World nations, as in the classical and factor endowment theories of trade, is to blind ourselves to the realities of the contemporary world economy.

Fixed, freely available technology and consumer sovereignty

Just as capital resources are rapidly growing and being dispersed to maximise the returns of their owners throughout the world, so too is rapid technological change (mostly in the West) profoundly affecting world trading relationships. One of the most obvious examples of the impact of developed-country technological change on Third World export earnings is the development of synthetic substitutes for many traditional primary products.

Over the past twenty years, synthetic substitutes for primary products such as rubber, wool, cotton, sisal, jute, hides and skins have been manufactured in increasing quantities. The Third World's market shares of these natural products in all cases has fallen steadily. For example, between 1950 and the late-1970s the share of natural rubber in total world rubber consumption fell from 62 to 28 per cent while cotton's share of total apparel fibre consumption dropped from 41 to 29 per cent. Combining these technological substitution forces with those of low income and price elasticities of demand for primary products and the rise of agricultural protection in the markets of developed nations, one can see why the uncritical adherence to the theoretical dictates of 'comparative advantage' can be a risky and often unrewarding venture for many LDCs.

The assumption of fixed world-wide consumer tastes and preferences dictating production patterns to market-responsive atomistic producers is another fiction of economic theory. Not only are capital and production technologies disseminated throughout the world by means of the multinational corporations often aided and abetted by their home governments, but consumption technologies (i.e. consumer preferences and tastes) are often created and reinforced by the advertising campaigns of the powerful financial giants who dominate local markets. By creating demands for imported goods, market-dominating international enterprises can manufacture the conditions for their own further aggrandisement. For example, it has been estimated that over 90 per cent of all advertising in many Third World nations is financed by foreign firms selling in the local market. As pointed out earlier, contemporary consumers are rarely 'sovereign' about anything, let alone what and how much major corporations are going to produce.

Internal factor mobility and 'perfect competition'

The traditional theory of trade assumes that nations are readily able to adjust their economic structures to the changing dictates of world prices and markets. Movements along production possibility frontiers involving the reallocation of resources from one industry to another may be easy to make on paper. But, they are extremely difficult to achieve in practice. This is especially true in Third World nations where production structures are often very rigid and factor movements largely restricted. The most obvious example of this is plantation and small farm commercial agriculture. In those economies which have gradually become heavily dependent on their primary product exports, the whole economic and social infrastructure (roads, railways, communications, power locations, credit and marketing arrangements) may be geared to facilitate the movement of goods from production locations to shipping and storage depots for transfer to foreign markets. Cumulative investments of capital over time may have been sunk into these economic and infrastructure facilities and cannot easily be transferred to different spatially located manufacturing activities. Thus the more dependent LDCs become on a few primary product exports, the more inflexible their economic structures become and the more vulnerable they are to the unpredictabilities of international markets. It may take many years to transform a less developed economy from an almost exclusive primary product, export-oriented reliance to a more diversified, multi-sector structure.

In short, the internal processes of adjustment and resource reallocation necessary to capitalise on changing world economic conditions are much more difficult for the less diversified economies of the Third World to realise than for their rich counterparts in the northern hemisphere. And yet, curiously enough, those LDCs that can expand their capacities to produce low-cost labour-intensive manufactured goods for export in industries such as textiles, shoes, sporting goods, handbags, processed foodstuffs, wigs and rugs, often find these exports blocked by the tariff and non-tariff barriers erected by developed countries to restrict the entry of such low-cost goods into their home markets. The reason usually given is that this low-cost foreign competition will create unemployment among the higher cost domestic industries of the developed country and that the problems of internal economic adjustment are too serious to permit such unfettered foreign competition. Thus, the internal factor mobility assumption turns out to have limited applicability, whether because of real or imagined rationales, in even the most diversified economies of the developed nations.

We need not dwell on the limitations of the perfectly competitive model here since this issue is discussed in Chapter 3 and elsewhere. But it is essential to point out two major limitations of the application of this model to the theory of international trade. First by assuming either fixed or diminishing returns to scale (i.e. fixed or increasing production costs as output is expanded), the labour cost and factor endowment theories of trade neglect one of the most important economic phenomena in international economic relations. This is the pervasive and income-widening effect of increasing returns to scale and, therefore, decreasing costs of production. Decreasing production costs mean simply that large existing firms are able to underprice smaller or new firms and thus exert monopolistic control over world markets. Far from being a rare exception, as the defenders of free trade would like to suggest, **economies of scale (increasing returns) and decreasing costs are a pervasive factor in determining trade patterns**, not the least of which is in the area of agriculture where huge agribusiness enterprises in developed countries are able to underprice the lower productivity family farm in Third World countries. Economies of large-scale production lead to monopolistic control of world supply conditions (just as they do for domestic markets) for a wide range of products. Moreover, this process of market domination and control is largely irreversible: poor country industries, once behind, simply cannot compete with giant corporations.

Monopolistic and oligopolistic market control of internationally traded commodities means that large individual corporations are able to manipulate world prices and supplies (and often demands as well) in their own private interests. **Instead of competition, one finds joint producer activities and oligopolistic bargaining among giant buyers and sellers as the most pervasive price and quantity determining force in international economic affairs.**

But from the viewpoint of Third World nations trying to diversify their economies and promote industrial exports in particular, the widespread phenomenon of increasing returns (decreasing costs) to large-scale production in addition to the non-economic power of large multi-national corporations (i.e. their political influence with many governments) means that those who are first to industrialise (the rich nations) are able to take advantage of these economies of scale and perpetuate their dominant position in world markets. It is another case of the rich getting richer by holding all the economic and non-economic cards.

The second major limitation of the perfectly competitive assumption of trade models is its exclusion of **risk** and **uncertainty** in international trading arrangements. Even if one were to accept all the unreal assumptions of the traditional trade model as applied to the LDCs, it may still not be in their long-run interest to invest heavily in primary product export promotion, due to the historical instability of world markets for primary commodities in comparison with manufactured goods.

As we have pointed out, concentration on one or two vital primary product exports can play havoc with LDC development plans when the variability of foreign exchange earnings is largely unpredictable from one year to the next. Thus following the dictates of static comparative advantage, even in the unreal world of traditional trade theory, may not be the best policy from the perspective of a long-run development strategy. This is one reason why developing nations are demanding international commodity price stabilisation agreements and buffer stocks to stabilise export earnings (see Chapter 21).

The absence of national governments in trading relations

In the context of domestic economies, the co-existence of rich and poor regions, of rapidly growing and stagnating industries, and of the persistent disproportionate regional distribution of the benefits of economic growth can, at least in theory, be counteracted and ameliorated by the intervention of the state in market forces. Thus, cumulative processes for inequality within nation-states by which 'growth-pole' regions may be enriched at the expense of the regions left behind can be modified by government legislation, taxes, subsidies, social services, regional development programmes, etc. But since there is no effective international government to modify and counter the natural tendency of the rich nations to grow, often at the trading expense of the poor, not only can the highly uneven gains from trade become self-sustaining, they can also be reinforced by the uneven power of national governments to promote and protect the interests of their countries. By focusing on the atomistic behaviour of competitive firms in the context of different commodities being produced in anonymous countries, standard trade theory has ignored the crucial role which states play in international economic affairs. They possess many instruments of commercial policy (tariffs, import quotas, export subsidies, etc.) to manipulate their trade position *vis-à-vis* the rest of the world. Moreover, when developed nation governments pursue restrictive economic policies designed to deal with purely domestic issues like inflation, they can have profound negative effects on the economies of poor nations.

The reverse, unfortunately, is not true. Third World domestic economic policies have little impact on the economies of rich nations. Moreover governments of developed countries often conspire to promote their joint interests through co-ordinated trade and other economic ventures. While these activities may not be intentionally designed to promote their own welfare at the expense of the welfare of poor countries, this nevertheless is often the result. Increasingly, however, poor nations are recognising the benefits of their own co-ordinated activities and are attempting to provide a united front in international bargaining arrangements, especially in the area of scarce natural resources and raw materials where some do have considerable leverage.

Our point, therefore, is quite simple. Traditional trade theories neglect the crucial role which national governments can and do play in the international economic arena. Governments often serve to reinforce the unequal distribution of resources and gains from trade by differences in their size and relative economic power. Rich country governments can influence world economic affairs by their domestic and international policies. They can resist countervailing economic pressures from weaker nations and can act collusively and often in conjunction with their powerful multinational corporations to manipulate the terms and conditions of international trade to their own national advantage. There is no agency or world government to protect and promote the interests of the weaker parties (the LDCs) in such international affairs. Trade theory makes no mention of these powerful government forces. Its prescriptions are therefore greatly weakened.

Balanced trade and automatic international price adjustments

The theory of international trade, like other perfectly competitive 'general equilibrium' models in economics, is not only a full employment model but also one in which flexible domestic and international product and resource prices always adjust instantaneously to conditions of supply and demand. In particular, the 'terms of trade' (international commodity price ratios) adjust to equate supply and demand for a country's exportable and importable products so that trade is always balanced, that is, the value of exports (quantity times price) is always equal to the value of imports. With balanced commodity trade and no international capital movements balance of payments problems never arise in the 'pure' theory of trade.

But the realities of the world economy in the 1980s, especially in the period following the skyrocketing of international oil prices in the 1970s, are such that balance of payments deficits and the consequent depletion of foreign reserves (or the need to borrow foreign funds to cover commodity deficits) are a major cause of concern for all nations, both rich and poor.

In poor nations in particular, a combination of declining terms of trade and sluggish international demands for their export products has meant chronic commodity trade deficits. With the gradual drying up of bilateral and multilateral foreign assistance and the growing concern of LDCs with the social costs of private foreign investment (see Chapter 22), this has meant that severe balance of payments problems necessitate even further departures from relatively free trade. As well as coping with chronic balance of payments deficits and rising debt burdens on former loans, Third World nations have faced a new and even more serious economic threat in the 1970s and 80s; the spreading effects of worldwide inflation. All in all, gross imperfections in the international economy and the prevalence of non-market-determined commodity pricing systems make the automatic adjustment mechanism of traditional trade theory seem somewhat ludicrous.

Country trade gains accrue to country nationals

The sixth and final major assumption of trade theory, that country trade gains accrue to country nationals, is more implicit than the other five. It is rarely spelled out, nor need it be if one accepts the assumption that factors are internationally immobile. But given the gross unreality of that assumption, we need to examine the implicit notion, rarely challenged, that if Third World countries do benefit from trade, it is the people of these countries who reap the benefits. The issue thus revolves around the question of who owns the land, the capital and the skills that are rewarded as a result of trade. Are they nationals or are they foreigners? If both, in what proportions are the gains distributed?

We know, for example, that in the 'enclave' Third World economies like those with substantial foreign-owned mining and plantation operations, foreigners pay very low rents for the rights to use land, bring in their own foreign capital and skilled labour, hire local unskilled workers at subsistence wages and, in general, leave a minimal impact on the rest of the economy even though they may generate significant export revenues. While such visible enclave type economies are gradually disappearing in the Third World, they are often being replaced by more subtle forms of foreign domination: the economic penetration of multinational corporations. The distinction, therefore, between gross domestic product (GDP), which is a measure of the value of output generated within defined geographic boundaries, and gross national product (GNP), which measures the income actually earned by nationals of that country, becomes extremely important. To the extent that the export sector, or for that matter any sector of the economy, is foreign-owned and operated, GDP will be that much higher than GNP and few of the benefits of trade will actually accrue to LDC nationals. It is even possible for the value of exports to be greater than GNP; that is, foreign export earnings may exceed the total value of domestically accrued income.

Our point here is an important one. With the proliferation of multi-national corporations and the international ownership of the means of production in a wide range of countries, aggregate statistics for LDC export earnings may mask the fact that LDC nationals, especially those in lower income brackets, may not benefit at all from these exports. The major gains from trade may instead accrue to nonnationals, who may repatriate large proportions of these earnings abroad. In effect, the trade which is being carried out may look like trade between rich and poor nations. But in reality such trade is being conducted between rich nations and **other nationals of rich nations** operating in foreign countries. Until recently the activities of most mining and plantation operations had this characteristic. More importantly, much of the recent import-substituting, export-oriented manufacturing activities in poor countries may merely have masked the fact that many of the benefits were still being reaped by foreign enterprises. In short, LDC export performances can be deceptive unless we analyse the character and structure of export earnings by ascertaining who owns or controls the factors of production that are rewarded as a result of export expansion.

Conclusions: trade and economic development – the limits of theory

We can now attempt to provide some preliminary general answers to the five questions posed at the beginning of Chapter 19. Again, we must stress that our conclusions are highly general and set in the context of the diversity of Third World nations. Many will not be valid for specific nations at different times and periods. But on the whole we believe that these conclusions represent the consensus of current economic thinking, especially among Third World economists, on the relationship between trade and development, as the latter term has been defined throughout this book.

First, with regard to the rate, structure and character of economic growth, our conclusion is that **trade can be an important stimulus to rapid economic growth**. This is borne out by the 1960s experiences of countries like Taiwan, Brazil, South Korea and by the OPEC experience of the 1970s. Access to the markets of developed nations (an important 'if' for those Third World nations bent on export promotion) can provide an important stimulus for the greater utilisation of idle human and capital resources. Expanded foreign exchange earnings through improved export performance also provides the wherewithal by which LDCs can augment their scarce physical and financial resources. In short, where real and lasting opportunities for profitable exchange arise, foreign trade can provide an important stimulus to aggregate economic growth along the lines suggested by the traditional theory.

But, as we have seen in earlier chapters, rapid growth of national output may have little impact on development. An export-oriented strategy of growth, particularly when a large proportion of export earnings accrue to foreigners, may not only bias the structure of the economy in the wrong directions (by not catering to the basic needs of the people), but it may also reinforce the internal and external dualistic and inegalitarian character of that growth. Therefore the fact that trade may promote expanded export earnings, even increase output levels, does not mean that it is a desirable strategy for economic and social development. It all depends on the nature of the export sector, the distribution of its benefits and its linkages with the rest of the economy.

As for the distributional effects of trade, we can state almost without reservation that **the principal benefits of world trade have accrued disproportionately to rich nations and within poor nations disproportionately to both foreign residents and wealthy nationals**. This should not be construed as an indictment of the inherent nature of trade *per se*. Rather it reflects the highly inegalitarian institutional social and economic ordering of the global system in which a few powerful nations and their multi-national corporations control vast amounts of world resources. The conclusion of traditional trade theory, that free trade will tend to equalise incomes, is no more than a theoretical curiosity. Trade, like education, tends to reinforce existing inequalities. But it has the added defect of being conducted at the international level where the absence of a supranational state eliminates the possibility, which at least exists in theory at the national level, of redistributing the gains or investing them to promote development in disadvantaged regions. Factors such as the widespread existence of increasing returns, the unequal international distribution of economic assets and power, the growing influence of large multi-national corporations, the often blatant collusion among a few powerful governments and their giant corporations, and the combined ability of both to manipulate international prices, levels of production, and patterns of demand: all these factors, assumed not to exist in the traditional theory of trade, are crucial. Together, they lead us to the general conclusion that **Third World countries have benefited disproportionately less from their economic dealings with developed nations and may have in fact even suffered absolutely from this association.**

It should be apparent by now that the answer to the third question – under what conditions can trade help LDCs to achieve their development aspirations? – is to be found largely in the ability of Third World nations (probably as a group) to extract favourable trade concessions from the developed nations, especially in the form of the latter's elimination of barriers to LDC exports of labour-intensive manufactured goods and their willingness to stabilise primary commodity prices and export earnings. (We discuss the economic effects of tariffs and commodity agreements in the next chapter.)

Secondly, the extent to which LDC exports can efficiently utilise scarce capital resources while making maximum use of abundant but currently underutilised labour supplies will determine the degree to which export earnings benefit the ordinary citizen. Here linkages between export earnings and other sectors of the economy are crucial; for example, small farm agricultural export earnings will expand the demand for domestically produced simple household goods while export earnings from capital-intensive manufacturing industries are more likely to find their way back to rich nations in payment for luxury imports. Finally, much will depend on how much LDCs can influence and control the activities of private foreign enterprises. Their ability to deal effectively with multi-national corporations in guaranteeing a fair share of the benefits to local citizens is, therefore, extremely important.

The answer to the fourth question, whether LDCs can determine how much they trade, can only be speculative. For most small and poor countries, the option of not trading at all by closing their borders to the rest of the world is not very feasible. Not only do they lack the resources and market size to be self-sufficient, but their very existence, especially in the area of food production, often depends on their ability to secure foreign goods and resources. Some thirty-two of the 'least developed' countries face annual threats of severe famine for which international assistance is not a choice but a necessity.

For those more fortunate Third World nations which at least do not face annual fears of mass starvation, the international economic system, however unequal and biased against their long-run development interests, still offer the only real source of scarce capital and technological resources. The conditions under which such resources are obtained will greatly influence the character of the development process. As we show in the next chapter, the long-run benefits from trade among Third World countries themselves through the creation of regional trading blocs similar to the European Economic Community (EEC) may offer better prospects for a balanced and diversified development strategy than the almost exclusive reliance on the very unequal trading relations that they now individually engage in with the developed nations. Finally, for the few countries rich in mineral resources and raw materials, especially those that have been able to provide an effective international bargaining stance against the large corporations which purchase their exports (e.g. OPEC), trade has been and continues to be a vital source of development finance.

The fifth question – whether on balance it is best for Third World countries to look outward towards the rest of the world or inward towards their own internal capacities for development – turns out not to be an 'either-or' question at all. The consensus among most development economists, expecially those from the Third World, is leaning in the direction of a greater degree of 'collective' self-reliance. Their basic argument goes like this: Trade in the past has not been a great help to most developing nations and it has been positively harmful to some. Given the present imbalance in international power and wealth, pursuit of so-called 'free trade' policies and a more equitable distribution of the benefits of trade will more than likely be subverted by the wealthy to further their own private or national interests. Therefore, LDCs have to be very selective in their economic relations with the developed countries. They need to guard against entering into agreements and joint production ventures over which they are likely to relinquish control. While not shutting themselves off from trade with the rest of the world, Third World countries should seek ways to expand their share of world trade and extend their economic ties with one another. For example, by pooling their resources small countries can overcome the limits of their small individual markets and their serious resource constraints while still retaining an important degree of autonomy in pursuing their individual development aspirations. While it may not be possible for most LDCs to be self-reliant on an individual country by country basis, some form of trade and economic co-operation among equals is probably preferable to continued exposure to the dominating international power of rich nations and their potent multi-national corporations.

There is thus a consensus in the developing world

that a 'new international economic order' needs to be established in which developing countries can begin to reap the sizable benefits of international trade which they have long been denied. Early in 1975 a joint resolution among 150 Third World and developed countries (with only the United States casting a negative vote) was passed in Lima, Peru, setting as a target a 25 per cent share of world output for the LDCs by the year 2000 as opposed to the 7 per cent now being produced. At the Fourth Conference of the United Nations Committee on Trade and Development (UNCTAD IV) held in Nairobi in May 1976, Third World demands for more equitable and more profitable trading arrangements with the developing world within the context of a restructured world economy were pressed even further. In addition a consensus of opinion is now growing that Third World countries should begin to look both outward *and* inward – outward towards new forms of economic co-operation and trade with each other and inward to a greater degree of group self-reliance through the intelligent economic use of their own joint resources, both human and physical. The new experiment in co-operation among the five Andean nations in South America (Bolivia, Chile, Colombia, Ecuador and Peru) is a real world manifestation of this outward–inward search for collective self-reliance. (In the next chapter we deal in detail with the various arguments for and against economic integration among Third World countries.) It remains to be seen whether political obstacles will continue to inhibit such effective forms of economic co-operation as they have in the past for such regional groupings as in the Latin American Free Trade Association and the East African Community, or whether the powerful economic logic of such co-operation will transcend and overcome political inhibitions.

In the absence of such political roadblocks, it seems clear that increased economic co-operation among diverse Third World nations at roughly equal stages of development offers a real alternative to their present pursuit of separate and therefore very unequal trade relationships with the rest of the world. Thus, even though a new economic order may not be immediately forthcoming, it may still be possible for LDCs to capture some of the real potential gains from specialisation and trade (among themselves) without the need to expose themselves to the continual backwash effects of a contemporary world economy and trading system which is dominated by a wealthy clique of rich nations and powerful multi-national corporations.

Concepts for review

'vent for surplus' theory of trade	increasing returns and decreasing costs
synthetic commodity substitutes	growth poles
monopolistic and oligopolistic market control	balanced trade
collusion	enclave economies
	'collective' self-reliance

Questions for discussion

1. What factors – economic, political and/or historical – do you think will determine whether or not a particular Third World nation is more or less dependent on international exchange? Explain your answer giving a few specific examples of different LDCs.
2. Explain some of the reasons why the non-oil-producing countries of the Third World seem to have benefited relatively less than the developed nations over the past 25 years from their participation in international trade.
3. Traditional free trade theories are based on six crucial assumptions which may or may not be valid for Third World nations (or for developed nations for that matter). What are these crucial assumptions and how might they be violated in the real world of international trade?
4. Traditional free trade theory is basically a *static* theory of international exchange leading to certain conclusions about the benefits likely to accrue to all participants. What *dynamic* elements in real world economies will tend to negate the widespread distribution of the benefits of free trade? Explain this dynamic process.
5. Third World critics of international trade sometimes claim that present trading relationships between developed and underdeveloped countries can be a source of 'antidevelopment' for the latter and merely serve to perpetuate their weak and dependent status. Explain the apparent meaning of this argument. Do you tend to agree or disagree and why?

Further reading

For a critique of the traditional theory of trade as applied to underdeveloped nations, see: H. Myint, 'The "classical theory" of International Trade and Underdeveloped Countries', *Economic Journal*, lxviii, 1958; H. Kitamura, 'Capital Accumulation and the Theory of International Trade', *Malayan Economic Review*, iii, 1, 1958; G. Myrdal, *The Challenge of World Poverty*, Pantheon, New York, 1970, ch. 9; H. Myint, 'International Trade and the Developing Countries', in P. A. Samuelson, ed., *International Economic Relations*, Macmillan, 1969; T. Balogh, 'Fact and Fancy in International Economic Relations, Part I', *World Development*, i, 1 and 2, February 1973, and the special issue on Trade and Poor Economies contained in the *Journal of Development Studies*, 15, No. 3, April 1979.

Chapter 21 The balance of payments and commercial policies

> What the Third World must ask of the international order is protection of its legitimate interests in the trade field, not trade concessions, and a genuine transfer of real resources, not the present 'aid' charade.
> *Santiago declaration of Third World Social Scientists, April 1973*

Introduction

In the previous chapter we examined the scope and limitations of the traditional theory of international trade as applied to the contemporary position of less developed nations in the world economy. Our focus was primarily on international commodity trade in theory and practice and its likely effects on Third World growth, efficiency, equity and stability in comparison to the developed world. In this chapter and the next we extend this analysis in two ways. First, in this chapter we examine the range of LDC commercial and financial policies (e.g. import tariffs, physical quotas, export promotion versus import substitution, exchange rate adjustments, international commodity agreements and economic integration) within the broad framework of 'outward' versus 'inward' looking strategies of development. In Chapter 22 we go beyond simple commodity trade to examine the international flow of financial resources. Traditionally this flow has been almost exclusively a 'north–south' phenomenon: financial resources have been transferred from the developed to the less developed countries. However, the need to recycle the vast new OPEC oil wealth opens up new possibilities for intra-Third World resource transfers, possibilities to be examined in the next chapter.

The flow of financial resources has two main components: the flow of **private foreign investment** funds and other resources primarily via the carrier of the modern multi-national corporation and the flow of **public resources** in the form of bilateral and multilateral foreign aid. Within the context of the flow of private foreign investments and public foreign aid, we shall review some alternative Third World policy approaches towards its financial dealings with the developed world. But first we look more closely at the nature of a country's balance of payments and some of the issues surrounding various trade strategies for development.

The balance of payments

The extension of our analysis beyond simple commodity trade into the area of the international flow of financial resources permits us to examine the **balance of payments** position of Third World nations *vis-à-vis* the rest of the world. A balance of payments table is designed to summarise a nation's transactions with the outside world; for example Table 19.1 showed changes over a period of time for the Third World as a whole and the sources and uses of funds. A more analytically convenient way to present such a table is to divide it into three components. The **current account** component portrays the flow of goods and services in the form of exports and imports for a country during a given year. It allows us to analyse the impact of various commercial policies on commodity trade. The **capital account** shows the volume of private foreign investment and public grants and loans from individual nations and multilateral donor agencies such as UNDP and the World Bank. It permits us to examine the relative importance of international flows of financial resources in augmenting a nation's domestic savings. Finally, the **cash account** shows how cash balances (foreign reserves) and short-term claims have changed in response to current and capital account transactions. The cash account is thus the balancing item which is lowered (i.e. a net outflow of foreign exchange) whenever total disbursements on the current and capital account exceed total receipts. In practice the dividing line between the capital and cash accounts is arbitrarily set so that claims and debts maturing in more than a year (or those that have no fixed maturity date as in the case of grants) are listed in the capital account. All other short-term financial claims and debts (i.e. those that mature in one year or less) are normally included in the cash account.

A balance of payments table for a hypothetical Third World country is shown in Table 21.1. We see that there is a net negative balance of $15 million on current account. Commodity imports (primarily manufactured consumer, intermediate and capital goods) plus payments to foreign shipping firms exceed commodity exports (primary agricultural and raw material products) by these $15 million. On the capital account, we see that there is a net inflow of $7 million of private foreign investments (mostly from multi-national corporations who build factories in the LDC). There is also a net positive $3 million inflow of public loans and grants in the form of foreign aid and multilateral donor agency assistance. Note that the gross inflow of $6 million in public loans and grants is partially offset by a $3 million capital outflow representing amortisation and interest payments on former loans. In a number of Third World countries these debt service repayments on former loans are now at a point where they often exceed new public financial inflows. If forced to repay all these loans, many poor countries may soon on balance actually be transferring financial resources to rich nations! Finally, private transfer payments of $1 million (e.g. monetary outflows of private individuals to friends and relatives living in another country) bring the capital account into a net positive balance of $9 million. This means that the combined net balance on current *and* capital accounts is a negative $6 million. This amount represents the balance of payments **deficit** of our hypothetical LDC. If the balance on current and capital account were positive it would be a balance of payments **surplus**.

Table 21.1
An hypothetical balance of payments table for a less developed nation (millions of dollars)

Item		
A. Current account		
Commodity exports		+35
Primary products	25	
Manufactured goods	10	
Commodity imports		−45
Primary products	10	
Manufactured goods	35	
Services (e.g. shipping costs)		− 5
Balance on current account		−15
B. Capital account		
Private foreign investment (net)		+7
Government and multilateral flows (net)		+3
Loans		+5
Grants		+1
Debt repayments		−3
Private transfer payments (net)		−1
Balance on capital account		+9
Balance on current and capital accounts		−6
C. Cash account		
Net decrease in official monetary reserves		+6
Balance on cash account		+6

Financing payments deficits: the international monetary system and special drawing rights

In order to finance this $6 million negative balance on combined current and capital accounts, our hypothetical country will have to draw on its Central Bank holdings of official monetary reserves. Such reserves consist of gold and a few major foreign currencies such as the US dollar, the British pound sterling, the Swiss franc, the German mark and, increasingly, the Japanese yen. They also include a new international currency called Special Drawing Rights (see below). We see, therefore, that the balance on current account *plus* the balance on capital account must always be offset by the balance on cash account. This is shown by the net *decrease* of $6 million in official monetary reserves. If the country is very poor it is likely to have a very limited stock of these official monetary reserves. This overall balance of payments deficit of $6 million, therefore, may pose severe strains on the economy and greatly inhibit its ability to continue importing needed capital and consumer goods. In the least developed nations of the world, which have to import to feed a hungry population and which possess very limited stocks of monetary reserves, such payments deficits may spell disaster for many millions of people.

Faced with existing or projected balance of payments deficits on combined current and capital accounts, Third World nations have a variety of policy options. They can seek to improve the balance on current account by promoting export expansion and/or limiting imports. In the former case, there is the further choice of concentrating on primary or secondary product export expansion. In the latter case, policies of import substitution (i.e. the protection and stimulus of domestic industries to replace manufactured imports in the local market) and/or selective physical quotas or bans on the importation of specific consumer goods may be tried. Alternatively they can seek to achieve both objectives simultaneously by altering their official foreign exchange rates through currency devaluation. We will examine the controversy over export promotion, import substitution and exchange rate adjustment in the next section.

A second alternative, though often not exclusive of the first, is for Third World countries to try to improve the balance on their capital account by encouraging more private foreign investment and seeking more public foreign assistance. But since neither private foreign investment nor more than a small proportion of foreign aid comes in the form of gifts (i.e. outright grants), the receipt of such loan assistance implies the necessity of future repayments of principal and interest. In the case of directly productive foreign investments in, say, building local factories, it entails the potential repatriation overseas of sizable proportions of the profits of the foreign-owned enterprise. Moreover, as we show in the next chapter, the encouragement of private foreign investment has much broader development implications (many negative) than the mere transfer of financial and/or physical capital resources.

Finally, developing nations can seek to modify the detrimental impact of chronic balance of payments deficits by expanding their stocks of official monetary reserves. One way of doing this is through the acquisition of a greater share of a new international 'paper gold' known as Special Drawing Rights (SDRs). Traditionally, under the working of the international monetary system, countries with deficits in their balance of payments were required to pay for these deficits by drawing down on their official reserves of the two principal international monetary assets, gold and US dollars. But, with the phenomenal growth in the volume and value of world trade, a new kind of international asset was needed to supplement the limited stock of gold and dollars. Consequently, in 1970 the International Monetary Fund (IMF) was given the authority to create $10 billion of these Special Drawing Rights. These new international assets perform many of the functions of gold and dollars in settling balance of payments accounts (see Table 19.1). By the end of 1980 the total value of SDRs actually allocated was in excess of $18 billion of which $3.6 billion was earmarked for the non-oil exporting less developed nations. Eventually, the IMF would like to see all international financial settlements conducted in SDRs with gold and dollars dropped as official mediums of exchange.

A major issue of great concern to Third World countries, therefore, is the distribution of the benefits of SDRs. The present formula for distributing SDRs gives 75 per cent of the total to the 25 industrial nations. This leaves only 25 per cent to be distributed among the 90 or so Third World countries who participate in the international monetary system. Dissatisfied with this situation, these countries acting as a group are now exerting pressure on the developed nations to agree to the creation of supplementary special drawing rights which would be allocated in preferential amounts and/or preferential terms to developing nations. The issue of these supplementary SDRs could have greatly helped to solve the short-run financial crisis faced by most Third World nations, particularly the 40 or so least developed, as a result of the rapid rise in international oil and food prices in the 1970s.

More generally, Third World nations acting as a group are beginning to exert increasing pressures on the developed nations for a greater voice in the shaping and control of a reformed international monetary system. Before 1972, LDCs had virtually no role and no voting power in the monetary system. It was run by a so-called 'Committee of Ten' which consisted of ten rich nations whose decisions rarely took into account the plight of the vast majority of the world's peoples. More recently this committee was increased on a permanent basis to the new IMF Committee of Twenty with increased representation of Third World nations. It is to be hoped that future reforms of the international monetary system will increasingly reflect the needs and desires of these poor nations. At least they now have a forum to express their views and to air their grievances. Most importantly, however, if Third World nations can present a unified stance, they now possess the voting power to veto any monetary reform which they believe is not in their best economic interests.

Having summarised some basic balance of payments concepts and issues as they relate to both commodity trade and international flows of financial resources, we can now turn to the question of alternative trade policies for development.

Trade policies for development: to look outward or inward or outward and inward?

A convenient and instructive way to approach the complex issues of appropriate trade policies for development is to set these specific policies in the context of a broader LDC strategy of looking outward or looking inward.[1] In the words of Professor Streeten, outward-looking policies 'encourage not only free trade but also the free movement of capital, workers, enterprises and students, a welcome to the multi-national enterprise, and an open system of communications'. On the other hand, inward-looking policies stress the need for LDCs to evolve their own style of development and to be the masters of their own fate. This means policies to encourage indigenous 'learning by doing' in manufacturing and the development of indigenous technologies appropriate to a country's resource endowment. Such greater self-reliance can be accomplished, according to proponents of inward-looking trade policies, only if 'you restrict trade, the movement of people and communications, and if you keep out the multi-national enterprise, with its wrong products and wrong want-stimulation and hence its wrong technology'.[2]

Within these two broad philosophical approaches to development, we can place specific commodity trade strategies analytically, in a fourfold division:

1. primary outward-looking policies (encouragement of agricultural and raw material exports);
2. secondary outward-looking policies (promotion of manufactured exports);
3. primary inward-looking policies (mainly agricultural self-sufficiency);
4. secondary inward-looking policies (manufactured products self-sufficiency through import substitution).

Keeping this typology of trade strategies in mind, let us look at four broad areas of commercial and financial policy:

1. Export promotion.
2. Import substitution.
3. Tariffs, physical quotas and foreign exchange rate adjustments.
4. Economic integration.

Export promotion: looking outward and seeing the trade barriers

Export promotion of LDC exports, either primary or secondary, has long been considered a major ingredient in any viable long-run development strategy. The colonial territories of Africa and Asia with their foreign-owned mines and plantations were classic examples of primary outward-looking regions. It was partly in reaction to this 'enclave' economic structure and partly due to the industrialisation bias of the 1950s and 1960s that newly independent states as well as older LDCs put

[1] For an excellent discussion of these issues see P. P. Streeten, 'Trade strategies for development: some themes for the seventies', *World Development*, i, 6, June 1973, pp. 1–10.

[2] *Ibid.*, p. 2.

great emphasis on the production of manufactured goods first for the home market (secondary inward-looking) and then for export (secondary outward-looking). Let us, therefore, look at the scope and limitations of LDC export expansion, first in primary products and then in manufactures.

Primary commodity export expansion

As we saw in the previous chapter, the Third World still relies on primary products for over three-quarters of its export earnings. With the notable exception of petroleum exports and a few needed minerals, primary product exports have grown more slowly than total world trade. Moreover, the LDC share of these exports has been falling over the past two decades. Since food, food products and raw materials make up almost 40 per cent of all LDC exports and, for the vast majority of the Third World nations, constitute their principal source of foreign exchange earnings, we need to examine the factors affecting the demand for and supply of primary product exports.

On the demand side there appear to be at least five factors working against the rapid expansion of Third World primary product, and especially agricultural, exports to the developed nations (their major markets). First, the per capita income elasticities of demand for agricultural foodstuffs and raw materials are relatively low compared with fuels, certain minerals and manufactures. For example, the income elasticities of demand for sugar, cocoa, tea, coffee and bananas have all been estimated at less than unity with most in the range of 0.3 to 0.5.[3] This means that only a sustained high rate of per capita income growth in the developed countries can maintain even modest export rates of these particular commodities from the LDCs. Such high growth rates that prevailed in the 1960s were not matched in the 1970s. Second, developed-country population growth rates are now at or near the replacement level so that little expansion can be expected from this source. Third, the price elasticity of demand for most non-fuel primary commodities appears to be relatively low, although the data on this point are far from convincing. When relative agricultural prices are falling as they have during most of the last two decades, such low elasticities mean less total revenue for agricultural exporting nations (recall our discussion of the relationship between price elasticity and total revenue in Chapter 3). But when commodity prices are rapidly rising, as they did for sugar during the 1973–1974 period, those 19 or so LDCs which together supply 80 per cent of world sugar exports stand to gain substantial short-run revenues.

A widely used device to modify the tendency for primary product prices to decline relative to other traded goods is the establishment of *international commodity agreements*. The primary purposes of such agreements are to set overall output levels, to stabilise world prices and to assign quota shares to various producing nations for such diverse items as coffee, tea, copper, lead and sugar. Commodity agreements can also provide greater protection to individual exporting nations against excessive competition and the overexpansion of world production. Such overexpansion of supply tends to drive down prices and curtail the growth of earnings for all countries. In short, commodity agreements are intended to guarantee participating nations a relatively fixed share of world export earnings and a more stable world price for their commodity. It is for this reason that the United Nations Committee on Trade and Development (UNCTAD) advocated, at its fourth international conference in May 1976, the establishment of an 11 billion dollar fund to support the prices of some 18 primary commodities including sugar, tea, copper, tin, and lead produced by Third World nations. It also called for the establishment of 'buffer stocks' of commodities to stabilise prices whenever supply and demand become grossly imbalanced.

The fourth and fifth factors working against the long-run expansion of LDC primary product export earnings – the development of synthetic substitutes and the growth of agricultural protection in the developed countries – are perhaps the most important. Synthetic substitutes for commodities such as cotton, rubber, sisal, jute, hides and skins, act both as a brake against higher commodity prices and as a direct source of competition in world export markets. As we saw in the previous chapter, the synthetic share of world market export earnings has steadily risen over time while the share of natural products has fallen.

In the case of agricultural protection in the form of tariffs and quotas in developed countries against

[3] See A. Maizels, *Exports and Economic Growth of Developing Countries*, Cambridge University Press, 1968.

food and fibre exports, the effects can be most devastating to Third World export earnings. The common agricultural policy of the European Economic Community, for example, is much more discriminatory against LDC food exports than that of each individual EEC nation before the agreement to integrate their economies was finalised.

On the supply side, there are also a number of factors working against the rapid expansion of primary product export earnings. The most important, however, is the structural rigidity of many Third World rural production systems. We discussed these rigidities, which take the form of limited resources, poor climate, bad soils, antiquated rural institutional, social and economic structures and non-productive patterns of land tenure in Chapter 16. Whatever the international demand situation for particular commodities (and these may certainly differ from commodity to commodity), little export expansion can be expected when rural economic and social structures militate against positive supply responses from peasant farmers who are averse to risk. Furthermore, in those developing nations with markedly dualistic farming structures (i.e. large corporate capital-intensive farms, existing side by side with thousands of fragmented low productivity peasant holdings) any growth in export earnings is likely to be distributed very unevenly among the rural population.

We may conclude that the successful promotion of primary product agricultural exports first necessitates a reorganisation of rural social and economic structures along the lines suggested in Chapter 16 to raise total agricultural productivity and distribute the benefits more widely. The primary objective of any Third World rural development strategy must be to provide sufficient food to feed the indigenous people of the nation first and then be concerned about export expansion. But having accomplished this most difficult internal development task, LDCs will only be able to realise the potential benefits of their comparative advantage in world commodity markets (especially with regard to raw materials and non-food cash crops) if they can co-operate with one another, be assisted by developed nations in formulating and carrying out international commodity agreements and price stabilisation programmes, and secure greater access to developed country markets. This is why UNCTAD IV, where these issues were discussed, was so critical for Third World participants. On the whole, however, given the structure of world demand for primary products, the threat of local food shortages, and thus the desire for agricultural self-sufficiency, the inevitability of further technological developments of synthetic substitutes and the unlikelihood of lower levels of agricultural protection among developed nations, the real scope for primary product export expansion in individual LDCs *vis-à-vis* the developed nations at present seems rather limited.

Nevertheless, such pessimism about the export of primary products should not entail a retreat from emphasis on rural development. The rapid expansion of local food and cash crop production is or should be a major component of any national development strategy whether or not a country seeks to export its surplus to the rest of the world. Finally, it should be pointed out that for certain primary commodities like food grains, timber products, fish, meat and certain fruits and vegetables, world demand is better suited for rapid export expansion than for most others, as both income and price elasticities of demand are relatively high. Ultimately, one cannot really talk about primary product export expansion without reference to particular commodities and specific countries. Such a specific commodity and country analysis is unfortunately beyond the scope of this book.[4]

Expanding exports of manufactured goods

The expansion of Third World manufactured exports was given great stimulus by the spectacular export performance of countries like South Korea, Singapore, Hong Kong, Taiwan and Brazil during the 1960s. For example, Taiwan's total exports grew at an annual rate of over 20 per cent during the 1960s while exports from South Korea grew even faster. In both cases, this export growth was led by manufactured goods which constituted almost 75 per cent of both nations' foreign exchange earnings. For the Third World as a whole, manufactured exports grew from 6 per cent of their total merchandise exports in 1950 to 28 per cent by 1980. However, the LDC share of total world trade in manufactures has remained relatively unchanged at under 8 per cent over the past few decades.

[4] See Maizels, *op. cit.*, however, for a lengthy and detailed analysis of this issue.

The demand problems facing LDC manufacturing export expansion, though different in basic economic content from those facing primary products, are nonetheless similar in practice. Thus, although income and price elasticities of international demand for manufactured goods in the aggregate are higher than for primary commodities, they afford little relief to Third World nations bent on expanding their exports of manufactured goods. This is largely due to the growing protection in developed nations against the manufactured exports of LDCs – ironically caused, in part, by the successful penetration of low-cost, labour-intensive manufactures from countries like Taiwan, Hong Kong and Southern Korea during the 1960s and 1970s into developed nation markets. The Canadian economist, Gerald Helleiner, makes the point well when he observes that:

> Of fundamental importance to the issue of Third World manufacturing export prospects are the barriers which are erected by the developed countries to restrict entry of these products to their own markets. Tariffs, quotas and other barriers in the markets of the rich constitute a major impediment to large-scale industrial exports. The tariff structures of the rich nations are such as to offer the greatest degree of effective protection to their producers in the very industries in which poor countries are most likely to be competitive – light industries relatively intensive in the use of unskilled labour such as textiles, footwear, rugs, sporting goods, handbags, processed foodstuffs, etc. This is precisely because of these industries' inability freely to compete, unskilled labour-intensity putting them at a comparative disadvantage within the context of their relatively high wage economies.[5]

The growth of unemployment in developed countries, especially in traditional industries such as textiles where almost 40 per cent of Third World manufactured exports are concentrated, makes the prospects for lower trade barriers on LDC light manufactures for the remainder of the 1980s seem rather remote. Moreover, as more and more Third World countries attempt to emulate the spectacular manufactured export successes of a few in the 1960s, the competition for access to the narrowing developed-country markets is likely to lead to many unforeseen difficulties and disappointments. But, as in the case of agricultural production, this gloomy export outlook should be no cause for curtailing the needed expansion of manufacturing production to serve local markets in less developed countries. Moreover, as we argue below, there is great scope for mutually beneficial trade in manufactures among Third World countries within the context of the gradual economic integration of their national economies. Too much emphasis has been placed on the analysis of trade prospects of individual LDCs with the developed nations and not enough on the prospects for mutually beneficial trade with each other.

Import substitution: looking inward but still paying outward

In the 1950s and early 1960s many Third World countries faced with a declining world market for their primary products, a growing balance of payments deficit on current account, and a general belief in the mystique of industrialisation, decided to pursue what has come to be known as an 'import substitution' strategy of development. This entails an attempt to replace commodities, usually manufactured goods and formerly imported, with domestic sources of production and supply. The typical strategy is first to erect tariff barriers or quotas on the importation of certain commodities, then to try to set up a local industry to produce the goods that were formerly imported – items such as radios, bicycles or household electrical appliances. Typically, this involves co-operation with foreign companies who are encouraged to set up their plants behind the wall of tariff protection and given all kinds of tax and investment incentives. While initial costs of production may lead to higher retail prices than those of former imports, the economic rationale put forward for the establishment of import-substituting manufacturing operations is either that the industry will eventually be able to reap the benefits of large-scale production and lower costs (this is the so-called 'infant industry' argument for tariff protection) or that the balance of payments will be improved as fewer consumer goods are imported. Often a combination of both arguments is

[5] G. K. Helleiner, *International Trade and Economic Development*, Penguin, 1972, pp. 69–70.

advanced. Eventually, it is hoped and, in many cases, anticipated that the infant industry would 'grow up' and be able to compete in world markets. It could then generate export earnings once it lowered its average costs of production.

Two decades of import-substituting experience, especially in Latin America, have left a less than satisfactory record. Specifically, four undesirable outcomes have emerged. First, the main beneficiaries of the import substitution process have been the foreign firms who, well placed behind tariff walls, could take advantage of liberal tax and investment incentives. After deducting interest, profits, royalty and management fees, most of which are remitted abroad, the little that may be left over usually accrues to the wealthy local industrialists with whom foreign manufacturers co-operate and who provide their political and economic cover.

Second, most import substitution has been made possible by the heavy and often government-subsidised importation of capital goods and intermediate products by foreign (and domestic) companies. In the case of foreign companies many of these are purchased from their parent and sister companies abroad, with two immediate results. First, capital-intensive industries are set up, catering usually for the consumption habits of the rich and having a minimal employment effect (see our discussion of the output employment lag in Chapter 13). Second, far from improving the LDC's balance of payments situation, indiscriminate import substitution often worsens it by raising the requirements for imported capital goods and intermediate products while, as we have just seen, a good part of the profits is remitted abroad in the form of private transfer payments.

A third detrimental effect of many of the import substitution strategies of the 1950s and 1960s was its impact on traditional primary product exports. In order to encourage local manufacturing through the importation of cheap capital and intermediate goods, foreign exchange rates (i.e. the rate at which the Central Bank of a nation is prepared to purchase foreign currencies) were often artificially overvalued. This has the effect of raising the price of exports and lowering the price of imports in terms of the local currency. For example, if the 'appropriate' or free market exchange rate between Pakistini rupees and US dollars were, say, 20 to 1 but the official exchange rate were set at 10 rupees to the dollar, an item which costs $10 in the USA could be imported into Pakistan for 100 rupees (excluding transport costs and other service charges). If the free market exchange rate prevailed (i.e. the exchange rate determined by the supply of and demand for Pakistani rupees in terms of dollars) it would cost 200 rupees. Thus by overvaluing their exchange rate, LDC governments are able effectively to lower the domestic local currency price of their imports. At the same time their export prices are increased; for example, at an exchange rate of 10 to 1, US importers would have to pay 10 cents for every one-rupee item rather than 5 cents if the hypothetical free market ratio of 10 to 1 were in effect. Table 21.2 provides rough estimates of the extent of currency overvaluation in nine developing countries.

The net effect of overvaluing exchange rates in the context of import substitution policies is to encourage capital-intensive production methods still further (since the price of imported capital goods is artificially lowered) and to penalise the traditional primary product export sector by artificially raising the price of these exports in terms of foreign currencies. This causes local farmers to be less competitive in world markets. In terms of its income distribution effects, the outcome of such government policies may be to penalise the small farmer and the self-employed at the expense of improving the profits of the owners of capital both foreign and domestic. Industrial protection has the effect of taxing agricultural goods in the home market as well as discouraging agricultural exports. Import substitution policies in practice, therefore, are often said to have worsened the local distribution of income by favouring the urban sector and the higher income groups while discriminating against the rural sector and the lower income groups.

Fourth, and finally, import substitution which may have been conceived with the idea of stimulating self-sustained industrialisation by creating 'forward' and 'backward' linkages with the rest of the economy has often in practice inhibited that industrialisation. By increasing the costs of inputs to potentially 'forward' linked industries (those which purchase the output of the protected firm as inputs or intermediate products in their own productive process – e.g. a printer's purchase of paper from a locally protected paper mill) and by purchasing its inputs from overseas sources of supply rather than through 'backward' linkages to domestic suppliers of its inputs, inefficient import substituting firms may block the hoped-for process of self-reliant,

Table 21.2
Official and estimated free market exchange rates

Country		Year	Domestic Currency Units	Official Rate (c)	Degree of Overvaluation (percent)	Implied Free Market Exchange Rate
				Units of National Currency per $ US		
Argentina	(a)	1958	Pesos	18.0	100	36.0
Brazil	(a)	1966	Cruzeiros	2,220.0	50	3,330.0
	(b)	1966	Cruzeiros	2,220.0	27	2,819.0
Chile	(b)	1961	Pesos	1.053	68	1.769
Colombia	(d)	1968	Pesos	15.89	22	19.39
Malaya	(b)	1965	Dollars (M)	3.06	4	3.18
Mexico	(a)	1960	Pesos	12.49	15	14.36
	(b)	1960	Pesos	12.49	9	13.61
Pakistan	(a)	1963–64	Rupees	4.799	25	5.999
	(b)	1963–64	Rupees	4.799	50	7.199
Philippines	(a)	1965	Pesos	3.90	20	4.68
	(b)	1965	Pesos	3.90	15	4.49
Taiwan	(a)	1965	$N.T.	40.10	20	48.12

Source: Derek Healey, 'Development Policy: New Thinking About an Interpretation', *Journal of Economic Literature*, x, 3, September 1972, p. 781.

integrated industrialisation.

All things considered, we concur with Professor Helleiner, whose views seem to reflect a consensus among those development economists who have studied the process of import substitution that:

> It is difficult to find any rationale for the pattern of import substituting industrialization which has, whether consciously or not, actually been promoted. It has given undue emphasis to consumer goods in most countries; it has given insufficient attention to potential long-run comparative advantages, i.e. resource endowments and learning possibilities; and it has employed alien and unsuitable, i.e. capital-intensive, technologies to an extraordinary and unnecessary degree. If a selective approach to import substitution is to be pursued at all, and there is a strong case to be made for a more generalized approach, the selection actually employed in recent years has left a great deal to be desired. The consequence has too frequently been the creation of an inefficient industrial sector operating far below capacity, and creating very little employment, very little foreign exchange saving, and little prospect of further productivity growth. The object of policy must now be gradually to bring incentive structures and thus the relative efficiencies of various industrial activities into some sort of balance, thereby encouraging domestic manufacture of intermediate and capital goods at the expense of importable consumer goods and the development eventually of manufacture for export.[6]

Tariffs, physical quotas and exchange rates adjustments

Tariffs and quotas

Since import substitution policies are predicated on the protection of local industries behind tariff barriers and since tariffs and import quotas are an important instrument of Third World commercial policy, it might be worth while briefly to discuss the use and abuse of tariffs and quotas in many poor

[6] Helleiner, *op. cit.*, p. 105.

nations. Governments in less developed countries impose tariffs and physical quotas on imports for a variety of reasons. For example, tariff barriers may be erected in order to raise government revenue. In fact, given administrative and political difficulties of collecting local income taxes, fixed percentage taxes on imports (i.e. tariffs) collected at a relatively few ports or border posts often constitute one of the cheapest and most efficient forms of raising government revenue. In many LDCs, foreign trade taxes constitute the major source of government income and thus provide a central feature of the overall fiscal system. On the other hand, physical quotas on certain imports like automobiles and other luxury consumer goods, while more difficult to administer and more subject to delays, inefficiency and corruption (e.g. with regard to the granting of import licences), are nevertheless another effective means of restricting the entry of particularly troublesome commodities.

Tariffs may also be levied to restrict the importation of non-necessity products (usually expensive consumer goods) and thus improve the balance of payments. Like overvaluing the official rate of foreign exchange, tariffs may be used to improve a nation's terms of trade. However, in a small country unable to influence world prices of its exports or imports (in other words, most LDCs) the terms of trade argument for tariffs (or devaluation) has little validity. Finally, as we have just seen, tariffs may form an integral component of an import substitution policy of industrialisation.

Much of international trade theory, and most developed country trade economists, oppose the use of tariffs and other trade barriers as economically inefficient ways of stimulating industrial growth or achieving almost any other economic aim. Theoretically this is correct, if the questionable assumptions of the traditional free trade models are accepted. But apart from the revenue argument, the only really valid argument for the erection of barriers to most imports, and its is a fundamental philosophical as well as economic argument, is the desire of a nation or group of Third World nations to 'go it alone', or move alone, along the development path which they deem most desirable. Arguments for and against tariffs and import quotas are ultimately arguments for or against the desirability of pursuing inward-looking development strategies.

A country, or more likely a group of poor countries, may see their long-run development aspirations tied to their own ability to generate appropriate local institutions, patterns of consumption and production, technologies, products, entrepreneurship, etc. If they believe that an open policy of widespread contact with the outside world, whether in the field of trade or, as we shall shortly see, in the area of private and public foreign assistance, would in the long run be detrimental to their development aspirations, the erection of trade and other economic and non-economic barriers to international exchange need not be as harmful to national welfare as implied by traditional static or dynamic economic criteria based on a false or irrelevant set of assumptions. At the same time, we must not make the opposite mistake of assuming that by closing itself, whether partially or completely, to the rest of the world, a Third World nation will automatically be better able to achieve a more broadly based development. On the contrary, as we have seen with respect to import substitution policies, tariff and quota barriers may merely provide an economic shield behind which poverty, unemployment and inequality grow even worse.

Foreign exchange rates, exchange controls and the devaluation decision

In the section on import substitution, we briefly discussed the question of foreign currency exchange rates. Remember that a country's 'official' exchange rate is the rate at which its Central Bank is prepared to transact exchanges of its local currency for other currencies in approved foreign exchange markets. Official exchange rates are usually quoted in terms of US dollars – i.e. so many pesos, cruzeiros, pounds, shillings, rupees, Bhat, etc. per dollar. For example, the official exchange rate of Kenya shillings for US dollars in 1975 was approximately shs 7 per dollar while the Indian rupee was officially valued at approximately 7.6 rupees per dollar. If a Kenyan manufacturer wished to import fabrics from an Indian textile exporter at say a cost of 7 600 rupees, he would need shs 7 000 to make the purchase. However, since almost all foreign exchange transactions are conducted in US dollars, the Kenyan importer would need to purchase $1000 worth of foreign exchange from the Central Bank of Kenya for his 7 000 shillings and then transmit these dollars through official channels to the Indian exporter.

Official foreign exchange rates are not necessarily set at or near the economic 'equilibrium' price for foreign exchange – i.e. the rate at which the domestic demand for a foreign currency like dollars would just equal its supply in the absence of governmental regulation or intervention. In fact, as we saw in Table 21.2 the currencies of most Third World countries are usually 'overvalued' by the Central Bank in relation to this hypothetical 'supply-equals-demand' equilibrium exchange rate. Whenever the official price of foreign exchange is established at a level which, in the absence of any governmental restrictions or controls, would result in an excess of local demand over the available supply of foreign exchange, the domestic currency in question is said to be overvalued.

The economic results of pursuing an intentional policy of currency overvaluation have been succinctly summarised in the following extract from the 1968 *Economic Survey of Asia and the Far East*[7]:

> All exporters (who predominantly sold agricultural goods) were required to surrender foreign exchange earnings at the official rate of exchange. This clearly constituted a tax on the agricultural sector of the economy. At the official rate of exchange there existed a large unsatisfied demand for imports. Thus a strict rationing of the entitlement to import through licensing had to be made. The overvalued rate of exchange and the consequent unsatisfied demand for imports naturally meant domestic prices for imports substantially above international prices. This price differential was not absorbed by the government through license fees or import surcharges, but was allowed to be converted into monopoly profit for the license holder, and served as a major source of investable funds in the private sector. The excess demand generated by the strict quantitative control of imports further opened up high profit opportunities for investors in import substituting industries.

In such situations of excess demand, LDC Central Banks have three basic policy options designed to maintain the official rate of exchange. First, they can attempt to accommodate this excess demand by running down their reserves of foreign exchange and/or by borrowing additional foreign exchange abroad and thereby incurring further debts. Second, they can attempt to curtail the excess demand for foreign exchange by pursuing commercial policies and tax measures designed to lessen the demand for imports – e.g. tariffs, physical quotas, licensing, etc. Third, and finally, they can regulate and intervene in the foreign exchange market by 'rationing' the limited supply of available foreign exchange to 'preferred' customers. Such a rationing device is more commonly known as 'exchange control'. It is a policy in wide use throughout the Third World and is probably the major financial mechanism for preserving the level of foreign exchange reserves at the prevailing official exchange rate.

The mechanism and operation of exchange control can be illustrated diagrammatically with the aid of Figure 21.1. Under free market conditions the equilibrium price of foreign exchange would be P_e with a total of OM units of foreign exchange demanded and supplied. If, however, the government maintains an artificially low price of foreign exchange (i.e. an overvaluation of its domestic currency) at P_a, then supply of foreign exchange will amount to only OM′ units since exports are 'overpriced'. But at price P_a, the demand for foreign exchange will be OM″ units with the result that there is an 'excess demand' equal to M′M″ units. Some mechanism, therefore, will have to be devised to ration the available supply of OM′. If the government were to auction this supply, importers would be willing to pay a price of P_b for the foreign

Figure 21.1
The free market and controlled rate of foreign exchange

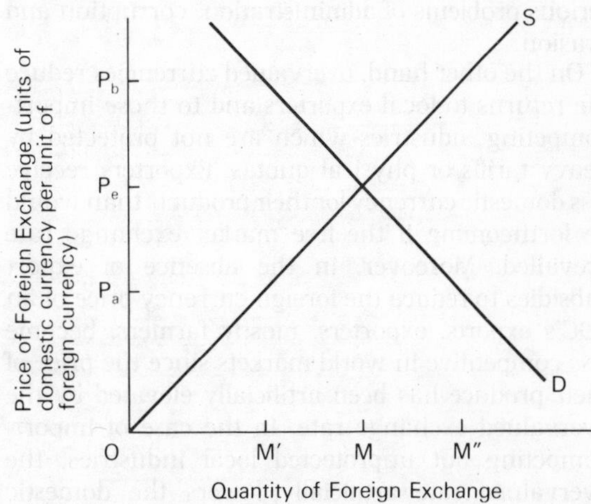

[7] UNECAFE, *Economic Survey of Asia and the Far East 1968*, Bangkok 1969, p. 67.

exchange. In such a case the government would make a profit of P_aP_b per unit. Typically, however, such open auctions are not carried out and limited supplies of foreign exchange are allocated through some administrative quota or licensing device. Opportunities for corruption, evasion and the emergence of 'black markets' are thus made possible since importers are willing to pay as much as P_b per unit of foreign exchange.

Why have most Third World governments opted for an overvalued official exchange rate? Basically, as we have seen, they have done so as part of widespread programmes of rapid industrialisation and import substitution. Overvalued exchange rates reduce the domestic currency price of imports below that which would exist in a free market for foreign exchange – i.e. by the forces of supply and demand. Cheaper imports, especially capital and intermediate producer goods, are needed to fuel the industrialisation process. But overvalued exchange rates also lower the domestic currency price of imported consumer goods, expecially expensive luxury products. Third World nations wishing to limit such unnecessary and costly imports often need, therefore, to establish import controls (mostly physical quotas) or to set up a 'dual' exchange rate system: one rate, usually highly overvalued to be applied to capital and intermediate good imports and the other, much lower, for luxury consumption good imports. Such dual exchange rate systems, therefore, make the domestic price of imported luxury goods very high while maintaining the artificially low and thus subsidised price of producer good imports. Needless to say, dual exchange rate systems like exchange controls and import licences present serious problems of administration, corruption and evasion.

On the other hand, overvalued currencies reduce the returns to local exporters and to those import-competing industries which are not protected by heavy tariffs or physical quotas. Exporters receive less domestic currency for their products than would be forthcoming if the free market exchange rate prevailed. Moreover, in the absence of export subsidies to reduce the foreign currency price of an LDC's exports, exporters, mostly farmers, become less competitive in world markets since the price of their produce has been artificially elevated by the overvalued exchange rate. In the case of import-competing but unprotected local industries, the overvalued rate artificially lowers the domestic currency price of foreign imports of the same product – e.g. radios, tyres, bicycles, household utensils, etc.

In the absence of effective government intervention and regulation of the foreign exchange dealings of its nationals, overvalued exchange rates have a tendency to exacerbate balance of payments problems simply because they cheapen imports while making exports more costly. As we mentioned in our discussion of the balance of payments, chronic payments deficits resulting primarily from current account transactions (i.e. exports and imports) can possibly be ameliorated by a *currency devaluation.* Simply defined, a country's currency is devalued or, more strictly depreciated, when the official rate at which its Central Bank is prepared to exchange the local currency for dollars is increased. For example, a devaluation of the Kenya shilling or Indian rupee would occur if their previous (1975) official exchange rates of approximately 7 shillings and 7.6 rupees to the dollar were changed to say 10 shillings and/or rupees per dollar. In both instances, US importers of Kenyan and Indian goods would have to pay fewer dollars to obtain the same products as they had to prior to the devaluation. On the other hand, US exports to Kenya and India would become more expensive (i.e. require more shillings and/or rupees to purchase) than before. In short, by lowering the *foreign* currency price of its exports (and thereby, it is hoped, generating more foreign demand) while raising the *domestic* currency price of its imports (and thereby lowering domestic demand) Third World nations which devalue their currency hope to improve their trade balance *vis-à-vis* the rest of the world.

An alternative to a currency devaluation would be to allow foreign exchange rates to fluctuate freely in accordance with changing conditions of international demand and supply. Freely fluctuating or flexible exchange rates are not thought to be desirable, especially in Third World nations heavily dependent on exports and imports, because they are unpredictable, subject to wide and uncontrollable fluctuations and susceptible to foreign and domestic currency speculation. Such unpredictable fluctuations can wreak havoc with both short- and long-range development plans. We see once again, therefore, that bowing to the free market forces of supply and demand (this time for local and foreign currencies) could subject a wide range of Third World nations to even greater instability and increased vulnerability than market intervention. The present international monetary system of 'floating' exchange rates, which was legalised at the January 1976 IMF meetings in Jamaica, represents a compromise between a fixed (artificially 'pegged') and a fully flexible exchange rate system. Under this 'managed' floating system major international currencies are free to fluctuate but erratic swings are limited through central bank intervention and international co-operation. Many developing countries, however, have decided to continue to peg their currencies to the world's major currencies, although some like Kenya have decided to peg their currencies to the movements of a weighted average of a large number of major currencies rather than to tie it to a particular currency like the US dollar or the pound sterling.

One final point about Third World currency devaluations, particularly in the light of previous chapter discussions, is their probable effect on domestic prices and, more importantly, on the domestic distribution of incomes. A currency devaluation has the immediate effect of raising domestic prices so that imported goods are now more expensive to purchase in terms of the local currency. Shirts, shoes, radios, records, foodstuffs, bicycles, etc., which formerly cost x pesos, now may cost $x+y$ pesos depending on the magnitude of the devaluation. If as a result of these higher prices, domestic workers seek to preserve the 'real' value of their purchasing power, they are likely to initiate increased wage and salary demands. Such increases, if granted, will raise production costs and tend to push local prices up even higher. A wage–price spiral of domestic inflation is thereby set in motion. In fact, a vicious circle of devaluation – domestic wage and price increases – higher export prices – worsened balance of trade – devaluation could result. In effect, the devaluation decision could simply exacerbate the balance of payments problem while generating galloping inflation domestically. The experience of Latin American nations with such uncontrollable inflation during the 1950s and 1960s and many other LDCs in the 1970s have made them reluctant users of the tool of currency devaluation.

As for the distributional effects of a devaluation, it is clear that by altering the domestic price and returns of 'tradable' goods (exports and imports) and creating incentives for the production of exports as opposed to domestic goods, devaluation will benefit certain groups at the expense of others. In general, urban wage earners, those with fixed incomes, the unemployed and those small farmers and rural and urban small-scale producers and suppliers of services who do not participate in the export sector stand to be financially hurt by the domestic inflation that typically follows a devaluation. On the other hand, large exporters (usually large land-owners and foreign-owned corporations) as well as the more medium-sized local businesses engaged in foreign trade, stand to benefit the most. While we cannot categorically assert that devaluation tends to worsen income distribution without reference to specific countries and situations, we may conclude that the more concentrated is the ownership and control over the export sector in private as opposed to public hands, the greater will be the likelihood of an adverse effect on income distribution. For this reason, among others, international commercial and financial problems (e.g. chronic balance of payments deficits) cannot be divorced from domestic problems (e.g. poverty and inequality) in Third World nations. Similarly, policy responses to alleviate one problem might improve or worsen others. This interaction between problems and policies will be discussed at length in Chapter 24.

Conclusions: trade policies and development

In the final analysis it is not a less developed country's inward- or outward-looking stance *vis-à-vis* the rest of the world that will determine whether or not it develops along the lines described in Chapter 6 and in many other parts of this book. Inward-looking protectionist policies that include tariffs, quotas, and exchange rate adjustments do not necessarily guarantee more jobs, higher incomes and health, clean water, and relevant education any more than do outward-looking non-interventionist policies. In fact, as Professor Streeten so skilfully pointed out when summarising a recent Cambridge University conference on trade and development:

> A curious paradox came out of the discussion [on the effects of trade on LDC inequalities]. It seemed that both inward-looking, import-substituting, protectionist, interventionist policies and outward-looking, market-orientated, non-interventionist policies tend to increase market imperfections and monopolies

and reduce the demand for labour-intensive processes, the latter because the market rewards most those factors that are relatively scarce (capital, management, professional skills) and penalizes those in abundant supply and because the market strengthens the ability to accumulate of those who have against those who have not. But though it is paradoxical that both a protectionist 'distorted' system of prices, interest rates, wages and exchange rates and a market-determined one should increase inequalities, there is no contradiction. It is plausible that within a certain social and political framework, both export-orientated market policies and import-substitution-orientated, interventionist, 'distorting' policies should aggravate inequalities, though one set may do this somewhat more than the other. Perhaps economists have been barking up the wrong tree when disputing which set of price policies contributes more to equality. In an inegalitarian power structure, both make for inequality; in an egalitarian power structure, both may make for equality.[8]

Economic integration: the potential benefits of looking both outward and inward

Some basic concepts

One significant variant of the free trade doctrine which can have important relevance to Third World countries is the theory of economic integration. The basic idea is for a group of nations in the same region, preferably of relatively equal size and at equal stages of development, to join together in an economic union by raising a common tariff wall against the products of non-member countries while freeing internal trade among members. Nations which levy common external tariffs while freeing internal trade are said to have formed a **customs union**. If external tariffs against outside countries differ among member nations while internal trade is free, the nations are said to have formed a **free trade area**. Finally, a **common market** possesses all the attributes of a customs union (i.e. common external tariffs and free internal trade) plus the free movement of labour and capital among the partner states.

The theory of customs unions and economic integration has a rather treasured place in modern literature on international trade. It is associated principally with the work of Jacob Viner in the 1940s. But the core of this theory, focusing on the static resource and production reallocation effects within highly integrated and flexible industrialised nations, is of limited value to contemporary developing nations intent on building up their industrial base. Yet many concepts of the theory of integration do provide valid criteria on which to evaluate the probable short-run success or failure of economic co-operation among Third World countries.

The basic economic rationale for the gradual integration of less developed economies is a long-term dynamic one. It is that integration provides the opportunity for industries which *have not yet been established* as well as for those that have to take advantage of the economies of large-scale production. Integration, therefore, needs to be viewed as a mechanism to encourage a rational division of labour among a group of countries, each of which is too small to benefit from such a division of labour. In the absence of integration, each separate country may not provide a big enough domestic market to enable local industries to lower their production costs through economies of scale. In such cases, import-substituting industrialisation will typically result, as we have seen, in the establishment of high-cost, inefficient local industries. Moreover, the same industry (e.g. textiles or shoes) may be set up in two or more adjoining small nations. Each will be operating at less than optimal capacity but will be protected against the imports of the other by high tariff or quota barriers. Not only does such duplication result in wasted scarce resources, it also means that consumers are forced to pay a higher price for the product than if the market were large enough for high-volume, low-cost production to take place at a single location.

This leads to a second dynamic rationale for LDC economic integration. By removing barriers to trade among member states, the possibility of **co-ordinated industrial planning** is created, especially in those industries where economies of scale are likely to exist, such as fertiliser and petrochemical plants, heavy industry like iron and steel, capital goods and machine tool industries, and small farm

[8] Streeten, *op. cit.*, pp. 3–4.

mechanical equipment. But the co-ordinated planning of industrial expansion which enables all member states to accelerate their rates of industrial growth by assigning given industries to different members takes the partners that much closer to full economic and, eventually, political union. Problems of sovereignty and national self-interest impinge at this stage. To date they have overwhelmed the economic logic of a close and co-ordinated union. However, as Third World nations, especially small ones, continue to experience the futility of either development in isolation (autarky) or full participation in the highly unequal world economy, it is likely that interest will increase, in coming decades, in the long-run benefits of some form of co-operation among groups of LDCs.

In addition to these two long-term dynamic arguments for integration, there are also the standard textbook *static* evaluative criteria known as **trade creation** and **trade diversion.** Trade creation is said to occur when external barriers and internal free trade lead to a shift in production from high to low cost member states. For example, before integration both country A and country B may produce textiles for their respective local markets. Country A may be a lower cost producer but its exports to country B are blocked by the latter's high tariff barrier. If A and B form a customs union, eliminating all barriers to internal trade, country A's more efficient low-cost textile industry will cater for both markets. Trade will have been created in the sense that the removal of barriers has led to a shift in country B's consumption from its relatively high cost textiles to the lower cost textiles of country A.

Similarly, trade diversion is said to occur when the erection of external tariff barriers causes production and consumption of one or more member states to shift from lower-cost non-member sources of supply (e.g. a developed country) to higher-cost member producers. Trade diversion is normally considered undesirable since both the world and member states are perceived to be worse off as a result of the diversion of production from more efficient foreign suppliers to the less efficient domestic industries of member states. But this argument ignores two basic facts. First, because of potential economies of scale, the creation of local jobs, and the circular flow of income within the integrated region, static trade diversion may turn out to be dynamic trade creation. This is simply a variant of the standard 'infant industry' argument for protection with the more likely possibility that the infant will grow up as a result of the larger market in which it operates. Second, if in the absence of integration, each member state were to protect its local import-substituting industry against cheaper foreign suppliers, the common external tariff of member states causes no more trade diversion than would have happened anyway. But, as we just saw, if there are scale economies the possibility of dynamic trade creation can emerge. Thus static but useful concepts like trade creation and trade diversion must be analysed in the dynamic context of growth and development based on the realities of current commercial policies of Third World nations rather than in the theoretical vacuum of traditional free trade models.

Third World regional integration in practice: some case studies[9]

Having outlined some basic economic aspects of regional integration, we can now formulate a set of specific issues against which one can evaluate the successes or failures of various recent integration schemes in the Third World. The questions are the following:

- Has integration stimulated a more rapid growth rate of internal trade among member states than in its absence?
- Has the growth of internal trade had the character of 'trade creation' or 'trade diversion', bearing in mind some of the limitations of these concepts discussed above?
- How has integration affected the trade of individual member countries?
- What effect has integration had on the aggregate economic growth rate of member countries?
- What have been the main obstacles hindering integration?

We can draw on Dr Pazos' detailed study to provide preliminary answers to these questions on the basis of the recent integration experiences of Third World countries in Latin America, the Caribbean and Africa. Seven regional groups of

[9] For a useful summary of Third World regional integration experiences, see Felipe Pazos, 'Regional integration of trade among less developed countries', *World Development*, i, 7, July 1973, pp. 1–12.

varying size, economic structure and levels of development have entered into arrangements to integrate their economies – some more closely than others – since 1960. They are (1) the **Latin American Free Trade Association** (LAFTA) formed in 1960 and consisting of 11 Latin American countries (see Table 21.3); the **Central American Common Market** (CACM) also formed in 1960 and comprising five Central American nations; (3) the **Andean Group** formed in 1969 and consisting of Bolivia, Chile, Ecuador, Colombia and Peru; (4) the **Caribbean Free Trade Area** (CARIFTA) formed in 1968 and consisting of 12 Caribbean nations. In 1973, CARIFTA was converted into a fully integrated **Caribbean Community**; (5) the **Central African Customs and Economic Union** (CACEU) formed in 1964 and comprising Cameroon, Central African Republic, Congo and Gabon; (6) the **East African Community** (EAC) which was in existence from colonial times until the mid-1970s and consisted of Kenya, Uganda and Tanzania; and finally (7) the newly formed (1975) **Economic Community of West African States** (ECOWAS) consisting of 16 countries – nine French, six English and one Portuguese speaking – with a total population of 136 million and an area of 6.5 million square km. ECOWAS is the largest economic union in Africa.

Table 21.3 summarises the expansion of trade among member states of the six integration groups between 1960 and 1970. It can be seen that in two of the four older groups, CACM and CACEU, internal trade grew at a phenomenal annual rate of 28.8 and 23.2 per cent respectively during the 1960s. The other two older groups (LAFTA and EAC) showed only moderate rates of growth of between 7 and 8 per cent annually. But it is important to note that in both cases this internal growth rate was significantly higher than the growth rate of total trade for each. This can be seen by the rise in internal trade as a percentage of total trade between 1960 and 1970 for both groups, from 8.5 to 10.6 per cent for LAFTA and from 14.6 to 17.3 per cent for EAC. The relatively slow growth of intra-trade within LAFTA and EAC can be attributed largely to the emergence of new forms of protective restriction in the 1960s designed to permit the weaker partners to catch up slowly with the stronger ones.

Table 21.3
Intra-trade of integration groups, 1960–1970

	Value of exports to area ($ million)				Share of exports to the area in total exports (%)				Annual growth rate of exports to the area (%)		
Integration group	*1960*	*1968*	*1969*	*1970*	*1960*	*1968*	*1969*	*1970*	*1960–68*	*1969*	*1970*
Latin America											
LAFTA[1]	564	999	1,206	1,254	8.5	10.7	11.7	10.6	7.4	20.7	3.9
Andean Group[2]	(40)	(60)	(84)	(109)	(2.5)	(2.2)	(2.9)	(3.3)	(5.2)	(40.0)	(29.8)
CACM[3]	33	247	250	286	7.5	26.0	25.7	26.1	28.8	1.2	14.4
Caribbean											
CARIFTA[4]	27	52	66	—	5.0	5.9	7.2	—	8.6	26.9	—
Africa											
CACEU[5]	3	16	21	—	1.7	4.0	4.6	—	23.2	31.2	—
EAC[6]	63	116	122	142	14.6	17.1	16.8	17.3	7.9	5.2	16.4

Notes
1. *Latin American Free Trade Association:* Argentina, Bolivia, Brazil, Chile, Colombia, Ecuador, Mexico, Paraguay, Peru, Uruguay, Venezuela.
2. *Andean Group:* Bolivia, Chile, Colombia, Ecuador, Peru.
3. *Central American Common Market:* Costa Rica, El Salvador, Guatemala, Honduras, Nicaragua.
4. *Caribbean Free Trade Area:* Barbados, Guyana, Jamaica, Trinidad and Tobago, Antigua, British Honduras, Dominica, Grenada, Montserrat, St Kitts-Nevis-Anguilla, St Lucia, St Vincent.
5. *Central African Customs and Economic Union:* Cameroon, Central African Republic, Congo, Gabon.
6. *East African Community:* Kenya, Uganda, United Republic of Tanzania.

Source: Pazos, 'Regional integration of trade among less developed countries', *World Development*, Vol. 1 No. 7, July 1973, p. 2, Table 1.

Both the Andean Group and CARIFTA, formed in the late 1960s, showed big jumps in their internal trade in 1969. But we must await further data to evaluate the trade expansionary effects of each group. However, the rapid pace at which trade began to expand in CARIFTA and the Andean group testifies to the potential capacity of Third World nations to conduct mutually beneficial trade among themselves. Finally, since the bulk of the increase in intra-trade among the various integration groups was concentrated in the manufacturing sector (e.g. in CACM 74 per cent of all intra-trade is in manufacturing categories), the scope for industrial growth can be greatly strengthened by economic co-operation among various LDCs. Instead of trying to compete with one another for access to heavily protected developed country manufactured goods markets, Third World nations may stand a better long-run chance to diversify their economies successfully by trading with one another behind the protective barrier of a common tariff.

With regard to the complex and in some cases irrelevant question of trade creation and trade diversion, Dr Pazos's analysis reveals evidence of the existence of both. But on the whole he concludes with respect to CACM (the most carefully analysed group) that 'integration has created competition among the producers of the five countries and has probably promoted industrial specialisation by types of products, thus permitting larger production scales and lower costs'.[10] Thus trade creation does seem to have pervaded CACM – the only group closely analysed by Dr Pazos.

Although the benefits of integration in terms of growth rates of member country exports, their GNPs and their intra-country trade balances are not uniformly distributed, especially when there is a dominant country in the group (e.g. Kenya in EAC), all participants of CACM appear to have benefited from an expansion of exports and have also received considerable net benefits in terms of national output and employment rates of growth.[11]

Dr Pazos concludes his analysis of the economic effects of integration with regard to CACM with the observation:

> The experience of Central America shows that, under appropriate circumstances, the eliminat-ion of restrictions on the mutual trade of a group of developing countries brings about considerable expansion in their commercial interchange, fuller use of industrial capacity, specialization of production, economies of scale, increased industrialization and faster economic growth, without any rise in the number of industrial failures or in the amount of unemployment.[12]

In spite of the impressive record of the Central American Common Market and the early favourable results of the Andean and CACEU experiences, there still remain major stumbling blocks, some real, others psychological and political, in the path of a more widespread Third World movement towards various forms of economic integration. The major problems relate to differences in levels of development among prospective mem-bers and the consequent expectation among smaller members that a uniform trade liberalisation will unduly benefit the more developed members at their expense. In short, a successful integration scheme must not penalise any members, while ensuring that the distribution of the benefits of co-operation are reasonably equitable. If there are severe imbalances among member countries at the outset (as in the case of Kenya *vis-à-vis* its two East African neighbours) the tendency for unequal gains from trade to emerge and for the widening of the income gap between rich and poor members as a result of free trade will be reinforced. Such unequal benefit distribution is entirely analogous to that between rich and poor nations described in our critique of traditional free trade theory.

However, in the case of regional integration, it is at least possible to redistribute the gains from trade or plan for the more rapid industrial development of weaker members to enable them to catch up through co-ordinated policy planning. This re-distribution or co-ordination is not possible at the international level. It had been attempted in the EAC (e.g. Kenya provided direct financial transfers to the other two members in the early 1960s) with mixed success, due largely to the fact that EAC member states were still able to pursue their own separate and often conflicting industrial development strategies and there was no really effective supra-

[10] *Ibid.*, p. 4.

[11] *Ibid.*, pp. 6–9.

[12] *Ibid.*, p. 9.

national agency to enforce compliance with the provisions of the integration scheme.

We may conclude that Third World countries at a relatively equal stage of industrial development, with similar market sizes, and with a strong interest in co-ordinating and rationalising their joint industrial growth patterns stand to benefit most from the combined inward- and outward-looking trade policies represented by economic integration. In particular, regional groupings of small nations like those of Central America and Central Africa can create the economic conditions (mainly in the form of larger internal markets) for acceleration of their joint development efforts. In the absence of such co-operation and integration, the prospects for sustained economic progress would be bleak. Moreover, by blocking trade to a large extent with the more powerful developed nations and perhaps also restricting or prohibiting the deep penetration of multi-national corporations (see below) into their industrial sectors, these nations can provide a better base for their long-run development efforts.

But, while such an integration strategy may seem logical and persuasive on paper (in fact, it may be the only long-run solution to the economic problems of small nations), in practice it requires a degree of statesmanship and a regional rather than nationalistic orientation that are often lacking in many countries. Nevertheless, as time goes on and developing nations begin to see their individual destinies more closely tied to those of their neighbours, and as the pursuit of greater self-reliance and self-sufficiency gathers momentum in the decade of the 1980s, one might speculate that the pressures for some form of economic integration will gradually overcome the forces of separation. Surely, the collective experience of the six regional groupings briefly reviewed in this section as well as the new West African Community will be closely watched by other Third World nations and may constitute a decisive factor in the latter's decisions whether or not to move towards economic integration.

Trade policies of developed countries: the need for reform

We have seen that a major obstacle to LDC export expansion, whether in the area of primary products or manufactures, has existed in the various kinds of trade barriers erected by developed nations against the principal commodity exports of Third World countries. In the absence of economic integration or even in support of it, the prospects for future LDC trade and foreign exchange expansion rest largely with the domestic and international economic policies of developed nations. While internal structural and economic reform may be essential to economic and social progress in many Third World nations, an improvement in the competitive position of those industries where LDCs do have a dynamic comparative advantage will be of little benefit either to them or the world as a whole so long as their access to major world markets is restricted by rich-country commercial policies. Four major areas where a developed country's economic and commercial policies stand out as the most important from the perspective of future Third World foreign exchange earnings are:

- Tariff and non-tariff barriers to LDC exports.
- Developed-country export incentives.
- The issue of **adjustment assistance** for displaced workers in industries hurt by freer access of labour-intensive, low-cost LDC exports.
- The general impact of rich-country domestic economic policies on Third World economies.

Rich-nation tariff and non-tariff trade barriers

The present tariff and non-tariff barriers (excise taxes, quotas, sanitary regulations, etc.) imposed by rich nations on the commodity exports of poor ones present a great obstacle to the expansion of the latter's export-earning capacities. Moreover, many of these tariffs increase with the degree of product processing – i.e. they are higher for, say, processed foodstuffs compared with basic foodstuffs (e.g. groundnut oil as compared with groundnuts) or for shirts as opposed to raw cotton. This practice inhibits LDCs from diversifying their own secondary export industries and thus acts to restrain their industrial expansion and diversification.

The effect of an import tariff or excise duty on the earnings of producing countries can be demonstrated quite easily by using simple demand and supply analysis. In Figure 21.2 a tariff levied at the rate of AB/BC (e.g. a uniform *ad valorem* tariff of say 100 per cent) lowers the demand curve facing all exporters of the commodity in question from DD_d (the domestic and former world demand curve) to DD_w (the new post-tariff world demand curve facing exporters). This in turn lowers the equilibrium price received by LDC exporters from OH to OG while the volume of their exports falls from OQ to OC.

Figure 21.2
The effects of developed-country tariffs and excise taxes on LDC export sales and prices received

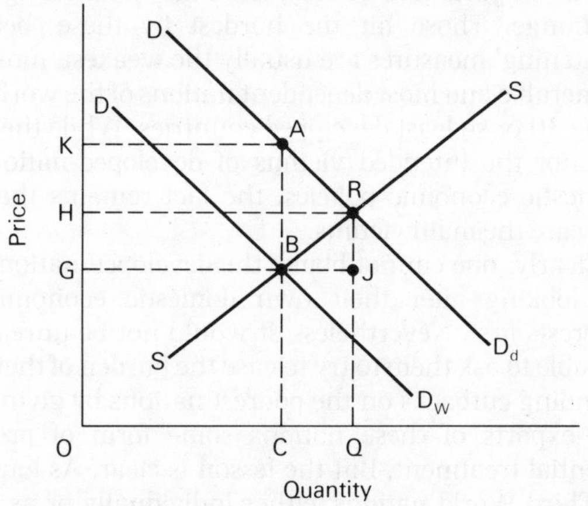

LDC exporters as a group, therefore, lose foreign exchange in an amount equal to the area OHRQ–OGBC. However, the actual real income loss is only HRBG since the area under the supply curve reflects the real resource costs of producing the export, and these total costs have also been reduced by an amount shown by the area CBRQ as a result of the export cutback. Note the area GKAB represents total developed-country tariff revenue.

Thus, the total effects of developed-country tariffs are to lower the effective price received by LDCs for their exports (i.e. worsen their terms of trade), reduce the quantity exported, and diminish Third World foreign exchange earnings. Although the burden which developed-country tariffs impose upon LDC primary and secondary product exports varies from commodity to commodity, the net impact of trade barriers on all products is to reduce Third World foreign exchange earnings by many billions of dollars. In the absence of widespread reductions in these trade barriers, and the establishment of special preferences for LDC primary product exports, there can be little optimism about the possibility of accelerating Third World export earnings through trade with the developed nations.

Export incentives

In addition to restricting the imports of Third World products, many developed countries provide generous financial incentives in public subsidies and tax rebates for their own export industries. The Japanese Government has made the greatest use of this policy by working closely in support of its export industries. Although LDC governments also provide export incentives, their limited fiscal capacity prevents them from effectively counteracting the impact of rich-country subsidies. The overall effect of this public support of private industries is to make rich-country industries more competitive in world markets and to delay the time when Third World industries are able to compete effectively. It is simply another instance of the disproportionate ability of the wealthy to stay on top.

Adjustment assistance

One of the major obstacles to the lowering of rich-nation tariff barriers against the manufactured exports of poorer nations is the political pressures exerted by those traditional light manufacturing industries which find their products underpriced by low-cost, labour-intensive foreign goods. Not only can this cause economic disruption for higher cost domestic industries, it can also lead to a loss of employment for its workers. In classical trade theory the answer to this dilemma would be simple: merely shift these rich-country workers with their complementary resources to those more capital-intensive industries where a comparative advantage still exists. Everybody will be better off as a result.

Unfortunately, even in the most industrialised and economically integrated societies of the world, the process of adjustment is not so simple. More important, the political power of many of these older industries is such that whenever they feel threatened by low-cost foreign imports they are able to muster enough support effectively to block competition from the LDCs. Such activities make a mockery of pious statements about the benefits of free trade.

Unless some scheme of 'adjustment assistance' is established by which the governments of developed nations financially assist industries and their workers in the transition to alternative and more profitable activities, trade barriers against competitive Third World exports will continue to be raised. Many such schemes have been proposed. To date, however, none has been really effective in persuading threatened industries and industrial workers to forgo their private interests in the interest of maximum world welfare. In fact, the typical response of developed-country governments has been to subsidise new investment in threatened industries to keep them afloat. Nevertheless, continuous efforts must be made to search for an acceptable programme of adjustment assistance. Without the introduction of such programmes in developed nations, the world market for Third World manufactured exports will always remain highly restricted both for new entrants and for the growth of existing suppliers.

Domestic economic policies

While it is far beyond the scope of this chapter to examine the myriad ways in which the economic welfare of many export-oriented poor nations is tied to the domestic fiscal and monetary policies of rich nations, the importance of this linkage must not be overlooked. The major factor determining the level and growth of Third World export earnings (and this was confirmed by their relatively good performance in the 1960s and their steep decline during the two recessions of the 1970s) has been the ability of rich nations to sustain high rates of economic growth without inflation. Even a low income elasticity of demand for LDC exports can be compensated for by a high rate of developed country income growth. It follows that Third World export performance is directly related to the growth and price stability of developed-country economies.

But just as the poor are often said to be 'the last to be hired and the first to be fired', so too when international economic disruptions occur, the world's poor nations feel the effects much sooner and more substantially than the rich nations. The worldwide inflationary spiral of the 1970s, caused by a combination of Keynesian-type excess aggregate demand-pull and natural resource (especially petroleum), cost-push provides a classic example of this phenomenon. Faced with rampant inflation at home, developed countries were able to call upon traditional macro-economic policies designed to restrict aggregate demand (e.g. lower government expenditure, higher taxes, higher interest rates, a slower growing money supply, etc.) while attempting to control wage and price rises. When rapid inflation is accompanied by growing balance of payments deficits and rising domestic unemployment, as in the 1970s, these deflationary general domestic fiscal and monetary policies tend to be reinforced by specific government actions to curtail imports and control the outflow of foreign exchange. Those hit the hardest by these 'belt tightening' measures are usually the weakest, most vulnerable and most dependent nations of the world – the 30 or so least developed countries. While they are not the intended victims of developed-nation domestic economic policies, the fact remains that they are the main victims.

Clearly, one cannot blame the developed nations for looking after their own domestic economic interests first. Nevertheless, it would not be unreasonable to ask them to try to ease the burden of their spending cutbacks on the poorest nations by giving the exports of these nations some form of preferential treatment. But the lesson is clear. As long as Third World nations, either individually or as a group, whether willingly or unwillingly, permit their economies to be linked too closely to the economic policies of rich nations, they will remain the chief though innocent victims in times of stress while in times of prosperity their rewards will be minimal. Even more disturbing is the loss of their capacity to control their own economic and social destinies.

The lessons of the 1970s therefore revealed to Third World nations as no economic model could have that they need to make every effort to reduce their individual and joint economic vulnerabilities. Perhaps the best way to do so is by pursuing policies of greater 'collective' self-reliance within the context of mutual economic co-operation and a more cautious and defensive attitude towards the further penetration of their economies by rich-country products, technologies and corporations. While not denying their interdependence with developed nations, many developing nations now realise that a reduced economic dependence is probably in their best long-run interest.

Concepts for review

balance of payments	export promotion
current account	import substitution
trade surplus v. trade deficit	tariffs
	quotas
capital account	non-tariff trade barriers
cash account	infant industry
commercial policies	export duty or subsidy
'learning by doing'	official exchange rate
autarky	overvalued exchange rate
adjustment assistance	
export incentives	forward and backward industrial linkages
outward- v. inward-looking development policies	

economic integration
customs union
free trade area
common market
trade creation
trade diversion

Questions for discussion

1. Draw up a balance of payments table similar in format to that of Table 21.1 but using the most recent available data from your own country. Explain the significance or non-significance of the various entries in the current and capital accounts. What happened to the level of your country's foreign reserves during the year in question?
2. Explain the distinction between primary and secondary inward- and outward-looking development policies. How would you classify your own country's economic policies according to these categories?
3. Briefly summarise the range of commercial policies available to Third World countries and why some of these policies might be adopted.
4. What are the possibilities, advantages and disadvantages of export promotion in Third World nations with reference to specific types of commodities (primary food products, raw materials, fuels, minerals, manufactured goods, etc.)?
5. Most less developed countries in Latin America, Africa and Asia have pursued policies of import substitution as major components of their development strategies. Explain the theoretical and practical arguments in support of import substitution policies. What have been some of the weaknesses of these policies in practice and why have the results often not lived up to expectations? Explain.
6. Explain some of the arguments in support of the use of tariffs, quotas and other trade barriers in Third World countries.
7. What are the basic static and dynamic arguments for economic integration in less developed countries? Briefly describe the various forms which economic integration can take (customs union, free trade areas, etc.). What are the major obstacles to effective economic integration in Third World regions?
8. How do the trade policies of developed countries affect the ability of less developed countries to benefit from greater participation in the world economy? How do non-trade domestic economic policies of rich nations affect the export earnings of Third World countries? What is meant by 'adjustment assistance' and why is it so important to the future of Third World manufactured exports prospects? Explain.

Further reading

Two of the best sources of thoughtful information on trade policies and strategies for development are: G. K. HELLEINER, *International Trade and Economic Development*, Penguin, 1972, and PAUL STREETEN, 'Trade strategies for development: some themes for the seventies', *World Development*, i, 6, June 1973.

Chapter 22 Private investment and foreign aid

> Two decades of experience with international economic cooperation have convinced many leaders in the developing countries that basic changes in their economies and social systems are more important than quantitative increases in external resource transfers.
>
> *Communiqué of Third World social scientists, March 1974*[1]

Introduction

We discovered at the beginning of Chapter 21 that a country's international financial situation as reflected in its balance of payments and its level of monetary reserves depends not only on its current account balance (its commodity trade) but also on its balance on capital account (its net inflow or outflow of private and public financial resources). Since almost all non-oil exporting developing nations incur deficits on their current account balance, a continuous net inflow of foreign financial resources represents an important ingredient in their long-run development strategies.

The international flow of financial resources takes two main forms: **private foreign investment** mostly by large multi-national corporations with headquarters in the developed nations and **public development assistance (foreign aid)** from both individual national governments and multi-national donor agencies. In this chapter we examine the nature and significance of private foreign investment and foreign aid and the controversy over it in the context of the changing world economy. Although our principal emphasis is on the traditional north–south flow of development finance (i.e. from developed to less developed nations), the emergence in the 1970s of wealthy OPEC oil nations with their vast surplus of 'petro-dollars' created exciting possibilities for intra-Third World development assistance. We explore this new phenomenon at the end of the chapter.

[1] 'Self reliance and international reform', *World Development*, ii, 6, June 1974.

Private foreign investment and the multi-national corporation

Few developments have played as critical a role in the extraordinary growth of international trade and capital flows during the past two decades as the rise of the multi-national corporation (MNC). These huge business firms with their far-flung networks of subsidiaries in dozens of Third World countries all marching to the drum of centralised global output maximising decisions of parent companies located in North America, Europe and Japan present a unique opportunity and a host of critical problems for those many less developed nations in which they conduct their business.

The growth of private foreign investment in Third World countries has been extremely rapid. It has risen from an annual rate of $2.4 billion in 1962 to over $10 billion by the early 1980s. But, as we have seen, direct foreign investment involves much more than the simple transfer of capital or the establishment of a local factory in a Third World nation. MNCs carry with them technologies of production, tastes and styles of living, managerial services, diverse business practices, including co-operative arrangements, marketing restrictions, advertising and the phenomenon of 'transfer pricing' to be discussed shortly. Unlike certain types of foreign aid, the purpose of MNC activities is far from charitable. In many instances, they have little to do with the development aspirations of the countries in which they operate. But before analysing some of the arguments for and against private foreign investment in general and multi-national corporations in particular, we outline the character of these enterprises.

Multi-national corporations: size, patterns and trends

Two central characteristics of multi-national corporations are their large size and the fact that their worldwide operations and activities tend to be centrally controlled by parent companies. Many MNCs have annual sales volumes in excess of the entire GNPs of the developing nations in which they operate. Table 22.1, for example, shows that in 1976, the three largest multi-nationals, Exxon, General Motors, and Royal Dutch/Shell, had gross sales greater than the GNPs of all but six developing nations (China, Brazil, India, Iran, Mexico and Turkey). By 1980 the twenty largest MNCs had annual sales volumes in excess of $10 billion, while more than 200 others had sales in excess of $1 billion. The largest US multi-nationals like Exxon and General Motors each sold over $60 billion in 1980 while Mobil, Texaco and Ford each had annual sales well in excess of $30 billion. The combined sales of these five MNCs alone exceeded the GNPs of many *developed* nations including Australia, Canada, Belgium, Sweden and Switzerland. In fact, the largest multi-national, Exxon, had total revenues in 1980 in excess of $90 billion, thus surpassing the entire gross national products of countries like Sweden, Belgium and Switzerland!

Such enormous size confers great economic (and sometimes political) power on MNCs *vis-à-vis* the countries in which they operate. This power is greatly strengthened by their predominantly oligopolistic market positions, that is, they tend to operate in product markets dominated by a *few* sellers and buyers. They are thus able to manipulate prices and profits, to collude with other firms in determining areas of control, and generally to restrict the entry of potential competition through their dominating influence over new technologies, special skills and consumer tastes as a result of product differentiation and advertising.

The largest MNCs have many foreign branches and overseas affiliates. Nearly 200 have subsidiaries in 20 or more countries. Eight of the ten largest are based in the United States while US firms exercise control over about 30 per cent of all foreign affiliates. Britain, Germany and France, together with the United States, control over 75 per cent of all MNC affiliates. Latest estimates put the book value of their total foreign investment in excess of 200 billion with over 80 per cent of that total owned by MNCs in these four countries. Of this total, approximately one-third is located in Third World countries. But, given their small size, the LDCs feel the presence of multi-national corporations more acutely than the developed countries.

Historically, multi-national corporations, especially those operating in Third World nations, focused on extractive industries, mainly mineral and raw material production. A few agribusiness MNCs became involved in export-oriented plantation agriculture and local food processing. Recently, however, manufacturing interests have occupied a greater share of their activities. At present, manufacturing accounts for almost 28 per cent of the estimated stock of foreign direct investment in LDCs, while petroleum and mining represent 40 and 9 per cent respectively. But the overall importance of MNCs in the economies of Third World nations, especially in the manufacturing and service sectors, is rapidly growing. In the 1960s, MNC private direct investments represented about one-fifth of the total flow of resources to LDCs. Moreover, this flow increased at an annual average rate of 9 per cent. Thus the stock of foreign private investment increased faster than the GNP of most poor countries during the past decade.

Given the above brief sketch of the size and importance of multi-national corporations, we can now discuss some of the arguments for and against their activities in the context of the development aspirations of Third World nations.

Private foreign investment: some pros and cons for development

Few areas in the economics of development arouse so much controversy and are subject to such varying degrees of interpretation as the question of

Table 22.1
Ranking of countries and multi-national corporations according to size of annual product, 1976

Rank	Economic Entity	Product[1] ($ billions)	Rank	Economic Entity	Product[1] ($ billions)
1.	United States	1,694.9	31	Indonesia	36.0
2.	USSR	717.5	32.	South Africa	33.7
3.	Japan	513.5	33.	Norway	32.0
4.	West Germany	461.8	34.	Venezuela	31.3
5.	France	355.9	35.	Nigeria	30.9
6.	China	307.1	36.	Rumania	30.0
7.	United Kingdom	233.5	37.	*Ford Motor*	28.9
8.	Italy	183.0	38.	Finland	27.9
9.	Canada	182.5	39.	*Texaco*	26.4
10.	Brazil	143.0	40.	*Mobil Oil*	26.1
11.	Spain	107.2	41.	South Korea	25.3
12.	Poland	99.0	42.	Hungary	24.8
13.	Australia	97.3	43.	Greece	23.6
14.	Netherlands	91.6	44.	Bulgaria	21.6
15.	India	87.9	45.	*Standard Oil (Cal.)*	19.4
16.	East Germany	75.8	46.	*British Petroleum*[2]	19.1
17.	Sweden	74.2	47.	Taiwan	17.1
18.	Iran	69.1	48.	*Gulf Oil*	16.4
19.	Belgium	68.9	49.	*IBM*	16.3
20.	Mexico	65.5	50.	Thailand	16.2
21.	Switzerland	58.1	51.	Portugal	16.1
22.	Czechoslovakia	56.5	52.	*Unilever*[2 3]	15.7
23.	*Exxon*	48.6	53.	*General Electric*	15.7
24.	*General Motors*	47.2	54.	Colombia	15.6
25.	Austria	42.2	55.	*Chrysler*	15.5
26.	Turkey	41.2	56.	Peru	13.5
27.	Argentina	40.7	57.	Pakistan	13.1
28.	Denmark	39.0	58.	*ITT*	11.8
29.	Yugoslavia	37.7	59.	*Standard Oil (Ind.)*	11.6
30.	*Royal Dutch/Shell*[2 3]	36.1	60.	*Philips*[3]	11.5
			61.	All other developing countries	less than 11.5

[1] Gross national product for countries and gross sales for corporations.
[2 3] Corporations based outside of the United States, in: [2] the United Kingdom; [3] the Netherlands.
Sources: Gross national product figures from the *World Bank Atlas* (Washington: World Bank, 1978).
Corporate sales figures from United Nations, Department of Economic and Social Affairs, *Transnational Corporations in World Development: A Re-Examination*, New York: United Nations, 1978, Table IV–1.

the benefits and costs of private foreign investment in the economies of the Third World. If, however, we look closely at the essence of this controversy, we find not so much disagreement about the influence of MNCs on traditional economic aggregates such as GNP, investment, savings and manufacturing growth rates (though these disagreements do indeed exist) as about the fundamental economic and social meaning of development as it relates to the diverse activities of MNCs. In other words, the controversy about the role and impact of foreign private investment in developing economies often has as its underlying (though usually unstated) basis a fundamental disagreement about the nature, style and character of a desirable development process. The basic arguments for and against the development impact of private foreign investment in the context of the type of development it tends to foster can be summarised as follows:

Traditional economic arguments in support of private investment: filling 'gaps'

The pro-foreign investment arguments mainly grow out of the traditional neo-classical analysis of the determinants of economic growth. Foreign private investment (as well as foreign aid) is typically seen as a way of filling in gaps between the domestically available supplies of savings, foreign exchange, government revenue and skills and the planned level of these resources necessary to achieve development targets. To give a simple example of the savings-investment gap analysis, recall that the basic Harrod–Domar growth model postulates a direct relationship between a country's rate of savings, s, and its rate of output growth, g, via the equation $g = s/k$, where k is the national capital/output ratio. If the planned rate of national output growth, g, is targeted at say 7 per cent annually, and the capital/output rate is 3, then the needed rate of saving is 21 per cent (since $s = g \times k$). If the saving that can be domestically mobilised amounts to only say, 16 per cent of GNP, then a savings gap equal to 5 per cent of GNP can be said to exist. If the nation can fill this gap with foreign financial resources (either private or public) it will be better able to achieve its target rate of growth.

Therefore, the first and most often cited contribution of private foreign investment to national development (i.e. when this development is defined in terms of GNP growth rates – an important implicit conceptual assumption) is its role in filling the resource gap between targeted or desired investment and locally mobilised savings.

A second contribution, analogous to the first, is its contribution to filling the gap between targeted foreign exchange requirements and those derived from net export earnings plus net public foreign aid. This is the so-called foreign exchange or trade gap. An inflow of private foreign capital can not only alleviate part or all of the deficit on the balance of payments current account, but it can also function to remove that deficit over time *if* the foreign owned enterprise can generate a net positive flow of export earnings. Unfortunately, as we discovered in the case of import substitution policies in practice, the overall effect of permitting MNCs to establish subsidiaries behind protective tariff walls is often a net worsening of both the current and capital account balance. Such deficits usually result both from the importation of capital equipment and intermediate products (normally from an overseas affiliate and often at inflated prices) and the outflow of foreign exchange in the form of repatriated profits, management fees, royalty payments and interest on private loans.

The third gap said to be filled by foreign investment is between targeted governmental tax revenues and locally raised taxes. By taxing MNC profits and participating financially in their local operations, LDC governments are thought to be better able to mobilise public financial resources for development projects.

Fourth and finally there is the gap in management, entrepreneurship, technology and skills which is presumed to be partially or wholly filled by the local operations of private foreign firms. MNCs not only provide financial resources and new factories to poor countries: they also supply a 'package' of needed resources, including management experience, entrepreneurial abilities and technological skills which can then be transferred to their local counterparts by means of training programmes and the process of learning by doing. Moreover, according to this argument, MNCs can educate local managers about how to establish contacts with overseas banks, locate alternative sources of supply, diversify market outlets and, in general, become better acquainted with international marketing practices. Finally, MNCs bring with them sophisticated technological knowledge about production processes while transferring modern machinery and equipment to capital-poor Third World countries. Such transfers of knowledge, skills and technology are assumed to be both desirable and productive to the recipient nations.

Arguments against private foreign investment: widening gaps

There are two basic arguments against private foreign investment in general and the activities of MNCs in particular: the strictly economic and the more philosophical or ideological.

On the economic side, the four 'gap filling' pro-private foreign investment positions outlined above are countered by the following arguments:

- Although MNCs provide capital they may lower domestic savings and investment rates by stifling competition, failing to reinvest much of their profits, generating domestic incomes for those groups with lower savings propensities, inhibiting the expansion of indigenous firms who might otherwise supply them with intermediate products by their practice of importing these goods from overseas affiliates, and imposing high interest costs on capital borrowed by host governments.

- Although the initial impact of MNC investment is to improve the foreign exchange position of the recipient nation, its long-run impact may be to reduce foreign exchange earnings on both current and capital accounts. The current account may deteriorate as a result of substantial importation of intermediate products and capital goods while the capital account may worsen because of the overseas repatriation of profits, interest, royalties, management fees, etc.
- While MNCs do contribute to public revenue in the form of corporate taxes, they can also diminish that revenue as a result of liberal tax concessions, investment allowances, disguised public subsidies and tariff protection provided by the host government.
- The management, entrepreneurial skills, technology and overseas contacts provided by MNCs may have little impact on developing local sources of these scarce skills and resources and may in fact inhibit their development by stifling the growth of indigenous entrepreneurship as a result of the MNCs dominance of local markets.

But the really significant criticism of MNCs is usually conducted on more fundamental levels than those briefly outlined above. In particular, Third World countries have commonly raised the following objections[2]:

1. Their impact on development is very uneven and in many situations MNC activities reinforce dualistic economic structures and exacerbate income inequalities. They tend to promote the interests of the small number of well-paid modern sector workers against the interests of the rest by widening wage differentials. They divert resources away from needed food production to the manufacture of sophisticated products catering primarily for the demands of local elites. And they tend to worsen the imbalance between rural and urban economic opportunities by locating primarily in urban areas and contributing to the accelerated flow of rural–urban migration.
2. MNCs typically produce **inappropriate products** (those demanded by a small rich minority of the local population), stimulate **inappropriate consumption patterns** through advertising and their monopolistic market power, and do this all with **inappropriate (capital-intensive) technologies of production**. This is perhaps the major area of criticism of MNCs.
3. As a result of 1 and 2 above, local resources tend to be allocated towards socially undesirable projects. This in turn tends to aggravate the already sizable inequality between rich and poor and the serious imbalance between urban and rural economic opportunities.
4. MNCs use their economic power to influence government policies in directions unfavourable to development. They are able to extract sizable economic and political concessions from competing LDC governments in the form of excessive protection, tax rebates, investment allowances and the cheap provision of factory sites and essential social services. As a result, the private profits of MNCs may exceed social benefits. In some cases, these social returns to host countries may even be negative! Alternatively, a MNC can avoid much local taxation by means of artificially inflating the price it pays for intermediate products purchased from overseas affiliates, so as to lower its stated local profits. This phenomenon, known as 'transfer pricing', is a major practice of MNCs and one over which host governments can exert little control so long as corporate tax rates differ from one country to the next.
5. MNCs may damage host economies by suppressing domestic entrepreneurship and using their superior knowledge, worldwide contacts, advertising skills and range of essential support services to drive out local competitors and inhibit the emergence of smaller scale local enterprises.
6. Finally, at the political level, the fear is often expressed that powerful multi-national corporations have the ability to gain control over local assets and jobs. They can then exert considerable influence on political decisions at all levels. In extreme cases, they may even subvert the very political process of host nations (e.g. the International Telephone and Telegraph Co. experience in Chile).

Reconciling the pros and cons

While the above list provides a range of conflicting

[2] See P. P. Streeten, 'The Multinational Enterprise and the Theory of Development Policy', *World Development*, i, 10, October 1973.

arguments, the real debate ultimately centres on different ideological and value judgments about the nature and meaning of economic development and the principal sources from which it springs. The advocates of private foreign investment tend to be 'free-market, private enterprise, *laissez faire*' doctrinalists who firmly believe in the efficacy and beneficence of the free market mechanism where this is usually defined as a 'hands-off' policy by host governments. As we have seen, however, the actual operations of MNCs tend to be monopolistic and oligopolistic in practice. Price setting is achieved more as a result of international bargaining and collusion than as a natural outgrowth of free market supply and demand.

Those who argue against the activities of MNCs are often motivated more by a sense of importance of national control over domestic economic activities and the minimisation of dominance/dependence relationships between powerful MNCs and Third World governments. They see these giant corporations not as needed agents of economic change but more as vehicles of 'anti-development'. MNCs, they argue, reinforce dualistic economic structures and exacerbate domestic inequalities with wrong products and inappropriate technologies. Some opponents, therefore, call for the outright confiscation (without compensation) or the nationalisation (with some compensation) of foreign-owned enterprises.[3] Others advocate a more stringent regulation of foreign investments, a tougher bargaining stance on the part of host governments, a willingness on the part of LDCs to 'shop around' for better deals, and finally, a greater co-ordination of LDC strategies with respect to terms and conditions of foreign investment. An example of such co-ordinated strategies was the 1971 decision by the Andean Group in Latin America to require foreign investors to reduce their ownership in local enterprises to minority shares over a 15 year period. Tanzania adopted a similar policy of securing a controlling share of foreign enterprises in line with its Arusha Declaration of 1967 on socialism and self-reliance. As might be expected, however, the annual flow of private foreign investment declined as a result of these more stringent conditions.

In view of the strong anti-MNC sentiment being aired in the capitals of many Third World nations and the 'demonstration effect' of the power of the OPEC cartel to gain increasing control over foreign oil companies, it appears that the phenomenal growth of MNC influence in less developed countries in the 1950s, 1960s and early 1970s will not be matched in the 1980s. The arguments both for and against private foreign investment have a certain empirical validity while reflecting important differences in value judgments. Perhaps the only really valid conclusion is that private foreign investment can be an important stimulus to economic and social development so long as the interests of *both* MNC and host country governments coincide (assuming, of course, that they do not coincide along the lines of dualistic development and widening inequalities). As long as MNCs see their role in terms of global output or profit maximisation with little interest in the long-run domestic impact of their activities, the accusations of the anti-private investment school of thought will gain increasing Third World acceptance. Perhaps there can be no real congruence of interest between the objectives of MNCs and the priorities of LDC governments. On the other hand, a strengthening of the relative bargaining powers of host country governments through their co-ordinated activities, while probably reducing the overall magnitude and growth of private foreign investment in the Third World, may make that investment better suited to the real long-run development needs and priorities of poor nations. The net social benefits of this trade-off between quantity and relevance is likely to have a positive

[3] The question whether or not 'nationalised' foreign enterprises or confiscated domestic private property (e.g. large but unproductive land holdings) should be compensated and, if so, at what amount is typically a political issue. In general, however, such compensation should depend on (1) the manner in which the enterprise or property was acquired; (2) the historical and replacement costs of the assets confiscated: (3) the nature and record of the enterprise's relations with the government and people of the confiscating country prior to confiscation; and (4) the financial benefits and economic returns which have already been reaped prior to confiscation. Compensation should be based on a careful evaluation of the above four factors with (1) and (3) providing the political criteria and (2) and (4) the economic rationale for the overall decision. For an economic defence of policies of confiscation and nationalisation of foreign-owned property in Third World countries, see Martin Bronfenbrenner, 'The appeal of confiscation in economic development', *Economic Development and Cultural Change*, April 1955, pp. 201–208.

impact on national development. Whatever the outcome, it will certainly be interesting and instructive to see what happens to the magnitude, direction and nature of private foreign investment and the role of MNCs during the 1980s.

Foreign aid: the development assistance debate

In addition to export earnings and private foreign investment, the final major source of Third World foreign exchange is public bilateral and multilateral development assistance, known also as foreign aid. The volume of official development assistance, which includes bilateral grants, loans and technical assistance as well as multilateral flows, has grown from an annual rate of about $4.6 billion in 1960 to approximately $21 billion in the early 1980s. However, in terms of the percentage of developed-country GNPs allocated to official development assistance, there has been a steady decline from 0.51 per cent in the early 1960s to slightly less than 0.35 per cent in 1979–1980. The United States is still the major supplier of public aid to Third World nations but its proportion of total development assistance has declined from 53 per cent in 1960 to approximately 27 per cent in the year 1980. Tables 22.2 and 22.3 provide recent data on the flow of aid resources from the developed market economies to the developing world while Table 22.4 provides similar information on aid from the USSR, Eastern Europe and China from 1970–1976. Finally, Table 22.5 shows the flow of assistance from international organisations to developing countries over a similar period.

Quoting statistics on the volume, direction and

Table 22.2

Net flow of resources from DAC countries to developing countries and multilateral institutions ($ millions)

	1964–66 Average[1]	1970[1]	1975	1979	1980
Official	**6,146.9**	**7,929.2**	**16,608.7**	**25,114.1**	**32,047.9**
Official Development Assistance (ODA)	5,913.0	6,790.5	13,585.1	22,420.2	26,768.2
Bilateral	5,550.0	5,666.7	9,815.3	15,917.9	17,620.8
Grants[2]	3,732.6	3,309.2	6,268.0	11,289.6	13,639.2
Loans[3]	1,817.1	2,357.4	3,547.1	4,628.4	3,981.6
Contributions to multilateral institutions	363.1	1,123.8	3,769.6	6,502.2	9,147.4
Grants	204.2	551.7	2,028.7	3,603.3	3,678.0[6]
Capital subscription payments	157.3	540.6	1,731.6	2,846.1	4,719.8[6]
Concessional loans	1.6	31.5	9.3	52.8	36.9[6]
Other official flows[4]	233.9	1,138.7	3,023.6	2,693.9	5,279.7
Private flows	**3,928.1**	**6,875.1**	**22,427.6**	**49,062.7**	**42,428.0**
Direct and portfolio investment[5]	3,016.6	4,733.2	18,285.6	39,018.1	n/a
Private export credits	911.4	2,141.9	4,141.9	10,044.5	n/a
Grants by Private Voluntary Agencies	**n/a**	**857.5**	**1,341.8**	**1,996.8**	**2,360.7**
Total	**10,075.0**	**15,662.1**	**40,378.1**	**76,836.7**	**76,836.4**
(as % of GNP)	*0.75*	*0.78*	*1.05*	*1.18*	*1.07*

[1] Figures prior to 1974 do not include New Zealand and Finland.
[2] Technical assistance, food aid, and other grants.
[3] New development lending, food-aid loans, debt reorganization and equities and other bilateral assets.
[4] Official export credits (including official funds in support of private export credits), debt relief, equities and other bilateral assets, and contributions to multilateral institutions on terms not concessional enough to quality as ODA.
[5] Includes bilateral and multilateral portfolio investment.
[6] Figures exclude France.

NOTES: Figures include capital subscriptions to multilateral organizations made in the form of notes payable on demand; however, after 1975, such subscriptions are reported in the year in which they are issued rather than the year in which they are cashed by the recipient organizations.

Source: Overseas Development Council, *U.S. Foreign Policy and the Third World Agenda 1982*, Table F-12.

Table 22.3
Net flow of official development assistance from DAC countries as a percentage of GNP 1960, 1970, 1976–81

	1960	1970	1976	1977	1978	1979	1980*	1981*
Australia	.37	.59	.41	.42	.54	.52	.47	.49
Austria	—	.07	.12	.24	.29	.19	.22	.25
Belgium	.88	.46	.51	.46	.55	.56	.48	.55
Canada	.19	.41	.39	.48	.52	.47	.42	.43
Denmark	.09	.38	.56	.60	.75	.75	.72	.74
France	1.35	.66	.62	.60	.57	.59	.62	.62
Germany	.31	.32	.36	.33	.37	.44	.43	.43
Italy	.22	.16	.13	.10	.14	.09	.15	.18
Japan	.24	.23	.20	.21	.23	.26	.32	.31
Netherlands	.31	.61	.83	.86	.82	.93	.99	1.02
New Zealand	—	.23	.41	.39	.34	.30	.27	.26
Norway	.11	.32	.70	.83	.90	.93	.82	.90
Portugal	1.45	.67	—	—	—	—	—	—
Sweden	.05	.38	.82	.99	.90	.94	.76	.90
Switzerland	.04	.15	.19	.19	.20	.21	.24	.25
United Kingdom	.56	.41	.40	.46	.48	.52	.34	.48
United States	.53	.32	.26	.25	.27	.19	.27	.26
DAC Totals								
ODA ($ billion) nominal prices	4.6	7.0	13.8	15.7	20.0	22.3	26.6	30.3
ODA as % of GNP	.51	.34	.33	.33	.35	.34	.37	.38
ODA ($ billion) constant 1978 prices	13.1	14.9	17.3	18.0	20.0	20.3	22.2	23.1
GNP ($ trillion) nominal prices	.9	2.0	4.2	4.7	5.6	6.5	7.1	7.9
ODA deflator	.35	.47	.80	.87	1.00	1.10	1.20	1.31

* Estimated.

Source: *World Development Report, 1981*, Annex table 16.

trends in development assistance, however, is of little relevance without an understanding of the meaning of foreign aid and its role and/or limitations in promoting economic and social development. But this presents difficulties. For the definition of aid and the meaning and motives attached to it may vary from donor country to donor country and from one multilateral development assistance agency to another. More importantly there are likely to be fundamental differences in attitudes and motivations between donor and recipient countries. Aid is thus a complex and confusing term, especially when it is used to cover a variety of resource transfers from one country to another. Many of these may be military or political in nature and have nothing to do with promoting economic development.

Because of the complex and often conflicting nature of foreign aid is seen differently by donor and recipient countries, we must first analyse the giving and receiving of aid from these two often contradictory viewpoints. One of the major criticisms of the literature on foreign aid is that it has concentrated almost exclusively on the motives and objectives of donor countries while devoting little attention to why LDCs accept aid and what they perceive it will accomplish. We therefore examine the aid question first from these differing perspectives.

We subsequently summarise the conflicting views of the effects of traditional aid relationships over the past two decades, look at the emerging new aid role of OPEC oil nations and conclude with an analysis of how development assistance can be made more effective.

Why donors give aid

Countries give aid primarily because it is in their political, strategic and/or economic self-interest to do so. While some development assistance may be motivated by moral and humanitarian reasons to assist the less fortunate, there is no historical evidence to suggest that over longer periods of time donor nations assist others without expecting some benefits (political, economic, military, etc.) in return. We can therefore separate the motivations of donor nations into two broad, but often inter-related, categories: political and economic.

Political motivations

This has been by far the primary motivation of aid-granting nations, especially the two major competing donor countries, the United States and the Soviet Union. Foreign aid in America has been viewed from its very beginnings in the late 1940s under the Marshall Plan, when it set out to reconstruct the wartorn economies of Western Europe, as a means of containing the international spread of Communism. When the balance of 'cold war' interests shifted from Europe to the Third World in the mid-1950s, the policy of containment embodied in the US aid programme dictated a shift in emphasis toward political, economic and military support for 'friendly' less developed nations, especially those considered most strategic. Most aid programmes to developing countries were therefore oriented more towards purchasing their security and propping up their sometimes shaky regimes than promoting

Table 22.4
Economic aid from USSR, Eastern Europe and China to developing countries, gross commitments, 1970–1976 ($ millions)

	1970	1972	1975	1976
Donors				
USSR	194	581	1,299	875
Eastern Europe	188	655	422	496
Peoples Rep. of China	709	499	273	108
Total	1,091	1,735	1,994	1,479
Recipients				
Africa	589	419	444	504
Asia	395	940	1,308	223
Middle East	—	—	25	296
Latin America	107	331	217	156
Total	1,091	1,690	1,994	1,179

Sources: Department of State, Bureau of Intelligence and Research, 'Communist states and developing countries: aid and trade in 1973,' Research Study INR RS-20, 10 Oct. 1974.
Based on data from US Central Intelligence Agency, *Communist Aid to the Less Developed Countries of the Free World, 1976.* Docket No. ER77-10296, Aug. 1977, and *International Policy Report*, Vol. 11, No. 1, April 1976. Published by the Institute for International Policy, Washington, D.C.

Table 22.5
Net flow of resources from multilateral institutions to developing countries, 1970 and 1976–1979 ($millions)

	Concessional				Total			
	1970	1976	1978	1979	1970	1976	1978	1979
World Bank Group	**163**	**1,326**	**1,083**	**1,385**	**739**	**3,243**	**3,245**	**4,339**
International Development Association (IDA)	163	1,310	1,007	1,278	163	1,310	1,007	1,278
International Finance Corporation	—	—	—	—	68	193	58	108
World Bank	—	16	76	107	508	1,740	2,180	2,953
IMF Trust Fund	—	—	**864**	**680**	—	—	**864**	**680**
United Nations	**498**	**1,252**	**1,730**	**2,214**	**498**	**1,252**	**1,730**	**2,214**
Regional Banks	**225**	**369**	**552**	**531**	**326**	**936**	**1,239**	**1,355**
Inter-American Development Bank (IDB)	224	282	332	335	308	567	707	782
Asian Development Bank	1	62	161	116	16	294	390	394
African Development Bank and Fund	—	11	39	55	2	55	122	147
European Communities	**210**	**501**	**805**	**1,124**	**221**	**559**	**883**	**1,286**
Arab/OPEC Funds	—	**419**	**966**	**264**	—	**554**[1]	**1,446**[1]	**n/a**
Total	**1,096**	**3,867**	**6,000**	**6,198**	**1,784**	**6,544**	**9,407**	**10,398**[1]

[1] OECD secretariat estimate.

Source: Overseas Development Council, *U.S. Foreign Policy and the Third World Agenda 1982*, Table F-5.

long-term economic development. The successive shifts in emphasis from South Asia, to Southeast Asia, to Latin America, the Middle East and back to Southeast Asia during the 1950s and 1960s and then towards Africa and the Persian Gulf in the late 1970s and Central America in the early 1980s reflect the changes in US strategic and political interests more than changing evluations of economic need.

Even the Alliance for Progress, inaugurated in the early 1960s with such fanfare and noble rhetoric about promoting Latin American economic development, was in reality formulated primarily as a direct response to the rise of Fidel Castro in Cuba and the perceived threat of communist take-overs in other Latin American countries. As soon as the security issue lost its urgency, however, and other more pressing problems came to the fore (the war in Vietnam, the growing dollar crisis, the rise in US domestic violence, etc.) the Alliance for Progress stagnated and began to fizzle out. Our point is simply that where aid is seen primarily as furthering donor country interests, the flow of funds tends to vary in accordance with the donor's political assessment of changing international situations and not the relative need of different potential recipients.

The experience of other major donor countries like Great Britain and France has been similar to that of the United States. Although obvious exceptions can be cited (e.g. Sweden, West Germany, perhaps Japan), it is widely agreed that donor countries have utilised foreign aid largely as a political lever to prop up or underpin 'friendly' political regimes in Third World countries which were perceived to be in the national security interests of Western nations. Most socialist aid, especially that of the Soviet Union, grew out of the same political and strategic motivations (e.g. Cuba and Angola) although the form and content of that aid may have been different.

Economic motivations

Within the broad context of political and strategic priorities, foreign aid programmes of the developed nations have had a strong economic rationale. In fact while the political motivation may have been of paramount importance, the economic rationale was at least given greater lip-service as the overriding motivation for assistance.

The principal economic arguments which have been advanced in support of foreign aid are:

1. External resources (both loans and grants) can play a critical role in supplementing domestic resources to meet target levels of saving, investment and foreign exchange. This is the familiar 'gap' analysis of foreign assistance discussed in the previous section on private investment. Targets such as 1 per cent of developed country GNPs to be set aside for aid are regularly put forward by international commissions and just as regularly disregarded in most donor countries.
2. External assistance is assumed to facilitate and accelerate the process of development by stimulating and generating additional domestic savings as a result of the higher growth rates which it is presumed to induce. Eventually the need for aid disappears. Local resources then become sufficient to make the development process self-sustaining.
3. Financial assistance needs to be supplemented by technical assistance in the form of high level manpower transfers to ensure that aid funds are most efficiently utilised to generate economic growth. This manpower gap-filling is thus analogous to the financial gap-filling process mentioned above.
4. Finally, the amount of aid should be determined by the recipient country's 'absorptive capacity', a euphemism for its ability to use aid funds wisely and productively (i.e. the way donors want them to be used). Typically, it is the donor countries which decide which LDCs are to receive aid, how much, in what form (i.e. loans or grants, financial and/or technical assistance), for what purposes and under what conditions on the basis of their (the developed countries') assessment of LDC absorptive capacities. But the total amount of aid rarely has anything to do with Third World absorptive capacities; typically it is a residual and low priority element in donor country expenditure. In most instances the recipient countries have had little say in the matter.

These economic arguments on behalf of foreign aid as a crucial ingredient for LDC development should not mask the fact that even at the strictly economic level definite benefits accrue to donor countries as a result of their aid programmes. The increasing tendency towards providing loans instead of outright grants (interest-bearing loans now constitute about 70 per cent of all aid as compared to less than 40 per cent in earlier periods), and towards tying aid to the exports of donor countries has saddled many LDCs with substantial debt repayment burdens. It has also increased their import costs, often by as much as 20 to 40 per cent. These extra import costs arise because aid which is tied to donor country exports limits the receiving nation's freedom to shop around for low-cost and suitable capital and intermediate goods. As one former US aid official candidly put it:

> The biggest single misconception about the foreign aid program is that we send money abroad. We don't. Foreign aid consists of American equipment, raw materials, expert services, and food – all provided for specific development projects which we ourselves review and approve ... Ninety-three percent of AID funds are spent directly in the United States to pay for these things. Just last year some 4,000 American firms in fifty states received $1.3 billion in AID funds for products supplied as part of the foreign aid program.[4]

In a similar vein, a former British Minister of Overseas Development noted that 'About two-thirds of our aid is spent on goods and services from Britain ... trade follows aid. We equip a factory overseas and later on we get orders for spare parts and replacements ... [aid] is in our long-term interest.'[5]

Why LDCs accept aid

The reasons why Third World nations at least until recently have been eager to accept aid even in its most stringent and restrictive forms have been given much less attention than why donors provide aid. This is especially puzzling in view of the many instances where both parties may have conflicting rather than congruent motives and interests. Basically, however, one can identify three reasons, one major and two minor, why LDCs have sought foreign aid. The major reason is clearly economic in concept and practice. Third World countries have tended to accept uncritically the proposition, typically advanced by developed country economists, taught in all university 'development' courses, and supported by reference to 'success' cases like Taiwan, Israel and South Korea to the exclusion of many more failures, that aid is a crucial and essential ingredient in the development process. It supplements scarce domestic resources; it helps to transform the economy structurally; and it contributes to the achievements of LDC take-offs into self-sustaining economic growth. Thus, the economic rationale for aid in LDCs is based largely on their acceptance of the donor's perceptions of what the poor countries require to promote economic development.

The basic area of conflict arises, therefore, not out of any disagreement about the role of aid but about its amount and conditions. LDCs, naturally, would like to have more aid in the form of outright grants or low-cost loans with a minimum of strings attached. This means the abolition of tying aid to donor exports and the granting of greater latitude to recipient countries to decide for themselves what is in their best long-run development interests.

The two minor though still important motivations for LDCs to seek aid are political and moral. In some countries aid is seen by both donor and recipient as providing greater political leverage to the existing leadership to suppress opposition and maintain itself in power. In such instances assistance takes the form not only of financial resource transfers but military and internal security reinforcement as well. While South Vietnam represents the most dramatic illustration of this aid phenomenon in the 1960s, a number of other Third World nations share this political motivation. The problem is that once aid is accepted, the ability of recipient governments to extricate themselves from implied political and economic obligations to donors and to prevent donor governments (both capitalist and socialist) from interfering in their internal affairs can be greatly diminished.

Finally, we come to the moral motivation. Whether on grounds of basic humanitarian responsibilities of the rich towards the welfare of the poor, or because of a belief that the rich nations owe the poor 'conscience money' for past exploitation, many proponents of foreign aid in both developed and less developed countries believe that rich nations have an obligation to support the economic and social development of the Third World. They go on to link this moral obligation with the need for greater LDC autonomy with respect to the allocation and use of aid funds.

[4] William S. Gaud, 'Foreign aid: what it is; how it works; why we provide it', *Department of State Bulletin*, lix, 1537, December 1968, p. 603.

[5] Statement by Earl Grinstead, reported in *Overseas Development*, November 1968, p. 9.

The effects of aid

The controversy over the economic effects of aid, like that related to private foreign investment, is fraught with disagreements. On one side are the 'economic traditionalists', who argue that aid has indeed helped to promote growth and structural transformation in many LDCs.[6] There are others who have argued that aid does not promote faster growth but may in fact retard it by substituting for, rather than supplementing domestic savings and investment and by exacerbating LDC balance of payments deficits as a result of rising debt repayment obligations, and tying aid to donor country exports.[7]

Aid is further criticised for focusing on and stimulating the growth of the modern sector, thereby increasing the gap in living standards between the rich and the poor in Third World countries. Some would even assert that foreign aid has been a positive force for 'anti-development' in the sense that it both retards growth[8] and worsens income inequalities through reduced savings. Rather than relieving economic bottlenecks and filling gaps, aid (and for that matter, private foreign assistance) not only widens existing savings and foreign exchange resource gaps but may even create new ones (e.g. urban–rural or modern sector–traditional sector gaps).

On the donor side, there has been growing disenchantment in recent years with foreign aid as domestic issues like inflation, unemployment and balance of payments problems gain increasing priority over international cold war politics. One often hears the expression 'aid weariness' used to describe developed country attitudes towards foreign assistance. Taxpayers have become more concerned with domestic economic problems, especially as they realise increasingly that their tax moneys allocated to foreign aid may be benefiting primarily the small elites of LDCs who may in fact be richer than themselves.

OPEC's surplus 'petrodollars' and Third World development assistance

Instead of looking only at the traditional aid

Table 22.6
Concessional assistance by OPEC members in 1977* ($ millions and percentages)

	Commitments			Net disbursements			
Donor country	Bilateral	Multi-lateral	Total	Bilateral	Multi-lateral	Total	As % of GNP
Algeria	10.0	51.5	61.5	10.0	36.7	46.7	0.24
Iran	85.1	205.1	290.2	140.0	62.1	202.1	0.24
Iraq	108.6	27.0	135.6	25.0	28.4	53.4	0.28
Kuwait	1,039.4	212.7	1,252.1	792.0	649.8	1,441.8	10.18
Libya	24.6	111.8	136.4	25.0	84.4	109.4	0.63
Nigeria	—	60.7	60.7	1.4	62.2	63.6	0.19
Qatar	104.6	47.6	152.2	100.0	17.6	117.6	4.71
Saudi Arabia	2,515.0	449.2	2,964.2	1,660.0	713.0	2,373.0	4.82
UAE	968.3	108.1	1,076.4	1,010.0	251.8	1,261.8	10.97
Venezuela	—	147.2	147.2	—	71.5	71.5	0.20
Total	4,855.6	1,420.9	6,276.5	3,763.4	1,977.5	5,740.9	2.01

* Provisional data, in particular bilateral disbursement data are partly OECD Secretariat estimates.

Source: OECD, *1978 Review*, Table G.3.

[6] See, for example, Chenery and Carter, 'Foreign Assistance and Development Performance', *American Economic Review*, lxiii, 2, May 1973.

[7] For example, by the end of 1975, the Third World was in debt to the tune of over $90 billion compared with $61 billion at the end of 1973. Amortisation and interest payments were more than 9 per cent of gross foreign exchange earnings compared with 7 per cent in 1974. These debt claims continued to rise rapidly for the remainder of the 1970s.

[8] See, for example, Keith Griffin and J. L. Enos, 'Foreign Assistance: objectives and consequences', *Economic Development and Cultural Change*, April 1970, pp. 313–27.

relationships between the developed 'North' and the less developed 'South', we should also take into account the vast new potential for intra-Third World development assistance growing out of the enormous surplus oil revenues currently being generated by the 13 members of the Organisation of Petroleum Exporting Nations (OPEC). In 1974 alone, a total of $54 billion of *surplus* oil revenues were available for recycling to the non-oil-exporting nations. Some estimates are that these surplus revenues may total as much as $100 billion during the early 1980s. While by far the greatest proportion of surplus petrodollars were recycled back to the developed industrial nations, in 1977 a total of $6.7

Table 22.7
Recipients of bilateral aid from OPEC countries, 1975 and 1978 ($ millions and percentages)

	Net flow in 1975 ($ millions)	(as % of total)	Net flow in 1978 ($ millions)	(as % of total)
Middle East	**3,297.8**	**66.7**	**1,441.5**	**57.1**
Bahrain	21.7	0.4	44.1	1.8
Egypt[1]	2,072.7	41.9	508.2	20.1
Jordan[1]	249.8	5.0	239.1	9.5
Lebanon	1.3	—	120.6	4.8
Oman[1]	203.0	4.1	16.7	0.7
Syria[1]	535.5	10.8	339.0	13.4
Yemen[1]	139.4	2.8	122.5	4.9
Yemen, Democratic[1]	34.1	0.7	27.4	1.1
Asia	**772.4**	**15.6**	**375.0**	**14.9**
Afghanistan	21.6	0.4	18.4	0.7
Bangladesh	61.1	1.2	26.8	1.1
India	203.7	4.1	183.9	7.3
Indonesia	0.0	0.0	27.4	1.1
Pakistan	421.2	8.5	67.7	2.7
Sri Lanka	23.0	0.5	3.6	0.1
Vietnam	40.0	0.8	0.0	0.0
Africa	**625.4**	**12.6**	**400.0**	**15.9**
Algeria[1]	50.0	1.0	−4.5	—
Cameroon	17.4	0.4	3.3	0.1
Djibouti	0.0	0.0	60.0	2.4
Ghana	0.0	0.0	18.4	0.7
Mali	23.5	0.5	3.6	0.1
Mauritania[1]	24.7	0.5	107.4	4.3
Morocco[1]	97.9	2.0	34.3	1.4
Niger	14.1	0.3	16.2	0.6
Somalia[1]	72.9	1.5	26.8	1.1
Sudan[1]	174.1	3.5	53.2	2.1
Tunisia[1]	68.0	1.4	24.9	1.0
Latin America	**0.7**	**—**	**2.4**	**0.1**
Europe	**15.9**	**0.3**	**0.0**	**0.0**
Arab countries, unallocated	**233.5**	**4.7**	**134.4**	**5.3**
Other unallocated	**1.1**	**—**	**171.1**	**6.8**
Total	**4,946.8**	**100.0**	**2,524.4**	**100.0**
Arab countries	4,018.9	81.2	1,824.5	72.3
Least developed countries	409.9	8.3	497.8	19.7

[1] Arab country as defined by membership in Arab League.

Source: Overseas Development Council, *Agenda 1980*, Table E–20, p. 236.

billion were earmarked for loans and investments in Third World nations, with almost $4.9 billion going into direct bilateral assistance (see Table 22.6). It is to be hoped that an even greater proportion of future surplus oil revenues will find its way back to the non-oil-exporting developing nations whose total import bill rose by more than $13 billion in 1974 and another $10 billion in 1980 as a direct result of OPEC price increases.

There are a number of possible ways in which the major oil exporters can play a new and significant role in assisting less fortunate Third World countries. To a large degree they are already initiating such a role. For example, the principal Arab member of OPEC, Saudi Arabia, has been extending sizable grants and credits to a number of needy Arab states like Egypt and Jordan. Although much of this assistance is in the form of military and political support, a good deal of it is for genuine economic development. Beyond that, Arab oil producers have created an Arab Fund for Economic and Social Development with an initial capital endowment of $300 million as well as a Fund for African Development with an initial outlay of $250 million. A few of the Persian Gulf oil states which have close religious and technical ties with Pakistan are stepping up their development assistance to this country. Outside the Middle East, Venezuela has embarked on an ambitious aid programme to assist needy Latin American nations while Nigeria has recently established an $80 million Special African Aid Fund to be administered by the African Development Bank, and to provide low-cost long-term loans to the poorest African nations.

Table 22.6 provides a detailed breakdown of bilateral and multilateral OPEC aid commitments and disbursements in 1977, whereas Table 22.7 shows the major recipients of OPEC bilateral aid in 1975 and 1978. Note in particular that four countries Egypt, Syria, Jordan and India – received over 60 per cent of all OPEC commitments. Finally, Figure 22.1 shows how much more active OPEC nations have already become in the aid field in comparison with the developed countries – at least in terms of the percentage of their GNPs being devoted to development assistance.

Of even greater potential significance than all these outlays, however, was the 1975 decision of

Figure 22.1
Comparison of per capita GNP and aid commitments and disbursements of selected OPEC and developed countries, 1979

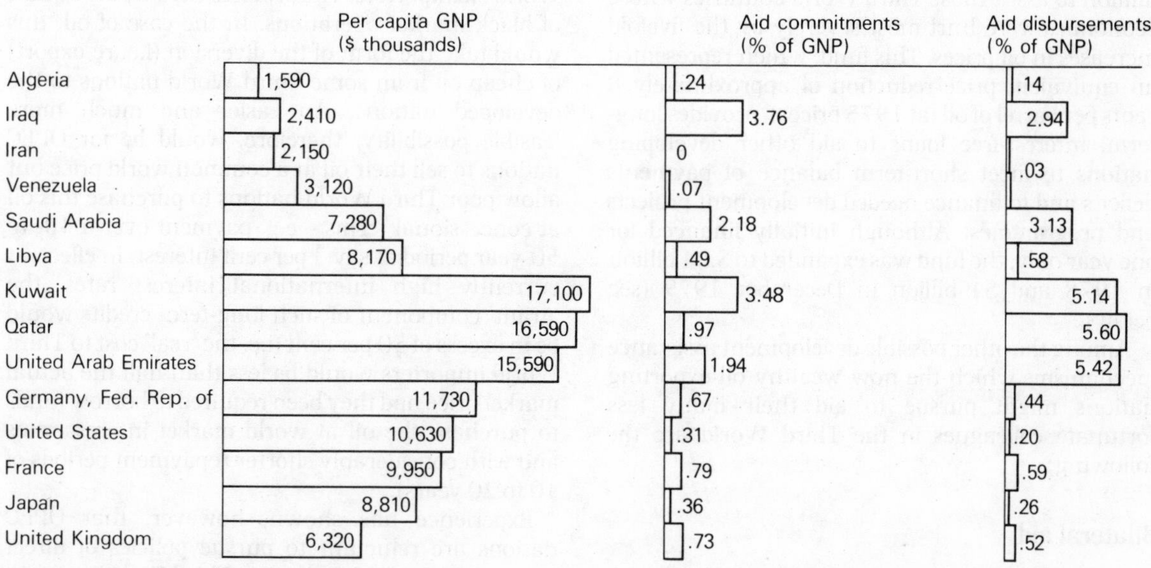

Sources: *IBRD, World Development Report, 1981*, Table I. OECD, *Development Co-operation*, 1980, Tables A-12, G-4.

OPEC countries led by Saudi Arabia to initiate and contribute $600 million towards the establishment of a new $1.2 billion International Fund for Agricultural Development. The other $600 million was contributed by the developed nations. The fund doubled the external resources being given or loaned at low interest for long-term agricultural development in Asia, Africa and Latin America. It became operational in January 1976 and its financial resources are to be replenished each year with Saudi Arabia being the largest single contributor. The voting power within the new fund will be divided one-third for OPEC countries, one-third for the developing nations and one-third for the developed world. Thus, for the first time in history there now exists a major international financial institution which is *controlled* by the Third World! This, indeed, is a remarkable breakthrough in a global economic system which has in the past been totally dominated by the rich nations of the world. It is hoped that it will provide a precedent for future aid relationships in which economically more fortunate developing nations begin to assume increased responsibility for the welfare of their less fortunate colleagues in other parts of the Third World.

A second major OPEC initiative, sponsored jointly by Iran and Venezuela, was the decision taken in January 1976 to set aside an annual fund of $800 million to assist those Third World countries whose economies were hurt most severely by the fivefold increases in oil prices. This fund, which represented an equivalent price reduction of approximately 8 cents per barrel of oil (at 1975 prices), provides long-term, interest-free loans to aid other developing nations to meet short-term balance of payments deficits and to finance needed development projects and programmes. Although initially financed for one year only, the fund was expanded to $2.4 billion in 1978 and $4 billion in December 1979 (see below).

Among the other possible development assistance mechanisms which the now wealthy oil-exporting nations might pursue to aid their many less fortunate colleagues in the Third World are the following:

Bilateral aid

Expanded bilateral assistance programmes ranging from outright grants to low-interest, long-term concessional loans would obviously be one of the most important mechanisms for recycling surplus petrodollars to needy Third World nations. Moreover, direct private or public investment projects in fertiliser and energy production in underdeveloped countries would substantially assist these nations to meet their current and future food requirements.

Expanded financial support for international assistance agencies

An alternative to direct intra-Third World bilateral assistance would be the channelling of more of the surplus oil revenues into the major international and regional financial institutions such as the World Bank, the International Monetary Fund, and the Asian and Inter-American Development Banks. Such indirect assistance would have the advantage that all multilateral aid has over bilateral assistance: the minimisation of political and/or ideological strings.

Concessional oil sales

A third possibility would be for OPEC to establish a two-tier or dual price system for their oil sales: a much higher market price for rich industrial nations and a considerably lower subsidised price for Third World oil importers. The problem here would be that of black market operations. In the case of oil, this would take the form of the diversion (i.e. re-export) of cheap oil from some Third World nations to the developed nations. An easier and much more feasible possibility, therefore, would be for OPEC nations to sell their oil at a common world price but allow poor Third World nations to purchase this oil at concessional terms – e.g. payment over a 40- to 50-year period at say 3 per cent interest. In effect, at currently high international interest rates, the 'grant' component of such long-term credits would be in excess of 50 per cent (i.e. the 'real' cost to Third World importers would be less than half the actual market price had they been required to borrow funds to purchase the oil at world market interest rates and with considerably shorter repayment periods of 10 to 20 years).

Experience has shown, however, that OPEC nations are reluctant to pursue policies of direct concessional oil sales to other Third World nations. The most recent evidence of this was in November 1979 when non-oil LDCs were persuaded by OPEC to stop pressing for special oil price concessions and to seek further aid instead. This was then followed by an OPEC decision at their annual meeting held in Caracas in December of 1979 to increase their aid to other Third World countries from $2.4 to $4 billion. The money would be collected by setting aside a few cents on every OPEC barrel of oil sold.

In spite of the serious economic hardships which the phenomenal rise in international oil prices has had on most less developed nations (see Chapter 25), the oil exporting countries are nevertheless riding a crest of popularity among their Third World colleagues. They are experiencing this strong sense of identification from other developing nations largely because they have shown that it is possible for small nations, acting together, to bring the big industrial giants to their economic knees. But such goodwill and peer group identification will quickly vanish if wealthy OPEC nations do not rapidly seize the opportunity to step into the foreign aid vacuum and assume their important new role of economic leadership within the Third World.

Conclusions: towards a new view of foreign aid

When all is said and done, the combination of 'aid disillusionment' on the part of many Third World recipients and 'aid weariness' on the part of traditional developed country donors does not augur well for the continuation of past relationships. But we would argue that this is desirable rather than depressing. Dissatisfaction on both sides creates the possibility of new arrangements and new relationships of greater congruence of interest and motivation on the part of both donor and recipient. The OPEC-sponsored International Fund for Agricultural Development and the new fund for balance of payments adjustments are two outstanding examples of such new aid relationships. A lower total volume of aid from the developed nations but one which is geared more to the real development needs of recipient nations and which permits them a greater degree of flexibility and autonomy in meeting development priorities would on balance represent a positive step. The rising proportion of development assistance funds now being channelled through multilateral assistance agencies like the World Bank and various regional Development Banks, whose political motives are presumably less narrowly defined compared with those of individual donor countries, is a welcome development.

More aid is better than less aid for some of the reasons outlined above. But from the viewpoint of LDC recipients, whatever the source and volume of aid, the more it takes the form of outright grants and concessional loans, the less it is tied to donor exports, the more local autonomy is permitted in its allocation and the more it is supplemented by the reduction of donor-country tariff and non-tariff barriers against Third World exports, the greater will be the development impact of this foreign assistance. Although it may seem wishful thinking to imagine that rich Western countries (both capitalist and socialist) will move in the direction of such real development-oriented aid policies that at first glance appear to be against their economic self-interests, on closer examination this viewpoint may not be so far-fetched after all.

As the realities of global interdependence slowly penetrate the political perceptions of developed-nation governments, and perhaps eventually their populace as well, it may begin to dawn on them that their real long-run economic and political interests do in fact lie with the achievement of broad-based development in Third World nations. Eliminating poverty, minimising inequality and in general raising levels of living for the masses of LDC peoples may just turn out to be in the most fundamental self-interest of developed nations, not because of any humanitarian ideals (though one would hope that these are present) but simply because in the long run there cannot be two futures for mankind – one for the very rich, the other for the very poor – without the proliferation of global conflicts.

Enlightened self-interest, therefore, may be the only peg on which to build the hope for a new world order, one in which foreign assistance, both public and private, can begin to make a real and lasting contribution to Third World development.

Concepts for review

private foreign investment	private transfer payments
foreign aid	strong currencies
grants v. loans	savings-investment gap

foreign monetary reserves
multilateral donor agencies
bilateral donor agencies
debt burden
foreign exchange gap
'tied' aid
absorptive capacity
multi-national corporations
petrodollars
transfer pricing
inappropriate products
technical assistance
aid weariness

Questions for discussion

1. The emergence of giant multi-national corporations over the past two decades is said to have altered the very nature of international economic activity. In what ways do these MNCs affect the structure and pattern of trading relationships between the developed and underdeveloped world?
2. Summarise the arguments for and against the role and impact of private foreign investment in less developed countries. What strategies might LDCs adopt to make private foreign investment fit their development aspirations better without destroying all incentives for foreign investors?
3. How important is foreign aid for the economies of the Third World in relation to their other sources of foreign exchange receipts? Explain the various forms which development assistance can take and distinguish between bilateral and multilateral assistance. Which do you think is more desirable and why?
4. What is meant by 'tied aid'? Both capitalist and socialist nations have increasingly shifted from grants to loans and from untied to tied loans and grants during the past decade. What are the major disadvantages of tied aid especially when this aid comes in the form of interest-bearing loans?
5. Under what conditions and terms do you think LDCs should seek and accept foreign aid in the future? If aid cannot be obtained on such terms do you think LDCs should accept whatever they can get? Explain your answer.
6. Aid from OPEC countries has amounted to much less annually ($9.5 billion) than the annual increased oil import costs of all other developing nations ($13 billion). And yet OPEC countries are rarely criticised by their Third World colleagues. Why do you think this is so and do you feel that OPEC countries can do more to assist those developing countries whose economies were hit hardest by recent oil price increases? Explain.

Further reading

On private foreign investment and the role of multinational corporations, see: SANJAYA LALL, 'Less Developed Countries and Private Foreign Direct Investment: a review article', *World Development*, ii, 4 and 5, April–May 1974; PAUL STREETEN, 'The Multinational Enterprise and the Theory of Development Policy', *World Development*, i, 10, October 1973; and United Nations, *Transnational Corporations in World Development: A Re-Appraisal*, New York, 1978.

On the question of the benefits and costs of foreign aid see: LESTER B. PEARSON (chairman), *Partners in Development, Report of the Commission on International Development*, Praeger, New York, 1969, chs 1, 6, 7, 8, 9 and 11; GUNNAR MYRDAL, *The Challenge of World Poverty*, Pantheon, New York, 1970, chs 10 and 11; J. BHAGWATI and R. S. ECKAUS, eds, *Foreign Aid*, Penguin Modern Economic Readings, 1970; GEORGE C. ABBOT, 'Two concepts of foreign aid', *World Development*, i, 9, September 1973.

Part Four Possibilities and prospects

Chapter 23 Development planning: theory and practice

Planning is the exercise of intelligence to deal with facts and situations as they are and find a way to solve problems.
Jawaharlal Nehru

If we could first know *where* we are, and *whither* we are tending, we could better judge *what* to do, and how to do it.
Abraham Lincoln

Introduction

The planning mystique

In the three decades since the Second World War, the pursuit of economic development among Third World nations has been crystallised by their almost universal acceptance of development planning as the surest and most direct route to economic progress. Until recently few in the Third World would have questioned the advisability or desirability of formulating and implementing a national development plan. Planning has become a way of life in the government ministries of most less developed nations and every five years or so the latest development plan is paraded with the greatest of fanfare.

But why, until recently, has there been such an aura and mystique about development planning and such universal faith in its obvious utility? Basically, because centralised national planning was widely believed to offer the essential and perhaps the only institutional and organisational mechanism for overcoming all obstacles to development and for ensuring a sustained high rate of economic growth. In some cases central economic planning even became regarded as a kind of 'open sesame' which allows Third World nations to pass rapidly through the barrier dividing their pitiably low standards of living from the prosperity of their former rulers. But in order to catch up, poor nations were persuaded and became convinced that they required a comprehensive national plan. The planning record, unfortunately, has not lived up to its advance billing and scepticism is now growing about the planning mystique.

In this chapter we examine the role and limitations of development planning as practised in Third World nations, both in its own right and in the broader framework of national economic policy formulations. We start with a brief review of the nature of economic planning and its widespread practice in the world's economies. We then summarise the main arguments for and against the role of planning in less developed countries and conclude with a review of the recent history of LDC planning in practice. In Chapter 24 we take up the broader questions of economic policy for development and examine some of the positive and negative factors (both economic and non-economic) of substantial state intervention in economic activities.

The nature of economic planning and its differential role in the world's economies[1]

Economic planning may be described as the conscious governmental effort to influence, direct and in some cases, even control changes in the principal economic variables (consumption, investment, savings, exports, imports, etc.) of a certain country or region over the course of time in order to achieve a predetermined set of objectives. The

[1] Portions of the material in this and the following two sections are drawn from the author's earlier book, *Development Planning: models and methods*, Oxford University Press, Nairobi, 1971, Chapter 1.

essence of economic planning is summed up in these notions of governmental influence, direction and control. Similarly, we can describe an **economic plan** as a specific set of quantitative economic targets to be reached in a given period of time. Economic plans may be either comprehensive or partial. A **comprehensive plan** sets its targets to cover all major aspects of the national economy. A **partial plan** covers only a part of the national economy – industry, agriculture, the public sector, the foreign sector and so forth.

In one of its first publications dealing with developing countries in 1951, the United Nations department of economic affairs distinguished four types of planning, each of which has been used in one form or another by most LDCs.

> First it ... [planning] refers only to the making of a program of public expenditure, extending over from one to say ten years. Second, it refers sometimes to the setting of production targets, whether for private or for public enterprises, in terms of the input of manpower, of capital, or of other scarce resources, or use in terms of output. Thirdly, the word may be used to describe a statement which sets targets for the economy as a whole, purporting to allocate all scarce resources among the various branches of the economy. And fourthly, the word is sometimes used to describe the means which the government uses to try to enforce upon private enterprise the targets which have been previously determined.[2]

Proponents of economic planning in developing countries argue that the uncontrolled market economy can, and often does, subject these nations to economic stagnation, fluctuating prices and low levels of employment. In particular, they claim that the market economy is not geared to the principal operational task of poor countries: how to mobilise limited resources in a way that will bring about the structural change necessary to stimulate a sustained and balanced growth of the entire economy. Planning has come to be accepted, therefore, as an essential and pivotal means of guiding and accelerating economic growth in all Third World countries.

Before examining these issues further, we consider the various aspects and characteristics of economic planning as it is practised in different situations and at different stages of economic maturity in the world's economies. Unfortunately, the usual division of economic systems into market economies and planned economies can be very misleading when viewed in an overall perspective. In the real world there are no completely planned or completely unplanned economies; planning is obviously a matter of degree. Therefore, in order to avoid confusion we may distinguish among three fundamental but distinct types of economic planning.

Planning in market economies

First, we must recognise that even in predominantly private enterprise economies like those of the United States, the United Kingdom and Japan, planning plays a vital although relatively indirect role in the economic process. In the context of these economies, planning usually consists of the conscious effort by the government to attain rapid economic growth with high employment and stable prices through its various fiscal and monetary policies. Recognising that the completely unfettered play of the market mechanism can lead to highly unstable economic situations, these governments actively attempt to create conditions that will prevent economic instability while still stimulating economic growth. The policy instruments used are primarily those in the fields of monetary, fiscal and foreign trade relations. Greater employment and higher incomes for a growing population are induced by expansionary monetary policy, increased government spending and tax rate adjustments. Inflation and deflation are held in check by countercyclical fiscal policies, interest rate adjustments and wage-price guidelines. Balance of payments fluctuations are counteracted by tariff adjustments, exchange controls, import quotas and tax incentives. In all the above methods **the instruments of policy are active but indirect**. They are active in that they push the economy in a desired direction. They are indirect in that they are intended merely to create favourable conditions which will influence private decision makers to behave in ways that are likely to promote stable economic grow[th.] Although no detailed economic plan in the [sense of a] set of specific targets is drawn up [...]

[2] United Nations Department of Economic Affairs, *Measures for the Economic Development of Underdeveloped Countries*, New York, 1951, p. 63.

economies, limited government planning is nevertheless carried out on the basis of analysis of past trends and projections of future economic conditions.

Planning in command economies

The second category of economic planning is associated mainly with the Soviet Union and those Soviet-type economies of Eastern Europe where the government actively and directly controls the movements of the economy through a central decision-making process. A specific set of targets predetermined by central planners forms the basis of a complete and comprehensive national economic plan. Resources, both material and financial, are allocated in accordance not with market prices and conditions of supply and demand, as in idealised market economies, but with the material, labour and capital requirements of the overall plan. Thus **the essential difference between planning in market and command economies is one of inducement versus control**. While the former merely attempts to prevent the economy from straying from a desired path of stable growth by active but indirect instruments of policy, the latter not only draws up a specific set of targets representing a desired course of economic progress, but also attempts to implement its plan by directly controlling the activities of practically all productive units in the entire national economy. In short, the command economy plan dictates the future position of all economic variables. However, not even the economies of command socialist countries are 100 per cent centrally planned. For example, in the Soviet Union, aspects of the market economy are becoming increasingly evident in the production, distribution and pricing of a wide variety of consumer goods.

Planning in mixed developing economies

Finally, the third, and for our purposes, most important, example of economic planning lies in the realm of development planning within the framework of the mixed economies of most Third World countries. These economies are characterised by the existence of an institutional setting in which part of the productive resources are privately owned and operated while the other part is controlled by the public sector. The actual proportionate division of public and private ownership varies from country to country. However, unlike market economies where there is usually only a small degree of public ownership, LDC mixed economies are distinguished by a substantial amount of government ownership and control. The private sector of these economies typically consists of four distinct forms of individual ownership: (1) the traditional subsistence sector consisting of small-scale private farms selling a part of their produce to local markets; (2) small-scale individual or family-owned commercial business and service activities; (3) medium-sized commercial enterprises in agriculture, industry, trade and transport owned and operated by local entrepreneurs; and (4) large jointly owned or completely foreign owned manufacturing enterprises, mining companies and plantations primarily catering to foreign markets but sometimes with substantial local sales. The capital for such enterprises usually comes from abroad while, as we saw in the previous chapter, a good proportion of the profits tends to be transferred overseas.

In the context of such an institutional setting, we can identify two principal components of development planning in mixed economies:

1. The government's deliberate utilisation of domestic saving and foreign finance to carry out public investment projects and to mobilise and channel scarce resources into areas that can be expected to make the greatest contribution towards the realisation of long-term economic objectives (e.g. the construction of railways, schools, hydroelectric projects and other components of economic infrastructure, as well as the creation of import-substituting industries).
2. Governmental economic policy (e.g. taxation, licensing, import quotas, wage and price policy) to stimulate, direct, and in some cases, even control private economic activity in order to ensure a harmonious relationship between the desires of private businessmen and the social objectives of the central government.

The compromise nature of this situation between the extremes of market inducement and collectivist control is readily evident from the above simplified characterisation of planning in mixed-market economies. Since most Third World countries fall into this category, let us look now at some of the economic and institutional reasons that have led many to conclude that planning is necessary if these poor countries are to accelerate their pace of development.

The rationale for planning in Third World economies

The widespread acceptance of planning as a development tool rests on a number of fundamental economic and institutional arguments of which the following four are most often put forward.

The market failure argument

Markets in LDCs are permeated by imperfections both of structure and operation. Commodity and factor markets are poorly organised and the existence of 'distorted prices' often means that producers and consumers lack the necessary information to act in a way conducive to efficient production and distribution. Secondly, well-organised capital markets based on the existence of specialised financial institutions performing a great variety of monetary functions (such as the channelling of private savings into loan markets to provide capital funds to finance investment projects) are either non-existent or poorly developed in most Third World countries. In short, the inefficiency or absence of well organised commodity, factor and capital markets is said to reduce considerably the ability of the LDC economic system to function effectively without some form of external interference.

The failure of the 'market' to price factors of production correctly is further assumed to lead to gross disparities between social and private valuations of alternative investment projects. In the absence of governmental interference, therefore, the market is said to lead to a misallocation of present and future resources or, at least, to one which may not be in the best long-run social interests. This market failure argument is perhaps the most often quoted reason for the expanded role of government in less developed countries.

A clear statement of this viewpoint was presented in a 1965 report of a United Nations Conference on Planning which asserted that:

> It is an integral task of planning to achieve the best possible use of scarce resources for economic development. . . . The need for using appropriate criteria for selecting projects arose because of the failure of the market mechanism to provide a proper guideline. In less-developed economies, market prices of such factors of production as labour, capital and foreign exchange deviated substantially from their social opportunity costs and were not, therefore, a correct measure of the relative scarcity or abundance of the factor in question.[3]

A more recent publication of the United Nations Industrial Development Organisation (UNIDO) provides the following explicit market failure rationale for planning in LDCs:

> Governments cannot, and should not, take a merely passive role in the process of industrial expansion. Planning has become an essential and integral part of industrial development programmes, for market forces, by themselves, cannot overcome the deepseated structural rigidities in the economies of developing countries. . . . Today the need for some degree of economic planning is universally recognised. It is, of course, an integral part of the economy of the Soviet Union and the other centrally planned countries. . . . In developing countries, planning is more feasible and more desirable than in developed market economies. The greater feasibility is a result of the smaller number of variables that must be taken into consideration, and the greater desirability stems from the fact that the automatic mechanisms for co-ordination of individual actions function less satisfactorily in developing than in developed economies. Planning in developing countries is made necessary by *inter alia*, the inadequacies of the market as a mechanism to ensure that individual decisions will optimise economic performance in terms of society's preferences and economic goals. . . . The inadequacy of the market mechanism as a means of allocating resources for industrial development sometimes results from government policy itself or because the theoretical

[3] United Nations, *Planning the External Sector: techniques, problems and policies*, September 1965, p. 12.

assumptions (particularly with respect to the mobility of the factors of production) do not apply to the actual economic situation. Even more importantly, the market mechanism cannot properly allow for the external effects of investment.[4]

The resource mobilisation and allocation argument

Third World economies cannot afford to waste their limited financial and skilled manpower resources on unproductive ventures. Investment projects must be chosen not only on the basis of a partial productivity analysis dictated by individual industrial capital/output ratios, but rather in the context of an overall development programme which takes account of external economies, indirect repercussions and long-term objectives. Skilled manpower must also be utilised where its contribution will be most widely felt. Economic planning is assumed to help modify the restraining influence of limited resources by recognising the existence of particular constraints and by choosing and co-ordinating investment projects so as to channel these scarce factors into their most productive outlets. On the other hand, it is argued that competitive markets will tend to generate less investment, to direct that investment into socially low-priority areas (e.g. consumption goods for the rich) and to disregard the extra benefits to be derived from a planned and co-ordinated long-term investment programme.

The attitudinal or psychological argument

It is often assumed that a detailed statement of national economic and social objectives in the form of a specific development plan can have an important attitudinal or psychological impact on a diverse and often fragmented population. It may succeed in rallying the people behind the government in a national campaign to eliminate 'poverty, ignorance and disease'. By mobilising popular support and cutting across class, caste, racial, religious or tribal factions with the plea to all citizens to work together towards building the nation, an enlightened central government through its economic plan is thought to be best equipped to provide the incentives needed to overcome the inhibiting and often divisive forces of sectionalism and traditionalism in a common quest for widespread material and social progress.

The foreign aid argument

The formulation of detailed development plans with specific sectoral output targets and carefully designed investment projects has often been a necessary condition for the receipt of bilateral and multilateral foreign aid. In fact, some cynics would argue that the real reason why LDCs construct development plans is to secure more foreign aid. With a 'shopping list' of projects, Third World governments are better equipped to solicit foreign assistance and persuade donors that their money will be applied as an essential ingredient in a well-conceived and internally consistent plan of action. To a certain extent, this is a charade, but one whose origin lies as much with developed-country desires for sophisticated and detailed project descriptions within the framework of a comprehensive development plan as with LDC desires to secure foreign aid at any cost.

The nature of development planning: basic types of planning models

The planning process: six basic characteristics

While there exists a great diversity of development plans and planning techniques throughout the Third World, there are some basic characteristics of 'comprehensive' development planning that are common to most countries. Professor Tony Killick has listed the following six characteristics of a development plan as being representative.[5]

[4] R. Helfgoth and S. Schiavo-Campo, 'An Introduction to Development Planning', *UNIDO Industrialisation and Productivity Bulletin*, 16, 1970, p. 11.

[5] T. Killick, 'The Possibilities of Development Planning', *Institute for Development Studies, Oxford Economic Papers*, July 1976.

1. Starting from the political views and goals of the government, planning attempts to define policy objectives, especially as they relate to the future development of the economy;
2. A development plan sets out a strategy by means of which it is intended to achieve the objectives, which are normally translated into specific targets;
3. The plan attempts to present a centrally co-ordinated, internally consistent set of principles and policies, chosen as the optimal means of implementing the strategy and achieving the targets, and intended to be used as a framework to guide subsequent day-to-day decisions;
4. It comprehends the whole economy (hence it is 'comprehensive' as against 'colonial' or 'public sector' planning);
5. In order to secure optimality and consistency, the comprehensive plan employs a more-or-less formalised macro-economic model (which, however, will often remain unpublished), and this is employed to project the intended future performance of the economy;
6. A development plan typically covers a period of, say, five years and finds physical expression as a medium-term plan document, which may, however, incorporate a longer-term perspective plan and be supplemented by annual plans.

Although the formulation of a comprehensive plan is the goal of most poor countries, it is sometimes necessary to base such plans on a more partial sectoral analysis. In very poor countries with limited data and minimal industrial diversification, partial plans may be the most that can be accomplished. Three basic planning models can be distinguished.

Three types of planning models

Development plans, as we have just seen, are typically based on some more or less formalised macro-economic model. Such planning models may be divided into three categories according to the degree of structural complexity and the particular use to which the model is being put. They are (1) the aggregate growth model; (2) the sectoral projection model; and (3) the comprehensive inter-industry model.

The aggregate growth model

The first and most elementary type of planning model, the **aggregate growth model**, deals with the entire economy in terms of such macro-economic variables as consumption, production, investment, saving, exports and imports. Aggregate growth models are usually used to determine possible growth rates of national output under simplifying assumptions about savings and investment. The simplest and most commonly used is the Harrod-Domar model which, as we saw in Chapter 6, assumes that limited savings and investment constitute the major constraint on aggregate economic growth. Given targeted GNP growth rates, the model is used to specify the amount of domestic saving necessary to generate such growth. In countries where inadequate foreign exchange reserves are felt to be the principal bottleneck inhibiting economic growth, the aggregate model might concentrate more on exports, imports, terms of trade fluctuations and sources of foreign financial assistance. In either case, the aggregate growth model usually provides only a rough first approximation of the general directions which an economy might take. As such, it rarely constitutes the operational development plan. In most instances, the projection of aggregate components of GDP merely provides a general overall framework or initial stage in the formulation of a comprehensive development plan.

The sectoral projection model

The so-called **'sectoral' growth or projection model** really comprises two fundamentally different approaches to development planning. The first attempts to divide the economy into two or more 'main-sectors' such as agriculture and non-agriculture, or the consumption-goods sector, the investment-goods sector, and the export sector. The objective is to formulate an internally consistent plan for the whole economy by focusing on the growth prospects of a limited number of its principal sectors. This more detailed approach is often called a **complete main-sector planning model**.

A second and less ambitious sectoral approach concentrates on levels of production and consumption so as to investigate the possibility of growth in a single individual sector of the economy. This approach, sometimes referred to as a **single-sector project model**, analyses growth prospects in isolated sectors of the economy (agriculture, transportation, construction) with a view to identifying specific industrial investment projects which then might be funded with either domestic or foreign resources. The major analytical tool for 'appraising' alternative sectoral investment projects is the cost/benefit methodology discussed in Chapter 4.

The single-sector project approach is most often undertaken in those economies where statistical data for either an aggregate or a complete main-sector model are lacking, but where detailed information may exist for one or more individual sectors. The main drawback is that the development plan, if based exclusively on a sectoral project approach, often loses its desirable characteristics of internal consistency, and more important, overall feasibility. Rather than a well co-ordinated programme of action, such partial plans could easily emerge as no more than a haphazard collection of assorted development projects with no apparent interconnections.

The single sector project approach to planning has been used primarily in African-type economies where the industrial sector is still in its infancy and statistical data are often crude and incomplete. The earlier five-year plans of Ghana (1959–1964), Nigeria (1963–1968), Kenya (1964–1969/1970), Tanzania (1964–1969/1970) and Uganda (1961/1962–1965/1966), could be described generally as **public sector project plans**. Considerable effort, however, was exerted by the Planning Ministries of these countries to co-ordinate as best they could the individual investment projects in light of limited statistical information.

The comprehensive inter-industry model

The third and most sophisticated approach to development planning is to utilise some variant of the inter-industry or **input–output model** in which the activities of *all* productive sectors of the economy are interrelated through a set of simultaneous algebraic equations expressing the specific production processes or technologies of each industry. All industries are viewed both as producers of **outputs** and utilisers of **inputs** from other industries. For example, the agricultural sector is both a producer of output (e.g. wheat) and user of inputs from, say, the manufacturing sector (e.g. machinery, fertiliser, etc.). Thus, direct and indirect repercussions of planned changes in the demand for the products of any one industry on output, employment and imports of all other industries are traced throughout the entire economy in an intricate web of economic interdependence. Given the planned output targets for each sector of the economy, the inter-industry model can be used to determine intermediate material, import, labour and capital requirements with the result that a comprehensive economic plan with mutually consistent production levels and resource requirements can, in theory, be constructed.

Inter-industry models range from simple input–output models, usually consisting of from 10 to 30 sectors in the developing economies and from 30 to 400 sectors in advanced economies, to the more complicated 'linear-programming' or 'activity-analysis' models where checks of feasibility (i.e. what is possible, given certain resource constraints) and optimality (what is best among different alternatives) are also built into the model. But the distinguishing characteristic of the inter-industry or input–output approach is the attempt to formulate an internally consistent, comprehensive development plan for the entire economy.[6]

Unfortunately, sophisticated inter-industry models require an inordinate amount of statistical information and are primarily applicable in economies that have achieved a considerable degree of industrial development as evidenced, for example, by a significant volume of inter-industry transactions. They are thus of limited value for developing economies. Nevertheless, simple input–output models have been put to a number of useful tasks in those developing economies which have begun to diversify their industrial sectors.

Important considerations in choosing planning models

As indicated earlier, there are a number of different

[6] For a detailed mathematical description of input–output and linear programming models with hypothetical illustrations of their use in development planning, see M. P. Todaro, *op. cit.*, Chapters 2, 3 and 5.

types of economic models and planning approaches from which a developing nation can choose. A country about to draw up a development plan will have to decide which method, or combination of methods, is most suitable to its own special needs and objectives. An intelligent and informed choice will depend on the answers to a number of important questions which must be specifically analysed before reaching a final decision. Some of the more relevant considerations which have been suggested are the following:

1. Stage of development

The choice of a particular plan strategy obviously depends on the existing level of a country's economic development. If the economy is still permeated by small-scale subsistence agriculture, a limited monetary sector, and little or no inter-industry relations, then detailed quantitative planning can have little applicability. It would probably be more appropriate to concentrate on individual 'social overhead' public investment projects aimed at creating the necessary conditions to initiate economic transformation. Some general idea of possible overall rates of growth of GDP and its major components as well as considerations of population growth, and in the case of most small economies, possibilities of export expansion loom more important at this early stage. In the later stages the likely path of development is often more clearly discernible, and greater detail in planning methods may become more feasible.

2. Institutional structure

Another important consideration concerns the institutional structure of the economy and the relative roles envisaged for the public and private sectors in the development process. Where the private sector is not very influential and is expected to play a relatively passive role, the public sector will ordinarily be expected to take up the slack and provide the initial stimulus and continued overall direction. Accordingly, more attention will be devoted to public investment projects and sources of government finance. However, if the private sector is considerably more active, then the plan is more likely to concentrate on the creation of favourable conditions in which private economic activity is free to flourish in a manner that contributes to the social good. A corollary of this public-versus-private consideration concerns the general attitude and willingness of the private sector to co-operate with the central government in a joint effort to promote national development. Where conflicts between public and private interests arise, the former will normally take precedence over the latter.

3. Availability and quality of statistical information

The availability and reliability of statistical information necessary to initiate and formulate a development plan represents a third important influence on the choice of particular planning approaches. To the extent that existing data are poor and unreliable, there will be considerably less scope for the more refined type of analysis required by some mathematical programming models. However, while the complete absence of certain statistical information may preclude the use of particular models, economic planners are often advised to resort to 'educated guesses' or to the adaptation of empirical information from economies in similar circumstances rather than to forego completely a particularly useful approach merely for lack of full statistical data.

4. Resource constraints

The character of the development plan is often greatly influenced by the particular resource constraints or bottlenecks impinging on the economy. The nature and character of resource constraints are often related to the stage of a country's economic development. However, in general, capital and foreign exchange scarcity have been regarded as the principal bottlenecks limiting rapid economic development. If capital constitutes the crucial constraint, every care must be taken to ensure its most effective and productive utilisation. Labour-intensive investment projects may have to be stressed so that limited capital funds can be distributed into diverse channels in the economy. When depleted foreign exchange reserves emerge as the operative constraint, export promotion and/or some form of import control will assume increased importance in the plan. Other possible economic bottlenecks that might appear during the course of the development process include limited supplies of high-level manpower, inadequate transport facilities, and limited government finance. Economic planning is conceived, therefore, as an efficient means of dealing with different resource constraints as they arise during the development process.

5. Priorities and objectives

Finally, the specific long-run social and economic goals and objectives which the less developed nation deems most important must provide the conceptual basis for the entire plan. Economic goals most commonly mentioned include:

- a rapid increase in per capita income,
- a high level of employment,
- a relatively stable price level,
- a reduction of poverty and income inequalities,
- a favourable balance of payments situation, and
- a diversified and self-reliant economy.

While each of the above objectives may be desirable in itself serious conflicts may easily arise if all are pursued with equal intensity. Therefore, it often becomes necessary to determine, in the light of existing social, economic and institutional conditions and constraints, the specific objective, or combination of objectives, which should receive special priority in the development plan. The remaining targets might then constitute some form of associated 'side conditions' or secondary priorities to be realised as far as possible in the course of seeking fulfilment of the priority objectives.

This completes our brief review of the character and role of development planning as it has been traditionally presented by its proponents. We now consider some of its limitations and shortcomings.

The crisis in planning: problems of implementation and plan failures

After more than two decades of experience with development planning in Third World countries, the results generally have been disappointing. In the most comprehensive and exhaustive study of the development planning experience in some 55 countries, Albert Waterson concluded that:

> An examination of postwar planning history reveals that there have been many more failures than successes in the implementation of development plans. By far the great majority of countries have failed to realize even modest income and output targets in their plans except for short periods. What is even more disturbing, the situation seems to be worsening instead of improving as countries continue to plan.[7]

In a similar vein, Derek Healey, in a review article on development policy over the post-war decades, concluded that the results of planned development have been 'sadly disillusioning for those who believed that planning was the only way'.[8]

What went wrong? Why has the early euphoria about planning gradually been transformed into disillusionment and dejection? We can identify two interrelated sets of answers, one dealing with the gap between the theoretical economic benefits and the practical results of development planning and the other associated with more fundamental defects in the planning process, especially as it relates to administrative capacities, political will and plan implementation.

Theory v. planning practice

The principal economic arguments for planning that were briefly outlined earlier (market failure, divergences between private and social valuations, resource mobilisation, investment co-ordination, etc.) have often turned out to be negated by the actual planning experience. Commenting on this planning failure, Killick has noted that

> it is doubtful whether plans have generated more useful signals for the future than would otherwise have been forthcoming; governments have rarely, in practice, reconciled private and social valuations except in a piecemeal manner; because they have seldom become operational documents, plans have probably had only limited impact in mobilizing

[7] Albert Waterson, *Development Planning: lessons of experience*, Johns Hopkins University Press, 1965, p. 293.

[8] Derek T. Healey, 'Development Policy: new thinking about an interpretation', *Journal of Economic Literature*, x, 3, September 1973, p. 761.

resources and in coordinating economic policies.[9]

To take the specific case of the market failure argument and the presumed role of governments in reconciling the divergence between private and social valuations of benefits and costs, the experience of government policy in many LDCs has often been one of exacerbating rather than reconciling these divergences. We have touched on these issues in several of the preceding problem-focused chapters, but to illustrate the point we recapitulate here four crucial problem areas where private and social valuations tend to diverge and where the impact of government policy has often tended to increase rather than reduce these divergences.

1. Factor-prices, choice of technique and employment creation

A presumed conflict between two major planning objectives – rapid industrial growth and expanded employment opportunities – has typically resulted in the neglect of employment creation in the interest of industrial growth. As we saw in Chapter 13, there need be no such conflict if government policies were more geared to adjusting factor price signals to the real resource scarcities of developing societies. But in fact these private price signals have increasingly diverged from their implicit social valuations, partly as a result of public policies which have raised the level of wages above labour's scarcity value by various policies such as minimum wage legislation, tying wages to educational attainment, and structuring rates of remuneration at higher levels on the basis of comparable international salary scales. Similarly, we saw how various investment and tax allowances, over-valued exchange rates, low import duties and credit rationing at low interest rates served to lower the private cost of capital far below its scarcity or social cost.

The net effect of these factor price distortions has been the tendency to encourage private and public enterprises to adopt more capital-intensive production methods than would exist if public policy attempted to 'get the prices right'. In short, private valuations of benefits and costs often dictate more capital-intensive methods of production while true social valuations would point to more labour-intensive technologies. This divergence between private and social valuations of productive factors is, as we have seen, one of the major reasons for the slow growth of employment opportunities. Within the mystique of development planning, the more powerful mystique of forced industrialisation has remained a high priority for many years. Contrary to the expectations of its most vocal advocates, therefore, planning has had a far from salutary effect on efficient resource allocation in most developing countries. These planning advocates would probably claim that their arguments still hold; the problem has been bad planning and not the mere fact of planning.

2. Rural–urban imbalances and migration

A second major area of divergence between private and social valuations where until recently LDC economic policy appears to have been counterproductive to social concerns is with regard to widespread and rapid rural–urban migration. As we discovered in Chapter 14, government policies which are strongly biased in favour of urban development, as revealed by the existence of sizable urban–rural income differentials and disparities in locational economic opportunities, have stimulated an excessive outflow of rural migrants in search of limited but highly paid urban jobs. With growing urban unemployment and stagnating agriculture, the continued heavy influx of rural migrants represents a net social loss to society in the context both of lost agricultural output and higher social costs of their urban accommodation. However, from the private viewpoint of the typical migrant, the existence of urban unemployment and thus a less than unitary probability of finding an urban job is more than compensated for by high urban–rural wage differentials. The 'expected' urban wage still exceeds expected rural incomes. It is therefore 'privately' rational for rural dwellers to continue to migrate to the cities in spite of high and rising levels of urban unemployment. However, from the social viewpoint such continued migration is undesirable.

Again, the heavy urban industrialisation bias of most LDC development plans in the 1950s and 1960s combined with relative rural and agricultural neglect, created the conditions and distorted the price signals and economic incentives which contributed to the urban employment crisis. Rather

[9] Killick, *op. cit.*

than narrowing the gap between private and social valuations, the planning experience seems to have widened them. It may thus have exacerbated the misallocation of human resources in many Third World countries.

3. The demand for education and the employment problem

In Chapter 17 we discovered how economic signals and incentives in many LDCs have served to exaggerate the private valuations of the returns to education to a point where the private demand for ever more years of schooling is greatly in excess of the social payoff. The tendency to ration scarce highly paid employment opportunities by level of completed education in combination with the policy of most LDC governments to subsidise the private costs of education, especially at the higher levels, has led to a situation in which the social returns to investment in further quantitative educational expansion seem hardly justified in comparison with alternative investment opportunities (e.g. creation of productive employment projects). But, so long as private benefit/cost valuations show high returns, and in the absence of effective policies like those suggested in Chapter 18 to alter these signals in accord with social valuations, LDC governments will continue to face extraordinary public pressure to expand school places at all levels.

As a result, even greater proportions of government recurrent expenditures will be earmarked for educational expansion. Such outlays often amount to no more than an investment in idle human resources. The government's ability to undertake other public investment activities will be correspondingly reduced. Educational planning appears, therefore to have contributed little to reconciling divergences between social and private valuations of investment in schooling.

4. The structure of the economy

As a final example of the way in which planning and development policy have often contributed to the maintenance or exaggeration of socially 'incorrect' signals and incentives, consider the emphasis of the 1950s and 1960s on rapid industrialisation through import-substitution. We saw in Chapter 21 how a wide range of external and internal pricing policies including special tax concessions to foreign investors, overvalued exchange rates designed to lower the cost of capital and intermediate goods imports, subsidised interest rates and credit rationing to new industries, together with a whole array of bureaucratic industrial licensing arrangements, have all served to provide an artificial stimulus to import-substituting industrial expansion. But we also learned that for the most part the experience of import substitution, especially in Latin America, has failed to meet planned expectations in terms of the eventual realisation of low-cost efficient production by local industries. Moreover, the heavy emphasis on urban industrial growth and the concomitant creation through economic policy of distorted signals and incentives rewarding private industrial activity has greatly contributed to the stagnation of the agricultural sector.

To take a single case, overvalued exchange rates designed to lower import prices of intermediate goods also raise export prices. If the country and the vast majority of its rural people must rely on primary product export earnings, such exchange rate policies designed to stimulate industrialisation can make agricultural exports less competitive and be a drain on agricultural expansion. Similarly, most other policies designed to stimulate industrial growth tend to work against the interests of the rural sector. The net result of such relative rural neglect in most development plans, especially during the first two decades of planning, has been the phenomenon of agricultural stagnation and rural poverty described in Chapters 15 and 16. But, as we saw, the lessons of such rural neglect have not been lost on LDC governments and planning for agricultural growth is increasingly gaining priority attention.

Reasons for planning failures

In view of the preceding examples, we may conclude that the gap between the theoretical economic benefits of planning and its practical results in most developing countries has been large. The gap between public rhetoric and economic reality has been even greater. While professing to be concerned with eliminating poverty, lowering inequality and creating employment, many LDC planning agencies have in fact unknowingly contributed to their perpetuation. Some of the major explanations for this have to do with the failures of the planning process itself. These failures include[10]:

1. Deficiencies in plans and their implementation

Plans are often over-ambitious, trying to accomplish too many objectives at once without consideration of conflicting and competing objectives; they are often grandiose in design but vague on specific policies needed to achieve stated objectives; and, finally, the gap between plan formulation and its implementation is often enormous – i.e. many plans, for reasons to be discussed below, are never implemented.

2. Insufficient and unreliable data

The economic wisdom of a development plan depends to a great extent on the quality and reliability of the statistical data on which it is based. When these data are weak, unreliable or simply non-existent as in many poor countries, the quality and accuracy of quantitative comprehensive plans are greatly diminished. Moreover, where these unreliable data are compounded by an inadequate supply of qualified economists, statisticians and other planning personnel (as is also the situation in most poor nations) the attempt to formulate and carry out a comprehensive and detailed development plan is likely to be frustrated at all levels. In such situations, it is both foolish and a waste of scarce high-level human resources to engage in an extensive planning exercise.

3. Unanticipated economic disturbances both external and internal

Since most LDCs are open economies with considerable dependence on external variables such as changes in international commodity prices, fluctuating trade, the domestic economic policies of developed-nation purchasers of their exports, and the irregular flow of private and public development assistance, it becomes exceedingly difficult for them to engage in even short-term forecasting, let alone long-range planning, in the face of such manifest uncertainty. The oil price increases of the 1970s obviously caused havoc in LDC development plans. But the energy crisis was only an extreme case of a general tendency for economic factors over which most LDC governments have little control to determine the success or failure of their development policies. Given such vulnerability to external factors, LDC governments need to retain a maximum flexibility in their economic plans and be ready to make adjustments as the occasion arises. In the long run a policy of greater self-reliance and less external dependence provides an obvious but often difficult answer to this dilemma. As was pointed out in Chapter 21, economic integration offers an attractive alternative to both strictly outward- and inward-looking development policies.

4. Institutional weaknesses

Much has been written about the institutional weaknesses of the planning processes of most Third World countries. These include among others, the separation of the planning agency from the day-to-day decision-making machinery of government; the failure of planners, administrators and political leaders to engage in a continuous dialogue and internal communication about goals and strategies; and the international transfer of institutional planning practices and organisational arrangements which may be appropriate to local conditions.

In addition, much has been written about incompetent and unqualified civil servants; cumbersome bureaucratic procedures; excessive caution and resistance to innovation and change; interministerial personal and departmental rivalries (e.g. finance ministries and planning agencies are often conflicting rather than co-operative forces in LDC governments); lack of commitment to national goals as opposed to regional, departmental or simply private objectives on the part of political leaders and government bureaucrats, and, finally, in accordance with this lack of national as opposed to personal interest, the widespread phenomenon of political and bureaucratic corruption that is a pervasive problem of many Third World governments.

While it is beyond the scope of this chapter to deal further with these substantial institutional weaknesses, one should not minimise their importance in holding back the necessary structural and institutional reforms to accelerate the process of

[10] Killick, *op. cit.*

economic and social development. They are critical factors, in addition to the three previously mentioned, in explaining the widespread failures of contemporary development planning.

5. Lack of 'political will'

The ultimate cause of LDC planning failures is not simply lack of economic potential, nor even inadequate administrative capacity. Rather, poor plan performance and the growing gap between formulation and implementation is largely attributed to a lack of commitment and 'political will' on the part of many Third World leaders and high level civil servants. Waterson summarises his analysis of the development planning experience thus:

> The available evidence makes it clear that in countries with development plans, lack of adequate government support for the plans is the prime reason why most are never carried out. Conversely, the cardinal lesson that emerges from the planning experience of developing countries is that the sustained commitment of a politically stable government is the *sine qua non* for development. Where a country's political leadership makes development a central concern, the people can also be interested through a judicious use of economic incentives. And, although it is never easy to reform administrative and institutional inefficiency, commitment by political leaders is a necessary condition for reform; without it, reform is impossible.[11]

One might add, parenthetically, that such a political will to develop on the part of national leaders (assuming that by 'development' we mean eliminating poverty, inequality and unemployment as well as promoting aggregate per capita GNP growth) will require an unusual ability to take a long-term view and to elevate national social interests above factional class, caste or tribal interests. It will also necessitate the co-operation of the economic elites who may correctly see their privileged positions challenged by such a 'development' posture.

Thus, a political will to develop entails much more than high-minded purposes and noble rhetoric. It requires unusual ability and a great deal of political courage to challenge powerful elites and vested interest groups, and to persuade them that such development is in the long-run interests of *all* citizens. In the absence of their support, whether freely offered or coerced, a will to develop on the part of politicians is likely to meet with continuous frustration and growing internal conflict.

[11] Waterson, *op. cit.*, p. 367.

Concepts for review

- economic planning
- economic plan
- planning model
- comprehensive v. partial plans
- inducement v. control in planning
- centralised v. decentralised planning
- development planning
- economic infrastructure
- market failure
- policy objectives
- plan targets
- internal plan consistency
- short-, medium- and long-term planning
- aggregate, sectoral and interindustry planning models
- project planning
- stage of development in relation to choice of planning technique
- plan implementation
- 'incorrect' signals and incentives
- external economic disturbance
- political will

Questions for discussion

1. Why do you think so many Third World countries were persuaded of the necessity of development planning? Were the reasons strictly economic?
2. Some forms of economic planning are said to exist in *all* contemporary economies. Compare and contrast the main aspects of planning in so-called capitalist and socialist economies. How does development planning in most Third World nations compare with these two models?
3. Explain and comment on some of the major arguments or rationales, both economic and non-economic, for planning in Third World economies.
4. Planning is said to be more than just the formulation of quantitative economic targets. It

is often described as a 'process'. What is meant by the planning process and what are some of its basic characteristics?

5. Compare and contrast three basic types of planning models. What do you think are some of the strengths and weaknesses of using mathematical planning models in developing nations?
6. 'A developing country should choose the most sophisticated quantitative planning model when drawing up a comprehensive plan.' Comment on this statement, being sure to include in your answer a discussion of the types of consideration which should be taken into account when choosing a particular kind of planning model.
7. There is much talk today of a 'crisis in Third World planning'. Many have even claimed that development planning has for the most part been a failure. List and explain some of the major reasons for plan failures. Which reasons do you think are the most important? Do you think that development planning has in fact been a failure? Explain.

Further reading

On the nature and role of development planning see: JAN TINBERGEN, *Development Planning*, World University Library, Weidenfeld and Nicolson, London, 1967; MICHAEL P. TODARO, *Development Planning: models and methods*, Oxford University Press, Nairobi, 1971; HOLLIS CHENERY, ed., *Studies in Development Planning*, Harvard University Press, 1971.

On the planning experience of Third World countries during the last decade as well as a critique of the 'planning mystique' see: ALBERT WATERSON, *Development Planning: lessons of experience*, Johns Hopkins University Press, 1965; MIKE FABER and DUDLEY SEERS, eds, *The Crisis in Planning*, Chatto and Windus, 1972, 2 vols, especially article by Seers on 'The prevalence of pseudo-planning; TONY KILLICK, 'The Possibilities of Development Planning', *Oxford Economic Papers*, July 1976.

Chapter 24 Monetary and fiscal policies

> There are extremely powerful structural factors in Latin America which lead to inflation and against which traditional monetary policy is powerless.
> *Raul Prebisch*[1]

> The taxation potential in underdeveloped countries is rarely fully exploited . . . no more than one-fifth or possibly one-tenth of what is due [is collected].
> *N. Kaldor, Cambridge University*

Introduction

Although development planning represents the most visible aspect of public economic policy in Third World nations, the actual day-to-day policy decisions of LDC governments typically represent unplanned and often *ad hoc* responses to emerging and unforeseen economic crises. Within the broad framework of development objectives, diverse macro-economic policies and public investment projects tend to have less internal consistency and economic rationality than many textbook planning models would lead us to believe. The very real physical, human and administrative resource limitations of most developing countries are sufficient to prevent comprehensive planning from being more than a paper exercise, although much can be learned about the economy and its major constraints as a result of such an exercise. Therefore in this chapter we take a broader yet more eclectic view of economic policy in Third World countries by looking at two traditional aspects of government activity in mixed market economies: monetary and fiscal policy. Reviewing the nature and possible shortcomings of these macro policy instruments in the context of the special economic and structural circumstances of less developed countries will help us to discuss both the role and the limitations of government economic policy in guiding Third World development.

[1] Director General of the Latin American Institute for Economic and Social Planning, United Nations, Santiago, Chile.

Some components of macro-economic policy in Third World nations

A fruitful way to examine the economic impact of public policies in Third World countries is to pick specific development problems and then analyse how economic policies have affected them in the past and in what ways such policies might be improved in the future. Our discussion throughout Parts Two and Three of this book has followed this problem-oriented approach. We have seen that major development problems such as poverty, inequality, population growth, unemployment, migration, education, rural development and foreign trade and finance are all affected by and affect government policies. In many cases, policies designed to ameliorate one problem only serve to worsen another. But, by and large, the interdependence between problems and policies is of a complementary rather than a conflicting nature. For example, measures to eliminate poverty and reduce inequality will probably be consistent with stimulating rural development, curtailing rural–urban migration and counteracting the incentives to raise large families. Conversely, measures to promote rural development, to improve educational access, to create urban and rural job opportunities and to expand foreign exchange earnings are likely to contribute towards less poverty and lower inequality.

We return to this theme of the interdependence between problems and policies in a people-oriented development strategy later in this chapter when we summarise the preceding analyses. At this point it may be useful to examine some of the main aspects of LDC economic policy by utilising the traditional textbook division between 'monetary' and 'fiscal' policies.[2] But rather than merely providing a 'shopping list' of components of monetary and fiscal policy, we concentrate on how LDC monetary and fiscal policies can promote or retard a broad-based strategy of economic and social development.

Monetary and financial policies: the limitations of traditional macro-measures

In developed nations, monetary and financial policy plays a major direct and indirect role in government efforts designed to expand economic activity in times of unemployment and excess capacity (economic recessions) and to contract that activity in times of excess demand and inflation. Basically, monetary policy works on two principal economic variables: the aggregate supply of money in circulation and the level of interest rates. The supply of money (basically currency in circulation plus commercial bank deposits[3]) is thought to be directly related to the level of economic activity in the sense that a greater money supply induces expanded economic activity by enabling people to purchase more goods and services. This in essence is the so-called 'monetary' theory of economic activity. Its advocates argue that by controlling the growth of money supplies through Central Bank operations, governments can regulate their nation's economic activity.[4]

On the other side of the monetary issue are the so-called Keynesian economists who argue that an expanded supply of money in circulation increases the availability of loanable funds. A supply of loanable funds in excess of demand leads to lower interest rates. Since private investment is assumed to be inversely related to prevailing interest rates, businessmen will expand their investments as interest rates fall. More investment in turn raises aggregate demand via the Keynesian mechanism of income determination described briefly in Chapter 13. This added investment will lead to a higher level of economic activity (i.e. more employment and a higher GNP). Similarly in times of excess aggregate demand and inflation, governments pursue 'restrictive' monetary policies designed to curtail the expansion of aggregate demand by reducing the growth of the national money supply, lowering the supply of loanable funds, raising interest rates and thereby inducing a lower level of investment and less inflation.

Although this description of monetary policy in developed countries grossly simplifies a complex process, it does point out two important aspects of monetary policy which developing countries lack. First, the ability of developed country governments to expand and contract their money supplies and to raise and lower the costs of borrowing in the private sector (i.e. the level of interest rates) is made possible by the existence of highly organised, economically independent and efficiently functioning money and credit markets. Financial resources are continuously flowing in and out of savings banks, commercial banks and other nationally controlled public and private 'financial intermediaries' with a minimum of interference. Moreover, interest rates are regulated both by administrative controls and by market forces of supply and demand, so that there tends to be a consistency and relative uniformity of these rates in different sectors of the economy and in all regions of the country.

By contrast, money markets and financial in-

---

[2] In reality, LDC governments have at least *four* major 'policy instruments' at their disposal: (1) fiscal policy, (2) monetary and financial policy, (3) legislative controls (e.g. on foreign exchange, prices, wages, industrial licensing, immigration, etc.) and (4) miscellaneous policy interventions including creation of 'para-statal' organisations, (e.g. marketing boards, public utilities, research institutions), nationalisation, exhortation for voluntary action, requests for foreign aid, anti-monopoly laws and reform, etc. In this chapter, we focus only on (1) and (2). Instruments (3) and (4) have been dealt with elsewhere.

[3] Commercial banks are privately owned financial institutions whose main functions are to receive deposits and make short-term loans to private individuals, companies and other organisations.

[4] A central bank, sometimes referred to as a banker's bank and a 'lender of last resort', acts primarily as the government's bank. Briefly, its main functions are to issue and control the supply of currency, accept deposits from and make loans to commercial banks, set interest rates on loans to banks, influence the structure of domestic interest rates and conduct foreign exchange transactions with central banks in other countries. Almost all developing nations have a central bank.

stitutions in most developing countries are highly **unorganised**, often externally **dependent** and spatially **fragmented**.[5] Many commercial banks are merely overseas branches of major private banking institutions in developed countries. Their orientation therefore, like that of multi-national corporations, may be more towards external and less towards internal monetary priorities. The ability of Third World governments to regulate the national supply of money is further constrained by the 'openness' of their economies and by the fact that the accumulation of foreign currency earnings through current account surpluses is a significant but unpredictable and uncontrollable source of their domestic monetary resources. Most importantly, the commercial banking system of most LDCs is restricted almost exclusively to rationing scarce loanable funds to 'credit-worthy' medium and large-scale enterprises in the modern sector, both in manufacturing and in agriculture. Small farmers and indigenous small-scale entrepreneurs and traders in the manufacturing and service sectors must normally seek finance elsewhere, usually through local moneylenders and 'loan sharks' who charge exorbitant rates of interest.

Thus, most less developed countries operate under a dual monetary system: a small and largely externally controlled or influenced *organised* money market catering for the financial requirements of a small group of middle- and upper-class foreign and local businesses in the modern industrial and agricultural sectors, and a large but amorphous *unorganised*, uncontrolled and often usurious money market to which most low-income individuals are obliged to turn in times of financial need. This is just another manifestation of the dual structure of many LDC economies and their tendency, whether intentional or not, to serve the needs of wealthy elites while neglecting the requirements of the ubiquitous poor.

The second major limitation of standard (Western) monetary policy as applied to the structural and institutional realities of Third World nations is the assumption of a direct linkage between lower interest rates, higher investment and expanded output. In reality, as we discovered in Chapter 13 when discussing Keynesian macro theory, there may be severe 'structural' supply constraints inhibiting the expansion of output even when the demand for it increases. These constraints may relate to inadequate management, lack of essential intermediate products, bureaucratic rigidities, licensing restrictions and, in general, a lack of interdependence within the industrial sector. Whatever the reasons, structural supply rigidities mean that any increase in the demand for goods and services will not be matched by increases in supply. Instead, the excess demand (in this case for investment goods) will merely bid up prices and lead to or worsen inflation. In some Latin American nations, this structural inflation has been a chronic problem made even worse on the cost side by the upward spiral of wages as workers attempt to protect their 'real' income levels.

The emergence of development banking

In their attempts to secure systematic finance for sustaining planned industrial expansion, many less developed countries have established a new type of financial institution known as 'development banks'. These banks are specialised financial institutions which supply medium- and long-term funds for the creation or expansion of industrial enterprises. They have arisen in many Third World nations because the existing banks usually concentrate either on relatively short-term lending for commercial purposes (commercial and savings banks) or the control and regulation of the aggregate supply of money (central banks). Moreover, existing commercial banks usually set loan conditions which are inappropriate for establishing new enterprises or for financing large-scale projects.Their funds more often are allocated to 'safe' borrowers – established industries, many of which are foreign-owned, or run by well-known local families. True 'venture capital' for new industries rarely finds approval.

In order to facilitate industrial growth in economies characterised by a scarcity of financial capital, development banks have sought to raise capital from two major sources: (1) bilateral and multilateral loans from national aid agencies like the United States Agency for International Development (USAID) and from international donor agencies like the World Bank ; (2) loans from their own

[5] One of the earliest descriptions of unorganised and fragmented money markets in Third World countries can be found in U. Tun Wai, 'Interest Rates Outside the Organized Money Markets', *IMF Staff Papers*, November 1957.

governments. However, in addition to raising capital, development banks have had to develop special skills in the field of industrial project appraisal where modern techniques of cost-benefit analysis are widely employed. In many cases their activities go far beyond the traditional banker's role of merely lending money to credit-worthy customers. The activities of development banks often even encompass direct entrepreneurial, managerial and promotional involvement in the enterprises they finance. Development banks have thus played an important role in the industrialisation process of many LDCs.

Although development banks are a relatively new phenomenon in Asia, Africa, the Middle East and Latin America, their growth and spread has been substantial. In the mid-1940s there were no more than 10 to 12 such institutions. By the end of the 1960s their numbers had increased to hundreds and their financial resources had burgeoned into billions of dollars. Moreover, although initial sources of capital came from agencies like the World Bank, as well as bilateral aid agencies and local governments (for example, the Industrial Credit and Investment Corporation of India was established in 1954 with a 30-year interest-free advance of 75 million rupees from the Indian Government), the growth of development bank finance has often been further facilitated by growing participation by private investors, both institutional and individual, foreign and local. For example, almost 20 per cent of the share capital of these banks was foreign-owned in 1970 with the remaining 80 per cent derived from local investors.

In spite of their impressive growth and their growing importance for Third World industrial expansion, development banks have come under increasing criticism for their excessive concentration on large-scale loans. Some privately owned finance companies (also categorised as development banks) refuse to consider loans of less than \$20 000 to \$50 000. They argue that lesser loans do not justify the time and effort involved in their appraisal. As a result, development finance companies almost totally isolate their activities from the field of aid to small enterprises, even though in most countries such aid is of major importance to the achievement of broadly based social and economic development. In many regions it may constitute the bulk of assistance needed in the private sector, both formal and informal. Small-scale entrepreneurs often lacking technical, purchasing, marketing, organisational and accounting skills as well as access to bank credit are thus forced to seek funds in the exploitive unorganised money markets. Unless these small enterprise financial and technical needs can begin to be served, the long-run impact of development banks, public as well as private, will be mainly confined to assisting a relatively few private individuals and those who run state enterprises to concentrate their combined economic power even further.

We may conclude, therefore, that in spite of the growth of development banks in almost every developing nation, a need remains for the establishment of new types of savings institutions and financial intermediaries. Such institutions should not only mobilise domestic savings from small as well as large savers but, more importantly, they should begin to channel these financial resources to those small entrepreneurs, both on the farm and in the marginal or informal sector of urban areas, who until now have been almost totally excluded from access to needed credit at reasonable rates of interest.

Fiscal policy for development

Taxation: direct and indirect

In the absence of well organised and locally controlled money markets, most developing countries have had to rely primarily on fiscal measures to mobilise domestic resources. The principal instruments of such public resource mobilisation have been government tax policies. Typically direct taxes – those levied on private individuals and corporations (income tax) and mainly on property – vary between 20 to 40 per cent of total tax revenue for most LDCs and range from between 2 and 5 per cent of GNP (see Table 24.1). On the other hand, indirect taxes – import and export duties levied on foreign trade and excise taxes levied on the direct domestic consumption of different commodities like petrol, cigarettes, liquor, consumer durables, etc. – comprise the major source of fiscal revenue. Table 24.1 shows the tax structure and revenue sources of twenty-two selected LDCs.

Traditionally, taxation in Third World countries has had two purposes. First, tax concessions and similar fiscal incentives have been thought of as a means of stimulating private enterprise. Such

Table 24.1
The tax structure and revenue sources of selected less developed nations, (Percentage of total public revenue)

	(Percent of total Public Revenue)					
	Direct taxes			Indirect taxes		
Country	Personal and corporate	Property	Total direct	Foreign imports and export duties	Domestic (excise taxes)	Total indirect
Ethiopia	15.6	8.3	23.9	33.3	42.8	76.1
India	19.8	9.3	29.1	17.8	53.1	70.9
Somalia	7.2	1.1	8.3	58.1	33.6	91.7
Indonesia	28.8	2.1	30.9	43.3	25.8	69.1
Congo	14.1	0.1	14.2	62.0	23.8	85.8
Kenya	42.6	0.7	43.3	34.2	22.5	56.7
Pakistan	15.7	5.7	21.4	24.2	54.3	78.5
Korea	33.8	8.3	42.1	16.2	41.0	57.2
Sri Lanka	20.7	2.9	23.6	47.6	28.4	76.0
Thailand	13.6	2.1	15.7	41.5	42.8	84.3
UAR	20.4	8.2	28.6	21.8	31.3	53.1
Philippines	23.9	8.2	32.1	21.4	43.4	64.8
Morocco	29.7	5.5	35.2	19.9	42.4	62.3
Tunisia	29.7	3.8	33.5	13.3	52.0	65.3
Paraguay	11.7	5.8	17.5	50.8	29.0	79.8
Ecuador	11.5	9.9	21.4	56.7	21.6	78.3
Brazil	11.4	1.4	12.8	3.5	70.1	73.6
Honduras	27.2	2.0	29.2	38.4	32.4	70.8
Ghana	23.2	2.7	25.9	49.1	25.0	74.1
Guatemala	12.4	5.6	18.0	32.5	49.4	81.9
Costa Rica	23.1	6.3	29.4	34.2	36.4	70.6
Chile	35.3	6.4	41.7	12.2	45.9	58.1

Source: Montek Ahluwalia, The scope for policy intervention', in Chenery, Duloy and Jolly, eds, *Redistribution with Growth: an approach to policy*, mimeo, August 1973, Table 1.

concessions and incentives have typically been offered to foreign private investors to induce them to locate their enterprises in the developing country. While such tax incentives may indeed increase the inflow of private foreign resources, we discovered in Chapter 22 that the overall benefits of such special treatment of foreign firms is by no means self-evident.

The second purpose of taxation, the mobilisation of resources to finance public expenditures, is by far the more important. Whatever the prevailing political or economic ideology of the less developed country, its economic and social progress largely depends on its government's ability to generate sufficient revenues to finance an expanding programme of essential, non-revenue yielding public services such as health, education, transport, communications and other components of the economic and social infrastructure. In addition, most Third World governments are directly involved in the economic activities of their nations through their ownership and control of public corporations and state trading agencies. Direct and indirect tax levies enable the government to finance the capital and recurrent expenditures of these public enterprises, many of which often operate at a loss.

In general, the taxation potential of a country depends on the following five factors:

- the level of per capita real income;
- the degree of inequality in the distribution of that income;
- the industrial structure of the economy and the importance of different types of economic activity (e.g. the importance of foreign trade, the significance of the modern sector, the extent of foreign participation in private enterprises, the

degree to which the agricultural sector is commercialised as opposed to subsistence-oriented):
- the social, political and institutional setting and the relative power of different groups (e.g. landlords as opposed to manufacturers, trade unions, village or district community organisations):
- the administrative competence, honesty and integrity of the tax-gathering branches of government.

We now examine the principal sources of public tax revenues in the context of this fivefold classification. We can then consider how the tax system might be used either to redistribute incomes or simply to expand government economic activity.

As can be seen from Table 24.1, there are basically two categories of taxes – direct and indirect. Direct taxes consist primarily of income taxes on individuals and corporations, and property taxes. Indirect taxes largely comprise taxes on foreign trade (import and export duties) and excise taxes on the local consumption of commodities.

Personal income and property taxes

The personal income tax yields much less proportionate revenue in the less developed than in the more developed nations. In the latter, the income tax structure is said to be 'progressive', that is, people with higher incomes theoretically pay a larger percentage of that income in taxes. In practice, however, the average level of taxation in countries like the United States does not vary much between middle and upper income groups. This is because of the many tax loopholes which the wealthy are able to take advantage of. In less developed countries a combination of more exemptions, lower rates on smaller incomes, and a general administrative weakness in collecting income taxes means that less than 3 per cent of Third World populations pay income tax compared with between 60 and 80 per cent of the populations of developed nations.

In spite of this limited coverage and the fact that it is administratively too costly and socially unfair to attempt to collect income taxes from the poor, it is nevertheless true that most LDC governments have not been persistent enough in collecting taxes from the wealthy. Since it is the highest income groups that offer the greatest potential yield to the tax collector, the large income inequalities prevailing in most Third World countries mean that there is great scope for expanding income tax revenues. Moreover, in those countries where the ownership of property is heavily concentrated and therefore represents the major determinant of unequal incomes (e.g. most of Asia and Latin America), property taxes can be an efficient and administratively simple mechanism both for generating public revenues and correcting gross inequalities in income distribution. But, as can be seen from Table 24.1, in none of the 22 countries listed does the property tax constitute more than 10 per cent of total public revenues. Moreover, in spite of much talk about reducing income inequalities, the share of property taxes as well as overall direct taxation has remained roughly the same for the majority of Third World countries over the past two decades. Clearly this phenomenon cannot be attributed to government tax-collecting inefficiencies as much as to the political and economy power and influence of the large landowning classes in many Asian and Latin American countries. The political will to carry out development plans must include the political will to extract public revenue from the most accessible sources to finance development projects. Where the former is absent, so too will be the latter.

Corporate income taxes

Taxes on corporate profits, both of domestically and foreign owned companies, amount to less than 2 per cent of GDP in most developing countries, compared with more than 6 per cent in most developed nations. The main reason why these taxes raise so little revenue in Third World countries is that there is relatively less corporate activity in the overall economy, combined with a tendency of LDC governments to offer all sorts of tax incentives and concessions to manufacturing and commercial enterprises. Typically, new enterprises are offered long periods (sometimes up to 15 years) of tax exemption and thereafter take advantage of generous investment depreciation allowances, special tax write-offs and other measures to lessen the incidence of their taxation.

In the case of multi-national foreign enterprises, the ability of LDC governments to collect substantial taxes is often frustrated. These locally run enterprises are able to shift profits to partner companies in those countries offering the lowest levels of taxation through transfer pricing (discussed in Chapter 22).

When local subsidiaries of multi-national corporations buy from or sell to partner companies in other countries, the prices in such transactions are merely internal accounting prices of the overall corporation: it makes no difference to the calculation of 'total' corporate profits what price one subsidiary charges another since the cost of one will be offset by the income of the other. For example, in high tax nations, MNC exports to branches in low tax countries can be invoiced at artificially low prices. This practice reduces corporate profits in the high tax country and raises them in the low tax nation. The latter is often referred to as a 'tax haven'. Thus, by means of transfer pricing, multi-national corporations are able to shift their profits from one place to another in order to lower their overall tax assessment while leaving their total profits unchanged. So long as such tax havens exist, this profit-shifting practice greatly limits the ability of individual LDCs to increase public revenues by raising taxes on foreign corporations.

Indirect taxes of commodities

The largest sources of public tax revenues in less developed countries are the taxes on commodities – import, export and excise duties (see Table 24.1 for details). These indirect taxes, by which individuals and corporations are taxed indirectly through their purchase of commodities, are relatively easy to assess and to collect, especially in the case of foreign traded commodities which must pass through a relatively few frontier ports and are usually handled by a few wholesalers. This ease of collection is one reason why countries with extensive foreign trade typically collect a greater proportion of public revenues in relation to their GNPs than do those countries with limited foreign trade. For example, in open economies with up to 40 per cent of their GNP derived from foreign trade (most African nations come into this category), an average import duty of 25 per cent will yield a tax revenue equivalent of 10 per cent of GNP. By contrast, in countries like India and Brazil, with only about 8 per cent of their GNP derived from exports, the same tariff rate would yield only 2 per cent of GNP in equivalent tax revenues.

Although we discussed import and export duties in the context of LDC trade policies in an earlier chapter, one further point about these taxes, often overlooked, needs to be mentioned. It is that import and export duties, in addition to representing the major sources of public revenue in many LDCs, can also be an efficient substitute for a corporate income tax. To the extent that importers are unable to pass on to local consumers the full costs of the tax, an import duty can serve as a proxy tax on the profits of the importer (which is often a foreign company) and only partially a tax on the local consumer. Similarly, an export duty can be an effective way of taxing the profits of producing companies, including those locally based multi-national firms which practise transfer pricing. But export duties designed to generate revenue should not be raised to the point of discouraging local producers from expanding their export production.

In selecting commodities to be taxed, whether in the form of duties on imports and exports or excise taxes on local commodities, certain general economic and administrative principles need to be followed to minimise the cost of securing maximum revenue. First, the commodity should be imported or produced by a relatively small number of licensed firms so that evasion can be controlled. Second, the price elasticity of demand for the commodity should be low so that total demand is not choked by the rise in consumer prices that results from the tax. Third, the commodity should have a high income elasticity of demand so that as incomes rise, more tax revenue will be collected. Fourth, for equity purposes it is best to tax those commodities like motor cars, refrigerators, imported fancy foods, household appliances, etc., which are consumed largely by the upper income groups, while foregoing taxation on items of mass consumption like basic foods, simple clothing and household utensils, even though these may satisfy the first three criteria set forth above.

Problem of tax administration

In the final analysis, a developing nation's ability to collect taxes needed for public expenditure programmes, and to use the tax system as a basis for modifying the distribution of personal incomes, will depend not only on the enactment of appropriate tax legislation but more importantly on the efficiency and integrity of the tax authorities who must implement these laws. As Professor Kaldor noted two decades ago:

> In many underdeveloped countries the low revenue yield of taxation can only be attributed to the fact that the tax provisions are not properly enforced, either on account of the inability of the administration to cope with

> them, or on account of straightforward corruption. No system of tax laws, however carefully conceived, is proof against collusion between the tax administrators and the taxpayers; an efficient administration consisting of persons of high integrity is usually the most important requirement for obtaining maximum revenue, and exploiting fully the taxation potential of a country.[6]

Thus, the ability of Third World governments to expand their 'tax nets' to cover the higher income groups and to minimise tax evasion by local and foreign individuals and corporations will largely determine the efficiency of the tax system in its dual function of generating sufficient public revenues to finance development programmes and reducing poverty and income inequalities. Much will depend on the political will to enact and *enforce* such egalitarian tax programmes.

Fiscal policy and inflation

The spiralling inflation that often exceeded 30 per cent per annum in the 1970s affected every nation in Africa, Asia, the Middle East and Latin America. In the more developed countries, inflation rates of 12 to 25 per cent per annum were the highest recorded in many decades. The very economic and political stability of countries like Great Britain and Italy were threatened more by this inflation than by any other event since the Second World War. Economists have variously attributed the inflation of the 1970s to two major factors, the upward 'demand pull' of prices as a result of a decade of expansionary fiscal and monetary policy (and in the United States, the heavy expenditure on the war in Vietnam) and the upward 'cost push' of raw material and commodity prices resulting from the unprecedented 400 per cent rise in oil prices and the worldwide failure of agricultural production to keep pace with rising demand. Given the traditional economic factors of a simultaneous demand pull and cost push inflation, psychological factors also entered the picture as workers' expectations of continuing price rises and a further eroding of their real incomes caused them to press for ever higher wage increases. These spiralling wage increases exerted further upward pressure on production costs, leading to even higher consumer prices. Thus, inflation has a way of becoming self-generating and extremely difficult to stop. A number of Latin American nations were aware of this fact long before the global inflation of the 1970s.

Faced with rising prices and higher levels of unemployment (a combination of forces unprecedented in modern Western economic history and which contradicted the traditional macro-economic theories that postulated an inverse relationship or trade-off between inflation and unemployment), most developed countries, as we have seen, pursued a combination of economic policies. These included (1) slowing monetary growth and raising interest rates, (2) curtailing the growth of government expenditure, (3) raising taxes especially for middle and upper income groups, (4) establishing wage and price guidelines in an effort to control the upward movement of costs and prices, and (5) manipulating foreign exchange rates, raising tariff and non-tariff barriers to imports and, in general, attempting to cut back specifically on oil imports in an effort to reduce payments deficits and prevent the further erosion of their foreign exchange positions. While such restrictive monetary, fiscal and commercial policies impose severe economic hardships, especially on poor families in the developed countries, their governments at least possessed the economic tools to cope with the unique inflationary forces of the 1970s.

But what about the less developed countries? Can their domestic monetary and fiscal policies also act as an effective brake on the inflation which they too experienced with even more severe economic dislocations and hardships than the developed countries? Or must they resign themselves to remaining 'non-players' standing on the sidelines, making only minor efforts to modify their domestic rates of inflation, while the developed countries participate in the fight against inflation? This second question better describes the position of most contemporary Third World nations.

Unlike the inflationary experience of a number of Latin American countries in the 1960s which mostly grew out of expansionary domestic demand policies combined with production supply inelasticities, the inflation of the 1970s and 80s was for most LDCs largely *external* in origin. Being much more dependent than developed countries on the importation of oil, capital goods, raw materials,

[6] N. Kaldor, 'Taxation for Economic Development', *Journal of Modern African Studies*, i, 1, 1973.

intermediate products and consumer goods over whose prices they have virtually no control, the non-oil-exporting developing nations found themselves with equally high or higher rates of inflation but without many of the economic policy tools with which to combat this price spiral. Most LDCs had therefore to content themselves with policies to control the importation of certain non-essential goods, to stimulate and promote greater exports to pay for increased imports, to seek special international foreign exchange credits, to ration limited credit from both domestic and foreign sources to essential industrial uses, to hold the line on wage increases while attempting to expand the tax net, and to seek ways to control the rising prices of essential foodstuffs and basic subsistence commodities consumed by the urban and rural poor, often by means of costly government food subsidy programmes.

While the above components of anti-inflationary LDC economic policies can help to modify the impact of rising prices, especially for those income groups who can least afford it, they are nevertheless insufficient to control domestic inflation. Third World dependence on the world economy in general and on developed-country domestic and international economic policies in particular (not to mention the policies of their oil-producing OPEC colleagues), was never more dramatically illustrated than by the inflation and resource squeeze crisis of the 1970s. The most lasting impact of this experience was probably the realisation by many LDCs of the real need for increased co-operation among themselves in the pursuit of a greater degree of national or regional self-reliance. Finally, Third World nations discovered the value of a strong international bargaining stance *vis-à-vis* the developed world, especially with regard to the pricing and utilisation of those mineral and raw materials over which they as a group can now exert some effective control.

The interrelationship between problems and policies

It has been convenient for teaching purposes throughout Parts Two and Three to isolate major development problems and to identify an appropriate range of corresponding fiscal, monetary and other public policy alternatives. In reality, however, all these problems and many of the policy responses are highly interrelated. Problems of Third World poverty and inequality cannot be separated from problems of rapid population growth, rising urban unemployment, stagnating agriculture and unequal and inappropriate educational systems. Similarly, problems of excessive rural–urban migration and rising urban unemployment cannot be analysed in isolation from problems of mass rural poverty, highly unequal land tenure arrangements, rapid population growth and the elitist, urban-oriented structure of most formal systems of education. One could go on indefinitely demonstrating the many ways in which Third World development problems and policies are linked in an intricate web of cause and effect.

For illustrative purposes, however, and by way of summarising much of what has been said in Parts Two and Three, we look again at five critical development problems analysed separately in earlier chapters, along with some of their major policy implications. Table 24.2 provides a brief summary of the major domestic policy options suggested for coping with the problems of poverty and inequality, population growth, urban unemployment, rural underdevelopment and inappropriate educational structures.

It may be seen that for the most part policies designed to deal with one problem often contribute to the solution of one or more of the others. Thus, for example, policies designed to eliminate poverty, such as land reform, asset redistribution, tax and subsidy policies, the provision of rural social services and the creation of widespread job opportunities, are also policies which should help to curtail rapid population growth, reduce rural–urban migration and promote agricultural progress and rural development. Similarly, policies designed to boost rural development such as institutional reforms to aid the small farmer, rural public works programmes, the provision of rural social services and economic infrastructure and the restructuring of rural educational systems and training programmes also contribute to the alleviation of urban unemployment (e.g. through lowering the incentives to migrate), the reduction of rural fertility levels, and the amelioration of living conditions where 80 per cent of Third World poverty is located. Finally, policies

Table 24.2
The interrelationship between problems and policies

Problem	Policy
Poverty and inequality	Asset redistribution (mainly from growth) Land reform Provision of rural social services Poverty-focused investments (target groups) Tax and subsidy policies Job creation urban and rural Improved educational access
Excessive population growth	Eradicate poverty Provide family planning services Monetary incentives and disincentives Education and job opportunities for women Improved maternal and child nutrition and health
Urban unemployment	Reducing migration by eliminating artificial urban-rural incentive and economic opportunity imbalances Getting factor prices right Choosing and/or developing appropriate labour-intensive technologies Poverty focused rural investments Modifying urban incentive effects of inappropriate educational systems Slowing population growth
Agricultural stagnation and rural underdevelopment	Rural institutional reforms (land tenure, small-farmer access to credit, information, biological and chemical farm inputs, crop insurance, new seeds) Improved rural education, health, sanitation, water supplies and other social services Specialised rural training programmes Rural public works Export promotion
Inappropriate and unequal education	Modification of educational demands by reorientation of economic signals and incentives towards rural sector Improved access through system of loans, subsidies and tuition according to ability to pay Minimising excessive credentialisation Promoting non-formal, out-of-school lifetime education Reorientating curricula

designed to make education more relevant for development (e.g. by giving it a more functional and rural-oriented structure or by improving access to lower income groups) can be a major force in promoting rural development, reducing urban unemployment, lowering population growth rates (especially as more women are educated) and providing realistic earning opportunities for children of low-income families.

Note that in Table 24.2 we have left out the whole range of international issues and policies dealing with problems of trade, aid and foreign investment. This was done for convenience of exposition. Clearly, policies designed to minimise the harmful effects of trade, aid and foreign investment while maximising their beneficial potentialities will have a direct and indirect impact on the five major problem areas depicted in the table. The reader should consider whether he or she can show how policies designed to deal with private foreign investment can help to alleviate the urban unemployment crisis, or how trade policies might promote rural development.

Public administration: the scarcest resource[7]

Throughout this chapter and in previous ones, we have tended in our policy discussions to gloss over one of the most critical shortages in the development process. This is the very real and often binding constraint on economic progress that arises out of the shortage of public (and private) administrative capability. Many observers would agree that the lack of such managerial and administrative capability is the single scarcest resource in the developing world. The problem is not only a lack of training or experience. It also arises out of the political instability of numerous Third World nations. When power is constantly changing hands, considerations of efficiency and public welfare are likely to be subordinated to political loyalty. Moreover, the larger the group of officials affected by a change of power, the more difficult it will be to maintain any continuity in the formulation and execution of policy.

Public administration is unlikely to function efficiently when the rule of law is in question; where there is public disorder; or where there is little consensus on fundamental issues. Acute conditions of class, tribal or religious conflict within a society will usually be reflected in the management and operation of government departments and public agencies. In a highly traditional society, where kinship ties are strong and such concepts as statehood and public service have not yet taken firm root, there is little place for a merit system. Similarly, where the dominant values are religious or transcendental, traditional incentives to perform in the wider public interest may not have much appeal.

Many LDC governments may also have civil service goals other than performance: to break up traditional elites; to 'nationalise' the service; ideological correctness; to reflect or favour an ethnic ratio; to include or exclude minorities. Most governments also are organised in the traditional hierarchical form. But some have experimented with negative hierarchy (from bottom to top), ad hocracy (temporary arrangements), and polyarchy (co-operation with outside organisations – this latter particularly when some special form of expertise is concerned).

Virtually all LDC bureaucracies are hopelessly overstaffed at the bottom and hopelessly understaffed at the top. There is a chronic and desperate shortage of skilled competent managers capable of independent decision-making. The more parastatal organisations are set up, the more nationalised industries, quasi-governmental bodies, development corporations, training institutions – the thinner will this layer of managers be spread.

In the case of nationalised industries, most such experiments have been economically disastrous and have resulted in all kinds of strains within the central civil service. Personnel systems within the public service are usually not adequate for the increased management complexities of an industrial enterprise. So parallel personnel systems have been set up, multiplying the public service systems, draining skills, leading to disparities in terms and conditions of service and affecting the availability of manpower and morale. Political considerations often affect the ability to recruit competent managers with special technical skills. In short, nationalisation in many instances has often just added to the financial burden of the government budget.

But whatever the organisational and political problems of public administration, the sheer difficulty of efficiently managing complex modern economic systems is often cited when referring to critical public policy issues in the Third World. To give but one striking example of the administration problem, consider the case of the Tan-Zam railroad in East Africa.

The Tan-Zam railway, giving Zambia access to the sea at Dar es Salaam, was built in less than 5 years by the Chinese, and was formally opened in July 1976. In October 1978 President Kaunda of Zambia announced that, effective immediately, despite UN sanctions, OAU pressures, and the civil war in Zimbabwe-Rhodesia, he was reopening Zambia's border with Rhodesia and resuming the interrupted rail link with the South. The reason: massive administrative breakdowns had so impaired the functioning of the railway that it was threatening to strangle the entire Zambian economy.

In early 1978 the EEC had granted Zambia \$8m for fertilizer desperately needed by its ailing agricultural sector. The first consignments from the US were unloaded at Dar es Salaam, where the railway was unable to handle them and they were left in the

[7] I am grateful to a former graduate student, Diana Boernstein, for assistance in preparing this section.

open to rot. As the pile-up increased, Tanzania was reported to have increased storage and demurrage charges by 1000%. Zambia then ordered the fertilizer to be rerouted through Beira, whence it went by rail to Moatize, and by road through Malawi and Zambia. After 60 000 tons had been transported it became clear that Mozambique's railways and Zambia's transporters, already short of fuel and spare parts, could not cope. Shippers refused to take the remaining 90 000 tons to Dar es Salaam, because of the congestion there. Zambia then suggested it go to Maputo, from which it could be carried by South African railways via Pretoria and Mafeking to Francistown, where an armada of small Zambian truckers would carry it across the Kazungulu ferry. But the Dunkirk did not materialise. By the end of September Zambia had spent an extra $250 000 in transport costs; Maputo and Francistown were drowning in fertilizer; only some 2 000 tons had arrived in Zambia; and the ploughing season had begun.

In addition, some 100 000 tons of Zambian copper was either awaiting transportation or trapped somewhere on the line. Further stockpiles at the mines reached 70 000 tons by early October, causing cash shortages to the copper companies who do not get paid until the copper is on the high seas. Production was hampered by shortages of spare parts and lubricating oil, which were held up elsewhere.

In four years' time Tanzania and Zambia would have to start repaying their $400m debt to China. About 100 Chinese specialists were brought back to try and restore the line to working order; but they saw little chance of it paying its way unless its administration was completely overhauled. More than half the locomotives were under repair. A quarter of the 2 100 freight cars were off the line at any one time. The accounts department weren't getting the bills out, and the railway was owed millions of dollars. Without huge spending on new equipment and training programmes there was little possibility of Tan-Zam handling even a fraction of its capacity; and even such spending would not necessarily guarantee results.

This is a dramatic example of an administrative shortfall in one sector – unanticipated in any feasibility study or economic blueprint – whose effects were felt not only in other sectors of the Zambian economy but also in neighbouring states. It serves to illustrate the crucial importance of the administrative component in economic development planning; not only in relation to the particular project under consideration, but also in relation to the functioning of the entire economic system.

Development policy and the role and limitations of the state: concluding observations

Mindful of the seriousness of the public administration problem, we conclude this chapter with some generalisations on the actual formulation of economic policy in the Third World and speculations about the future role and limitations of the state in the mixed market economies characteristic of most countries of Asia, Africa, the Middle East and Latin America.[8]

In view of the somewhat disappointing development record of the past two decades, most economists would agree that their early and almost mystical belief in the efficacy and benefits of central planning in comparison to market forces has not been validated by Third World experience. Moreover, economic policies have more often than not tended to be *ad hoc* responses to recurring and often unexpected crises rather than the playing out of a grand economic design for development. We should never forget that political leaders and decision makers are human beings like the rest of us with all the human idiosyncrasies, foibles and weaknesses. Except in very unusual cases, they will tend to take a 'parochial' (class, caste, tribal, religious, ethnic, regional, etc.) rather than a 'national' point of view. In democracies, politicians will respond first to their political constituencies and the vested interest groups within their home areas. In more autocratic forms of government, whether military dictatorship or strict one-party rule, political leaders will still have a natural tendency to

[8] Although, based on the Chinese experience and the growing pressures for egalitarian reforms, some Third World countries are likely to turn to even greater public ownership and control over domestic resources in the coming decades, it is fair to assume that the vast majority will remain mixed in overall economic structures with a probable increasing direct and indirect role being played by the state.

respond to those groups to whom they owe their power or on whom their continued power depends. We must always bear in mind that economic policies are made, not by economists or planners, but by politicians who are likely to be more interested in 'muddling through' each emerging crisis and staying in power than necessarily in instituting major social and economic reforms. But if, as many now believe, the coming development crisis is one whose solution will necessitate economic and social reform, we should not dismiss the possibility that the present dilemmas can and will be overcome.

We therefore need to be pragmatic about the role and limitations of economic policies in developing (or, for that matter, developed) nations. On the one hand, we should avoid the tendency to assume that political leaders and decision makers place the national interest above their own private interests or base their policies on some notion of social welfare as opposed to the private welfare of those groups to whom they are primarily indebted. On the other hand, we should equally avoid the cynical view that the social interest, and especially the interest of the poor, the weak and the inarticulate, will never be considered short of revolution. Social and political revolutions are notorious vehicles by which one elite replaces another while the welfare of the poor remains largely unaffected (China and more recently Cuba being probably the most notable exceptions). It appears more reasonable, therefore, to base our discussion of the role and limitations of the state on the proposition that most Third World governments are beset by conflicting forces, some elitist, others egalitarian, and that their economic policies will be largely a reflection of the relative power of these competing interests. Although narrow elitist interests have tended to prevail in the past, the groundswell for a more egalitarian development process has now reached the point where politicians and planners can no longer ignore it or camouflage it behind noble but empty rhetoric.

Whatever one's ideological preconceptions about the proper role of government, there can be no denying that over the past two decades, governments in developing countries have increasingly claimed responsibility for the management and direction of their economies. It has been said that in many countries, especially in Africa, if the government does not induce development, then it probably will not happen at all. If nothing else, governments in these countries are the most important users of trained manpower. How they deploy these limited human resources thus becomes a crucial issue for the success or failure of the development effort. Moreover, how governments are structured and how they manage development has been vitally important and will continue to be even more so in the future.

In classical economics the role of government was conceived simply in terms of maintaining law and order, collecting taxes and generally providing a minimum of social services. With the Keynesian revolution, the economic role of government was greatly expanded. Governments were assigned prime repsonsibility within a market economy for stabilising overall economic activity by means of countercyclical monetary and fiscal policies with the objective of maintaining full employment without inflation. At the same time that the Keynesian revolution in Western economic thought was occurring, the Soviet Union was demonstrating to the world the power of central planning to mobilise resources and accelerate industrial growth.

As indigenous leadership replaced colonial leadership in many developing nations, these two models of the role of the state were presented. Impressed by the Soviet planning performance yet still imbued with a history of private enterprise from colonial days, most LDCs adopted a mixed market economy, with a relatively heavy emphasis on central planning and public participation in all aspects of economic activity. Given the growing concern with questions of poverty and inequality, however, the role of the state today has increased to an even greater extent in spite of the consensus that planning has not worked the magic that some believed it would, and that many public corporations are notoriously inefficient users of valuable financial and human resources.

Thus there seems to be a general agreement today among economists and others that LDC governments should *not* do *less*, but that they should do *more* and do it better than in the past. Most would agree that the machinery of many Third World governments has become too cumbersome. There are too many ministries, often with competing interests, too many public corporations and too many boards of one kind or another. Governments are criticised for being too centralised and too urban-oriented in both staff and outlook. Civil servants and other trained personnel are often poorly utilised, badly motivated and in many respects less productive than they should be. There is too much corruption and too little inventiveness and innovation. Bureaucratic red tape and ossified procedures and processes sap originality and flexibility. In short, contemporary LDC governments are criticised for being not too different from almost any other government around the world!

But whether one likes it or not, Third World governments must inevitably bear a greater responsibility for the future well-being of their countries than do those in the more developed nations. As their primary tasks of nation-building (in the newly independent countries) and generating rapid economic growth (in all LDCs) are gradually supplemented by preoccupations with problems of poverty, unemployment and inequality, Third World governments are forging a new role, one that will require innovation and change on a scale that has rarely occurred in the past. Central to this new role will be institutional and structural reform in the fields of land tenure, taxation, asset ownership and distribution, educational and health systems, credit rationing, labour market relations, the organisation and orientation of technological research and experimentation, the organisation of state trading corporations and public sector enterprises, and the very machinery of government and planning itself. Whether or not such a transition from a purely growth-oriented development strategy to one also emphasising the elimination of poverty and the reduction of inequality will require major political transformations, as some have suggested,[9] or whether the existing leadership can respond to the new environment of development by initiating and carrying out major institutional reforms, is a moot point. One can certainly predict that the public sector, whether centralised or decentralised, whether jointly with private enterprise or on its own, will in the coming decades continue to claim increasing responsibility for the 'commanding heights' of most Third World economies.

Concepts for review

- monetary and fiscal policies
- unorganised money markets
- inflation: cost push, demand pull and structural
- restrictive v. expansionary monetary policy
- financial intermediary
- organised money markets
- Central bank
- commercial banks
- development banks
- money supply
- direct v. indirect taxes
- progressive v. regressive taxation
- tax loopholes
- expansionary fiscal policies
- contractionary fiscal policies
- recession

Questions for discussion

1. The current debate on the role and limitations of development planning in Third World mixed economies turns on the age-old economic question of how much economic activity should be guided by market forces and how much state intervention there should be. Where do you stand in this debate in relation to planning v. the market in terms of your own country? Explain the reasoning behind your answer.
2. Keynesian-type macro *monetary* and *fiscal* policies have proved to be effective instruments of government economic policy in developed nations but their relevance and effectiveness in most Third World economies is greatly limited. Comment on this statement, being sure to include in your discussion a description of various types of monetary and fiscal policies.
3. What is meant by the terms 'inflation' and 'recession'? Is it possible for an economy to experience an inflation and a recession simultaneously? If so, can you give some recent examples of this phenomenon, explaining how such 'reflation' could come about? If not, explain why not.
4. Distinguish between 'demand pull', 'cost push' and 'structural' inflation. Is it possible to have them all occuring simultaneously? Explain.
5. What policy alternatives (both fiscal and monetary) do Third World governments possess in coping with the type of worldwide inflation which occurred during the first half of the 1970s? Is it possible for most LDCs to control this type of inflation completely, or must they attempt

[9] See, for example, A. Shourie, 'Growth, Poverty and Inequalities', *Foreign Affairs*, li, 2, January 1973.

to contain its excesses while relying ultimately on the effectiveness of developed-nation anti-inflationary policies? Explain your answer.

Further reading

On fiscal and monetary policy for Third World nations, see: W. ARTHUR LEWIS, *Development Planning: the essentials of economic policy*, Harper & Row, New York, 1966: DEREK T. HEALEY, 'Development Policy: new thinking about an interpretation', *Journal of Economic Literature*, x, 3, September 1972; R. I. McKINNON, *Money and Capital in Economic Development*, The Brookings Institution, Washington, 1973; E. S. NASSEF, *Monetary Policy in Developing Countries*, Rotterdam University Press, 1972; J. H. ADLER, 'Fiscal policy in a developing country', in K. Berril, ed., *Economic Development with Special Reference to East Asia*, St Martin's Press, 1965; R. J. CHELLIAH, 'Trends in Taxation in Developing Countries', *IMF Staff Papers*, July 1971; J. TOYE (ed.), *Taxation and Economic Development*, Frank Cass, London, 1979.

An excellent introduction to the economics and politics of public policy in developing nations can be found in TONY KILLICK, *Policy Economics: a text for developing countries*, Heinemann, 1980.

Chapter 25 Global interdependence in the 1980s: food, energy and the new international economic order

I believe that with all the dislocations that we are now experiencing there also exists an extraordinary opportunity to form for the first time in history a truly global society, carried by the principle of interdependence.
Henry Kissinger, US Secretary of State, 1975

The time has come for the dominant powers to renounce their desire for national advantages, to proclaim an end to all unequal relationships which developing countries have had to accept . . . and to create a 'new international economic order'.
Ferdinand Marcos, President of the Philippines[1]

Introduction

The new interdependence

We live today in an increasingly interdependent world and, perhaps some day, a 'world without borders', to borrow the title of a provocative book by Lester R. Brown.[2] For Third World countries, this dependence on rich nations is and has always been a stark fact of their economic lives. It is the principal reason for their growing interest in promoting greater individual and collective self-reliance. At the same time, the developed countries of the world, who once prided themselves on their apparent self-sufficiency, are rapidly discovering that in an age of increasingly scarce natural and mineral resources they too are growing more economically dependent on the policies of certain groups of developing countries. All indications point to the fact that by the beginning of the twenty-first century no nation or region will be able to survive economically in complete isolation from others. It would therefore be foolish to analyse the contemporary problems of underdevelopment without placing Third World nations squarely in the context of the interdependent, yet highly unequal, global economy.

In this final chapter, we review the aspects of Third World economic and non-economic dependence touched on in previous chapters and point out some emerging new areas of interdependence between rich and poor nations. We then examine some of the major global economic issues likely to affect the less developed nations in the last two decades of the twentieth century and conclude with an analysis of the Third World's growing demand for a new international economic order. But before engaging in such a crystal ball exercise, we need to set out an analytical framework to outline and review the many ways in which the development of poor nations, as this concept has been defined throughout the book, is influenced by and dependent on the international activities of the industrialised nations.

A schematic framework for analysing the international developmental dependence of Third World countries

In Chapter 6 we attempted schematically to illustrate and describe the intimate two-way

[1] Speaking on behalf of 110 Third World countries at UNCTAD IV meeting in Nairobi, May 1976.

[2] Lester R. Brown, *World Without Borders*, New York, Random House, 1972.

linkages between the three principal components of our definition of underdevelopment: low levels of living, low self-esteem, limited freedom from external dominance and limitations of choice. In this section we extend that basically domestic framework to recognise the many ways in which each of these components is affected by forces which are external to both the nation and to the individual. Figure 25.1 is a simplified presentation of the international social system from the viewpoint of most Third World nations.

The inner circle reproduces the principal components of and linkages within the domestic social system from Figure 6.1 (p. 100). This inner circle

Figure 25.1
Underdevelopment in a global social system: a suggested schematic framework

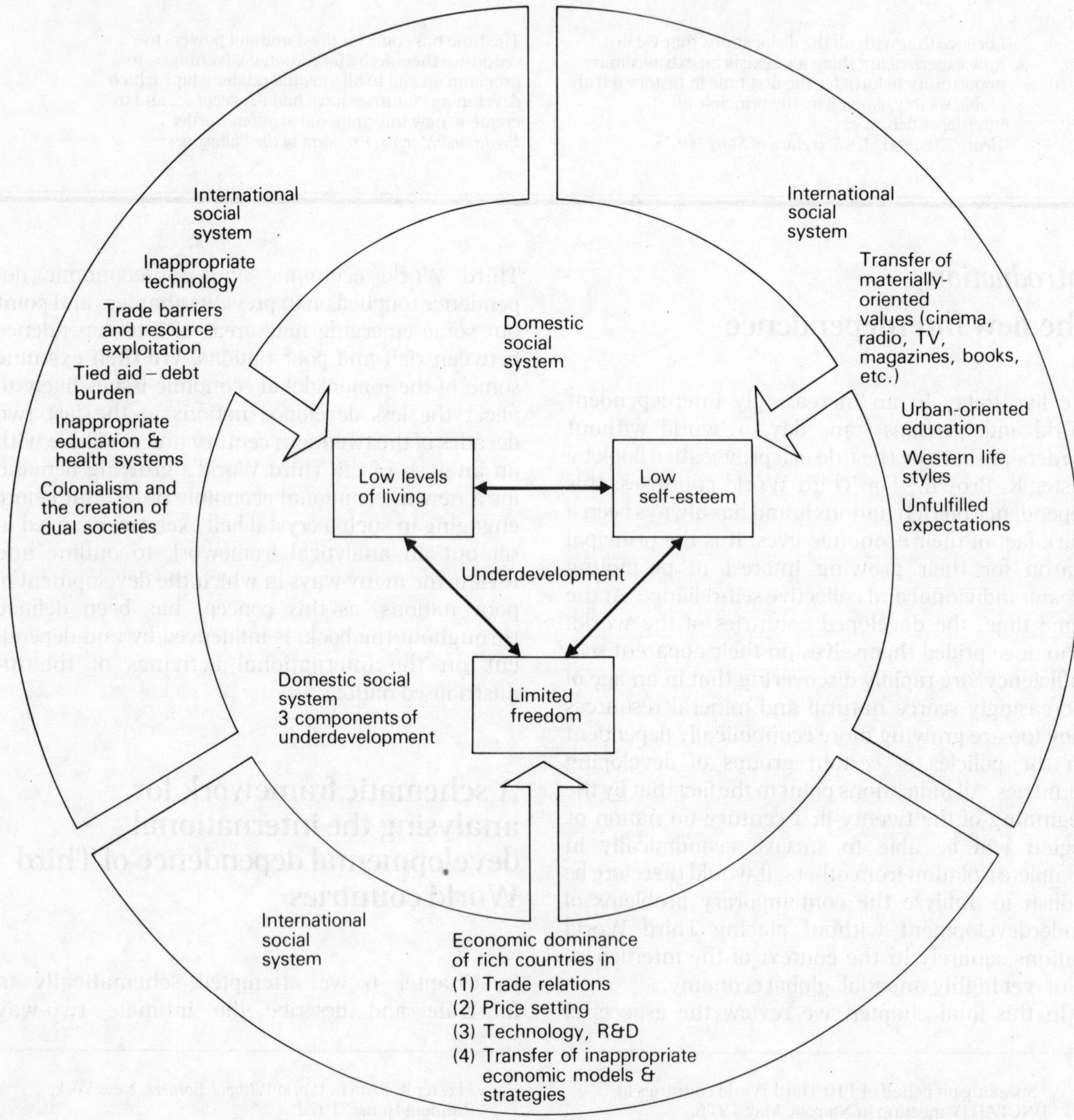

represents the forces of underdevelopment in most Third World countries. The outer circle represents aspects of the international social system of which each underdeveloped country is a part, whether willingly or not. This wider system is controlled largely by rich-country interests and economic policies. Arrows point from the outer circle to each of the three 'components of underdevelopment' boxes in the inner circle. At the origin of each arrow is a sample list of the many ways in which rich country institutions and activities can influence levels of living, esteem and freedom in poor countries. The degree to which these external activities will determine the internal outcome of development strategies will obviously vary from nation to nation. But, as we have seen in Parts Two and Three, almost every developing country is subject to one or more of the external forces portrayed in Figure 25.1.

Low levels of living

Take first the various external influences contributing to low levels of living. Each of the three main components – low incomes, limited education and poor health (the famous triad of poverty, ignorance and disease) – is strongly influenced by outside forces. For example, low incomes are perpetuated and exacerbated by a whole array of international economic policies of rich nations (including technological transfer, trade, aid, private assistance, etc.) which tend to focus on the modernisation of a small industrial urban sector, often at the expense of the masses of people outside this narrow elite. The economic impact of these forces and their corresponding development (more accurately 'anti-development') philosophies is the accentuation of the dualistic nature of many Third World societies. Inadequate health conditions, reinforced by inappropriate facilities, are partly the result of the wholesale transfer of Western systems of health care and excessive professional credentialisation to developing countries. These systems typically emphasise curative rather than preventive medicine, inappropriate and often irrelevant medical training and the location of most modern health facilities in urban areas catering for small and wealthy elites while most people in rural areas receive little or no medical attention.

In education the situation is analogous to that of health. LDC educational systems, curricula and philosophies copy those in the developed nations, even though their relevance and functional utility to Third World nations are questionable. We discuss each of the above phenomena relating to incomes, health and education in more detail later in this chapter.

Low self-esteem

The external factors contributing to low levels of living in Third World countries obviously thereby contribute to low self-esteem, confused cultural identity and a lessened sense of dignity and personal worth. But the principal reason why such self-depreciating attitudes become widely experienced by the very poor, who in the past were probably no better off in material terms, is that along with industrial technologies, educational systems and health practices, the values, ideals and symbols of material-oriented life styles have been transferred from rich to poor countries. Today a man often feels poor in spirit if he is poor in material goods, not solely because poverty and low esteem are necessarily connected, but because of the widespread adoption of Western social conventions and attitudes towards modernisation and material well-being in most Third World countries. It is difficult enough for parents who are very poor to see their children starving, sick and helpless. It wounds their dignity and self-respect even further when the society around them begins to hold them accountable for their unfortunate condition or when they contrast their situation with the relative affluence of others. The principal transmission mechanisms for these value transfers from developed to less developed countries are the cinema, magazines, television, radio programmes and books, most of which originate in or are greatly influenced by the economically dominant cultures of the northern hemisphere.

Limited freedom

To a large extent, our third component of underdevelopment – limited freedom – in fact *defines* the dominance and dependence relationship in which poor countries often find themselves *vis-à-vis* the rich nations. Their range of economic choice, whether in the pursuit of labour-intensive industrial growth or the promotion of export-oriented agricultural strategies, is greatly circumscribed. For example, the only methods of production that may be available are the labour-saving techniques of rich labour-scarce countries, and the prices which agricultural primary commodities can fetch in world markets have tended to fall in relation to the manufactured goods which must be imported. As we have seen, their freedom to dictate the terms and conditions of foreign aid and private foreign assistance may be restricted also by their economic vulnerability and their pressing need for development finance. In short, LDC governments must often contend with the fact that the development strategies they might prefer to pursue in order to achieve real social and economic progress are the very ones that may not be in the best interests of foreign nations or powerful multi-national corporations. As an unfortunate result, Third World countries are often forced to pursue a second or third-best strategy (e.g. capital-intensive industrialisation) which may ultimately exacerbate the very conditions they seek to improve (e.g. reducing unemployment).

Some manifestations of LDC dependence: a retrospective review

For illustrative purposes this international dependence can be divided into four broad categories: economic, technological, institutional and socio-cultural.

Economic dependence

Subsistence economies which produce all they consume are by definition independent of the rest of the world. For hundreds of years most African societies functioned in this way, and even today there are remote parts of Africa, Latin America and the South Pacific which have little or no ties with the outside world. But as newly independent nations are formed, and as others attempt to accelerate their economic progress, it becomes inevitable for them to engage in economic transactions with other nations. The more modernised the economy becomes, the more it is likely to be integrated into the global economic system.

Countries attempting to raise levels of living and to provide a wide range of material goods and social services are often obliged to seek those products which they themselves are incapable of producing through international trade. Their incapability may be because of a lack of resources, both physical and human, or a need to concentrate on a few products which they are in an advantageous position to produce. A country like China was able to cut itself off economically from the rest of the world and pursue what appears to have been a successful independent development strategy largely because of its vast endowments of land, natural resources, raw materials and human resources.

Few other Third World countries can realistically follow the Chinese economic model, let alone adapt the crucial cultural, political and ideological foundations for that social and economic policy. An important fact of economic life in the last two decades of the twentieth century for less developed countries, and increasingly for developed countries, is that the capacity of most national governments to improve the well-being of their people cannot be separated from their ability first to find profitable foreign markets for the products they can produce most efficiently and, second, to have access to the necessary technology, energy supplies and raw materials from abroad in order to produce these products. If it is unable, or cannot afford, to draw widely on the world's resources, a less developed country will be severely disadvantaged in seeking to improve the levels of living of its people significantly.

Recognising the great difficulty of avoiding economic relations with the outside world in general and with the developed countries in particular, even as a policy of greater collective self-reliance is pursued, less developed countries today find themselves handicapped by their economic dependence on rich-country policies in four areas: trade, foreign aid, private foreign assistance and world-wide inflation in association with the international backwash effects of rich-country macro-economic policies. We review these areas very briefly, as earlier chapters have dealt with them in depth.

1. International trade

One often hears the term 'open economy' applied to

many, especially small, Third World countries. As we saw in Chapter 19, the term means that their economies and national incomes are greatly dependent on their sale of exports to and purchase of imports from other nations. Many countries in Africa, Asia and Latin America derive anything from 25 to 90 per cent of their GNP from international trading activities. Trade accounts for almost 80 per cent of the flow of total foreign currency earnings into the developing countries. But during the last 20 years, the less developed nations' share of world trade (excluding oil exports) has dropped from over 15 per cent to less than 12 per cent. This has been due not only to a relatively slower growth in their *volume* of exports but also because the *prices* they receive for their exports (mostly raw materials and basic agricultural commodities) have grown at a slower pace than the prices of goods they must import from rich nations (mostly manufactured and semi-manufactured goods). Since net commodity foreign exchange earnings (total value of exports minus total value of imports) depend both on the volume and price of exports and imports, the declining relative prices of LDC exports compared with their imports (the terms of trade) means that most Third World countries have found themselves over the years paying more money per unit import while receiving less money and expending more real resources per unit of exports.

It is easy to blame the weak international trading position of poor nations on the fact that they are relatively more efficient exporters of primary products for which the international demand is unfortunately income- and price-inelastic. As we saw in Chapter 21, this argument is commonly used to justify policies of rapid industrialisation and import substitution to reduce the vulnerability of LDCs to their very disadvantageous international trading positions. While this argument, at least in theory, appears to be generally valid, it neglects an equally important aspect of international economic relations, namely the ability of the powerful rich nations to manipulate world commodity and manufactured goods prices for their own self-interest (see Chapter 20). They can further frustrate the export promotion strategies of poor countries by means of tariff and non-tariff barriers placed on primary product exports.

The developed countries are not nearly as vulnerable or dependent on the trade and tariff policies of less developed countries. Only 23 per cent of their total exports go to poor nations. Third World countries on the other hand have to rely on rich countries for 74 per cent of their export markets. But LDC imports from rich countries, even if only 23 per cent of the latter's total, still amount to a very sizable proportion of their GNPs. The combination of this dependence on international trade and their limited bargaining power makes the international economic position of individual Third World countries highly vulnerable to the foreign economic policies of developed nations. This dependence in turn greatly limits their ability to manipulate important domestic economic variables like saving, investment, commodity prices and levels of employment, since these efforts can often be frustrated by external factors beyond their control. In Chapter 21 we discussed possible LDC strategies for lessening this dependence on both foreign trade and the trading policies of foreign countries.

2. Foreign aid

Given the difficulties of generating sufficient foreign exchange to finance needed equipment and materials for development projects through international commodity trade, Third World countries have had to rely on foreign assistance from developed nations to fill the gap between investment targets and the domestic and international funds needed to finance these investments. But even more than trade, foreign aid carries with it connotations of charity and dependence, both psychological and monetary. Financial dependence arises from the basic fact that most foreign aid in the form of loans must be repaid. The burden of this debt accumulated by less developed countries has now reached a point where some poor countries may soon have debt repayments that *exceed* new lending so that there will be a net reverse financial flow from these poor countries to the rich donor nations. Often the terms and conditions of foreign aid are also, as we have seen, restrictive. Recipient nations are typically required to use the loans to purchase equipment and materials from the lending countries themselves (the phenomenon of 'tied aid') even though they might be able to buy these items cheaper in other countries. While such tied aid may be better than no aid at all since these loans tend to carry lower interest charges than those prevailing in world money markets, the economic benefits of such 'second best' assistance may be negligible. Moreover, aid funds, especially those given on a 'bilateral', country-to-country basis, carry with them subtle and sometimes not so subtle political implications which needy countries would prefer not to have. Whatever its presumed economic benefits to both donor and recipient nation, the present structure of international aid relationships, at least in the opinion of many Third World observers, tends to intensify the economic, psychological and political dependence of the less developed on the more developed nations of the world.

3. Multi-national corporations and private foreign investment

Rapid technological advances in transportation, communication and management over the past 25 years have greatly increased the size of private corporations. In the process they have been transformed from purely domestic business firms to multi-national or global enterprises. They not only operate in a diversity of nations, but also purchase inputs from many different countries. This internationalisation of production is becoming increasingly dominant in global economic relations to the point where traditional concepts of the nature and benefits of international trade are being extensively re-examined.

Many multi-national corporations have now reached a stage where they are larger, in economic terms, than many of the countries in which they operate. For example, Exxon generates more total income than Argentina, General Motors more than Nigeria, IBM more than Colombia, Gulf Oil more than Peru, Unilever more than Pakistan and so on down the list (see Table 22.1).

The emergence of these multi-national corporations as dominant global institutions is in many ways challenging the very existence of nation states. MNCs have in the past had the power to dictate to needy countries the terms and conditions of their operations. Their economic influence on the outcome of national development policies can therefore be decisive, not to mention their political influence (e.g. the role of ITT in Chile). In Chapter 22 we discussed this powerful new force in international economic and political relations and the pros and cons as well as the future of their financial activities in the Third World.

4. The transmission of international inflation and the impact of rich-country domestic policies

The 1970s witnessed a worldwide inflationary spiral that had few peacetime precedents in modern history. Annual consumer price increases of 15 to 20 per cent were common in the developed as well as the less developed nations of the world. This is in contrast to the former's historical rates of price increase which had averaged 3 to 5 per cent annually. While the steep rises in international oil prices by the Organisation of Petroleum Exporting Countries (OPEC) were a major contributing factor, the ultimate inflationary sources can be traced to the economic policies of the developed countries themselves. Whatever the origin of these unprecedented price increases, however, the fact remains that those which can least afford it – the least developed countries of Africa, Asia and Latin America – are typically the hardest hit. As the prices of their manufactured imports rocket, their real incomes decline. The real problem, however, is that in countries so dependent on foreign trade and so exposed to fluctuations in international prices, the actual range of economic policy choices to combat these adverse external effects are severely limited. In effect, Third World nations are dependent on the ability of the developed nations to control their own inflationary spiral before any relief can be anticipated.

But the problem is compounded further by the fact that in attempting to control inflation, developed countries often need to adopt policies that are directly and indirectly harmful to the economic welfare of poor nations. Tariff and non-tariff controls on imports to protect domestic workers and producers, cutbacks in foreign financial and technical assistance, and a general policy of economic austerity all contribute to worldwide economic repercussions which make the precarious positions of many developing countries even more uncertain. As a result, many more people in the LDCs may be made much worse off as a result of the bettering of the economic conditions of the relatively few people in rich nations.

Many people therefore argue that the welfare and even the economic viability of many Third World nations largely depend on the economic policies pursued by developed nations in their efforts to improve the welfare of their own people. The converse is clearly not true.

Technological dependence

One of the most significant areas of Third World international dependence lies in the twin fields of science and technology. This is because the process of scientific and technological advance in all its stages, including basic and applied research and machinery and equipment development, has been in the past and now continues to be heavily concentrated in and for the richer countries of the world. Almost 98 per cent of total world expenditure on science and technology originates in the economically developed countries. This would not be such a problem, in fact, it would be an obvious advantage to poor countries, were it not for the fact that the scientific and technological priority problems of developed nations are *not* the same as those of the less developed nations. The latter sorely need efficient production techniques which will take maximum advantage of their abundant supplies of labour and limited quantities of capital. However, equipment research and development in the rich countries specialise in methods and processes which economise on labour so as to take advantage of their abundantly available supplies of physical capital and scientific expertise.

In other words, for two-thirds of the world's population 98 per cent of the world's technological research is focused on the wrong problems, using the wrong methods, in order to bring about the wrong results (e.g. the importation of foreign technologies often results in rising instead of falling levels of unemployment). For those Third World countries who have neither the resources nor the current capability to develop their own more 'appropriate' technologies, this dependence almost guarantees that poorer countries will be at a competitive disadvantage with rich nations in the manufacture and sale of many products. We analysed this vital issue at a number of points in Part Two, especially in Chapter 13 where we explored the relationship between technological transfer and the LDC employment question.

Institutional dependence: education and health

The educational and health systems of most Third World countries are largely replicas of those in the developed nations. In addition to borrowing inappropriate production technologies (over which they have little control), less developed countries initially borrowed (or, better, were given) equally inappropriate systems of education and health services (over which they do have considerable control). For example, we saw in Chapter 17 that the formal educational system of most poor countries is largely oriented towards student progression via examinations from primary to secondary to university education. The ultimate objective of this system, whether intentional or not, is the training of students for jobs in the highly paid, modern urban sector of the economy. Unfortunately, in contrast to developed nations where such systems and curricula do have some bearing on the likely occupations of graduating students, there are only a limited number of these modern sector opportunities in most developing nations. In fact, the urban modern sector typically employs at most 10 to 20 per cent of the total labour force (except in some Latin American and East Asian countries). Moreover, only about one student in fifty who begins primary school is likely to complete secondary education, and perhaps one in two hundred will complete university education. For that vast majority of students who will not receive more than three or four years of schooling and who are likely to have to earn their living in traditional agricultural or informal urban activities, the functional relevance of most educational curricula to these activities is now being widely questioned.

On the health side, we find a similar dependence phenomenon operating in less developed countries. Given the low levels of per capita income and abundant supplies of labour, we might expect that with their limited financial resources and the need to spread medical services as widely as possible, health systems in LDCs would stress prevention rather than cure and would use labour-intensive rather than capital-intensive techniques. Unfortunately this is not the case in most parts of Asia (with the notable exception of China), Africa and Latin America. On the contrary, health systems typically cater for a small urban elite and stress curative rather than preventive medicine. They favour capital-intensive construction techniques (e.g. expensive hospitals with sophisticated equipment) with highly skilled doctors rather than simple clinics with a few doctors and many medical auxiliaries.

Moreover, Western medicine dispensed by private rather than publicly employed doctors has been stressed to the exclusion of traditional medicine. In addition to catering disproportionately for the urban elite, health programmes, medical schools and delivery systems in most LDCs are often uncritically modelled on those in the developed countries. This is usually the result either of historical colonial ties with the mother country or the 'demonstration effect' of elaborate hospitals and sophisticated training programmes which captivate the minds of young Third World medical students studying overseas. Whatever the reason, the predominantly urban-based, curative and capital-intensive health systems found in most underdeveloped countries are inappropriate 'transplants' of Western medical practices and rely on Western methods of training for their continuation.

Like urban-oriented educational systems, LDC health systems typically reflect the biases and special interests of the dominant developed nations of the world. Whether this intellectual and institutional dependence persists will depend on the degree to which developing countries make a genuine commitment to the widespread improvement in the health and living conditions of their peoples.

Socio-cultural dependence

A final component of international dependence affecting not only levels of living but also individual self-esteem and dignity is the transfer of the values, ideals, symbols and attitudes of Western societies. As we have seen, a major aspect of this transfer phenomenon is the almost universal adoption of material living standards to measure the worth of a human being. In societies where the majority of people are unable to attain even the lowest of these standards, the primacy of such material-oriented values can serve to perpetuate the consciousness of underdevelopment rather than to elevate development aspirations. This is not to deny the importance of motivating people to improve their material well-being (although such motivation is rarely necessary). Rather it is to accentuate the more important task of gearing rising aspirations to economic realities and guaranteeing that the domestic gap between rich and poor does not continually widen.

The transfer of Western institutions and standards (socialist and capitalist) can also create or aggravate obstacles to development not only in education, health and consumption. It also affects the nature of trade unions and labour legislation, social services, including means of transport and communications, bureaucracies, political and party systems, attitudes towards extended and nuclear families, land tenure patterns and military institutions. Many of these can be positive forces for social and economic development, but uncritical acceptance and adoption of them by Third World countries, especially by the educated elites, not only reflect their current state of international dependence but, more importantly, can raise serious barriers to the realisation of the very development goals they presumably were adopted to achieve.

Manifestations of emerging global interdependence: energy, food and natural resources

If the 1950s and 1960s could be described as the era of nationalism and cold war politics, the 1970s and 1980s will probably come to be known as the decades of global interdependence. The world-wide inflation which began in the early 1970s pushed the world economy to the brink of chaos. Global food scarcities caused by a combination of rising wealth in the developed countries and increasing population growth in the poor countries, along with severe drought conditions in parts of Africa and Asia, alerted the world to the fact that massive starvation was not a remote possibility. Grain and soyabean prices doubled and tripled, largely to the detriment of the very poor in Asia, Africa and Latin America and to the benefit primarily of the United States which currently accounts for almost three-quarters of the world's net grain exports. On top of these food price rises, the countries of the Persian Gulf and their colleagues in OPEC dramatically increased international oil prices by 800 per cent thus threatening the viability of the world economy as no other event had since the Great Depression. Rising oil prices in turn caused the prices of fertiliser (for which petroleum is a significant input) to increase sharply. This exacerbated an already dangerous world food situation. While this inflation in the prices of basic goods affected rich and poor nations alike, it fell most heavily on the poorest of the Third World nations, thereby further increasing the gap between them and the rest of the world.

But even though world price inflation demonstrated once again the enormous vulnerability of the poorest Third World nations to international economic setbacks, the vulnerability of rich country economies to rapidly rising natural resource prices dramatically illustrated that, at least in the case of minerals and basic raw materials, their dependence on access to Third World resources is far greater than anyone had thought. In all probability, it will be even greater in the future. Let us therefore examine this growing global interdependence with reference to three critical commodities: energy, food and natural resources.

Energy and the world economy

If anyone ever doubted that energy and energy supplies (e.g. oil, coal, natural gas and hydro-electric power) are the foundations of the modern industrial economies, the 'energy shock' of the 1970s dramatically proved the point. In 1970 the developed nations, comprising one-third of the world's population, were consuming annually almost 85 per cent of world energy production. But the non-oil-producing Third World countries also rely heavily on oil to fuel their growing industrial and agricultural economies. The massive and unprecedented 400 per cent increase announced by members of the Organisation of Petroleum Exporting Countries in 1974 resulted in enormous additions to their total export revenues, rising from some $14.5 billion in 1972 to over $110 billion in 1974. Admittedly the high proportion of these revenues is derived from the principal oil-importing developed nations like Great Britain, France, Italy, Japan and the United States. But the oil import bill of the non-OPEC developing countries, numbering about 90, rose from$4 billion in 1973 to over $17 billion in 1975, an increase of more than $13 billion or 300 per cent. Further price increases in 1979–80 added another $10 billion to the total import bill. **These increases alone amounted to more than the total value of all official foreign aid provided to these countries by the developed nations during the same years.**

The oil price explosion, irrespective of its eventual outcome, clearly demonstrated the following points about the world economy of the 1980s.

1. Almost all the developed countries are net importers of oil. Their ultimate dependence upon the pricing policies of an organised group of Third World nations was thus vividly revealed. Japan, for example, depends on imports for 99 per cent of its petroleum, while Western Europe imports 96 per cent of its requirements. Their economies were shaken in a manner attributable to no single event in the previous 30 years. For the foreseeable future, therefore, the oil-exporting countries are in positions of immense power. The six Middle East nations, for example, account for little more than one per cent of world's population but control over half of the world's known reserves of petroleum and a far greater share of total exportable reserves. The nature of their newly discovered economic power is not being lost sight of by other Third World nations. Many LDCs are now attempting to form OPEC-like cartels for other minerals, raw materials and primary products over which they exert some substantial control.
2. The non-oil-exporting LDCs, especially those with limited export markets also are vulnerable to rapid increases in the price of fuels. For illustrative purposes, however, we can distinguish among four groups of Third World countries according to their vulnerability to rapid energy cost increases. The first group consists of countries like Colombia, Mexico, Bolivia and Peru which are largely self-sufficient in oil and are therefore not directly affected. The fortunes of other raw material exporters like Malaysia, Morocco, Zambia and Zaïre depend on the price fluctuations of their principal commodity – first higher in the mid-1970s, then sharply lower in the early 1980s. A third category consists of nations like South Korea, Hong Kong, Brazil, Taiwan and Singapore. These countries are all closely integrated into the world economy, primarily through their import of raw and intermediate materials for processing into manufactured goods. The energy component of their imports is therefore large, but they are able to pass on most of their extra energy and raw material costs in the form of higher prices to buyers of their manufactured export products. Moreover, the dynamism of their economies assumes relatively good access to export credits and foreign lending.

The fourth and last category of nations consists

of those 40 or so Third World countries which are extremely vulnerable to rapid world price increases for petroleum and other products (see the category of 'low income countries' in the Appendix to Chapter 5). Included among these countries are most of those in sub-Saharan Africa, South Asia (India, Pakistan and Bangladesh), Central America, and a few separate countries like Uruguay, Chile and possibly the Philippines. Together they constitute almost 50 per cent of the population of Third World countries, excluding China. For them, the economic consequences of rising resource and commodity prices are overwhelmingly adverse. They are the poorest of countries, with the lowest anticipated economic growth rates and the most limited margin for economic manoeuvre. Having large accumulated debt burdens and limited foreign exchange earning capacities, they are unlikely to have any access to short-term credit. This is the most dependent and vulnerable group of all.

3. The direct dependence of both developed and less developed nations on energy imports is compounded in the case of the less developed countries by the indirect effects of their economic dependence and vulnerability to the economic policies of rich nations. This indirect dependence is manifested in the latter countries' ability to adjust their economies to the altered international circumstances. For example, in their efforts to combat the negative effects of higher import prices for energy and raw materials and the more general inflationary trend, wealthy countries are likely to cut back on foreign travel and foreign assistance. These and related policies can exacerbate an already difficult foreign exchange position for the least developed nations.
4. Finally, as we discovered in Chapter 22, much will depend on how the newly discovered 'petrodollar' wealth of OPEC nations is recycled in world financial markets (i.e. how they invest their enormous surplus of oil revenues). If it almost all goes to the developed countries, as most of it has and probably will, then the overall result may be a transfer of scarce financial resources from poor to rich nations through the intermediary of the oil-producing states. For example, if 90 per cent of Arab oil revenues come from developed countries and 10 per cent from the LDCs, and if, after domestic use, 95 per cent of the excess revenue is reinvested in rich country economies, then in effect the non-oil-producing LDCs are financing Arab investments in rich countries. On the other hand, if the 13 OPEC countries reaffirm their historical ties with other Third World nations and use their surplus funds to invest in the economies of poor nations, then their extraordinary wealth could greatly help to stimulate economic and social improvements in less fortunate nations.

Raw materials and mineral resources

No nation or continent is endowed with *all* the raw materials essential for the functioning of a modern industrial economy. As these materials become increasingly scarce, their very uneven distribution throughout the world could thrust previously weak nations into positions of considerable economic power in much the same manner as that experienced by the oil-producing states. World mineral interdependence and, especially, the growing raw material dependence of rich nations on poor ones, is a new and vital component of the growing economic interdependence of all nations. Raw material interdependence in particular has two main aspects.

First, the consumption of nearly all essential minerals, both metallic and non-metallic, is rapidly rising. Those countries of North America and especially Western Europe which industrialised earliest have almost depleted many of their indigenous supplies of basic raw materials. According to Lester Brown:

> The rich countries, particularly the United States, Japan and those of Western Europe, with their steadily rising consumption of minerals required to support their affluence, are becoming increasingly dependent on the poor countries with their largely unexploited mineral reserves. In western Europe, consumption of eleven basic industrial raw materials – bauxite, copper, lead, phosphate, zinc, chrome ore, manganese ore, magnesium, nickel, tungsten and tin – exceeds production. In the case of copper, phosphates, tin, nickel, manganese ore and chrome ore, nearly all needs must now be met from imports.[3]

[3] Brown, *op. cit.*, p. 193.

Table 25.1 shows that the United States' dependence on raw material imports in 1970 included the need to import more than half its supplies of aluminium, manganese, nickel, tin, zinc and chromium. By 1985 iron, lead and tungsten will probably be added to the list, bringing it to a total of nine of the basic 13 industrial raw materials. By the year 2000 the United States will more than likely be dependent primarily on foreign sources for all its basic industrial raw materials, with the probable exception of phosphate. Its total imports of energy fuels and minerals, which cost $8 billion in 1970, is projected to increase to almost $64 billion by the turn of the century. As competition for dwindling reserves of high grade minerals sharply increases over the coming decades, the United States as well as the other industrialised countries will become increasingly vulnerable to external forces beyond their control. These forces will originate from supplier nations, mostly in the Third World, whose international bargaining power will be on the rise, especially if organisations similar to OPEC are formed for other scarce minerals.

The second aspect of raw material interdependence, therefore, is the fact that known reserves of a number of minerals are highly concentrated in a few, mostly Third World, locations around the globe. For example, four less developed countries (Chile, Peru, Zambia and Zaïre) supply almost all of the world's exports of copper. Three others (Bolivia, Malaysia and Thailand) supply over 70 per cent of all tin traded in international markets. Mexico, Peru and Australia account for almost 60 per cent of the world traded supply of lead. With regard to phosphate and potash, two of the three principal nutrients (potash, phosphates and nitrogen) in the chemical fertilisers so important to international agricultural production, we find that Canada supplies most of the world's potash while Morocco, Tunisia, Senegal, Togo and the United States control most of the phosphates. The range and concentration of important LDC suppliers of these and other essential minerals to the United States (and, even more so, to other developed countries) is indicated by Table 25.2.

The above discussion reveals that the prospect of economic **collective bargaining** by major Third World suppliers of scarce raw materials emphasises the very real nature of the growing dependence of rich countries on the poor ones. Growing resource scarcities promise to modify the current international economic and political relationships among nations with the likely elevation of the relative influence and power of certain Third World countries in the international hierarchy. Whatever the probable outcome, however, it can no longer be said that international dependence runs only from poor countries to rich countries.

Table 25.1
US dependence on imports of principal industrial raw materials, with projections to year 2000

Raw material	1950	1970	1985	2000
		% imported		
Aluminium	64	85	96	98
Chromium	n/a	100	100	100
Copper	31	0	34	56
Iron	8	30	55	67
Lead	39	31	62	67
Manganese	88	95	100	100
Nickel	94	90	88	89
Phosphorus	8	0	0	2
Potassium	14	42	47	61
Sulphur	2	0	28	52
Tin	77	n/a	100	100
Tungsten	n/a	50	87	97
Zinc	38	59	72	84

Source: Lester R. Brown, *World Without Borders*, p. 194.

World food shortages

The 1970s also witnessed the transition from a previous era of commercial food surpluses to one of global shortages, rising prices and growing national concern primarily among the least developed of Third World countries. While droughts in parts of Africa and Asia exacerbated the short-term seriousness of the world food problem, its long-term trend has been in the direction of a narrowing gap between total world production and world consumption. Food prices are likely to remain much higher than they were during the previous decade and, one continent, North America, is emerging as the only major world source of exportable food supplies. Almost half the world's population will continue to be overwhelmingly dependent on North American food surpluses. But rising prices of petroleum and fertilisers, major imports of most poor countries, greatly deplete those foreign exchange funds that would ordinarily be used to buy food from these large grain suppliers.

Table 25.2
US imports of selected minerals from principal LDC suppliers

Mineral	Major LDC suppliers with % supplied by each		Total % supplied by LDCs
Aluminium bauxite	Jamaica	53.5	88.2
	Surinam	27.4	
	Guyana	7.3	
Cobalt	Zaire	34.5	43.0
	Zambia	8.5	
Copper	Peru	23.2	37.9
	Chile	14.7	
Iron ore	Venezuela	30.6	30.6
Lead	Peru	22.0	31.7
	Mexico	9.7	
Manganese	Gabon	26.3	55.5
	Brazil	18.8	
	Zaire	10.4	
Tin	Malaysia	64.3	96.5
	Thailand	23.3	
	Bolivia	8.9	
Tungsten	Bolivia	18.0	39.0
	Peru	12.0	
	Thailand	9.0	

Source: Overseas Development Council, *Agenda for Action: 1974*, Washington, Table C–10.

Table 25.3
Indicators of world food security, 1966–1979 (million tonnes and days)

	Reserve stocks of grain	Grain equivalent of idled US cropland (million tonnes)	Total reserves	Reserves as days of annual grain consumption
1966	167	53	220	82
1967	189	60	249	89
1968	220	74	298	103
1969	206	71	277	92
1970	166	48	214	69
1971	183	65	248	78
1972	142	35	177	54
1973	147	3	150	44
1974	131	3	134	40
1975	138	3	141	42
1976	194	1	195	55
1977	191	24	215	59
1978	226	24	251	65
1979	200	0	200	51

Source: Overseas Development Council, *Agenda 1980*, New York, Praeger, 1980, p. 178.

Although high food prices and periodic grain shortages represent at most an inconvenience to the affluent in both rich and poor nations, to the very poor they may mean the difference between life and death. For the approximately 700 million people in 32 Third World countries who already survive on the margin of nutritional subsistence or who spend 80 per cent of their incomes on food, there are no second chances when prices double, or a crop fails, or the rains do not come. Moreover, when global food reserve stocks are low (they had fallen from 26 per cent of annual world grain consumption in 1961 to less than 10 per cent by 1980), the capacity of developed nations collectively to respond with food aid to emergency areas of drought, floods or crop failures is severely diminished. This was dramatically illustrated by the general failure of the World Food Conference held in Rome in 1974 to come up with more than token transfers of food grains to starving nations. Table 25.3 shows how rapidly the annual days of grain reserves have fallen since 1966 while Table 25.4 shows the degree to which developing countries have become large net importers of grain during the latter part of the 1970s.

What are the principal factors behind the dramatic alteration of the world food situation? We can identify four. On the demand side, we have

1. the combined effects of rising population and affluence.

On the supply side, there are the four critical resource constraints of land, water, energy and fertiliser as manifested in:

2. the limited scope for expanding areas of cultivation.
3. the growing shortage of water for agricultural production and
4. rising energy costs slowing down the growth of high energy and fertiliser-intensive agriculture.

Together, rapidly rising demand and slowly growing supply are pushing up the international prices of vital foods. We now turn to discuss specifically the international determinants of world food demand and supply.[4]

Determinants of demand: population and affluence

In the 1960s the world food problem was perceived primarily as a race against time between rising numbers of people in developing countries and total food supplies. The race always seemed to remain fairly close but there was a general optimism that new breakthroughs in the technology of food production (the so-called Green Revolution) would ultimately declare food the winner. In the long run population growth would have to be reduced. But for the immediate future it appeared that famine and starvation were an unlikely occurrence.

What these watchers of the race between food and population failed to realise, and what the 1970s vividly revealed, was the fact that, in addition to Third World population growth, rising affluence in the developed nations was becoming a major factor in the annual increases in food demands. While population growth still remains the dominant source of expanding demand (e.g. with world population growing at approximately 2 per cent per year, maintaining current levels of world per capita consumption will require a doubling of food production every thirty or so years), rising income levels account for an ever-increasing proportion of this demand. For example, in terms of the demand for basic food grains (wheat, maize and rice) which dominate world consumption patterns, people in the less developed nations consume approximately 181 kg per person per year. Nearly all of this is consumed *directly* as bread, maizemeal and rice to meet minimum energy requirements. On the other hand the average North American consumes over 450 kg per year, but out of this total only 65 kg is consumed directly in the form of bread, pastry and breakfast cereals. The remaining 385 kg per capita is consumed *indirectly* in the form of meat, milk and eggs, that is. 385 kg of cereal grains per capital are used to feed livestock and poultry, the products of which are then consumed by the North American public.

The agricultural resources (mainly land, water, energy and fertilisers) required to produce this output for an average North American are often five to seven times that required for an Asian or African. Moreover, as per capita incomes rise, a significant share of this additional income is spent on high quality beef and poultry, which in turn means greater indirect consumption of feed grains and soyabeans, much of which will have to be imported.

[4] For a more comprehensive discussion of these determinants, see Lester R. Brown and Erik P. Eckholm, 'Food: growing global insecurity', in ODC, *Agenda for Action*, 1974, ch. 4.

Table 25.4
World net grain trade in the 1970s (million metric tonnes – negative figures represent imports)

	1969/70–1971/72 Average	1977/78	1978/79	1979/80
Developed market economies	**26.4**	**74.8**	**79.5**	**104.5**
North America	54.1	104.7	107.9	129.0
Western Europe	−24.2	−20.7	−15.1	−17.0
Australia and New Zealand	10.9	13.4	9.7	15.9
Japan	−14.4	−22.6	−23.0	−23.4
Centrally planned economies	**−13.3**	**−34.1**	**−34.1**	**−56.6**
People's Republic of China	−5.4	−7.4	−9.7	−8.5
USSR and Eastern Europe	−7.9	−26.7	−24.4	−48.1
Developing countries	**−19.7**	**−32.9**	**−36.7**	**−42.8**
Africa and Middle East	−8.1	−17.0	−16.9	−20.6
Asia	−11.5	−14.3	−14.7	−15.5
Latin America	−0.1	−1.6	−5.1	−6.7
Other	**−1.4**	**−1.7**	**−1.8**	**−2.1**
Total interregional exports[1]	**65.0**	**118.1**	**117.6**	**144.9**
Total world exports[1]	**105.1**	**166.0**	**172.7**	**194.3**

[1] Interregional exports includes only those grain exports which move from one region to another; world exports includes all exports of grain whether intra- or inter-regional.

NOTE: The world grains that are traded include wheat and wheat flour, milled rice, and coarse grains (corns, barley, rye, oats, and sorghum). Net exports are on a July to June year.

Source: Overseas Development Council, *Agenda 1980, op cit.*, p. 180.

This only exacerbates an already tight world food market and can mean less direct consumption for the poorest in Third World nations.

Constraints on supply: land, water, energy and fertilisers

We can conveniently invoke the fundamental concept of a 'production function' described in Chapter 4 to analyse the current constraints on world food supplies. Basically, there are four critical factors of modern agricultural production which are serious resource constraints on its expansion: land, water, energy and fertiliser. The principal mechanisms for expanding world food supplies fall into two basic categories:

1. increasing the total amount of land under cultivation;
2. raising yields on existing arable land through the more intensive use of water, energy and fertilisers.

Both cases represent increases in agricultural inputs which should lead to higher outputs in accordance with the basic economic theory of production. But, in the contemporary world, the possibilities of increasing these production inputs are restricted by the following factors:

(a) *Land expansion.* Historically this has been the traditional approach to expanding agricultural production. The potential for further expansion today is limited by the fact of the growing competition for its use by industrial development, urbanisation, new town development and transportation.

(b) *Fresh water expansion.* Water was once thought to be free, that is, it was thought to be present in such plentiful supplies that one person's use of it would not impair its availability to another. But it is far from free for modern agriculture. In fact, it is a scarce and critical input. There are many regions of the world, particularly in Africa, where the availability of sufficient water could turn unproductive land into a productive resource. The principal way of achieving this is through irrigation projects made possible by the damming up of natural waterways. But most of the world's rivers that are suitable for damming and irrigation have already been developed. Any future efforts to expand fresh water supplies for agriculture will require alternative techniques, such as river diversion (this creates serious problems when a river flows between more than one country), desalting ocean water, digging expensive bore holes to tap underground water or cloud-seeding to create and manipulate rainfall in dry agricultural areas. Unfortunately, the outlook for these efforts is, at present, not very promising.

(*c*) *Energy expansion.* An alternative source of intensifying agricultural production on existing land is through the application of greater energy inputs, such as the use of mechanised farm equipment (tractors, seeders, reapers and combines). However, as we have already seen, the sharp international price increases in energy supplies make such efforts extremely costly. In fact, high energy prices are more than likely to hold down total food production, especially in energy-intensive areas like North America and the Soviet Union, unless food prices rise equally fast.

(*d*) *Fertiliser expansion.* In addition to land, fresh water and energy, supplies of fertilisers are becoming more and more scarce as a result of higher prices and alternative uses for the petroleum inputs into fertiliser production. The process of manufacturing chemical fertilisers requires large amounts of costly energy inputs. In the face of these rising costs and the enormous expansion of world demand for fertilisers, it is clear that future prices will continue to rise. In 1974, for example, prices rose very rapidly, and Third World countries had to pay many hundreds of millions of dollars more for their fertiliser imports than in previous years. Worse still, many nations could not even obtain adequate supplies at any price. Included among these nations were the very populous and food-scarce countries of South and South-east Asia (e.g. India, Pakistan, Bangladesh and the Philippines). A continuation of high prices and limited supplies of chemical fertilisers means lower per capita outputs and increased food import needs for these nations over the coming years. Unfortunately, this increase in basic food needs has come at a time when world food prices are also high and global grain reserves are at dangerously low levels.

It should be evident from the preceding description of the prospects for world food demand and supply that many of the least developed Third World countries are likely to become even more dependent on future food imports from the developed regions, mainly the United States, but also Canada and the Soviet Union. With world demand outpacing supply, rising prices will mean greater burdens on the very poor. Worse still, shortages of vital agricultural resource inputs like energy and fertilisers will probably lead to some form of world food rationing. With the United States controlling almost three-quarters of exportable world grain supplies, the use of food as a new and deadly weapon of political blackmail against hungry Third World nations becomes a distinct, and frightening, possibility.[5]

It becomes all the more urgent, therefore, for such populous food-short nations as Bangladesh, India, Indonesia and much of sub-Saharan Africa as well as parts of Latin America to intensify their efforts to promote labour-intensive and energy-saving small- and medium-scale commercial farm development. This is where the greatest and least costly output potential lies. We discussed and reviewed the possible nature of such labour-intensive agricultural and rural development strategies in Chapters 15 and 16.

International resource interdependence: the political economy of cooperation or conflict

Our discussion in this final chapter has touched on many of the economic and non-economic manifestations of the growing interdependence of nations. Whereas a decade or so ago this interdependence was perceived primarily in terms of the dependence

[5] In fact, a 1974 report of the US Central Intelligence Agency (CIA) entitled *Potential Implications of Trends in World Population, Food Production and Climate*, specifically addresses itself to the possibility of using food as a political lever to influence the policies of needy nations.

of poor nations on the rich ones, today developed countries are rapidly discovering that in a world of growing mineral and raw material scarcities, their future economic well-being will depend increasingly on the international economic policies of many Third World countries. Let there be no misunderstanding. The poor nations are and will continue to remain considerably more vulnerable to the economic events and policies of rich nations than the other way round. But their international bargaining power is undoubtedly rising.

Before concluding with a review of the 'new international economic order' debate, we take up the question of the future implications of growing world resource interdependence. Our purpose is not only to stress its crucial importance to the future economic situations of many Third World countries but also to illustrate once more the manner in which simple economic analysis can illuminate important 'real world' issues.

Emerging resource scarcities: the pricing, rationing and 'access' problem

The events of the 1970s highlighted the fact that the world is in the middle of a fundamental and profound economic transformation. For decades, the developed nations experienced continuous economic progress based on expanding industrial production and rising exports to each other and to the less developed countries. Raw material inputs were cheap and in plentiful supply. It was a buyers' market: sellers (mostly LDCs) had to compete vigorously with each other to find markets for their abundant raw materials. More simply, supply increases continuously exceeded demand expansion.

Today, for the first time since the Great Depression of the 1930s, there is a worldwide seller's market for many goods – i.e. more buyers (demands) must compete with one another to obtain limited supplies. The growing list of scarce items goes beyond oil, food and fertiliser. It includes timber, minerals, cotton and man-made textiles among others. What will happen to countries both rich and poor, in such a situation of scarcity?

One thing is clear. The new era of scarcity is bound to alter international economic relations. It may even lead to a major revision of the international economic system as demanded by Third World nations and as adopted by the Special Session of the UN General Assembly in April 1974 in the form of the controversial Declaration and Action Programme on the Establishment of the New International Economic Order. Those countries rich in minerals and basic raw materials, both rich and poor, will discover a greater or, at least, a new economic power. Those without such natural resource supplies, especially those in Third World countries, will find their already economically vulnerable position even weaker. As scarcities become more pronounced, there will be the ever-present threat of 'economic warfare' among nations: individual resource-rich countries may use this as a weapon to extract exorbitant demands from economically desperate nations with limited resources.

But here we confine our discussion to the simple economics of resource scarcity. Recall from Chapter 3 that a very scarce resource can be described as having a relatively inelastic or vertical supply curve; that is, the total amount which can be supplied to potential purchasers at different prices is not very variable. This is especially the case for non-renewable resources like minerals and basic raw materials. Once they have been extracted from the ground, they can never be replaced. This is in contrast to renewable resources like timber or fish which can regenerate themselves after a period of years. As industrial economies expand and newly developing countries initiate rapid industrialisation programmes, the demand for these resources grows more rapidly over time: there is a rightward shift in

Figure 25.2
World resource scarcity: the free market solution

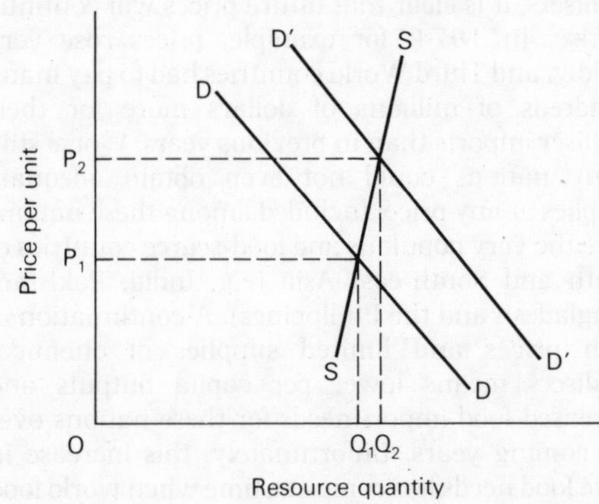

the world demand curve from say D–D to D′–D′ as shown in Figure 25.2.

If prices were allowed to be determined solely by the forces of supply and demand, the result would be a rise in resource prices from P_1 to P_2 with a corresponding increase in quantities produced and purchased from Q_1 to Q_2.

But remember (Chapter 3) that the position of demand curves is based on income levels: the higher the income level, the further to the right the demand curve (i.e. those with more incomes are willing to pay a higher price for a given quantity of a commodity than those with lower incomes). The only way one can talk realistically about a 'world demand' curve for a resource, however, is to try to add up or aggregate in some way the individual country demand curves.

Consider, for example, Figure 25.3. Assume the 'world' consists of only two countries, or two groups of identical countries. Country A is a poor, Third World country. Its demand curve for the resource in question is shown in Figure 25.3(*a*). Being poor, it simply cannot afford to buy this resource at any world price higher than 3. But as the world price falls from, say, 3 to 1, its quantity demanded rises rapidly from 5 to 40 units. In other words, within the low price range of 3 to 1, Country A's demand curve is highly elastic; for example, if the resource, such as oil, is very cheap it will pursue a rapid energy-intensive industrial and agricultural development strategy; if oil is expensive, it will 'economise' on the use of this resource input.

Figure 25.3(*b*) portrays the hypothetical demand curve for Country B (a rich nation) showing that it is prepared to purchase 50 units of the resource in question at a price of 5 per unit, 65 units at a price of 4 per unit, 75 units at a price of 3, and so on. We see, therefore, that over the relevant price range of 5 to 1, Country B's demand curve is relatively inelastic. (Can you verify this from the numbers?)

Figure 25.3
Aggregating individual country demand curves: an hypothetical illustration

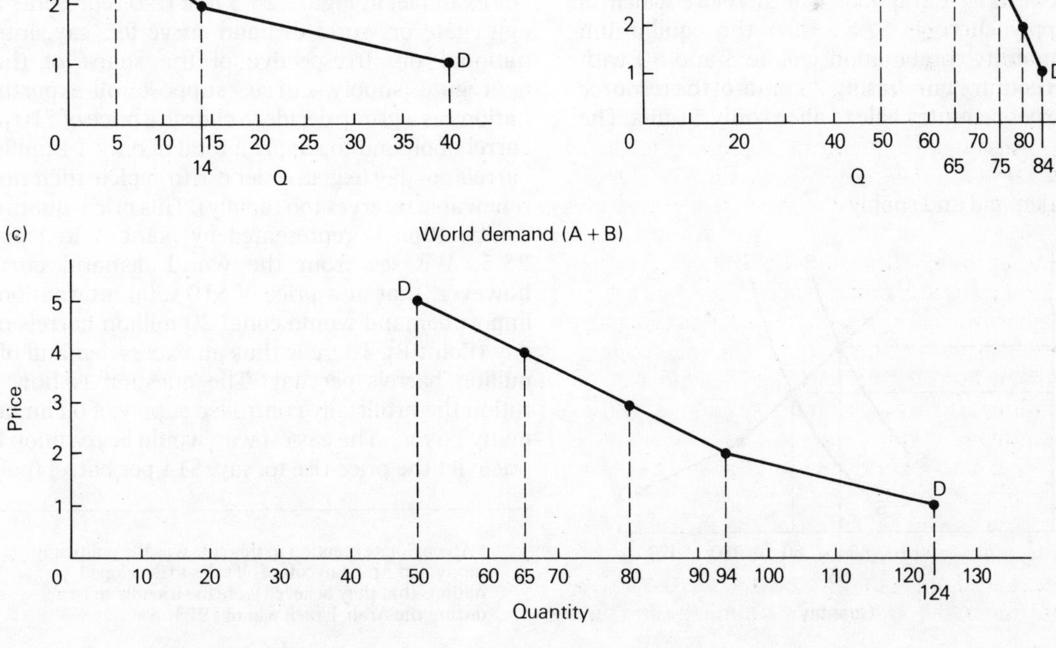

We can now add together the demand curves of Country A and B to arrive at an approximation of the 'world' or aggregate demand curve for this resource simply by adding the quantities demanded at each price for both countries. This is shown in Figure 25.3(*c*). For example, at prices 5 and 4, the world demand curve is the same as the rich country individual demand curve; at these high prices the poor country cannot afford to buy any of the resource. At a price of 3 per unit, however, world demand will be equal to 80 units, the sum of the LDC demand of 5 and the developed country demand of 75. Similarly, at a price of 2 per unit, world demand will equal 94 units of the resource. Finally, at a price of 1, total demand is 124 units.

Now suppose we superimpose a hypothetical inelastic world supply curve for this resource (assume only one country is the supplier) on our world demand curve as is done in Figure 25.4. We see that if S–S is the supply curve, the competitive equilibrium price will settle at 4 with the quantity supplied equalling quantity demanded at 65 units. But in such a situation the poor country has been priced out the market – that is, the whole of the resource supply will go to the rich country, which can afford to pay higher prices. As a result, the rich country is able to produce more manufacturing output using this essential input while the poor nation's industries stagnate. The income and output gap between rich and poor will therefore widen. If the supply curve is S′–S′, then the equilibrium price–quantity combination will be 3 and 80 with the rich country purchasing 75 units of the resource and the poor country able to afford only 5 units. The net result will be much the same as with the supply curve S–S.

Figure 25.4
World demand and supply

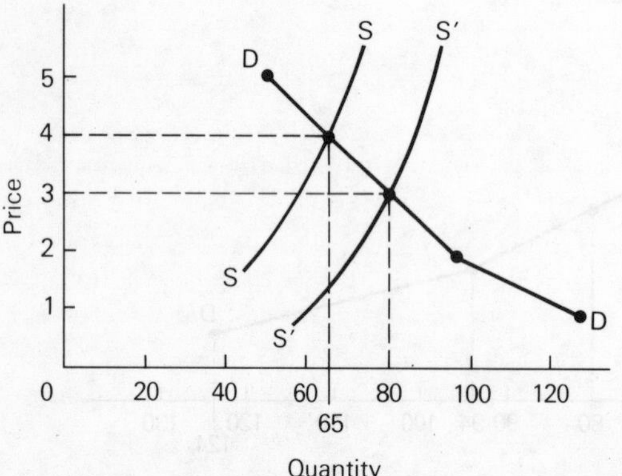

Instead of allowing the forces of international supply and demand to determine equilibrium prices and quantities of this resource, we could simply have assumed that the sellers' market is such that the resource supplier or suppliers have the bargaining power to set the world price at almost any level they wish (or believe they can get away with). This in fact is closer to the reality of the contemporary world economy than the simple interacting supply and demand analysis. The outcome is much the same.

Suppose suppliers decide to set the international price at 4 units. World demand will still be 65 and this will determine total sales. If the price were set at 3, total sales would equal 80 units as before. We can conclude, therefore, that in a purely sellers' market in which prices are established not by supply and demand but by the individual (monopoly) or collective (oligopoly) decisions of suppliers, the world demand curve will determine total output and the distribution of this output among various demanding nations.[6] Clearly, in a sellers' market, the wealthy nations have an immense advantage in the scramble for limited supplies.

Suppose now that the sellers are able to determine unilaterally both the price they will charge and how much they are prepared to sell of their commodity. For example, in Figure 25.5 line D–D represents an aggregate or world demand curve for, say, international oil. Irrespective of the shape of their aggregate supply curve, suppose oil-exporting nations as a group decide to charge a price of $10 per barrel of oil and to supply a total of only 14 million barrels per day (e.g. in order not to deplete their non-renewable reserves too rapidly). This price–quantity combination is represented by point A in Figure 25.5. We see from the world demand curve, however, that at a price of $10 total international import demand would equal 20 million barrels per day (Point B). There is thus an excess demand of 6 million barrels per day. The question is how to ration the artificially controlled supply of oil among many buyers. The easiest way would be to ration by price: let the price rise to, say, $14 per barrel (point

[6] An obvious exception to this rule was the politically motivated Arab boycott of oil sales to developed nations that they believed were too friendly to Israel during the Arab–Israeli war of 1973.

Figure 25.5
Seller price and quantity fixing: the problem of rationing and access

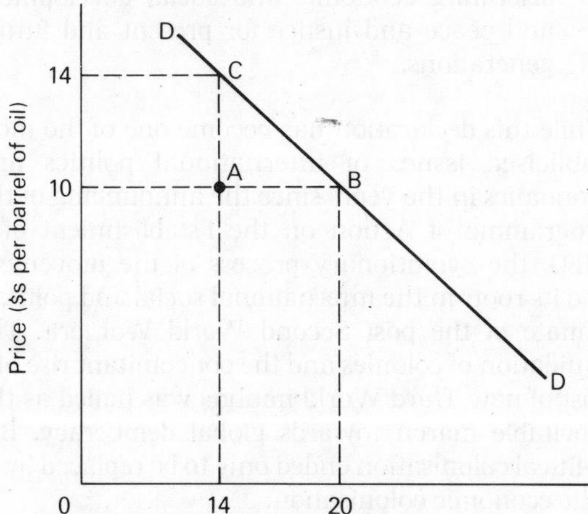

C) and let only those who can pay these exorbitant prices purchase the oil. But such blatant international economic extortion would be politically very dangerous and invite severe retaliation. Such economic warfare would be against the best interests of everyone concerned. An alternative way would be to engage in 'non-price' bargaining with potential buyers by agreeing to sell them the oil, or other vital resource, in return for economic, political and/or military considerations. A final alternative would be for the suppliers to decide arbitrarily who will be able to purchase the resource by means of export quotas or embargoes to different countries based on either political or economic motives.

Global interdependence and the new international economic order

Evidence of present inequities

The 1970s were also marked by a major challenge by Third World nations against an international economic order which they believed to be strongly stacked against their economic interests. Although we have identified and analysed the fundamental areas of contention in our chapters on international trade, private investment and foreign assistance, it is useful to reiterate the impressive and growing evidence that demonstrates how poor nations are being disadvantaged by existing market structures.[7]

First, there is the substantial imbalance in the distribution of international monetary reserves. Although Third World nations constitute over 70 per cent of the world's population, they received less than 4 per cent of the international reserves of $131 billion during the first half of the 1970s. Since rich nations control the creation and distribution of these reserves (e.g. through their own monetary expansion – mainly dollars – and through their effective control over actions of the International Monetary Fund), they have the power to manipulate these international financial assets to their own benefit.

Second, rich nations benefit disproportionately in the distribution of the value added of the products traded between themselves and the poor nations. Unlike the developed countries, Third World nations receive back only a small fraction of the final price obtained from international purchases of their products. The reason is simple: LDCs are often too weak and powerless to exercise any substantial control over the processing, shipping, and marketing of their primary products. Often they themselves must purchase back at substantially marked up prices the final products processed from their own raw materials.

Third, in order to protect and perpetuate their affluent life-styles, rich nations typically resort to all types of tariff and non-tariff protection of inefficient domestic industries in combination with restrictive practices. Thus, their rhetoric in support of the 'free' working of the international market mechanism belies the reality of their market management and control. Third World countries contend, therefore, that any competitive successes they may realise from international trade become nullified by the restrictive trade policies of protectionist industrial nations.

Fourth, most of the contracts, leases, and concessions that the multi-national corporations have negotiated in the past with the developing countries have unfairly benefited the MNC at the expense of the host country. Because of royalty payments, tax

[7] Mahbub ul Haq, 'A view from the south: the second phase of the north–south dialogue', in M. McLaughlin *et al.*, *The United States and World Development: Agenda 1979*, New York, Praeger, 1979, pp. 116–17.

concessions, transfer pricing, capital allowances, etc., LDC host governments contend that they receive only a small fraction of the benefits derived from the exploitation of their own natural resources by the MNCs.

Fifth, and finally, when it comes to critical economic decisions affecting the workings of the world economy, Third World nations have only a pro forma participation in the decision-making process. Their advice is rarely solicited by the industrial powers in key decisions relating to the future of the world economy. More importantly, although they represent a large majority of the world's population, developing countries have less than one-third of the total votes in such key international economic institutions as the World Bank and the International Monetary Fund. Their numerical majority in the United Nations General Assembly carries no influence on international economic decisions.

Given this background of international inequities in economic power and influence, Third World nations launched a major drive in the 1970s to try to reshape the world economic order to better serve their own interests. Like so many social and political movements, their rhetoric was often unnecessarily inflammatory and many charges and allegations were patently unfounded. But it is informative to trace the New International Economic Order (NIEO) movement and to highlight some of its key provisions. Although its origins can be traced back to the 1950s and early 1960s, the NIEO movement received its first formal political endorsement at the sixth Special Session of the UN General Assembly in 1974. Let us look briefly at how the NIEO emerged and what specifically it is all about.

Origins and content of the New International Economic Order (NIEO)

The United Nations General Assembly, in a Sixth Special Session convened in April 1974 in the immediate aftermath of the petroleum crisis, concluded its deliberations by committing itself

> to work urgently for the establishment of a new international economic order based on equity, sovereign equality, common interest and cooperation among all states, irrespective of their economic and social systems, which shall correct inequalities and redress existing injustices, make it possible to eliminate the widening gap between the developed and the developing countries and ensure steadily accelerating economic and social development and peace and justice for present and future generations.

While this declaration has become one of the most publicised issues of international politics and economics in the years since the announcing of the Programme of Action on the Establishment of a NIEO, the evolutionary process of the movement had its roots in the international social and political climate of the post Second World War era. The liquidation of colonies and the concomitant rise of a host of new Third World nations was hailed as the inevitable march towards global democracy. But political colonisation ended only to be replaced by *de facto* economic colonisation.

To this day, non-oil exporting LDCs account for less than one-fifth of the world's trade; and that figure decreases every year. Three-fourths of their exports are bound for the developed markets, often the former colonial power. Four-fifths of all export earnings are generated by about a dozen commodities, excluding oil. The developing countries account for less than 7 per cent of world industrial production and are particularly vulnerable to fluctuations in commodity pricing, inflation and recession. This, they claim, is the heritage of the colonial venture.

The effects of colonialism are also felt in financing. Foreign investment, often by a single capital-rich country and typically controlled by a foreign based multi-national corporation is seen as being an absolute necessity for rapid growth. But it can severely limit any sense of autonomy or freedom to choose. Developing countries are also dependent on foreign sources for technology in nearly all fields; about 98 per cent of the world's research and development capability is located in the developed world along with 94 per cent of all patents.

The pattern of colonial dependent development – economic, political and social – could not be set aside by fiat. The historical process which gave the majority of the world's population equal status in the realm of States left them still in a position of economic dependence. The newly granted sovereignty triggered a 'revolution of rising expectations'. Governments desiring rapid social and economic development set about ambitious plans for national development. Most followed the pattern set by the industrialised west and reviewed earlier in this book.

A series of programmes and targets in the early 1960s created a mood of optimism. The launching of the first UN Development Decade, the Alliance for Progress in 1961, and the Yaunde Convention in 1963 all fired expectations. By the late 1960s, however, enthusiasm waned as the unintended side-effects of rapid economic growth became evident – uncontrolled growth of cities, neglect of rural areas, and increasing social stratification, among others. Outward looking policies based upon the benefits of free international trade failed, as the nature of the primary commodity markets in relation to manufactured goods could not sustain the flow of foreign capital necessary for development projects. Inward looking policies of import substitution also failed largely because of inefficiencies of production, reliance on foreign capital investment and lack of intermediate goods.

The Second UN Development Decade of the 1970s therefore incorporated a more sober assessment of development prospects, but even these revised expectations were falling short. Then came the sudden and unexpected rise in Third World economic power in the wake of OPEC's 1973 oil embargo and subsequent pricing policies. These actions conclusively demonstrated that the world economy was truly a world, i.e. an interdependent, economy. It was in this light that the NIEO was created in which Third World countries attempted to utilise their newly found economic leverage to demand a new structure of international economic relations and a new set of rules affecting trade, industrialisation, transfer of technology and foreign assistance.

Four main points of the Programme for Action deserve special attention:

1. Renegotiating the debts of developing countries
2. Redefining the terms of trade and assuring greater access to developed country markets
3. Reforming the International Monetary Fund and its decision making process, and
4. Attaining UN official development assistance targets

1. Renegotiating the debts of developing countries

At the heart of most developing countries' plans for rapid economic progress is the need for a continuous flow and stable stock of foreign currency. By far the most serious drain on these stocks is the ever increasing debt burden. The Programme for Action calls for urgent action to 'mitigate adverse consequences for the current and future development of developing countries arising from the external burden of debt contracted on hard terms.' It further demands 'Debt renegotiation ... with a view to concluding agreements on debt cancellation, moratorium, rescheduling or interest subsidisation'.

The major concern is to halt the drain of foreign currency which debt repayment aggravates, often to the point where large percentages of foreign exchange earnings go solely to the repayment of past debt, thereby crippling current development projects. It is hoped that debt reorganisation would enable a developing country to continue debt servicing payments and so restore its position in international financial markets. On becoming a 'better risk', a developing country would then be better able to attract needed foreign private capital. One suggested method of reservicing was for the IMF to act as an international facility to 'finance part of the financial requirements of countries' deficits'.

2. Redefining the terms of trade and access to markets

The main purpose of these reforms related to trade and market access would be to secure a stable if not increasing amount of foreign currency. Faced with deteriorating terms of trade, the developing nations sought to stabilise their financial situation in several ways:

(*a*) through *indexation* – the tying of commodity prices to those of manufactured goods. This policy would arrest the tendency of primary commodities to lose ground to imported manufactured goods thus stabilising the real price of LDC exports

(*b*) through the creation of a *Common Fund* to help stabilise commodity price fluctuations of such products as tin, rubber, coffee and cocoa, partly by establishing *buffer stockpiles*. Although Third World countries initially demanded a $6 billion fund, in March 1979 agreement was reached with industrialised countries to establish such a fund with an initial subscription of $400 million.

(*c*) through *preferential treatment* of LDC exports by

a non-reciprocal lowering of tariff barriers by the developed West and Soviet 'Block' nations as well as reforms concerning non-tariff programmes, duties and restrictive import regulations, particularly those concerning processed goods.

With these reforms, the developing nations agree that they would be better able to compete with the developed countries and to expand and diversify their export capacities. Expansion and diversification would in turn allow for more rapid and continuous growth.

3. Reform of the IMF

Developing nations, like the end of a whip, are effected in the extreme by fluctuations in the developed economies upon which their development programmes ultimately depend. The proposal of the NIEO seeks to find a way to assure the stable and continuous flow of development assistance from the IMF whose major contributors are the OECD nations, and to be protected from the deteriorating effects of inflation and recession in the west.

In addition, the NEIO proposes a restructuring of the decision making process within the IMF to give a greater voice to the developing world when critical decisions are to be made.

4. Attaining UN official development aid targets

Set out in the objectives of the NIEO is the goal that each economically advanced nation should progressively increase its development assistance to 0.7 per cent of its GNP. In principle, this aid is to be untied and provided on a long and continuous basis. Several mechanisms have been put forward including the sale of gold held by the IMF and a development tax in developed countries. Major emphasis is on stable, concessional (i.e. grant or very soft) untied flows.

By 1979 only the Netherlands and Sweden met the 0.7 per cent GNP target. The US, Japan, Switzerland, Finland and Austria each contributed less than 0.3 per cent of their GNP. The average of all DAC countries was only 0.35 per cent of total GNP.

Observations on the NIEO

The programme of the NIEO is not a doctrine nor is it necessarily a document of confrontation. Rather, it is a proposal, a series of demands subject to negotiation. As with all documents, its true importance is not in its content but in how that content is used. The meanings and rhetoric, with which the Programme for Action overflows, can be changed, bent or 'interpreted'. At the time of writing this book, progress on the establishing of a NIEO *per se* has had little tangible result. In fact, many would claim that in the late 1970s and early 1980s, the old economic order was replaced not by a new order but by a new disorder. High oil prices, world-wide inflation and global recession simultaneously weakened the will of industrialised Western nations to be generous, while creating widening cracks in Third World solidarity. But just as with other major UN declarations, the NIEO does provide a rallying point, acting as a symbol of unity of purpose among the Third World nations in their increasing efforts for recognition by and often their struggle with the industrialised West.

Concluding remarks

Our discussion in this final chapter has touched upon many of the economic and non-economic manifestations of the growing interdependence of nations. We have seen that whereas a decade or so ago this interdependence was perceived primarily in terms of the dependence of poor nations on the rich ones, today developed countries are rapidly discovering that in a world of growing mineral and raw material scarcities, their future economic well-being will depend increasingly on the international economic policies of many Third World countries. Let there be no misunderstanding, however. The poor nations are and will continue to remain considerably more vulnerable to the economic events and policies of rich nations than the other way around. But their international bargaining power is undoubtedly on the rise.

The events of the 1970s and early 1980s underlined that the world is in the midst of a fundamental and profound economic transformation. For decades, the developed nations experienced continuous economic progress based on ever expanding industrial production and rising exports to each other and to the less developed countries. Raw material inputs were cheap and in plentiful supply. It was a 'buyers' market – i.e. sellers (mostly

LDCs had to compete vigorously with each other to find markets for their abundant raw materials. More simply, supply increases continuously exceeded demand expansion.

But today, for the first time since the Great Depression of the 1930s, there is a worldwide 'sellers' market for many goods – i.e. more buyers (demands) must compete with one another to obtain limited supplies. The growing list of scarce items goes beyond oil, food and fertiliser. It includes timber, minerals, cotton and man-made textiles among others. What will happen to countries, both rich and poor, in such a situation of scarcity?

One thing is clear. The new era of scarcity is bound to alter international economic relations. It may even lead to a major revision of the international economic system as first demanded by Third World nations in the form of the controversial Declaration and Action Programme on the Establishment of the New International Economic Order. Those countries rich in minerals and basic raw materials, both rich and poor, will discover either a greater or, at least, a new economic power. Those without such natural resource supplies, especially those in Third World countries, will find their already economically vulnerable position even weaker. As scarcities become more pronounced, there will be the ever present threat of 'economic warfare' among nations – i.e. individual resource-rich countries may use their resources as a weapon to extract exorbitant demands out of economically desperate resource-poor nations.

Our point here is that the question of how limited supplies of scarce resources, such as energy and certain raw materials, and commodities such as food grains are 'rationed' and who gets 'access' to these supplies will assume increasing economic and political importance in future years. The outcome will probably be determined by *both* economic and non-economic considerations. Over the last decade, the world has witnessed a rapid international shift, especially for the developed countries, from the basic question of how to get *access* to foreign markets (both developed and Third World) where finished products could be *sold*, to the very different present question of how to get *access* to markets (both less developed and developed) where raw materials can be *purchased*.

With this shifting world economic situation, the names and numbers of 'players' as well as the rules of the international economic power game have changed rapidly. No longer is it simply a competitive or co-operative game among a select group of rich countries vying for poor-country markets to sell their expensive manufactures in return for cheap primary products and natural resources. Resource-rich Third World nations will undoubtedly have a much greater impact on the future functioning and status of the world economy. Whether or not they act as spokesmen for the larger issues of Third World development on behalf of their less fortunate compatriots remains to be seen.

The crucial question is whether or not this emerging new economic interdependence among all nations, both developed and less developed, will lead to greater co-operation or greater conflict. The newly discovered resource and raw material bargaining potential of Third World nations may turn out to be the lever that has long been needed to make the more developed countries realise that the economic futures of both groups of nations are intimately linked. No longer can rich nations totally dominate the established international economic order without inviting harmful retaliation. Co-operation becomes essential. On the other hand, the potential for economic conflict will probably become even more pronounced if resource-rich developing countries attempt to over-exploit their real new strengths. Such a strategy may merely invite heavy retaliation from the still more powerful rich nations who, as we have seen, may begin to use food as a counter-weapon against the Third World's raw materials. The only feasible outcome of this emerging new international interdependence is one in which *everyone* either wins or loses. In the interdependent world of the last quarter of the twentieth century, there cannot in an ultimate sense be simultaneous winners and losers.

With each passing year, rich and poor nations alike share an increasingly common economic destiny. The world community must begin to realise that a 'new international economic order' is not only possible; it is *essential.* Such a new international order should be based on the principle that *each* nation and *each* individual's development is intimately bound to the development of *every* nation and *every* individual. The future of all mankind is linked more closely today than ever before, and all indications are that it will become even more interdependent in the coming decades.

Let us hope, therefore, that reason and good sense will prevail so that the 'First', 'Second' and 'Third' worlds can truly become part of ONE WORLD, forged together by a common economic destiny and guided by the humane principles of peace, brotherhood and mutual respect.

Concepts for review

curative v. preventive medicine	international collective bargaining
value transfers	indirect grain consumption
economic dependence	resource interdependence
internationalisation of production	
institutional transfers	oil revenue recycling
	buyers' v. sellers' markets
	non-renewable resources
world demand curve	
rationing and access	
economic conflict	

Questions for discussion

1. Some, mainly Third World, social scientists argue that the pursuit of a more self-reliant social and economic development strategy requires LDCs to minimise their *dependence* on and *vulnerability* to external forces and decisions emanating from the First and Second World. Comment on this argument, including in your discussion a summary statement of the meaning of concepts like dependence and vulnerability.
2. Summarise the various economic, technological, institutional, intellectual and cultural manifestations of Third World international dependence. Do you think that these forms of dependence are as serious as some assert? If so, what types of policies might LDC governments pursue to minimise their *negative* effects while maximising their *positive* contributions to development? Explain.
3. The 1970s ushered in an era in which, for the first time, developed nations began to recognise their growing dependence on and vulnerability to the policies of certain Third World groups of nations. Briefly describe this new source of developed country dependence. Can you think of areas other than oil where such dependence might emerge in the future?
4. The actions of OPEC in 1973–1974 dramatically demonstrated that co-ordinated action by Third World nations in the area of physical resource control could substantially benefit a diverse group of LDCs. Do you think the future will bring greater co-operation among Third World nations in the area of international collective bargaining? What are some of the major obstacles?
5. 1974 was also a year in which the first World Food Conference was held in Rome, bringing all nations together to discuss the world food crisis. Do you believe that there is such a global food crisis and, if so, what are its origins?
6. How are the world food and energy crises interrelated? What is meant by global 'food reserves'? Who controls these reserves and what position might Third World nations adopt with regard to assuring access to these reserves? Explain your answer.
7. In an era of growing mineral and raw material resource scarcities, problems of non-price rationing and access assume increasing importance while traditional allocations by the international pricing mechanism become relatively less important. Explain the meaning of, and comment on, this statement.
8. Can the growing objective of greater self-reliance in Third World nations be reconciled with the tendency towards greater global economic and non-economic interdependence? Explain.
9. What international attitudes and policies do you think your nation should adopt in light of the dramatic energy, food and price developments of the mid-1970s? Is there much room for a choice among alternative strategies given your country's size, history and /or stage of development? Explain your answer.

Further reading

In addition to current newspaper and magazine articles which almost every day have some piece on energy, food and/or inflation, a good, non-technical discussion of global interdependence can be found in: LESTER R. BROWN, *World Without Borders*, Random House, New York, 1972 and, more recently, BARBARA WARD, *Progress for a Small Planet*, W. W. Norton, New York, 1979.

For an analysis of the world food and energy crises

as these affect Third World nations see: JAMES P. GRANT, 'Energy Shock and the Development Prospect' in *Agenda for Action: 1974*. ODC, Praeger, New York, 1974 and LESTER R. BROWN and ERIK P. ECKHOLM, 'Food: growing global insecurity' in the same volume.

Among the many good books on the New International Economic Order, the following are most noteworthy: J. BHAGWATI, *The New International Economic Order*, MIT Press, Cambridge, Mass., 1976; J. SINGH, *The New International Economic Order*, Praeger, New York, 1977; E. LAZSLO *et al, The Objectives of the New International Economic Order*, Pergamon Press, New York, 1978; and, M. MCLAUGHLIN *et al, The United States and World Development: Agenda 1979*, Praeger, New York, 1979, especially Chapters 2 and 4 by John Sewell and Mahbub ul Haq.

Glossary

The following glossary of terms is designed to cover most of the major concepts and organisations, both regional and international, discussed in the text. Note that the *italicised* words which appear in any definition are themselves defined elsewhere in the glossary.

absolute (cost) advantage: if country A can produce more of a commodity with the same amount of real *resources* than country B (i.e. at a lower absolute *unit cost*), then country A is said to have an absolute cost advantage over country B. See also *comparative advantage*.

absolute poverty: a situation where a population or section of a population is able to meet only its bare *subsistence* essentials of food, clothing and shelter in order to maintain minimum *levels of living*. See also *international poverty line* and *subsistence economy*.

absorptive capacity: the ability of a country effectively to 'absorb' foreign private or public financial assistance – i.e. to use the funds in a productive manner.

adjustment assistance: the process of providing public financial assistance to workers and industries hurt by the importation of lower-cost competitive foreign goods. Such assistance allows them to 'adjust' to a new occupation during a transitional period.

'advanced' capitalism: *economic system* characterised by private ownership but with a major role played by the *public sector*. Most developed *market economies* like those in North America, Western Europe, Japan and Australia are examples of advanced capitalism.

A.I.D.: see *USAID*

age structure (of population): the age composition of a given population. For example in LDCs, the age structure of the population is typified by a large portion of population under 15 years old, a slightly smaller proportion aged between 15 and 45 years and a very small proportion above 45 years old.

aggregate consumer demand: that part of the total demand (*aggregate demand*) for goods and services in the economy attributed to the demands of households for consumer goods and services within a specific period, usually one year. See also *consumption*.

aggregate demand: a measure of the real purchasing-power of the community. Commonly referred to as the total effective demand or total expenditure, it normally comprises private *consumption* (C) private and public *investment* (I) government expenditure (G) plus net exports (X–M).

agrarian system: the pattern of land distribution, ownership and management; also the social and *institutional* structure of the agrarian economy. Many Latin American and Asian *agrarian systems* are characterised by concentrations of large tracts of land in the ownership of a few powerful *landlords*. *Rural development* in many LDCs may require extensive reforms of the existing *agrarian system*.

agricultural extension services: services offered to farmers usually by the government in the form of transmitting information, new ideas, methods and advice about, for instance, the use of fertilisers, control of pests and weeds, appropriate machinery, soil conservation methods, simple accounting, etc., in a bid to stimulate high *farm yields*.

agricultural labour productivity: the level of agricultural output per unit of labour input, usually measured as output per man-hour or man-year. It is very low in LDCs compared to developed countries. See also *labour productivity* and *farm yields*.

agricultural mechanisation: the extensive use of machinery in farm production activities thereby reducing the amount of labour input necessary to produce a given level of output. See also *labour-saving technological progress*.

'appropriate' technology: the 'right type' of *production technique*, i.e., one that employs *factors of production* in their 'least cost' or 'correct' proportions. For example, a technology that employs a higher proportion of labour relative to other factors in a labour abundant economy is in general more appropriate than one which uses smaller labour proportions relative to other factors. See also *factor price distortion* and *principle of economy*.

A.D.B.: **Asian Development Bank**: a regional development bank located in Bangkok whose major objective is to assist the development of Asian nations through the provision of *loans* and *technical assistance*.

asset ownership: the ownership of land and *physical capital* (factories, buildings, machinery, etc.) which are employed to generate income for their owners. The distribution of asset ownership is a major determinant of the distribution of personal income in any non-socialist society. See also *income distribution.*

autarky: a *closed economy* that attempts to be completely *self-reliant.*

average cost: the total cost of production of a commodity incurred by a producer during a period divided by the number of units of output produced in that period. See also *unit cost.*

average propensity to consume (APC): the proportion of total income expended on *consumption*; derived by dividing total consumption expenditure, C, by total income, Y, – i.e. APC = C/Y. See also *marginal propensity to consume.*

average propensity to save (*APS*): the proportion of total income, Y, that is set aside as *savings*, S – i.e. APS = S/Y. See also *marginal propensity to save* and *savings ratio.*

balance of payments (table): a summary statement of a nation's financial transactions with the outside world. See also *current account, capital account* and *cash account.*

balanced trade: a situation where the value of a country's exports and the value of its imports of visible items are equal.

barter transactions: the trading of goods directly for other goods in economies not fully monetised.

basic science and technological innovation (relationship between): basic science refers to a systematic, scientific and objective investigation aimed at bringing into existence 'new' knowledge or tools – while technological innovation has to do with the application of *inventions* of basic science (such as the new tools or knowledge) to perform tasks in a more efficient way.

'big push theory' of development: theory stating that all LDCs require to 'take off' into a period of self-sustaining *economic growth* is a massive investment programme designed to promote rapid *industrialisation* and the building up of *economic infrastructure.*

bilateral assistance (aid): see *foreign aid.*

birth rate, crude: number of children born alive each year, per thousand population – e.g. a crude birth rate of 20 per thousand is the same as a 2 per cent increase. See also *general fertility rate* and *death rate.*

black market: a situation in which there is illegal selling of goods at prices above a legal maximum set by the government. It occurs due to relative *scarcity* of the goods concerned and the existence of an excess demand for them at the established price. See also *rationing* and *exchange control.*

brain drain: the emigration of highly educated and skilled professional and technical manpower from the developing to the developed countries.

C.A.C.M.: Central American Common Market: an economic union formed in 1960 and consisting of five central American nations: Costa Rica, El Salvador, Guatemala, Honduras and Nicaragua.

capital: see *physical capital* and *human capital.*

capital account: that portion of a country's *balance of payments table* which shows the volume of *private foreign investment* and public *grants* and *loans* that flow into and out of a country over a given period – usually one year. See also *current account* and *cash account.*

capital accumulation: increasing a country's stock of real *capital*, i.e. net investment in fixed assets. To increase the production of capital goods necessitates a reduction in the production of consumer goods. 'Economic' development largely depends on the rate of capital accumulation.

capital-intensive technique: more capital-using process of production – i.e., that which uses a higher proportion of capital relative to other *factors of production* such as labour or land.

capital-output ratio: a ratio which shows the units of *capital* that are required to produce a unit of output over a given period of time. See *Harrod-Domar equation.*

capital-saving technological progress: arises as a result of some *innovation* which facilitates achievement of higher output levels using the same quantity of capital inputs.

capital stock: total amount of physical goods existing at a particular time which have been produced for use in the production of other goods (including services).

capitalism: see *pure market capitalism* and *advanced capitalism.*

cash account: the 'balancing' portion of a country's *balance of payments* table showing how cash balances (*foreign reserves*) and short term financial claims have changed in response to *current* and *capital account* transactions.

cash crops: crops produced entirely for the market, e.g. coffee, tea, cocoa, cotton, rubber, pyrethrum, jute, wheat, etc.

centralised planning: the determination by the State of what shall be produced and how *factors of production* shall be allocated among different uses. In a free enterprise economy consumers decide what shall be produced through their demands. While maximum amount of central planning is found in Soviet type economies, LDCs and developed countries do show increasing state planning in an attempt to maintain *full employment*. Central planning is done at the 'centre' and then dictated to various sections in the economy.

ceteris paribus: a Latin expression widely used in economics meaning 'all else being equal' – i.e., all other variables are held constant.

'character' of economic growth: the distributive implications of the process of *economic growth*; for example, participation in the growth process, *asset ownership*, etc. In other words, how that *economic growth* is achieved and who benefits.

Chinese People's Commune: a multi-purpose political, administrative and organisational unit covering the full range of economic, social and administrative activities necessary and feasible in a rural community. The People's Agricultural Communes are the basis of *rural development* in China. Communal ownership includes all the rural land, all means of agricultural production and commune-owned industries.

closed economy: an economy in which there are no foreign trade transactions or any other form of economic contacts with the rest of the world. See also *autarky* and *'inward-looking' development policies.*

cognitive skills: the ability to perceive and understand abstract concepts and think logically; to have knowledge and/or be aware of a range of relevant information.

collusion: an agreement among sellers of a commodity (or commodities) to set a common price and/or share their commodity market.

'Command' Socialism: a type of *economic system* where all *resources* are state-owned and their allocation and degree of utilisation are determined by the centralised decisions of planning authorities rather than by a *price system*. The USSR is the most outstanding example of a command socialist economy.

commercial policy: policy encompassing instruments of 'trade protection' employed by countries to foster industrial promotion, export diversification, employment creation and other desired development oriented strategies. They include *tariffs, physical quotas* and *subsidies.*

common market: a form of *economic integration* in which there is free internal trade, a common external tariff, plus the free movement of labour and capital among partner states. The *European Economic Community* (EEC) provides an example. See also *customs union* and *free trade area.*

comparative advantage: a country has a comparative advantage over another if in producing a commodity it can do so at a relatively lower *opportunity cost* in terms of the foregone alternative commodities that could be produced. Taking two countries, A and B, each producing two commodities, X and Y, country A is also said to have comparative advantage in the production of X if its *absolute advantage* margin is greater or its absolute disadvantage is less in X than in Y.

complementary resources: *factors of production* that are necessarily used along with others to produce a given output or to accomplish a specific task, e.g., man-hours of farm labour are complementary to a hectare of land in the production of maize; machinery and equipment are complementary to labour in the construction of a road, etc.

comprehensive plans: those *economic plans* that set their targets to cover all the major sectors of the national economy.

contraints: see *economic constraint.*

consumer sovereignty: the notion central to *'Western' economic theory* that consumers determine what and how much shall be produced in an economy. The free play of the *price system* and *market mechanism* is then assumed to equilibrate consumer demand with producer supply of that commodity.

consumption: that part of total *national income* devoted to expenditure on *final goods* and services by individual consumers during a given period of time, typically one year. Total private consumption is assumed to be directly related to the level of aggregate personal income.

consumption 'diseconomies': problems (costs) that occur to individuals or society as a whole as a result of the unpopular consumption habits of another individual. Examples include alcoholism, poor individual hygiene, drug addiction, etc.

consumption 'economies': advantages (benefits) that accrue to individuals or society as a whole as a result of increases in the consumption of certain types of goods or services by other individuals – e.g., education, health care, etc.

consumption possibility line: in international *free trade* theory a locus of points showing the highest possible consumption combinations that can be attained as a result of trade. Graphically, the consumption possibility line is represented by the international price line at its tangency to the domestic *production possibility curve* of a country.

cost/benefit analysis: a basic tool of economic analysis in which the actual and potential *costs* (both *private* and *social*) of various economic decisions are weighed against actual and potential *private* and *social benefits*. Those decisions or projects yielding the highest benefit/cost ratio are usually thought to be most desirable. See also *project appraisal*.

cost-push inflation: *inflation* that results primarily from the upward pressure of production costs, usually because of rising raw material prices (e.g., oil) or excessive wage increases resulting from trade union pressures. See also *demand-pull* and *structural inflation*.

current account: that portion of a *balance of payments table* which portrays the market value of a country's 'visible' (e.g. commodity trade) and 'invisible' (e.g. shipping services) exports and imports with the rest of the world. See also *capital account* and *cash account*.

curative medicine: medical care which focuses on curing rather than preventing disease. Requires extensive availability of hospitals and clinics. See also *preventive medicine*.

customs union: a form of *economic integration* in which two or more nations agree to free all internal trade while levying a common external *tariff* on all non-member countries. See also *common market* and *free trade area*.

death rates, crude: yearly number of deaths per thousand population – e.g., an annual crude death rate of 15 per thousand or 1.5 per cent of the population. See also *birth rate* and *infant mortality*.

decentralised planning: regionalised or sectoral planning as opposed to planning at the centre. See *centralised planning*.

decile: a 10 per cent proportion of any numerical quantity – e.g., a population divided into deciles would be one which was divided into 10 equal numerical groups. See also *quintile*.

decreasing costs: if *increasing returns* exist then a given proportionate change in output will require a smaller proportionate change in quantities of factor inputs thus implying a fall in cost per unit of output because input costs will be expected to rise less than proportionately with output. In short, a fall in *average costs* of production as output expands.

deficit expenditure: amount by which planned government expenditure exceeds realised tax revenues. *Deficit expenditure* is normally financed by borrowed funds and its major object is to stimulate economic activity by increasing the purchasing power within an economy (i.e., its *aggregate demand*).

demand curve: graphical representation of the quantities of a commodity or resource that would be bought over a range of prices at a particular time, when all other prices and incomes are held constant. When demand curves of all consumers in the market are aggregated a 'market demand' curve is derived showing the total amount of the good which consumers are willing to purchase at each price.

demand-pull inflation: *inflation* that arises because of the existence of excess Keynesian *aggregate demand* – i.e., when total effective demand exceeds the productive capacity (aggregate supply) of the economy.

demographic transition: the phasing out process of *population growth rates* from a virtually stagnant growth stage characterised by high *birth* and *death rates*, through a rapid growth stage with high birth rates and low death rates, to a stable, low growth stage in which both birth and death rates are low.

demonstration effects: the effects of transfers of alien ways of life upon nationals of a country. Such effects are mainly cultural and attitudinal in nature, e.g., *consumption* habits, modes of dressing, patterns of education, leisure and recreation, etc.

dependence: a corollary of *dominance*; a situation where the LDCs have to rely on developed country domestic and international *economic policy* to stimulate their own *economic growth*. *Dependence* can also mean that the LDCs adopt DC education systems, their technology, economic and political systems, attitudes, *consumption* patterns, dress, etc.

dependency burden: that proportion of the total population of a country falling in the ages of 0–15 and 64+ which is economically unproductive and therefore not counted in the labour force. In many LDCs the population under the age of 15 accounts for almost as much as half of the total population thus posing a burden to the generally small productive labour force and to the government which has to allocate *resources* on such things as education, public health, and housing for the *consumption* of people who don't contribute to production.

devaluation: a lowering of the 'official' *exchange rate* between one country's currency and those of the rest of the world – e.g., a ten per cent devaluation of the Kenya shilling would entail a change from its present rate of approximately shs. 8.2 per dollar to shs. 9.02 per dollar.

development (meaning of): the process of improving the quality of all human lives. Three equally important aspects of development are: (1) raising people's living levels – i.e., their incomes and *consumption* levels of food, medical services, education, etc. – through 'relevant' *economic growth processes*, (2) creating conditions conducive to the growth of people's *self-esteem* through the establishment of social, political and *economic systems* and *institutions* which promote human dignity and respect, and (3) increasing people's *freedom to choose* by enlarging the range of their choice variables – e.g., increasing varieties of consumer goods and services.

development banks: specialised public and private *financial intermediaries* providing medium and long-term credit for the creation or expansion of industrial enterprises in developing countries.

development plan: the documentation by a government planning agency of the current national economic conditions, proposed public expenditures, likely developments in the *private sector*, a macro-economic projection of the economy, and a review of government policies. Many LDCs publish five-year *development plans* to announce their economic objectives to their citizens and others.

diminishing returns: the principle that if one *factor of production* is fixed and constant and additions of other factors are combined with it, the *marginal productivity* of *variable factors* will eventually decline. The major assumptions of this principle are that at least one factor is fixed, units of the variable factors are identical, and there exists no *technical progress*. For example, if a fixed land area is combined with constant additions of labour using simple tools to produce coffee, output will initially increase but as more and more labour units are added, average output per man-hour/year declines as also do marginal additions to total product. See also *'surplus' labour*.

disguised underemployment (unemployment): a situation in which available work tasks are split among *resources* (typically labour) such that they all seem fully employed, but in reality much of their time is spent in unproductive activities.

disposable income: the income that is available to households for spending and saving after personal income taxes have been deducted.

division of labour: allocation of tasks among the workers such that each one engages in tasks that he performs most efficiently. *Division of labour* promotes worker specialisation and thereby raises overall *labour productivity*. It has its historical origins in Adam Smith's *Wealth of Nations*.

dominance: in international affairs, a situation in which the developed countries have much greater power than the less developed countries in decisions affecting important international economic issues – e.g., the prices of agricultural commodities and raw materials in world markets. See also *vulnerability* and *dependence*.

doubling time (of population): period that a given population size takes to increase itself by its present size. *Doubling time* is approximated by dividing any numerical growth rate into 72 – e.g. a population growing at 2 per cent per year will double in size approximately every 36 years.

dualism: the coexistence in one place of two situations or phenomena (one desirable and the other not) which are mutually exclusive to different groups of a society – e.g., extreme poverty and affluence, modern and traditional economic sectors, growth and stagnation, university education among a few and mass illiteracy, etc.

dual price system: government-operated pricing mechanism whereby producers of, say, a staple crop are paid a different price from the one consumers (mostly urban consumers) are charged. In short, any two-price system, one for sellers and the other for buyers.

EAC: East African Community: a now defunct economic grouping of the three East African countries – Kenya, Uganda and Tanzania – established by the Treaty of East African Cooperation of 1967 following the Philip Commission Report of 1966. Cooperation took the form of running jointly a number of common public services by the three governments (railways, airways, ocean and lake transport, research) and a *customs union* in which there was internal *free trade* and a common external *tariff* on imports. Cooperation in East Africa dates back to colonial times.

ECA: Economic Commission for Africa: a regional branch of the *United Nations'* system located in Addis Ababa, Ethiopia, and devoted to the analysis of economic developments and trends in African nations. Statistical bulletins and technical analyses of economic trends in individual countries and groups of countries in various regions of Africa are regularly published. See also *ECLA* and *ESCAP*.

ECLA: Economic Commission for Latin America: A regional branch of the *United Nations'* system located in Santiago, Chile, and devoted to the regular publication of technical and statistical analyses of economic trends in Latin America as a whole and in individual Latin American nations. See also *ECA* and *ESCAP*.

economic 'constraint': a barrier to the attainment of a set target (e.g. *economic growth*) in a particular period of time. For example, *physical capital* has long been thought of as the major 'constraint' on *economic growth* in LDCs.

economic disincentives (for fertility reduction):

economic disadvantages (costs) and risks of having small families, e.g. parents' insecurity during their old age (no children or too few children to care for them), shortages of parents' farm labour supply, etc.

economic efficiency (in production): in traditional *Western economic theory*, a situation in which all *resources* are fully employed and no *resource* can be reallocated to another use without some loss of output. This condition is satisfied when the *marginal products* of all real *resources* in use are equal. See also *optimisation* and *economy, principles of.*

economic good: any commodity or service which yields 'utility' to an individual or community and which must be paid for in money terms in a monetary economy, or 'in kind' in a non-monetary economy.

economic growth: the steady process by which the productive capacity of the economy is increased over time to bring about rising levels of *national income*. Rapid economic *growth* has been a major preoccupation of economists, planners and politicians in LDCs in the last two or three decades because it has been thought to be a major precondition determining *levels of living.* Emphasis is now shifting to problems of *income inequality, poverty* and *unemployment.*

economic incentives (for fertility reduction): economic motivations aimed at encouraging parents to limit their families to a specified size. Such economic incentives include: free or subsidised education for children of families within the specified family size, free or subsidised medical treatment for small families, high wages for mothers with few children, etc.

economic infrastructure: the underlying amount of *capital accumulation* embodied in roads, railways, waterways, airways and other forms of transportation and communications plus water supplies, financial institutions, electricity and public services such as health, education, etc. The level of infrastructural development in a country is a crucial factor determining the pace and diversity of economic development.

economic integration: the merging to various degrees of the economies and economic policies of two or more countries in a given region. See also *common market, customs union, free trade area, trade creation* and *trade diversion.*

economic plan: a written document containing government policy decisions on how *resources* shall be allocated among different uses in order to attain a targeted rate of *economic growth* over a certain period of time. See also *economic planning, centralised planning, planning model* and *plan implementation.*

economic planning: a deliberate and conscious attempt by the State to formulate decisions on how the *factors of production* shall be allocated among different uses or industries, thereby determining how much of total *goods* and services shall be produced in the ensuing period(s). See also *economic plan* and *centralised planning.*

economic policy: statement of objectives and the methods of achieving these objectives (policy instruments) by government, political party, business concern, etc. Some examples of government economic objectives are maintaining *full employment*, achieving a high rate of *economic growth*, reducing *income* and regional development *inequalities*, maintaining price stability, etc. Policy instruments include fiscal policy, monetary and financial policy and legislative controls (e.g. price and wage control, rent control, etc.).

economic principles: basic concepts of economic theory which provide the tools of economic analysis. Examples of economic principles are the principle of substitution, the *principle of economy*, the principle of *diminishing returns*, the concept of *scarcity*, etc.

economising spirit: the act of minimising the real *resource* costs of producing any level of output. In general, allocating scarce *resources* with great care. See also the *optimisation principle.*

economic system: the organisational and institutional structure of an economy including the nature of *resource* ownership and control (i.e. private v. public ownership and control). Major economic systems include *subsistence economy, pure market capitalism, advanced capitalism, market socialism, command socialism* and *'mixed' systems* that characterise most LDCs.

economic 'variable': a measure of economic activity such as *income, consumption* and *price* that can take on different quantitative values. Variables are classified either as 'dependent' or 'independent' in accordance with the economic model being used.

economies of scale: these are economies of growth resulting from expansion of the scale of productive capacity of a firm or industry leading to increases in its output and decreases in its cost of production per unit of output.

economy, principle of: see *principle of economy.*

ECOWAS: Economic Community of West African States: A recently formed (1975) economic community of 15 West African countries – 9 French, 5 English and 1 Portuguese – with a total population of over 125 million and a land area of 6.5 million square miles. It is the largest example of *economic integration* in Africa and includes such countries as Nigeria, Ghana, Upper Volta, Senegal, Niger and Chad.

educational certification: the phenomenon by which particular jobs require specified levels of education. Applicants must produce 'certificates' of such completed schooling in the *formal educational system*.

EEC: European Economic Community: a European economic federation (*common market*) established under the Treaty of Rome in 1957 with a view of abolishing inter-state *tariffs* within the federation in order to increase trade volume (and hence *GDP*) of member states. The current membership of EEC includes: West Germany, Luxembourg, Great Britain, Italy, Denmark, Austria, Greece, Switzerland, France and the Netherlands.

elasticity of demand: see *price elasticity of demand* and *income elasticity of demand*.

elasticity of factor substitution: a measure of the degree of 'substitutability' between *factors of production* in any given *production process* when relative factor prices change.

employment 'gap': (1) *deflationary*: amount by which employment at equilibrium national output falls short of employment that would obtain at capacity output. (2) *inflationary*: amount by which prices at equilibrium national output exceed that which would obtain at capacity or *potential output* level. The employment gap is a major *Keynesian* concept but one that has limited relevance for many LDCs.

enclave economies: those economies found among LDCs in which there exist small pockets of economically developed regions (often due to the presence of colonial or foreign firms engaged in plantation and mining activities) with the rest of the larger outlying areas experiencing very little progress. See also *dualism*.

equilibrium price: the price at which the quantity demanded of a good is exactly equal to the quantity supplied. It is often referred to as the price at which the market clears itself. See also *price system*.

equilibrium wage rate: the wage rate that equates the demand for and supply of labour – i.e. the wage at which all the people who want to work at that wage are able to find jobs and also at which the employers are able to find all the workers they desire to employ. In other words, it is the wage rate that clears the labour market.

ESCAP: Economic Commission for Asia and the Pacific: a regional branch of the *United Nations'* system located in Bangkok, Thailand, and devoted to the technical and statistical analysis of economic developments and trends in the diverse countries of Asia and the Far East. See also *ECA* and *ECLA*.

exchange control: a governmental policy designed to restrict the outflow of domestic currency and prevent a worsened *balance of payments* position by controlling the amount of *foreign exchange* which can be obtained or held by domestic citizens. Often results from *overvalued exchange rates*.

exchange rate: the rate at which central banks will exchange one country's currency for another (i.e. the 'official' rate). Rates are normally expressed in terms of dollars – e.g. X pesos per dollar. See also *overvalued exchange rate* and *devaluation*.

export dependence: a situation where a country relies heavily on exports as the major source of finance needed for carrying out development activities. This is the situation of many LDCs who must export *primary products* to earn valuable *foreign exchange*.

export incentives: public *subsidies*, tax rebates and other kinds of financial and non-financial measures designed to promote a greater level of economic activity in export industries.

export promotion: purposeful governmental efforts to expand the volume of a country's exports through *export incentives* and other means in order to generate more *foreign exchange* and improve the *current account* of its *balance of payments*.

external diseconomies of production: these are the increased costs that a single firm or a group of firms faces in increasing its output beyond a certain level, because of problems for which the firm or the group of firms concerned is not responsible. Such diseconomies include: increases in cleaning costs due to pollution of other firms, transport delays due to too many vehicles on the road, etc.

external economies of production: increases in output (or decreases in costs) of an individual firm over a certain range of production and plant scale due to production advantages it derives from the expansion activities of other firms – e.g. its use of new equipment that has been invented by an outside group of growing firms. See also *internal economies of production*.

factors of production: *resources* or *inputs* required to produce a *good* or service. Basic categories of *factors of production* are: land, labour and *capital*.

factor endowment trade theory: the neo-classical model of *free trade* which postulates that countries will tend to specialise in the production of those commodities which make use of their abundant *factors of production* (land, labour, *capital*, etc.). They can then export the surplus in return for imports of the products produced by factors with which they are not sufficiently endowed. The basis for trade arises because of differences in relative factor prices and thus domestic price ratios as a result of differences in factor supplies. See also *comparative advantage*.

factor mobility: the unrestricted transference or free voluntary movement of *factors of production* between different uses and geographic locations.

factor-price distortions: situations in which *factors of production* are paid prices which do not reflect their true *scarcity* values (i.e. their competitive market prices) because of institutional arrangements which tamper with the free working of market forces of supply and demand. In many LDCs the prices paid for *capital* and *intermediate producer goods* are very low because they are either duty-free or are subject to very low rates of duty, while labour is paid a wage above its competitive market value because of trade union and political pressures. *Factor-price distortions* can lead to the use of inappropriate techniques of production. See also *neo-classical price incentive model*.

factor price equalisation: in *factor endowment trade theory* the proposition that because countries trade at a common international price ratio, factor prices among trading partners will tend to be equalised assuming identical technological possibilities for all commodities across countries. The prices of the more abundantly utilised *resources* will tend to rise while those of the relatively scarce factors fall. Over time, international factor payments will tend towards equality – e.g. real wage rates for labour will be the same in Britain or Botswana.

'false paradigm' model of underdevelopment: the proposition that *Third World* countries have failed to develop because their development strategies (usually given to them by Western economists) have been based on an 'incorrect' model of development – one that overstressed *capital accumulation* without giving due consideration to the necessary social and *institutional* changes.

family planning programmes: public programmes designed to help parents to plan and regulate their family size in accordance with their ability to support such a family. Programme usually includes supply of contraceptives to adult population, education on the use of birth control devices, mass media propaganda of benefits derived from smaller families, etc.

FAO: Food and Agricultural Organisation: a department of *United Nations* based in Rome, Italy, whose major concern is to expand world food production in order to meet food intake requirements of the growing world population. FAO researches into modern methods of increasing *farm yields* and educates farmers on their use. It also works in collaboration with such bodies as the World Food Council, Overseas Food Organisation, etc.

farm yields: a quantitative measure of the productivity of a given unit of farm land in producing a particular commodity – usually measured in terms of output per hectare (e.g. so many kilos of rice per hectare).

farmer cooperatives: associations of farmers mainly engaged in cash crop production to enable them to reap the benefits of *economies of scale*. Large tracts of farm land are jointly owned and operated by the cooperative with profits being shared in accordance with a pre-arranged pattern of distribution (not necessarily equal for all farm families).

fertility rate, general: yearly number of children born alive per thousand women within the child-bearing age bracket (normally between the age of 15 and 49 years). See also *crude birth rate*.

final goods: commodities that are *consumed* to satisfy wants rather than passed on to further stages of production. Whenever a *final good* is not *consumed* but is used as an *input* instead, it becomes an *intermediate good*.

financial intermediary: any financial institution, public or private, which serves to channel loanable funds from savers to borrowers. Examples include commercial banks, savings banks, *development banks*, finance companies, etc.

First World: the now economically advanced *capitalist* countries of Western Europe, North America, Australia, New Zealand and Japan. These were the first countries to experience sustained and long-term *economic growth*.

fixed inputs: *inputs* which do not vary as output varies. A hectare of land for example is a *fixed input* on a small family farm because it can be used to produce different quantities of, say, maize output without its size changing. See also *variable inputs*.

fixed input coefficients: a phenomenon in the economics of production in which any level of output requires a fixed ratio of *factor* inputs – e.g. 3 units of labour are always required to produce 10 units of output so that in order to produce 50 units of output, 15 units of labour will be required. The labour (input) coefficient (L/Q) in this case would be 0.3 ($= \frac{3}{10}$).

flexible institutions: *institutions* that are self-responsive or can be made to respond to changing *development* requirements. For example, a system of land tenure that can adjust itself or be adjusted to allow for a more equitable redistribution of land would represent such a flexible institution. See also *rigid institutions.*

flexible wages: wages that adjust upwards or downwards depending on the directions of forces of demand for and supply of labour – e.g. if the demand for labour increases (decreases) or its supply decreases (increases), all other things being equal, wages will increase (decrease).

foreign aid: the international transfer of public funds in the form of *loans* or *grants* either directly from one government to another (*bilateral assistance*) or indirectly through the vehicle of a *multilateral assistance agency* like *IBRD (World Bank).* See also *tied aid.*

foreign exchange: claims on a country by another held in the form of currency of that country. Foreign exchange system enables one currency to be exchanged for (or be converted into) another, thus facilitating trade between countries. See also *exchange rate* and *foreign reserves.*

foreign reserves: the total value (usually expressed in dollars) of all gold, dollars and *Special Drawing Rights (SDRs)* held by a country as both a reserve and a fund from which international payments can be made.

'formal' educational system: the organised and 'accredited' school system with qualified teachers, standard curricula, regular academic years and recognised certification. Encompasses primary, secondary and tertiary educational institutions. See also *non-formal educational system.*

free market: see *pure market capitalism, price system* and *market mechanism.*

free trade: trade in which goods can be imported and exported without any barriers in the form of *tariffs, physical quotas* or any other kind of restriction.

free trade area: a form of *economic integration* in which there exists free internal trade among member countries but each member is free to levy different external *tariffs* against non-member nations. See also *customs union, common market* and *LAFTA.*

freedom to choose (of a society): a situation in which a society has at its disposal a variety of alternatives from which to satisfy its wants. See also *development* (meaning of).

full employment: (1) a situation where everyone who wants to work at the prevailing wage rate is able to get a job, or alternatively (2) a situation whereby some job seekers cannot get employment at the going wage rate but *open unemployment* has been reduced to a desired level, e.g. 2 per cent.

functional distribution of income: the distribution of income to *factors of production* without regard to the ownership of the factors. See also *factor shares* and *marginal productivity.*

gains from trade: the increase in output and *consumption* resulting from specialisation in production and *free trade* with other economic units including persons, regions or countries.

GATT: General Agreement on Tariffs and Trade: an international body set up in 1947 to probe into the ways and means of reducing tariffs on internationally traded goods and services. Between 1947 and 1962 GATT held about seven conferences but met only with moderate success. Its major success was achieved in 1967 during the 'Kennedy Round' of talks when tariffs on primary commodities were drastically slashed.

Gini coefficient: an aggregate numerical measure of *income inequality* ranging from zero (perfect equality) to one (perfect inequality). It is graphically measured by dividing the area between the perfect equality line and the *Lorenz curve* by the total area lying to the right of the equality line in a Lorenz diagram. The higher the value of the coefficient the higher the *inequality of income distribution* and the lower it is the more equitable the *distribution of income.* See also *Lorenz curve* and *'skewed' distribution of income.*

good: see *economic goods*; also *final goods.*

grant: an outright *transfer payment* usually from one government to another (*foreign aid*) – i.e. a gift of money or *technical assistance* which does not have to be repaid. See also *loans* and *tied aid.*

green revolution: the revolution in grain production associated with the scientific discovery of new hybrid seed varieties of wheat, rice and corn which have resulted in high *farm yields* in many LDCs.

gross domestic product (GDP): the total monetary value calculated at market prices of all final *goods* and services produced in an economy over a given period of time, typically one year. See also *gross national product, national income* and *national expenditure.*

gross national product (GNP): the sum total of all incomes that accrue to the *factors of production* in a particular geographical region over a given time period – i.e. *GDP* 'plus' all incomes that accrue to residents of that region from their investments in foreign countries 'less' incomes that accrue to foreigners as a result of their investments in that region.

growth: see *economic growth.*

'growth poles': more economically and socially advanced regions than others around them – e.g. urban centres *vis-à-vis* rural areas in LDCs. Large scale economic activity tends to cluster around such 'growth poles' due to economies of agglomeration – i.e. lower costs of locating an industry in an area where much *economic infrastructure* has been built up.

'hard' loan: see *loans.*

Harrod–Domar equation: this is a functional economic relationship in which the growth rate of *gross domestic product (g)* depends directly on the national *savings ratio (s)* and inversely on the national *capital/output ratio (k)* so that it is written as $g = s/k$. The equation takes its name from a synthesis of analyses of growth process by two economists (Sir Roy Harrod of Britain and E. V. Domar of the USA).

hidden momentum (of population growth): a dynamic latent process of population increase that continues even after a fall in *birth rates* because of a large youthful population that widens the population's parent base. Fewer children per couple in the succeeding few generations will not mean a smaller or stable population size because at the same time there will be a much larger number of childbearing couples. Thus a given population will not stabilise until after two or so generations.

hidden unemployment (of labour): a situation in which labour is fully employed but is unproductive either because the workers are incapacitated, sick, uneducated, hungry, unmotivated or are using unsuitable tools in their tasks. See also *underemployment* and *disguised unemployment.*

hybrid seeds: seeds produced by cross-breeding plants or crops of different species through scientific research. See also *green revolution.*

human capital: productive *investments* embodied in human beings. These include skills, abilities, ideals, health, etc., that result from expenditures on education, on-the-job training programmes and medical care. See also *physical capital.*

IBRD: International Bank for Reconstruction and Development: (*World Bank*): an international financial institution forming part of the *United Nations* system and based in Washington DC (United States). One of its main objectives is to provide 'development funds' to needy *Third World* nations (especially the poorest countries) in the form of *interest*-bearing *loans* and *technical assistance.* The *World Bank* operates with funds borrowed primarily from rich nations but increasingly from *OPEC* countries as well. See also *IDA.*

IDA: International Development Association: an international body set up in 1960 to assist the *World Bank* (*IBRD*) in its efforts to promote economic development of the underdeveloped countries by providing additional *capital* on a low *interest* basis (i.e. through *'soft' loans*) especially to the poorest of the poor developing countries.

IFC: International Finance Corporation: an international financial institution that was set up in 1956 to supplement the efforts of *World Bank* in providing development *capital* to private enterprises (mainly industrial) of the underdeveloped countries.

ILO: International Labour Organisation: one of the *United Nations* functional organisations based in Geneva whose central task is to look into problems of world manpower supply, its training, utilisation, domestic and international distribution, etc. Its aim in this endeavour is to increase 'world output' through maximum utilisation of available human *resources* and thus improve *levels of living* for people.

IMF: International Monetary Fund: an autonomous international financial institution that originated from the Bretton Woods Conference of 1944. Its main purpose is to regulate the international monetary exchange system that also evolved at the same conference but has since been modified. In particular, one of the central tasks of *IMF* is to control fluctuations in *exchange rates* of world currencies in a bid to alleviate severe *balance of payments* problems.

imperfect competition: a market situation or structure in which there are relatively few buyers and sellers of similar but differentiated products. Examples include *monopoly* and *oligopoly.* See also *perfect competition.*

imperfect market: a market where the theoretical assumptions of *perfect competition* are violated by the existence of, for example, a small number of buyers and sellers, barriers to entry, non-homogeneity of products and imperfect information. The three imperfect markets commonly analysed in economic theory are *monopoly, oligopoly* and monopolistic competition.

import substitution: a deliberate effort to promote the emergence and expansion of domestic industries by replacing major imports such as textiles, shoes, household appliances, etc., with locally produced substitutes. Requires the imposition of protective *tariffs* and physical *quotas* to get the new industry started. See also *infant industry.*

income distribution: the way in which total *national income* is divided among households and/or major *factors of production* in the economy. See also *functional distribution of income* and *size distribution of income.*

income effect: the implicit change in *real income* resulting from the effects of a change in a commodity's price on the quantity demanded.

income elasticity of demand: the responsiveness of the quantity demanded of a commodity to changes in the consumer's income, measured by the proportionate change in quantity divided by the proportionate change in income.

income 'gap': the gap between the incomes accruing to the bottom poor and the top rich sectors of a population. The wider the gap the higher the inequality in the *income distribution.* Also used to refer to the gap between *income per capita* levels in rich and poor nations.

income in 'kind': a household's or firm's income in the form of goods or services instead of in the form of money. Payments in a *barter* and *subsistence economy* are mainly made in 'kind'.

income inequality: the existence of disproportionate distribution of total *national income* among households whereby the share going to rich persons in a country is far greater than that going to the poorer persons (a situation common to most LDCs). This is largely due to differences in the amount of income derived from ownership of property and to a lesser extent the result of differences in earned income. Inequality of personal incomes can be reduced by steeply *progressive income* and *wealth taxes.* See also *Gini coefficient* and *Lorenz curve.*

income per capita: total *GNP* of a country divided by the total population. Per capita income is often used as an economic indicator of the *levels of living* and *development.* It, however, can be a 'biased' index because it takes no account of *income distribution* and the ownership of the *assets* which are employed to generate part of that income.

increasing returns: a disproportionate increase in output which results from a change in the scale of production. In traditional economic theory, increasing returns (and thus *decreasing costs*) will occur until a certain output level has been reached and thereafter *diminishing returns* (increasing costs) are assumed to set in. Some industries (e.g. utilities, transportation) are characterised by increasing returns over a wide range of output. This leads to *monopoly* situations. See also *economies of scale.*

increasing opportunity cost: in a state of *full employment* the shifting away of increasing amounts of productive *resources* from the production of one commodity, e.g. automobiles, to another, e.g. food, involves an *opportunity cost.* The *opportunity cost* of producing a given increase in automobiles is the amount of food production foregone. As more and more cars are produced at the expense of food there will be *increasing opportunity costs* of additional car production. This gives rise to the phenomenon of the 'concave' *production-possibility curve* in economic theory.

indirect taxes: taxes levied on goods purchased by the consumer (and exported by the producer) for which the taxpayer's liability varies in proportion to the quantity of particular goods purchased or sold. Examples of indirect taxes are customs duties (*tariffs*), excise duties, sales taxes and export duties. The indirectness of such taxes arises because the consumer or producer can avoid paying them by not consuming or producing the taxed goods. They are a major source of tax revenue for most LDCs as they are easier to administer and collect than *direct taxes* (e.g. income and property taxes).

industrialisation: the process of building up a country's capacity to 'process' raw materials and to manufacture goods for *consumption* or further production – e.g. setting up firms and acquiring plant and equipment (including *human capital*) to process agricultural products and extracted raw materials or to make manufactures such as radios, cars, tinned foods, ploughs, clothes, etc.

infant industry: a term given to a newly established industry usually set up behind the protection of a *tariff* barrier as part of a policy of *import substitution.* Once the industry is no longer an 'infant', the protective tariffs are supposed to disappear but they often do not.

infant mortality: the deaths among children between birth and one year of age. *Infant mortality rate* measures the number of these deaths per 1 000 live births.

inferior good: a good for which demands fall as consumer incomes rise. The *income elasticity of demand* of an inferior good is thus negative.

inflation: a period of above normal general price increases as reflected, for example, in the consumer and wholesale price indices. More generally, the phenomenon of rising prices. See also *cost-push, demand-pull* and *structural inflation.*

informal sector: that part of the urban economy of LDCs characterised by small competitive individual or family firms, petty retail trade and services, *labour-intensive* methods of doing things, low *levels of living*, poor working conditions, high *birth rates*, low levels of health and education, etc. But it is often thought of as providing a major source of urban employment and economic activity.

infrastructure: *see economic infrastructure.*

innovation: the application of *inventions* of new production processes and methods into production activities as well as the introduction of new products. *Innovations* may also include the introduction of new social and institutional methods of organisation and management commensurate with modern ways of conducting economic activities. See also *inventions* and *modernisation ideals.*

inputs: goods and services – e.g. raw materials, man-hours of labour, etc. – used in the process of production. See also *factors of production* and *resources.*

institutions: norms, rules of conduct and generally accepted ways of doing things. **Social** institutions refer to well defined and formal organisations of society that govern the way that society operates – e.g. class system, private v. communal ownership, educational system, etc., while **economic** institutions include the banking systems, the mechanism of resource allocation, the *economic system* and general role of public v. private activity. Finally, **political** institutions refer to the systems that govern the operations of the government of a particular society – e.g. formal power structures, political parties (e.g. Socialist and Democratic parties), mechanism of getting into power, etc.

integrated rural development: the broad spectrum of rural development activities encompassing the simultaneous fostering of small-farmer agricultural progress; improvement of *levels of living* (incomes, employment, education, health and nutrition, housing and other social services) for the rural people; reducing inequality in the distribution of rural incomes and urban–rural imbalances in incomes and economic opportunities; and the capacity of the rural sector to sustain and accelerate the pace of these improvements over time.

integration: see *economic integration.*

interdependence: interrelationship between *economic* and *non-economic variables*. Also in international affairs, the situation in which one nation's welfare depends to varying degrees on the decisions and policies of another nation, and vice-versa. See also *dependence, dominance* and *vulnerability*.

interest: the payment (or *price*) for the use of borrowed funds. See also *interest rate, social discount rate, time preference*, etc.

interest rate: the amount that a borrower must pay a lender over and above the total amount borrowed expressed as a percentage of the total amount of funds borrowed – e.g. if a man borrowed 100 rupees for one year at the end of which he had to repay 110 rupees, the *interest rate* would be 10 per cent per annum.

intermediate producer goods: goods that are used as *inputs* into further levels of production, for example, leather in shoe manufacture, iron ore into steel production, etc. See also *final goods.*

internal economies (diseconomies) of production: these are the advantages (lower costs) in the case of economies or the *constraints* (additional costs) in the case of diseconomies to a single firm as its scale of production expands. They include: decreasing or increasing administrative costs, improved or worsened coordination problems, shortages of appropriate manpower skills, etc. See also *external economies* and *diseconomies of production.*

international poverty line: an arbitrary international *real income* measure, usually expressed in constant dollars (e.g. $50), used as a basis for estimating the proportion of the world's population that exist at bare levels of *subsistence* – i.e. those whose incomes fall below this poverty line.

invention: the discovery of something new, for example, a new product (e.g. *hybrid corn*) or a new production process (e.g. a cheaper and more efficient way of producing synthetic rubber). See also *innovation.*

investment: that part of *national income* or *expenditure* devoted to the production of *capital goods* over a given period of time. 'Gross' investment refers to total expenditure on new *capital goods*, while 'net' investment refers to the additional *capital goods* produced in excess of those that wear out and need to be replaced.

'investment' in children (process of): the process by which parents raise the 'quality' and hence the 'earning capacity' of children by providing them with an education in expectation of future returns. In this sense, children in poor societies are viewed as *capital goods* and a source of old age security. See also *human resources.*

invisible hand: this term has its origin in Adam Smith's famous book *Wealth of Nations* written in 1776. It argues that the unbridled pursuit of individual self-interest automatically contributes to the maximisation of the social interest. See also *laissez faire, perfect competition* and *pure market capitalism.*

'inward' looking development policies: policies that stress economic *self-reliance* on the part of LDCs, including the development of indigenous *'appropriate'* technology, the imposition of substantial protective *tariffs* and *non-tariff trade barriers* in order to promote import substitution and the general discouragement of *private foreign investment*. See also *autarky* and *outward-looking development policies*.

Keynesian economics: that branch of *Western macro-economic theory* focusing on the determination of aggregate income and employment in an *advanced capitalist, market economy*. Named after its originator, John Maynard Keynes, the famous British economist of the 1930s.

Keynesian model: model developed by John Maynard Keynes in the early 1930s to explain the causes of economic depression and hence the unemployment of that period. The model states that unemployment is caused by insufficient *aggregate demand* (AD) and it can be eliminated by, say, government expenditure that would raise AD and activate idle and/or underutilised resources and thus create jobs.

labour or capital-augmenting technological progress: the *technological progress* that adds to the effectiveness (productivity) of the existing quantity of labour (or capital) – e.g. labour by general education, on-the-job training programmes, etc.; and capital by *innovation* and new *inventions*. See also *labour-saving technological progress*.

labour-intensive technique: more labour-using method of production – i.e. that which uses proportionately more labour relative to other *factors of production*. See also *capital-intensive technique*.

labour productivity: the level of output per unit of labour input, usually measured as output per man-hour or man-year.

labour-'saving' technological progress: associated with the achievement of higher output using unchanged labour inputs as a result of some *invention* (e.g. the computer) or *innovation* (such as assembly line production).

labour theory of value: in classical international trade theory, the proposition that relative commodity prices depend on relative amounts of labour used to produce those commodities. Much of Marxist economics is based on the labour theory of value.

LAFTA: Latin American Free Trade Association: an economic federation of eleven Latin American states formed in 1960 and within which all commodities are traded free of *tariff*. Each member state, however, may levy *tariffs* and legislate other trade restrictions on goods entering it from countries that are not members of the federation. The primary purpose of LAFTA is to encourage *trade creation* in the economically integrated area; its current membership includes: Brazil, Argentina, Chile, Venezuela, etc.

laissez faire: literally 'allow to do', an expression often used to represent the notion of free enterprise, market *capitalism*. See also *perfect competition* and *pure market capitalism*.

landlord: a proprietor of a freehold interest in land with rights to lease out to tenants in return for some form of payment for the use of the land.

land reform: deliberate attempt to reorganise and transform existing *agrarian systems* with the intention of improving the distribution of agricultural incomes and thus fostering *rural development*. Among its many forms, *land reform* may entail provision of secured tenure rights to the individual farmer; transfer of land ownership away from small classes of powerful land owners to tenants who actually till the land; appropriation of large estates for establishing small new settlement farms; instituting land improvements and irrigation schemes, etc.

latifundios: very large landholdings in Latin American *agrarian system*, capable of providing employment for over 12 people each, owned by a small number of *landlords* and comprising a large proportion of total agricultural land. Holders of *minifundios* are often required to offer unpaid seasonal labour to latifundios.

'laws' v. tendencies: a law is a universal truth – i.e. it holds in all situations and its validity is independent of the social and/or political context in which it is observed – e.g. in the physical sciences, the law of gravity holds whether an experiment is conducted in North America, the USSR, China, Botswana or Brazil. On the other hand, *tendencies* (as in the case of economics) are only inclinations of behaviour or phenomena that may occur under similar conditions but are not always true in different social contexts.

levels of living: the extent to which a person, a family or group of people can satisfy their material, social and spiritual wants. If they are able to afford only a minimum quantity of food, shelter and clothing their levels of living are said to be very low. On the other hand if they do enjoy a greater variety of food, shelter, clothing and other things such as good health, education, leisure, etc., then clearly they are enjoying relatively high levels of living. See also *development* (meaning of).

life expectancy (at birth): time period, normally in years, that a baby is expected to live after it has been born alive. In LDCs, this time period is roughly 48 years for male children and 52 years for female children. In developed countries, it is approximately 70 years for male children and 72 years for female children. See also *birth rate.*

life sustenance: those basic goods and services like food, clothing and shelter that are necessary to sustain an average human being at the bare minimal *level of living.*

literacy: the ability to read and write. Literacy rates are often used as one of the many social and economic indicators of the state of *'development'* within a country.

loans: the transfer of funds from one economic entity to another (e.g. government to government, individual to individual, bank to individual, etc.) which must be repaid with *interest* over a prescribed period of time. *'Hard'* loans refer to those given at 'market' rates of interest whereas *'soft'* loans are given at 'concessionary' or low rates of *interest.* See also *grant.*

Lorenz curve: a graph depicting the variance of the *size distribution of income* from perfect equality. See also *Gini coefficient.*

luxury goods: goods whose demand is generated in large part by the higher income groups within a country. Luxuries are regarded as suitable objects of taxation from the social point of view (in order to 'improve' *income distribution*) as they are not considered 'necessary' for 'life maintenance'. Examples of luxuries in a less developed economy are very expensive motor cars, imported expensive clothing, cosmetics, jewellery, television sets, etc.

macro-economics: that branch of economics which considers the relationships between broad economic aggregates such as *national income,* total volumes of *saving, investment, consumption* expenditure, employment, *money supply,* etc. It is also concerned with determinants of the magnitudes of these aggregates and their rates of change through time. See also *Keynesian economics.*

'macro' population – development relationship: a general cause-and-effect relationship between development process and population growth. *Development* causes population growth rates to slow down and stabilise by providing *economic incentives* that motivate people to have smaller families. Population growth (in the absence of population problem) in turn, affects development in many ways – e.g. it increases *aggregate demand* that stimulates increases in national output, provides more people for national defence, etc.

malnutrition: a state of ill-health resulting from an inadequate or improper diet – usually measured in terms of average daily protein consumption.

Malthusian population 'trap': an inevitable population level envisaged by the Reverend Thomas Malthus (1766–1834) at which population increase was bound to stop because after that level the life-sustaining resources that increase at an arithmetical rate would be insufficient to support human population which increases at a geometrical rate. Consequently, people would die of starvation, diseases, wars, etc. The Malthusian population 'trap' therefore represents that population size that can just be supported by the available resources.

manpower planning: the long range planning of skilled and semi-skilled manpower requirements and the attempt to gear educational priorities and investments in accordance with these future *human resource* needs.

marginal cost: the addition to total cost incurred by the producer as a result of varying output by one more unit.

marginal product: the increase in total output resulting from the use of one additional unit of a *variable factor of production.*

marginal propensity to consume (MPC): the change in *consumption,* C, divided by the change in income, Y, that brought it about – i.e. $MPC = \Delta C/\Delta Y$.

marginal propensity to save (MPS): the change of *saving,* S, that results from a given change in income, Y, that is, the ratio of change in saving to the change in income so that $MPS = \Delta S/\Delta Y$ or dS/dY in calculus. By definition $MPC + MPS = 1$. See also *marginal propensity to consume (MPC).*

marginal utility: the satisfaction derived by consuming one additional or one less unit of a good. A consumer's marginal utility is said to be maximised if his marginal utility per last unit of expenditure on that good is equal to marginal utilities of all other goods available to him, divided by their respective prices.

market economy: a free private enterprise economy governed by a *price system* and *market mechanism.* See also *perfect competition* and *pure market capitalism.*

market failure: a phenomenon which results from the existence of market imperfections (e.g. *monopoly* power, factor immobility, lack of knowledge, etc.) which weaken the functioning of a free *market economy* – i.e. it 'fails' to realise its theoretical beneficial results. Market failure often provides the justification for government interference with the working of the free market.

market mechanism: the system whereby *prices* of commodities or services freely rise or fall when the buyers' demand for them rises or falls or the sellers' supply of them decreases or increases. See also *price system.*

market socialism: *economic system* in which all *resources* are owned by the State but their allocation in the economy is done primarily by a market *price system.* See also *'Command' Socialism.*

mass production: large scale production of goods or services achieved primarily through automation, specialisation and the *division of labour.*

micro-economics: that branch of economics which is concerned with individual decision units – firms and households – and the way in which their decisions interact to determine relative prices of goods and *factors of production* and how much of these will be bought and sold. The 'market' is the central concept in micro-economics. See also *price system* and *traditional economics.*

micro-economic theory of fertility: an extension of the theory of economic behaviour of individual firms and households to the family formation decisions of individual couples. The central proposition of this theory is that family formation has costs and benefits and thus the sizes of families formed will depend on these costs and benefits. If the costs of family formation are high (low) relative to its benefits, the rates at which couples will decide to bring forth children will decline (increase). See also *'opportunity cost' of a woman's time, (general) fertility rate, (crude) birth rate, economic incentives* and *disincentives of fertility reduction,* etc.

microfundios: very small landholdings in Latin American *agrarian system* which are further divisions of *minifundios* as a result of growing populations on crowded areas of poor land, e.g. in Guatemala microfundios yield an average income that is less than one third of that provided by the *minifundios.*

minifundios: landholdings in the Latin American *agrarian system* which are considered too small to provide adequate employment for a single family. They are too small to provide the workers with a *level of living* much above the bare survival minimum. Holders of minifundios are often required to provide unpaid seasonal labour to *latifundios* and to seek outside low-paid employment to supplement their meagre incomes. See also *latifundios* and *microfundios.*

mixed commercial farming: the first step in the transition from *subsistence* to *specialised farming.* This evolutionary stage is characterised by the production of both staple crops and *cash crops* and, in addition, simple animal husbandry.

'mixed systems': *economic systems* that are a mixture of both *capitalist* and *socialist* economies. 'Mixed' economic systems characterise most developing countries. Their essential feature is the coexistence of substantial *private* and *public* activity within a single economy. See also *market socialism* and *advanced capitalism.*

model: an analytical framework used to portray functional relationships among economic *variables.*

modernisation ideals: ideals regarded by some as necessary for sustained *economic growth.* They include *rationality, economic planning,* social and economic equalisation, and improved *institutions* and attitudes.

money income: the income accruing to a household or firm expressed in terms of some monetary unit – e.g. 1 000 rupees or pesos per year.

money supply: sum total of currency in circulation plus commercial bank demand deposits (M_1) plus sometimes savings bank time deposits (M_2).

moneylender: in Asia, a person who lends money at higher than market rates of *interest* to peasant farmers to meet their needs for seeds, fertiliser and other *inputs.* Activities of moneylenders are often unscrupulous and can help to accentuate landlessness among the rural poor.

monopoly: a market situation in which a product which does not have close substitutes is being produced and sold by a single seller. See also *perfect competition* and *oligopoly.*

monopolistic market control: a situation in which the output of an industry is controlled by a single producer (or seller), or a joint group of producers governed by joint decisions.

multilateral assistance agency: see *foreign aid.*

multi-national corporation (MNC): an international or transnational corporation with headquarters in one country but branch offices in a wide range of both developed and developing countries. Examples include General Motors, Coca Cola, Firestone, Philips, Renault, British Petroleum, Exxon, ITT, etc.

national expenditure: total expenditure on *final goods* and services in an economy over a given time period. National expenditure (E) includes: *consumption* expenditure (C), *investment* expenditure (I) government expenditure (G) and expenditure on exports by foreigners (X) less expenditure on imports by domestic residents (M). Thus $E = C+I+G+X-M$.

national income: total monetary value of all *final goods* and services produced in an economy over some period of time, usually a year. See also *gross national product (GNP)* and *national expenditure.*

necessary condition: a condition that must be present although need not be enough for an event to occur – e.g. *capital* formation is a necessary condition for sustained *economic growth* (i.e. before increase (growth) in output can occur, there must be tools to produce it). But for this growth to be continued, social, *institutional* and attitudinal changes must also occur.

necessity goods: life-sustaining items, e.g. food, shelter, protection, medical care, etc. These are essential for a good life. See also luxury goods.

'neo-classical' price incentive model: model whose main proposition is that if market prices are to influence economic activities in the right direction, they must be adjusted to remove *factor price distortions* by means of subsidies, taxes, etc., so that factor prices may reflect the true *opportunity cost* of *resources* being used. See also *'appropriate' technology.*

neo-classical economics: see *traditional (Western) economics.*

neo-colonial model of underdevelopment: model whose main proposition is that *under-development* exists in *Third World* countries because of exploitive economics, political and cultural policies of developed nations towards less developed countries, e.g. inappropriate transfers of technology, unequal trading relationships, misdirected assistance programmes, etc.

non-economic variables: elements of interest to economists in their work, but which are not given a monetary value or expressed in numerals because of their intangible nature. Examples of these include: beliefs, values, attitudes, norms and power structure. Sometimes *non-economic variables* are more important than the quantifiable economic variables in promoting *development.*

'non-formal' education: basically, any 'out of school' programme that provides basic skills and training to individuals. Examples include adult education, on-the-job training programmes, agricultural and other extension services, etc. See also *'formal' educational system.*

non-renewable resources: natural resources whose quantity is fixed in supply and cannot be replaced. Examples include petroleum, iron ore, coal and other minerals. See also *renewable resources.*

'non-tariff' trade barrier: barriers to *free trade* that take forms other than *tariffs* such as *quotas*, sanitary requirements for imported meats and dairy products, etc.

normal and superior goods: goods whose purchased quantities increase as the incomes of consumers increase. Such goods have a positive *income elasticity of demand.* See also *inferior goods.*

normative economics: the notion that economics must concern itself with what 'ought to be'. Thus, it is argued that economics and economic analysis always involve *value judgments*, whether explicit or implicit, on the part of the analyst or observer. See also *positive economics.*

OECD: Organisation for Economic Cooperation and Development: an organisation of 20 countries from the Western World, including all those in Europe and North America. Its major objective is to assist the economic growth of its member nations by promoting cooperation and technical analysis of national and international economic trends.

oligopoly: a market situation whereby there are a few sellers of similar but differentiated products. *OPEC* provides a good example of international oligopoly. See also *imperfect competition.*

oligopolistic market control: exists when a market structure has a small number of rival but not necessarily competing firms dominating the industry. Thus, all recognise the fact that they are interdependent and can maximise their individual advantages through explicit (cartel) or implicit (collusion) joint actions.

OPEC: Organisation of Petroleum Exporting Countries: an organisation consisting of the 13 major oil-exporting countries of the Third World who act as a 'cartel' or *oligopoly* to promote their joint national interests. Members are Saudi Arabia, Nigeria, Algeria, Venezuela, Libya, Kuwait, United Arab Emirates, Iran, Iraq, Equador, Qatar, Gabon and Indonesia.

open economy: an economy that engages in foreign trade and has financial and non-financial contacts with the rest of the world – e.g. in areas such as education, culture, technology, etc. See also *closed economy* and *outward-looking development policies.*

open unemployment: includes both *voluntary* and involuntary *unemployment.* Voluntarily unemployed persons are those unwilling to accept jobs for which they could qualify probably because they have means of support other than employment. Involuntary unemployment is a situation in which job-seekers are willing to work but there are no jobs available for them. *Open unemployment* is most conspicuous in the cities of less developed countries. See also *under-employment, surplus labour* and *disguised unemployment.*

opportunity cost: in production, the real value of *resources* used in the most desirable alternative – e.g. the *'opportunity cost'* of producing an extra unit of manufactured good is the output of say, food that must be foregone as a result of transferring *resources* from agricultural to manufacturing activities; in *consumption*, the amount of one commodity that must be forgone in order to consume more of another. See also *increasing opportunity cost.*

'opportunity cost' of a woman's time: real or monetary wage or *profits* that a woman sacrifices by deciding to stay at home and raise children instead of working for a wage or engaging in profit-making self-employed activities. The higher the opportunity cost of a woman's time involved in bearing children, the more unwilling she will be to bring forth more children – at least in terms of the *micro-economic theory of fertility.*

optimisation, principle of: a principle which states that in order to minimise costs in production or maximise 'satisfaction' in *consumption*, scarce *resources* should be used in the economically most 'efficient' manner while *goods* and services should be consumed so that the last unit of expenditure yields the same *marginal utility* for all individuals. See also the *principle of economy, appropriate technology, economic efficiency*, etc.

'organised' money market: the formal banking system in which loanable funds are channelled through recognised and licensed *financial intermediaries*. See also *'unorganised' money market.*

output-employment lag: a phenomenon in which employment growth 'lags' substantially behind output growth – normally, when output grows at a rate of three to four times that of employment as it has in most modern sectors of 'developing nations'.

outward-looking development policies: policies that encourage *free trade*, the free movement of capital, workers, enterprises and students, a welcome to *multi-national corporations* and an open system of communications. See also *open economy.*

'overvalued' exchange rate: an *exchange rate* that is 'officially' set at a level higher than its real or 'shadow' value – i.e. 9 Indian rupees per dollar instead of say, 15 rupees per dollar. Overvalued rates cheapen the real cost of imports while raising the real cost of exports. They often lead to a need for *exchange control.*

'package' of policies: a set of multi-dimensional economic and social policies aimed for example at removing inequalities and improving living standards for the masses. In short, a set of different but mutually reinforcing policies designed to achieve a single or multiple objective.

partial plans: those that cover only a part of the national economy, e.g. agriculture, industry, tourism, etc.

per capita food production: total food production divided by the total population.

per capita income: see *income per capita.*

perfect competition: a market situation characterised by the existence of (1) very many buyers and sellers of (2) homogeneous goods or services with (3) perfect knowledge and (4) free entry so that no single buyer or seller can influence the price of the good or service. See also *price system, laissez faire, Western economic theory* and *pure market capitalism.*

personal income: the amount of *money income* received by households over a given period of time. Note that some incomes are earned (as a result of rendering productive services) but not currently received, (e.g. undistributed profits and contributions for social insurance), while some incomes received by the household sector are not earned through current productive activity, e.g. *transfer payments*. Personal income is derived by adding to *national income* the various incomes received by the households but not earned, and subtracting those that are earned but not received.

physical capital: tangible investment goods, e.g. plant and equipment, machinery, buildings, etc. See also *human capital.*

plan: see *economic plan* and *development plan.*

plan implementation: the practical carrying out of the objectives set forth in the *development plan*. Some of the difficulties encountered in attempting to attain plan targets result from insufficient availability of economic *resources* (physical and financial capital, skilled manpower, etc.), insufficient *foreign aid*, the effects of *inflation*, and, most importantly, lack of *political will.*

planning model: a mathematical *model* (e.g. an input–output or 'macro' planning model) designed to simulate quantitatively the major features of the economic structure of a particular country. *Planning models* provide the analytical and quantitative basis for most national and regional *development plans*. See also *economic plan* and *plan implementation.*

policy: see *economic policy.*

policy instruments: see *economic policy.*

political economy: the attempt to merge economic analysis with practical politics – i.e. to view economic activity in its political context. Much of 'classical' economics was political economy and today 'political economy' is increasingly being recognised as necessary for any realistic examination of development problems.

political will: a determined, deliberate, purposeful, independent decision, conclusion or choice upon a course of action by persons in the political authority such as elimination of inequality, poverty and unemployment through various reforms of social, economic and *institutional* structures. Lack of 'political will' is often said to be one of the main obstacles to *development* and the main reason for the failure of many *development plans*. See also *plan implementation*.

population density: the number of inhabitants per unit area of land, e.g. per square mile.

population increase (rate of): rate at which a given population size grows over a period of time, say, one year. Part of this rate, that which results entirely from increases in the number of births is called the *rate of natural increase of population*, to distinguish it from the rate resulting from, say, immigration.

'positive' economics: The notion that economics should be concerned with 'what is', was, or will be. It addresses itself to questions such as, what government policies will generate faster GNP growth; what government policies will reduce unemployment, inflation, inequality, etc. Answers to these questions are supposedly based on facts or empirical observation. See also *'normative' economics*.

potential output: the aggregate capacity output of a nation – i.e. maximum quantity of goods and services that can be produced with available *resources* and a given state of technology.

poverty: see *absolute poverty*.

poverty line: see *international poverty line*.

preventive medicine: medical care that focuses on the prevention of sickness and disease through immunology and health education. See also *curative medicine*.

present consumption: expenditure on goods and services that satisfy short-term wants – e.g. expenditures on food, cinema, entertainment, etc. Future consumption refers to expenditures on consumer items that yield want-satisfying benefits over a long time period, normally beyond one year, such as expenditure on cars, residential houses, furniture, etc. See also *consumption*.

price: monetary or real value of a *resource*, commodity or service. The role of prices in a *market economy* is to *ration* or allocate resources in accordance with supply and demand; additionally, relative prices should reflect the relative scarcity values of different resources, goods or services. See also *price system*.

price elasticity of demand: the responsiveness of the quantity of a good demanded to changes in its price, expressed as the percentage change in quantity demanded divided by the percentage change in price.

price elasticity of supply: the responsiveness of the quantity of a commodity supplied to changes in its price, expressed as the proportionate change in quantity supplied divided by the proportionate change in price.

price system: the mechanism by which scarce resources, goods and services are allocated by the free upward or downward movements of prices in accordance with the dictates of supply and demand in *a market economy*. See also *perfect competition* and *pure market capitalism*.

primary industrial sector: part of the economy that specialises in the production of agricultural products and the extraction of raw materials. Major industries in this sector include: mining, agriculture, forestry and fishing.

primary products: products derived from all extractive occupations – farming, lumbering, fishing, mining and quarrying – viz. foodstuffs and raw materials.

principles: see *economic principles*.

principle of economy: the proposition in *perfect competition* that for a given level of *resources* (inputs), producers will tend to minimise costs for a given level of output or maximise output for a given cost. The need to 'economise' arises because resources are 'scarce' and are therefore not free.

private benefits: gains that accrue to a single individual – e.g. profits received by an individual firm. See also *social benefits*.

private cost: the direct monetary outlays or costs of an individual economic unit, e.g. the private costs of a firm are the direct outlays on *fixed* and *variable inputs* of production.

private foreign investment: the investment of private foreign funds in the economy of a developing nation, usually in the form of *import substituting* industries by *multi-national corporations (MNCs)*.

private sector: that part of an economy whose activities are under the control and direction of non-governmental economic units such as the households or firms. Each economic unit owns its own *resources* and uses them mainly to maximise its own well-being.

production function: a technological or engineering relationship between the quantity of a good produced and the minimum quantity of *inputs* required to produce it.

productivity gap: the difference between per capita product of, say, the agricultural population, i.e. *agricultural labour productivity*, in LDCs and that in developed countries. It has tended to be wide because of differences in the application of technological and biological improvements.

production process: see *production technique.*

production-possibility curve: a curve on a graph indicating alternative combinations of two commodities or categories of commodities (e.g. agricultural and manufactured goods) that can be produced when all the available *factors of production* are efficiently employed. Given available *resources* and technology, the P–P curve sets the boundary between which combination is attainable and which it is unobtainable. See also *opportunity cost* and *production function.*

production technique: method of combining *inputs* to produce required output. A production technique is said to be *appropriate* ('best') if it produces a given output with the least cost (thus being economically efficient) or with the least possible quantity of real resources (technically efficient).
A technique may be *labour-intensive* or *capital-intensive.*

profit: the difference between the market value of output and the market value of *inputs* that were employed to produce that output. Alternatively, a firm's or farm's profits can be defined as the difference between total revenue and total cost.

profit maximisation: making as large as possible the profits of a firm or farm. Producers often desire to find the level of output which results in maximum profits, at least according to a fundamental assumption of 'Western' economic theory.

progressive income tax: a tax whose rate increases with increasing personal incomes – i.e. where the proportion of personal income paid by a rich person in taxes is higher than that paid by a poorer person. A progressive tax structure therefore tends to improve *income distribution.* See also *regressive tax.*

project appraisal: the quantitative analysis of the relative desirability (profitability) of investing a given sum of public and/or private funds in alternative projects – e.g. building a steel mill or textile factory. *Cost/benefit* analysis provides the major analytical tool of project appraisal.

public sector: that portion of an economy whose activities (economic and non-economic) are under the control and direction of the State. The State owns all *resources* in this sector and uses them to achieve whatever goals it may have – e.g. to promote the economic welfare of the ruling elite or to maximise the well-being of society as a whole. See also *private sector.*

pure market capitalism: *economic system* in which all *resources* are privately owned and their allocation is done exclusively by a *price system.* See also *perfect competition, market economy, invisible hand* and *laissez faire.*

quintile: a 20 per cent proportion of any numerical quantity – e.g. a population divided into quintiles would be one which is divided into five equal numerical groups. See also *decile.*

quota: a physical limitation on the quantity of any item that can be imported into a country – e.g. so many automobiles per year.

rate of natural increase (of population): see *population increase, rate of.*

rationality: one of the foundations (with regard to people's behaviour) upon which traditional or *Western economic theory* is built. An economically 'rational' person is one who will always attempt to maximise satisfaction or profits, or minimise costs. The notion of rationality as one of the *modernisation ideals* means the replacement of age-old traditional practices by modern methods of 'objective' thinking and logical reasoning in production, distribution and consumption. See also *rational choice, principles of economy* and *optimisation* and *profit maximisation.*

rationing: a system of distribution employed to restrict the quantities of goods and services that consumers or producers can purchase or be allocated freely. It arises because of excess demand and inflexible prices. *Rationing* can be by coupons, points or simply administrative decisions with regard to commodities, by academic credentialisation with regard to job allocation, by industrial licences with regard to *capital good* imports, etc. See also *black market.*

'rational' choice: a choice commensurate with logical reasoning. In economic theory it is often assumed that everyone behaves rationally in his economic activities. See, for example, the *principle of economy, profit maximisation, principle of optimisation* and *rationality.*

real income: the income that a household or firm receives in terms of the real goods and services it can purchase. Alternatively, it is simply *money income* adjusted by some price index.

recession: a period of slack general economic activity as reflected in rising unemployment and excess productive capacity in a broad spectrum of industries.

redistribution policies: policies geared to reducing inequality of incomes and economic opportunities in order to promote '*development*'. Examples include *progressive tax* policies, provision of services financed out of such taxation to benefit persons in the lower income groups, *rural development policies* giving emphasis to raising *levels of living* for the rural poor through *land reform* and other forms of *asset* and wealth redistribution, etc.

regressive tax: if the ratio of taxes to income as income increases tends to decrease, the tax is called 'regressive' – i.e. relatively poor people pay a larger proportion of their income in taxes than do relatively rich people. A regressive tax therefore tends to worsen *income distribution*. See also *progressive tax*.

renewable resources: natural resources which can be replaced so that the total supply is not fixed for all time as in the case of *non-renewable resources*. Examples include timber and other forest products.

rent: in the context of *macro-economics* it refers to the share of *national income* going to the owners of the productive *resource*, land (i.e. *landlords*). In everyday usage, the price paid for rental property, e.g. buildings and housing. In the theory of *micro-economics* it is a short form for 'economic rent' – i.e. the payment to a *factor* over and above its highest *opportunity cost*.

replacement fertility: level of *fertility* at which child bearing women have just enough daughters to 'replace' themselves in the population. This keeps the existing population size constant through an infinite number of succeeding generations. See also *fertility rate, general*, and *birth rate*.

research and development (R and D): a scientific investigation with a view towards improving the existing quality of human life, products, profits, *factors of production* or just plain knowledge. There are two categories of R and D. (1) 'basic' R and D – i.e. one without a specific commercial objective and (2) 'applied' R and D – i.e. one with a commercial pursuit.

resources, physical and human: *factors of production* used to produce goods and services to satisfy wants. Land and capital are frequently referred to as *physical resources* and labour as the *human resource*. See also *fixed* and *variable inputs*.

resource endowment: a nation's supply of *factors of production*. Normally such endowments are supplied by nature, e.g. mineral deposits, raw materials, timber forests, labour, etc. See also *factor endowment theory of trade*.

rigid institutions: *institutions* that are designed in such a way that they cannot be adjusted or adjust of themselves to accommodate *development* requirements, e.g. a social system – typically a clan unit – that has conservative values which render it resistant to *modernising ideals*.

risk: a situation in which the probability of obtaining some outcome of an event is not precisely known, that is, known probabilities cannot be precisely assigned to these outcomes but their general level can be inferred. In everyday usage a risky situation is one in which one of the outcomes involves some loss to the decision maker, for example, changes of demand, weather and tastes. See also *uncertainty*.

rural development: see *integrated rural development*.

rural support systems: systems which need to be created to stimulate the productivity of both small- and large-scale agricultural farms. These include making more effective and efficient the rural *institutions* directly connected with production, e.g. banks, *moneylenders*, public credit agencies, seed and fertiliser distributors; and provision of services such as technical and educational *extension services*, storage and marketing facilities, rural transport and feeder roads, water, etc.

savings: that portion of *disposable income* not spent on *consumption* by households plus profits retained by firms. Savings are normally assumed to be positively related to the level of income (personal or national).

savings ratio: savings expressed as a proportion of *disposable income* over some period of time. It shows the fraction of *national income* that is saved over any period. The savings ratio is sometimes used synonymously with the *average propensity to save*. See also *Harrod–Domar equation*.

'scale-neutral' technological progress: *technological progress* which can lead to the achievement of higher output levels irrespective of the size (scale) of the firm or farm – i.e. it is equally applicable to small as well as to large-scale production processes. An often cited example is the *hybrid seeds* of the *green revolution* which theoretically can increase yields on both small and large farms (if *complementary resources* such as fertiliser, irrigation, pesticides, etc., are available).

scarcity: in economics, the term referring to a situation which arises when there is less of something (e.g. an *economic good, service* or *resource*) than people would like to have if it were free. The quantity of goods and services are scarce relative to people's desire for them because the economy's resources used in their production are themselves scarce. Scarcity therefore gives rise to the need for efficient allocation of resources among alternative competing uses through, for example, the free *market mechanism* in *capitalist* economies or through a centralised *command system* in planned economies.

scatter diagram: a two-dimensional graph on which numerical values of statistically observed *variables* are plotted in pairs, one measured on the horizontal axis and the other on the vertical axis.

Second World: the now economically advanced *socialist* countries. Major *Second World* countries include: the Soviet Union and other Soviet type economies of eastern Europe such as Poland, Czechoslovakia, Yugoslavia, etc. See also *First World* and *Third World*.

secondary industrial sector: the 'manufacturing' portion of the economy that uses raw materials and *intermediate products* to produce *final goods* or other *intermediate products*. Industries such as motor assembly, textile and building and construction are part of this sector.

self-esteem (of a society): feeling of 'human worthiness' that a society enjoys when its social, political and *economic systems* and *institutions* promote human respect, dignity, integrity, self-determination, etc. See also *development* (meaning of).

self-reliance: reliance on one's own capabilities, judgment, resources, skills in a bid to enhance political, economic, social, cultural, attitudinal and moral independence. Countries may also desire to be self-reliant in particular aspects such as food production, manpower and skills, etc. Increasingly, the term 'collective' self-reliance is being used in the *Third World*.

shadow price: *price* that reflects the true *opportunity-cost* of a *resource*.

sharecropper: in the *agrarian systems* of LDCs the tenant peasant farmer whose crop produce has to be shared with the *landlord*. The *landlord* usually appropriates a large share of the tenant's total crop production.

shifting cultivation: peasant agricultural practice in Africa in which land is tilled by a family or community for cropping until such time that it has been exhausted of fertility. Thereafter the family or community moves to a new area of land which is prepared for cropping as the previous one was. This is left to regain fertility until eventually it can be cultivated once again.

size distribution of income: the distribution of income according to size, class of persons, e.g. the share of total income accruing to say the poorest 40 per cent of a population or the richest 10 per cent, without regard to the sources of that income (e.g. if it comes from wages, *interest, rent* or *profits*), See also *functional distribution of income, Lorenz curve* and *Gini coefficient*.

'skewed' distribution of income: skewness is a lack of symmetry in a 'frequency distribution'. If income is perfectly distributed such a distribution is said to be symmetrical. A skewed distribution of income is one diverging from perfect equality. Highly 'skewed' distribution of income occurs in situations where the rich persons, say the top 20 per cent of the total population, receive more than half of the total *national income*. See also *Lorenz curve* and *Gini coefficient*.

small farmer: farmer owning a small family-based plot of land on which he grows *subsistence* crops and perhaps one or two *cash crops*, relying almost exclusively on family labour.

small-scale industry: industry whose firms or farms operate with small-sized plants, low employment and hence have small output capacity. *Economies of scale* do not normally exist for such firms or farms but they often tend to utilise their limited *physical, human* and financial *resources* more efficiently than many large-sized firms or farms.

social benefits: gains or benefits that accrue or are available to the society as a whole rather than solely to a private individual – e.g. the protection and security provided by the police or the Armed Forces; the *external economies* afforded by an effective health care system; and the widespread benefits of a literate population. See also *private benefits*.

social cost: the cost to society as a whole of an economic decision, whether private or public. Where there exist *external diseconomies* of *production* (e.g. pollution) or *consumption* (alcoholism), social costs will normally exceed *private costs* and decisions based solely on private calculations will lead to a misallocation of resources.

'social' discount rate: the rate at which the society 'discounts' potential future *social benefits* to find out whether such benefits are worth their present *social cost*. The rate used in this discounting procedure is usually the social *opportunity cost* of the funds committed.

social science: that branch of study that concerns itself with human society, its behaviour, activities and growth, e.g. sociology, history, philosophy, political science, economics, etc.

social system: term used to refer to the *organisational* and *institutional* structure of the society including its *value premises*, attitudes, power structures and traditions. Major social systems include: political set-ups, religions, clans, etc.

socialism: see *command socialism* and *market socialism*.

'soft' loan: see *loans*.

special drawing rights (SDRs): new form of international financial asset – often referred to as 'paper gold' – created by the *International Monetary Fund (IMF)* in 1970 and designed to supplement gold and dollars in settling international *balance of payments* accounts. At present 75 per cent of the total SDR issue is distributed to 25 industrial nations while only 25 per cent is distributed among the more than 100 developing countries that participate in the international monetary system.

specialisation: a situation in which *resources* are concentrated in the production of a relatively few commodities rather than a wider range of commodities. See also *comparative advantage* and *division of labour*.

specialised farming: the final and most advanced stage of the evolution of agricultural production in which farm output is produced wholly for the market. It is most prevalent in advanced industrial countries. High farm yields are ensured by a high degree of *capital formation, technological progress* and scientific *research and development*. See also *subsistence farming* and *commercial farming*.

spread effects: impacts that are felt beyond the initial place of action. Sometimes referred to as 'echo' effects. The spread effects for example of increasing medical services are: a reduction in *death rates*, a rise in *life expectancy* at birth, healthy and productive labour force, etc.

'stages of growth' theory of development: this theory of development is associated with the American economic historian W. W. Rostow. According to Rostow, before a country can achieve development, it must inevitably pass through the following stages: (1) traditional and stagnant low per capita stage, (2) transitional stage (in which the 'pre-conditions for growth' are laid down), (3) the 'take-off' stage (beginning of *economic growth* process), (4) industrialised, mass production and consumption stage (*development* stage).

staple food: a leading or main food consumed by a large section of a country's population, e.g. maize meal in Kenya, Zambia and Tanzania, rice in South-East Asian countries, yams in West Africa, mandioca in Brazil, etc.

structural inflation: *inflation* that arises as a result of supply inelasticities and structural rigidities (e.g. inefficient marketing and distribution systems) in the industrial sectors of the economy. A form of *demand-pull inflation* but can exist with considerable excess capacity and unemployment.

structural theory of underdevelopment: hypothesis that *underdevelopment* in *Third World* countries is due to underutilisation of *resources* arising from structural and/or *institutional* factors that have their origins in both domestic and international *dualistic* situations. *'Development'*, therefore, requires more than just accelerated *capital* formation as espoused in the *stages of growth* and *'false paradigm'* models.

structural transformation: the process of transforming the basic industrial structure of an economy so that the contribution to *national income* by the manufacturing sector increasingly becomes higher than that by the agricultural sector. More generally, an alteration in the industrial composition of any economy. See also *primary, secondary* and *tertiary industrial sectors*.

subsidy: a payment by the government to producers or distributors in an industry to prevent the decline of that industry (e.g. as a result of continuous unprofitable operations), an increase in the prices of its products, or simply to encourage it to hire more labour (as in the case of a wage subsidy). Examples of subsidies are export subsidies to encourage their sale abroad, subsidies on some foodstuffs to keep down the cost of living especially in urban areas, farm subsidies to encourage expansion of farm production to achieve *self-sufficiency* in food production, etc.

subsistence economy: an economy in which production is mainly for own consumption and the standard of living yields no more than the basic necessities of life – food, shelter and clothing. See also *subsistence farming*.

subsistence farming: farming in which crop production, stock rearing, etc., is mainly for 'own-consumption' and is characterised by low productivity, *risk* and *uncertainty*. See also subsistence economy.

sufficient condition: a condition which causes an event to occur – e.g. being a university student is a sufficient condition to get a loan under university education loan schemes. See also *necessary condition*.

supply curve: a positively sloped curve relating the quantity of a commodity supplied to its *price*.

'surplus' labour: the excess supply of labour over and above the quantity demanded at the going 'free' market wage rate. In Arthur Lewis' two-sector model of economic development, surplus labour refers to that portion of the rural labour force whose *marginal productivity* is zero or negative. See also *underemployment*.

synthetic commodity substitutes: commodities that are artificially produced but of like nature with and substitutes for the natural commodities, e.g. those involving rubber, cotton, wool, camphor, pyrethrum, etc. Producers of raw materials, mainly LDCs, are becoming more and more vulnerable to competition from synthetics from industrialised countries as a result of the latter's more advanced state of scientific and technical progress.

tariff (ad valorem): a fixed percentage tax (e.g. 30 per cent) on the value of an imported commodity levied at the point of entry into the importing country.

technical assistance: *foreign aid* (either *bilateral* or *multilateral*) which takes the form of the transfer of expert personnel, technicians, scientists, educators, economic advisors, consultants, etc., rather than a simple transfer of funds.

technological progress: increased application of new scientific knowledge in form of *inventions* and *innovations* with regard to *capital*, both *physical* and human. Has been a major factor in stimulating the long-term *economic growth* of contemporary developed countries. See also *labour-augmenting, labour-saving, capital-augmenting* and *scale-neutral technological progress.*

tenant farmer: one who farms on land held by a *landlord* and therefore lacks secure ownership rights and has to pay for the use of that land, e.g. by surrendering part of his output to the owner of the land. Examples are found in the Latin American and Asian *agrarian systems.* See also *sharecropper.*

terms of trade (commodity): the ratio of a country's average export price to its average import price. A country's *terms of trade* are said to 'improve' when this ratio increases and to 'worsen' when it decreases – i.e., when import prices rise at a relatively faster rate than export prices (the experience of most LDCs over the past two decades).

tertiary sector: the 'services' and commerce portion of an economy. Examples of services include: repair and maintenance of *capital goods*, haircuts, public administration, medical care, transport and communications, teaching, etc. See also *primary* and *secondary sectors.*

Third World: the present 143 or so developing countries of Asia, Africa, the Middle East and Latin America. These countries are mainly characterised by *low levels of living,* high rates of *population growth,* low levels of *per capita income* and general economic and technological *dependence* on *First* and *Second World* economies.

Third World or 'development' economics: the economics of the less developed nations of Africa, Asia and Latin America which addresses itself mainly to problems of *economic growth, poverty, unemployment* and inequality

tied aid: *foreign aid* in the form of *bilateral loans* or *grants* which require the recipient country to use the funds to purchase goods and/or services from the donor country – thus the aid is said to be 'tied' to purchases from the assisting country.

'total' factor productivity: total monetary value of all units of output per unit of each and every *factor of production* in an economy. It is a measure of the average productivity of all factors employed in an economy.

trade (as an engine of growth): *free trade* has often been described as an 'engine of growth' because it encourages countries to *specialise* in activities in which they have *comparative advantages* thereby increasing their respective production efficiencies and hence their total outputs of goods and services.

trade creation: a situation in the theory of *customs unions* that occurs when, following the formation of the union, there is a shift in the geographic location of production from higher-cost to lower-cost member states. See also *trade diversion.*

trade diversion: occurs when the formation of a *customs union* causes the locus of production of formerly imported goods to shift from a lower cost non-member state to a higher cost member nation. See also *trade creation.*

trade-off: the necessity of sacrificing ('trading off') something in order to get more of something else – e.g. sacrificing *consumption* now for *consumption* later by devoting some present *resources* to *investment.* See also *opportunity cost.*

traditional (Western) economics: the economics of *capitalist market economies* characterised by *consumer sovereignty, profit maximisation, private enterprise* and *perfect competition.* The major focus is on the efficient allocation of *scarce resources* (see *economic efficiency*) through the *price system* and the forces of supply and demand. See also *micro-economics, macro-economics, Keynesian economics, laissez faire, invisible hand, market economy* and *'Western' economic theory.*

transfer payment: any payment from one economic entity to another that takes the form of a 'gift' – i.e. it is not for a service rendered and it need not be repaid. Examples include unemployment insurance, food stamps, welfare payments, *subsidies,* bilateral *grants,* etc.

transfer pricing: an accounting procedure usually designed to lower total taxes paid by *multi-national corporations (MNCs)* in which intra-corporate sales and purchases of goods and services are artificially invoiced so that *profits* accrue to those branch offices located in low tax countries ('tax havens') while offices in high tax countries show little or no taxable profits.

'trickle down' theory of development: the prevalent view of the 1950s and 1960s in which *development* was seen as purely an 'economic' phenomenon in which rapid gains from the overall growth of *GNP* and *per capita income* would automatically bring benefits (i.e. 'trickle down') to the masses in the form of jobs and other economic opportunities. The main preoccupation was therefore to get the growth job done while problems of *poverty, unemployment* and *income distribution* were of secondary importance.

UN: United Nations: a global organisation set up at the end of World War II with the basic aim of cultivating international cooperation among countries and hence ensuring that any conflicts or misunderstanding between or among countries would be resolved by peaceful means. At present the UN has a membership of 172 countries drawn from both the developed and less developed nations. The United Nations has its headquarters in New York, but many of its organs have headquarters elsewhere.

uncertainty: a situation in which the probability of obtaining the outcome(s) of an event is not known. There is thus a plurality of possible outcomes to which no objective probability can be attached. See also *risk.*

UNCTAD: United Nations' Conference on Trade and Development: a body of *United Nations* whose primary objective is to promote international trade and commerce with a principal focus on trade and *balance of payments* problems of developing nations. Its first Secretary General was Raul Prebisch of Latin America.

underdevelopment: economic situation in which there are persistent *low levels of living* with the following characteristics: *absolute poverty,* low *per capita incomes,* low rates of *economic growth,* low *consumption* levels, poor health services, high *death rates,* high *birth rates, vulnerability* to and *dependence* on foreign economies, and limited *freedom to choose* between *variables* that satisfy human wants. See also *development.*

underemployment: a situation in which persons are working less, either daily, weekly, monthly or seasonally, than they would like to work. See also *open unemployment* and *surplus labour.*

underutilisation of labour: operation of labour force at levels below their capacity or potential output. See also *open unemployment, underemployment, disguised underemployment, voluntary unemployment,* etc.

UNDP: United Nations' Development Programme: a member of the *United Nations* family system of world bodies whose major function is to promote *development* in *Third World* countries. Major development oriented projects financed and carried out by UNDP include: initiation of nutrition, health and education programmes, building up agricultural, industrial and transport infrastructure, etc.

UNESCO: United Nations' Educational, Scientific and Cultural Organisation: a major organ of the *United Nations* system located in Paris and charged with the responsibility of promoting 'international understanding' by (1) spreading ideas or knowledge through the educational process, (2) encouraging multi-racial coexistence through reconciliation of cultural values of different societies, and (3) sponsoring educational, cultural and scientific exchange programmes that make it possible for educators, artists, writers and scientists from a wide variety of countries and cultures to meet and exchange ideas and knowledge.

unit cost: the average total cost per unit of output of any *economic good* or service.

'unorganised' money market: the informal and often usurious credit system that exists in most developing countries (especially in rural areas) where low income farms and firms with little collateral are forced to borrow from *moneylenders* and 'loan sharks' at exorbitant rates of *interest.* See also *'organised' money market.*

urbanisation: economic and demographic growth process of urban centres.

USAID: United States Agency for International Development: a *bilateral assistance agency* of the United States government whose primary objective is to assist *Third World* countries in their *development* efforts as part of United States foreign policy. The 'economic' assistance given by USAID normally takes the form of educational *grants,* special interest *loans* and *technical assistance.* However, much of AID's activity also consists of 'non-economic' (mostly military) assistance to 'friendly' LDC governments.

values and value premises: principles, standards or qualities considered worthwhile or desirable. A value judgment is one based on or reflecting one's personal or class beliefs. See also *normative economics.*

variable: see *economic variables.*

variable inputs: *inputs* or *resources* whose required use in a *production function* will vary with changes in the level of output. For example, in the production of shoes, labour is usually a variable input because as more shoes are produced, more labour must be used. See also *fixed inputs.*

'vent for surplus' theory of trade: states that the opening up of world markets to developing countries through international trade provides them with the opportunity to take advantage of formerly underutilised land and labour resources to produce larger *primary product* outputs, the surplus of which can be exported to foreign markets. Such economies will usually be operating at a point somewhere inside their *production possibility frontiers* so that trade permits an outward shift of such a production point.

vested interest (groups): group of persons that have acquired rights or powers in any sphere of activities within a nation or in international affairs which they often struggle to guard and maintain. Examples of powerful *vested interest* groups in developing countries include *landlords*, political *elites*, and wealthy private local and foreign investors.

vicious circle: a self-reinforcing situation in which there are factors which tend to perpetuate a certain undesirable phenomenon – e.g. low incomes in poor countries lead to low *consumption* which then leads to poor health and low labour productivity and eventually to the persistence of *poverty*.

voluntary unemployment: a situation in which people can get work at the going wage rate but choose to remain out of work either because they hope to get better paid jobs or they want to enjoy leisure by remaining temporarily out of their jobs. See also *open unemployment*, *underemployment* and *hidden unemployment*.

vulnerability (of LDCs): a situation in which LDCs find themselves in a *dominance* and *dependence* relationship *vis-à-vis* the developed countries. LDCs are said to be economically 'vulnerable' to the decisions of rich nations in areas such as trade, *private foreign investments*, *foreign aid*, technological *research* and *development*, etc. See also *dominance* and *dependence*.

welfare indices (GNP index, equal weights index, poverty weighted index): indices used to measure the material well-being of the population. The *GNP* index is derived from the *size distribution of income* in which each income group receives a weight equal to its share of total income. The equal weights index is derived by assigning each 'size group' of the population equal welfare weights. In the poverty weighted index the (poor) bottom size groups of the population are given higher weights than the rich.

'Western' economic theory: a body of economic principles based on the economics of *advanced capitalist market economies* and built upon a specific set of assumptions about economic behaviour that largely reflect the *institutional* nature of these societies. See also *traditional economics*, *laissez-faire*, *invisible hand* and *market economy*.

World Bank: see *IBRD*.

Index